The Teaching
of Reading

REVISED

EDITION

The Teaching of Reading

John J. DeBoer
UNIVERSITY OF ILLINOIS

Martha Dallmann
OHIO WESLEYAN UNIVERSITY

HOLT, RINEHART and WINSTON, Inc.

New York • *Chicago* • *San Francisco* • *Toronto* • *London*

Preface to the Revised Edition

Public and professional interest in the teaching of reading has not abated since the appearance of the first edition of this book. Newspapers and general magazines continue to report the activities of schools and school systems in their efforts to improve the quality of instruction in reading. Interesting accounts of research in reading have appeared in the professional magazines. Several new books, addressed to teachers, have been published.

Although the first edition of *The Teaching of Reading* appeared only four years ago, there appears to be ample need of a new edition that takes account of the rapid developments which have occurred. Perhaps no field in education is receiving more attention than reading in the decade of the sixties. The authors of this book hope that the current revision will be of material assistance in keeping the reader informed of significant new emphases and innovations in the teaching of reading.

The basic structure and much of the text material in the book remain the same. Attention has been given, however, to the growing interest in the implications of the science of linguistics for the teaching of reading, the spread of programs of individualized reading, the significance of programed learning and teaching machines, the special reading problems of the gifted child, and new reports on the role of phonics in reading instruction. The discussions of reading in the content fields, so vital to the entire reading program, have been expanded in various parts of the book. Bibliographies and sources for teaching aids have been brought up to date. More space has been given to suggestions for classroom activities, particularly in the descriptions of reading games. New material on children's interests and children's literature has been included.

The changes will go on, and there will be no end to the need for constant revision of such books as these. We must work with what we know, or think we know, today, and keep alive the hope that some day most of our present problems in reading will be solved. We may be sure, however, that when that day comes there will be new problems and new books about reading!

In addition to the individuals and organizations mentioned in the preface to the first edition, the following authors and publishers are due our thanks for their courtesy in permitting us to quote from their materials: Luella Cole, Mrs. E. W. Dolch, the Educational Testing Service, and Scott, Foresman & Co.

J. J. DeB.
M.D.

February, 1964

Preface to the First Edition

This book is designed to introduce the student to the problems of reading instruction in the elementary school and to provide him with facts and ideas that he can use in dealing with these problems. It strives to bring together the many viewpoints and techniques that have been described in recent books and articles on the teaching of reading. When viewpoints are in conflict, as in the case of phonic instruction in the initial stages of reading, the authors have not hesitated to take a position and to support it with evidence and arguments. New emphases, such as the current enthusiasm for individual instruction and the use of visual aids, are given due recognition. (For example, as this book goes to press, experiments in individualized reading instruction are being conducted in all parts of the country. Controversy as to the nature and extent of the individualization desirable is being reflected in books and magazine articles. The most recent of these are included in the bibliographies at the end of the appropriate chapters in this book.) These emphases are considered in the light of the fact that sound principles may find varying applications in the years ahead. It is hoped that this volume encourages teachers to experiment with the new ideas as they at the same time keep informed about prevailing practices. The discussion has been geared, however, to the needs of students who are making their first acquaintance with the field.

Part I, intended as a general introduction to the teaching of reading, stresses the relation between reading and society, and between reading and the general development of the child. It considers the place of reading in the school program, the nature of the reading process, and the elements essential to growth in reading.

Part II discusses the specific reading abilities that need to be cultivated in school. This section is unique in the fact that it is divided into "A" and "B" chapters—the former discussing the skills in general terms, and the latter providing specific teaching aids for the development of these skills. This separation between general principles and specific teaching practices is designed to facilitate the use of this book both in teacher education courses and among teachers in service. The teacher of classes in reading will find this organization especially useful when classroom instruction is accompanied by various types of direct experience with children. Experienced teachers, familiar with the general principles, will find numerous ideas in the "B" chapters for ways of developing the various reading skills.

Part III, "The Reading Program in Action," draws together the specific elements in reading instruction and shows how they function in the program as a whole. Chapter 15, which deals with the school-wide program in reading, is intended primarily for the administrator, supervisor, and reading coordinator.

For the many centuries since the invention of movable type, reading has been the major instrument of mass communication. Today, as we see the beginnings of an "exploding" world population and the return of oral-aural communication through electronics, we may, as an editorialist in the *Saturday Review* recently suggested, witness the decline of reading and books as the chief means of transmitting the cultural heritage. At present, reading is keeping pace with its rival media; but if this decline should occur in the future, the loss will be great. Books like this one are designed to help the oncoming generations to share in the unique heritage that only the printed word can bequeath.

We acknowledge our debt to the many individuals whose works are named in this volume, and to many others whom it was not possible to mention. Special thanks are extended to the following writers, editors, and publishers who have permitted us to quote longer passages: Walter B. Barbe; Emmett A. Betts; the Children's Book Council of New York City; E. W. Dolch; Harper & Brothers; J. N. Hook; Thomas D. Horn; the International Reading Association and the *Reading Teacher* (Russell G. Stauffer, Editor); May Lazar; Helen Rand Miller; the National Council of Teachers of English, chiefly for quotations from its magazine, *Elementary English*; the Board of Education of the City of New York and its Bureau of Educational Research; Mary O'Rourke; the Superintendent of Public Instruction, Springfield, Illinois; the University of Chicago Press; Lester Wheeler; and Edwin H. Smith. Appreciation is expressed also to those schools and school systems that made photographs available to us. Individual credits appear with each picture. We are especially grateful to Professor Ruth Strickland of Indiana University for her careful reading of the manuscript and her thoughtful commentary on it. Her suggestions have improved the book, but she should not be held responsible for its point of view or for any errors that may appear in it.

J. J. DeB.
M.D.

Champaign, Illinois
Delaware, Ohio
January, 1960

Contents

PREFACE TO THE REVISED EDITION   *v*
PREFACE TO THE FIRST EDITION   *vii*

PART ONE / Reading and Child Development   *1*

  1.   The Challenge of Reading   *3*
  2.   The Setting for Reading   *11*
  3.   The Nature of Reading   *17*
  4.   Elements Essential to Growth in Reading   *26*

PART TWO / Cultivating Growth in Reading Abilities   *39*

  5A.   Readiness for Reading   *41*
  5B.   Developing Readiness for Reading   *60*
  6A.   Word Recognition   *83*
  6B.   Developing Skill in Word Recognition   *109*
  7A.   Reading with Comprehension   *130*
  7B.   Developing Comprehension in Reading   *146*
  8A.   Reading Rates   *170*
  8B.   Developing Appropriate Reading Rates   *182*
  9A.   Locating Information   *195*
  9B.   Developing Ability To Locate Information   *211*
  10A. Oral Reading   *227*
  10B. Developing Skill in Oral Reading   *236*
  11A. Children's Interests in Reading   *249*
  11B. Developing Children's Interests in Reading   *269*
  12.   Providing for Individual Differences   *293*
  13.   Helping the Retarded and the Unusually Gifted Child in Reading   *306*

PART THREE / The Reading Program in Action   *349*

  14.   The Reading Program in the Primary Grades   *351*
  15.   The Reading Program in the Intermediate Grades   *372*
  16.   The School-wide Program in Reading   *383*
  17.   The Social Uses of Reading   *403*

INDEX   *411*

Reading
and
Child Development

1

The Challenge of Reading

Our age has been variously called the Age of Science, the Atomic Age, the Space Age, the Age of Crisis. We must leave to future historians the choice of a name that will most completely describe our times. They might say, "It was the best of times; it was the worst of times," but if they should unearth a copy of Dickens' *A Tale of Two Cities,* for instance, they would find that this description also fits an earlier period.

For readers of this book it would be useful to think of the present period as the Age of Communication. We can talk directly to people who live on the far side of the globe. The air waves everywhere vibrate with words. Scientific discoveries have made possible a succession of inventions which have overcome the barriers to communication among the nearly three billion human inhabitants of this planet. Telephone, telegraph, radio, television, teletype, and various methods of voice recording are examples of the ways in which language symbols have now become the means of bringing human beings together.

The Values of Reading

Yet technology has not replaced reading. The printed page reaches millions still untouched by electronics, and for those who can take advantage of the newer devices, reading still serves unique purposes. It is many things to many people. It is a telescope, because through it we can look at the distant stars and speculate about life upon them. It is a microscope, because through it we cannot only examine the chromosomes and the atoms, but also infer those minute particles which even the finest lenses cannot reveal. It is a never-ending widescreen film on which the human pageant passes in review. It is still the only known time machine that can recreate the events of the past and open up the vistas of the future. Primitive man calls reading magic, and he is right.

Reading meets needs which the newer media cannot fully satisfy. Gray and Rogers have expressed this thought well:

> It is an indispensable factor in modern life, interwoven with work, recreation, and other activities of young people and adults. Its great value lies in two facts: printed materials provide the most illuminating and varied records of human experience that are now available; and they can be examined and restudied time and again at the reader's convenience in acquiring clear understandings, in developing rational attitudes, and in reaching sound conclusions. Some of these values cannot be attained so effectively through other media because the individual is not free to pause and deliberate at will.[1]

Not since the invention of the printing press has direct communication, most of it involving reading in one way or another, played so large a part in human affairs. Today's situation is admirably described in a report of the Allerton House Conference on Education:

> America's largest industry is communication—reading, writing, listening, speaking. That fact is seldom recognized because communication is an integral part of every industry and business in America and has a separate existence only in such things as newspapers, magazines, radio, television, telephone, and telegraph. Here are three examples of the importance of communication in America's economic life.
>
> Item: A major railroad has estimated that about two-thirds of its annual payroll is expended for sending and receiving spoken and written messages. . . .
>
> Item: In the manufacture of an automobile, communication begins playing a part when a foreman in the Mesabi Iron Range gives instructions to his men. . . . The advertising that helps sell the car is communication. . . . The raw materials of which the car is made are ordinarily worth only two or three hundred dollars. The physical labor and the cost of plant and equipment represent considerably more. But when all the communication costs are totaled, it becomes apparent that the greatest share of the cost of the automobile is for words. It does not seem unreasonable to estimate that for an automobile costing three thousand dollars, fifteen hundred is spent for words. He who buys a three-thousand-dollar automobile is driving fifteen hundred dollars worth of words over the highway.
>
> Item: The major expenditures of government are for words. Tens of

---

[1] William S. Gray and Bernice Rogers, *Maturity in Reading*, p. 8. Chicago: The University of Chicago Press, 1956.

thousands of stenographers in Washington, Springfield, the county court-
house, and the city hall immortalize these words in quadruplicate. . . .
When expenditures of all branches of the government total one hundred
billion dollars, it seems rather conservative to say that sixty billions of those
dollars are spent for communication. . . . Communication *is* America's
biggest industry.[2]

Reading, one of the major avenues of communication, is essential to the
existence of our complex system of social arrangements. But it is more than that.
It is the means by which every age is linked to every other. It makes possible
man's capacity for "time binding," the ability to perceive himself in the historic
process and the fluid universe around him. If all the inventions of a hundred
years were destroyed and only books were left, man could still be man, in the
sense intended by the idealists, the poets, the great creators. Teaching reading is
a humanizing process.

Public Interest in Reading Ability

In view of these values, it is not surprising that there has always been so
much concern over the question whether Johnny is learning to read. In our own
country, from the days of the *New England Primer* to the present, adults have
eagerly watched their young take their first faltering steps in the world of print.
Each year they spend hundreds of millions of dollars to make reading instruction possible. Each year more than 10 percent of all new books published are
for children. Today, the public concern with reading ability is reflected in many
popular books, magazine articles, pamphlets, newspaper columns, and editorials
devoted to the subject. Surely the teacher of reading is engaged in work of vital
importance to the public.

Efforts at the Improvement of Reading

The teaching profession has responded to the public interest by constant
intensive efforts to discover ways of improving reading instruction. Four major
reports of the National Society for the Study of Education (1925, 1937, 1949,
and 1961) have been devoted to the subject. Conferences devoted to reading and
the language arts are annually sponsored by colleges and universities, many of
which (*e.g.,* The University of Chicago, the University of Pittsburgh, Temple
University, Claremont College) publish regular volumes of proceedings. Numerous organizations, notably the National Council of Teachers of English, the

---

2 "The Teaching of English in Illinois," *Educational Press Bulletin,* February 1958. Office
of the Superintendent of Public Instruction, Springfield, Illinois. Quoted from J. N. Hook.

National Conference on Research in English, the American Educational Research Association, and the International Reading Association, devote much or all of their attention to problems in the teaching of reading. Large school systems issue bulletins and detailed course outlines on reading. Publishers supply, with their basal reading series, manuals which are often practically equivalent to textbooks on the teaching of reading. Special monographs provide bibliographies and research summaries dealing with reading. Educational periodicals regularly publish articles describing newer practices or viewpoints or reporting and summarizing research in the field. Among these are the *Journal of Educational Research*, the *Elementary School Journal*, the *Reading Teacher*, the *English Journal, Elementary English*, the *Journal of Developmental Reading*, and *Education*. All of these are in addition to the various magazines dealing with libraries and children's literature. More than 4000 individual research studies in reading have been published in England and America since 1880, most of them in the last thirty years.

All of these discussions, investigations, and reports have not led to complete agreement about methods of teaching reading. Indeed, the differences of opinion are often sharp and the debates are sometimes acrimonious. Nevertheless, there is a substantial body of agreement on many important issues. For example, it seems clear from the research that no one method is best for all children under all circumstances, that children differ widely in the kinds of instruction they need. It seems clear also that a wide variety of approaches must be used in order to get best results with most children. Moreover, we have learned much about the psychology of reading, about the role of emotion, motivation, home background, and other factors in reading retardation. We have learned most of all, perhaps, about the nature and extent of individual differences in reading.

Individual Differences in Reading

Individual differences among children provide perhaps the greatest challenge to the teacher of reading. Although all teachers know there are differences among their pupils, many are not fully aware of the vast range of those differences. What they need to learn is the fact that these differences are normal, that they exist at birth and increase as the children grow older. Children differ in every identifiable characteristic—in height, weight, color of hair and eyes, intelligence, home background, emotional adjustment, and educational achievement, to name but a few examples.

The more complex a skill is, the greater the differences in ability are likely to be. Since reading is a highly complex skill, children differ greatly in their reading needs and achievement. They show variation in the extent to which they are prepared to begin reading when they first enter school. The range in reading ability among pupils in any grade is very wide. Indeed, the better the instruction, the greater the probable range in a classroom. Even among pupils who make equal scores on reading tests, the differences in the *nature* of reading problems and of the reading abilities which produced the scores are significant and numerous.

Individualization in silent reading does not imply, of course, that silent reading is unrelated to the social experiences of the children. Children will read aloud from books which they have enjoyed. They will dramatize stories they have read. The story hour will be enriched by anecdotes from their own reading. But the silent reading remains individual, as it must, without the harmful ritual in which the better readers embarrass the stumbling victim by showing him, amid waving hands, that they know what he does not.

The Complexity of Reading

Reading is a challenge to the teacher also because it is such a complex process. Reading is not a general ability, but a composite of many specific abilities. It is therefore necessary to break down general comprehension into the specific skills which together constitute it. It is necessary to inquire how well the child is able to grasp the general meaning of a passage; how well he can differentiate between fact and opinion; how well he can follow directions; how well he can interpret maps, graphs, and tables; how well he can organize what he reads and classify ideas; how well he can visualize what he reads; and how well he can locate information.

A single reading skill, although a very important one, well illustrates the complexity of reading. Any teacher who undertakes to cultivate, for instance, children's critical discrimination in reading finds that she is dealing with a whole cluster of abilities. Among these are classifying ideas, distinguishing between fact and fancy and between fact and opinion, establishing cause and effect, making generalizations, interpreting idiomatic and figurative language, making inferences, recognizing emotional reactions and motives, judging relevancy, and drawing general conclusions. These abilities must be taught, either with the aid of basal readers or the child's general experiences with research-type or recreatory reading, or both.[3]

Reading and Knowledge

Reading is an important means of introducing the child to the surrounding world. In this fact we find our opportunity as well as our challenge. Through

---

[3] Gertrude Williams, "Provisions for Critical Reading in Basic Readers," *Elementary English*, 36 (May 1959), 323–331. Also reprinted in Elona Sochor, *Teaching Critical Reading*, a bulletin of the National Conference on Research in English. Champaign, Illinois: The National Council of Teachers of English, 1959.

reading the child can view ever-widening horizons and explore ever-new areas in the world of things, people, and events. School need never be dull as long as there are books to tell about the earth, the sea, the sky, faraway places, events past and present, or the plants and animals and physical phenomena around us.

It must require some ingenuity to turn the study of our wonderful world into a dreary chore, but somehow we often succeed in doing so. Consider, for example, the plight of the fifth-grade child filling in the blanks of a workbook that demands in what part of West Virginia hay is raised or what the present population of New Jersey is. Very few elementary school children want to know these facts or have any idea of what to do with them when they find them. Such busywork is necessary only when the school has no books other than textbooks or when the teacher does not know how to teach the use of an atlas, an almanac, or an encyclopedia.

Contrast this picture of an elementary school child with that of one who has discovered a special issue of the *National Geographic Magazine* dealing with our Eastern states or become absorbed in a book about our national parks or the life of a great hero. The difference is that in the one case the pupil is engaging in an essentially purposeless activity; in the other he is actively reaching out for information to satisfy his curiosity and to find answers to his own questions.

The pupil's knowledge is the distillation of his impressions gained from abundant reading. The residue left by these impressions keeps growing and changing as his contact with the world of reality through experiences with books expands. For this reason, many teachers encourage their pupils to read whole books about important topics, rather than merely a few pages in a textbook. The availability of reliable, interesting children's books in nearly all areas of study has fundamentally altered the pattern of instruction in many elementary school subjects. The key to learning, therefore, is the cultivation not only of the ability to read, but also of the love of reading. Young children must be helped to think of reading as an activity with an inherent appeal. The child who loves to read is father to the man who keeps informed through reading.

Reading and Personality

Reading involves skill, it involves thinking, but considered in its broader sense it affects the entire personality. The world of people and events encountered on the printed page may shape a reader's attitude toward his fellows, toward school, toward parents, and toward life in general. It may heighten his appreciation of the physical world about him or give him a sense of excitement about the future. On the other hand, it may cause perplexity, fear, or anxiety. The teacher bears a great responsibility for the judicious selection of reading matter to which the learner is exposed and for providing expert guidance in the interpretation of what is read.

Especially to the young child in school, successful and happy experiences with reading will determine in great measure his feelings about himself and his social environment. He knows, often before he starts school, that success in reading is essential to success in school. He may be afraid of the reading task, or frustrated when he has difficulty, or rebellious to all adult authority. It is incumbent upon the teacher to make the child feel comfortable and at ease and to give him many opportunities for success experiences that build self-confidence.

Reading and Citizenship

Our age is one that constantly demands great decisions, decisions which affect the future—even the survival—of the human race. Never before in history has so much depended upon the knowledge and wisdom of both the rulers and the ruled. We need, of course, an informed electorate if government by the consent of the governed is to have real meaning. But perhaps even more, we need an informed leadership. The greatest of our statesmen have been well-informed men—men with a wide reading background, knowledge, and the ability to use the knowledge of others in specific areas. The future leaders of local, state, and national governments, of industry, finance, and the military are at this moment passing through the most critical stage of their apprenticeship in our elementary school classes. If their early experiences in school help them to lay the right foundations, we may look to wise and knowledgeable leadership later. The teacher of reading in the elementary school has indeed a heavy responsibility.

FOR FURTHER STUDY

Bobbitt, Franklin, *The Curriculum of Modern Education*, pp. 137–176. New York: McGraw-Hill Book Company, Inc., 1941.

Causey, Oscar S., ed., *The Reading Teacher's Reader*, pp. 255–267. New York: The Ronald Press Company, 1958.

Hildreth, Gertrude, *Teaching Reading*, pp. 1–14. New York: Holt, Rinehart and Winston, Inc., 1958.

LaBrant, Lou, "Personal Factors in Reading," *Reading in an Age of Mass Communication*, William S. Gray, ed., pp. 39–57. New York: Appleton-Century-Crofts, 1949.

Meeker, Alice M., *Teaching Beginners to Read*. Rinehart Education Pamphlets. New York: Holt, Rinehart and Winston, Inc., 1958.

Travers, John F., "Reading Teachers Are Made—Not Born," *Education,* 83 (September 1962), 15–19.

Tyler, Fred T., and William A. Brownell, "Facts and Issues: A Concluding Statement," *Individualizing Instruction,* pp. 316–328. Sixty-first Yearbook of the National Society for the Study of Education, Part I, Nelson B. Henry, ed. Chicago: The University of Chicago Press, 1962.

Witty, Paul, *Reading in Modern Education,* pp. 1–16. Boston: D. C. Heath and Company, 1949.

2

The Setting for Reading

This book will describe how a great miracle happens. It will tell of the transformation that takes place in a child who enters first grade at six, often unable to recognize one word in print, and emerges six years later able to read newspapers, magazines, and books.

Arthur is an example. When Arthur started school, he did not care whether he would ever learn to read. He was unaccustomed to taking part in group activities. He was not attracted to the library table with its many lovely picture books, which so many of the other boys and girls liked to examine. Arthur spent most of his time at the easel, drawing pictures of airplanes. He seemed happiest when no one spoke to him. Yet, six years later, he could read fluently and with understanding many parts of the *World Book Encyclopedia, Compton's Pictured Encyclopedia, Our Wonderful World,* and the *Junior Britannica.* He read *Boys' Life, Junior Natural History Magazine, My Weekly Reader,* and even some adult newspapers. He continued to be interested in aviation, but he also read, on his own, books about many other subjects, both fiction and nonfiction. A new world had been opened to him through books.

Then there was Judy, who upon entering first grade was eager to learn to read but was so shy that in the first week it taxed the ingenuity of her teacher to keep her from crying. Although Judy had learned to say the *abc's* through the persistent efforts of oversolicitous parents, she showed her immaturity for reading by the difficulty she had in differentiating between letters like *b* and *d* and *m* and *n*. However, after six years in the elementary school, Judy was reading about two books a week, in addition to the reading she was doing in school. She regularly read the magazine, *The American Girl,* and enjoyed books like

Amos Fortune, Free Man by Elizabeth Yates, *The Story of Clara Barton* by O. M. Price, and *Patrick Henry, Firebrand of the Revolution* by Nardi Reeder Campion.[1] Reading had become for Judy a source of both pleasure and much worthwhile information. Judy had developed effective methods of recognizing independently new words she met in her reading. She was reading with understanding at rates appropriate to her purposes, and she had learned the art of reading critically. She was also able to locate and use reference materials with dispatch and ease.

What brings about these great changes in the many boys and girls who, like Arthur and Judy, acquire reading ability in so short a time? A description of a few imaginary scenes, typical of those in modern elementary school classrooms, will give some hint of the climate in which reading ability grows.

A View of a Modern Elementary School Classroom

A visit in Miss Smith's first-grade room early in the fall revealed even to the casual observer many ways in which she indirectly interested the boys and girls in reading. In one corner of the room was a library table well equipped with picture books. On the top of a low bookcase was a papier-mâché cat, fully a foot in length, while near it was displayed the book by Wanda Gág, *Millions of Cats*. On a bulletin board was a picture of a boy seemingly happily absorbed while reading a book about pets. In the front part of the room in two concentric half circles were seated the 26 children who comprised the first grade, listening attentively to Miss Smith. She was reading *The Three Billy Goats Gruff*, preparatory to the pantomiming by the class of the encounters of the three goats.

Harold rushed to his second-grade room eager to show to his teacher a shell that his uncle had sent him from Florida. After he and Miss Taylor talked about it, Harold dictated some sentences about his shell, which the teacher wrote, first on small-sized paper and later on large lined paper. The completed chart had at the top of the piece of paper a large picture, in color, that Harold had drawn of his prized possession. Below was a report, entitled "My Shell." The next day Harold, who was still finding a preprimer difficult although he was in the second grade, was to be given the opportunity to show his shell to the other pupils in the room and to read to them the message on the chart.

In Miss Baxter's third-grade room the boys and girls were receiving meaningful practice in locating reading materials and finding passages bearing upon a given topic. They were given help in developing these locational skills while

---

[1] *Amos Fortune, Free Man* by Elizabeth Yates (New York: Aladdin, 1950); *Story of Clara Barton* by O. M. Price (New York: Grossett and Dunlap, Inc., 1954); and *Patrick Henry, Firebrand of the Revolution* by Nardi Reeder Campion (Boston: Little, Brown and Company, 1962).

My Shell

I have a shell.
It is pink.
It is a large shell.
My uncle gave the shell to me.
He sent it from Florida.
I like to listen to the shell.

they were working on a unit on transportation. In studying the aviation phase of the unit, the pupils wanted answers to such questions as these: (1) What makes airplanes stay up in the air? (2) What were the first airplanes like? (3) Who are the "heroes of the air"? After the pupils had formulated questions for investigation, they were given experience in finding books in the library dealing with aviation, readable by at least some of the boys and girls in the class. Among those selected were *The First Book of Airplanes* by Jeanne Bendick, *The Noon Balloon* by Margaret Wise Brown, *How Airplanes Are Made* by David C. Cooke, *Young America's Aviation Manual* by David C. Cooke, *Model Planes for Beginners* by H. H. Gilmore, *The Little Airplane* by Lois Lenski, *Helicopters: How They Work* by John B. Lewellen, *Jet Transports* by John B. Lewellen, *The Boys' Book of Space* by Patrick Moore, *The Story Book of Aircraft* by Maude and Miska Petersham, *Let's Find Out, A Picture Science Book* by Nina and Herrman Schneider, and *Wings in Your Future* by Leo Schneider and Maurice U. Ames.[2]

---

2 Jeanne Bendick, *The First Book of Airplanes* (New York: Franklin Watts, 1952); Margaret Wise Brown, *The Noon Balloon* (New York: Harper and Row, Publishers, 1952); David C. Cooke, *How Airplanes Are Made* (New York: Dodd, Mead and Company, Inc., 1956); David C. Cooke, *Young America's Aviation Manual* (New York: The McBride Company, 1954); H. H. Gilmore, *Model Planes for Beginners* (New York: Harper and Row, Publishers, Inc., 1942); Lois Lenski, *The Little Airplane* (New York: Oxford University Press, 1938); John B. Lewellen, *Helicopters: How They Work* (New York: Thomas Y. Crowell Company, 1954); John B.

The next problem was to find what information these books contained on the three questions already listed and on others that were suggested. Each book was assigned to one or more pupils who were responsible for collecting the information on the questions. At the same time, however, that the boys and girls were looking for answers to their questions, they were also searching for additional information on the topic of the unit. After all the books had been examined and read, at least in part, by someone, the questions were discussed in class. Each pupil reported on the answers he had found and, with the help of the teacher, committees of boys and girls recorded answers to the questions.

In another room Miss Olson read to her fourth grade a message she had just received from the principal asking them if they would be responsible for an assembly program on Lincoln's birthday. The pupils decided to comply with the request. After brief discussion they agreed that before they could come to a wise decision as to the content of the program, they would need to read extensively on the topic.

In Miss Whiteside's fifth-grade room the boys and girls were engaging in a variety of purposeful activities that promote growth in reading skills. A large map of the United States entitled "Who's Who in the U.S.A.?" was posted on a bulletin board. On it were written the names of the famous Americans about whom the pupils were studying in a unit on "Modern Americans." Attached to each place mentioned on the map was a ribbon that connected the name of the place with an object or model representative of the contribution of the person associated with the place. A model of the first kind of airplane used in the United States was connected with Kitty Hawk, North Carolina, to represent the work of the Wright brothers. A river boat carved out of wood was fastened to a ribbon that led to Hannibal, Missouri, the boyhood home of Samuel Clemens. Two boys and one girl were standing in front of the map and studying it intently. At a nearby table a second girl was drawing a picture of Hull House, which she said she planned to use to illustrate the work of Jane Addams, the founder of this famous Chicago settlement house. Several pupils were reading independently an encyclopedia for children. One was looking for material about Will Rogers, another about Clara Barton, and a third about Maud Ballington Booth. In one corner of the room four children on a committee were busily planning how they could present to the class the material that they had gathered about Thomas Edison. After considerable discussion they decided to make a poster illustrating many of his contributions.

In another part of the room five pupils were working on a dramatization

---

Lewellen, *Jet Transports* (New York: Thomas Y. Crowell Company, 1955); Patrick Moore, *The Boys' Book of Space* (New York: Roy Publishers, 1956); Maude and Miska Petersham, *The Story Book of Aircraft* (Philadelphia: Holt, Rinehart and Winston, Inc., 1935); Nina and Herrman Schneider, *Let's Find Out, A Picture Science Book* (New York: William R. Scott, Inc., 1946); Leo Schneider and Maurice U. Ames, *Wings in Your Future* (New York: Harcourt, Brace and World, Inc., 1955).

to illustrate scenes from the life of William Cody. Meanwhile Miss Whiteside was helping one girl, seriously retarded in reading, to read *George Carver, Boy Scientist*.[3] With the help of the art teacher, who had been called in as consultant, three boys were making a model, chiefly in clay, of the Panama Canal. The boys explained to the visitor that the group had been reading several sources describing the structure of the canal and that after they had completed their model, they would connect it on the large map on the bulletin board with the country of Panama. This part of the display, the boys said, was to help others in the room realize the great contribution of George W. Goethals, who made possible the construction of the canal through his laboratory studies and through his skill in making the results of his research quickly available to the public. Still another committee had just finished writing on the board the program they planned to give to the rest of the class the next day. Since their special work was on Helen Keller, they had listed this as their program:

Helen Keller, the Blind Woman Who Learned to "See"

1. Report on the early life of Helen Keller
2. Demonstration of braille
3. Dramatization of a scene from Helen Keller's life
4. "Quiz program" about Helen Keller.

In a sixth grade taught by Mrs. Spooner, David excitedly brought to school a letter from a pen pal in Germany. Since the letter was written in German, David, at his teacher's suggestion, asked Mr. Schmidt, the custodian, who grew up in Germany, whether he would have time to translate the letter. As Mr. Schmidt translated the letter, David jotted down the message. Before he left, Mr. Schmidt volunteered to write in German the reply that David would write in English. As David read the translated letter to the class, several questions were asked of him about Germany, some of which he could not answer. David agreed to try to find the answer to these questions: (1) Where is Heidelberg? (2) Was Heidelberg bombed during World War II? (3) For what is Heidelberg famous? After David had found the answers to the questions by consulting the encyclopedia, he posted the questions and answers on a bulletin board so that the information would be available to everyone.

Miss Burton's sixth-grade room also furnished an excellent example of how the individual pupil can thrive in the atmosphere of the modern elementary school. The pupils were all working on a unit on "Contributions of Greece to Civilization." Some were reading independently to gather more information on topics that they had volunteered to investigate. History textbooks, library books, and reference books were used. Four children were carving soap replicas

---

[3] Augusta Stevenson, *George Carver, Boy Scientist*. Indianapolis: The Bobbs-Merrill Company, Inc., 1944.

of various types of columns used in Old Greece. Three pupils were busy putting up an exhibit of materials they would need the next day when they would be reporting to the class their findings on the topic, "The life of an Athenian boy." Another group was discussing how they would present their material the following day on "The life of a Spartan boy." In the meantime, the teacher was giving special help to three boys and a girl. One of the boys was reading silently a selection from an easy book of Greek myths. To guide him in his study of the selection, the teacher had prepared questions in written form. Another of the boys, who lacked skill in using the index of a book, was preparing under the supervision of the teacher an index for a notebook on the unit that his committee had compiled. A third boy was working on an outline for a report that he was to give as part of the culminating activity. From time to time the teacher helped him, for she realized that in previous attempts at outlining he had shown marked deficiencies. Part of the time the teacher was listening to Sally, who was practicing for oral reading that she was to do later in the week as her committee presented their findings on Greek architecture. Since Sally had difficulty in oral reading, the teacher helped her diagnose her points of weakness and strength and gave her suggestions for making improvement as well as opportunity to put into effect the suggestions given.

In classrooms such as these, children are daily growing in their mastery of the process of reading. In the chapters to come, we will see how this miracle is accomplished.

3

The Nature of Reading

In former days, reading was considered to be a relatively simple mechanical skill. Even today this conception is still held by many people who are unfamiliar with the psychology of the reading act. Some think of reading as a sounding out of printed words, either with or without a comprehension of meaning. Others restrict their concept of reading to the ability to read aloud, assuming that good oral readers automatically make good silent readers.

Reading is a much more complex process. We know that effective reading involves all of the higher mental processes. It involves recall, reasoning, evaluation, imagining, organizing, applying, and problem solving. Good reading requires good thinking. When we teach reading, especially in the beginning stages, we must teach good thinking.

Some definitions of reading, however, are perhaps too broad. The Claremont College (California) conferences on reading follow the thesis that reading includes all perceptive observation of the real world around us. In this sense, reading becomes synonymous with education itself. While such a definition is justifiable if its terms are made sufficiently explicit, we must admit that most people today do not attach a similar connotation to the word "reading." In this book we shall think of reading as an activity which involves the comprehension and interpretation of ideas symbolized by written or printed language.

What Happens in Reading?

To understand the role of the various elements that are important to growth in reading, it is helpful to consider the question, "What really takes place when a person reads?"

The reader is looking at an object in the form of a book or a magazine or a billboard or a road sign. Most commonly the object consists of paper, usually white. On the paper appear certain marks made, as a rule, by the application of a dark-colored ink. That is all. Just ink marks on white paper. And yet looking at those marks may cause a person to turn pale, as in the case of a letter containing bad news, or to laugh, or to smile, or to cry, or to hold his breath in suspense. A laboratory test would reveal that a reader's pulse rate may at times rise sharply when he looks at those curious ink marks on paper. How can the seeing of these marks bring about such striking mental and physical experiences?

There is no *meaning* on the page, only ink. The meaning is in the reader's mind. Each mark is a signal that arouses some image or concept that is already in the mind of the reader. The order in which these images and concepts are evoked, the context in which they are called forth, and the relations between these images and concepts as revealed by the arrangement of these marks, make it possible for the reader to gain new meanings. But the process depends on what the reader brings to the printed page and on the questions he asks.

It has often been said that reading is an *active* process. Good reading is a reaching out, a searching for meaning. The child must go to the printed page with anticipation, with questions, with specific intent. A person turns to a newspaper with the purpose of finding out what has happened recently. He searches the headlines and chooses a story that arouses his curiosity. He reads the story in order to find out what the headline means. He gets real meaning from what he reads because he has asked questions as he has gone along.

The following conversation[1] never took place, but it illustrates the need for an active, creative approach to reading:

> *Book:* Won't you please ask me a question?
> *Man:* Why do you ask that?
> *Book:* Because I can only ask you to ask me questions and can only answer the questions you ask.
> *Man:* Why don't you just tell me what you have to say?
> *Book:* I can't. I have nothing to tell you except answers to your questions.
> *Man:* Haven't you the same thing to say to every reader, all put down in black and white?
> *Book:* No! I never say the same thing twice. Black letters on white paper are nothing in themselves. You can only read meaning, and so much of that is in you. You never ask the same question twice because you are living and that means changing all the time. Your experience and your interests grow if you are alive.
> *Man:* I'll read you from cover to cover; I'll read every word. I won't miss a thing. I'll pass an examination on you!

[1] By Helen Rand Miller, from *Creative Reading*, by Helen Rand Miller and John J. DeBoer. Seymour, Ind.: Graessle-Mercer Company, 1950.

Book: Oh, vain, stupid, foolish little man, to say that you will get out of me all that is in me. You can't. There is nothing in me except as you bring me to life in your living mind, imagination, and heart.

Man: So you don't live except as you live with living people?

Book: That's right. Nothing does. You don't yourself.

Man: But how can I ask you questions before I know what you have to say?

Book: Use your brain. Think of what I might be able to tell you. I didn't say that you had to ask all your questions before you began to read. Let's have a little cooperation. Ask me one question at a time and look for my answer. Keep on asking questions as you read. Think ahead as you look ahead when you drive your car. What happens when you don't know where you are driving? It's your responsibility to ask me the questions that will let me be at my best in answering you.

Man: I don't always want to work when I read. Sometimes I just want to enjoy my reading. I'd like to relax while you entertain me.

Book: And I want you to enjoy yourself whether you are working or just enjoying yourself. You'll have more fun if you are a bit companionable. It won't tire you to go along with a character and ask, "Does he love me? Will he come?"

Man: So I must play along with the characters in a story I'm reading for pleasure.

Book: Of course, if you are to share their pleasure. If you don't do your part, you let me down.

Man: And what if you don't answer the questions I want answered?

Book: Then I let you down. Don't waste your time and wear me out unless I have what you want.

Man: Don't I have to read you to find out whether you have what I want?

Book: No, not if you know how to have a good look at me.

Man: So, I must learn to ask questions?

Book: Yes, everything depends upon that.

Reading as Symbolic Behavior

Man communicates through symbols. A symbol may be a physical act, such as a grimace, a smile, a nodding of the head, or an upraised hand in a discussion. Traffic lights and highway signs are symbols. Spoken language is a complex set of symbols consisting of various combinations of speech sounds. Any representation perceptible to the senses may serve as a symbol.

In reading we employ visual symbols to represent auditory symbols. The basic task in reading is therefore to establish in the mind of the reader automatic connections between specific sights and the sounds they represent. Since the sounds themselves are symbols of meanings, the process of reading involves a hierarchy of skills ranging from auditory and visual discrimination to such higher order mental activities as organizing ideas, making generalizations, and drawing inferences.

By the time they first enter school, most children have learned to use the symbols of the spoken language to the extent of their needs and their level of development. Some evidence indicates that they have already mastered all the basic sentence patterns of their native tongue. Some children, in fact, have already made a beginning in the substitution of visual for auditory symbols. They have started on the road to reading. In any case, the teacher of primary reading has a strong foundation on which to build.

Eye Movements in Reading

The visual symbol of the written or printed word is the means by which the appropriate sounds and images are evoked in the mind of the reader. Contrary to the common belief, reading does not take place while the eyes move across the line. If a letter, a word, or a phrase is to be perceived, the eyes must pause long enough to take it in. Since in fluent reading the pauses or "fixations" may be as brief as one-fourth of a second, the reader has the illusion that he is reading as the eyes move from left to right on the page. Actually, the movement of the eyes from one stopping point to the next takes a fraction of a second, so that in effect the view of the words in a line seems continuous. The interruptions between the pauses may be likened to the breaks between the individual photographs that make up a motion picture. When we look at a movie, we are not conscious of the fact that we are really seeing an extremely rapid succession of still pictures. So, too, it is when we read a line of type. We cannot "see" while our eyes are in motion.

The important point in the reading act, then, is the instant when the eyes fix upon a specific spot in the line. All else depends on what the reader sees and perceives in this instant. If he sees and perceives only individual letters or small groups of letters, he will not be reading, because meaning is constructed, not from letters, but from whole words. This is not to say that individual letters will not often help in the perception of the word as a whole. It means only that the reader must perceive the whole word or group of words while the eyes pause. Unless he does so, he is not really reading.

Various methods have been employed in reading laboratories and clinics to study the eye-movement behavior of readers. One of the most common methods has been the photographic method. One instrument, known as the ophthalmograph, makes motion-picture records of eye movements in the process of silent reading. The subject is asked to read a passage on a card. As he reads, a ray of light is directed toward his eyes. As the light reaches the eyes, the corneas reflect it upon a moving film. The film thus records the movements of the eyes as the latter pass from left to right on the line and as they return to the beginning of the next line. It records the number of "fixations" on each line, the order in which the reader fixes upon each word or phrase, the duration of each fixation, the number of "regressive movements" (return to previous points of fixation), "periods of confusion" (points of difficulty which are revealed by numerous regressive movements), and the accuracy of the "return sweep" (the movement of the eyes to the beginning of the next line).

In the initial stages of reading, the child's eyes may wander over the page in search of familiar words. As competence grows, under the skilled guidance of the teacher, he learns to confine his observation to one line at a time and to move in a habitual progression from left to right. At first, duration of each fixation will tend to be relatively long—perhaps as much as nine-tenths of a second. There will be many fixations per line. There will be many regressive movements in which the reader will make return movements to words that were not recognized or comprehended the first time. When a word gives special difficulty, there will be many regressions, and the ophthalmograph film would show a period of confusion. After much experience, and especially when interest is high, the duration of each fixation will decrease and the number of fixations per line will become steadily smaller. Eventually, as the child masters the basic skills and increases his stock of words recognized at sight, he becomes able to read each line in a fairly regular, rhythmical series of fixations, with a minimum number of regressive movements. By the fourth grade, the frequency of fixations and the number of regressions commonly tend to level off somewhat (always provided that the material is within the reader's comprehension), and the basic eye-movement habits have become reasonably well established. Some studies seem to show an additional spurt at the beginning of the high school period and indicate that the normal growth in rate of reading may continue until grade 10. Individual differences and training will, of course, affect each child's rate of growth, and it must be emphasized that improvement in both rate and comprehension may be brought about at any age.

Regular eye movements, however, are a symptom rather than a cause of good reading. The efforts that have been made in some instances to "pace" a child's eye movements or to change his reading habits by means of mechanical devices appear to have doubtful value. No doubt many boys and girls improve in their ability to recognize words at sight as a result of exercises with such devices, for any method which will enable a child to recognize a word quickly and accurately will contribute effectively to his reading ability, provided it is accompanied by procedures which sustain and stimulate his genuine interest in the content. But the basic efforts in instruction should be to focus on meaning and to provide abundant opportunity for contact with the printed word in normal, well-motivated reading situations.

Visual Shapes, Sounds, and Meanings

In approaching written or printed material, the child typically converts the visual shapes of letters and words into their corresponding sounds. At the beginning he probably utters the sounds aloud or to himself. The sounds then evoke in his mind the images and meanings which they represent. As he gains proficiency, he depends less and less on the sound "bridge" between visual stimulus and meaning, although a faint awareness of speech sounds is probably always present in reading. If the sound images continue to be prominent in the child's reading, he will develop habits of vocalization and possibly lip-movement. Both speed and comprehension will then suffer. The connection between visual stimulus and meaning must become as direct as possible, as soon as possible.

In order to establish habits of meaningful reading at the outset, most teachers begin reading instruction with the whole word, which is the smallest meaning-bearing unit, as contrasted with the phoneme, the smallest sound-bearing unit, which by itself ordinarily carries no meaning. The child can identify many short words as quickly and easily as he can individual letters. As we have seen, the mature reader does not read letter by letter, but rather in a series of relatively few, brief fixations of the eye per line. Effective reading, then, involves instantaneous recognition of whole words or even phrases. For this reason, the beginning reader is introduced to whole words which appear again and again in ordinary printed discourse. Reading must become as soon as possible a process of thought getting. It is of the utmost importance that, especially in the initial stages, reading should be relatively fluent, rather than a laborious process of deciphering the sounds of words. Basic habits of meaningful reading should be established at the very beginning of instruction.

It is clear, however, that it would be impossible for a child to learn to recognize at sight all the words he is likely to encounter. He must master certain skills which will enable him to recognize new words independently. The nature of these skills and the methods of teaching them will be discussed in Chapters 6A and 6B.

The term "phonics," which is based on the Greek word meaning "sound," is used to designate the practice of sounding out a word in order to identify it. Naturally, if the sounding out is to help in getting meaning, the word must already be a part of the child's vocabulary. In contrast to the alphabet method, phonics deals with *phonograms*, or visual symbols for speech sounds. Since the individual letters of the alphabet may have more than one sound, and since some sounds are made by combinations of letters, the phonics method must be distinguished from the alphabet method. Thus *a* in *cat* is a different phonogram from *a* in *late*. Thus also the letters *ph* and *gh* constitute individual phonograms.

Some linguists and some educators look upon phonics as the natural method of teaching reading. They reason that since words are made up of sounds in various combinations, a child will be able to read if he knows all the symbols which stand for the various sounds of the English language. For example, the late Leonard Bloomfield recommended that the child be introduced first to the letters of the alphabet, one phonetic value at a time. He urged that the child be taught to read by means of a sequence of four stages, in which the aim would be to develop the habit of connecting letters with sounds.

A contrary view is expressed by James E. McDade, who opposes "sounding" in beginning reading. He explains his position in the following way:

> Students of reading now generally agree that word-by-word reading is an evil, because it is the grouping and the relations of words, rather than single words, that express meanings. If the child is kept continually in the active attitude of seeking for meanings in his reading, his eyes sweep forward to search out the sense of phrases and sentences. He unconsciously forms from the beginning perceptual habits that never have to be unlearned. To give the beginning reader the contrary habit of lingering on the single word as a word, or, still worse, on the separate parts of the single word, is to thwart the formation of effective perceptual habits, and build up a complex of frustrations which will become clinical materials for later years of "remedial work." Phonetics in beginning reading move continually, not forward to the meaningful phrase and sentence, but backward in the direction of the meaningless phonogram and the meaningless alphabet. It is not an adequate defense to say that this work prepares the child to get meaning at some future time. Phonetic procedure as a part of beginning method is disastrous in turning away from meaning at the most significant time, when habits are being formed. Thus it shatters the child's earliest reading perceptions into a chaos of meaningless fragments, so numerous as to exceed many times over the twenty-six of the old alphabet method.
>
> Phonetics may well be useful to older children as a means of dealing with an occasional puzzling word, if their habit of reading for meaning is already well established, but at the beginning the effect on the child's reading can be only harmful. . . . If it is desirable that children should love to read, and that libraries should be used more freely and intelligently, every reader's first experiences in reading should be made meaningful, and consequently pleasurable.[2]

Good teachers do not generally follow dogmatic theories in planning their reading programs. They want children to learn to read and to grow as rapidly as possible in their reading ability. They know that young children can learn to recognize some whole words as readily, as quickly, and with as much satisfaction as individual letters. They know also that these children need soon to master skills of word recognition involving the analysis of unfamiliar words into their component parts. For these teachers the questions are simply when, how, and how much for which child.

For many years efforts have been made to take the subject of phonics out of the realm of rhetorical debate and to determine the proper role of phonics by

---

[2] James E. McDade, *Next Steps in Non-Oral Reading*, p. 9. West Palm Beach, Fla.: Palm Beach Press, 1946.

means of controlled experimentation. "If the proof of the pudding is in the eating," it was said, "why not test various methods under scientifically controlled conditions, and thus settle the question once and for all?" However, in spite of extensive experimentation over a period of forty years, the conflict over phonics continues. The difficulty seems to lie in the complexity of the problem. Investigators encountered many difficult questions. Under what conditions, for what children, and at what stage of development is the phonics method useful? What kind of phonics method is most effective? Should the element of speech sounds be considered at all in the teaching of silent reading? Because of the contradictory and sometimes inconclusive results of the experiments, research workers were frequently obliged to fall back on psychological theory. Nevertheless, by combining what is known about children's learning with the results of scientific investigations in reading, students of the problem were able to arrive at a rough general agreement on classroom use of phonics.[3]

Kinds of Reading

It will be emphasized in this book that reading is not a general ability. The term "reading" embraces a wide variety of tasks, activities, skills, and mental processes. For many of these, special kinds of instructional assistance are needed.

The kind of reading a person does will usually depend upon his purpose. He may read for pure recreation and enjoyment or he may read to study. Ideally he will find pleasure in study-type reading too, but his approach, attitude, and technique will be different. He may read to find the answer to a question or the solution of a problem, to learn the main idea of a selection or some specific items of information, to discover the outcome of a series of events or to follow directions in making a model airplane or baking a cake. For all of these purposes he employs different methods in his reading.

Sometimes the reader weighs, tests, and challenges what he reads. At other times he gives himself over to "the willing suspension of disbelief" as he follows an imaginary narrative, or he lets the mood of a poet take possession of him. He reads to be enlightened, or comforted, or inspired. Life is varied, and reading is as varied as life.

Reading occurs at different levels. A child may read easy materials fluently and without help. This is the independent reading level. He may read harder materials, calling for concentration and special effort. This is the level of challenge. He may read materials which require outside help. This is the instructional level.

_____
[3] The term "phonics" usually refers to a method of teaching reading. "Phonetics" means the science of speech sounds, a branch of linguistics. In educational discussions the terms are sometimes used interchangeably, but in general the word "phonics" means phonetics as applied to reading.

The diversity of reading tasks, skills, and challenges appears in almost all the areas of the school curriculum. How the school may best deal with them is the essential theme of this book.

FOR FURTHER STUDY

Harris, Albert J., *Effective Teaching of Reading*, pp. 1–21. New York: David McKay Company, Inc., 1962.

Hildreth, Gertrude, *Teaching Reading*, pp. 64–83. New York: Holt, Rinehart and Winston, Inc., 1958.

Smith, Henry P., and Emerald V. Duchant, *Psychology in Teaching Reading*, pp. 20–83. Englewood Cliffs, N.J.: Prentice-Hall, Inc., 1961.

4

Elements Essential to Growth

in Reading

Teaching may be defined as the process of supplying the conditions favorable to learning. The teaching of reading is no exception. This chapter describes some of the conditions needed by children to make maximum progress in learning to read.

These conditions include:

1. Physical health
2. Mental health
3. Sight and hearing
4. Intelligence
5. Background of experience
6. Knowledge of language
7. Desire to read
8. Purposes for reading
9. Interest in reading
10. Reading skills

Fortunately, nearly all children come to school already possessing most of these elements in some degree. A minority of children learn to read in spite of the lack of some of these elements. Blind children, deaf children, and sick children can learn to read. But to the extent that children are lacking in the elements named, they will be handicapped in the process of learning to read.

The teacher and the school do not bear exclusive responsibility for providing all the necessary conditions. Other agencies, especially the family, bear major responsibility for some of them. The school, however, is inevitably involved, in one degree or another, in helping to create all the conditions that contribute to growth in reading.

When we specify those factors in child development which are basic to success in reading, we are not suggesting a hierarchy of educational values. Physical and mental health, for example, are ends in themselves. They do not become important merely because they contribute to good reading, as though reading were the supreme purpose of the school. But since this book is concerned with methods of teaching reading, it must necessarily take the broad developmental context into account.

Physical Health

We know that a reasonable measure of physical health is essential to all school learning. Physical discomfort, languor, a low energy level, and similar symptoms of health problems may often interfere with normal progress in reading. Nervous tension and even ordinary physical fatigue can reduce enjoyment and interest in reading, with consequent decline in efficiency. Vitamin deficiencies and endocrine disturbances have been associated with poor reading. Smith and Dechant mention adenoids, infected tonsils, poor teeth, rickets, asthma, allergies, tuberculosis, rheumatic fever, and other prolonged illnesses as possible factors in reading retardation.[1] Frequent absence from school resulting from illness necessarily retards progress in reading and may produce attitudes of aversion or indifference toward reading.

We must let the clinician determine whether a case of extreme reading retardation may be attributed to physical causes. For our part as teachers we must do all we can in the classroom to promote the physical well-being of our pupils. Free and inexpensive school lunches help to provide needed nutrition. (In one school, a pupil who was considered "just lazy" proved to be just hungry.) We can help to provide a healthful physical environment in school— good light, proper humidity and temperature, appropriate seating. We can arrange for periods of rest and of exercise.

Mental Health

Among the basic developmental needs of children that affect growth in reading is a feeling of security, of being accepted and loved, and of being

---

[1] Henry P. Smith and Emerald V. Dechant, *Psychology in Teaching Reading*, pp. 154–155. Englewood Cliffs, N.J.: Prentice-Hall, Inc., 1961.

adequate to the tasks they are expected to carry out. Everyone performs better in any activity if he has self-confidence, a feeling of successful performance, and a strong desire to achieve. One cannot learn well, in reading or in anything else, if he is distracted by anxieties, frustrations, and the sense of failure. For this and other reasons, every effort is made in modern schools to build wholesome attitudes in children, to give them a sense of belonging and a feeling of being accepted and respected, and to provide many success experiences. Good reading is best carried on in a classroom atmosphere that is warm, friendly, and relaxed.

A success experience need not be in reading activity in order to result in growth in reading. Any experience which builds the child's feeling of general adequacy will help to increase his zest in attacking difficult reading situations and to remove the distractions and anxieties which result from the fear of failure in school. The following anecdote illustrates the value of developing the latent interests and abilities of children:

> One little girl who had not succeeded at all in any other classroom activity suddenly began to read with her group after dancing had been introduced in her classroom. Up to that time she had been timid and shy; but when the children danced, she joined them. She was so graceful that her ability was recognized by other children.[2]

Increasingly, teachers are realizing the significance of the relationship between social and emotional factors and beginning reading. They recognize that the child accustomed to the give-and-take of a social group, especially of his peers, will be likely to adjust more quickly to the school situation and consequently will be more likely to be ready to read sooner than the child who has lacked contacts with other boys and girls. Also, since reading is taught primarily in group situations, the child who does not feel at ease with others is less likely to be able to attend to the reading. Teachers also realize that such a child is less likely to enjoy what he reads when reading in a group than the child who feels comfortable with his agemates.

In one study[3] maladjusted homes or poor family relationships were found to be contributing causes in more than half of the cases of reading disability that were investigated. As one writer has put it, "Children bring their families to school." They come with all the attitudes and predispositions which were formed in the home and neighborhood during those influential first years of life. Children who are overprotected or the victims of parents who are over-

---

[2] From *Fostering Mental Health in Our Schools.* Yearbook of the Association for Supervision and Curriculum Development. Washington, D.C.: National Education Association, 1950.

[3] Helen Mansfield Robinson, *Why Pupils Fail in Reading.* Chicago: The University of Chicago Press, 1946.

ambitious for their children, boys and girls who are unwanted or neglected or insecure because of conflict between parents or because of the loss of one or both of them, are often handicapped in their efforts to learn. On the other hand, children who come from stable homes, who are accepted and loved by their parents, clearly approach the reading task with a great advantage.

When home conditions are unfavorable to the child, it is the responsibility of the school to take these conditions into account and to compensate for them as much as possible. Some children of normal or superior intelligence fail to learn to read because of emotional difficulty, severe anxiety, or insecurity that develops at the time they are first faced with the reading task. The cause may be the arrival of a new baby, parental hostility, or a feeling of anxiety on the part of the parents concerning the child's reading progress—an anxiety which is easily communicated to the child. Worries of this kind interfere with the concentration so necessary in making the fine discriminations involved in reading. Moreover, children who face serious emotional problems frequently have difficulties with such other aspects of language communication as articulation or listening comprehension. Such shortcomings, in turn, contribute to retardation in reading.

The cause-and-effect relationship between emotional and social immaturity and poor reading is sometimes reversed. Often, to be sure, lack of various characteristics of the maturing emotional and social life can have a detrimental effect upon reading, but the fact must not be overlooked that frequently inability to read well is a cause of personality defects. The child who cannot read, no matter how normal he was in his emotional reactions when he entered school, is likely to develop undesirable personality traits if he cannot enter into the reading activities that form a large part of the typical elementary school day. Aggression, withdrawal, irritability, and other forms of unsocial or antisocial behavior are often the visible manifestations of a personality thwarted because it cannot engage in activities satisfying to others in the classroom.

Sight and Hearing

SIGHT. It has been estimated that about one fourth to one half of elementary school children are in need of visual correction. One of the first questions the reading clinician asks about the nonreader is, "Does this child have satisfactory eyesight?" The child who must strain his eyes to read is not likely to enjoy the process and will, usually, try to avoid reading. If his vision is so poor that even with considerable effort it is difficult or impossible for him to differentiate between the forms of letters, success in reading will be delayed until he is given reading materials printed in type that he can read comfortably. All teachers should be alerted to signs of visual difficulties among their pupils.

It must not be assumed, however, that poor vision is generally the chief cause of poor reading. Cases of nearsightedness, farsightedness, astigmatism, muscular imbalance, and lack of fusion are found among both good and poor readers. Nevertheless, in good readers as well as in poor readers such conditions tend to result in fatigue and consequent loss in reading ability. Quite probably nearly all readers—slow, normal, and superior—who have visual defects would improve in reading ability if their defects were corrected.

Visual handicaps among children may be of many kinds. While the classroom teacher should not undertake to make a diagnosis of the difficulty in any individual case, she should be aware of the common types of visual deficiencies in order that she may know when a child should be referred to a specialist. In addition to the more usual phenomena of nearsightedness, farsightedness, and astigmatism, the eye specialist often encounters cases of monocular vision. In normal vision, both eyes receive the image of an object, and the two images are fused in the process of perception. This kind of seeing is called binocular vision. Some individuals, however, ignore or suppress the image received by one eye, and consequently "see" with only one eye. In some cases the individual alternates between one eye and the other; in other cases he alternates between monocular and binocular vision.

Since most reading involves near-point vision, it is important for the teacher to recognize the difference between far-point and near-point vision. A child whose vision tests normal when looking at a distant object but who has great difficulty in seeing an object singly and clearly at a distance of fourteen inches or less is in need of attention. Preschool children tend to be farsighted. For this reason, teachers in the first and second grades should place heavy reliance upon the chalk board and on large charts. Children who have visual difficulties should be seated near the chalkboard. Long periods of near-point reading should be avoided.

The Snellen Chart, while useful in the hands of an oculist, has definite limitations as a screening device for primary reading. Teachers should be alert to outward signs of visual difficulties, such as facial contortions, thrusting and tilting of the head, and holding a book too close to the face. When they observe such behavior, they should recommend consultation with an oculist.

HEARING. A child who suffers from hearing loss is at a distinct disadvantage. He will, for example, have difficulty in benefiting from the teacher's oral explanations. Especially if the child is taught by predominantly oral-phonetic methods, auditory acuity is important in the process of learning to read. The child with hearing loss will have inadequate or inaccurate auditory images of the words he reads, and consequently may encounter difficulty in word recognition.

As in the case of visual defects, hearing loss may be no more common among poor readers than among good readers. Nevertheless, all readers who have deficient hearing ability would probably be aided in reading performance if they received appropriate attention from parents, teachers, and physicians.

Estimates vary as to the number of children who have significant hearing defects. One of the most conservative estimates places the percentage of children with considerable hearing loss at $1\frac{1}{2}$ to $3\frac{1}{2}$ percent of all children. Other findings suggest as much as 30 percent for girls and 50 percent for boys. Whatever the precise figures may be, we are safe in concluding that careful attention should be given to the hearing ability of all pupils.

Intelligence

It is known that a fairly close relationship exists between intelligence and the ability to read. This relationship may be ascribed, in part, to the fact that intelligence tests and reading tests set many tasks that are similar. The fact that the correlation between performance in intelligence tests and reading tests usually tends to be very high may mean merely that a large part of an intelligence test calls for abilities closely related to the ability to read. Moreover, it must be remembered that cultural background and present environment are likely to affect performance in both reading and intelligence tests. Then, too, our general notion of intelligence places a high value on reading ability. Nevertheless, whatever the reasons may be, it has been demonstrated that in our culture, and under present conditions in American schools, a child has a better chance of success in reading if he has average or above average intelligence. Furthermore, if we define a child's intelligence as the rate at which he is able to learn, we may assume that the rate of his growth in reading is affected by and limited by his intelligence.

If intelligence is thought of as an inherited ability, the school and the teacher cannot significantly affect this factor. But there is reason to believe that in the early years of a child's life, environment may have an effect upon what is commonly considered as intelligence. Certainly a rich environment, one which offers many opportunities for learning, can help a child with limited intellectual endowment to make much greater use of his native ability than he could if he were deprived of intellectually stimulating surroundings.

Background of Experience

If it is true that success in reading depends on what the reader brings to the printed page, much significance must be attached to the body of direct and indirect experiences which he has accumulated in advance of the reading. The child's prior stock of impressions will determine in large measure how much meaning he will derive from the visual symbols before him. These impressions will include both the things that have happened to him directly and the symbolic experiences he has had with reading, listening, viewing of motion pictures and television, and the like.

A simple example illustrating the point that written symbols acquire meaning for the reader because of his previous experiences is that of a reader who encounters what to him is a new word, the word *hogan*. The writer states that a hogan is a circular house used by the Navaho Indians as a dwelling. He may go on to give further details—the materials of which these houses are built, the presence or absence of windows and doors, and similar information. The reader has had previous experience with the letters of which the word is composed and he is able to pronounce it, but he has never before encountered the word *hogan*, nor has he ever seen a hogan. How can this curious visual symbol have meaning for him?

Hogan acquires meaning for him because he has had direct experience with other words and ideas in the sentence. These words arouse images in his mind because he has encountered in personal experience the ideas and images they represent. He has seen a circle, and he has had experience with houses. Encountering the concepts of *house* and *circle* in a specific relation to each other, the reader is enabled to create a new image in his mind—an image approximating a hogan—which he has never seen. Thus, through the combination and recombination of familiar words, images, and concepts, the reader builds new meanings which in turn provide the basis for further understandings.

It becomes apparent that the fundamental elements in reading comprehension derive from direct experience. References to such concepts as anger, love, hate, reconciliation, warmth, pain, light and dark, can have meaning for the reader only in the degree to which he has in one way or another had experience with them. But not only does direct experience facilitate the acquisition of meaning from the printed page, it also creates the conditions for that keen interest in reading which is so essential to reading growth. For example, a person who has visited the headquarters of the United Nations will read with redoubled insight and pleasure a story in *The New Yorker* about a reporter's visit to the same place; a boy who is assembling a stamp collection will read a book about stamp issues with an intensity of interest which would not exist in a boy who does not pursue this hobby. Thus the reading of recent history also takes on significance and life as the reader recognizes in historical scenes the flesh and blood realities he knows from his own past. The depth and range of his comprehension will depend in part upon the length and richness of that past.

Basic to all the reading experience through which children learn is the direct contact with things, people, and events. It has been argued that the concepts usually encountered in reading material are common to the experience of most or all children, and that the instructor's primary task is to teach the recognition of the printed symbol. Such argument overlooks the wide diversity of the environments of children in the country, in the city, in mining or industrial towns, in slums or wealthy suburbs, in cattle country or fishing villages. For example, an excellent story, "Black Storm," by Thomas C. Hinkle,[4] begins as follows: "Near a frontier cattle town of old Kansas on the memorable morning, John McDonald, the cattle-owner of the Chisholm Range, stood in the center of a corral holding the reins of a beautiful horse—a coal-black gelding." Consider the difference in the understanding which a country boy, especially one from the west, and a city boy would bring to this passage!

Reading is, of course, in itself an important kind of experience. Through the synthesis of the direct impressions which can be brought about in the process of reading, the reader develops new images and concepts which enable him to extend the range of his vision of reality. The amount of direct experience that even the most privileged person may enjoy is necessarily limited. Through reading we may range in imagination over the globe, over the known universe, and over the centuries, and each new reading experience provides the background for further understanding in reading.

Knowledge of Language

If direct experience is to be of substantial aid in reading, it must be accompanied by an adequate fund of experience with language. Children who visit a fire station and see the engines, the ladders, the fire extinguishers, and the other equipment, but do not hear the words which identify the objects, have not been adequately prepared for reading about firemen and fire fighting. It is necessary to introduce them to the verbal symbols in association with the observation of the objects and the processes. Much discussion and explanation of terms should therefore accompany the direct experiences which the school provides.

That a good knowledge of language is necessary in preparation for the reading experience illustrates the close interrelations of the various aspects of language communication. Evidence shows that there is a strong relationship between linguistic ability and reading achievement, and that a child's ability to understand and use language orally is an important factor in beginning reading.[5] All we know about children's language learning points to the interrelatedness of the four facets of language—reading, writing, speaking, and listening. We may conclude, therefore, that wide experience with all kinds of language, including extensive contacts with words and sentences in meaningful situations, contributes effectively to the improvement of reading. Growth in reading usually is produced best, not from a program of isolated drills, but from a rich, diversified, and stimulating language environment and a curriculum which provides for many kinds of highly motivated language experiences.

---

[4] In E. M. Orr, E. T. Holston, and Stella S. Center, *Discovering New Fields in Reading and Literature*. New York: Charles Scribners' Sons, 1955.

[5] Gertrude Hildreth, "Interrelationships among the Language Arts," *Elementary School Journal*, 48 (June 1948), 538–549.

Desire and Purpose

The *desire* to read is the motivating force that leads to reading. It may simply be the desire to do what others around us are doing. It may be the desire to have needed information or to spend a pleasant leisure hour. In any case, the desire to read arises from a sense of need for reading. The sense of need can be cultivated by creating the necessary conditions.

Desire eventuates in purpose, which clarifies the direction effort shall take. Thus the emphasis in reading guidance should be placed not upon arbitrary teacher-direction, but upon the awakening of pupil desire, the release of pupil energy, and the development of pupil self-direction. The teacher's aim is to guide, to lead—not to coerce; but the pupil must supply the voluntary effort if real learning is to take place.

Especially in the initial stages of reading, the factor of good motivation is of prime importance. Motivation is not a mere mechanical preliminary to the reading itself, but is the result of the teacher's providing or helping the pupil to discover clear goals. If the child's first experiences with reading are purposeful, he will be started on the road to meaningful reading. We cannot start him with a set of skills, mechanically acquired without reference to meaning, and then expect him later to put them to use in meaningful reading.

The principle of reading with a purpose, of *active* reading, has clear implications for reading assignments. We must not send children to the printed page without adequate preparation for the reading. A good assignment, as a rule, includes a discussion which will orient the pupil to the material he will encounter. It helps him to formulate questions to be answered and to visualize clearly the uses to which the information is to be put. It gives him some notion of the nature of the material to be read and the manner in which the material is to be approached. It helps him to anticipate some of the key words and perhaps the pronunciation of unfamiliar proper names. In short, the good assignment helps the pupil to establish clear purpose for the reading. Perhaps the best assignments are self-assignments. Such assignments arise out of problems, discussions, and activities that call for further information. The search may be initiated by the individual himself, by a committee, or by the class as a whole.

The reading connected with a unit of instruction may involve various purposes. Reading may be done as preliminary exploration, or browsing, in a variety of books for the purpose of general orientation to the subject of the unit. This would be a period of "sampling," a get-acquainted period to indicate the nature of the area to be studied. It may be done as differentiated research, where each pupil pursues some special aspect of the main topic. Reading may also be done for the purpose of outlining and organizing what has been read in various sources.

The number and types of purposes for which individuals read are almost unlimited. Children and young adults have so many things that they want, and need, to know. They want to know what the good radio and television programs and movies are, and what makes them good; how to apply for a position and how to behave in an interview; what makes wars and how they can be prevented; how they can be more popular among their friends; what they can believe in the newspapers; how they can get along better at home; where they can get the truth about the trouble spots around the world. They want to know about labor, prices, employment, and new scientific advances. They want to know what they must do to be safe when riding a bicycle, driving a car, or repairing a light switch. They want to know what attitudes they should assume toward sex, courtship, and marriage, ethics and religion. Many would like to know how they can help to secure more and better schools and libraries for all children and youth.

The task of the school is to assist the reader in carrying out his purposes. If he is frustrated by obstacles too numerous and too great in the form of vocabulary burden or complexity of thought, he will soon give up his purposes or seek to achieve them by means other than reading. Too many young readers have abandoned the spontaneous search for meaning in books because they did not receive appropriate guidance. But if they are given the encouragement and opportunity, they will often avidly explore every aspect of experience, asking more questions than the wisest and most learned can answer.

Interest in Reading

Closely related to purpose in reading is interest. Children are most likely to read with comprehension those materials which deal with topics of interest to them. In fact, it has been found that some pupils are able to read stories at a level of reading difficulty far beyond their normal abilities if the subject is one in which they are vitally interested. Thus a boy who follows professional baseball closely may successfully read a sports story in a newspaper even though it is several years beyond him in reading difficulty.

Certain studies have suggested that the interest of a story is closely related to its "readability." For example, a group of pupils was asked to compare two stories which had been rewritten to make them equivalent in reading difficulty as measured by three well-known formulas. One was a version of Hawthorne's *The House of Seven Gables*; the other was "The Get-away Boy," by David Vincent Sheehan. The pupils reported that they found the former to be the "harder" reading because they considered it less interesting. Yet from the evidence of the readability formulas, the two selections were equal in difficulty.[6] It is therefore necessary for the teacher to discover pupils' genuine interests in

---

[6] David Bernstein, "Improved Reading through Interest," *School Review*, 62 (January 1954), 40–49.

order to provide them with appropriate guidance in the selection of things to read.

Children's interests are at least in part the result of the experiences they have had. They are closely related to the activities of play and work which constitute their daily living. Many of these interests are common to all boys and girls. Others are common only to boys or only to girls. Some are related to the earlier, others to the later, ages. Still others arise out of individual experience and are affected by the special aptitude or background of the individual. Since interests are learned, rather than inherited, it is possible to extend both their range and their quality. Any activity which will open new fields of exploration to children can help to expand a pupil's reading interests and his mastery of the printed page. Reading should, therefore, be taught in the setting of a wide variety of purposeful enterprises designed to expand the child's range of interests. Radio, television, films, field trips, class projects, group discussion involving the exchange of experiences—all these are methods by which the ground may be prepared for ever more zestful and meaningful reading.

An example of the effectiveness of interesting activities is reported by Kathleen Hester.[7] A first-grade teacher, overwhelmed by the great variety of individual differences among her pupils, hit upon a system of "reading by invitation." By creating a classroom environment rich in stimulation, she succeeded in arousing the interest of all the children in books. Some began to read later than others. Some made more progress than others. Formal reading instruction was given only to those who gave evidence of being ready. All, however, had begun to read by January. The setting is described as follows:

> To inaugurate the program, several interest centers were set up in the room. Peg boards, colored pegs, colored beads and strings, puzzles, clay, and drawing paper were provided. A library corner was set apart, with two portable screens, two tables, four chairs, two davenports, two bookcases (all constructed from orange crates and painted royal blue and cherry red), and a floor lamp. Attractive books were placed on the table and in the bookcases. A doll, a doll buggy, and play dishes were put in a playhouse in this corner, also. A painting easel afforded even the spoiled baby opportunity to express himself.

Reading Skills

The omission thus far of a discussion of the specific skills involved in the act of reading itself has been intentional. We felt that because so much of formal reading instruction has stressed the mechanical skills of word recognition and sentence comprehension, a heavy emphasis upon the background factors

---

[7] Kathleen B. Hester, "Every Child Reads Successfully in a Multiple-level Program," *Elementary School Journal,* 53 (October 1952), 86–89.

in reading growth was needed here. Nevertheless, no consideration of the development of reading competence would be complete without careful attention to the matter of specific reading skills. Later chapters will discuss these in detail.

Some children, of course, acquire the necessary skills without formal instruction. Given the various conditions described earlier in this chapter and an environment which is in every respect conducive to reading growth, they learn from the beginning to get meaning from the printed page and almost unconsciously develop the habits of word recogition and comprehension of sentences and longer units. For such children the analytical reading drills can be more harmful than helpful.

Most children, however, can be materially aided by specific instruction in reading skills. They can make more rapid improvement if they can be shown how to recognize letters and phonic elements, how to discover familiar elements in the longer unfamiliar words, how to use context clues, how to note details, how to find the main idea of a longer passage, how to compare, evaluate, and visualize the author's meaning, how to locate and utilize needed information, how to follow printed directions, and how to adapt approach and speed of reading both to the nature of the material read and to their purpose. These skills can be learned through guided practice. In no case must there be neglect of either the factor of interest or the factor of skill in reading.

Study of the elements that make up the ability to read has revealed how complex the process of reading is. Dr. Bernice Leary has summed it up well:

> It is no light matter to acquire the wide range of abilities and skills basic to reading, even in a mechanical sense. Nor is it any light matter to convert into meaning the language of mathematics, science, literature, and the social studies; to maintain a critical attitude toward what is read; to develop the habit of relating written experience to our own experiences; and to adjust reading abilities to different materials by grasping the author's intent, his use of words, and his style of writing, and by defining clearly one's own reading purposes.[8]

The preceding survey of growth factors has illustrated how intimately reading is related to the total development of the child. When we speak of "developmental" reading, therefore, we may be referring to any one of three aspects of the problem of reading instruction. First, we may be considering the effect of the various growth factors on the child's progress in reading. Second, we may be thinking of the ways in which reading affects the child's general intellectual, emotional, and social growth. Third, we may have in mind the orderly progression of reading skills as new needs emerge from the growing life of the child. In whatever sense the term is used, it focuses attention on the fact that reading

---

[8] *Improving Reading in Content Fields*, p. 10. Compiled and edited by William S. Gray, Supplementary Educational Monographs, No. 62. Chicago: The University of Chicago Press, 1947.

is a continuous process, that it is a part of an intricate pattern of growth, and that each factor and each specific skill must be considered in relation to all others.

FOR FURTHER STUDY

Almy, Millie C., *Children's Experiences Prior to First-Grade and Success in Beginning Reading.* New York: Bureau of Publications, Teachers College, Columbia University, 1949.

Burton, William H., *Reading in Child Development,* pp. 413–448. Indianapolis: The Bobbs-Merrill Company, Inc., 1956.

Causey, Oscar S., ed., *The Reading Teacher's Reader,* pp. 255–293. New York: The Ronald Press Company, 1958.

Dawson, Mildred A., and Henry A. Bamman, *Fundamentals of Basic Reading Instruction,* rev. ed., pp. 17–28. New York: David McKay Company, Inc., 1963.

Ephron, Beulah Kanter, *Emotional Difficulties in Reading.* New York: Julian Press, Inc., 1953.

Gray, William S., ed., *Reading in Relation to Experience and Language.* Chicago: The University of Chicago Press, 1944.

Hester, Kathleen, *Teaching Every Child to Read,* pp. 17–83. New York: Harper and Row, Publishers, 1955.

Monroe, Marion, *Growing into Reading,* pp. 22–169. Chicago: Scott, Foresman and Company, 1951.

Russell, David H., "Language Arts and Personality," *Elementary English,* 30 (March 1953), 167–180.

Schubert, Delwyn G., "Visual Immaturity and Reading Difficulty," *Elementary English,* 34 (May 1957), 323–325.

Witty, Paul, and David Kopel, *Reading and the Educative Process,* pp. 225–232, 239–243. Boston: Ginn and Company, 1939.

Cultivating Growth
in
Reading Abilities

5a

Readiness for Reading

When is a child ready to read?

In some countries, as in England, the compulsory school attendance age is five years; in others, as in the Soviet Union and in Sweden, it is seven years. In the United States it is typically six years. Not all children in all countries are required to learn to read at the outset, but the general expectation is that formal instruction begins when school begins.

In this country some children begin to read before they come to school. In a group of 5,103 beginning first-grade children, Dolores Durkin found 49 who had some ability in reading. She concluded tentatively from her study (now going on in another school system) that the slower readers especially might benefit from an earlier start in reading.[1] This judgment runs counter to prevailing opinion on the subject, and will doubtless bring about a re-examination of a point of view long thought to be well established.

In spite of the varying and sometimes contradictory counsels of research workers and expert observers, we can be reasonably confident of the validity of several generalizations affecting reading readiness. (1) Teachers are now spending a disproportionate amount of time and effort in teaching reading to children who lack the necessary maturity to make a successful beginning in reading. (2) Children differ widely in their rates of growth. In the ten months of chronological age which typically spans beginning groups of first-grade pupils, the differences among the children reflect a range of several years in general ma-

---

[1] Dolores Durkin, "An Earlier Start in Reading?" *Elementary School Journal*, 63 (December 1962), 147–151.

turity. Even one month of growth at age six represents twice the gain made in one month by the same child at age twelve. (3) Other things being equal, most children who have reached a mental age of six and one-half to seven have a better chance of making a successful beginning in reading than one with a lower mental age. Some children with a mental age of six or even less, however, do make satisfactory progress in reading, especially when the reading materials provided are on a very easy level. (4) Reading readiness depends on many factors in addition to mental age.

The advanced student who wishes to consult the research studies bearing on the subject of reading readiness should examine some of the excellent summaries of the literature that have been made. Following are a few of these:

Anderson, Irving H., and Walter F. Dearborn, *The Psychology of Teaching Reading*, pp. 50–100. New York: The Ronald Press Company, 1952.

Betts, Emmett A., *The Foundations of Reading Instruction*, Part III. New York: American Book Company, 1950.

Blair, Glenn M., and R. Stewart Jones, "Readiness," in *Encyclopedia of Educational Research*, Chester W. Harris, ed., 3rd ed., pp. 1081–1086. New York: The Macmillan Company, 1960.

Smith, Henry P., and Emerald V. Dechant, *Psychology in Teaching Reading*, pp. 84–119. Englewood Cliffs, N.J.: Prentice-Hall, Inc., 1961.

The annual summaries of research on reading by Theodore L. Harris in the *Journal of Educational Research*.

The extensive research literature on reading readiness to which reference has been made proves, if nothing else, that the problems, like those of human learning in general, are complex and that the need for further investigation is endless. We must remember, however, that we are not dealing with objects on an assembly line, but with human beings. The principal object is not to achieve efficiency in "putting out a better product," in this case a child who makes better scores on standardized tests. The fullest development, well-being, and happiness of the child is the ultimate end, and reading is but a means to that end.

There is a school of thought, unhappily a diminishing one, that considers children worthwhile for their own sake and that refuses to use them to prove that our nation and our society are stronger and more intelligent than other nations and other societies. It is a deeply ingrained principle of democracy that the school, and society itself, exist for the welfare of the individuals who comprise them, not the reverse. This principle has pertinence to the problem of reading readiness.

If we press reading instruction upon the child who gives every sign that he is not ready for such instruction and will experience anxiety and frustration as a result, we are not merely making a pedagogical error but are in effect committing an offense against the child. If we withhold reading instruction from a child, whether he be three years or eight years of age, when he could clearly find success and enjoyment in reading, we are withholding from him his birthright. It follows that there should be reading instruction for some children in the preschool and that some children in the primary grades, particularly in the first grade, should not be given formal reading instruction.

The difficulty is that we can not always recognize readiness with certainty. We do not have an infallible formula for determining whether a child is ready to read. We must continue to depend on teachers' judgments. But teachers can be measurably aided in making these judgments by making use of criteria which are reliably associated with readiness to read.

If the teacher has serious doubts about the readiness of an individual child, she will be wise to delay reading instruction for a time and to encourage the child to spend his time and energy on other activities that he can do successfully. Too early instruction is not only wasteful of the teacher's effort; it may also give rise to a lasting aversion to reading on the part of the child.

Is This Child Ready To Read?

One significant indication of a child's readiness is his initial attitude toward reading.

On the opening day of school the first-grade teacher will find that her pupils vary greatly in their attitudes toward reading. There will be boys and girls like Tommy, who, pencil and tablet clutched tightly, go to the teacher and exclaim enthusiastically, "I want to learn to read. I want to learn to read." Fathers, mothers, and possibly sisters and brothers have been reading fascinating stories to them. So they come to school, wanting to learn to read in order to be independent of others for their stories. They may have discovered, too, that a great deal of information is found in books. They will insist on being taught to read in a hurry.

But not all the children in the room will be like Tommy. There will probably be a Susan, who has enjoyed hearing others read or tell stories to her, but who has not looked forward to learning to read. She prefers not to learn, because she thinks it more fun to have her mother read to her than to read by herself. However, the teacher may wonder whether, in spite of lack of interest at the time, Susan may not become ready for reading before Tommy.

Then, too, there is Peggy, who enters school with fear and trepidation because she has heard disconcerting tales about what happens at school. The teacher may ask herself, "If I can get Peggy to overcome her fear, will it be wise to put her into a reading group?"

Another familiar figure in a first-grade room at the beginning of the year is

Jim, who is greatly disturbed at the thought that now he can no longer spend the entire day playing cowboy. He is in no mood to be interested in what is done at school, for he anticipates only boring experiences.

In the average first grade, then, the children's attitudes toward learning to read may range from disinclination, to indifference, to anticipation. There are many other respects, however, in which first-grade children reveal great differences. They differ in mental, physical, social, emotional, and other educational or psychological factors of great importance in beginning reading.

Numerous factors, therefore, contribute to reading readiness. The presence of any or even all of them will in itself not guarantee reading success. Further, it is not necessary that all these factors be present in equal degree, although most of them should be present in at least moderate degree. One useful and fairly comprehensive list of these factors is presented by Gray, who based it on the work of the English scholar Fred J. Schonell (opposite page).

Mental Age

A pupil's readiness to read and the methods and materials that should be used in teaching him are determined in part by his mental maturity. It is therefore necessary to know as much as possible about the child's mental characteristics. One way of getting such information is through the use of dependable mental tests. However, it should be remembered that even the best mental test provides an imperfect measure of native ability or intelligence. A child who had many rich and intellectually stimulating experiences will do better on an intelligence test than a child of equal innate ability who has been brought up in a very limiting environment.

Tests should not ordinarily be given a child immediately upon his entrance into the first grade, when he is still unaccustomed to the school environment. Many teachers like to wait until several weeks after school starts before they give any kind of standardized tests. The practice of having pupils come before the opening day of school, sometimes in the preceding spring, to take tests to determine their fitness for entrance into the first grade or to aid in their placement is probably questionable, chiefly because the accuracy of the test results is doubtful. Furthermore, if taking a test is the child's first or one of his first school experiences, he may think of going to school as a not especially intriguing adventure.

STANDARDIZED TESTS OF MENTAL ABILITY. Perhaps the best known individual test of mental ability is the *Terman Revision of the Stanford-Binet Intelligence Scale*, available in two forms, published by Houghton Mifflin Company, Boston. Since this test involves some knowledge of language, it may not fully reflect the real abilities of children with language handicaps.

Another now frequently used individual intelligence test is the *Wechsler-*

READING READINESS CHART

Name of child

Date of birth   Age in years   and months

Results of tests, if any are given:

    Mental age   Intelligence Quotient

    Reading Readiness Score

Estimates of child's development

1   2   3   4   5

General mental ability

Background of previous experience

Range of speaking vocabulary

Accuracy of pronunciation and related speech habits

Ability to express oneself clearly to others

Habit of observing details and forming associations with things
    seen or heard

Ability to perceive likenesses and differences

Ability to recognize relationships

Ability to keep in mind a series of events or other items

Ability to think clearly and in sequence

Ability to make good choices and decisions

Good health

A well-nourished body

Freedom from undue fatigue

Visual efficiency and discrimination

Auditory efficiency and discrimination

Emotional balance

Social adjustment and feeling of security

Ability to focus on specific learning activities

Ability to follow directions

Ability to work effectively in a group

Interest in pictures and the meaning of written or printed
    symbols

A desire to learn to read

---

1 = *well below average*; 2 = *below average*; 3 = *average*; 4 = *above average*; 5 = *well above average*.

SOURCE: William S. Gray, *The Teaching of Reading and Writing*. UNESCO. Chicago: Scott, Foresman and Company, 1956.

Bellevue Intelligence Scales, published by the Psychological Corporation, New York. In it, as in the *Terman Revision of the Stanford-Binet Intelligence Scale,* the factor of language ability is involved.

An example of a nonlanguage individual psychological test is the *Arthur Performance Scale,* published by C. H. Stoelting and Company, Chicago. It can be used with children with language handicaps, as for example, some who come from non-English-speaking homes. The use of the *Arthur Performance Scale,* however, is not restricted to children with language problems.

A much-used group test is the *Pintner-Cunningham Primary Test,* Form A, Form B, and Form C, published by Harcourt, Brace and World, Inc., New York. The subtests, which together are devised to test general mental ability, give an indication of the nature of the abilities tested. They are: Test 1, Common Observation; Test 2, Aesthetic Differences; Test 3, Associated Objects; Test 4, Discrimination of Size; Test 5, Picture Parts (in which the pupil is tested in ability to find among several pictures one like a designated one); Test 6, Picture Completion (in which the pupil is asked to indicate which of a number of parts is needed to finish an incomplete picture); Test 7, Dot Drawing (in which the pupil is asked to connect dots so that a picture like a given one will be drawn). Although all seven tests are composed entirely of pictures, an understanding of language is required for taking the test since all the directions are given verbally.

The California Test of Mental Maturity, Pre-Primary Battery, published by the California Test Bureau, Los Angeles, California, is available in a long and short form. Certain of the subtests require a minimum use of language, while other sections reveal how adequately the child understands relationships expressed in words. Since a pupil's score in a nonlanguage test is often considerably higher or lower than in language tests, it is of great value to obtain test scores on the types of mental ability tested both by language and by nonlanguage tests. *The California Test of Mental Maturity, Pre-Primary Battery* is concerned with the following mental factors: memory, spatial relationships, logical reasoning, numerical reasoning, and verbal concepts.

The *Davis-Eells Test of General Intelligence or Problem-Solving Ability, Primary-A,* for grades 1 and 2, called *Davis-Eells Games* on the pupils' booklets, is published by Harcourt, Brace and World, Inc., New York. Mental capacity is considered synonymous in this test with problem-solving ability. In constructing the test the authors took special care to choose content equally familiar to all economic-social cultures within an urban environment. No reading skill is required, for all the exercises consist of pictures to be checked in answer to thought questions given orally by the examiner. Rate of response is not checked in the test.

The Pintner Non-Language Primary Mental Test, published by the Bureau of Publications, Teachers College, Columbia University, New York, can also be used with children with language handicaps.

Other widely used group intelligence tests are: the *Kuhlmann-Anderson Intelligence Test, Grade IA,* published by the Educational Test Bureau, Inc., of Minneapolis, Minnesota, and the *Detroit Beginning First Grade Intelligence Test,* distributed by Harcourt, Brace and World, Inc., New York.

SUBJECTIVE DATA ON MENTAL ABILITY. Intelligence tests, however, are not the only means by which the teacher can gain insight into the child's intelligence. Long before psychological tests were available there were rough methods of estimating a person's intelligence. Although mental tests are probably more reliable indexes of intelligence than more informal methods, the latter should also be used. Informal observation may serve as a valuable check on the accuracy of test scores. If no mental test has been given, the observant teacher may compare the child's reactions with those usually expected of children of his age. By consulting books on child growth and development the teacher can find out what types of behavior are characteristic of children at various age levels. Information about an individual child's customary behavior can also be obtained from others who know him well, especially his parents. And, of course, the teacher should realize that environmental deprivations may make the child seem less intelligent than he is.

Physical Fitness

The teacher of the beginning reader should always consult such data as may be available in the doctor's or nurse's offices. Information that can be obtained through conferences with parents is also often helpful. Through observation of the child the teacher can frequently get clues to the child's physical well-being which may alert her to the need for referral to the nurse or doctor. If there is no school nurse, symptoms of illness or handicap may be discussed with the parents, who may be encouraged to consult a physician, dentist, or oculist. Rather easily observable factors like sleepiness, listlessness, irritability, and languor often are signs of difficulties that may seriously interfere with learning to read.

Unfortunately, during the critical period of getting ready to read and of beginning reading, children are often absent from school because of illness. Not much can be done by the teacher to prevent such illness, except to provide frequent rest periods and frequent periods of physical activity, to check room temperature and ventilation, and to suggest that a child be sent home at the first sign of a cold or other illness. Since frequent interruptions are to be expected, the teacher should plan her work accordingly. Much repetition and review of earlier activities are necessary. When a child returns after an absence of several days, the teacher should do everything possible to make him feel that he still belongs, has his own seat, and follows the familiar routine. He should be greeted with pleasure by teacher and class.

VISION. Since probably no phase of the physical well-being of the child affects reading as much as eyesight, the vision of a child who is about to learn to read should be checked as carefully as possible.

The screening test for vision that is most commonly used in schools is the Snellen Letter chart or the Snellen Symbol E chart, which is an adaptation of the letter chart, for use with nonreaders. On the letter charts are seven rows of the letter *E*, printed in various sizes, decreasing from the top row to the bottom. While the examinee is being tested, he stands 20 feet from the chart and reads as far down the Snellen Letter chart as his vision permits. On the Snellen Symbol E chart the pupil indicates by the fingers of one hand the positions, like **E, m, Ǝ,** and **ɯ**, in which the letter *E* occurs on that chart. If the rating on a Snellen chart for either eye is below 20/20, referral should be made to a competent eye doctor. Teachers should guard against concluding, if a child's vision for reading at the "far-point" is good, that his vision for reading at the "near-point," as required when reading books, is satisfactory. Many persons see well at a distance but have difficulty at the near-point. The Snellen charts commonly test only the clearness of vision at a distance of 20 feet. As Schubert has pointed out,[2] nearsightedness, which is the only visual anomaly detected by the Snellen chart, is more commonly associated with good rather than poor reading ability.

Some investigators believe that the eyes of the average child are not sufficiently mature for near-point reading until the age of eight. This estimate coincides with other estimates which place the ideal age for beginning reading at later than six. Indeed, the phenomenal success claimed for such programs in beginning reading as the one at New Castle, Pennsylvania, may be attributable in part to the fact that major reliance was placed upon filmstrips, charts, and other large-type material to be read at far-point.

The Visual Sensation Tests of the "Betts Ready to Read" battery make a more comprehensive visual analysis than is possible through the use of the Snellen charts. Like the latter they test clearness of vision at the far-point, and they also make it possible to detect some problems of binocular vision. By means of a telebinocular, a stereoscopic machine developed by Emmett A. Betts and associates, with accompanying stereoscopic slides or stereographs, these tests check distance fusion, binocular visual efficiency at a far-point (clearness of vision), left-eye efficiency, right-eye visual efficiency, vertical balance, depth perception, lateral balance, fusion at the reading distance, and sharpness of image.

Other tests of near-point vision are:

The Eames Eye Test. New York: Harcourt, Brace and World, Inc. (Measures visual acuity, nearsightedness, farsightedness, fusion, and astigmatism.)

---

2 Delwyn G. Schubert, "Visual Immaturity and Reading Difficulty," *Elementary English,* 34 (May 1957), 323–325.

The Orthorater. Bausch and Lomb Optical Company, New York.

The Keystone Visual Survey Tests. Keystone View Company, Meadville, Pennsyl.
vania.

The Sight Screener. American Optical Company, Southbridge, Massachusetts.

Before choosing any test for checking visual efficiency teachers are advised
to study carefully the literature furnished by the publishers of the tests to note
what they purport to test and how the tests operate. In no case should the
teacher or school nurse use vision tests to try to *diagnose* eye defects. The tests
should be used in the schools merely as screening tests. If the results of the testing indicate that there is a possibility of a difficulty in vision, a referral for
diagnosis and possible remediation should be made to a competent specialist
in the field of vision.

Even without tests some symptoms of visual difficulties, like inflamed eyelids,
scowling, and frowning, can be detected. The distance from the eye at which a
child holds his books may also be a sign of trouble. Complaints of headaches
after reading, too, are frequently significant in discovering vision problems.

HEARING. Because hearing ability may have an important effect on reading,
in many schools an effort is made to secure accurate information about children's auditory acuity. In these schools the health service often checks hearing
by means of an audiometer. Some audiometers are made for group, others for
individual, testing. Audiometers are obtainable from:

The Graybar Electric Company, New York. (Distributes the Western
    Electric 4C group audiometer.)

The Maico Company, Minneapolis, Minnesota.

Aurex Corporation, Chicago, Illinois.

Medical Acoustic Instrument Company, Minneapolis, Minnesota.

Dakon Corporation, New Hyde Park, New York.

Otarion Listener Corporation, Ossining, New York.

C. H. Stoelting Company, Chicago, Illinois.

Sonatone Corporation, Elmsford, New York.

Further information on audiometers is given in Emmett A. Betts, *The
Foundations of Reading Instruction.* New York: American Book Company,
1950.

The use of an audiometer requires specialized training. Moreover, in many
schools teachers do not have access to clinics in which audiometers are used.
They should therefore be alert to observable signs of hearing loss, which frequently goes undetected and which can seriously interfere not only with reading progress but with learning in general. Inattention, monotonous or un-
natural pitch, lack of clear and distinct speech, frequent requests for repetition

of questions, turning one ear to a speaker, head tilting, and rubbing of the ear are among the indications of possible defects of hearing.

The classroom teacher can also make a rough check of children's hearing by means of the "watch-tick" test. The examiner holds a watch of medium size and quietness in the palm of his hand and stands behind the child being examined. The child covers one ear with the palm of his hand. The watch is held about three feet from the child and moved closer until the child indicates that he hears its tick. Both ears are tested in this way. By comparing one child's responses with another's, the teacher knows which children should be examined by a nurse or doctor. Whisper tests and low-voice tests may also offer clues as to whether hearing difficulty may be suspected.

Social and Emotional Development

The social maturity of a child can be determined in part by observing his "at-homeness" in group situations. It is of special importance to note his ability to cooperate with others in a group. Emotional maturity can roughly be gauged by the child's reaction to conditions that to him are unpleasant, his willingness to consider the rights of others, and his ability to sacrifice immediate pleasures for future gains.

To the child in the prereading period, school is still a strange place calling for many adjustments which had not been required of him at home. Teachers will often observe signs of fear, anxiety, withdrawal, or belligerence in children as a result. Getting ready to read requires the growth both of self-confidence and of confidence in the teacher.

Educational Factors

Educational factors that have decided bearing upon beginning reading can be measured through the use of tests frequently referred to as reading readiness tests as well as by means of a variety of nonstandardized procedures.

READING READINESS TESTS. Many, though not all, of the educational factors related to beginning reading can be measured by means of reading readiness tests.

Many reading readiness tests appraise the child's background of information, either in a subtest so labeled or in one by some other name in which other characteristics of reading readiness are also tested. The breadth of background of a pupil's information, which reflects the richness of experience he has had, can be tested by asking him such questions as "How many cents are there in a nickel?" It is also tested directly in some tests, when, for example, the child is asked to make the association between a picture and printed symbols.

The ability to discriminate between objects, words, and letters is also measured in many reading readiness tests. A common method for evaluating the ability to discriminate among objects is to present a series of four or five pictures in a row, all but one of which is like the first one. The series may consist of pictures of five houses all alike except one in which no chimney is shown. The child is asked to cross out the one that is unlike the first one. Similar exercises are devised for testing the pupil's ability to discriminate between letters or words. Pupils are not expected to read the words or letters; all they are to do is to recognize which letter or word is different from others in the same row, or which are alike.

Comprehension of the meaning of words is also tested in many reading readiness tests. In some tests the pupil is asked to give words that mean the opposite of the words named by the examiner. If, for example, the teacher says *summer,* the pupil is to answer *winter;* if the teacher says *up,* the pupil is to say *down.*

One widely used readiness test is the *Gates Reading Readiness Test,* published by the Bureau of Publications, Teachers College, Columbia University, New York. It is divided into five subtests which measure specific skills important in learning to read. The skills tested are the ability to follow directions, to discriminate between words that are similar, to differentiate between sounds, and to identify letters and numbers by name. The ability to follow directions is tested by asking the pupil to mark pictures as instructed. Two subtests measure the ability to discriminate between words. One does so by requiring the child to indicate which two words in each group of four are alike. The other asks the child to state which word in a series of four is like the one shown to the child on a word card. In the fourth subtest the pupil marks the picture the name of which rhymes with a word the examiner names. The first four subtests are group tests, but the fifth subtest, in which the pupil names as many of the capital and small letters and the given numbers as he can, must be given to one pupil at a time.

The Van Wagenen Reading Readiness Test, published by the Betts Reading Clinic, Haverford, Pennsylvania, has two forms, both within the same test booklet. It tests range of information, perception of relations, vocabulary, memory span for ideas, word discrimination, and word learning. The subtest entitled "Perception of Relations" evaluates the child's ability to make analogies of this type: "Birds, sing: dogs, ———." Under "Memory Span for Ideas" the child is asked to repeat verbatim after the examiner sentences of increasing length and complexity. The part on "Word Discrimination" tests visual discrimination, which is the ability to differentiate between two or more forms. The subtest "Word Learning" tests the rapidity with which a child can learn a new word when symbols with which the word is to be associated are given. Cards with a series of symbols (not letters of the alphabet) are shown to the pupil, and he is told what word to associate with that card. After a series of cards has been presented several times, the pupil is asked to name the words as he looks at the cards. The *Van Wagenen Reading Readiness Test* is usable only as an individual test.

The *Metropolitan Readiness Tests,* which are group tests published by Harcourt, Brace and World, Inc., New York, and available in two forms, consist of six subtests, entitled "Word Meaning," "Sentences," "Information," "Matching," "Numbers," and "Copying." All six subtests are made up of pictures which the pupil is asked to mark or copy according to oral instructions by the teacher. The first subtest is a test to measure the child's ability to understand words. In the second subtest the pupil's comprehension of phrases and sentences is checked. The informational background of the child is tested in the third test. In the fourth test his power of visual perception is measured as revealed by his ability to select the letter, figure, word, or picture that is similar to a specified one. The fifth subtest measures many abilities related to numbers, such as knowing the vocabulary of numbers, writing numbers, recognizing written numbers, understanding number terms, telling time, and knowing the meaning of fractional parts. In the sixth subtest, "Copying," the pupil's power of visual perception and his motor control are tested. One special value of this subtest, in terms of reading skills, is that it helps detect tendencies toward reversing parts of letters or words that may be indicative of difficulties in reading.

The *Lee-Clark Reading Readiness Test,* published by the California Test Bureau, Los Angeles, is a group test printed in only one form. The three subtests measure the ability to match letters, to follow directions, to understand the meaning of words, and to note similarities among given words.

The *Classification Test for Beginners in Reading,* by Clarence R. Stone and C. C. Grover, distributed by the Webster Publishing Company, St. Louis, Missouri, is a group test, in which the pupil's ability to observe likenesses and differences between word forms is tested. No more than about twenty minutes is required for giving the test.

In the choice of reading readiness tests, as in the selection of other kinds of standardized tests, attention needs to be given to validity, reliability, ease of administering and of scoring, availability in more than one form, and reasonableness of cost. Since many teachers find it valuable to know a child's achievement in a variety of abilities related to beginning reading, they welcome the fact that many readiness tests are divided into subtests. When averages or norms are computed for the subtests, the teacher can determine in which of the characteristics tested each child is average, above average, or below average.

Although readiness tests alone are far from perfect means of determining whether a pupil is ready for beginning reading, the use of sufficiently reliable and valid ones is an asset in evaluation. However, the results must be interpreted with caution. The correlation of scores made by groups of children who have taken several readiness tests has not been very high. Nevertheless, it is probably true that a teacher can learn more about how ready a child is for beginning reading by giving him a reading readiness test than she could learn by spending the same length of time on other means of evaluation.

INFORMAL MEANS OF EVALUATION. Even though standardized tests throw considerable light on factors that are important in deciding whether it is advisable to begin the teaching of reading to a child, much can be done without them in trying to make that decision wisely. Informal tests, constructed by the teacher, can also be of decided help.

1. *Testing visual and auditory discrimination.* The ability to discriminate between letter and word forms and between letter and word sounds, which constitutes an essential to reading, can be tested in a variety of ways through teacher-made tests. In devising these tests the teacher must have clearly in mind the meaning of the terms *visual discrimination* and *auditory discrimination* and the importance to reading of the development of these skills. She must not confuse *visual discrimination* with *vision* nor *auditory discrimination* with *hearing.* By *visual discrimination* is meant the ability to *differentiate* between two or more forms, such as objects, written words, or written letters. Although a child's vision may be excellent, he may be unable to make fine differentiations between similar objects, pictures, words, or letters presented in visual form. In order to succeed in reading, the child should be able to differentiate between forms as nearly alike as *m* and *n.* If an individual cannot see such differences readily, he is likely to be greatly handicapped when learning to read. Some entering pupils do not possess this ability to the extent needed for beginning reading, but fortunately it can be developed through training.

By *auditory discrimination* is meant the ability to note the differences between sounds. A high degree of correlation has been found between auditory discrimination and success in reading.[3] A child's hearing may be excellent, even though he is unable to distinguish between the sound of the bells of the Presbyterian Church and the Lutheran Church. In order to be successful in reading, especially when it is taught chiefly by means of phonetic approaches, pupils should be able to recognize the difference between sounds as similar as the *b* and the *p* sounds as they occur in words. As in the case of visual discrimination, auditory discrimination may be improved through practice.

To test visual discrimination the teacher may make a test similar to one used frequently in standardized reading readiness tests. She may ask the pupils, for example, which word in the following row is different from the others:

man man man men man.

Or she may ask the boys and girls to find the word, in a row like the following, that is different from the first one in the row:

fine fine find fine fine.

---

[3] Bertha Boyd Thompson, "A Longitudinal Study of Auditory Discrimination," *Journal of Educational Research,* 56 (March 1963), 376–378.

A test of this type can be duplicated for the pupils on sheets of paper containing many rows of words arranged like those in the examples.

To test auditory discrimination the teacher can ask the pupils to indicate, for example, which of these pairs of sounds which she gives are alike and which are different: *m,n; n,m; n,n; m,m; b,p; p,p; p,b; b,b.* Or she can ask the pupils to name other words that begin with the same sound as the one with which, for example, the word *mother* begins. Another variation is to ask the pupils which pairs of words like the following begin with the same sound: *mother, man; cat, came; bark, pie.*

2. *Appraising other factors.* Through teacher-made tests, in many cases similar to those found in standardized tests, the teacher can get an approximation of the child's vocabulary, his ability to follow directions, his ability to remember, his power to do critical thinking, as well as of many other skills or abilities related to reading.

A significant test to determine a child's ability to retain words presented in written form can easily be devised. The teacher can present on cards a series of three or four or more words and spend several minutes providing the pupil with practice on them. She can give the practice by first naming the words and then asking the pupils to repeat them. Then she may have the pupil match the cards with words written in manuscript writing on the board. Further practice can be provided by having a pupil point to the words on the list on the board as the teacher or another child names them in an order different from the one in which they are written. To check the ability to remember the words the teacher can ask the pupil, after an interval of an hour or longer, to name the words earlier presented as the teacher points to them on the board or shows cards on which they are written.

Valuable information can also be collected through careful observation of the children. To get insight into a child's background of experience, the teacher may wish to talk with him concerning his interests. A rough measure of his attitude toward reading can be gained by observing how often he looks at books on the reading tables, whether he asks for stories to be read to him, and whether he is interested in finding out what the written word says. Whether he has acquired the top-to-bottom and left-to-right sequence can be determined in part by observing him as he looks at pictures and as he "reads" captions and other labels. An index of his vocabulary can be gained by listening to him talk and by gauging roughly how well he understands what he hears. Many teachers keep a written record of those characteristics of a child that have a bearing upon his ability to learn to read. Whether a written record is kept or not, informal observation of children in classroom and school ground situations serves as a useful supplement to standardized reading readiness tests.

Thus, during the first weeks of school, the teacher will want to study the characteristics of each child that relate to success in beginning reading. She can do so by means of mental tests, reading readiness tests, informal observations of children, conferences with children, consultation with parents and others, and examination of records. Some factors that she should consider are intelligence, hearing, vision, visual and auditory discrimination, experience background, vocabulary, emotional and social maturity, ability to remember, ability to follow directions, power to do critical thinking, and interest in reading. On the basis of her best judgment, as she weighs all the data that she has collected, the teacher will decide which pupils are ready for reading and which pupils are not.

Guidelines for Helping the Child Get Ready to Learn to Read

After the first-grade teacher has decided whether her pupils are ready to learn to read, she is confronted with the problem of what to do with those who are not ready for systematic instruction in reading. Should she have them postpone participation in all activities that pertain to reading in the hope that as they mature they will overcome their shortcomings? Clearly the answer is "No."

It is true that some children who are not ready for reading at the beginning of the school year will be ready in a few months even without special instruction. They need merely to wait for the further maturing of their various powers. Others, however, will respond quickly to specific guidance. There is no justification for the attitude of the teacher who, when asked why one child sat by himself in the back of the room throughout most of the school day, answered, "Oh, he is waiting for his reading readiness."

What then are the guidelines that the teacher should follow when planning a program for the prereading period?

The teacher should have clearly in mind the objectives of the prereading period. The general purpose of the prereading period is, of course, to guide the child in such a way that he will become better prepared for beginning reading. More specifically, the objectives of the prereading program can be stated as follows:

1. To determine whether the child is ready to learn to read, and if he is not ready, to find out how he can best be helped.

2. To assist the child in becoming adjusted to life in school.

3. To broaden the child's background of experience.

4. To help the child to gain greater emotional and social maturity.

5. To help the child increase his speaking and understanding vocabulary.

6. To provide an environment in which the child will have an opportunity to develop the skills essential to beginning reading.

7. To increase the child's interest in reading and to make him aware of the functions of reading.

Unless the child is cognizant of needs that can be satisfied through reading, he is not likely to be strongly motivated to read. In many ways the teacher can help him see that through reading he can learn to increase his store of information and that reading can be a source of pleasure for him.

Reading readiness activities should be an integral part of the total first-grade program. By means of many of the activities that the children carry on in any good first-grade program many of the goals of the prereading period can be attained. For example, characteristic activities of a first grade, such as story-telling, the examination of picture books, music and art activities, and excursions, can contribute greatly to the development of readiness for reading.

Direct help in the form of practice activities should be provided for some boys and girls. Although many of the activities of a good first-grade program, even when not designed specifically to prepare children for reading, are instrumental in fostering reading readiness, some boys and girls seem to require additional practice on certain skills which are essential to beginning reading. For example, practice periods set up to help children gain proficiency in discriminating between word forms are valuable when not enough meaningful repetition can be provided by incidental means. Such practice should not, however, replace abundant incidental instruction, which is afforded, for instance, when the children look for a name on a chart listing the children who have special responsibilities for the week. The teacher may at that time say, "No, that word is not *John* (as the teacher points to *Jim* and then *John*) although it begins like *John*. It is *Jim*." "Find Mathilda's name. Is it longer or shorter than Mary's?"

The activities of the prereading period should provide background for the initial reading tasks. Unfortunately, the reading textbooks, which must be written for the child population as a whole, cannot take account of the many variations in the social, cultural, geographical, and vocational backgrounds of all the children. The characters and situations portrayed in most reading text-books are, therefore, usually drawn from the environments of fairly typical middle-class homes and communities. To be sure, the popularity of television has had an equalizing effect upon the background information that many boys and girls have. The city child who watches television has a better understanding of the farm and the farm child of the city than was formerly the case. Nevertheless, this knowledge as obtained through television is often superficial. The slum-dwelling child or the child living on a Wyoming ranch or an Indian reservation is still likely to have some difficulty in recognizing the Bob and Sue of the suburbanite family in the basal reader. Furthermore, to the country child the incidents may be quite dull in comparison with the killing of a rattlesnake or the rounding up of cattle escaping through a break in the fence.

Nor can it be taken for granted that the city child will understand references to a farm. He may not ever have seen a cow, and the illustration in the book may give him a misleading impression of her size.

Preparing the children for the basal reading series can therefore, in some instances, be a formidable task. Storytelling, discussion, and the use of various audio-visual aids may be used to prepare the child for the situations encountered in the readers. A rich "experience" program in the prereading period, including possibly a visit to a farm, will provide the foundation upon which the initial reading skills may be built.

Even in schools where no basal reading series is used and the program is individualized as the teacher attempts to help every child read material on his level, problems similar to those mentioned in relation to the textbook program persist. In such an individualized reading program it is still necessary to provide appropriate experiences in preparation for reading. Experiences such as field trips, discussions, and at times word study can help assure greater effectiveness for an individualized reading program as well as for one based in part on textbooks.

The length of the reading readiness period should vary. Many boys and girls can begin to read almost as soon as they start school. Many will be ready to begin within a few weeks of that time. Some will probably not be well equipped for reading until some months have passed. For others, occasionally, it may be desirable to wait still longer. However, in a school system in which the teaching of reading is part of the first-grade curriculum, as it almost always is, a child should not be deprived of reading instruction throughout the school year unless he is clearly too immature to undertake the task with facility and pleasure. If he is not learning to read at some time during the year when most of his classmates are doing so, he may develop a poor attitude toward reading or serious feelings of inferiority. Usually, after sufficient preparation for the reading task, the child will find experiences of success in reading if the teacher employs methods and materials appropriate to his needs.

In explaining to parents why reading instruction has been delayed for their children, teachers sometimes use the analogy of infants' teething, walking, and talking. They point out that some children start later than others, but that after they have their teeth, and have learned to walk and to talk, they get along as well as the others. They explain that it is not in the child's interest to bring pressure upon him to read before he is ready. There is merit in this analogy, because maturational factors play a large part in reading readiness. However, one important difference should be recognized. Parental guidance plays a relatively small part in determining when a child begins to walk, and none at all in determining when his first teeth make their appearance. On the other hand, parent and teacher guidance and environmental conditions generally have an enormous effect on the cultivation of genuine reading readiness. Reading readiness cannot be brought about before a child is mature enough to read, but it can be delayed by failure to provide the necessary guidance early enough.

A child should be taught to read as soon as he is ready. If he is ready before he starts school he should be permitted, even encouraged, to learn to read. The experience of reading, for the child who can read with success and pleasure, enriches his life and contributes to his general development. On the other hand, it is an error to assert, as certain writers have done, that a child who starts to read late has lost one or more years of his life and that he will always be one or more years behind his capacity to read. First, there are many experiences besides reading that a young child can have to enrich his life. Second, a considerable amount of evidence shows that some children who do not receive reading instruction until the second year of school outstrip their counterparts who learned to read in the first grade, even before the end of the elementary school period.

A large variety of appropriate materials should be made available during the prereading period. Since one important objective of the prereading period is to develop and maintain an interest in reading, the children should have access to a large number of attractive books. Some of these may be placed on a library table, of height appropriate for the first-grade child, while others may be arranged on low bookcases. Included should be books to which the pupils have been introduced as the teacher showed them or talked about them or read from them to the class. The display should not, however, be limited to books with which the pupils are familiar. There should also be some that are new to the children, so that through them interest in exploring books can be developed. To help the boys and girls realize that books are valuable not only for the stories but also for the information they contain, the book collection should include both stories and informational material.

Books that boys and girls have made can also stimulate interest in reading. On the library table may be placed large books that other children have made in preceding years. For example, if the first grade the year before made as a class project a big picture book telling about a visit to a farm, the children can see how by means of the book it is possible to share information with others. Such a book is especially helpful if there are captions or simple story material accompanying the pictures. The new class, too, might bring pictures on a subject like "Our School" or "Our Pets" and mount them to form a big book. Under each picture the teacher might write a sentence or two suggested by the children. It is easy to interest children in a book they have helped to make.

Displays on bulletin boards can be of much value. A bulletin board on which are mounted leaves, with captions telling the kind, may help extend the experiences of some of the children. It can also give them further proof that learning to read is worthwhile, since the words below the leaves give significant information. Pictures of the means of transportation that some of the boys and girls have used, like the bicycle, the truck, the automobile, and the airplane, can serve similar purposes.

Many publishing companies that sell textbooks for elementary school reading also have reading readiness booklets that can serve a helpful purpose for some children. Some of the booklets provide specific preparation for a certain series of readers, while others can be used profitably by some boys and girls regardless of the reading books that will be used later.

Duplicated materials made by the teacher can also be valuable. For instance,

exercises in noting likenesses and differences among groups of pictures, or geo-
metric designs, or letters, or words can be provided in this manner.

*The learner should be ready for each stage in learning to read before he
begins it.* For a long time the term *readiness,* when used in connection with
reading, referred only to the prereading period. Now, however, it is realized
that *readiness* should be considered with each stage of reading instruction. Before any new task in reading is presented, the question of readiness on the part
of the child to learn it should be studied. Before instruction on how to use a
dictionary is begun, for example, the teacher should make certain that the
child has the requisite skill for undertaking the new learning. One requirement
in that case is that he must know alphabetical order. Since a good reading
program is developmental in nature, readiness for any stage in learning to read
is usually acquired in the preceding stage. In such a program the skills acquired in one stage form the background for learnings that take place in succeeding stages.

Probably in every lesson the teacher should consider whether the pupils
are ready for the activities to be performed in it. Preparation sometimes needs
to be made long before a lesson is taught—for example, by having the pupils
take a trip to a farm before a unit on the farm is begun. At other times readiness for the main part of the lesson can be developed during the first few
minutes of the class period, through questions that set the mood for the story,
or through explanations that will make clearer the concepts to be developed
or through pictures or other visual aids shown to the group. But always,
whether as introduction to one day's reading activities or as a preliminary to a
new unit of work in reading or a next stage in reading, the problem of having
the child ready for reading should be given serious consideration.

5b

Developing
Readiness for Reading

So far we have discussed in some detail the theory basic to a sound prereading program. Now let us see how it can be applied in the classroom.

Fostering Emotional and Social Maturity

As the first-grade teacher adjusts her procedures to the emotional and social maturity of her pupils and strives to help them reach higher levels, she will keep certain principles in mind: (1) The teacher herself should act like an emotionally and socially mature person. (2) An atmosphere of calm, courtesy, industry, and happiness should prevail in the room. (3) Respect should be shown for the personality of each person. (4) Restrictions should serve a purpose and be relatively few in number. (5) Directions and suggestions should generally be positive rather than negative. (6) Praise is usually more effective than blame, but praise must be deserved to be of value. (7) In all school activities, the devel-opment of the entire child should be taken into consideration. (8) Every individual needs security, approval, success, and means of self-expression. (9) The help and cooperation of parents should be secured whenever possible. (10) The teacher should not necessarily postpone reading instruction until a child is well adjusted socially and emotionally, because success in reading can contribute greatly to a feeling of security.

The teacher will encounter numerous problems of emotional and social maturity which directly affect a child's readiness for reading. Some children are shy, others over-aggressive; some are "spoiled" or overprotected. What can the teacher do for them?

Often the shy child is the immature child. Insecurity may result from many causes. One of the common characteristics of the shy child is his fear of not being accepted by his peer group. If he has had little previous experience with participation in group activity, he may need gradual and patient introduction to group enterprises of many types. Certainly he should be made to feel, by every possible means, that he is liked. He should be brought into contact with other children who are friendly to him. He should receive praise for successful efforts at social adjustment. He should be encouraged to contribute constructively to the work of the group, and thus secure the approval of his peers.

In the case of the child who cries easily or loses his temper on slight provocation, careful attention should be given to his general physical well-being. Has he been getting enough rest and wholesome food? Does he show signs of illness? Where the crying may have become a habit, the teacher should be ready to supply suitable distractions and try to avoid situations that may give rise to crying. The positive approach is usually the more effective. Thus when a child exhibits self-control in a situation, the teacher, instead of ignoring such desirable behavior, may say, "I noticed that Phyllis did not become angry when George broke her clay bowl. She helped George pick up the pieces and said she would try to make another bowl."

Although the aggressive child may be the most troublesome, he usually presents a less serious problem than the shy and retiring one. Tactful discussions with the group as a whole about respecting the rights of others may be helpful, and it may be necessary to provide experiences that teach the child he cannot get what he wants through aggressive behavior. Most aggressive children are merely seeking to gain recognition which they cannot get by more constructive methods. They should be given frequent opportunities to obtain such recognition by means that are socially approved.

The teacher will also encounter the overprotected and the "spoiled" child. Wherever possible, she should seek the cooperation of the oversolicitous parents. The overprotected child, while feeling secure in the affections of the teacher, should be encouraged to assume ever-increasing independence in making and carrying out decisions. The teacher should insist on his doing for himself the things he can learn to do without adult assistance and should praise him when he succeeds. The "spoiled" child usually insists on having his own way in all matters. When thwarted, he may engage in pouting, crying, or various forms of aggressive behavior. Most "spoiled" children can be taught to "take turns" in group activities. They can be made to understand that no one is able to have his own way at all times and that thoughtfulness of others creates pleasant relationships. In extreme cases it may be necessary to isolate the child temporarily from the group, if only for the sake of the other children. Such disciplinary measures should, however, be regarded as exceptional.

Developing Educational Readiness

As the teacher pays attention to the emotional and social development of boys and girls, she can at the same time help them grow in other characteristics that have a marked bearing upon success in beginning reading. How this can be done through attention to the experience background, auditory and visual discrimination, and other factors is explained in the remaining pages of this chapter.

Enriching the Child's Background of Experience

One way in which children's readiness for reading can be cultivated is through the extension of their experience background. Experience is important, not merely because children must get ready for reading, but because appropriate, wholesome, and varied experiences are an important part of each person's life, at any age. Even for the many children in the primary school who have already enjoyed a wide variety of experiences with places, persons, things, processes, and events, new and interesting school experiences are desirable. The school should provide all children with an interesting environment in which to grow up. Although many —perhaps most—of the children who enter first grade have a sufficient experience background to learn to read, the school should continue to open new worlds of experience to all children. For those children whose experiences have been severely limited, it may be desirable to postpone formal reading instruction until they have had the opportunity to enjoy a variety of direct experiences.

For all children it is well to make sure that the situations encountered in their first reading books are familiar. Most children's books, especially reading textbooks, present scenes and incidents familiar to the great majority of children. A boy and a girl, parents, a dog or a cat, simple toys, and perhaps a tractor or a mechanical crane constitute the major "props" of the primers. Nevertheless, the wider and richer the child's previous experience has been, the greater his chances of approaching the reading with confidence and pleasure. Building background should therefore not be limited to the kind of situations encountered in the first reading book.

Experienced teachers are familiar with the wide variety in the range and types of backgrounds found among school children. They know it is necessary to study the children carefully in order to meet the multifarious individual needs. In some cases it will be possible to distinguish between different groups in the first-grade class. Thus, for example, those children who have not attended kindergarten may be selected for an exploratory trip through the school building. If an individual child has never had a pet, the teacher may talk with him about animals, show him pictures of pets, or better still, arrange for the class to acquire one.

Socio-economic level will often affect the nature of the child's previous experiences, but not necessarily their extent. Children from middle-class homes have often traveled considerably, even to distant countries. They are likely to see more movies, have more toys and books at home, and have more opportunity for gardening, experimentation with pencils, crayons, and paper and construction materials than lower-class children. On the other hand, the slum-dwelling child knows a world that is quite unfamiliar to his more fortunate classmate. He may have developed, through the necessities of his life, a greater maturity and independence and often even a tragic sophistication about the ways of the adult world.

The ideal school environment for preparing boys and girls for reading, then, is one in which many things are going on. A primary class may be building a large model airplane, operating a store, viewing a film, making a terrarium, or caring for a pet. The child's background of experience can be extended by going on field trips, examining objects, looking at pictures, observing or participating in demonstrations and experiments, and listening to stories.

The following list exemplifies the many kinds of things that went on in one third grade:[1]

1. Two children were typing thank-you notes on the typewriter.

2. Several boys were piloting a good-sized, homemade, wooden airplane.

3. There was a piano and Nancy was showing Erma how to play.

4. The "Movie Man," Mr. Moore, was letting two boys help him fix the machine for us.

5. There were three cages with small animals. Yes, one cage would do, but can't you generalize better with three animals, or see exceptions to generalizations?

6. There were the scales with the seven

---

[1] Elsie Butler, "Living Together in Third Grade," *Elementary English*, 28 (January 1951), 2–3.

little weights. Some children were weighing various objects.

7. There was a child fixing a ten-watt light bulb over which some leaves were drying.

8. There was a bucket of papier-mâché. Two girls were making puppets. One little boy was painting the face of a dry puppet.

9. There was a pretty chest with dress-up clothes. It is seldom used now. A few days ago it was quite a busy chest.

10. There was a big sewing basket which the children had made and filled with scraps of cloth, thread, scissors, needles, pins, buttons, etc.

11. There were Cleo and Harvey with a fruit jar, a pie tin, sand, some begonia leaves, and a book on plants. Cleo was reading the directions and Harvey was following them.

12. There were paper sacks of various sizes. Girls were making dolls of these sacks and dresses for them of colored crepe paper.

13. There were many plants. Some were to make the room attractive. Some were for experimental purposes. Bean seed and grass seed were planted in various ways.

14. There were two easels with brushes and paints and a child at each easel. One child told you she was painting a picture of her house and herself with a green pocketbook. The other child showed signs of not wanting to talk about his painting.

15. Several children were working on individual newspapers. The teacher wished several had been working on one newspaper, but that had been voted down.

16. There were exhibits on a table with labels or signs by each:

A. In this jar are ant eggs and ants—Barbara.

B. Here are two cocoons. My sister found them—Betty.

C. This is bamboo. It came off of a tree at the greenhouse—Joan.

D. This bird's nest fell out of a tree during the storm—Harvey.

17. There was a low table with pie tins and fourteen little hands busy with clay.

In such a rich and active environment, chil-dren's curiosities are whetted and reading experiences take on new meaning.

GOING ON FIELD TRIPS. The eagerness of most first-grade children to learn more about the part of the world near them should be fully utilized. There are many places in or near school that boys and girls enjoy seeing. Trips through the school, examination of playground equipment, walks to gather leaves or stones, trips to look at trees and birds— all can be made real learning experiences, contributing not only to reading but also helping the child find out more about the world in which he lives. But such trips must be carefully planned if the maximum value is to be obtained. Part of the planning should usually involve preparing the pupils for the trip so that they will know better what to look for. For instance, before the boys and girls go on a walk to gather leaves, some pictures of pretty leaves may be shown and brief comments made. The purpose of the children in going on the walk, possibly to see how many different kinds of leaves each child can find, should be one that is whole-heartedly accepted by the group. During the trip itself help should also be given frequently in the form of suggestions or questions or directions. At this time the teacher may ask the pupils to notice if many leaves have fallen, and whether more green leaves are on the trees than on the ground. After the trip it is important to have a follow-up, when the pupils may engage in one or more activities such as showing their leaves, expressing rhythmically how the leaves fall, mounting them, drawing pictures suggested by their walk, making up a poem about leaves, or planning the words for a chart telling about their trip.

EXAMINING OBJECTS. By means of objects displayed in the room or otherwise brought to the attention of the boys and girls, the pupil's fund of information can be greatly extended. Discussion of material on a science table can be encouraged. The children can be encouraged to bring to school objects in which they are interested, like stones or model airplanes or toy boats, and to explain them to the other children. Thus through wise direction many significant facts can be learned as the children show a new doll, a strange-looking acorn, or a knife that was recently received as a birthday present.

LOOKING AT PICTURES. Pictures serve as an important means of broadening the experience background of the children. If motion-picture equipment is available, the teacher can select motion pictures that will fit the needs and interests of her group. Slides and filmstrips, too, some of which are specifically planned for several of the basic reading series, can be used to make concrete the things that might otherwise be rather meaningless abstractions. Mounted pictures, post cards, and snapshots, brought either by the pupils or the teacher, can be a source of pleasure and of learning. Exhibiting them attractively will encourage children to study them and can also serve as a means of teaching them how to display pictures effectively. If the children share the responsibility of arranging the materials in an orderly fashion, they can develop skill in mounting pictures and arranging attractive displays.

OBSERVING OR PARTICIPATING IN DEMONSTRATIONS AND EXPERIMENTS. Demonstrations and experiments are of special interest to many children, and they can be the source of much information. Many experiences in science lend themselves well to use in the first grade; these include finding out what happens to plants when they have and when they do not have sunlight, discovering what effect salt has on ice, noticing how steam becomes water, and discovering that air is necessary for a candle to burn. Often the teacher can let the pupils take part in the experiments.

LISTENING TO STORIES. Storytelling at all ages can open vistas to the first-grade child. Realistic stories, in particular, are appealing to children of five and six. Although children should share in the story telling and self-expression for the child telling a story is important, the welfare of the listener should also be considered. Consequently, the quality of the story and the method of telling it should be matters of concern not only for the sake of the storyteller but also for that of the listener.

ENGAGING IN OTHER ACTIVITIES. The teacher has at her disposal many other means of preparing boys and girls for beginning reading through extending their experiences. She can do this by providing records to which the children can listen, encouraging creative expression through music and art, interesting the children in putting on plays or puppet shows, and making provisions for discussions and conversation that is interesting, elevating, and informative.

Stimulating Growth in Language Abilities

Since there is a close relationship between reading and other language abilities, much can be done to help the pupil develop in all the linguistic skills. Both during the pre-reading period and after the child has begun reading in books, his development in language can be stimulated in a variety of ways so that he will become more ready for reading or will become a more efficient reader. The teacher can effect growth in reading skill or in abilities related to reading by wisely guiding activities that deal with speech, listening, and writing.

One period of the school day that can contribute richly to the development of language efficiency is the "sharing period." In a large number of primary grades a short period, popularly called "sharing time" or "telling time," is set aside daily so that the pupils will have an opportunity to "share" some of their experiences with others in their group. They do so by telling their classmates and the teacher experiences of interest to them. During this period many teachers like an informal seating arrangement, often in circular or semicircular formation.

Typically during the "sharing period," one pupil at a time, either while seated or while standing at a place where others can see him, tells in a sentence or more something that he thinks will interest others. At times he has something to show to the class as he makes his explanation. A child showing a stone that he found on his way to school may say, "I found a pretty stone." With or without questioning by the teacher or the rest of the group he may add, "I found it on the way to school. I am going to keep it." Other typical bits of information given by first-grade pupils are:

"We have a new baby. It is a baby sister."
"Mother is taking me to the five-and-ten-cent store tonight. I will buy a doll."
"I fell yesterday. This is where I hurt my leg. A dog chased me."

In conducting a "sharing period" these are points many teachers find profitable to observe: (1) Good English should be encouraged but not to the point of inhibition of spontaneity in talking. (2) Participation should be well distributed. Although frequently not every child can have a "turn" during every "sharing time," no one should be slighted day after day and nobody should monopolize the time. (3) Opportunities to increase the pupils' vocabulary should be utilized. This can often be done if after a pupil has used a word unfamiliar to many, the teacher makes the term clearer. For example, if one child says, "I found this piece of marble," the word *marble* can be explained through comments or questions by the teacher. (4) "Sharing time" should be a happy time. (5) The "sharing period" should not be a long period, probably not more than about twenty minutes in length. (6) A good

time for a "sharing period" is at the beginning of the day when the pupils are eager to tell what has happened since they were last with the others.

Many values can be gained through effective use of "sharing time," some of which are directly related to reading abilities. Besides having an opportunity to improve the understanding vocabulary, the children can grow in self-confidence, in power to relate events in sequence, in ability to predict outcomes, in attentiveness when listening, in growth in number and complexity of concepts, in interest in reading more about some of the topics discussed, and in many other ways. The relationship of many of these learnings to getting ready for reading is evident.

Developing Speech

One of the chief objectives of first-grade programs, before and after reading instruction is begun, is to help the pupil express himself well orally. Skill in speech plays a significant part in learning to read. The child embarrassed by ridicule because of baby talk is not likely to want to participate freely in group discussions based on reading activities. The boy or girl unable to talk in short, simple sentences is frequently unable to anticipate the meaning of a sentence, even of the type found in beginning reading books. In these and other ways skill in reading and in speech often go hand in hand.

The following points should serve as guidelines in the selection of procedures for the development of speech:

1. Most speech improvement comes about through informal classroom activities.
2. Provision should be made for a large number of enriching experiences that give opportunity for improved oral expression.
3. Attention should be given to various phases of speech, such as proper enunciation and pronunciation, adequate speaking vocab-

ulary, and interest in speaking with or to others, with an understanding of courtesies and proprieties in speaking.

4. Pupils who need help in speech should be given opportunity for special practice.

5. The teacher's own speech habits should be a suitable model for the children.

6. Poor speech habits may be caused by feelings of insecurity.

7. Special attention should be given to children who come from homes where a foreign language is spoken.

8. The teacher should not do all the talking.

9. The physical features of the room and the activities carried on by the class should be made so interesting that the children will have vital topics for discussion and conversation.

10. The atmosphere of the classroom should encourage children to converse freely at appropriate times.

The following are some ways in which the teacher can help pupils to improve the pattern of their expression:

1. Providing many opportunities for free discussion during various activities, such as planning a project or making the schedule for the day.

2. Encouraging the pupils to tell stories that they have heard or experienced or made up.

3. Asking pupils to explain pictures they have drawn.

4. Placing on the bulletin board pictures which the pupils can interpret orally to others.

5. Setting aside time for dramatizing some of the stories read or told by the teacher to the group.

6. Helping the boys and girls put on simple puppet shows.

7. Providing opportunities for dramatic play—for example, playing house.

8. Helping the children do choral reading or otherwise saying poems in unison.

9. Making provisions for many opportunities for singing.

10. Talking individually to the boys and girls when they come to school in the morning, during the noon hour, when they leave in the afternoon, or during periods set aside for individual or committee work.

11. Encouraging all pupils to participate in a "sharing period."

12. Asking pupils to talk about group experiences, like class trips to the bakery or the post office or the fire station, or to report on trips they have taken when not under the supervision of school.

13. Displaying in the room objects that are likely to stimulate discussion.

14. Setting time aside for the children to tell about what they enjoy doing, like caring for an animal, playing a game, or doing some cooking.

Improving Listening

One aspect of the language arts that has not been emphasized sufficiently in many schools is listening. Frequently it has been taken for granted. Because of its close relationship to reading and to many other significant activities both in and out of school, increased attention should be given to this ability.

In trying to help children develop better habits of listening, the teacher should utilize regular classroom activities whenever possible. The following are ways in which children can be helped to become better listeners:

1. As the teacher tells or reads stories to the boys and girls, she can stop occasionally to ask questions that test their attentiveness —for example, "Why did Bobby want to get some apples for his mother?"

2. After the teacher has told or read part of a selection to the class, she may say, "When

I finish the story, see if you can find out what happened to the snowman."

3. The pupils can be encouraged to listen carefully to stories so that they can tell them to others.

4. The pupils can draw up standards for good listening, such as looking at the person talking, not talking while someone else talks, and not playing with anything while someone is talking.

5. Evaluations of how well the pupils are listening, according to standards like those mentioned in (4) above, can be made by the class.

6. Listening can be encouraged by means of dramatization of stories or incidents.

7. At times some pupils may be given exercises in improving and testing their ability to listen.

Improving the Speaking and Understanding Vocabulary

Closely related to the improvement of both speaking and listening is the development of the speaking and understanding vocabulary. Since the vocabulary of beginning books and the sentence structure used in these books are necessarily below the understanding and speaking level of many of the children, it is important to extend their knowledge and use of words through listening and talking. Although much of the work on vocabulary development may be carried on by incidental instruction, it should nevertheless be carefully planned. Direct practice may sometimes be needed. Growth in children's speaking and listening vocabulary can be fostered in many ways:

1. Providing opportunity to engage in activity on significant units of work. New words should be introduced as need for them arises.

2. Reading or telling stories that include some unfamiliar words. The meaning of new words should of course be explained.

3. Writing a group letter.

4. Dramatizing words like *walked, ran, crept, raced.*

5. Calling attention to children's use of new or especially colorful words.

6. Drawing pictures illustrating such new words as *funnel, burrow, tractor.*

7. Playing games in which children make up sentences that refer to a new word. A sentence might be, "I am thinking of something a rabbit does. He does it when he makes a hole. The word begins with the *b* sound."

8. Using motion pictures, slides, and filmstrips.

9. Bringing interesting objects to the room. If a rock exhibit is set up, for instance, children may enlarge their vocabulary by learning terms like *marble, granite, sandstone.*

10. Taking children on excursions and helping them become familiar with terms that give more meaning to their trip, like *cash register, sales, customer.*

11. Introducing songs and poems that contain new words.

In helping children to add words to their understanding and speaking vocabulary, the teacher may follow these steps:

1. Introduce the word in a meaningful situation.

2. Draw attention to the new word by giving its meaning, asking someone in the group who knows the word to give the meaning, or questioning the others so that they can tell what the word means.

3. Let some of the children use the word in a sentence.

4. Make certain that the pupils pronounce the word correctly.

5. Use the word in later conversation or discussion.

6. Encourage the pupils to use the word.

Developing a Reading Vocabulary

Even during the prereading program the

teacher can help the pupils acquire a reading vocabulary that will assist them greatly when they begin reading in a book. She can do so by labeling shelves where articles like scissors, paste, and crayons are kept. Attaching the children's names to their lockers and desks can also be of value. But merely labeling articles is not enough, for looking at a word, without the intent to remember it, frequently does not result in learning on the part of the child. For this reason, attention should be called to the labels and the children should be given an opportunity for associating the words with objects. At times the pupils may be asked to match the appropriate cards with the labels or they may name cards containing the words without comparing them with the cards used as labels. Labeling objects like a table, a desk, or a chair is of little value unless a real purpose is served thereby. It may be profitable, for example, to place words on a table to show what is to be exhibited on it.

Picture-word cards, cards on which the picture and the name of the item pictured are given, like *mother, father, sister, brother, cat, dog, school,* and *home,* can be displayed and used in practice exercises for pupils who seem to need such repetition. On the back of the card may be written the word that goes with the picture, so that pupils may practice recognizing words without looking at the illustrations. Sets of small cards like these, possibly four inches by six inches, can be used by the pupils individually. Similarly, both large cards for group use and small cards for individual practice can be made, with the names of the primary and the secondary colors corresponding to the color illustrated on the reverse side.

There are many other means of adding words to the children's vocabulary. The teacher may put on the chalkboard or on large sheets of paper directions often used in the classroom, such as "Please get your wraps," or "Please form a circle." Instead of giving the directions orally, the teacher

may sometimes point to these. Plans for the day may also be written on the board daily before school: "We will take a walk," or "We will hear a good story today." A chart with the names of the children in the room can be used in a game in which one child points to a name while another says it.

Learning to Write

The simple writing experiences of children during the prereading period can be of help in later reading instruction. Usually their writing during this stage is confined to the writing of their names or the copying of sentences from the board or from sheets of paper. Brief invitations to parents or short sentences to accompany illustrations they have made may be copied. Through writing of this type, children can be made more aware of the function of the written word both as writing and as reading. Moreover, as the pupils are writing they can become familiar with the configuration of words, by noting which words are short words, which are long words, and which begin or end in the same way. Since many children enjoy reading what they have written, they should have opportunity to read to others in the room or to their parents the captions under their pictures or the notes they write.

Developing Auditory and Visual Discrimination

Among the most important prerequisites for successful reading are the ability to differentiate between sounds of words and letters and the ability to see the differences between written words and between letters. Since improvement in making such discriminations can be brought about through training, suggestions for their development are given in the following pages.

AUDITORY DISCRIMINATION. In helping children to discriminate between sounds they hear, teachers should remember that:

1. *There is great variation among first-grade children in powers of auditory discrimination.* The difference is not necessarily due to degrees of auditory acuity. Two children, for example, may plainly hear the words *weather* and *whether,* but only one may be able to note the difference in the sound.

2. *Instruction in auditory discrimination should take individual differences into account.* Many children will have developed the needed skill in auditory discrimination before they first come to school. For them the exercises in discrimination would be wasteful and stupid. On the other hand, the child who cannot tell whether *dog* and *cat* begin with the same sound or with different sounds needs help in learning to discriminate between sounds that are quite unlike. The same is true of those children who have little difficulty in distinguishing sounds at the beginning of words but have trouble with sounds at the end of words.

3. *Instruction in auditory discrimination should be an integral part of the regular classroom activities.* As children take part in the usual classroom activities, like playing with their toys or pets, their attention can be drawn to the differences in sounds. When, for example, a child fails to distinguish between *car* and *cars,* the teacher may try to help him detect the difference. At times there is value in providing separate exercises in noting which pairs of words are alike and which different, as in the case of *car* and *cars,* and *car* and *car.* Or a child may be asked to supply the last word of the second line of a jingle in order to make it rhyme with the first line.

Some of the ways in which auditory discrimination can be developed during the prereading period consist of having the pupils do the following:

1. Giving orally the beginning sounds of words with initial consonants, like the *r* sound in *rabbit.*

2. Giving orally words beginning with the same sound with which another word begins. The teacher may write on the board the words named by the pupils, even though the pupils cannot read them.

3. Telling which pairs of words named by the teacher, like *mother, man* or *little, ball,* begin with the same sound.

4. Naming the word in a list given by the teacher, like *mother, man, many, few, market,* that does not begin with the same sound as the others.

5. Telling which pairs of words given by the teacher end in the same sound, like *walks, sings,* or *runs, play.*

6. Naming the word in a list, like *at, talk, fit, get,* that does not end with the same sound as the others.

7. Telling which pairs of words, like *rat sat,* or *bat, sit,* are rhyming words.

8. Telling which word in a list does not rhyme, as in *cat, bat, sat, sit.*

9. Naming rhyming words.

10. Telling which pairs of sounds, like *m, n,* or *n, m,* are alike.

11. Making up rhymes.

12. Playing the game, "I spy." In this game, pupils guess what object a child refers to in a statement like, "I spy something that begins with the same sound as *Mary,*" or "I spy something that ends with the same sound as *took.*"

13. Naming the objects in a picture that begin with the same sound as a word that is named by the teacher.

14. Naming the objects in a picture that rhyme with a word that is named by the teacher.

15. Supplying the last word for a two-line jingle of which the teacher gives all but the last word. The pupils would name the words that rhyme with the last word of the first line.

VISUAL DISCRIMINATION. In planning procedures for the development of visual discrimination during the prereading period, certain general observations should be kept in mind: (1) Some beginning first-grade pupils do not have enough skill in visual discrimination to undertake the reading task with ease. (2) Instruction should be adapted to individual differences. (3) So far as possible, skill in visual discrimination should be furthered in connection with meaningful classroom activities. (4) Not all deficiencies in visual discrimination need to be removed before reading instruction is begun. As the child learns to read, opportunities for making finer discriminations will present themselves.

Some suggestions for methods of providing growth in the ability to distinguish between word forms and letter forms during the prereading period are:

1. Asking the pupils to find the word in a written series, like *big, boy, big, big, big,* which is unlike the other words.

2. Asking the pupils to draw a line under each word in a written series, like the following, which is the same as the first word in a row:

    man   mother   man   man   man.

At first, practice should be given in differentiating between words that are decidedly different in appearance, like *man* and *mother.* Later, the pupil should be asked to discriminate between words almost alike in appearance, like *man* and *men.*

3. After pupils have dictated to the teacher a record of some experience they have had, like taking care of a pet, asking one child to draw a line under all the words in the story that begin with the same letter as a word indicated by the teacher.

4. Listing two parallel columns of words, in which the same words are used but in a different order. The pupils may draw lines connecting the like words in the two columns.

5. Asking the pupils to cross out a given word, like *dog,* each time that it occurs in a group of sentences in which the word is used several times.

6. Having the pupils match tagboard cards, on which single words are written, with words as they are written on the board.

7. Having the pupils draw a circle around a word in a list on the board that is the same as a word on a card shown to the class.

8. Having the children find on a chart all the names of pupils in the room that begin with a specified letter.

9. Having the pupils find the part of a longer word that is like a shorter word. For example, the boys and girls might be shown, on the chalkboard, the words *walk* and *walking* and be asked to underline in the second word the part that is like the first.

walk   *walk*ing

10. Helping the boys and girls judge the length and shape of words by means of configuration clues as lines are drawn around each of two words that have been written on the chalkboard. The pupils could then tell whether the outline of the two words is alike or different. For example, the "boxes" drawn around the words *run* and *see* would be similar, but those drawn around the words *sing* and *play* would be different.

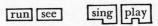

Improving the Ability to Remember

The ability to remember plays an important role in reading.

One cause of inadequate retention in reading is found in poor habits of attentiveness: a child who does not pay careful attention to what is going on cannot be expected to remember. The teacher can attack this problem by assisting boys and girls to become more attentive. Some ways in which children can be helped to attend better, and therefore to remember better, have been discussed earlier in this chapter under the related topic, "Improving Listening." Here are some additional suggestions for increasing a pupil's memory span:

1. Making the work interesting enough so that the pupil will have reason to want to pay attention.

2. Making sure that the work is on the level of the pupil.

3. Varying the activities frequently enough so that the child's power of attention will not be overtaxed. At the same time children should be helped to develop an ever longer span of attention.

4. Developing in pupils the desire to remain with an activity until it is completed, unless there is good reason not to do so.

5. Keeping in the room reasonable orderliness conducive to good attention.

6. Requiring pupils to keep to the topic of discussion.

7. Keeping each child responsible for remembering the answer to a question that he asked a community helper on a trip to the post office or police station or fire department.

REMEMBERING A SEQUENCE OF IDEAS. To help the boys and girls to remember a sequence of ideas encountered in reading or listening, the teacher may wish to follow some of these suggestions:

1. After the teacher or a pupil has told a story, the teacher may ask such questions as, "What was the first thing Nancy did when she saw that her dog had followed her?" "What did she do next?"

2. After the teacher has given directions for a simple experiment, like showing that plants need light, she may ask the pupils, "What is the first thing we need to do?" and "What do we need to do next?" After the experiment has been completed, the pupils may be asked to enumerate the steps that were followed.

3. Retelling stories can be a helpful means of developing the ability to remember a sequence of ideas. The pupil should relate the incidents in the correct order.

4. The boys and girls, with the assistance of the teacher, might build a topical outline for the dramatizing of a story. The pupils decide upon the events to be included in the dramatization and the teacher lists these on the chalkboard. They could then arrange these events in logical sequence.

5. The teacher might place on a flannel board, in mixed-up order, a series of pictures illustrating a story known to the boys and girls and then ask the pupils to rearrange the pictures in correct order.

6. The group may make a "movie" either to illustrate a story that the teacher has told or read to them or to portray activities in which they have engaged. Such an activity furnishes excellent practice in remembering events in sequence and cultivates other abilities important in reading, such as critical thinking, good work habits, skill in following directions, and ability to work with others.

A "movie" theater can be simply constructed. A large cardboard box can be used as the stage. An opening can be cut into one side of the box, possibly 12 inches high and 18 inches wide, through which the "movie" is viewed. The roller can be two ends of broom handles, to which the "movie" roll is attached. Each of the rollers can be inserted into the "theater" through two holes, one cut at the top and the other at the bottom of the box near the front corners of the "theater." Flaps of the box at the two sides of the "theater" (as it stands with the "stage" side to the front) through which the "movie" is put into it can be closed by means of a string at each opening tied around two brass fasteners. The "theater," when placed on a table, will need to project far enough over the edge so that the bottom parts of the rollers are free of the table.

Steps in planning a "movie" on a story told to the class may be these:

a. Discussing the story.

b. Deciding to make a "movie" of the story.

c. Retelling the story.

d. Deciding on pictures to include.

e. Working out a sequence of the pictures to be drawn.

f. Assigning pictures to be drawn.

g. Drawing the pictures.

goats at the side of the hill, (2) the green hill that they saw in the distance, (3) the stream they would have to cross, (4) the bridge they would have to cross, (5) the ugly troll who lived under the bridge, (6) the youngest billy goat starting to cross the bridge, (7) the troll roaring at the youngest billy goat, (8) the youngest billy goat talking with the troll, (9) the youngest billy

The troll roaring at the youngest billy goat

h. Deciding on captions or longer explanations of the pictures to be written for the "movie" by the teacher.

i. Arranging the pictures and the writing in the proper sequence.

j. Fastening the pictures to a roll.

k. Practicing telling the story of the "movie."

If the story of "The Three Billy Goats Gruff" were made into a "movie," these are pictures that might be drawn: (1) three billy

goat feeding on the hillside, (10) the second billy goat starting across the bridge, (11) the troll roaring at the second billy goat, (12) the second billy goat talking with the troll, (13) the second billy goat going across the bridge, (14) the first and the second billy goats feeding on the hillside, (15) the big billy goat starting across the bridge, (16) the troll roaring at the big billy goat, (17) the big billy goat talking with the troll, (18) the fight between the big billy goat and the troll, (19) the end of the troll, (20) the big billy goat going across the bridge, and (21) the three billy goats feeding on the hillside.

If there are fewer pupils than pictures to be drawn, some children could draw two. If the number of pictures is less than the number of pupils, two children could each draw a picture on the same topic. In that case one of the pictures, not necessarily the better, could be used in the "movie" and the other displayed with pride elsewhere, possibly as part of a big book or on the bulletin board.

FOLLOWING DIRECTIONS. The ability to follow directions involves considerable skill in remembering. So many directions are given to children in school that, as a rule, no special exercises are needed for practice in this skill. Usually the problem is to reduce. rather than increase, the number of teacher mandates. To facilitate learning, the teacher's directions should be clear. Although at first the directions should be very simple, they should become more complex as the pupils develop. At times the teacher may need to demonstrate how to follow a rather involved set of directions. At other times she can help pupils by having the class follow directions together.

Stimulating Growth in Critical Thinking

There are several methods of stimulating the power of critical thinking among children. The teacher can help the pupils increase in ability to think critically by means of the questions she asks when she reads or tells stories to them. For example, as she reads the story *Millions of Cats* by Wanda Gág, she may ask, "What do you think the little old woman will say when the little old man comes home not with one cat, but with millions of cats?" Or after she has told "The Tale of Peter Rabbit," she may ask, "Why was Peter Rabbit happy at the end of the story even though his mother had punished him?" Questions about what will happen next force children to think as they listen. Pantomine or dramatization of stories also calls for certain kinds of critical thinking, as does interpretation of a story by drawing pictures. The teacher can further encourage critical thinking by giving the boys and girls a part in planning activities, in deciding upon the better course of action in a given situation, and in determining why some of their actions were wise or unwise.

One excellent opportunity for the development of the power to think is provided by the "planning period," which is part of the daily program in an increasing number of primary grade rooms. During this period, which is usually at the beginning of the school day, the pupils, with the direction and guidance of the teacher, make plans for the day. The role of the teacher in planning will vary, depending upon the ability of the pupils to map out a good schedule, the complexity of the planning, and other factors. Always, however, without seeming authoritarian, the teacher maintains her role as a leader responsible in major part for the planning of the day's adventures.

The planning period is often divided into two parts. In the first part of the period, the pupils and the teacher consider the schedule for the day. The teacher may write on the board the suggestions of the class along with her own. Often the teacher starts the planning period by inquiring what items of business were not completed during the preceding day or days. Decision can then be reached as to what should be on the agenda for the day. Other suggestions can be made and discussed. The teacher may want to make a chart for a check list of the schedule for the day. Such a chart might contain items like these:

What Should We Do Today?

1. Listen to a story.
2. Tell stories.
3. Play house.

4. Draw or paint.
5. Write.
6. Play games.
7. Look at picture books.
8. Make things.
9. Sing.
10. Rest.
11. Have lunch.
12. Go to the washroom.

At first, as each item is considered the teacher will usually need to read it, but before long some of the children will be able to read at least some of the items orally to the rest of the group. As the schedule for the day is planned, the teacher may find it best to have more specificity in the items than the check list offers. For example, instead of stating one point of business for the day as "Play games," it may be stated, "Learn a new game and play some we know."

After the teacher thinks a justifiable listing has been completed, she and the pupils can decide on the sequence or the time of day when each activity shall take place. Frequently it will be found that too many activities have been planned.

The planning period offers a variety of ways by which the children can develop readiness for reading. Some of these are: noting the left-to-right and top-to-bottom sequence in reading; being aware of the fact that reading helps one know what to do next; learning to read some words that are used often in a written list; developing self-expression; and listening to others.

Increasing Skill in Handling Books

Skill in handling books, another ability to which attention should be given in the pre-reading period, can be developed in the following ways through precept and practice:

1. The teacher should handle all books with care.

2. The teacher may help the boys and girls draw up a list of specifications for taking care of books, such as:

a. Have clean hands when you handle a book.

b. Do not fold the pages of a book.

c. Do not tear the pages of books.

d. Do not put pencils or other objects in a book.

e. Do not write in a book.

f. Turn the pages of a book carefully.

3. The pupils may demonstrate proper ways of holding books.

4. The desirability of arranging books neatly on shelves and on the library table may be discussed and demonstrated.

5. Responsibility for care of books can be developed by rotating appointments of pupils serving as librarians.

6. The teacher might make a little bookman, whose body is in the shape of a book, who at times speaks to the boys and girls about how he likes to be treated.

7. Two pupils might present a short skit in which one child takes the part of a well-handled book and the other of a poorly-handled one. The two characters might tell how people treat them.

Orienting to Left-to-right and Top-to-bottom Sequence

Some children entering first grade require help in observing a left-to-right and top-to-bottom sequence in reading pictures or print. Some need to be shown which is their right and which is their left hand. Others, who do know left from right, have not yet discovered that reading, in English, proceeds from left to right and from top to bottom. Special practice in left-to-right and top-to-bottom reading may sometimes be needed.

The following are suggestions for helping children develop this directional orientation to reading:

1. As the teacher reads a book to the

class, she can point out where she starts reading and in what direction she progresses.

2. As the teacher or children reread from charts or the chalkboard stories that have been dictated, the teacher can run her hand rhythmically under the lines. Or she can ask a pupil to point to the word with which she should begin reading. In time, a pupil can sweep his hands below the line he is reading from a chart or from the chalkboard. Care must be taken in the latter case that word pointing with consequent "word calling" does not result.

3. At times, when the teacher writes on large sheets of paper or on the board, she can ask the pupils where she should begin writing and in what direction she should proceed.

4. As some pupils are placing a picture story on a flannel board, they should be guided to arrange the pictures from left to right in each row and from top to bottom by rows.

5. The pupils might be encouraged, as they draw "add-on" pictures, to proceed from left to right.

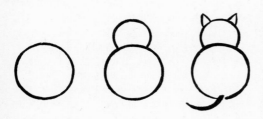

Developing and Maintaining Interest in Reading

The importance of access to an abundance of interesting reading materials has already been stressed in this book. Other ways in which the teacher can try to interest the children in books are: taking them to the school or public library where they can browse among the books and where, probably, the librarian will be willing to tell them a story; inviting one or more children from a second

or third grade to entertain the first grade by reading an interesting story to them; taking boys and girls to other rooms in the elementary school in which they can see books being used for various purposes; reading stories and informational material to the class.

The "sharing period," discussed earlier in this chapter, can serve to interest children in reading. They can be encouraged to show and talk about books they like. Some of these may be picture books for which the child reporting makes up the story. Or the books may contain a simple text, which someone has read beforehand to the pupil reporting.

Use of little booklets containing children's stories, written by the teacher at the dictation of the pupils, gives added incentive to learning to read. In these booklets may be recorded reports planned by the class as a whole on an activity in which they have engaged, such as a trip to a farm. Or the material may consist of individual accounts about each child—for example, reports on the work of each child's father. Some teachers, too, for recording in these books, make up stories in which the vocabulary is well controlled. Although making such a book is time-consuming, it is worthwhile in the long run, since the book can often be used not only once with a given group but also later on with classes of succeeding years.

Keeping records on charts of some of the experiences of the group, such as visiting the grocery store, can also stimulate interest in reading. How these charts can be constructed and utilized is explained below.

Using the Experience Chart in the Prereading Period

The term *experience chart* ordinarily refers to a written record of an experience a class has had, is having, or is intending to have. An experience chart is planned cooperatively by the pupils and the teacher and, in the primary grades, is usually recorded by the teacher. First-grade children who found pretty leaves may make an experience chart telling about their leaves, or those about to have a party may plan a chart to help remember points about the proposed party. Two examples of such charts follow:

Leaves
We found many pretty leaves.
We found them on our walk.
We found some red leaves.
Some of our leaves are brown.
Some of our leaves are yellow.

Our Party
We will have a party.
We will have the party on Monday.
We will have it in the afternoon.
Mary and Susan will bring cookies.
We will drink milk.
We will play games.

Experience charts serve a variety of purposes. The teacher's objective in helping plan a chart may be primarily to give children an opportunity to learn to express themselves well. Sometimes they are used chiefly to provide an opportunity for co-operative planning. Such charts are called language charts. Experience charts that are used primarily for reading purposes, either to get the child more nearly ready for beginning reading or to supplement the reading experiences that he has already had, are known as reading charts. Various purposes can, however, be served by the same chart. As the pupils construct and use a reading experience chart, they can also improve their expression and learn to plan cooperatively. The differentiation between the two kinds is made because in the so-called language experience chart it is not important to restrict the vocabulary as in the chart that serves primarily as a prereading or reading experience. The following discussion of experience charts refers essentially to those that help in

reading, either in the prereading period or later.

Many children profit from reading charts when they begin first grade. The exceptions are those children who have had a rich background of experience and are therefore ready to do the simple reading provided in pre-primers without the aid of reading charts. Their work with experience charts can be largely limited to language charts, in which reading is not the primary objective.

Experience charts are usually recorded on large pieces of paper, often 24 by 36 inches or 18 by 24 inches. They can, however, be made on smaller sheets, as they often are when they are designed for individual use rather than for group purposes. If the chart is to be preserved for a considerable time, it is often made on tagboard or mounting board. A record that is to be used for only a short time may well be kept on less expensive paper, like newsprint. Sometimes the charts are assembled, punched at the top, fastened by rings, and attached to a chart holder, which often is on a tripod base. Upon the tripod there is frequently an adjustable metal pole, across the top of which is a crossbar which holds the chart. Some experience records are kept in large notebooks, often made of butcher paper, probably 24 by 36 inches. The records kept in a notebook usually are on one theme, such as "Our Pets" or "Our Schoolroom" or "The First-grade Boys and Girls."

STEPS IN MAKING AND USING EXPERIENCE CHARTS. Experience charts are used in a variety of ways during the prereading period. Outlined below are steps similar to those that many teachers follow when detailed study of the chart is done as a prereading exercise. The chart is set up for two successive school days, although a shorter or longer time may be devoted to work on it. In considering these steps, the reader must bear in mind that many stories on charts or on the chalkboard have usually been made and utilized in a class before any one chart is given the detailed study that is here described.

FIRST DAY

1. The boys and girls participate in an interesting and significant experience.

2. The children discuss the experience.

3. The pupils, with the help of the teacher, plan the title, general content, and the exact sentences for the chart as the teacher does the writing on the board.

4. The chart as a whole is read first by the teacher, then by the pupils and the teacher together, and finally by the boys and girls alone.

SECOND DAY

5. Before class the teacher has copied onto chart paper the writing for the experience chart that she had put on the board the preceding day. The teacher has also copied on separate strips of tagboard each of the lines of the chart, so that they can be matched later with the writing on the chart. These are placed on the chalk tray or in a word-card holder. On word cards made of tagboard the teacher has also written a few of the words on which she plans to give special practice.

6. The new chart is then read by the teacher and pupils together.

7. The teacher reads sentences for the pupils to find, and they point to each one as they read it.

8. After the teacher has read the sentences out of the regular order, the pupils match the sentence strips with the sentences on the chart and read them.

9. As the teacher shows the boys and girls each of the several word cards, containing those words on which she thinks it is important to provide practice, she pronounces the word and has the pupils say it after her. A pupil then matches the word on the card with the same word on the chart. Further practice on the words can be given if before class the teacher writes these words on the board. In that case the pupils can name the words as the teacher points to them.

10. Review of words used in the chart that the boys and girls have studied earlier can then be made.

11. Before the period is over one or more pupils can read the chart alone.

DESCRIPTION OF SOME OF THE STEPS IN MAKING AND USING EXPERIENCE CHARTS. Since some of the steps already outlined need no further explanation, they are not included in the comments that follow.

1. *Motivation for making a chart.* After the pupils have engaged in an experience and have discussed it, there are many ways in which the teacher can interest the pupils in making, and then reading, an experience chart. The teacher may suggest to the pupils that they make a chart so that visitors coming into the room can read, or have read to them, what the class has done. Or the boys and girls may make one so that they can go to other rooms to read the chart to the children.

2. *Planning the chart.* In planning the chart, the teacher should keep in mind that: (a) Care needs to be taken that many, preferably all, of the children take part in the planning. (b) The teacher can, by questioning, help the pupils suggest significant items. (c) She can be of assistance in helping formulate sentences that are correct in structure. (d) She can help decide on the sequence. (e) She can guide the work so that the vocabulary used in the chart is fairly simple. She can also see that some words, on which she wants children to have practice, are used more than once and that appropriate "review" words also appear in the text. (f) She can give the pupils help in vocabulary building by asking for more colorful or more descriptive words to be substituted for given ones. (g) After the first draft is writ-

ten, she can assist the children in revising the sentences so that they may create a more unified composition.

3. *Constructing the chart.* Care should be taken to make the manuscript writing as nearly perfect as possible in the time available. Neatness, letter form, alignment, size, slant, and spacing between letters, between words, and between lines should receive adequate attention. If a picture is needed, it should be supplied by the teacher or a pupil or taken from a discarded publication.

4. *Making the sentence strips and the word cards.* The precautions given in connection with the writing of the chart should also be observed in the making of sentence strips and word cards. Teachers find it desirable to keep sentence strips and word cards of the same width, often about four inches wide, for uniformity when they are used with other cards and for ease in filing. For the same reasons some teachers also cut most of the word cards of the same length, approximately ten inches. Words that cannot be written without crowding on this size of paper are written on longer cards.

Usually no more than three or four new words should be included on one chart. These should be selected on the basis of their likely usefulness to the children. Some teachers prefer to choose words from the pupils' first reading books.

5. *Follow-up activities.* In addition to the culminating activity, already suggested, of reading the chart to visitors or pupils in other rooms, the teacher may make copies available to the children. She may leave space near each of the words that can be illustrated, so that the pupils can draw a picture that goes with the word; for example, opposite the word *leaves*, the pupils may draw a picture of leaves. This activity may help the children recall the word more easily later. The children can make the charts into a booklet and draw an appropriate picture for the cover. After a child has learned to "read"

the chart, he may take his booklet home and read it to his parents.

ILLUSTRATION OF WORK ON AN EXPERIENCE CHART. The following is a description of possible procedures in the development of an experience chart.[2]

The children had had a good time decorating the Christmas tree in their room. They were happy that every boy and girl had had the opportunity to put an ornament on the tree. Of special interest to them was the lighted star that they placed on the tip of the tree.

After the children finished decorating, they discussed various plans for enjoying their tree. One was to invite the second-grade children to join them as they sang Christmas songs. The teacher's suggestion to write a story about the tree, which would be read to the guests, was enthusiastically received.

The teacher helped the children to plan the story. When "Our Tree" was suggested as the title, she asked another pupil if he could think of a title that would tell what kind of tree it was. When the boy responded by suggesting "Our Christmas Tree," she wrote that title on the board. Then the

---

[2] The observance of Christmas in public schools is opposed by many persons, who believe that it violates the principle of separation of church and state. The United States Supreme Court has generally supported their position, although its rulings have not been specific with respect to Christmas celebrations. The observance of the Christmas festival in American public schools is common throughout the land. Parents who are offended by the use of the Christmas theme should be encouraged to express their sentiments. Usually all elements of the community that include both Christian and Jewish families will be pleased if the Christmas symbols are supplemented with the Hannukah celebration, which occurs at about the same time. The season should be made the occasion for the promotion of goodwill among people of all kinds of religious belief, as well as those who do not accept any formal religion.

pupils discussed informally some of the things they wanted to do. Comments like these were made:

"We want to tell them that we have a pretty tree."

"We want to tell who decorated it."

"We should tell about the star."

As the pupils suggested the wording for the sentences, the teacher showed them how to make complete sentences, how to observe good sequence, and how to use the words that were new to the children's reading vocabulary. Thus the following sentences, which the teacher wrote on the board, evolved:

We have a pretty tree.
We made our decorations.
We made angels.
We made balls.
We made stars.
We have a lovely star at the top of the tree.

Before the teacher began writing the first sentence, she asked a pupil to show where on the board she should write the first word. She asked this question to draw attention to the top-to-bottom and left-to-right sequence in reading.

We, a, ball, at, and *the* were words that the children had formerly acquired as part of their reading vocabulary. New words, which the teacher planned to teach in connection with the work on this chart were *tree, our, made,* and *have.* These were words that were found in their first-grade reading books.

Next followed practice in "reading" the chart. First, the teacher read the chart alone. Then she and the pupils read it together.

For an illustration on the chart several suggestions came from the children. Someone suggested cutting a picture of a Christmas tree out of a magazine. Another child thought that drawing one would be better. After further discussion it was agreed that

each pupil should cut, free hand, a tree out of a sheet of green construction paper and then decorate it as he saw fit. A committee was then to select one for the chart that the teacher agreed to have ready by the following day.

The next day the teacher brought with her the chart, separate strips of tagboard on which were written the title and each of the sentences used in the chart, and cards on which the new words *tree, our, made,* and *have,* and the review words *we, a, ball, at,* and *the* were written.

Practice was then given in reading the new materials. First, the teacher alone read the chart as she moved her hand across each line of writing. After the pupils had read it twice in concert, several children read it alone. Thereupon the pupils matched the sentence strips with the chart, by holding each strip next to the corresponding sentence on the chart and reading it. As the teacher read a sentence out of its normal order in the story, a pupil found the correct strip and read it orally.

To give practice on the words on the cards, the teacher began by asking someone to find the word *tree* in the title. Then the pupils pronounced the word *tree* as the teacher showed them the word card for *tree* and as she placed it in a card holder. A pupil pointed to the word *tree* in the last sentence and pronounced it. In a similar manner the teacher presented the words *our* and *have.* When she introduced the word *made,* before telling the pupils the word, she wrote *mother* and *made* on the board, explaining that the new word began with the same sound as the word *mother,* which they had already learned to read. After the class had identified the *m* sound in *mother,* the teacher pronounced the word *made* and asked the pupils to notice that both of these words began with the *m* sound. Next the pupils named other words beginning with the *m* sound, like *man* and *Mary,* which the teacher wrote on the board. As the teacher showed the cards for the review words *we, a, ball, at,* and *the,* the pupils named them and located them on the chart. The word cards containing the new words and the review words were then mixed, and pupils, individually, named them as the teacher showed the cards. Before the period was over several children again "read" the chart.

For follow-up work, on the third day of the lesson, the teacher brought to class duplicate copies of the chart, one for each child, on paper 8½ by 11 inches. She also had sheets of paper of the same size on each of which were the four new words *tree, our, made,* and *have.* Above the word *tree* space was left in which the pupils then drew a tree. The teacher also distributed to each boy and girl a piece of tan construction paper to which the pupils could paste the free-hand trees that they had cut out of green paper two days before. Thereupon the pupils made the sheets into booklets, fastening them with brass fasteners. Several children then read the story orally. The rule was made that as soon as a child could read the story without error he could give his booklet to his parents and read it to them. The boys and girls who did not have an opportunity to read the booklet orally on that day were given a chance to do so the next few days either during class time or at other times. When need for additional practice was indicated, it was provided. As further follow-up work one of the pupils read the chart to the second-grade boys and girls a few days after it was made, when the second grade joined the first to sing Christmas songs around the pupil-decorated Christmas tree.

ARGUMENTS FOR AND AGAINST THE USE OF EXPERIENCE CHARTS. There is disagreement concerning the use of experience charts. Most of the controversy centers on the question, "To what extent should experience charts be used in first-grade reading?" Especially controversial is the question as to whether they should be used as substitutes for the commercial reading readiness books.

Some of the arguments given for the use of experience charts as reading readiness materials are these: (1) The valuable experiences that boys and girls get can be made more meaningful by basing charts on them. (2) Reading about their own experiences is more interesting to them than using reading readiness books. (3) The relationship between reading and two other language arts, talking and writing, is made evident to the boys and girls. (4) The children acquire a reading vocabulary, the value of which they easily recognize.

Persons who do not favor the extensive use of experience charts try to refute the arguments given for their frequent use by claiming that: (1) The valuable experiences that boys and girls get will enrich their background of information and understanding without their necessarily writing a chart about the experiences. (2) Reading one's own story is not as interesting, in some cases, as reading the published prereading materials. (3) The relationship between reading and the other language arts can be made evident to the boys and girls without using experience charts extensively. (4) The pupils are able to recognize the value of the reading vocabulary they acquire when reading well-graded and well-written reading readiness books.

Among the most significant arguments advanced against extensive use of experience charts as reading materials is that the words that appear in the charts are not as well selected as those that are found in published reading readiness books. Writers of textbooks in reading for the primary grades have spent much time and energy in attempts to secure a suitable vocabulary. An effort is made by them to use words the pupils will meet frequently in other reading, to introduce only a few new words in each selection, and to give systematic review of words learned, by providing for repetition in the reading, at spaced intervals, both in the book in which the word is presented and in later books in the series. Those favoring the use of experience charts claim that the teacher can help in selecting words for a chart so that there will be included those that the children will be likely to encounter in other reading. However, if the teacher does much of the selecting of the words for a chart, it is evidently the teacher's, rather than the pupils', account.

Another argument against extensive use of experience charts as reading material in the first grade is that boys and girls do not get practice of the type needed for independent reading later on. Reading should be, it is argued by persons opposed to the wide use of reading experience charts, a process of thought getting, not a process of "reading" what one already knows—as is the case in experience charts when used as outlined on pages 75–80. Furthermore, criticism is directed at the fact that there is memorization of what is written on the chart, not reading in the true sense of the word.

A point the teacher must consider when deciding upon the number of experience charts to use is the fact that to make many charts is very time consuming.

No one formula can be given for the proportionate amount of emphasis that should be placed on experience charts. There will, in many classes, be some boys and girls who will need few, if any, reading experiences with charts or with published reading readiness materials before they begin regular book reading. With others it will be advantageous to use either or both types. What the proportion of charts and reading readiness books should be with those children for whom either type or both are indicated will vary with the skill of the teacher, the books available, and the needs of these pupils.

These, then, are some of the ways in which the first-grade teacher can help boys and girls become ready for the great adventure of the school, learning to read.

FOR FURTHER STUDY

Almy, Millie C., *Children's Experiences Prior to First Grade and Success in Beginning Reading.* Teachers College Contributions to Education, No. 954. New York: Bureau of Publications, Teachers College, Columbia University, 1949.

Artley, A. Sterl, *Your Child Learns to Read.* Chicago: Scott, Foresman and Company, 1953.

Baker, Emily, "Reading Readiness Is Still Important," *Elementary English,* 32 (January 1955), 17–23.

Betts, Emmett A., *Foundations of Reading Instruction,* pp. 103–369. New York: American Book Company, 1954.

Bond, Guy L., and Eva Bond Wagner, *Teaching the Child to Read,* pp. 93–145. New York: The Macmillan Company, 1960.

Boney, C. DeWitt, "A New Program for the Late Reader," *Elementary English,* 38 (May, 1961), 316–319.

Carroll, Marjorie W., "Sex Differences in Reading Readiness at the First Grade Level," *Elementary English,* 25 (October 1948), 370–375.

Carter, Homer L. J., and Dorothy J. McGinnis, *Teaching Individuals to Read,* pp. 27–40. Boston: D. C. Heath and Company, 1962.

Cowin, Shirley H., "Reading Readiness Through Kindergarten Experience," *Elementary School Journal,* 52 (October 1951), 96–99.

Harris, Albert J., *Effective Teaching of Reading,* pp. 43–68. New York: David McKay Company, Inc., 1962.

Harrison, M. Lucille, *Reading Readiness,* rev. ed. Boston: Houghton Mifflin Company, 1939.

Henig, Max S., "Predictive Value of a Reading-Readiness Test and of Teachers'

Forecasts," *Elementary School Journal,* 50 (September 1949), 41–46.

Homer, J. Roy, *Reading in Your School,* pp. 65–62. New York: McGraw-Hill Book Company, Inc., 1960.

Karlin, Robert, "The Prediction of Reading Success and Reading-Readiness Tests," *Elementary English,* 34 (May 1957), 320–325.

Peeler, Ruth B., "Helping the Kindergarten Get Ready for First Grade," *Elementary English,* 32 (April 1955), 221–223.

Russell, David H., *Children Learn to Read,* pp. 167–199. New York: Ginn and Company, 1961.

Smith, Henry P., and Emerald V. Dechant, *Psychology in Teaching Reading,* pp. 84–177. Englewood Cliffs, N.J.: Prentice-Hall, Inc., 1961.

Smith, Nila B., ed., *Readiness for Reading and Related Language Arts.* A Research Bulletin of the National Conference on Research in English. Champaign, Ill.: The National Council of Teachers of English, 1950.

Tomlinson, Ethel, "Language Arts Skills Needed by Lower Class Children," *Elementary English,* 33 (May 1956), 279–283.

Tooze, Ruth, *Your Children Want to Read.* Englewood Cliffs, N.J.: Prentice-Hall, Inc., 1957.

Williams, Gertrude H., "What Does Research Tell Us About Readiness for Beginning Reading?" *The Reading Teacher,* 6 (May 1953), 34–40.

6a

Word Recognition

Although, contrary to the popular view, reading involves much more than word recognition, the ability to recognize the sound and meaning of the printed symbol is basic to the reading process. This chapter will describe various procedures that are employed in the development of independence in the recognition of written and printed words.

The term *word recognition* as used in this book refers to the ability to recognize the sound and meaning of words as they appear on the printed page. This ability includes not only the recognition of words which are a familiar part of the speech of the reader, but also skill in "unlocking" words that are unfamiliar to him either as visual or auditory symbols.

Skills Needed for Independence in Word Recognition

Five major skills are necessary for the development of independence in word recognition. These are: (1) recognizing whole words by sight, (2) using context clues, (3) analyzing words phonetically, (4) using structural analysis of words, and (5) using the dictionary. These skills will be discussed in turn, although they will often be employed simultaneously in an attack upon a given word.

For example, in the sentence, "Susan is playing with her doll," the child may use all the clues for recognizing the word *playing*. If the word is not already a part of the child's sight vocabulary, he can use context, analyze it phonetically, note the suffix in structural analysis, and look it up in the dictionary.

Recognition of Words as Sight Words

The predominant method of teaching reading fifty and more years ago was to teach the child the individual letters first and then to teach him how to combine these letters into syllables and whole words. The reading of phrases and sentences was presumed to follow naturally. This method seemed the most simple and logical.

Later research on perception, however, revealed that most people tend to recognize the larger visual shapes first and examine details only when the larger configuration can not be readily identified. Thus it is easier for a child to recognize the word *cat* as a unit than to discover the phonetic values of the three letters and to combine them. He recognizes his pet, Muff, without adding up the colors and characteristics of the individual parts—legs, ears, eyes, etc. Only when two cats resemble each other in most details does he look more closely at the parts to make an identification.

Early eye-movement studies in reading by Dearborn, Judd, Buswell, and others confirmed this view. In a single fixation the reader recognizes whole words and even phrases which have become familiar through frequent exposure to them.

Consequently, most reading systems today begin with whole words and introduce the child to them by telling, association with pictures, using experience charts, and similar methods. An obvious advantage of this approach is the fact that a child is immediately started on the road to reading for meaning. The words so taught at the outset are known as "sight words," words that a child recognizes at once without deciphering the parts. To mature readers, of course, the great majority of written or printed words are sight words, regardless of the method by which they were first learned.

Lists such as the Dolch list of 220 words (see page 106), which contain words common to the International Kindergarten Union List, the Gates List, and the Wheeler-Howell List, have been compiled to indicate those words which are greatly needed by pupils during the initial period of reading instruction. Another useful list of words and word groups belonging to children's reading vocabularies, to be learned by the sight method as well as analytic methods, has been compiled by Helen Bachmann Knipp at the University of Pittsburgh. It was originally designed to be used with the Keystone Tachistoscope, an overhead projector with a device for controlling the speed of exposure of glass slides. However, the list, which is divided into five levels, may be used in any program of reading instruction.[1] Such lists as these may form the basis of instruction by means of charts, tachistoscopic exercises, and word cards.

---

[1] Helen Bachmann Knipp, *Basic Vocabulary, Phrases, and Sentences for Early Reading Instruction.* Meadville, Pa.: Keystone View Company, 1952.

Learning Words by the Sight Method

The procedure commonly followed in teaching by the sight method is as follows: When the pupil meets a word he cannot recognize, the teacher or another pupil tells him the word as it occurs as an isolated word, in a word list, or in a sentence. The child repeats the word, and further practice on it follows either then or later.

Presentation of new words to be added to the pupil's sight vocabulary is generally made both in meaningful context and out of context. The purpose is to make the pupil's response automatic when he sees the word. In this connection the chalkboard and teacher-made or commercial charts are most useful. Labeling of objects in the room is helpful if it is made functional. Thus the shelves in the cupboard may be labeled *Scissors, Paste, Brushes,* and *Cloths* to aid the child in finding materials. Words learned out of context should as soon as possible be encountered in context. Reading-card drills in which whole words are presented should be preceded and followed by the use of these words in speaking and reading. The task is made easier if the words are selected from those which the child uses in his own speech and from those "service" words, like prepositions, pronouns, connecting verbs, which account for a large majority of all words read.

Dolch and Bloomster[2] found that children do not profit greatly from word analysis much before they have reached a mental age of seven, although they can often make successful mechanical responses to phonics instruction before that time. However, other factors may strongly influence a child's readiness for word analysis. In any case, it would appear that the emphasis in the early stages of reading should be on meaningful wholes. The teacher will do well to take advantage of the child's informal discovery of words-by-sight, such as he makes by looking at labels on boxes, word games, chalkboard announcements, or reading charts. Even the commercials on his favorite TV programs may help him to accumulate a small stock of sight words.

The basis of the procedure is repetition of the desired words in different situations. If the child's reading vocabulary is consequently impoverished, as many of the critics of the sight-word method complain, the use of abundant voluntary reading in children's trade books can serve as supplement and corrective.

The chief aim here is to instill in the child the habit of looking at words as meaningful wholes, symbols of the speech arsenal he already possesses. Reading to learn and enjoy cannot wait until the child has mastered the phonic families.

It has been suggested that a stock of 50 to 100 words is necessary before work in phonetic analysis can be successfully begun. However, there seems to

---

2 Edward M. Dolch and M. Bloomster, "Phonic Readiness," *Elementary School Journal,* 38 (November 1937), 201–205.

be no good reason why the teaching of sight words cannot be accompanied earlier, if children are ready, by some phonic helps. The important consideration is that sounding should generally not take place apart from real words.

Not too many "new" words should be presented at one time. Individual differences among the children should determine the number attempted and the teacher should not inhibit the gifted reader in a successful quest for a growing reading vocabulary. For the average pupil, however, a firmer foundation is laid if only a very few words are thoroughly fixed in mind from day to day.

NOTING THE CONFIGURATION. After a pupil has been told a word by the sight method, he may at times find it helpful in recognizing the word when he encounters it again to observe the general configuration or outline of the word. Observation of the configuration of a word can be a valuable procedure not only during the period of reading readiness and initial reading instruction but in all stages of reading, including adult reading. In fact, for rapid reading it is essential. Through noting the outline of the word, the reader is saved from the necessity of painstakingly deciphering many words that he meets, especially if this clue is used in conjunction with the verbal context in which a word appears. Frequently, too, attention to the configuration can be given to good advantage along with a study of phonics. It is probably safe to say that the majority of pupils would profit from guidance in the use of this means of word recognition. One way in which the child in the early stages of learning to read can be aided in developing skill in the use of the configuration clues is through questions and comments by the teacher concerning the length of a word. If a child reads *mother* when he sees the word *man*, the teacher may say, "This word could not be *mother*, for *mother* is a longer word than this."

The following cautions should be observed in using the configuration of a word as a method of recognition: (1) Pupils should not be expected to remember a large number of words through configuration clues only, for many words closely resemble one another in general appearance. Overuse of this practice is likely to result in guessing. (2) The teacher should be on guard against making wrong use of the striking characteristics of a word as a means to word recognition. Not infrequently a teacher tries to help a child remember the word *monkey* by the "tail" letter on *monkey*. This is a most confusing practice, since many words other than *monkey* end in *y*.

Use of Context Clues

Often teachers use a combination of the sight method and context clues when they introduce the children to a new word. For example, a teacher may use the sight method plus the method of visual context when she helps a pupil learn the word *mother* as it appears with a picture of a woman. When using both of these procedures in teaching a child to identify the word, she may tell him the word is *mother* and then lead him to notice that the word goes with the picture. Or she may ask him what the word under the picture might be. If he says *mother*, she needs to let him know that he is right.

A word can also be presented by the sight method combined with the use of verbal context clues. For example, if the pupils know all the words except *bat* in the sentence "Bob has a ball and a bat," the teacher might tell them that she thinks many of them can figure out the new word in the sentence as they read it to see what word would fit where the new word appears. If the pupils suggest that the word might be *bat,* she will need to tell them that they are right. If the pupils do not name the correct word, the teacher should tell them the word and help them to see that *bat* fits with the meaning of the rest of the sentence.

Skill in making use of verbal context clues is significant to all stages of reading instruction, even to adult reading. In the earlier stages it is of great help in providing boys and girls with needed practice on words which they have identified at a previous time but which they still do not recognize instantly without other aids. Before the pupils have learned to identify and remember words through word analysis, they can, by means of skill in use of verbal clues, frequently get from the context the aid in recalling the word that they need. Even after they have developed facility in the use of structural and phonetic analysis they can, through efficient use of verbal context clues, be aided greatly in their rate of reading. Often through the context a reader can recognize a word faster than through analytic methods. For example, a person who comes across the sentence, "Geometry is one branch of mathematics in which I am greatly interested," can use a context clue in recognizing the word *mathematics*. After he has read the first five words of the sentence he observes that here is a long word beginning with *m* and ending in *ics* that is likely in that setting to be *mathematics*. A further reason for the importance of acquiring skill in the use of verbal context clues is that there are many words in the English language whose pronunciation depends upon the context, like *read, lead, bow*, and *refuse*.

As indicated in the illustration in the preceding paragraph, an adequate background of experience is essential for success in use of context clues. A person who does not know what geometry is would receive little help from context in the sentence, "Geometry is one branch of mathematics in which I am greatly interested." Consequently, it is the teacher's responsibility to provide sufficient experiences with the subjects about which the pupils will be reading. The teacher can help boys and girls get the needed background by a variety of means—discussions, explanations, demonstrations, experiments, field trips and other visual aids, and reading. Once he has read fairly easy material on a given subject, the pupil can often be helped to understand more difficult reading done subsequently on the same topic. At times, guidance can be given just before the class begins reading a selection in which concepts are discussed with which the pupils are not familiar. At other times, preparation for the reading may have taken place days or even weeks before. A wide background of experience is one assurance that the child will have less difficulty not only in reading in general, but also in making intelligent use of verbal context clues.

If a reader is to be expected to get help through the verbal context in the identification of a word, the proportion of unfamiliar to familiar words should be kept small. If a first-grade child comes to the sentence, "The boy has a ball and a bat," without recognizing either *boy* or *ball* or *bat*, no intelligent use of context clues can be made. The exact ratio of unknown to known words, as far as recognition of the word is concerned, cannot, of course, be ascertained because it will differ according to difficulty of the concepts discussed, the intelligence, maturity, background, and reading ability of the reader, and the skill of the teacher.

The identification of a word does not necessarily have to take place in context in order that the pupil may recognize it later by context clues. A teacher may write on the board the word *mother* when she tells the child the word, and later on, when he again encounters the word in his reading, help him make use of the context to recall the word. Sometimes it is desirable first to present a word in isolation, since more attention can be given it then.

Use of Phonic Analysis

The reader who must rely entirely on the sight method, the configuration of a word, and context clues will never develop proficiency in reading. To become a successful reader, he must develop skill in word analysis, both phonic and structural.

The place of phonics in reading instruction, as has been noted earlier, has been the subject of heated controversy and of much experimental research. Although the subject has been discussed by teachers for many years, it has today excited partisan interest not only within the teaching profession, but also among the public at large, in part because of the publication of such books as *Why Johnny Can't Read*.[3]

So great, indeed, has been the general concern that Dr. James B. Conant, engaged in a nation-wide study of American public education, called a conference of well-known writers on the teaching of reading to discuss the matter. Thus, on September 22 and 23, 1961, a group of reading specialists, representing a divergence of views on the question of phonics in reading instruction,

---

[3] Rudolf Flesch, *Why Johnny Can't Read And What You Can Do About It*. New York: Harper and Row, Publishers, 1955.

met in New York to discover areas of agreement among them on this subject. The conference was financed by the Carnegie Corporation of New York, and its report was later distributed by the Educational Testing Service.[4]

Twenty-seven members of the committee signed the report; one submitted a minority report. The group consisted of university professors, school superintendents, supervisors of reading instruction, and authors of widely used specialized phonics materials. It is reasonable to assume that it was representative of the opinions of leaders in research and teaching throughout the country.

What were the major generalizations about phonics that the members of the conference found that they could agree upon? The following quotations from the report provide an answer:

> It is not true that our schools, in general, use primarily a "sight-word" method. It is not true that our schools, in general do not teach phonics.
>
> We hold that reading cannot be taught by "sight-words" (look-say) alone. Such teaching would require our children to memorize, word by word, the mass of printed words. No reading authority advocates so impossible a procedure. . . .
>
> It should be remembered that when children come to school they want to learn to read. It is good sense to capitalize on this desire at once. Therefore, as the children begin to learn the reading skills, it is rather standard practice for good teachers to see to it that they simultaneously learn a few printed words that are common in children's speaking vocabularies and that they will thereafter recognize when they see them. With these few words as a base, the children can begin utterly simple reading almost immediately—for instance, a sentence of only two or three words. . . .
>
> The learning of these few initial words is not a mere feat of memory but is the result of the composite procedure by which in the very early stages of reading instruction children begin to learn how to identify printed words. Because of their use in the very beginning reading, these words are usually called "sight-words"—that is, they are words that once learned will thereafter be recognized whenever they are seen. They are the beginning of the "reading vocabulary" that all persons must possess who are going to read well. . . .
>
> However, many children at that age do not know what *sounds* are represented by the *letters* in the printed word. Therefore, they have to learn to relate the letters in the printed word to the sounds in the spoken word. With the variety of sounds that most letters have, this is not a small task. It is here that phonics enters in, for phonics is the study of the relationship of the letters and letter combinations in words on the printed page and the sounds in the spoken words. . . .
>
> But the whole purpose of reading is to get meaning. That is why good

---

[4] *Learning to Read: A Report of a Conference of Reading Experts.* With a Foreword by James B. Conant. Princeton, N.J.: Educational Testing Service, 1962.

teachers insist upon uniting phonics instruction with instruction in the word recognition skills through which meaning is ascertained.

The mastery of the skills that lead to recognition and meaning of words may not be left to chance or haphazard practice. If this seems obvious, then it should be equally obvious that learning the word recognition skills should be carefully planned and expertly guided if it is to be effective. This means that the heart of the reading instruction program really is a competent, dedicated teacher who knows both the theory of reading instruction and the ways different children learn. . . .

The following statements express the beliefs of the members of the Conference concerning the nature of the primary and elementary reading program as it exists in schools today and ways to strengthen it.

1. From our experience, we know that the constituent parts of the reading instruction program throughout our country are those that we have presented in this report as indispensable to a good, acceptable program. We know this, also, from the results of a survey made especially for our Conference by the Bureau of Applied Social Research, Columbia University.

The evidence from the Columbia Survey shows that:

a. classroom teachers of reading are in practically unanimous agreement on the importance of these constituent parts, and they report that they practice them in the classroom;

b. extremes of "no-phonics" or "all-phonics" programs are exceptions;

c. a predominantly sight-word method is practically nonexistent.

The dispute, therefore, is not over the *whether*, but over the *how* and the *when*.

A critical point of difference is the question whether the approach to word recognition should be *synthetic* or *analytic*. Advocates of the synthetic method favor teaching letters and graphemes, or phonograms, first, and then teaching children to combine the sound elements into words. Those who believe in the analytic method favor presenting children with whole words first and then teaching them to analyze words into the sound elements that comprise them. This second method is sometimes called the whole-part-whole method. It is probably the dominant method in American schools.[5]

Over the years, children have learned to read by various methods, including the synthetic. The problem has been one of finding a general approach which would be effective with the largest possible number of children and which would lead to strong and continuing interest in good reading throughout life. On this ground, the numerous methods which may be described as analytic have been most widely accepted. There is no meaning in phonemes. Only when they have been combined into word parts, whole words, phrases, and sentences

---

[5] See, for example, *The Torch Lighters,* by Mary C. Austin, pp. 127–128. Cambridge, Mass.: Harvard University Press, 1961.

do they yield meaning. And since there can be no true reading without the apprehension of meaning, the process should begin with the perception of the larger units—words and their affixes. Moreover, as soon as possible the child should be confronted with phrases and sentences in order to avoid the habit of word-by-word reading. Quick perception of the larger units is important, not primarily for the development of speed, but for the development of comprehension.

Most people will concede that an intelligent, able, sympathetic teacher, one who is flexible enough to adapt her procedure to individual needs, is more important than the method, but this fact in no way relieves us of the necessity of weighing the relative advantages of one method over another.

A second point of difference arises over the question whether instruction in phonics should be systematic or incidental. Granted that there is an essential body of phonics skills to be mastered, should these skills be taught sequentially to all children, whole words being deliberately chosen to illustrate a phonics principle? Or should the phonics principles be taught to each child as the need arises in his reading? Most reading specialists and classroom teachers prefer the former approach.

An objection to the sequential, isolated teaching of phonic principles is the fact that many good young readers discover the principles themselves in the course of highly motivated meaningful reading, and for them class instruction in phonics tends to be wasteful. On the other hand, in guided individualized reading programs there is danger that many children will fail to encounter or to master essential phonic elements.

In an important recent study, Durrell and others found that:

> Most reading difficulties can be prevented by an instructional program which provides early instruction in letter names and sounds, followed by applied phonics and *accompanied by suitable practice in meaningful sight vocabulary and aids to attentive silent reading.* . . .[6]

It should be noted that the plan which Durrell and his associates found to be superior provided for meaningful reading experiences simultaneously with instruction in "applied phonics."

LINGUISTICS AND READING. Suggestions for the application of phonetic principles to the teaching of reading have recently been made by a number of eminent linguists. The linguist emphasizes the fact that reading and writing are relatively recent inventions and that they are derivative from the spoken language. He therefore regards the study of speech sounds, or phonetics, as central to any defensible theory of reading instruction.

---

[6] Donald D. Durrell and others, "Success in First Grade Reading," *Journal of Education*, 140 (February 1958). Italics added.

For example, the late Leonard Bloomfield, in a series of two articles,[7] described a plan for initial reading instruction which is based upon the reproduction of speech sounds through the use of visual symbols. In Bloomfield's theory, the early stages of reading instruction should be concerned exclusively with mastery of the mechanics of reading. Nonsense words may serve very well in fixing the skills required for later meaningful reading. He suggests the following four stages in a sequence designed to promote the development of the essential mechanical skills that will lead eventually to fluent, effective reading:

1. The recognition of the letters of the alphabet. These are to be presented in two-letter and three-letter words, in groups arranged according to the five vowel letters. Each letter in a group should represent a single phonetic value. Thus only the short *a* or only the hard *g* should be included in a word-group. Work in this stage should be continued until the pupils are thoroughly trained.

2. Learning regular spellings in which double consonants and other digraphs appear in consistent uses.

3. Learning words whose spellings may be called *semi-irregular*, as in the word-groups *line, shine, mile,* and *while,* or *bone, stone, hole, pole.*

4. Learning irregularly spelled words, such as *father, mother, night, all, rough, cough,* and *through.* Unfamiliar words may be used. At this stage, however, each word is a separate item to be memorized so that it may be available for reading.

Bloomfield's ideas have recently been more fully developed in a book by Barnhart, intended to facilitate experimental use of the method in schools.[8]

Clarence Barnhart has carried on Bloomfield's work with the intention of facilitating the experimental use of his method. However, the one classroom experiment in which the Bloomfield approach was compared with a conventional phonic approach revealed no significant differences in pupil achievement. Clearly, further experimentation would be desirable.

Another well-known linguist, C. C. Fries, advocates a procedure not unlike that of Bloomfield's. Reviewing the history of linguistic science over a long period and of changes in theories of reading instruction, he outlines the implications of modern linguistics for the teaching of reading.[9] Although he recognizes that the ultimate purpose of reading instruction is reading for meaning, Fries believes that the child's introduction to reading should not be complicated by the search for meaning in words. The child's primary task is to make a transfer from auditory language signs in speech to a set of corresponding visual signs in reading. The ability to identify and distinguish the graphic shapes

---

[7] "Linguistics and Reading," *The Elementary English Review,* 19 (April, May 1942), 125–130, 183–186.

[8] Leonard Bloomfield and Clarence Barnhart, *Let's Read: A Linguistic Approach.* Detroit: Wayne State University Press, 1961.

[9] Charles C. Fries, *Linguistics and Reading.* New York: Holt, Rinehart and Winston, Inc., 1963.

which supply the visual symbols must first be brought to the level of instant and automatic response to the visual signals. Substituting visual for auditory signals implies clearly that the early reading experiences should be confined to words and meanings already a part of the child's speaking repertory.

Fries distinguishes three steps in teaching a child to read:

1. The child first learns to discriminate among letters instantaneously through recognition of contrasts of two or more letters. No connection should be made between letters and their sounds or between words and their meanings. Even the names of the letters are not essential at this stage.

2. The child learns to recognize contrastive sequences of phonemes which identify for him certain word-patterns of the language. The selection and ordering of the material in the exercises are the key to effective transfer from the use of auditory to that of visual associations, or language "signals." The progression of the materials should be so programed that each new item is tied by contrast to an item formerly practiced. An example of such a progression follows:

AT — CAT
A CAT — A RAT
PAT A CAT
A FAT CAT
PAT A FAT CAT

There should be no concern with meanings at this point. The purpose is to master the mechanics of reading. A child's interest grows, not out of meaning, but out of his success in recognizing the spelling-sequences. There should be much oral reading and use of pitch and stress and other signals not represented by graphic devices.

3. In the third stage, the reading process will have become so automatic that the reading will stimulate vivid imaginative realization of vicarious experience.

A major difference between the plans proposed by the linguists and the conventional initial phonics approaches is in the manner in which the phonic elements are first presented to the child. The linguists introduce the phonetic elements in whole words, either real words or nonsense words, presumably on the ground that the phonetic values of letters, especially vowels, cannot be determined in isolation. In both cases, however, the basis is laid by means of drills on language form and structure and on spelling patterns rather than on meanings.

The question is not whether children can learn to read by either or both of these methods. Under suitable conditions and with intelligent teaching most children can learn to read, as they have done through the years, by any of a great variety of methods. What concerns educators most is which method or methods over the long run will help the greatest number of readers to make the greatest progress in reading, develop keen and continuing interest in reading, and achieve the highest possible levels of comprehension. Quite possibly for some children the phonetic approach is the most effective, while for others another approach or combination of approaches is the most effective.

To the linguist, concerned with the spoken language, it seems logical to begin with the phoneme. Most educators hesitate to subject the young child, eager to read stories for himself, to long periods of drill with isolated letter sounds and nonsense syllables. They regard the visual associations with specific sounds as only one kind of aid, along with configuration and context and whole-word perception, in converting graphic signs accurately and speedily into meanings.

EVALUATION OF THE ROLE OF PHONICS INSTRUCTION. After examining a large number of studies relating to phonics, Witty and Sizemore drew the following general conclusions:[10]

> From this review one may conclude that the nature and amount of phonic instruction to be given is still a debatable question. Adherents to any one of a number of positions may find justification for their views in published sources from the devotees of the doctrine of "no phonics" to the advocates of a highly artificial approach. . . . .
>
> Moreover, many phonic systems appear to be difficult for most five- and some six-year-old children. Such children frequently become hopelessly confused and discouraged after exposure to involved systems of phonics instruction. Mental age and other factors are important in determining the propriety of using a phonics approach. . . .
>
> Phonic systems may develop in children a tendency to recognize a word piecemeal. This emphasis results, particularly when the method is used apart from a meaningful approach, in very slow reading. . . .
>
> Another limitation of phonics instruction is that it does not utilize other techniques that bring about quick, accurate word recognition. Children and adults often recognize words quickly, as wholes, and often recognize groups of words with rapidity too. The good reader does not see each letter or all the letters . . . Accordingly, a soundly conceived program of word recognition is not limited to phonic procedures. . . .
>
> Many children do need help in the mastery of phonic skills although some appear to have made satisfactory progress in reading without formal instruction. Therefore, a system of careful diagnosis of individual needs should precede the introduction of instruction in word analysis at all levels. Many workers believe that phonics instruction is particularly effective with some disabled or very retarded readers. It is, however, not the only procedure employed nor the sole procedure used with such readers.

---

[10] Paul Witty and Robert Sizemore, "Phonics in the Reading Program: A Review and an Evaluation," *Elementary English,* 32 (October 1955), 355–371.

We conclude from the foregoing and other studies that ear training, sounding, and phonic analysis represent essential skills in reading, whether teacher-taught or self-taught, and that careful provision must be made for the development of these skills, especially during the first years of reading instruction. We conclude further that phonic analysis is but one aid in the recognition of new words and that in instruction it should not be mistaken for the process of reading itself.

Every teacher should clearly recognize the limitations of phonics in the recognition of English words. For example, since English spelling is relatively unphonetic, many words cannot be "unlocked" by means of phonetic analysis. The word *sight* defies phonetic analysis until the word has been recognized as a whole, and even the word *cat* would yield no sense if a child approached it with only the letter names. Many letters have more than one sound, and in many instances the same sound can be symbolized by more than one letter or combination of letters. Thus the *g* has a hard and a soft sound; the sound of long *a* is symbolized by *a, ay, ey, ai, ei,* and others. Even the letter *o* may represent the phoneme [*i*], as in *women*. The frequent occurrence of silent letters, consonant digraphs (like *th*), and vowel digraphs (like *ou*) complicates the problem of phonic word-analysis. As a result, relatively few phonic elements can be depended upon to be represented constantly by the same letters.

Prolonged work on phonics independently taught not only diverts the child from the process of getting meaning from the printed page, but also reduces the time available for genuine reading. Some children will find drills in phonic distinctions like *at, an, am, ab,* and *ar* less than exciting. Others, by cultivating the habit of concentrating on a very narrow section of the printed line, may become slow readers. All of these, of course, are limitations, not arguments against the use of phonics. Reading should be from the outset an interesting experience to the child, and only as phonics contributes to interest in reading can it be considered a genuine help to learning.

PRINCIPLES OF TEACHING PHONICS. Certain generalizations can be drawn from the preceding discussion.

1. *Phonic analysis should follow experiences with sight-words, and it should be introduced as soon as it appears useful in helping to bring about instantaneous recognition of whole words.* The child should continually be encouraged to add new words to his sight vocabulary, but instruction in the likenesses and differences in phonetic elements in words should begin fairly early in the process of learning to read. There is no magic in the number 75 as the minimum number of words learned before phonics can be introduced. The vast majority of six-year-old children are able, at least under instruction, to discriminate among the shapes of letters.

2. *Instruction in phonics should be functional.* Only those generalizations

about differences and likenesses of words should be taught which apply to the simple words the beginner encounters in his reading or in presentations by the teacher.

3. *For most pupils, instruction in phonics should be systematic.* The progression should be from the simpler, more widely used elements and generalizations to the more difficult and less generally applied learnings, with well-distributed practice.

4. *The work in phonics should be adapted to individual differences.* Any program in word recognition should be geared to the developmental level of the children. Pupils within a given grade may be expected to be on varying levels in many respects, including the various phases of phonetic analysis. Some will not be ready as soon as others. Some will be able to deal with simple abstract learnings; others will profit more from concrete experiences. Moreover, progress will vary greatly after initial instruction has begun. Some pupils will need practically no help beyond that provided by the material they are currently reading, while others will benefit greatly from additional practice in workbooks or teacher-made materials and games or drills that focus attention on certain needed skills.

5. *Rules and generalizations should be taught inductively.* By presenting three or more familiar words that have the same initial, medial, or final letter, the teacher can call attention to the similarity and help the pupil to fix the appropriate sound in mind in such a way as to enable him to recognize the same sound in another word. For example, if the pupil has learned the similar beginning of the words *make, mother,* and *man,* he is equipped to attack the word *mouse* by applying a generalization to a new grouping of letters. Chalkboard, chart, and workbook can supply practice in making such applications, and of course the rule, which the pupil himself has been led to formulate, can then be used in his own "silent" reading. Similar generalizations can be made and applied with the medial vowel in words ending in a silent *e*.

ELEMENTS OF PHONICS TO BE TAUGHT.

1. *Definitions.*

    a. *Phonetics and Phonics. Phonetics* is the science of speech sounds. *Phonics* is phonetics applied to reading.

Since the individual letters of the alphabet may have more than one sound, and since some sounds are made by combinations of letters, the phonics method must be distinguished from the alphabet method.

    b. *Phonemes.* The basic sounds of speech.

    c. *Digraphs.* Written or printed symbols made up of two letters representing one phoneme or speech sound. They are of two kinds: consonant digraphs, like *th, ng,* and *ck,* and vowel digraphs, like *ei, ie, ea,* and *ay.*

    d. *Diphthongs.* Written or printed symbols representing two vowels so nearly blended that they almost produce a single speech sound, like *oy, ou,* and *ew.*

e. *Consonant blends.* Combinations of two or three consonants, *br, gr,* or *str,* blended in such a way that each letter in the blend still keeps its own identity.

f. *Phonograms,* or *graphemes.* The visual representation in writing or print of phonemes, or speech sounds.

2. *Outline of subject matter.* An examination of the teaching manuals accompanying many reading series will indicate, in spite of minor discrepancies, essential agreement as to the phonetic elements to be taught. They usually include all or most of the following:

Single consonants in monosyllabic and polysyllabic words
    a. In initial positions in words
    b. In final positions in words
    c. In medial positions in words
Consonant blends, like *st, gr, br, cr, tch, pl*
Consonant digraphs, like *ch, th, sh*
Single vowels
    a. "Short"
    b. "Long"
    c. Vowels modified when preceding *r*
    d. The *a* when preceding *l* or *w*
    e. Other vowel sounds
Vowel digraphs, like *ea, oa, ai, ay, ee, oo*
Diphthongs, like *oy, oi, ou, ow*
Silent letters

3. *Generalizations to be learned.* There seems to be more diversity of opinion as to what rules or generalizations related to phonetic analysis should be learned than there is concerning the phonic elements to be taught. The following are among the generalizations more commonly recommended:

A single vowel in a syllable is usually short unless it is the final letter in the syllable. (Examples: b*a*by; b*a*t)

If there are two vowels together in the same syllable, the first vowel is usually long and the second silent. (Example: b*oa*t)

If a final *e* in a syllable is preceded by a single consonant, a single vowel preceding the consonant is usually long and the *e* is silent. (Example: r*a*te)

The sound of a single vowel preceding an *r* is usually modified by the *r.* (Example: col*o*r)

The sound of a single *a* preceding an *l* or a *w* is affected by the *l* or *w.* (Examples: f*a*ll; cl*a*w)

A final *y* in words of more than one syllable is usually short. (Example: bab*y*)

A *c* before *e, i,* or *y* has, as a rule, the soft sound. (Example: *c*ity)

A *g* before *e, i,* or *y* has, as a rule, the soft sound. (Example: *g*em)

SEQUENCE. One caution needs to be expressed at this point. The listing of phonic elements and generalizations in the preceding section of this chapter is not to be considered as the sequence in which they are to be taught.

Grade levels are an undesirable criterion for determining sequence. Since the accomplishments of boys and girls and their readiness for any phase of reading instruction varies so much from grade to grade, it is better to express in terms of levels of achievement the sequence of phonic skills to be studied.

There is no one best sequence for teaching the various aspects of phonic analysis. Numerous acceptable orders of presentation have been worked out. The succession should be based on principles such as these: (1) There should be progression from the simple to the more complex. (2) Other things being equal, the more frequently used elements and generalizations should be taught before the less frequently used. (3) Provisions should be made on each level for the maintenance of skills acquired, at least in part, on the preceding level.

One of the best sources of suggestions as to the sequence to follow in phonic analysis is to be found in the teachers' manual accompanying the series of readers. Any teacher using one of these should acquaint herself with the program outlined in the manuals. However, the suggestions should not be followed slavishly. The recommendations are, for the most part, made in terms of the average child in a grade. The teacher must make adaptation to individual differences.

A suggested sequence for phonics instruction follows:

1. Provide needed work on auditory and visual discrimination.

2. Teach the sounds of consonants before those of vowels. Start with the single consonant sounds that have but one sound, namely, *b, h, j, l, m, p, t,* and *v.* Teach them as they occur in initial and then in final positions in words, before teaching them in medial positions. Finally, teach common consonant digraphs, then two-letter consonant blends, then three-letter consonant blends.

3. Teach the vowel sounds, the short sounds first, then the long.

4. Teach vowel digraphs and diphthongs and silent letters.

5. Teach rules governing long and short vowels.

Although exact stipulations as to the grade in which an element should be taught cannot be given, in general it should be noted that it is probably wise to complete almost all of the new work on phonetic elements and generalizations by the end of the third grade. However, much should be done in the intermediate grades to maintain and to make further application of learnings acquired earlier.

Use of Structural Analysis

Phonetic analysis is not the only type of word analysis. A second method of analyzing words is through the use of structural analysis. While in phonetic analysis the reader deciphers a word by means of sounds represented by the letters or combination of letters in a word, in structural analysis he recognizes the meaning or pronunciation units of a word.

Structural analysis deals with both word variants and word derivatives. By a word variant is meant a word that deviates from the root word according to grammatical usage. Word variants show inflections according to the case, number, and gender of nouns, the tense, voice, and mood of verbs, and the comparison of adjectives and adverbs. Thus variants of the noun *prince* are *princes* and *princess*; of the verb *walk* are *walks, walked, walking;* of the adjective *small* are *smaller* and *smallest*. Word derivatives are words formed from root words through the addition of prefixes and/or suffixes—for example, *likeable* and *uncomfortable*. Learning compound words—for example, *something*—through identification or recognition of the parts, and polysyllabic words through the aid of syllabication, is also part of structural analysis.

The question may be asked, "Why teach structural analysis of word variants or word derivatives when these words could be studied through phonetic analysis?" To be specific, "Why should the teacher bother teaching children to use structural analysis when learning the word *unhappy* after they can recognize the root *happy* and can analyze the word phonetically?" The answer is that phonetic analysis is a slower form of word analysis than structural analysis. The child who has learned to recognize instantly the prefix *un* in *unhappy* does not have to engage in the uneconomical procedure of first analyzing *un* phonetically. The reader who can quickly identify the common prefixes and suffixes reads with more speed than the one who has to use phonics in this process.

In succeeding paragraphs the following questions will be discussed: (1) What are the basic principles that should be observed in teaching structural analysis? (2) What should be taught to boys and girls in the elementary school about structural analysis? (3) In what sequence and at what levels should the various elements of word structure be taught? (4) What are some additional suggestions for teaching children to identify and recognize words by means of structural analysis? The fourth question will be answered primarily in Chapter 7B, where many specific illustrations are presented.

PRINCIPLES OF TEACHING STRUCTURAL ANALYSIS. The following principles warrant special emphasis in relation to analyzing words by means of their structure.

1. *Overemphasis on structural analysis should be avoided.* Structural analysis should be seen in relationship to other methods of word recognition. When

a word can be recalled by means of quicker methods, such as configuration or context clues, the reader should not resort to word analysis. If too much attention has been paid to locating root words, prefixes, and suffixes, it is possible for reading to become ineffective because the reader approaches too many words by trying to locate word parts. Consequently it is undesirable to have all "new" words analyzed either phonetically or structurally.

2. *As a rule, the reader should examine a "new" word to see if he can analyze it structurally before he tries to unlock it by means of phonics.* This principle is sound because structural analysis is usually a quicker method of word recognition than phonetic analysis. Consequently rate in reading as well as quality of comprehension can be improved if the more tedious methods involving phonics are employed only when other means fail.

3. *The analysis of "new" words should not be isolated from reading as a meaningful process.* Frequently it is advisable to present in context a "new" word that is to be analyzed structurally. The context can help the reader decide what the word is. For example, if the reader comes across the sentence, "Sam is walking home," and he knows the root word *walk*, he can often tell without really studying the ending that the "new" word is *walking*, not *walks* or *walked*.

4. *The sequence in teaching a new word by means of structural analysis should, as a rule, be from the whole word to the word part and then back to the whole word.* Specifically, it is usually desirable to present the word first—for example, *walking*—next to ask the pupils to identify the root word and the ending, and then to have them combine the root with the ending. This procedure is recommended because it more nearly resembles the situation in which the pupil is likely to encounter a word. Nevertheless, occasional special practice in which a child forms variants or derivatives of a word are helpful, as, for example, having the pupils form the words *walks, walked,* and *walking* from *walk.*

5. *Structural analysis should not be confused with "finding little words in big words."* One rather common method used to help boys and girls analyze words structurally is to ask them to "find little words in big words." This practice may be misleading. For example, finding *at* in *mat* could lead a child also to look for *at* in *mate* and therefore confuse him. Furthermore, even in *mat*, if the reader looks for *at*, he is likely to pronounce it *mŭ-at*. Anyone accustomed to searching for "little words in big words" might easily pronounce *together* as *to-get-her* or *some* as *so-me*, and in the word *furthermore* he might be led to a wrong identification if he isolates *the* or *he* or *her.*

6. *Generalizations should be developed with pupils.* They should not be presented as rules to be memorized. For instance, when teaching that words ending in *y* preceded by a consonant change the *y* to *i* before adding *es*, the teacher may write on the board a few nouns ending in *y*, some preceded by a consonant, others by a vowel, like *boy, boys; lady, ladies; day, days; candy, candies;* and *toy, toys.* The pupils may observe how the plural of each of the

singular nouns in the list was formed, writing in one column the singular words ending in *y* preceded by a vowel and in the other the singular words ending in *y* preceded by a consonant. Next the pupils may summarize their observation that to the words in the first column ending in *y* preceded by a vowel, an *s* only was added. The teacher may then explain that this generalization holds true in other cases. Similarly the boys and girls may summarize their finding that in the words in the second column—those ending in *y* preceded by a consonant—the *y* was changed to *i* before *es* was added. The teacher may then explain that this generalization, too, holds true in other cases. To make this original learning permanent, the pupils should be helped to note the application of these rules in their later reading and in their spelling. This method of procedure in developing a generalization is much more likely to be effective than that in which the teacher gives the rule and the pupils memorize it.

7. *There should be a developmental program that provides for training in structural analysis.* Skill in analyzing words structurally is such a significant phase of skill in word recognition that it cannot be left to chance. While incidental methods should be used whenever they help foster a better understanding of words on the part of boys and girls, the teacher should make certain that all the essential elements of structural analysis are presented and that provisions are made for the maintenance of these skills through meaningful distributed practice. Suggestions as to the elements to include in such a program are given in the next paragraphs.

DEVELOPMENTAL PROGRAM IN STRUCTURAL ANALYSIS. Exactly which elements and generalizations in structural analysis should be taught in the elementary school is a question that has not been determined. In trying to decide on the points to be studied, the teacher should keep these criteria in mind: (1) the frequency of occurrence of the structural form, (2) the ease with which the learner can identify the form, and (3) the value of the element to the development of speed and independence in word recognition.

The following elements in structural analysis of words are frequently considered important enough to be taught somewhere in the elementary school:

1. *Skill in identifying or recognizing words ending in* able, ance, d, ed, er, es, est, ful, ible, ies, ily, ing, ish, less, ly, ment, ness, *and* s *in words in which the root is known to the reader*. Pupils should be familiar with the application of the following generalizations about the endings of words:

Words ending in *y* preceded by a consonant change the *y* to *i* before adding *es* to form a variant of the root word.

Words ending in *y* preceded by a consonant change the *y* to *i* before *ed, er, est,* or *ly* is added.

Many words ending in a consonant double the final consonant before *ed* or *ing* is added.

Many root words ending in *e* drop the *e* before adding *ing* to form a variant.

2. *Skill in identifying or recognizing words with the prefixes* ab, ad, com, de, dis, ex, im, in, pre, pro, re, sub, *and* un *in words in which the root is known to the reader.* The more advanced pupils in the elementary school may also be helped to recognize the fact that a variation of the prefix *im* occurs in words like *illegal* and *illegible*, where instead of the *m* of the prefix *im* the first consonant of the root of the word is doubled so that the consonant preceded by *i* forms the prefix to the root of the word.

3. *Skill in identifying or recognizing compound words where one or both parts of a compound or hyphenated word are known to the reader.*

4. *Skill in identifying or recognizing the possessive form when the word without the possessive ending is known to the reader.*

5. *Skill in identifying or recognizing common contractions like* he'll, I'll, I'm, it's, there's, they're, that's, she'll, we'll, we're, what's, where's, *and* you'll *and those ending in* n't, *like* don't.

6. *Skill in identifying or recognizing polysyllabic words partly by means of syllabication.* Syllabication can aid in the identification and recognition of words. It is usually helpful to pupils to understand that there are as many syllables in a word as there are vowel sounds. It is not essential to the recognition or pronunciation of a word to know exactly where some of the breaks between syllables occur. For instance, a child does not have to know whether the division of syllables in the word *tumble* comes before or after the *b* in order to pronounce the word correctly, even though, of course, for written syllabication that knowledge is essential. However, if rules for syllabication are to be studied, these are some that may be helpful to elementary school children:

If the initial vowel in a word is followed by two consonants, the first of the two consonants usually ends the first syllable of the word, as in *big' ger.*

If the initial vowel in a word is followed by a single consonant, the consonant usually begins the second syllable of the word, as in *ma' jor.*

If the last syllable of a word ends in *le,* the consonant preceding *le* usually begins the last syllable, as in *ta' ble.*

SEQUENCE AND ALLOCATION TO LEVELS OF READING. The order in which the elements significant in structural analysis should be taught cannot be stated authoritatively for all grades or for all individuals within a grade. Factors like the following will need to be taken into consideration in working out the sequence in which the elements should be taught: (1) The items included in a list of points to be developed in stressing facility in word recognition through structural analysis should not, as a rule, be taken up in the order in which they occur in the reading. (2) One factor that should help determine the order of development is the occurrence or presentation in the reading textbook of words representative of the form to be studied. Most reading books for the elementary school provide definite guidance in the teachers' manual for a program of word recognition. (3) The difficulty of a point to be learned should be one of the criteria for deciding the order in which the items should be taught. Other things being equal, those points easier to learn and to apply should be taught first.

Use of the Dictionary

Effective use of a dictionary for purposes of word identification, pronunciation, and meaning is one of the most important skills in word recognition that need to be acquired in the elementary school. In Chapters 9A and 9B, dealing with the locational skills, a somewhat detailed account is given of how to help pupils develop skill in the use of the dictionary.

The Reading Vocabulary

The selection of words for inclusion in the pupil's reading vocabulary, especially in the primary grades, is a matter of considerable consequence. It is for this reason that makers of textbooks in reading have spent time and effort in the selection of words used in their books. In publishing reading books for the beginning primary grades they have tried to choose words whose meaning the boys and girls know. They have rightfully insisted that it is unwise to try to teach children in the first grade to read words with which they are unfamiliar, when there are several thousand words in their understanding vocabulary that they cannot recognize in print. It is not until the later primary grades that most authors of basal reading books try to introduce words that will extend the child's understanding vocabulary. In order to provide a vocabulary suitable for the child to read, authors of reading series have based their vocabulary selection on carefully compiled lists of words.

Description of Word Lists

One of the earliest studies of children's vocabulary was "The Kindergarten Union" list published in 1928 by the International Kindergarten Union, which is now the Association for Childhood Education International.[11] It contains the 2596 words which according to that study were used the most frequently by the young children whose parents or kindergarten teachers recorded the words the boys and girls used. Although this list does not indicate which words are encountered most in reading by beginning readers, it does throw light on the problem of vocabulary selection for first-grade books, since the words in the early reading material should be chosen from the words whose meaning presents no problem to the children.

---

[11] Association for Childhood Education International, "The Kindergarten Union List." New York: Bureau of Publications, Teachers College, Columbia University, 1935.

The much-used *A Teacher's Wordbook of 20,000 Words*, compiled by Edward L. Thorndike,[12] contains words selected from a large variety of sources of reading material, some for children, others for adults. Thorndike tabulated these so that the frequency with which each word is used is indicated by its placement in groups of 500 or 1000. It is of only limited value for work on vocabulary control for the primary grades, however, since the frequency with which words are used by adults in reading is not a good index of the words that can best be used in primary grade reading. *A Teacher's Wordbook of 30,000 Words*, by Edward L. Thorndike and Irving Lorge,[13] published in 1944, includes not only the results of the research reported in the earlier *A Teacher's Wordbook of 20,000 Words*, but also three other counts made of more than four million running words. Since it indicates the frequency with which some of the words are used in reading materials for children, it is more useful than its predecessor for writers of children's books and for teachers who construct some of their own instructional materials.

One of the most widely used lists by makers of textbooks for children in grades 1 through 3 is *A Reading Vocabulary for the Primary Grades* by Arthur I. Gates.[14] It is based in part on Thorndike's studies and gives 1811 words frequently used in primary grade reading materials. The relative frequency of words arranged in groups of 500 is shown.

A more up-to-date list, *Stone's 1941 Graded Vocabulary for Primary Reading*,[15] contains 2164 words selected on the basis of a vocabulary study of textbooks from the preprimer level through the third reader and of other lists compiled earlier. All the readers used in the study were published between 1931 and 1941.

The Author's Word List for the Primary Grades[16] is based on the study of the vocabulary of 84 preprimers, 69 primers, 84 first readers, 85 second readers, and 47 third readers. Among the preprimer and primer words were included only those that were found in one third or more of all the books studied on that level. The words are graded and their frequency of use is indicated.

A list that is based on words used in writing by children of the elementary school, through grade 8, is Rinsland's *A Basic Vocabulary of Elementary School*

---

[12] Edward L. Thorndike, *A Teacher's Wordbook of 20,000 Words*. New York: Bureau of Publications, Teachers College, Columbia University, 1926.

[13] Edward L. Thorndike and Irving Lorge, *A Teacher's Wordbook of 30,000 Words*. New York: Bureau of Publications, Teachers College, Columbia University, 1944.

[14] Arthur I. Gates, *A Reading Vocabulary for the Primary Grades*. New York: Bureau of Publications, Teachers College, Columbia University, 1935.

[15] Clarence R. Stone, *Stone's 1941 Graded Vocabulary for Primary Reading*. St. Louis, Mo.: Webster Publishing Company, 1941.

[16] L. L. Krantz, *The Author's Word List for Primary Grades*. Minneapolis, Minn.: Curriculum Research Company, 1945.

Children.[17] It consists of 14,571 words each of which occurred at least three times among the 6,112,359 words that the children in the elementary school used in their writing.

A Basic Sight Vocabulary by E. W. Dolch[18] consists of 220 words, exclusive of nouns, which are used with greatest frequency in reading books for the primary grades. Although no nouns are given in this list, Dolch has compiled a separate list of 95 nouns commonly used in the lower grades in basal reading books. Dolch's study shows that approximately two thirds of the words in reading material for the primary grades are among the 220 words listed by him. Almost as large a percentage of words found in the intermediate grade reading books that were examined in the Dolch study are in the list. Because of the frequency of the use of the words, they are words that many teachers think every child should learn to recognize with facility during the initial period of reading instruction. The list of 220 words is given on the opposite page.

Use of Word Lists

Although a great service has been done by the compilers of word lists, these points should be considered:

1. When making use of word lists based in part or in entirety upon occurrence of words in writing of or for adults, the teacher should not conclude that the words used most frequently in writing for adults are the ones that should appear in the books for children in the lower grades.

2. If a word list is based on the material written for adults as well as on some for children, unless the two parts of the study are kept discrete it is questionable to what extent the list is useful in determining the vocabulary that should be used in reading material for children.

3. The words that boys and girls should be taught to read should not be confined to a list of words that they write. The reading vocabulary of a child is almost invariably greater than his writing vocabulary.

4. Whenever a new reading series bases its vocabulary extensively on a list which expresses current practice in vocabulary selection among materials already in print for children, there is the likelihood that whatever imperfections in vocabulary there are in other books will be perpetuated.

5. There is danger of lack of rich content if the vocabulary is too strictly controlled. This is true especially in books in the content areas like social studies and science. As a rule, the children's books in these fields have a greater vocabulary burden than those in basal reading series. While in many respects this is fortunate, cognizance must be taken of the resulting reading problems.

---

17 Henry Rinsland, *A Basic Vocabulary of Elementary School Children*. New York: The Macmillan Company, 1945.

18 Edward W. Dolch, *Methods in Reading*, pp. 373–374. Champaign, Illinois: The Garrard Publishing Company, 1955.

A BASIC SIGHT VOCABULARY OF 220 WORDS[19]

a	come	had	many	round	together
about	could	has	may	run	too
after	cut	have	me		try
again		he	much	said	two
all	did	help	must	saw	
always	do	her	my	say	under
am	does	here	myself	see	up
an	done	him		seven	upon
and	don't	his	never	shall	us
any	down	hold	new	she	use
are	draw	hot	no	show	
around	drink	how	not	sing	very
as		hurt	now	sit	
ask	eat			six	walk
at	eight	I	of	sleep	want
ate	every	if	off	small	warm
away		in	old	so	was
	fall	into	on	some	wash
be	far	is	once	soon	we
because	fast	it	one	start	well
been	find	its	only	stop	went
before	first		open		were
best	five			take	what
better	fly	jump	or	tell	when
big	for	just	our	ten	where
black	found		out	thank	which
blue	four	keep	over	that	white
both	from	kind	own	the	who
bring	full	know		their	why
brown	funny		pick	them	will
but		laugh	play	then	wish
buy	gave	let	please	there	with
by	get	light	pretty	these	work
	give	like	pull	they	would
call	go	little	put	think	write
came	goes	live		this	
can	going	long	ran	those	yellow
carry	good	look	read	three	yes
clean	got		red	to	you
cold	green	made	ride	today	your
	grow	make	right		

[19] SOURCE: Edward W. Dolch, *Methods in Reading*. Champaign, Illinois: The Garrard Publishing Company, 1955, pp. 373–374. "A Basic Sight Vocabulary of 220 Words" may not be reproduced in any form without the express permission of the copyright owners.

6. Because of the great differences in reading ability among pupils within a grade, even rigid control of vocabulary does not make provisions for adapting the instructional materials to individual differences.

7. As a rule, as soon as boys and girls begin reading books of their own choice—trade books, for example—they are likely to read some in which the vocabulary is not best suited to their needs. Sometimes the vocabulary is more limited than necessary and at other times too advanced either because of the number and difficulty of the new words or because of lack of repetition of words. Wise guidance in helping boys and girls select books for outside reading is essential. The teacher should help all children learn new words "on their own" as they make use of the great wealth of supplementary material in reading that becomes available as the child progresses toward independence in reading.

8. Words on vocabulary lists usually give an index not of the difficulty of a word but of the frequency of its use.

The Vocabulary Burden

When deciding upon the reading materials for boys and girls, particularly in the lower grades, the teacher should consider not only the choice of the words included but also the proportion of new words and the amount of repetition provided at appropriately spaced intervals. The tendency has been to reduce the number of different words used in readers during the initial stage of reading instruction. No conclusive research is available on the optimum number of new words per page, but it is questionable whether it is desirable to introduce on the average more than one new word per page in preprimer material and more than two per page in the primer and first reader stages. The number of new words to be presented on a page, however, is dependent upon so many factors that it is doubtful whether research can establish the optimum number for either the primary or the intermediate grades. It is usually conceded that as the child progresses in his ability to read, he can encounter, without reaching a level of frustration, more new words in proportion to the running words than he could earlier. In this connection it is important to bear in mind that while the number of new words given on a page in an intermediate grade book is often considerably larger than the number in first-grade books (one reason being, of course, that the average length of the page increases from the primary to the intermediate grades), in reality many of the so-called "new" words in the intermediate grade reader are new only insofar as they have not been used before in the series; they may be words which the pupils have identified through other reading.

A bright child may not need nearly as many repetitions as the average child. Furthermore, the method of presentation of a new word by the teacher determines in part how many repetitions are desirable. It would seem that probably in the books for the primary grades adequate repetition is provided for the average child. However, many reading textbooks for the intermediate grades do not repeat words often enough for many boys and girls to be able to learn them without undue difficulty. This point is particularly serious when the words are new not only to the child's reading, but also to his understanding, vocabulary. A teacher can, however, solve this problem in part by supplying significant supplementary practice on the words, most of which should as a rule be done in context.

The proportionate number of new words and the amount of repetition desirable, too, should not be determined mechanically, without reference to the individual, to the method of presentation of words, and to the supplementary reading that the child does. The learning of words should not be dependent solely upon repetition in a textbook. If considerable emphasis is put in reading instruction on developing power to decipher new words and upon meaning, it becomes less important to rely greatly on word lists.

6b

Developing
Skill in Word Recognition

Specific suggestions for classroom practices in developing skill in word recognition are presented in this chapter. The classifications used in Chapter 6A are used here.

Teaching Words as Sight Words

The following suggestions may be helpful in teaching children to use a sight method in recognizing words.

1. *Present new words before reading a selection.* Let us assume that the new word to be encountered is *summer*. The teacher has written it on the chalkboard in manuscript and now points to it, saying it clearly —several times, if necessary. She invites the class to repeat it with her in unison. She turns next to a card holder or to word cards placed on the chalk ledge and asks individual children or the class as a whole to select the word *summer* from the numerous words on view. On the board are several sentences, one or more of which include the word *summer*. Children are called upon to

select those sentences containing the word and to point to the word. They then find the word in the selection to be read. Work with "review" words follows.

2. *Studying new words after a selection has been read.* At times the teacher may prefer to have the children read a selection before she helps them with the new words in it. She is justified in doing so if she has reason to believe that most of the pupils will be able to figure out the new words by themselves. If the selection to be read contains many new words, however, it is usually advisable not to rely upon children's ability to deal with them independently. After the reading, the children may be asked to identify the words with which they had difficulty, so that the teacher may present them in the manner suggested in the preceding paragraph.

3. *"Telling" the word to save time.* After a child has acquired some efficiency in analyzing words phonetically and structurally, it may still be desirable to present a word to him as a "sight" word. Stopping to puzzle

out the sound of a word may interfere seriously with the flow of the narrative and thus produce irritating interruptions in what should be a pleasurable process of getting meaning. In such instances the sensible teacher supplies the word so that the pupil may get on with the story.

4. *Reading "new" words orally from the board.* A list of numbered words written on the board may sometimes be used as a brief exercise in the building of a sight vocabulary. Members of the class volunteer to indicate by number the words they know. Thus the presentation of new sight words by the teacher is supplemented by class participation. Obviously such an exercise should be both very brief and relatively infrequent.

5. *Using configuration clues.* When presenting a word by the sight method, the teacher can refer to the general shape of the word by asking pupils to note its length, the pattern of ascending and descending letters, and other striking characteristics of the word. Thus in the case of the word *is*, she may call attention to its shortness; in the case of the word *elephant*, she may ask the class to note the high and the low points. The circular letters in *look*, for instance, are a valuable clue in the identification of the word.

6. *Distinguishing between words of similar length and shape.* Words which bear a general resemblance to each other in the eyes of a young child may be placed on the board in a row, with all the words alike except the one that is to be distinguished from the others. Thus in the following list of words:

when, where, where, when, where, when

pupils may be asked to draw a circle around each word that says "where." The exercise may be repeated for the identification of the word *when*. Brief exercises may be arranged for other words of similar general appearance, such as *say* and *may*, *man* and *can*, *make* and *cake*, *mat* and *sat*.

7. *Distinguishing between words presented in pairs.* Words often confused by young readers may sometimes be presented in pairs. Thus the following words may be written on the board together:

when, where   thought, through
why, what   on, no
then, there   went, want

The teacher points to each pair in turn, saying the words and calling on pupils to draw a line under the appropriate word or pair of words. Or she may write an incomplete sentence, calling on pupils to supply the missing words:

I ————————— a new ball. *(went, want)*

8. *Matching words and pictures.* Both to provide practice in recognizing words and to test the ability to do so, the teacher can give each pupil a sheet of paper on which there is one column of words and another of pictures. Pupils are then asked to draw lines from the words to the matching pictures. Or, instead of single words, groups of words or whole sentences can be supplied along with matching pictures. For example, pupils may be asked to draw a line from a picture of a boy with a ball to the one of three sentences that is illustrated by the picture:

Tom has a ball.
Tom has a bat.
Mary has a ball.

9. *Copying the word to be learned.* Some children who have difficulty in remembering the appearance of a word by means of the sight method find it helpful to get practice in writing the word. There are many ways in which practice can be provided through a visual-motor approach. For example, the child is presented with the written or printed word *sister*. He is told what the word says and then proceeds to copy it. If he has made an error, he draws a line under the part of the model word that he did not copy correctly. Then he takes a second look at the word, thinking of its sound as he does so. He knows that next he will be asked to write the word without looking at the model. After he has written the word from memory, he compares it with the original copy and takes note of any differences. After a certain amount of such practice, he tries to identify the word in a list and in context.

By no means do all children need to use this slow and rather cumbersome method for learning new words. Nevertheless, it has been used successfully when other methods have failed. It is useful also with children who normally respond readily to the sight method but have difficulty with certain words, such as *them, then, why, what, where,* and *when.*

Developing Word Recognition through Context Clues

Context clues are most effective when they are employed along with other methods of word attack. The following suggestions should be read with this principle in mind.

1. *Using pictures in connection with the presentation of a word.* If the teacher wishes to present the word *ball* to the young child, she may first show a picture of a ball and carry on a brief conversation about it. In this way she is able to create in the child's mind the impressions of reality that give meaning to the verbal symbols. First comes the referent, then the symbol for it. The symbol can then evoke the referent when the reader encounters it in verbal context. To reinforce the context clues, the teacher may call attention to the length and contour of a word and confront the reader with whole sentences in which it is used.

2. *Introducing new words, in advance of reading, with the aid of pictures.* Before either the class or a single pupil begins to read a selection, the attention of the children may be called to the accompanying pictures.

Discussion of the pictures will naturally lead to the new words in the text, which can be pointed out and emphasized. In such preliminary discussion, the teacher may encourage the class to anticipate the story from an examination of the pictures.

3. *Using picture-word cards.* Some teachers have quite successfully made extensive use of picture-word cards in teaching word recognition. Sets of cards, each one of which carries on one side a picture with the appropriate label and on the other the word alone, are given to all pupils. Sometimes larger versions of the picture cards are mounted along the walls, and the children make a game of matching their own cards with those they find there. It should be emphasized that such games in word recognition should be combined with abundant experience in encountering the words in sentence context.

4. *Using picture dictionaries.* In this connection the reader is referred to pages 121–122 for a discussion of the great value of the many new picture dictionaries.

5. *Using picture clues on the bulletin board.* The bulletin board should be a source of constant pleasure and stimulation to the pupils. Pictures, clipped from old magazines, drawn or contributed by pupils, or secured from various other sources (not from library periodicals!) are a most effective means of introducing children to the printed word. For example, a picture of a Christmas tree, attractively labeled, is a powerful device for drawing attention to the appearance of familiar words and for leading into a brief study of the structure of those words.

6. *Selecting words that are already in the child's vocabulary.* The new word to be learned should preferably be one that is already a part of the child's speaking or understanding vocabulary. To make certain that the word and its meaning are familiar to the pupils, the teacher may arrange for direct experiences and group discussions which will help to establish the needed word or words in the working vocabulary of the children. Thus if the word *zoo* is to be encountered in the reading, it may in some classes be desirable to arrange a trip to a zoo, look at a film or filmstrip about a zoo, look at pictures of animals in a zoo, or at least talk about zoos. Some of the fine picture books describing unfamiliar animals should be displayed on the book table or on the shelves of the classroom library.

7. *Anticipating meaning through completion exercises.* Pupils can be asked to supply words that might fit in a blank in an incomplete sentence, such as, "Dick _____ home after school." The word to be supplied is *ran.* If the pupils suggest *walked, ran, hurried,* or *hopped,* the teacher may say, "Yes, all those words would fit into the sentence, but this one begins with the *r* sound. Which word is it?" The correct word is then written in the blank. A variation from this type of exercise is one in which the pupils choose from a group of words the one that fits the meaning, for example,

Sam played—. (*ball, boy, bat, work, sing*)

8. *Discussing with the class appropriate techniques of identifying words through context.* Although the suggestions will necessarily vary with the pupil's stage in learning to read, certain general hints may prove helpful to children in various grades: (a) Read the entire sentence before trying to determine the meaning of the new word. (b) Look at the beginning and ending sounds of the word to note whether these match a word that would make sense in the context. (c) Read for meaning. If your first impression of a word, derived from its appearance, does not make sense, give it a second and more careful look. (d) If sentence clues do not help, read the whole paragraph. The broader context may provide the key.

9. *Becoming acquainted with words related to the theme of the selection.* If the teacher will introduce children to interesting new words in advance of the reading, vocabulary difficulties may be substantially diminished. Thus in a story about Eskimos, a preliminary discussion of such words as *igloo, kayak, whale, walrus, glacier,* and *frigid* may markedly reduce the child's word-recognition problems.

10. *Learning to recognize synonyms and antonyms.* Word meanings may frequently be obtained from reference to neighboring words. Thus in the sentence, "These are the nomothetic, or institutional, dimensions of our goal-structure, as distinguished from the idiographic, or individual dimensions," we have both synonymic and antonymic clues to the unusual words, *nomothetic* and *idiographic.* Phonic and structural clues are essential, and an elementary knowledge of Greek would help us a great deal, but the sentence contains its own built-in keys to the new words. At the child's level, the following sentences illustrate the value of contextual clues in the form of synonyms and antonyms:

The picture showed an *ocelot,* a member of the cat family, in a charming pose.

While the princess moved among the guests with a friendly smile for everyone, the prince offended many with his *dour* expression.

As the game was about to begin, the principal announced over the loud-speaker that the coach and *mentor* of the team would be present, after all.

Unlike the *torrid* winds of his homeland, the cool breezes from this picturesque harbor invigorated and inspired Sapu.

For various and *sundry* reasons, the squire delayed building his new home.

Neither the rich nor the *indigent* failed to find a welcome at the bishop's home.

11. *Using a word in a sentence to summarize the thought of a preceding sentence or group of sentences.* If this method is used, the pupil must know the words in the sentence(s) preceding the one containing the word that is unfamiliar in print.

The underlined word *friends* in the second

of the two sentences given below is clarified by the sentence that precedes it.

> Mary and Ann like each other.
> They are good *friends*.

12. *Having pupils find the word in a group of words which means the opposite or almost the opposite of the first word in the row.*

> *kind*: sad, happy, good, mean

13. *Writing on the chalkboard a sentence with a "new word" that a pupil has given orally.* As the teacher writes the sentence on the board, she might underline the "new word" and ask someone to read the sentence and to name the underlined word.

14. *Giving riddles, in written form, for the pupils to solve.* A number of simple riddles like the following might be written on the chalkboard:

> I give milk.
> I eat grass.
> What am I?

Opposite the riddle might be placed a series of words, like *apples, cow, house,* from which the children are to select the one that answers the riddle.

15. *Providing pupils with pictures to complete so that they fit sentences that accompany them.* Each child could be given a sheet of paper on which there is a series of sentences or groups of sentences, each containing an indication as to what needs to be done to a picture in order to have it fit the sentence containing the new word, which is underlined. For example, one group of sentences might be:

> Ted likes to play *ball*.
> His *ball* is red.

To the right of these two sentences might be given an outline picture of a ball.

16. *Giving the pupils duplicated pictures on which various words that they are learning are illustrated.* For example, there could be a picture of a Christmas scene, with these words illustrated in it: *mother, father, tree, book, doll, candy, ball.* The words could be written along the sides and bottom of the picture. The pupils could then draw a line from each of the words to the part in the picture illustrating that word.

17. *Using visual aids.* Some reading series are accompanied by films and filmstrips which introduce children to new concepts and new words. Teacher-made slides, based upon the reading materials, have also proved to be effective in helping children to cope with new vocabulary.

18. *Taking advantage of typographical aids.* Among the various types of context clues, some of the most helpful are the mechanical typographical devices. Punctuation marks, italics, bold print, parentheses, indentations, footnotes, and other similar devices provide helps in the recognition and interpretation of new words.

19. *Making effective use of context to aid in pronunciation.* Children may be given practice in recognizing the correct one of alternative pronunciations of words. In the following two sentences the context provides the essential clue:

> The *lead* in my pencil is broken.
> *Lead* the way, please.

Boys and girls enjoy making up sentences in which words like the following are pronounced in two different ways, depending upon the context: *read, tear, use, wound, wind, bow.*

Developing Word Recognition through Phonic Analysis

Suggestions given here for the use of phonics in the teaching of word recognition are intentionally confined to a relatively small number. The teachers' manuals which accompany the better reading series contain many excellent suggestions for applying the phonics principles stated in Chapter 6A. These suggestions are based upon the special vocabularies which are a part of the developmental programs described in specific series. Methods of teaching phonic skills described in the following paragraphs should, of course, be adapted to the specific needs of children, whether a basal reading series is used or not.

1. A child should not receive phonics instruction before he is "ready"—that is, until he is able to make the necessary visual and auditory discriminations with ease. The stage of readiness will vary with different children. It involves not only physiological maturity but also experience in making fine distinctions between shapes of printed symbols. Some research evidence points to a mental age of six and one-half to seven as essential to successful work with phonics.[1] These studies, however, deal with averages and should not be used as a substitute for the trained observation of the teacher in determining whether a given child is ready to receive phonics instruction. The important thing to remember is that the initial experiences with phonics should be successful ones.

2. One of the most elementary of the phonic skills is that of knowing the sounds commonly associated with single consonants in initial position in a word. In the first work on phonics, the teacher should teach consonants which, unless they are silent letters or blended with others, can be depended upon to have the same sound always—namely, *b, h, j, l, m, p, t,* and *v.* Practice

can be provided by means of procedures like these:

(a) After the pupils have had some practice in, for example, associating the letter *m* in the initial position in a word with the corresponding sound, they may name words in addition to the ones already mentioned that begin with the same letter. These words may then be listed on the board and attention drawn to the letter *m* in those words.

(b) The teacher may wish to write on the board two letters, such as *m* and *h,* with which the pupils have had some familiarity and illustrate them as they occur in initial position in a word. Then a pupil may point to the correct letter as the teacher names words that begin with either the sound of *m* or *h*—for example, *man, mother, hat, hair, many, had, has.* As a variation of this procedure, if the boys and girls can write the letters, each child could number a paper—possibly from 1 to 10—and then write *h* or *m* as the teacher names words beginning with these letters.

(c) The boys and girls might make sentences in which the initial sound is alike in many of the words in a given sentence, like:

Polly picked peas and put them near the flower pot.

3. To get practice in application of what they know about consonants in initial position in a word, as well as about the use of context clues, pupils could tell what word fits into sentences like this one, where only the initial consonant of the word is given:

Susan fed her d————.

Or the boys and girls might draw pictures to illustrate words missing in sentences of that type.

Similar types of practice might be provided for pupils to strengthen their recognition of the sounds of consonants in final position in a word.

[1] A. F. Watts, *The Language and Mental Development of Children,* p. 96. Boston: D. C. Heath and Company, 1944.

Fred J. Schonell, *The Psychology and Teaching of Reading.* Edinburgh and London: Oliver and Boyd, Ltd., 1945.

E. W. Dolch and Maurine Bloomster, "Phonic Readiness," *Elementary School Journal,* 38 (November 1937), 201–205.

4. Some boys and girls who can use phonetic clues secured through the recognition of consonants at the beginning and ending positions of a word are uncertain as to what to do when a consonant comes in a medial position within a syllable, as for instance in the word *late*. What can be done in the case of polysyllabic words is briefly described later in this section in the part on syllabication in connection with structural analysis of words. As a rule, in the case of monosyllabic words not much practice is needed on consonants in medial position if the pupils know well the role of the consonants in initial and ending positions. Nevertheless, an indication should be given to the child fairly early in his training in phonics that consonants can occur in other than beginning and ending positions.

5. As boys and girls meet in their reading consonant blends like *st, gr, tr, cr,* and *str,* they should learn that these and other consonant combinations are sounded in such rapid succession that they do not make two entirely separate sounds. They could be asked to name words beginning with whatever blend they are then studying or have studied. A phonic wheel like the one illustrated can help provide occasional drill not only on beginning consonant blends but also on initial single consonants.

The wheel can be made of two circles of tagboard, one a little smaller than the other, fastened together in the middle by a brass fastener so that the smaller wheel can spin around. Since the wheel here illustrated is to give practice on *st* in initial position in a word, the letters *st* are written on the inner circle next to an indentation in that circle made by cutting out a piece of the tagboard. The cut-out part should be of sufficient size so that endings like *ore* (to go with the *st* to form *store*) *one, op,* and *ick* written on the outer circle can be seen when the slot is moved in such a way that the opening in the smaller circle is opposite the place where

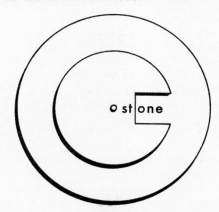

the ending in the larger wheel occurs. Then as the child spins the smaller circle he can read the words that begin with *st,* like *store, stone, stop,* and *stick.*

6. Another phonic device that helps provide needed practice is that of listing either consonant blends or single consonants on slips of tagboard about 1 by 3 inches, the consonant or consonant blend being written at the right of each of these cards. Attached by brass fasteners to the bottom of the pile of these smaller cards could be a larger one, possibly 2 by 5 inches, that contains all the letters of a word except the beginning consonant or consonant blend. If on the longer card the ending *ake* were given, then on the smaller cards might be written *b, r, c, t, m, f, l, s,* and *w.* To form different words for recognition, the pupils can lift up one card at a time to make a number of words ending in *ake.*

7. After boys and girls have learned the sound of *th,* both voiced as in *there* and voiceless as in *thin,* the teacher may wish to write on the board a list of words beginning with *th,* some with the voiced and some with the voiceless sound, such as *the, that, thick, think.* Then as the pupils pronounce each word they could, for instance, put a star in front of every word that begins with the sound of the *th* in *thin.*

8. When teaching vowel sounds the teacher may, for example, ask the pupils to identify the sound of the *a* in words like *at, bat, man, sand.* Or she may ask the boys and girls which words in a series like the following has an *a* with the same sound as the *a* in *at: ate, cat, am, air, can, arm, late, bat.*

sound of a vowel—for example, the sound of long and short *a—* the boys and girls could be given a sheet of paper on which are drawn squares about 2 by 2 inches. In each of the squares is a picture illustrating a short word containing the long or short sound of the letter *a.* Also in each square the teacher writes four or more words some of which contain the long *a* and some the short *a.* The pupils could then be instructed to draw a line under every word in a square that contains the same sound of the *a* as in the word illustrated by the picture. One row of the pictures with accompanying words might look like this:

Another, but similar, type of practice could be provided by asking the children to indicate which in a series of words listed on the chalkboard or on paper contains a given sound that is identified as the long sound or the short sound of a vowel. For example, the pupils might select words with the long *e* sound from among a group of words like the following, included among which are words with the long *e* sound, words with the short *e* sound, words with other sounds of *e,* and words with the silent *e: be, set, late, been, he, she.*

Another procedure is to have the pupils make new words by changing the vowel in a word to form other words, as when they substitute for the *a* in *hat,* the letters *i, o,* and *u* to form *hit, hot,* and *hut.*

9. To provide practice in identifying the

As a variation of the exercise just described, the pupils could indicate which words in a row like the following have the same sound of the vowel *a* as the first word in this row has: *bat rat rate made sat.*

10. To teach the boys and girls the sound of *ar, or, er, ir,* and *ur* as used in standard American speech, the teacher could have them give the sound of these letters as she pronounces them and writes words such as these on the board: *color, murmur, burglar, fir, orator.* Next the pupils can give the sound of those combinations of vowels with *r.* Then they can name other words containing an *ar, or, er, ir,* or *ur* combination. They should be helped to realize that a vowel preceding an *r* does not necessarily indicate such a combination, as, for example, in the case of *rare, figure, mire, deer, clear.*

In a similar way the teacher proceeds to develop inductively the sound of *a* when it precedes a *w* or an *ll*, as in *claw* and *fall*.

11. After the boys and girls have learned that in vowel digraphs, like *ea, oa, ai, ay, ee,* and *oo,* the sound of the first letter forming the digraph is usually long and the second silent, the teacher may list on the board examples that the pupils name. Then they can mark words, given on a list distributed to each child, which contain one of the digraphs that follow the rule. Some of the words on this list might be: *each, oats, may, eel*. What words are used will depend in part on the reading level on which the learner is. In a similar manner the pupils could practice on diphthongs like *oy, oi, ou,* and *ow*.

12. Although it is usually easy to develop the concept that some letters are silent, it is likely to be more difficult to teach the pupils *when* letters are silent. In this connection it is desirable that boys and girls recognize the difference between vowel digraphs, in which one letter is silent, and diphthongs, in which two letters together form one sound unlike either of the vowels. Practice may be provided by having the pupils tell in which words, in a list like the following, one of two letters in roman type is silent: *about, oil, boat, clean, cow, rail.*

To teach inductively the generalization that a final *e* in a syllable preceded by a single consonant is usually silent, the teacher could place on the board a numbered list of three or four words which are in harmony with the rule, like these:

1. rate
2. tame
3. hope
4. rule

For each word the pupils could be asked to (1) pronounce the word, (2) tell with what letter the word ends, (3) tell whether the *e* is silent or not silent, (4) indicate what kind of letter—vowel or consonant—precedes the

vowel and (5) state how many consonants precede the vowel. As a summary, the pupils could answer these questions about all the words in this list:

1. With what letter does each word end?
2. Is the *e* silent?
3. What kind of letter—vowel or consonant—precedes the final *e*?
4. How many consonants precede the final *e* in each of the words in the list?

Next the teacher could tell the pupils that usually when the final letter in a syllable is *e,* the *e* is silent if it is preceded by a single consonant. Thereupon she could give the pupils opportunity for applying the rule. They could tell in which of a list of words like these this rule applies: *came, ride, male, riddle, table.*

13. Practice could be provided in making substitutions of consonants in words. For example, if the pupil knows the word *fun,* he has merely to substitute the consonant *r* for *f* to be able to recognize the word *run*. The teacher can ask boys and girls who know the word *man,* when they come to the new word *can,* "What word that we know looks the same as this word except for the beginning letter?" When the boys and girls have replied *man,* the teacher can write *man* on the board directly below the word *can* and then ask with what sound that word (pointing at *can*) begins. She can continue by saying, "Let's name a word that begins with the *c* (hard *c*) sound and rhymes with *man*." Opportunity might also then be given for the boys and girls to name other words that are like *man* and *can* excepting for the beginning letter, like *tan* and *ran*. Attention needs to be drawn not only to the possibility of substitution of letters in initial position but also in ending and medial positions. For example, in learning the word *cat* when the word *can* is known, a similar procedure may be applied. The same holds true in words in which substitution of a vowel in medial position in a syllable is a possible means of deciphering a new word, as when *bit* is recognized when the word *bat* is known, by a substitution of the *i* for the *a*.

If special practice is needed to develop skill in identifying words through substitution of letters, an exercise like this might be used:

Direction: Draw a line under all words in each row that are exactly alike excepting for the beginning letter.

man   men   can   pan   ran   map

The following directions might be given with a page consisting of rows of words like those that are here listed.

Direction: Draw a line under all words in each row that are like the first word excepting for the ending letter.

has   hat   was   ham   had   his

14. To help the pupils remember sounds, the teacher could make a chart that gives the letters or combinations of letters that produce a sound, and a word illustrating each sound that the boys and girls have learned. Pictures which illustrate words containing a given sound are sometimes helpful. For example, the word *mother* with a picture of a mother would serve to help with the sound of *m*. Often, instead of using one big chart, tagboard cards, about 5 by 8 inches, are used, on each of which is one picture, one word, and one letter.

Another device is to have the boys and girls make individual books in which there is a page for each letter or letter sound that they have studied. On these pages they could paste pictures illustrating words that contain these sounds.

To get further practice in associating the written symbol and the sound, a box containing various consonants or consonant blends on slips of paper might be used. As a child draws a letter out of the box, he might name it and find objects in the room the names of which begin with that letter. Or

the pupils might match the written symbols with pictures arranged around the room that begin with a given sound. Or as the teacher holds up a picture, the children hold up a card with the letter or letters with which the name of the object in the picture begins.

15. Rhyming words can be used in teaching phonics. The teacher may repeat a nursery rhyme and ask the pupils to listen for words that rhyme, like *quick* and *candlestick*. Or the boys and girls might complete jingles that the teacher makes up, like:

At recess time on this day
All the children will want to ————.

As a variation the boys and girls might name pairs of rhyming words. Another procedure that might be used is naming of various words in pairs by the teacher, some of which rhyme and some of which do not rhyme, like:

meat, seat   take, talk.

The pupils could be asked which pairs rhyme.

16. To provide practice in becoming conscious of the position of sounds in a word, the teacher could tell the pupils, for example, that all the words she will give will contain the sound of *t*. After the teacher has given a word, a pupil may tell whether the sound of *t* comes at the beginning or end of a word or within it. Words like these can be pronounced: *hat, Tom, little.*

17. After the boys and girls have had work on blends, the teacher may draw four large circles on the blackboard, in one of which she has written, for example, the word *clock,* in another the word *tree,* and in still another *store.* Then as she gives, from a word card, the name of a word beginning with the sound of the *cl* in *clown,* a child can take the card and put it on the chalkboard ledge near the circle in which the word *clock* is written. Similarly when the teacher pronounces the word *stove,* a pupil should place the word card under the circle

containing the word *store.* The same can be done with the sound of *tr* in *tree.* If the word named does not begin with *st, cl,* or *tr,* it should be placed on the ledge below the circle not containing a word.

18. As the teacher names a word, the pupils may write the letter representing the sound with which the word begins.

19. The pupils may write on small slips of paper the vowels on which practice is needed, one vowel per piece of paper. If the practice is to be on the vowels *a* and *e,* the pupils may hold up the one of these two letters that is represented by a sound in each word as the teacher names it. For example, when the teacher says *name,* the pupils will hold up their papers with the letter *a* written on them.

20. When the boys and girls are ready to learn the diacritical markings of words, it is important to begin slowly enough so that the work will not be confusing to them. After they have worked on the long and short sounds of the vowels, the teacher may tell them that there is a way of indicating the sound of a letter in writing. Then she can tell them the markings for the long and short vowels and provide practice in their interpreting and writing these markings for words. One way in which she may wish to do this is by asking them to mark all the long and the short vowels in a list of words of which they already know the pronunciation. Later they can learn to decipher words by means of markings.

Since more than one set of diacritical markings are in common use, the system selected for practice should be the one most used in the pupils' glossaries or dictionaries. In the intermediate grades, however, boys and girls should be helped to decipher words when a system different from one they have been employing is used. They should know that at the bottom of the pages of a dictionary is given the guide for pronunciation that will help them interpret the markings of the words in that book.

Developing Word Recognition through Structural Analysis

Without resorting to the undesirable practice of having boys and girls "find little words in big"—for example, *as* in *has*—the teacher can in many ways aid the boys and girls in developing through structural analysis a method of identifying and recognizing some words more rapidly than through phonetic analysis. A few such methods are listed here.

1. As the teacher refers to compound words on the board, like *grandmother,* she may tell the boys and girls that the word is made up of two words and ask them to find these two words.

2. Use can be made of two columns of words in one of which is the first part of a compound word and in the other, the second part. The boys and girls can then draw lines connecting the words in the two columns which together form one word—for example,

grand	basket
worth	room
waiting	while
waste	mother

3. The boys and girls can make a collection of compound words for posting on the bulletin board. To the right of each compound word the words of which it is composed can be written.

4. The teacher might put into a cardholder a group of words, in mixed-up order, that might be used in forming compound words, like the following, which pupils will combine into compound words:

school	up
stairs	mother
book	grand
story	house

5. A crossword puzzle could be made by the teacher or pupils in which only compound words would serve as answers. Part of each word could be supplied in a numbered list while the other part could be chosen from an unnumbered list that is supplied with the puzzle.

6. The boys and girls can get help in unlocking words by looking for the root of a word that contains a suffix. For example, in the word *sings* the teacher may wish to draw a line under *sing,* stating that that much of the word the pupils already know. Then she can ask them to pronounce the root word and thereafter the new word.

7. The boys and girls can make a list of words containing a given root, like *walk, walks, walked, walking.*

8. When the pupils come to a word like *unwise,* if they have had the word *wise,* the teacher can draw a line under *wise* and ask what that part of the word is. The pupils can then give the prefix and, next, combine the prefix with the root of the word. Having the boys and girls make a list of common prefixes, like *mis, im,* and *ir,* with words in which they form a prefix, like *misuse, impossible,* and *irresponsible,* can help them both in word recognition and in word meaning.

9. On a sheet of paper each child can write the base words of a list of words containing either prefixes or suffixes or both that have been written on the board.

10. The teacher may write on the board a list of words with prefixes that mean *not,* like *unhappy, impossible,* and *irresponsible.* Then the boys and girls could name words to add to the list. Next they could draw a line under the different prefixes that mean *not.*

11. The boys and girls can supply the correct prefix for each word in a list, like the following, for which the meaning of the word to be formed has been given:

—— known   not known
—— like   not to like
—— kind   not kind

12. The pupils can be helped in the de-

velopment of the generalization that many root words ending in *e* drop the final *e* before adding *ing,* like *make, making.* They can give examples of words to which this generalization applies.

13. Each pupil can be given a card with a prefix or suffix, while the teacher has a series of cards containing root words to many of which a prefix or a suffix on a pupil's card could be added. As the teacher holds up a card, all pupils who have a card with a prefix or suffix that can be combined with the root word stand. Next the pupils who have the appropriate prefixes or suffixes can write on the chalkboard the words that can be formed from the root word with the addition of their prefixes or suffixes.

14. The class might make a chart with three columns, in the first of which are listed common prefixes. In the second column could be given a meaning of each prefix; and in the third column, examples of words in which the prefix has the designated meaning.

15. As the boys and girls acquire the essentials of syllabication, they should learn to divide words into syllables—first of all, as an aid to word recognition and, second, as a help in writing words when it is necessary to divide them into syllables. Some generalizations about syllabication, of value in word recognition, were given in Chapter 6A.

To give help in syllabication, the pupils might be given a list of words, some with one, others with two, and still others with more than two syllables. The boys and girls could indicate after each word the number of syllables it contains.

16. The class could make a list of contractions, with the words which were combined to form each contraction given opposite each contraction. Or a crossword puzzle could be made, the answers to which are contractions. The words from which the contractions are formed could constitute the numbered list of words for the puzzle.

Picture Dictionaries

The term *picture dictionary* usually refers to books in which a picture is used with every word entry to help the child identify and recall words. Often, but not always, the words are arranged in alphabetical order. To illustrate the letter *a*, a large picture of an apple, with the word *apple*, and a sentence containing the word may be given.

Some of the more widely used picture dictionaries are:

Clemans, Elizabeth, *Pixie Dictionary*. New York: Holt, Rinehart and Winston, Inc., 1960. 62 pp.

Courtis, Stuart, and Garnette Watters, *Illustrated Golden Dictionary*. New York: Simon and Schuster, Inc., 1951. 544 pp.

Gatcher, Dorothy, and Margaret Madden, *From A to Z Picture Dictionary*. Revised edition. New York: The Platt and Munk Company, Inc., 1960. 62 pp.

Guild, Marion, and Ruth Leder, *My Picture Dictionary*. New York: Maxton Publishers, Inc., 1949. 32 pp.

Guralnick, David B., and Staff, *Webster's New World Dictionary, Elementary Edition*. Cleveland: The World Publishing Company, 1962. 832 pp.

MacBean, Dilla W., *Picture Book Dictionary*. Chicago: Children's Press, Inc., 1962. 48 pp.

McIntire, Alta, *The Follett Beginning-to-Read Picture Dictionary*. Chicago: Follett Publishing Company, 1959. 32 pp.

Moore, Lilian, *The Golden Picture Dictionary*. New York: Golden Press, Inc., 1954. 38 pp.

Oftedahl, Laura, and Nina Jacobs, *My First Dictionary*. New York: Grosset and Dunlap, Inc., 1948. 140 pp.

O'Donnell, Mabel, and Willmina Townes, *Words I Like to Read, Write, and Spell*. New York: Harper and Row, Publishers, 1963. 224 pp.

Parke, Margaret B., *Young Reader's Color-Picture Dictionary for Reading, Writing, and Spelling*. Illustrated by Cynthia and Alvin Koehler. New York: Grosset and Dunlap, Inc., 1958. 93 pp.

Reed, Mary, and Edith Osswald, *My Little Golden Dictionary*. New York: Simon and Schuster, Inc., 1949. 56 pp.

Scott, Alice, and Stella Center, *The Giant Picture Dictionary for Boys and Girls*. New York: Doubleday and Company, Inc., 1958. 316 pp.

Walpole, Ellen Wales, and Mary Reed, *The Golden Dictionary*. New York: Simon and Schuster, Inc., 1944. 94 pp.

Warner, Jane, *The Golden Picture Book of Words*. New York: Simon and Schuster, Inc., 1954. 50 pp.

Watters, Garnette, and Stuart Courtis, *The Picture Dictionary for Children*. New York: Grosset and Dunlap, Inc., 1958. 383 pp.

Wright, Wendell W., ed., *The Rainbow Dictionary*. Cleveland: The World Publishing Company, 1959. 434 pp.

Some points that the teacher should keep in mind in connection with picture dictionaries are: (1) For the younger children, simplicity of arrangement of the words in the dictionary as well as simplicity of illustration of the words is imperative. (2) The children should be helped in understanding how to use the picture dictionary. (3) After the pupils know how to use the picture dictionary, it should be thought of primarily as a self-help device. (4) The picture dictionary should be made easily available to the children and displayed attractively, possibly on a reading table. (5) The school program should be so arranged that the boys and girls have time to make use of the dictionary.

Pupil-made picture dictionaries can be of much value to boys and girls. One type of picture dictionary is the one in which on separate sheets of paper the boys and girls either draw or paste a picture representing an entry word and then write the word, often used in a simple sentence, on the same page with the picture. These pages are arranged to good advantage in alphabetical order by means of a loose-leaf notebook. As the pupil meets a new word that can be illustrated, he writes it on a sheet of paper and pastes on the same sheet a picture that he has found or drawn himself. Sometimes the picture dictionary is a group project; at other times each pupil makes his own.

A picture dictionary may be in the form of cards, instead of sheets of paper, that contain the words and the illustrations of words. These cards can be arranged in a file, which can be expanded as the class progresses in knowledge of words. Another variation of the picture dictionary is often made in connection with the words that can be illustrated that occur in a story or a section of a book. As the pupil meets new words that can be illustrated in a given story or unit in a reader, he illustrates each one; he then can refer to the word as he finds the need of doing so. For example, if in a story the child meets the words *rabbit, tree, ran, squirrel,* and *into* he may divide a sheet of paper into four parts, using one of the four parts for the word *rabbit* under a picture of a rabbit and reserving another of the four parts for each of these words: *tree, ran,* and *squirrel. Ran* he may illustrate by a boy, a dog, or a rabbit running. Since words like *into* do not easily present themselves in a pictorial illustration, that kind of word usually is omitted from a picture dictionary.

Another teacher-pupil-made adaptation of the picture dictionary deals only with words used in a science or social studies unit.

As the pupil uses the picture dictionary to recognize words, the teacher can help him derive other benefits from it. Some of these values are: (1) help in spelling, (2) development of interest in words, and (3) development of skill in finding words in alpha-

betical order. If the picture dictionary is pupil made, these are additional values: (1) practice in arranging words in alphabetical order, (2) development of ability to draw, cut out, and paste pictures, and (3) development of skill in arranging words and pictures neatly on a page.

Workbooks as an Aid to Word Recognition

Workbooks of various types, when not used as busywork, can be of service in helping the child develop from dependence to independence in word recognition. One type, and probably the more useful, is that which accompanies reading series. The better reading series have a well-developed sequence of workbooks designed to be used in conjunction with the hardback books, the regular readers. Most of these are written to give the boys and girls practice after the material in the textbook has been read. In such instances the new words are presented in connection with the work in the reading books. After a story or part of a story has been read, the pupil is given more practice in recognizing the words in that and other selections by using the words in a variety of ways. At times the pupils are asked to draw a line under the word that completes the meaning of a sentence in which one of the new words has been left out. At other times the pupils may draw a line from a word to the picture which is used to illustrate it. An examination of any workbook accompanying a reader will reveal a variety of ways in which it provides practice on words and makes possible a test on the skills as well.

But not all workbooks published as part of a reading series are planned to be studied by the child after he has read a corresponding section in the textbook. Some are designed so that a child studies a number of pages in the workbook before he reads the material that corresponds to it in the reader.

In that case the new words for the selection in the reader are presented in the workbook and practice on their recognition is provided. In this type of arrangement the child thus meets in the workbook, before he even starts the regular book, all the new words in the story. The words are not, however, presented as a list of words, but are given in context, frequently in material of interest to the boys and girls.

Some teachers prefer making material of the workbook type themselves, believing that it is better suited to the needs of the particular boys and girls than that given in the workbooks. Although this practice has merit, it is time consuming and, today, not really necessary. It is true, however, that when workbook materials were sterile in content and poor in selection of objectives to be accomplished, it was not difficult to justify the large amount of time that many teachers, especially in the lower grades, spent in devising and duplicating materials to provide practice beyond that given in the reader on various skills of reading.

In using workbooks that are not made to accompany any one series of readers, there is the danger of lack of unity in objectives and procedures between reader and workbook. If the authors of the textbook series have in mind one program for the development of word recognition and the writers of the workbook follow a different sequence and observe other criteria, the articulation between the use of these two types of materials is often poor. This difficulty is especially likely to exist if the teacher is under pressure to require every pupil to do every page in a workbook, regardless of the appropriateness of the material to the rest of the program and to the needs of the boys and girls. Nevertheless, judicious use of workbooks that are made independently of any one series of readers can be helpful if the workbooks are based on sound principles of teaching reading.

Games and Word Recognition

In connection with the role of games in relation to the development of power in word recognition, these questions frequently concern teachers: (1) Under what conditions are games desirable? (2) What are some games that can aid in word recognition?

Criteria for Selection of Games

In determining the role of games in developing power in word recognition, the teacher needs to have her purposes clearly in mind. If the major purpose is to help the boys and girls become more skillful in identifying and remembering words, then a game, to be acceptable, must satisfy the requiremens for good drill. If the chief aim is to furnish recreation, then, of course, it is not essential that the characteristics of effective drill be present. Games that are not primarily designed to give help in reading can be scheduled during times of the school day set aside for recreational activities, such as before school, during the noon hour, during recess when better use of the time cannot be made, and during other periods when recreation is the primary aim.

One criterion for effective drill that is often not observed when games are used in learning to read is this: "Other things being equal, that drill is the better of two that provides the more practice on the skill in question in a given length of time." Other criteria of good drill for a game used primarily as a learning activity are: (1) The boys and girls should be cognizant of the purpose served by the drill. (2) The game should be on the interest level of the participants. (3) The game should not interfere with the development of good citizenship. (4) If competition is an element of the drill, it should be primarily competition with self, rather than with others. (5) The game should be a means to an end, not an end in itself.

List of Games Commercially Available

Some of the reading games are available through publishing companies, in variety stores, and in department stores. Use of most of these can be justified chiefly as recreational activities that may, however, provide opportunity for growth in reading. Many teachers like to place such games on a reading table, so that they will be accessible to the children in free periods during, before, or after school time.

The following list of games is merely illustrative of the large number now available.

1. *"Phonic Lotto," by E. W. Dolch. Champaign, Illinois: The Garrard Publishing Company.*

"Phonic Lotto," a game for two to ten players, consists of ten cards 7½ by 5½ inches, and sixty smaller cards, 2¼ inches square. Each of the larger cards is divided into six squares, on which there is printed a vowel or vowel combination accompanied by a picture, the name of which contains the vowel or vowel combination given in the square. The sixty smaller cards show pictures of objects whose names contain one of the vowel sounds found on the squares of the large cards. The sounds on which there is drill are the long and short vowel sounds, *a, e, i, o, u;* the digraphs, *ai, ay, ee, oa;* the diphthongs, *oi, oy, ou, ow, ew, oo;* and the vowels with the letter *r*, namely, *ar, er, ir, or, ur.* In the game the purpose is to match the small cards so that the pictures on them are placed on the pictures on the large card the names of which contain the same vowel sounds.

2. *"Group Word Teaching Game," by E. W. Dolch. Champaign, Illinois: The Garrard Publishing Company.*

The game consists of nine sets of cards each containing six like cards. On the cards of each set are listed 24 of the 220 basic sight words compiled by Dolch. The game is played much like Lotto. As a word from a

printed list is read by the leader, the players cover the word on their cards with small oblong pieces of paper.

3. *"Group Sounding Game," by E. W. Dolch. Champaign, Illinois: The Garrard Publishing Company.*

There are six cards, similar to Lotto cards, in each of the following sets: Set A—initial consonants; Set B—short vowels, *a, e,* and *i;* Set C—all short vowels; Set D—harder consonants: Set E—blended consonants; Set F—consonant digraphs; Set G—long vowels; Set H—vowels with *r*; Set I—diphthongs; Set J—miscellaneous consonants; Set K—closed syllables; Set L—open syllables; Set M—prefixes and suffixes; Set N—three syllables; and Set O—three syllables. The game can be played by six players, who cover the words the leader calls from a list of words on a given "set" that he is furnished.

4. *"What the Letters Say," by E. W. Dolch. Champaign, Illinois: The Garrard Publishing Company.*

This game, also called "A Beginning Sounding Game," consists of cards on which one sound for each letter is illustrated by a picture and a word. In the game the child gets practice in associating the name of a letter with one of its sounds and with three different words, on different cards that illustrate the sound.

5. *"Take," by E. W. Dolch. Champaign, Illinois: The Garrard Publishing Company.*

This is a self-teaching phonics game, in which the pupils match the sounds of the beginning, middle, or ending of words, with cards on which a picture and the name of that picture are given. This game is for boys and girls in the third grade and up.

6. *"The Syllable Game," by E. W. Dolch. Champaign, Illinois: The Garrard Publishing Company.*

In "The Syllable Game" there are three decks of sixty-four cards each, with two-syllable words in two decks and with words up to four syllables in the third deck. It is a game that a child can play either alone or with another person while learning to recognize many common syllables.

7. *"Phonic Rummy." Buffalo, N.Y.: Kenworthy Educational Service, Inc.*

"Phonic Rummy" comes in four sets: one for grades 1 and 2; another for grades 2 and 3; still another for grades 2, 3, and 4; and a fourth for grades 3, 4, and 5. In each set there are two packs of 60 cards. With these cards can be played a game in matching vowel sounds.

8. *"Junior Phonic Rummy." Buffalo, N.Y.: Kenworthy Educational Service, Inc.*

This game, similar to "Phonic Rummy," is also a matching game in which words used widely in first-grade readers are matched for vowel sounds.

9. *"Doghouse Game." Buffalo, N.Y.: Kenworthy Educational Service, Inc.*

"Doghouse Game" comes in twelve game envelopes, on the face of each of which are printed thirty-five phonograms as well as rules for pronunciation and sixty-four consonants and consonant blends. A variety of games can be played with these cards.

10. *"A B C Game." Buffalo, N.Y.: Kenworthy Educational Service, Inc.*

This game, designed for teaching letter, word, and picture recognition, is played by matching the cards in the set, on each of which are a picture, the name of the picture, and the letter with which the word begins. The game is played somewhat like "Old Maid," as the players try to find the mate for every card that they have until every player, excepting the person who has the card entitled "Mr. ABC," has given up all of his cards.

11. *"Phonic Quizmo." Chicago: Beckley-Cardy Company.*

This is another game that is similar to Lotto. The pupils cover on their cards the words beginning with the same letter or letter combination found in words that the teacher reads from a list supplied with the game.

12. *"Phonetic Word Wheel." Chicago: Beckley-Cardy Company.*

Various games can be devised with the phonetic word wheel in which the pupils are provided with practice in recognizing vowels, consonants, and blends.

13. *"Make-a-Word Game." Chicago: Beckley-Cardy Company.*

With the sixty-five green cards with consonants or consonant blends and the sixty-five orange cards with phonograms that are supplied in this game, matching games can be played.

14. *"Go Fish." Washington, D.C.: The Remedial Education Center.*

"Go Fish," a consonant sound game, consists of a series of three cards of each consonant, of three different colors, with a picture on each, the name of which begins with a consonant sound, the letter for which is also given on the card. Each player is given six cards, while the remaining cards are placed into the Fish Pile in the center. Each player in turn asks any other player for a card that begins with the consonant sound that he gives. If the player is unsuccessful in his attempt to get the desired card from a player, he goes to the Fish Pile to see if he can draw it from that. If he does not get the card at his first attempt, he loses his turn. Whenever a player has acquired all three cards beginning with the same consonant sound, he places the three cards in a pile in front of him, forming a "book." The person with the largest number of "books" wins the game.

15. *"Vowel Dominoes." Washington, D.C.: The Remedial Education Center.*

To play this game cards 1½ inches by 2½ inches, resembling dominoes, are used. On half of each card is a vowel and on the other half a picture of a word containing a vowel sound. For instance, on half of one card is the letter *o* and on the other half a picture of a drum, to represent the *u* sound. The game can be played much like dominoes. For example, a card with the letter *a* and a picture of a safety pin can be placed next to a card with the letter *i* and a picture of a top, so that the half of the first card on which the safety pin is drawn is next to the letter *i* of the second card, thereby placing the picture of a word with the *i* sound next to the letter *i*.

Other Reading Games

Many games other than those produced commercially can be used to develop reading skills. It is hoped that those listed here will suggest to the teacher many others that might be particularly suitable to the needs of her pupils.

1. *Pollyanna.* A board similar to the one pictured below can be made, with spaces marked off large enough so that a small word card can be placed on each, perhaps fastened to the board by "Ace" corners. The player spins the arrow, which will indicate the number of steps he can advance during his turn. The game can be played in a variety of ways, of which the following is one: If a player can pronounce each word in the steps that he is entitled to take, he places a button or

other small marker with which each player is supplied on the last word in his "turn." If he cannot pronounce all the words in the steps he is allowed, he is told the first word that halts his progress. Then he is required to place his marker on the word preceding the one he missed. The first player to arrive at "home" wins.

2. *Word Baseball.* One way in which to play "word baseball" is to designate one corner of the room as "home" and the other three corners as first, second, and third base. If the pupil who is "up for bat" can pronounce the word that the teacher shows him, he can go to first base. If he can say the next word, he may go to second base. If he can go on through third base to home, he scores a "home-run." However, if he is unable to pronounce his first word, he is "out" and an "out" is recorded for his team. If he cannot pronounce a word, other than the first one given to him when his turn comes, he proceeds to second base when the next batter on his side has pronounced the first word given to him. A similar procedure determines the length of his stay on third base. Scoring can be done in a variety of ways.

3. *A Reading "Spelldown."* The class can

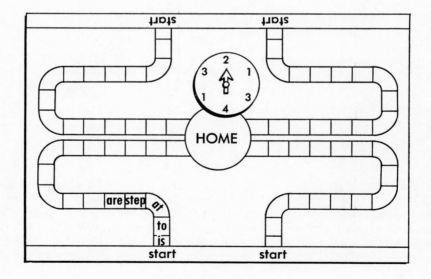

line up in two teams as they do for spell-downs. One child can be appointed score-keeper. The teacher should have a large number of word cards with words that the pupils have studied but on which they need further practice. As the teacher holds up the first card, the first pupil tries to pronounce it and use it in a sentence. If he is able to pronounce the word and use it in a sentence, he scores a point for his team; he then takes his place at the end of his line. If he cannot pronounce a word and use it in a sentence, he stays where he is and a score is recorded for the opposing team. In that case the card is shown to a member of the other team. If he, too, does not know the word or cannot use it in a sentence, the word "comes back" to the next pupil on the team who was first given the word. Each time a word is missed, the opposing team gets a point.

4. *Action Sentences.* The leader, who may be the teacher, places in a word holder or on a chalk ledge several sentences with directions such as "Get a book from the table." After a pupil has performed one of the directions, another child points to the sentence that tells what the other child did. He reads the sentence as he points to it.

5. *Checkers.* For this game a checkerboard about 16 by 16 inches may be used. "Ace" corners are fitted to each square on the board. On separate squares, the same size as the squares on the board, one word is written twice on each, in this manner:

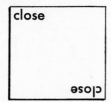

The game can be played in a variety of ways. One is that of having the player pronounce the word on the card he draws and then place it on the board.

6. *Ten-pins.* Ten-pins can be set up on the floor. From a stack of word cards placed face down, players take turns in picking up the top card. If a player can pronounce the word on his card, he gets a turn at trying to knock pins over with a ball. If he cannot pronounce a word, the person whose turn it is next pronounces it. Score is kept in terms of the ten-pins that are dislocated. This game is chiefly for recreational, not reading purposes.

7. *Ring-toss.* A variation of ten-pins is ring-toss. In this game, the person pronouncing his word correctly gets a turn at trying to toss a ring onto a hook. The winner is the one who has hooked the most rings by the time the hooks are filled. The chief value of this game is recreational.

8. *Flinch.* On cards similar to the one illustrated below may be written words from science, social studies, or a general word list. There need to be as many sets of cards, each containing the same number, as there are players. After the cards have been dealt face down, the first player turns over the top card. The cards numbered 1 are played in the center of the table while all others are played on the stack of an opponent if the number is consecutive, either up or down.

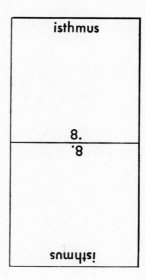

If a player is unable to play, he places the card in front of him face down at the bottom of his stack. If a player misses seeing a play, each opponent places a card face down on the player's stock. As he plays, each player says the number and word on the card.

9. *Sentence Game.* After word cards have been passed out to the class, the teacher reads a sentence using only words appearing on the cards. Each pupil who has a card on which a word used in that sentence is written goes to the front of the room. A pupil designated as "sentence maker" makes the sentence by arranging the children with their cards in the proper order as the teacher repeats the sentence. If a sentence maker forms the sentence incorrectly, another pupil is appointed in his place. The pupil who does not recognize that he has a needed word in his possession, or who thinks that he has one when he does not, can be "penalized" by his having to put his card into a center pile from which, with future sentences, the "sentence maker" selects the word if it is again needed for a sentence.

Distributors of Games

Teachers interested in securing reading games may, in addition to canvassing stores, wish to write to publishing companies for catalogues describing their reading games. Some companies that distribute games are: (1) Beckley-Cardy Company, Chicago, Illinois; (2) Cadaco-Ellis Company, Chicago, Illinois; (3) The Garrard Publishing Company, Champaign, Illinois; (4) Houghton Mifflin Company, Boston, Massachusetts; (5) Judy Company, Minneapolis, Minnesota; (6) Kenworthy Educational Service, Inc., Buffalo, New York; (7) Kraeg Games, Inc., St. Louis, Missouri; (8) Milton Bradley Company, Springfield, Illinois; (9) Remedial Education Center, Washington, D.C.; (10) Simon and Schuster, Inc., New York, New York; (11) Training Aids, Inc., Los Angeles, California;

and (12) Whitman Publishing Company, Racine, Wisconsin.

FOR FURTHER STUDY

Austin, Mary C., and Coleman Morrison, with others, *The First R: The Harvard Report on Reading in Elementary Schools*, pp. 27–35. New York: The Macmillan Company, 1963.

Beery, Althea, "Development of Reading Vocabulary and Word Recognition," *Reading in the Elementary School*, pp. 172–192. Forty-eighth Yearbook of the National Society for the Study of Education, Part II. Chicago: The University of Chicago Press, 1949.

Betts, Emmett A., *Foundations of Reading Instruction*, rev. ed., pp. 341–351. New York: American Book Company, 1954.

————, "Phonics: Practical Considerations Based on Research," *Elementary English*, 33 (October 1956), 357–371.

Bond, Guy L., and Eva Bond Wagner, *Teaching the Child to Read*, pp. 149–199. New York: The Macmillan Company, 1960.

Burton, William H., *Reading in Child Development*, pp. 232–309. Indianapolis: The Bobbs-Merrill Company, Inc., 1956.

Carter, Homer L. J., and Dorothy J. McGinnis, *Teaching Individuals to Read*, pp. 74–103. Boston: D. C. Heath and Company, 1962.

Causey, Oscar S., ed., *The Reading Teacher's Reader*, pp. 173–208. New York: The Ronald Press, 1958.

Clymer, Theodore, "The Utility of Phonic Generalizations in the Primary Grades," *The Reading Teacher*, 16 (January 1963), 252–258.

Cordts, Anna D., "And It's All Known As Phonics," *Elementary English*, 32 (October 1955), 376–378.

Durkin, Dolores, *Phonics and the Teaching of Reading*. Practical Suggestions for Teaching, No. 22, Alice Miel, ed. New

York: Bureau of Publications, Teachers College, Columbia University, 1962.

Gates, Arthur I., "Vocabulary Control in Basal Reading Material," *The Reading Teacher*, 14 (November 1961), 80–85.

Gray, William S., *On Their Own in Reading*. Chicago: Scott, Foresman and Company, 1960.

Hester, Kathleen B., *Teaching Every Child To Read*, pp. 136–193. New York: Harper and Row, Publishers, 1955.

Hildreth, Gertrude, "New Methods for Old in Teaching Phonics," *Elementary School Journal*, 57 (May 1957), 436–441.

———, "The Role of Pronouncing and Sounding in Learning to Read," *Elementary School Journal*, 55 (November 1954), 141–147.

———, "Some Misconceptions Concerning Phonics," *Elementary English*, 34 (January 1957), 26–29.

Kirk, Samuel A., and Winifred D. Kirk, "How Johnny Learns to Read," *Elementary English*, 33 (May 1956), 266–269.

McKim, Margaret G., and Helen Caskey, *Guiding Growth in Reading in the Modern Elementary School*, pp. 216–256, 351–363. New York: The Macmillan Company, 1963.

Monroe, Marion, *Growing into Reading*.

Chicago: Scott, Foresman and Company, 1951.

Russell, David H., "Teaching Identification and Recognition," *Handbook of Research on Teaching*, N. L. Gage, ed., pp. 868–883. Chicago: Rand McNally and Company, 1963.

Smith, Henry P., and Emerald W. Dechant, *Psychology in Teaching Reading*, pp. 183–211. Englewood Cliffs, N.J.: Prentice-Hall, Inc., 1961.

Smith, Nila B., "Phonics Then and Now," *Education*, 75 (May 1955), 560–565.

Strang, Ruth, Constance M. McCullough, and Arthur E. Traxler, *Problems in the Improvement of Reading*, 2d ed., pp. 283–295. New York: McGraw-Hill Book Company, Inc., 1955.

Elementary Reading Problems, pp. 7–11. Darien, Conn.: Teachers Publishing Corporation, 1957.

Wagner, Guy, and Max Hosier, *Reading Games*. Darien, Conn.: Teachers Publishing Corporation, 1960.

Wrightstone, J. Wayne and May Lazar, *Experience Charts: A Guide to Their Use in Grades 1–3*. Educational Research Bulletin No. 13. New York: Bureau of Educational Research, Board of Education of the City of New York, May 1952.

7a

Reading with Comprehension

A passage can properly be read with varying degrees of understanding. The scale of comprehension ranges from no meaning to complete understanding. The degree of desired comprehension will depend in part upon the purpose of the reader. The efficient reader will require from the printed page only what he is looking for. He may be distracted and charmed by other sounds and images, but he will not rest until he has discovered the answers to his questions.

Variations in degree of comprehension exist not only among but within individuals. Thus a sixth-grade pupil who reads every detail of the directions for performing an experiment may read a newspaper article only to find out whether anyone he knows is mentioned in it. In some cases, he may want only to get the general idea of a selection; in others, he may read not only to comprehend everything that is written but also to get the meaning "between the lines" and "beyond the lines." One of the characteristics of the efficient reader is the extent to which he can adjust the degree of his comprehension to his objective.

Besides the purpose of the reader, other factors have a bearing upon comprehension. The physical condition of the reader, his interest in the material, and the difficulty of the selection—all affect understanding.

Interrelationships of Comprehension Skills

The skills involved in reading comprehension are numerous and interrelated. Understanding of these interrelationships is needed for intelligent guidance of the pupil through the successive stages of reading growth.

130

COMPREHENSION AND WORD RECOGNITION. Word recognition is a prerequisite to comprehension, but it does not guarantee comprehension. Moreover, full recognition of all words in a passage is not always necessary for the degree of comprehension required. While reading a selection in order to give a detailed account of the contents may depend upon recognition of most or all of the words, reading to determine relevance to a given topic may not call for this amount of word recognition. Experience background, interest, and native intelligence may also play a part in determining how many and which individual words a reader may miss and still achieve high comprehension.

COMPREHENSION AND RETENTION. It is not at all uncommon for a reader to remember verbally some material that he does not understand. A nine-year-old girl, who lived far from a large body of water, was studying about New England and could glibly reproduce this sentence, which she remembered verbatim from her textbook: "New England has many good harbors." However, when the teacher asked her what the sentence meant, her ignorance of the meaning of the word *harbor* was revealed. The girl's retention of the sentence was perfect but her comprehension was zero.

COMPREHENSION AND RATE OF READING. In Chapter 3 on "The Nature of Reading" it was pointed out that the rate of reading and the degree of comprehension are not highly correlated. Although there is a positive correlation between rate of reading and quality of comprehension, it cannot be automatically assumed that because a person reads fast he necessarily comprehends well. The problem of the relationship between the two factors is complicated by the fact that an efficient reader will vary his rate of comprehension according to the type and difficulty of the material. Yet it is clear that in general, allowing for flexibility of approach, the better readers are also the faster readers.

COMPREHENSION AND SKILL IN USING REFERENCE MATERIALS. The reader with poor comprehension is also usually lacking in "locational" skills. He is not likely to make efficient use of an index. His ineffectiveness will often be caused, in part, by the fact that he has only a hazy idea of the material he has read. Furthermore, after he locates the needed data in a book, he may be unable to select the main points and the supporting details in what he reads or to follow the directions given. He may also have trouble when trying to summarize what he has found in reference books.

COMPREHENSION, A COMPLEX OF MANY SKILLS. A reader who is deficient in some aspects of comprehension may not necessarily have difficulty with all types of comprehension. He may be able to find the main idea of a selection with accuracy and dispatch, but have difficulty in following. Some children have good knowledge of word and sentence meanings but fail to understand longer selections like paragraphs or stories or articles. Others show proficiency in reading stories but cannot effectively read material in social studies or science or mathematics. Thus it becomes the responsibility of the teacher to discover the strengths and weaknesses in comprehension of her pupils, always remembering that there may be wide variations in individuals among the skills that constitute excellence in comprehension.

Causes of Difficulties in Comprehension

The teacher must understand the causes of difficulties in comprehension if she is to help individuals overcome their shortcomings in comprehending what they read. Moreover, knowledge of the causes may help the teacher to prevent the occurrence of serious deficiencies.

These are typical comments made by individuals who have difficulty in understanding what they read: "I am not able to concentrate as I read." "I have difficulty in figuring out the meaning of a selection because there are so many words that I do not recognize." "I often have trouble getting the meaning of the first page or two when I start reading. Often I have to read for a few minutes without really knowing what I am reading before it makes sense to me." "I can understand what I read but I cannot give a satisfactory summary of it."

LIMITED INTELLIGENCE. As we have seen, there is a substantial correlation between intelligence and reading ability. It is true that a child who is intelligent enough to go to school is intelligent enough to learn to read simple materials. Nevertheless, a child's ability to comprehend in reading is limited by the conceptual "load" that his mental ability enables him to carry. All the mechanical reading skills in the world will not enable him to read materials involving abstractions beyond the level of his mental development. While we should never underestimate a child's powers, we should adjust the task to his capabilities. The slowest learner can grow in comprehension, but in some cases we must expect the growth to be slow. The reader whose IQ is 65 may learn how to find the answer to a simple question, but he should not be required to interpret a complicated graph.

UNDESIRABLE PHYSICAL FACTORS. Noisy surroundings, inadequate lighting, high or low temperatures, uncomfortable chairs, and stimulating or distracting surroundings may interfere with maximum comprehension. Fatigue, malnutrition, or undernutrition may do the same. The successful teacher of reading is alert to such interfering physical factors.

OVEREMPHASIS ON WORD RECOGNITION. Methods of teaching that concentrate on the recognition of individual words to the exclusion of meanings derived from connected discourse may account for deficiences in comprehension. Bright children normally make the transition from word to phrase to sentence to paragraph with ease and with little aid from the teacher. Many boys and girls, however, are baffled by the task of finding meaning in word groups. They need to be encouraged to move rapidly on the line in order to discover what happened, or to find the answers to their questions. Exclusive use of phonic methods, for example, may result in mere word calling rather than intelligent reading. The aim is to equip the pupil with a variety of methods of attacking new words and at the same time to develop in him the power to get larger meaning from the printed page.

OVEREMPHASIS ON ORAL READING. Oral reading can have either a desirable or a detrimental effect on comprehension. Often oral reading of a selection that is particularly difficult for the reader increases his understanding of it, since he not only sees but also hears what he reads. Furthermore, in effective oral reading, if there is an audience, the reader is required not only to understand what he reads but also to interpret his understanding to others. In this process increased attention needs to be placed on comprehension.

Unfortunately oral reading, if not done well, can have an undesirable effect on comprehension. The reader can become so conscious of his audience that he will fail to understand what he is reading. Overemphasis on oral reading may also make a child so self-conscious while reading to others that his concentration may be on how, rather than on what, he is reading. There is a point to the familiar story of the child who, after he had read a passage orally, was asked by his teacher a simple question about the content of the selection. His response was, "I don't know. I wasn't listening; I was reading."

INSUFFICIENT BACKGROUND FOR READING A SELECTION. Another frequent cause of poor comprehension is lack of an experience background essential to the understanding of what is being read. A city child who has never been on a farm may have difficulty in fully comprehending a story about country life. A sixth-grade boy who has never worked with science materials may not be ready to follow the directions given for an experiment. Lack of understanding of the concepts involved in reading materials and of the words used is an additional limitation to comprehension. Semantic problems of pupils who know only one meaning of words like *fair, spring,* and *plain* also cause difficulties in comprehension.

FAILURE TO ADJUST READING TECHNIQUES TO READING PURPOSE AND TYPE OF READING MATERIAL. Good reading comprehension requires a flexible approach to the printed page. Stevie, for example, had been reading a great deal of fiction, and had derived great pleasure from the experience. However, when he encountered arithmetic problems, he had difficulty because he read them as if he were reading a story and so moved too rapidly over the lines. On the other hand, Bobby was a meticulous reader of science materials. When he tried to read stories, he failed to derive real satisfaction from his reading because he used the same reading methods for narrative that he was accustomed to employ with factual and expository prose. Similarly, a child may be unable to recognize the main idea of a passage because he is too absorbed in noting concrete details. The need is for versatility in adapting the reading method to the reading purpose and to the nature of the material read.

LACK OF APPROPRIATE TEACHER GUIDANCE. Difficulties in reading comprehension may frequently be overcome with the aid of a teacher who is skilled in observing the causes of the difficulties. Some of the possible causes have been suggested in the preceding paragraphs. They are, of course, only illustrative.

Alert teachers put forth great effort to find and eliminate or prevent the obstacles to meaningful reading. Problems of comprehension among pupils can sometimes be reduced by the effective use of questioning. By asking suitable questions before the pupils read a selection or after they have completed it, the teacher can help make otherwise obscure meanings clear. However, when teachers are unfamiliar with the nature and extent of the pupil's difficulties, the problems tend to multiply. The use of appropriate standardized reading tests,[1] informal teacher-made tests such as those suggested in the next chapter, and frequent oral reading by individual readers to the teacher are the common means of discovering some of the causes of poor comprehension. Careful observation of a pupil's reading behavior may offer valuable clues. The teacher may ask, "What type of material does the pupil read outside of class?" "How much spare time does he spend in reading?" "How does he attack new words?" "Does he have a limited vocabulary for his stage of development?" "Does he know how to get the main thought of a passage?"

School records are an essential source of information about the causes of poor comprehension. Attendance records, health records, previous school history, anecdotal records concerning the child's attitudes, problems, and earlier behavior, and similar records can give the teacher insight into his difficulties.

Comprehension Skills

To understand a child's problems in reading comprehension and to plan an effective developmental program in reading, the teacher needs to know the various skills that make up the ability to comprehend what is read. These specific skills may be classified (1) according to the reader's purpose, and (2) accord-

---

[1] A list is found in Chapter 13.

ing to the length and nature of the selection read. Let us consider first the skills dependent upon the reader's purpose.

READING TO FIND THE MAIN IDEA. One of the most common reasons for reading is to get the general idea of a selection. Reading of fiction is usually done for this purpose. Even in other types of reading, like science, it may often legitimately be the goal. In that field the primary grade pupil may read a page to find out whether it tells about helicopters. The more mature reader in an elementary school may read to find out whether it is advisable to include a certain chapter in a bibliography that he is preparing on "Our Solar System." The ability to determine the main idea of a part read is basic also to many other comprehension skills, such as the ability to summarize and organize. Skill in finding the main idea in a paragraph or a longer selection, and in not mistaking a detail for the major point, needs to be developed in many pupils not only through incidental means but often also through practice exercises.

READING TO SELECT SIGNIFICANT DETAILS. The ability to note important details is closely related to skill in finding the central thought or main idea of a selection. To be proficient in this respect, the reader needs to do more than differentiate between main points and supporting details; he must also be able to decide what points are important for the purpose he has in mind. In *Miss Hickory* by Carolyn Sherwin Bailey, the story about the little doll whose body is a twig of an apple tree and whose head is a hickory nut, the person who tells the story must be sure to remember exactly where the story takes place. However, the child who is reading the book solely for his own enjoyment may satisfy his purpose without taking special note of this detail. The reader who gives equal attention to all details that are presented may find himself so encumbered that he loses perspective. Practice may be needed to help him decide which details are worthy of special note and which should be ignored. Their relationship to the main idea of the selection will usually determine their value; the purpose of the reader will be another determinant. As the pupils work for improvement in noting details, they should be helped to realize that details are of value as they support a main idea or assist in arriving at a conclusion or serve some other purpose of the reader beyond that of merely taking note of details.

Care must be taken that practice in noting details does not decrease the ability to find the main idea or to generalize. Constant emphasis should be placed on the fact that details must be fitted into a setting in which they serve a purpose.

READING TO ANSWER QUESTIONS. At times, reading to answer questions is a means of improving the ability to note significant details.

Reading to find the answer to one or more questions is one of the common goals for reading in the elementary school. Even in high school and college and in life outside of school it often forms the purpose for reading. In school the teacher will often ask a question, as Mrs. Westlund did when she asked her first-grade children to read the story "Bobby and the Apples" to find out whether Bobby was able to get some apples to give to his mother. In the intermediate grades the teacher may ask the pupils to read a paragraph about cranberries in New England in order to find out what kind of soil is required for their growth. Or she may write on the board a list of questions which the pupils note before they read a selection.

Answers are relatively easy to find when the questions are partly couched in the exact words of the writer. With the immature reader or the one who has difficulty in reading to find the answer to a question, this type of question may be used at first. If the writer says, "Susan's father gave her a kitten for her birthday," the teacher may ask, "What did Susan's father give her for her birthday?" A sample of a question to which the answer can be found less easily is, "What reasons can you find for the actions of the heroine?"

Not only should the pupils gain skill in finding answers to questions that are stated by others. To avoid overdependence on the teacher they also need to develop in ability to formulate significant questions for themselves as purposes for reading. Questions by the teacher should serve chiefly as stepping stones to questions that the reader decides upon for himself.

READING TO SUMMARIZE AND ORGANIZE. Both the ability to select the main idea and to choose significant details are basic to another commonly sought goal of reading—that of summarizing and organizing. However, to make an adequate summary or to organize what has been read, it is not enough for the reader to know what the main idea is and what the significant details are. He must also be able to sense the relationship between the main point and the details as well as the interrelationships among the details. Furthermore, he oftens needs to know either how to make these relationships clear to others or how to record them for later rereading.

Frequently the efficient reader makes summaries and organizes what he reads without doing any writing. The person who reads a chapter and then asks himself what the main points are, what material constitutes significant details, and how all these parts are woven together is making a summary and organizing what he reads. In fact, skill in organizing or summarizing is ordinarily put to use without the writing of summaries or outlines. Practice in summarizing and organizing may lead to such skill in these activities that frequently the reader almost unconsciously summarizes and organizes what he reads.

READING TO ARRIVE AT GENERALIZATIONS. Formulating generalizations is in a sense a specialized form of summarizing. To arrive at generalizations the reader needs to note specific instances and then decide whether the data presented are sufficient to warrant a significant conclusion. If they are of the type on which a sound conclusion can be based, he must determine what the deduction from the instances discussed should be. If, for example, he reads about children in Holland who wore wooden shoes, he should realize that he would be wrong if he made the decision that Dutch children always wear wooden shoes. On the other hand, if a typical scene in a schoolroom in China were described and if the author indicated that the scene is representative, the reader may correctly conclude that Chinese schools in many respects are unlike the school he is attending.

One danger for the person not skillful in making generalizations is that he may generalize without sufficient evidence. Another is that he will make too broad a generalization. To avoid errors due to both of these causes a teacher can give specific guidance not only with material read but also with observations made in other situations.

READING TO FOLLOW DIRECTIONS. The ability to follow directions usually is a combination of many reading skills. The ability to note details, to organize, and to note the sequence of events are among the learnings essential to this type of reading skill.

READING TO PREDICT OUTCOMES. Another important comprehension skill is that of predicting outcomes. This skill may manifest itself in a variety of ways. For example, if the reader sees the sentence, "The farmers set no traps for any of the animals on the grounds, for they like animals," he can anticipate (unless a break in thought is indicated by words like *but* or *however* or *nevertheless*) that the next sentence in the paragraph will not contradict the thought that the farmers were kind to the animals. This skill is in effect an aspect of what we call "active" reading, in which the reader assumes an attitude of anticipation.

Skill in predicting outcomes is useful in helping the reader to note when he has misread a word or a sentence. It is also of value because the person who is adept at predicting outcomes as he reads can usually get the thought more quickly than others. This skill is helpful also in remembering what is read, for it enables the reader to take special note only of those points that are new to him or are different from what he would have expected, and the burden of recall is thereby lessened.

READING TO EVALUATE CRITICALLY. One of the most significant comprehension skills is that of making critical evaluations of what is read. By critical evaluation is not meant the attitude of suspecting every statement read of being false. The power of critical evaluation in reading involves numerous factors. The reader needs to learn to ask such questions as these: Is the material relevant? Can the facts alleged be verified? Is the author qualified to discuss the subject? Do the statements harmonize with what I know to be true? Does the author draw valid conclusions from the facts? Is the author omitting or suppressing any important facts? Are the statements expressions of fact, or inferences? Does the material contain any unstated assumptions? Can I accept these assumptions? Should I revise my own assumptions in the light of what I have read?

Critical discrimination in reading calls for a wide background of knowledge concerning the subject under discussion. Literally, the word "criticism" means the application of criteria, or standards of judgment. Such criteria can come only from some previous contact with the subject. The reader has no way of judging the truth of the statement, "Polio is seldom fatal," if he has not had some previous knowledge about polio. He must then be entirely dependent upon the reliability, competence, and honesty of the author. Moreover, critical reading involves the capacity for making comparisons and appraisals. Critical reading is active, creative reading. Children should develop the skills of critical independence in reading at the very outset.

The levels of criticism will vary with the age and maturity of the pupil. A primary school child may be asked to pick out a false statement in a series, such as "Horses can fly," while a sixth-grade pupil may be called upon to find editorial statements in a news story. Critical discrimination in reading can be cultivated through skillful training.

READING GRAPHS, TABLES, CHARTS, AND MAPS. Many readers do not recognize the value of tables, charts, graphs, and maps. Special instruction in the interpretation of these useful symbols is often necessary. With the increasing production of materials of this kind, this skill has become important as never before.

We turn now to another kind of classification of comprehension skills. Getting meaning from the printed page involves the ability to perceive and understand words *in relationship*. Thus the ability to recognize individual words is not enough. The young reader needs to learn how to get meaning from phrases, sentences, paragraphs, and longer selections.

PHRASE MEANING. Since a phrase can be said to be more than the sum total of the words in it, skill in comprehension of phrases is not synonymous with skill in word meaning. The expression *in the long run* means more than *in* plus *the* plus *long* plus *run,* even though the meaning of each of the words contributes to the total thought. Especially in the case of idiomatic expressions is there need to examine the words carefully in their composite setting in the phrase. Another cause of difficulty in phrase comprehension is that frequently an immature reader does not recognize a phrase as such and, therefore, does not read it in a meaningful grouping. In the sentence, "At long last the tired men arrived," if the reader pauses after the word *long* because he does not recognize the word *last* as belonging to the phrase, he will not get the meaning. Therefore it is necessary in the case of many learners to focus attention on the recognition and meaning of phrases.

SENTENCE MEANING. What has been said about a phrase being more than the sum total of the words comprising it can also be said about a sentence. While the comprehension of many sentences is often almost automatic with persons who are reading on their proper level, with others it is not. Often a reader can understand every word of a long or involved sentence without getting the meaning of the sentence. The understanding that sentences are thought units is often fundamental to the comprehension of a complex sentence. For this reason, a study of the interrelationships of the parts of a sentence is frequently of value. Because sentence comprehension is more than word recognition and because an understanding of sentences is essential to the comprehension of longer selections, the reader should become skillful in reading sentences as whole units.

PARAGRAPH MEANING. Many of the problems that are involved in the comprehension of paragraphs have already been referred to in the discussion of such skills as finding the main idea, selecting important details, answering questions, arriving at generalizations, and following directions. Some of the suggestions given in connection with predicting outcomes, evaluating critically, and summarizing and organizing also apply to paragraph comprehension. Frequently it is through reading a paragraph that the outcome is to be predicted. The paragraph may be one to be evaluated critically or to be summarized. Some problems of comprehension involve skills that are peculiar to the paragraph rather than to phrases or longer selections. Finding the topic sentence, if there is one, is one such problem. Another is that of seeing the relationship between the topic sentence and the other sentences. A realization of the purpose of each sentence in a well-constructed paragraph is still another. Because of these and other considerations unique to paragraph comprehension, special attention should be given to the means of understanding the paragraph.

COMPREHENSION OF LONGER SELECTIONS. Selections longer than paragraphs, such as articles, stories, chapters, or books, may present special problems. Among these are questions as to how to get the most value from center headings, side headings, and transitional words and phrases, or how to study the interrelationships between various types of paragraphs. Problems of sustained attention, too, arise with reading of this type. Since there are skills peculiar to comprehension of longer selections, special attention needs to be paid to the means of reading stories, articles, chapters, and books.

Problems of Comprehension in the Content Subjects

Careful studies have revealed that reading is not a general ability but a composite of specialized skills. These specialized skills are called for in the various curriculum areas and should be taught as the different types of reading materials require them. For example, the reading of historical material demands skills different from those essential in geography, science, or arithmetic. Giving the necessary instruction in these skills in connection with the subjects themselves will markedly improve learning in those subjects.

The readiness principle applies with special force to the reading in the content subjects. Before a pupil is asked to read a chapter or a selection in a textbook he should be mentally prepared for the task. The words which the pupil encounters on the printed page are abstract symbols to him unless he can bring a body of experience to the reading. Moreover, he should have had prior experience with the words which symbolize the images and concepts he is to learn. New words should be identified by the teacher and taught in context, not too many at a time. Audio-visual aids are valuable in communicating to the child the mental images which the words in the textbook are intended to evoke. Gradually he will develop skill in the use of context so that eventually he will be able to determine word meanings independently.

Pupils should learn to approach a reading assignment in the content fields with clearly conceived purposes. They must know what they are looking for, and why. Such purposes may arise out of previous class discussions, demonstrations, or experiments. They may be formulated in questions supplied by the teacher, but the teacher should make certain that everyone understands the meaning and significance of the questions. If the pupil's purpose for reading arises out of a keen interest of his own, the prospects of successful reading are greatest.

Appropriate techniques should be taught for the reading of specific types of material whenever new material is assigned. One of these techniques has to do with the art of previewing a selection. The pupil should learn to look at the whole of the selection to find out what it deals with, what its scope is, whether it is narrative or pure illustration or expository, what the larger ideas are, and what the supporting details are. For this purpose he examines the title, the subheadings, the topic sentences, and the introductory and concluding paragraphs. After this preliminary organization of the material he is ready to determine what parts are to be skimmed, scanned, or read carefully to be remembered.

The pupil is now ready to read the selection. As he goes along, he arranges the facts and ideas in his mind according to the plan he has observed in previewing the material. He searches for answers to questions which he has posed or which the teacher suggested at the beginning. He fixes in mind the illustrations which clarify the main ideas and the significant details which support them. In this active, selective process he learns to read in order to remember.

The effective teacher of the content subjects does not limit the reading materials to a single textbook. First, the textbook chosen for the class is usually too difficult or too easy for some of the pupils. Second, a pupil should have an opportunity to compare accounts of the same facts and events in different sources and thus make a beginning in the important process of critical reading. Third, the pupil should read widely at his own level of ability to reinforce the general understandings that are to be acquired, and to fire his interest in the subject. It is through the abundance of specifics that generalizations take on meaning.

In the hands of a wise and resourceful teacher, the textbook can serve a useful purpose for all pupils. It serves as a focus for class study, supplies a plan of organization, and specifies the scope of the subject in a way that individualized reading alone usually cannot do. But for full participation by all members of a class, for the enrichment of basic ideas, and for opportunities for sharing, the diversified readings are indispensable. Fiction, biography, travel stories, and anecdotes should be included in the readings for social studies. Even the readings in science can often appropriately include poetry. Fortunately the supply of such materials today is extensive.

The content subjects, particularly the social studies and science, provide excellent opportunities for instruction in library research. The teaching of locational skills is discussed elsewhere in this book. But the particular value of library research consists in the development of pupils' ability to synthesize materials from different sources, to interpret them, to evaluate their relevance, and to report the findings in a clear and interesting way. In the process the pupil not only learns how to use the reference aids found in the library, but also how to put together and to paraphrase what he has found. Moreover, research need not be confined to the library. Interviews with members of the school staff and individuals in the community may provide interesting and valuable documentation. The findings may be presented in an oral report, a paper, a chapter in a class book, or in a panel discussion. Thus reading can be effectively integrated with the other language arts.

SPECIALIZED VOCABULARY. One problem involving reading comprehension skills in the content areas relates to the specialized vocabulary employed.

In the social studies, the reader encounters such new words as *isthmus, legislative assembly, representative government.* In elementary school science, words of which the child previously had had no knowledge, like *planetarium, solar,* and *convection,* constantly occur. In arithmetic, words like *equation, dividend, quotient,* and in books about music and art, words like *percussion, bas relief,* and *perspective* frequently give difficulty. Words new to the reader will be found in any reading material likely to help the child increase in knowledge and power with words. Textbooks in reading beyond the beginning stages of reading instruction are, in fact, designed to present some words that are new to the child. The special point of difficulty in vocabulary in reading the content subjects is that the child is often confronted with a large proportion of words unknown to him.

Frequently, too, in the content areas a word may have a different meaning from the one that the child has been accustomed to associate with it. Neither the word *range* as used in the phrase *mountain range* nor the word *mouth* in the expression *mouth of the river* has the meaning that the child has previously given to it. Homonyms, particularly, often are a source of trouble. The steppes of some near-polar regions are not the steps with which the pupil has had contact.

It is often necessary for the teacher to help children to become ready to read material in a content area with which, without help with the meanings of words, they would have undue difficulty. Pupils should be helped to acquire the specialized vocabulary for permanent use, not merely for understanding of the material at a given time. One teacher asked the pupils to select words which they had met in their work on a unit on the Congo regions and then listed these words on a chart entitled "New Words." The pupils should be encouraged to use such words in their conversation and writing.

DIFFICULTY AND NUMBER OF CONCEPTS. Another source of trouble in the content areas lies in the number and the difficulty of the concepts. Expressions like *no taxation without representation* and *the consent of the governed* need to be made meaningful to pupils before they can comprehend fully the material they read in the social studies. The teacher, however, cannot expect children to comprehend the full meaning of many of the concepts all at once. *Liberty* can acquire added meaning to the child as he reads and discusses from year to year about more and more situations in which liberty or lack of it is evident, and as he notes again and again, with increasing insight, the beneficial effects of environments characterized by a spirit of liberty and the deleterious effects of regimentation. The first time the children read or hear the expression *scientific method* the teacher may find it wise to explain and illustrate the meaning of the term. Then, year after year, the children can be guided so that they will develop a more accurate understanding of its meaning and a deeper appreciation of its value. At each stage of development the pupil should be helped to increase his understanding until he finally comprehends what a mature educated adult understands when he reads or hears a term symbolizing such a concept.

NEED FOR CAREFUL READING. Much of the material in the content areas requires more meticulous reading than that which the pupil needs in his reading textbooks or in books of fiction. This is especially true of many of the

problems presented in arithmetic. Following directions for making an experiment in science, too, requires an attention to details that often is unessential—
in fact, even undesirable—for reading many other types of materials. Reading
with the intent to recall for a long time or possibly always is also often demanded of the reader who wishes to accomplish some of the worthwhile objectives that he may set for himself when reading in the content areas.

ABILITY TO MAKE GENERALIZATIONS. Reading materials in the social studies
and in science present many occasions when the reader is in special need of the
skills important in connection with making generalizations. If he arrives at a
wrong generalization or accepts one that is false, the reading can have dis-
astrous results. In the social studies, skill in reading depends to a very large
extent on the degree to which the reader can arrive at sound conclusions and
on the extent to which he can detect errors in reasoning of which the writer
may have been guilty. Skill in sensing cause-and-effect relationships also figures
prominently in the social studies, in science, and in literature.

Other skills that need to be noted in particular when reading in some of the
content areas are interpreting tabular and graphical material, including maps,
predicting outcomes, locating and making use of information given in reference
books, and judging the literary merit of a large variety of materials. Many boys
and girls need specific guidance in the development of these skills as they apply
to the various content areas.

General Procedures

Improvement in comprehension skills can be brought about in the same
manner that growth in almost all other reading abilities can be stimulated. It
can be achieved through reading in context during the regular reading period,
through reading activities during other parts of the school day, and through
reading out of class, as well as through the use of practice exercises specifically
set up to provide improvement in the skills. Activities other than reading, too,
can serve as an important means of improving comprehension in reading. Because of the close relationship between comprehension of material presented
orally and comprehension of material in written form, some procedures beneficial to the former type are also valuable in the development of the latter.

IMPROVEMENT THROUGH INCIDENTAL MEANS. If the term *incidental means*
is used to refer to all types of reading situations other than those involving practice exercises, there are many ways in which comprehension skills can be improved during the regular reading period by incidental means. Much of the
reading in the primary grades, for example, deals with reading to answer questions. The boys and girls may read a story in their textbooks in order to answer

a question that either the teacher or a pupil has raised. Or after the pupils have read a story they may practice selecting the main point by suggesting titles for a puppet show that they plan to base on the story. Similarly, practice in summarizing can be given when a pupil who has time to finish reading a selection summarizes the ending of the story for a child who has not completed it. During the process of reading a story there can be discussion as to what the children think will happen next. Skill in predicting outcomes can also be acquired by discussion of why certain developments in a story were the ones likely to take place. If the child reads the story of "The Three Billy Goats Gruff," after he knows how the little Billy Goat Gruff was allowed to cross the bridge, he can be asked what he would imagine the middle-sized Billy Goat Gruff would say when the troll threatened to eat him.

In classes other than reading, much opportunity can be given for improvement of comprehension skills simultaneously with learning the content. In the social studies there is almost unlimited chance for meaningful practice in reading maps. Boys and girls can be helped not only in reading political maps but also physical maps, temperature maps, rainfall maps, population maps, product maps, and others. Growing out of the work in social studies may be projects like one in which one fifth grade engaged. The teacher placed on a big bulletin board a variety of maps and a sheet of paper on which were listed significant and interesting questions under the caption, "Can You Find the Answers to These Questions?" The boys and girls were also encouraged to bring to school other types of maps, which, if appropriate, were posted.

The many tables given in geography books can be made to serve an important purpose in comprehension. Boys and girls who need to learn when to use a table and how to use it can be helped to acquire that learning during classes in the social studies and science. In these classes they can learn the importance of noting the titles of tables and the significance of the names of the columns and rows in a table. They may at times be asked to see how many of the questions that they have raised are answered in a table or graph or map in their own textbooks. They may also look into a reference book, such as a young people's encyclopedia, to find out what information bearing on their problems they may find there either in maps, tables, charts, or graphs. Use of literary maps in phases of literature for children can improve skill in using graphical materials and at the same time enhance the study of the literature.

There are also many ways in which the teacher can encourage the pupil to acquire skill in various types of comprehension outside of the classroom. She can stimulate the pupil to read widely and extensively. Incentive to note main points and significant details and to organize and summarize can be given by providing the children opportunity to report on some of the outside reading in a variety of ways. The reports may take the form of telling in a few sentences the gist of a book they have been reading or by describing in detail some favorite scene. Planning dramatizations based on books, giving puppet shows or television programs, or making "movies" can all help the learner to read with more comprehension.

The teacher can develop many of the comprehension skills through activities other than reading. She can ask the children to predict events in stories that she is telling or reading to them. She can encourage them to summarize reports they have heard, to enumerate in order the steps they followed in performing an experiment, to make plans for a project in which they are about to engage, to come to valid conclusions when they have listened to a series of remarks on related topics, and to decide whether certain information given to them orally is factual or a matter of opinion. The teacher's insistence on better concentration on whatever the children are doing can also bring about rewarding results. The individual who is in the habit of not concentrating when not reading is likely to find it difficult to refrain from letting his mind wander while reading.

IMPROVEMENT THROUGH PRACTICE EXERCISES. For some boys and girls a program of improvement in comprehension skills similar to the type just described will be sufficient. However, many will profit greatly if they are also given direct practice in the form of exercises to help them develop skills in comprehending what they read. Some pupils may need direct practice on all of the major types of comprehension skills, while others will require such help with only some or one of the skills. Ability in diagnosis on the part of the teacher is therefore necessary as she tries to determine which boys and girls need special practice in developing some or all of the comprehension skills.

In the use of practice exercises, the teacher must keep in mind certain basic principles. (1) *The teacher should have a clearly defined goal to be accomplished with each of the practice materials she uses.* She should decide what skills require direct practice and then provide the best type of exercises possible for achieving her goal economically. (2) *The boys and girls should know the purpose of each practice exercise.* Unless they know why they are doing a certain exercise, they are likely to get inferior results and lose interest. (3) *The boys and girls should be helped to see the importance of the skill to be developed by means of a given exercise.* Unless the pupils are helped to appreciate the worthwhileness of an activity, they are likely to perform it half-heartedly and consequently achieve poorly. In fact, it is often valuable to let them help determine, with teacher guidance, the number and types of exercises they need. (4) *Both the teacher and the pupil should know what, if any, progress is being made.* Knowledge of results, especially if they are encouraging, seems to be real incentive for learning. Through a study of results the teacher can also profit directly by securing evidence on the effectiveness of methods and procedures used.

7b

Developing
Comprehension in Reading

This chapter suggests ways in which the ideas developed in the preceding chapter can be put into practice.

Procedures for Developing Comprehension

Suggestions for developing the following types of skills are given in this first part of this chapter: (1) finding the main idea, (2) selecting significant details, (3) reading to answer questions, (4) making summaries and organizing material, (5) arriving at generalizations and coming to conclusions, (6) following directions, (7) predicting outcomes, (8) evaluating what is read, (9) reading graphical material, (10) getting the meaning of phrases, (11) comprehending sentences, and (12) comprehending paragraphs.

Developing Skill in Finding the Main Idea

Activities like the following may help the learner to find the main idea of a passage:

1. Stating the main idea of a selection.
2. Selecting from a list of sentences one that best expresses the main idea of a paragraph.
3. Selecting the best title from a list.
4. Naming a title to fit a given paragraph or longer selection.
5. Following directions, such as:

(a) Find the sentence that gives the main idea of the article.

(b) Draw a line under the words in the second paragraph that give the topic of that paragraph.

(c) Draw a line under the words that best describe the character discussed in the selection.

6. Reading a story to find out whether it is suitable to tell or read to others for a given purpose or to dramatize.
7. Reading a story a second time in order to determine what scenes should be dramatized.
8. Skimming a series or a group of trade books to decide which one to read, either for pleasure or some other purpose.

146

9. Telling which word of a series describes a character in a selection.

10. Making a "movie" or mural showing the main events in a story.

11. Noting certain phrases such as *the first* and *the most important* to see if they point out a main idea.

12. Matching a picture that illustrates a main idea with a paragraph that it illustrates.

ADDITIONAL ACTIVITIES. The following are illustrations of practice exercises based on the preceding suggestions:

1

Direction: After you have read the story, write an x on the line to show which one would make the best title.

We made many plans for Christmas. We decided to trim our Christmas tree. Each boy and girl will make a decoration. We also decided to have a party. We will place our presents under the tree. At our party we will play games. We will also sing songs.

———(a) Our Plans for Christmas
———(b) Our Christmas Tree
———(c) Decorations for Our Tree
———(d) Christmas in Our Town

2

Direction: On the line below the story write a good title for it.

Sir Edwin Landseer was one of the greatest animal artists of modern times. When he attended art school, he divided his time between his classes and the zoo, where he studied animals and drew pictures of them. Although Landseer drew pictures of many animals, probably his most famous ones are those of dogs. The best-known one undoubtedly is the one named "The Old Shepherd's Chief Mourner." It is the picture of a devoted dog sadly guarding the coffin of his master, a shepherd.

Learning to Select Significant Details

By performing activities like the following, boys and girls can get practice in noting details and choosing those that are significant for their purpose.

1. Indicating which of a series of ideas listed are brought out in a given selection.

2. Telling which of a series of details support the main idea of a selection.

3. Reading to note as many details as possible that support a main idea.

4. Making a list of details included in a selection.

5. Answering questions on details in a sentence, paragraph, or longer selection.

6. Completing sentences, copied by the teacher from a reading selection, in which blanks were left for words that test the comprehension of details.

7. Matching a series of details with a list of main ideas.

8. Giving a list of words to describe a character whose actions have been discussed in a story.

9. Taking special note of details of a story to be told to others.

10. Showing which word in a series of sentences or paragraphs does not belong in a paragraph.

11. Checking a list of materials to indicate which are needed for an activity or project.

12. Studying the regulations for use of equipment for the playground, the reading table, or the playhouse.

13. Looking at a picture and then describing it.

14. Drawing a picture illustrating details of what has been read.

15. Deciding what actions in a story should be performed by characters in a "movie" or play that the class plans to put on.

16. Making a list of details that occur in a story, as preparation for dramatizing the story.

17. Composing a paragraph by supplying

details to support a main idea that has been selected as theme.

18. Deciding which details are important to remember in terms of a stated purpose.

19. Preparing charts based on material that has been read—for example, a chart showing the growth in population in a state.

20. Taking notes on points read in order to report them to others in a group in connection with a unit of work.

21. Reading reference materials to answer questions raised by the class or by a committee in order to get information needed for a project.

22. Showing through outlining the relationship between details and a main point.

23. Indicating which details belong and which do not belong in an outline that has been made on a selection.

24. Reading material in science and mathematics in which careful note needs to be taken of many points in order to comprehend the meaning, and then answering questions on the material or using it in other ways.

25. Reading directions and then following them.

26. Doing editorial work on a class newspaper.

27. Deciding whether the facts given by a reporter include sufficient details to justify a given headline in a newspaper.

28. Discussing whether the author relates details through his own comments, by the characters' actions, or by reports by characters as to what happened.

29. Listing the details in a description of a room, a landscape, or some other setting, in preparation for making a drawing.

30. Writing a main idea for a paragraph and then writing details to support it.

31. Writing a paragraph describing a given object, which the pupils are to guess.

32. Keeping a news record.

33. Keeping a weather chart.

ADDITIONAL ACTIVITIES. Two types of pro-

cedure that can be used in order to develop skill in selecting details are illustrated in the following exercises.

1

Directions: After you have read the following paragraph, write *M* on the line to the left of the topic listed that expresses the main idea of the paragraph. Write *D* to the left of each topic that expresses a detail mentioned in the paragraph. Write *O* to the left of any item not mentioned in the paragraph.

One of the most interesting animals in the world is the great gray kangaroo, found in great numbers in Australia. One of its characteristics of special note is its size and shape. It is sometimes ten feet in length from the tip of the nose to the end of the tail and weighs as much as 200 pounds. Its long, strong tail is used as a prop when the kangaroo stands on its two hind legs. The kangaroo is a very swift runner. It can clear as many as twenty feet at one leap. It runs on its hind legs only. The development and care of the young is very interesting. Upon birth the baby kangaroo is only about an inch in length. It is then taken care of in the pouch to the front of the mother's hind legs. In this pouch it receives its nourishment from the milk of the mother. After the baby has lived in the pouch for about four months, it leans out of the pouch to eat grass while its mother, too, is grazing. Then for months thereafter, usually till the baby is about ten months old, the young kangaroo returns to the protection of the pouch even though it spends much of its time in the world outside. In fact, the baby likes the pouch so much that it stays in it until its mother refuses to carry it any longer.

_____ (a) The claws of the kangaroo.

_____ (b) The kangaroo, an interesting animal.

_____ (c) Australia, the home of the kangaroo.

_____ (d) How the kangaroo takes care of its young.

_____ (e) The leap of the kangaroo.
_____ (f) The value of the kangaroo.

2

Directions: The main topic of a paragraph is the food of the camel. Some of the sentences that are listed below are on that topic. Others do not deal with the topic and therefore should not be included in a paragraph on the food of the camel. Write *yes* on the line to the left of each sentence that can correctly be included in the paragraph and write *no* on the other lines.

_____ (a) The camel eats thistles that grow in the desert.
_____ (b) The camel is a lazy animal.
_____ (c) The mother camel is very tender toward her baby.
_____ (d) The camel can live for a long time without food.
_____ (e) The camel likes to eat baskets or saddles or newspapers.

Learning to Read to Answer Questions

Proficiency in finding the answer to a question can be helpful in a variety of reading situations. It is important at times in order to choose the main idea, to note details, to predict outcomes, to form generalizations, to follow directions, and to perform other activities connected with reading. Practice that can be of value in developing this important skill can be secured by performing the following activities.

1. Reading to answer questions stated by the teacher.
2. Indicating which of a series of questions listed by the teacher are likely to be answered in a given selection and then checking the responses after reading the selection.
3. Stating questions the reader would expect to find answered in a given selection and then checking to find the responses after reading the selection.

4. Indicating which of a series of questions that may possibly be answered in a given selection are formulated clearly, and rewording those that are not.
5. Reading to answer questions stated at the end of a selected reading.
6. Reading to answer questions brought out by viewing a film or filmstrip.

ADDITIONAL ACTIVITIES. The following exercises indicate two ways in which the pupils can get practice in deciding which questions are likely to be answered in a given selection. Since frequently it is important that the pupil rather than the teacher set a question or questions that he hopes will be answered in a selection, an exercise like the first one is often of value.

1

Directions: Before you read this selection on [title stated], make a list of questions that you may expect to find answered in it. Then read the selection to find the answer to as many questions as you can. After you have read it, on the lines provided after each question, write the answer to the questions that were answered in the paragraph. If a question was not answered, write the words *not answered*. (The selection may be chosen from the pupils' textbooks in social studies or science.)

1. Question 1. _____
   Answer: _____
   _____
2. Question 2. _____
   Answer: _____
   _____
3. Question 3. _____
   Answer: _____
   _____
4. Question 4. _____
   Answer: _____
   _____

2

Directions: Which of the following questions would you expect to find answered in the article on [title stated] given below? Before you read the selection, write *yes* on the line to the left of each question that you think may be answered. On the other lines write *no.* After you have read the selection, correct your *yes-no* answers by putting an *x* to the left of each of your answers that is incorrect. Then write the answer to each question that was discussed in the paragraph. Write it on the lines provided below the questions. (The selection may be chosen from the pupils' textbooks in social studies or science.)

1. _____ (Question 1 by the teacher is listed here.)

   Answer: _____

   _____

2. _____ (Question 2 by the teacher is listed here.)

   _____

   Answer: _____

3. _____ (Question 3 by the teacher is listed here.)

   _____

   Answer: _____

Making Summaries and Organizing Material

Skill in summarizing and organizing what is read can be developed through activities like these:

1. Telling which of several summaries best summarizes a paragraph or longer selection.

2. Answering questions like these: "What explorers helped Spain establish her claims to the New World? What did each of them do to give her a claim to the Americas?"

3. Organizing materials gathered from a variety of sources for an oral or written report.

4. Taking note of words like *first, second,* and *third* as they occur in context.

5. Classifying materials in the room for functional purposes—for example, putting all the books on one topic on a specified table or assembling, for use on two or more bulletin boards, pictures on different topics.

6. Telling what items belong in classifications like *food, clothing, shelter.*

7. Drawing pictures to tell the story of the main events in a story.

8. Arranging pictures in the order in which events pictured by them occurred in a story.

9. Learning the form for making outlines, including numbering and lettering, indentation, and capitalization and punctuation.

10. Organizing steps in a process demonstrated on a field trip, under topics such as "Steps in Baking Bread" or "The Manufacture of Flour."

11. Filling in main topics and subtopics of a selection when suggestions are given as to the number of main topics and the number of subtopics under each main topic.

12. Listing the questions on which information is needed to solve the problem of a unit, and then grouping the questions on similar topics.

13. Listing the topics on which information is needed to solve the problem of a unit, and then putting the list into outline form.

14. Placing subtopics, which are given in mixed-up order, under a list of main topics that are specified.

15. Making an outline, either in a group or individually, of parts of a story that one of the pupils will tell to another group of boys and girls.

16. Telling what is wrong with an incorrect outline that some pupil has made or one that the teacher has intentionally written incorrectly.

17. Arranging in correct order paragraphs

dealing with one topic given in mixed-up order.

18. Selecting the sentences that do not belong in a paragraph that is set up so that it contains some irrelevant sentences.

19. Writing headlines for a class paper.

20. Making a list of actions of characters to show what traits they possess.

21. Making charts giving information about topics studied, such as "Our Community Helpers," "How We Travel," "Famous Americans," "Greek Contributions to Civilization."

22. Studying the table of contents to note the organization of a book.

23. Learning where in a well-constructed paragraph a topic sentence, if there is one, is often found.

24. Reading to plan a dramatization.

25. Planning pictures for a "movie" or mural on a story or article read.

26. Telling under which of a series of circumstances outlining is of value.

27. Outlining the papers written by others in the group.

28. Checking a series of true-false statements like the following, to indicate which give good advice for making notes: (1) Take your notes in your own words, not in those of the writer. (2) If you do not understand what something means, be sure to include the point in your notes.

ADDITIONAL ACTIVITIES. Three additional ways in which practice can be given in summarizing or outlining are shown in these exercises.

1.

Directions: Make an outline that will give the information shown in this chart.

PURPOSES OF SETTLEMENT

For religious freedom   Jamestown
To help debtors   Plymouth
For commercial reasons   Pennsylvania
                         Georgia
                         New Amsterdam

2

Directions: The sentences in this paragraph are not in the correct order. Write *1* on the line to the left of the sentence that should come first. Write *2* on the line to the left of the sentence that should come second. Number the rest of the sentences in the same way.

_____ Stephen heard something call, "Caw! Caw!" _____ There lay a baby crow. _____ Stephen looked around. _____ One day Stephen went to the woods with his father. _____ When Stephen saw that the crow could not walk, he took it home with him. _____ The crow had a broken leg. _____ Stephen always took good care of his crow.

3

As the boys and girls are studying about the Missouri Compromise, they could be asked to fill in subtopics in this beginning of an outline.

THE MISSOURI COMPROMISE

A. Events leading up to the compromise
1.
2.
B. Provisions of the compromise
1.
2.
C. Effects of the compromise
1.
2.

Developing Ability to Arrive at Generalizations and Come to Conclusions

In addition to the following suggestions for activities that can be valuable in developing the ability to arrive at generalizations and come to conclusions, some of those recommended under "Making Summaries and Organizing Material" can be used.

1. Making and guessing riddles.

2. Checking which ones of several conclusions are warranted by data given and explaining why the unsound conclusions are invalid.

3. Stating as specific a conclusion as possible after reading data presented in a paragraph or longer selection and explaining, in some cases, why no broader conclusion could be reached.

4. Discussing questions like the following after reading a story: (a) "Why do you think _____ made his decision to go West?" (b) "Under what conditions do you think _____ would have been friendly to the strangers?"

5. Telling which of a list of statements are generalizations and which are specifics.

6. Listing facts heard or read that justify a given generalization or that prove that a given generalization is unsound.

7. After making a generalization based on what has been heard or read, checking the generalization against experiences or finding additional support for the generalization or experimenting to see if the generalization applies.

8. Discussing the effect that certain events in a story or in history had on individuals.

9. Stating the generalization that is justified on the basis of given facts.

10. Discussing the ideas contained in several stories to see if they give generalizations that were brought out in a story.

11. Formulating titles that indicate the generalization brought out in a series of stories.

12. Drawing a series of pictures that illustrate points leading to a generalization developed in a story or article.

ADDITIONAL ACTIVITIES. These exercises indicate how some of the above suggestions can be carried out.

1

After the teacher has read the following paragraph to the class, she asks the pupils, "What was Sally holding in her arms?"

It was Christmas Eve. Everybody in the family, Father, Mother, Bobby, and three-year-old Sally, were in bed, or were supposed to be in bed. Suddenly Mother awoke. She thought she heard the creak of a stair. Then she heard nothing. So she fell asleep again. Later she heard a sound that seemed to come from the living room. She thought she heard a thin voice say, "Ma-ma! Ma-ma!" It was not Sally's voice. It was not Bobby's voice. Then all was quiet again. But this time Mother did not fall asleep. She awoke Father. Father went downstairs to see what was happening. When he opened the door into the living room, he saw that the big Mama-doll that Santa Claus had left for Sally to find the next morning was gone. Then he looked into Sally's playroom. There he saw Sally sitting in her little rocker holding a bundle in her arms.

2

Pupils can make up and guess riddles like the following:

(a) "I have two legs and two wings. I can fly high into the air. I sing songs. I lay eggs. What am I?"
(b) "I lived in Minnesota when I was a boy. I am an aviator. I made one of the most famous airplane flights that has ever been made. My wife enjoys flying. Who am I?"

3

Directions: Below the following paragraph is a list of statements in the form of conclusions. On the blank to the left of each statement write *yes* if you think the reader can correctly come to that conclusion after reading the paragraph. Otherwise write *no*. If a conclusion is not correct for the paragraph, in the space provided state why you think it is not a sound conclusion. When you give your reasons, make certain to write the number of the conclusion to which you are referring.

On my last visit to the zoo, I spent part of my time watching two mother camels and their little colts. Both of the mothers stood near their young as if they wished to protect their babies from all harm. It seemed to me that there was a look of tenderness on the mothers' faces as they were looking at the little camels. I then remembered that my father had told me that the mother camel is often very kind to her young.

_____1. The camel is very gentle toward other animals.

_____2. The camel is very gentle toward people.

_____3. The mother camel is often very kind to her baby.

_____4. The mother camel is a very gentle animal.

Reasons. _____

_____

_____

_____

_____

Learning to Follow Directions

These methods may be helpful for an individual who is trying to improve his skill in following directions.

1. Observing written directions, such as, "Make one ball yellow. Make the other ball blue."

2. Following directions that the teacher has written on the chalkboard or on cards, such as, "Get ready for recess" or "Come to the reading circle."

3. Acting out an individually assigned sentence from a reading selection and then having the rest of the class tell which sentence it is.

4. Following written or oral directions for making things, such as a folder for papers or a papier-mâché globe.

5. Drawing a picture from directions given.

6. Drawing pictures based on descriptions that the boys and girls read.

7. Carrying out plans made by the class or a committee for work on a unit.

8. Writing directions for doing or making something.

9. Reading directions for a game and then following them.

10. Reading directions for doing tricks and then performing them.

11. Arranging in correct order the sentences for directions to do or make something.

12. Reading directions for work-type activities in various subject fields and then following them.

ADDITIONAL ACTIVITY. This type of exercise may be helpful to persons having difficulty either in giving or following directions for going from one place to another.

Directions: Draw a diagram showing how a person who is at the post office could get to the city hall.

From the post office walk north until you come to the end of the block. Then turn left and walk west for two blocks, crossing the street before you again turn right to walk another half block north. There in the middle of the block you will find the city hall.

Improving Ability to Predict Outcomes

Some of the suggestions given under "Developing Ability to Arrive at Generalizations and Come to Conclusions" may be added to the following list of activities for improving the ability to predict outcomes.

1. While looking at pictures of a story, stating what the outcome of the story is likely to be.

2. Indicating by means of multiple-choice questions what is likely to happen next in a story or article.

3. Telling what is likely to happen next in a story or article, without help of multiple-choice questions.

4. Discussing why things happened as they did in a story or other account.

5. Making up endings for stories, orally or in writing.

6. Estimating the answer in some types of arithmetic problems.

7. Comparing our present situation with a previous one in history and deciding what might happen as a result of present conditions.

8. Indicating what is likely to happen at the time when work on a science experiment is begun.

9. Evaluating plans the class is making, in terms of expected outcomes.

10. Predicting what will happen next after having listened to part of the account of an experience another pupil has had.

11. Listing on the board known points about a situation and possible outcomes and then discussing the probability of certain results and the unlikelihood of others.

12. Arranging in order pictures illustrating a story that the pupils have not heard or read in entirety.

ADDITIONAL ACTIVITY. After the boys and girls have learned that heat is more readily absorbed by dark objects than by light ones, they can predict what will happen after reading this set of instructions given in connection with the cans that are pictured.

The tin cans shown in the drawing have lids that fit tightly. One is painted black, or it may be darkened by holding it over a lighted candle so that the carbon will form on it, and the other is painted white, or it may be left with its tin surface unpainted. Each can top has a hole in it just a little larger than the thermometer that extends through to the inside. Set the two cans in the bright sunlight and keep a record of the thermometer readings.[1]

Developing Skill in Evaluating What Is Read

In addition to the means of developing critical evaluation that have been listed under suggestions for developing other comprehension skills, the following at times prove helpful.

1. Indicating which of a series of statements express facts only and then rewriting those that are not purely factual so that they do not express an opinion.

2. Deleting from paragraphs or longer selections statements that are not entirely factual.

3. Rewriting statements of fact that are mixed with statements of opinion, in such a way that instead of showing sympathy toward a person or event they will show antipathy (and vice versa).

4. Indicating which statements present only so limited a part of truth that an incorrect impression is given.

5. Differentiating between an editorial and other types of writing in a newspaper or magazine.

---

[1] Glenn O. Blough and Marjorie Campbell, *Making and Using Classroom Science Materials in the Elementary School,* p. 171. New York: Holt, Rinehart and Winston, Inc., 1954.

6. Deciding whether a story is real or fanciful and indicating the reason for the answer.

7. Deciding upon the purpose of an author in writing a given selection.

8. Determining whether an author is qualified, on the basis of the material presented, to come to the conclusions that he reaches.

9. Among books that were written long ago, indicating which books are highly valuable for a stated purpose, and which are not useful for the purpose.

10. Indicating which of a series of words arouse emotion.

11. Noting types of words often used to arouse emotions of sympathy or anger or love.

12. Adding to a list of words that express a given feeling.

13. Indicating which of a list of sentences reveal a sympathetic attitude and which an unsympathetic attitude toward a person or a situation.

14. Indicating which statements are relevant and which irrelevant to a given purpose.

15. Locating inconsistencies in a series of paragraphs or longer selections.

16. Matching a series of abstract statements with items in a list of incidents that illustrate the abstractions.

17. When reading abstract materials, thinking of incidents that illustrate the points.

18. Asking and, in other cases, answering thought-provoking questions about something that has been heard or read.

19. Choosing from a list of chapter titles those most likely to be valuable in connection with a given problem.

20. Setting up standards for a story to be chosen, such as listing points to consider when selecting a story to be read to others.

21. Giving book reviews in which emphasis is placed on the evaluation of the book rather than chiefly on the story itself.

22. Checking the authenticity of statements through use of various types of source materials.

23. Noting the copyright date of books that one reads.

24. Thinking of two persons, both qualified to speak or write on a given subject, but with a different experience background, and reporting how each might comment on it.

ADDITIONAL ACTIVITY. Directions like the following may be given to provide practice in discriminating between statements that are based entirely on facts and those which are based, in part at least, on opinion.

Directions: Some of the following sentences are statements of fact; others are, at least in part, expressions of opinion. On the line at the right of each sentence that is only a statement of fact, write an *F*, for *fact*. Write an *O*, for *opinion*, on the line if the statement is, at least in part, an expression of an opinion. Then in the space following the last sentence in this exercise, rewrite those sentences which reveal the writer's opinion. Rewrite them in such a manner that the rewritten sentences are statements of fact only. Number your sentences to correspond to the numbers of the printed sentences.

1. Lake Michigan cuts the state of Michigan into two parts. 1._____

2. The best place to be in winter is Florida. 2._____

3. The road from here to the next town is a gravel road. 3._____

4. The most beautiful place in the United States is Mount Rainier. 4._____

5. The best vacation spot in the Northwest is Portland, Oregon. 5._____

_____

_____

_____

_____

_____

Learning to Read Graphical and Tabular Material

The following types of activities can prove helpful in teaching boys and girls to read graphs, tables, charts, and maps with greater comprehension.

1. Answering questions about data on a calendar, such as "How many Thursdays are there in June?" or "On what day of the week is June 11?"

2. Making a calendar to record weather conditions.

3. Making graphs on individual or group achievements.

4. Making a map of the classroom or community.

5. Studying a map and map legend and then answering questions based on them.

6. Showing information of various types —for example, surface features, population centers, and political divisions—on maps that have been duplicated.

7. Making, in answer to a question, a list of important points that can be gained for a stated purpose from a given map, table, graph, or chart.

ADDITIONAL ACTIVITY. An exercise of this type may be used before pupils start keeping a similar record of their own achievement.

Directions: The graph shows how many spelling words out of the 15 in each weekly test Harold had correct during the first ten weeks of the school year. Answer the questions or follow the directions given below.

1. How many times did Harold have a perfect score? _____

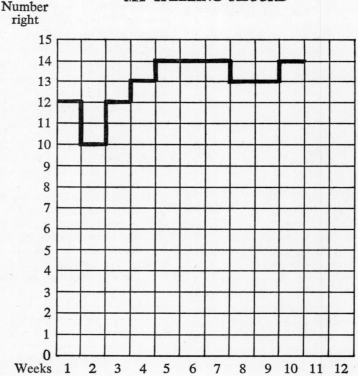

MY SPELLING RECORD

2. What was the largest number of words that Harold had wrong on any test?

———

3. During which week did Harold have the largest number of words wrong?

———

4. For how many more records of tests is there room on this graph? ———

5. Mark the graph for the eleventh week to show that Harold had two words wrong.

Developing Skill in Getting the Meaning of Phrases

Skill in the comprehension of phrases can be developed by a pupil by the following:

1. Giving the meaning of expressions used in sentences.

2. Matching phrases in one column with words with similar meaning in another column.

3. Finding in a selection phrases that answer certain questions, such as, "What group of words tells that Frank is happy?"

4. Discussing the meaning of commonly used idiomatic expressions.

5. Interpreting figures of speech.

6. Underlining the complete phrase in an exercise where the first word of the phrases is underlined.

7. Playing a game in which pupils read what is written on a phrase card.

8. Locating a phrase that is illustrated by a picture.

9. Making up a phrase that expresses the meaning of a given phrase.

10. Completing sentences by matching the beginnings of sentences given in one column with appropriate endings in a column of phrases.

ADDITIONAL ACTIVITY. An exercise like this may be used in the intermediate grades.

Directions: Each sentence in this exercise contains an expression in italics. To get the meaning of the expression, note the meaning of each word in it and study the context. If necessary, consult your dictionary. Then, in the space provided, explain what the expression means.

1. When the explorers came to the end of the path, they saw *a veil of spray* coming down from falls more than a hundred feet in height.

———————————————

2. General Grant asked his opponents for *unconditional surrender.*

———————————————

Improving Skill in Sentence Comprehension

Some pupils will find some of the following activities of value in improving their comprehension of sentences.

1. Drawing a line under one of a series of sentences that is illustrated by a picture in a workbook or teacher-made practice exercise.

2. Picking out in connection with an illustrated story the sentences that are well illustrated by a picture.

3. Answering, with *yes* or *no,* questions on which readers will agree if the meaning is clear to them, such as, (a) Is winter a colder season than summer? (b) Do all good people live in warm houses?

4. Arranging in correct order the parts of scrambled sentences.

5. Listing the sentences in a selection that help prove a given point.

6. Indicating which sentences in a series mean almost the same as specified sentences.

7. Making up sentences that describe a picture.

8. Finding in a book a sentence that suggests an appropriate title for a story or picture.

9. Getting practice in phrasing while reading so as to avoid difficulty in understanding a sentence. Difficulty would be likely to occur when a reader does not know, for example, that the end of a phrase in the following sentence comes after *happenings,* not after *unusual*: "One of the most unusual happenings occurred this morning."

10. Making sentences that show variety in structure, such as,

    a. Quickly the boys ran home.

    b. The boys ran home quickly.

11. Studying the thought of sentences in which the subject and predicate are in inverted order, and constructing some of that type.

12. Finding sentences that answer given questions.

13. Making up sentences that describe the same idea in different ways.

14. Studying sentences in which many adjectives or adverbs or phrases or clauses modify the subject and the predicate.

15. Interpreting the meaning of conjunctions and prepositions as they are used in sentences.

16. Answering questions about a sentence with which the pupils have difficulty and indicating which part of a sentence answers each question.

17. Making, in connection with a long sentence that presents comprehension difficulties, a sentence for every idea contained in it.

18. Establishing the relation in meaning among the parts of a sentence.

19. Deciding on the meaning of some sentences through the study of punctuation marks.

Developing Skill in Paragraph Comprehension

Many suggestions for improved comprehension of paragraphs have been given under various skills listed earlier in this chapter, as under "Developing Skill in Finding the Main Idea" and in "Making Summaries and Organizing Material." A few additional ones are given here.

1. Locating a paragraph on a stated page by means of directions such as, "Place a finger under the paragraph that begins with the words 'Evelyn ran home as fast as she could,'" or "Read the last sentence of the first paragraph on page _____ ."

2. Finding the paragraph that answers a question or contains a specified thought.

3. Finding the topic sentence of paragraphs that contain topic sentences.

4. Studying the topic sentence of a paragraph to help get the main idea of the paragraph.

5. Using the topic sentence of a paragraph as an aid when organizing as well as when skimming.

6. Studying the relationship of sentences within a paragraph.

7. Writing paragraphs on specified topics.

8. Arranging in order paragraphs that are not in the correct sequence.

9. Matching a series of paragraphs with summaries of these paragraphs.

ADDITIONAL ACTIVITY. An exercise like this can be particularly helpful since it is based on reading in the pupils' books. At least one of the paragraphs used in this exercise should have a topic sentence and at least one should not.

Directions: Read the three paragraphs in your [name of textbook supplied] on page _____ to answer these questions and to follow these directions. (The same questions as those given for the first paragraph should be asked about the other paragraphs.)

Paragraph 1. Does it contain a topic sentence? _____ If so, write the first three words of the sentence. _____

If there is a topic sentence in the paragraph, do all the details given in the paragraph support the topic sentence? _____

If the paragraph does not contain a topic sentence, would the paragraph be improved if it had one? _____ Give reasons for your answer. _____

_____

If the paragraph has no topic sentence

and if the paragraph could be improved if it contained one, write a sentence that would make a good topic sentence for the paragraph.

___

Developing Skill in Understanding the Meaning of Longer Selections

Since many suggestions for development of skill in comprehending longer materials were given under a variety of topics earlier in this chapter, we list here only the following three additional types of activities that pupils could profitably perform to gain more skill in comprehending materials of this type.

1. Finding the place in a story or article or book where specified parts begin.

2. Reading a story or article to decide where it can be divided into parts.

3. Taking a pretest, before reading a selection, on questions based on the selection and then, after reading it, taking the test again.

ADDITIONAL ACTIVITY. To help boys and girls make adequate use of center heads and sideheads, an exercise like this may prove of help.

Directions: Read the headings given in this exercise. Study them to find out what questions you would expect to find discussed under each. Then in the space to the right of each question write the number of the center head and the letter of the sidehead under which you would expect to find the question discussed. Write an *N*, for *not discussed*, in the space to the right of each question that you do not expect to find discussed under any of these headings.

CHRISTOPHER COLUMBUS

Center head:
Sideheads:

1. *The Boyhood of Columbus*
   a. Birthplace
   b. Work of his father
   c. His early interest in the sea

Center head:
Sideheads:

2. *The Plan of Columbus*
   a. His beliefs about the shape of the earth
   b. His disbelief in the stories of the dragons of the sea
   c. His belief that India could be reached by water

Center head:
Sideheads:

3. *Columbus in Search of Aid*
   a. Refusal of Spain to help him
   b. Plan to ask France for aid
   c. The help of the abbott
   d. Promise of help by Queen Isabella and King Ferdinand

Center head:
Sideheads:

4. *Getting Ready for the First Voyage*
   a. Getting men
   b. Getting ships and supplies

Center head:
Sideheads:

5. *First Voyage*
   a. Fears of the sailors
   b. Scarcity of food
   c. Length of the voyage
   d. Threat of mutiny
   e. Seeing land
   f. The landing

CHRISTOPHER COLUMBUS

       g. Exploring the land
       h. Return to Spain

Center head: 6. *Later Voyages and Death*
Sideheads: a. The second, third, and fourth voyages
          b. Return to Spain in chains
          c. Last days and death

1. Why were the sailors afraid they would fall off the edge of the earth? _____
2. How did the Spanish court treat Columbus upon his return after his fourth voyage? _____
3. Did the Norsemen discover America? _____
4. What did Columbus believe, even before 1492, was the shape of the earth? _____
5. Why did Spain at first refuse to give aid to Columbus? _____
6. Why was it hard to secure good men for the first voyage? _____
7. How many ships did Columbus have with him on his first voyage? _____
8. When was land first seen? _____
9. What did Columbus do to keep his men from mutinying on the first voyage? _____
10. Where did Columbus die? _____
11. What parts of America did the French explore? _____

The Development of Comprehension Skills through Reading Lessons

All of the comprehension skills can be developed in part through reading lessons without recourse to definite practice exercises. This section of the chapter is devoted to showing how growth in the various skills can be encouraged in these lessons. The material is based on selections from a second-grade, a fourth-grade, and a sixth-grade reader. The comprehension skills that a teacher will decide to develop in any of these lessons will depend upon the total develop-

mental reading program based upon the needs of the boys and girls. The suggestions enumerated in connection with any of these lessons are not necessarily the ones to be used. They are merely suggestive of the many possible ones from which a selection may be made. Nor should nearly all of the recommendations be used for any one selection, for the number is too large and there is overlapping among them. Excellent suggestions for the development of power in comprehension are also listed in the manuals for the teacher accompanying the basal textbooks.

A Second-grade Lesson

In the second-grade reader *We Are Neighbors*[2] is an adaptation of the story "Snipp, Snapp, Snurr, and the Red Shoes," written by Maj Lindman. It tells of three little boys who, after they found out that their mother would like some red shoes for her birthday, went out in search of work so that they could earn money to buy the gift. All three found work. Snipp finished painting a fence red, Snapp helped a man clean his chimney, and Snurr worked in a flour mill. When the boys had completed their work, they used the money they had earned to buy a beautiful pair of red shoes for their mother. Snipp in his clothes red with paint, Snapp in his suit that was black with soot, and Snurr looking like a snowman in his clothes that were covered with flour, rushed home

2 Odille Ousley and David Russell, *We Are Neighbors*. The Ginn Basic Readers. Boston: Ginn and Company, 1948.

happily to give their delighted mother the red shoes that they had purchased for her.

FINDING THE MAIN IDEA. The pupils may read the story in order to decide whether it would be a good one to read to another group or whether it would be suitable for using for a dramatization or a home-made "movie," if they had been planning to engage in one of these activities.

SELECTING IMPORTANT DETAILS. If the pupils decide to dramatize the story or to make a "movie" of it or to give a puppet play, they may read the story carefully in order to decide what scenes to include in the dramatization or "movie."

SUMMARIZING AND ORGANIZING. Although most work in writing summaries is usually postponed till grades later than the second, with some second-grade groups a simple file, possibly in the form of a loose-leaf notebook, of stories that they like particularly may be kept. For such a file the group could cooperatively plan a brief summary on this order: "Three boys, Snipp, Snapp, and Snurr, wanted to buy some red shoes for their mother for her birthday. They worked to earn the money. They earned enough money to buy her some red shoes. Their mother liked her present."

If the pupils decide to put on a play, they can help determine what the main parts of the play should be. The division might be as follows:

1. The boys ask their mother what she wants for her birthday.
2. The boys look for work.
3. The boys find work.
4. The boys buy the shoes.
5. The boys give the shoes to their mother. Then the pupils can decide on the details to be portrayed in connection with each main part.

ARRIVING AT GENERALIZATIONS. After discussing why the boys were so happy when they had spent their money to buy a gift for their mother, the teacher may guide the discussion, without undue moralizing, so that the boys and girls will tell of times when they, too, were happy when they had done something for someone else. It may be unwise in many instances to ask the pupils to state the generalization, that often a person becomes happy if he has made someone else happy; however, the teacher may make a statement that would serve as a generalization—for example, "Often people find that they become happy when they have done something nice for others."

PREDICTING OUTCOMES. During the course of the reading of the story, the teacher may at appropriate places make comments and ask questions like this: "Snipp's clothes were red after he had painted the fence and Snapp's were black after he had helped clean a chimney. What color do you imagine Snurr's were after he had finished working?" Then the boys and girls could be asked to read to find out whether they were right in their prediction.

EVALUATING CRITICALLY. The pupils may discuss whether they think the story is a fanciful tale. The likelihood of boys getting work of the types mentioned may be discussed in this connection.

ANSWERING QUESTIONS. The pupils may read the entire story, after a proper introduction by the teacher, to find out whether the boys were able to get some red shoes for their mother. After the pupils have read the part that tells that Snipp asked a man if he could paint the fence for him, the teacher may say, "Read the rest of the page to find out whether Snipp painted the fence for the man." After the pupils have read the parts that tell what kinds of work Snipp and Snapp had found, the teacher may say, "Read the next page to find out whether Snurr was able to find some work."

162 CULTIVATING GROWTH IN READING ABILITIES

FOLLOWING DIRECTIONS. The teacher may write on the board directions like these:

1. Finish reading the story.
2. Study the questions on the board.
3. Use your book to find answers to questions that you do not know.

SENTENCE COMPREHENSION. If the pupils have difficulty in comprehending the rather long sentence, "They were still thinking of ways they could earn money to buy red shoes," the teacher may ask them to tell in their own words what the boys were thinking about as they walked along. Or, after the children have read the sentence, she may ask them "Of what were the boys thinking as they were walking along?" Practice in formulating good sentences as they discuss what they read or as they make a summary can also indirectly help boys and girls in the comprehension of the meaning of the written sentences.

PARAGRAPH MEANING. To help the pupils become more familiar with the term *paragraph,* the pupils can be given a direction like this: "Read the last paragraph on page 131 [of the reader] to find out why the boys were happy."

COMPREHENSION OF A LONGER SELECTION. On the basis of a story like this one the pupils can be helped in learning to read longer selections more effectively by performing such activities as these: (1) finding where each of the parts of the story that were enumerated earlier under "Summarizing and Organizing" begins or (2) telling the story to another group of boys and girls.

A Fourth-grade Lesson

In the fourth-grade reader *Meeting New Friends,*[3] "The Wonderful Spectacles" tells

how two Dutch children, Jan and Gretchen, had an important part in the invention of the telescope. One day while their father, a spectaclemaker, had gone to another town, the two children accompanied by Malkin, the cat, had gone into their father's workshop and had examined many articles, his magnifying glasses among them. When they had looked at things in the shop through the magnifying lenses, they decided to go outdoors to examine things there. They noticed that a magnifying lens was helpful only when they looked at objects close to them. Then Jan, who happened to look at a weather vane through the two magnifying lenses held a distance apart, noticed that it seemed much larger and closer. When toward evening the children heard their father's voice, they rushed back into the shop to return the glasses before their father would miss them. In their hurry they knocked down and broke a pair of spectacles. Afraid of the punishment they would receive from their father, they were relieved momentarily when they noticed that again the cat was in the workshop, for they thought they might be able to let Malkin take the blame for the broken spectacles. When later in the evening the father reported that the spectacles had been broken and that evidently Malkin had caused the accident, Jan and Gretchen were still more relieved. But before long their consciences hurt them. Therefore they decided they would tell their father the truth. They also told him of their discovery of the effect upon the visibility of an object in the distance if it is viewed through two lenses held a ways apart. How the children's observation led to the invention of the telescope and what use Galileo made of their discovery are reported in the rest of the story.

This story is suited admirably to the development of any of a variety of comprehension skills. The following are a few possible ways in which improvement in comprehension can be brought about in

---

[3] Guy L. Bond and Marjorie C. Cuddy, *Meeting New Friends.* The Developmental Reading Series. Chicago: Lyons and Carnahan, 1951.

connection with a reading lesson based on this story.

FINDING THE MAIN IDEA. The boys and girls may decide to share some of the information they would get through the study of the section in their reader entitled "It Happened This Way," of which this story is the first. In that case they may, first of all, read this story and the others in the section in order to find out how they can best present to their audience the information gleaned from their reading. After they have read all the stories, they may decide that one would be suitable for telling, another for dramatizing, and another for a "movie." Still another may be used to demonstrate a process.

SELECTING IMPORTANT DETAILS. In connection with any of the activities suggested above it is important for the pupils to select important details.

SUMMARIZING AND ORGANIZING. The pupils may make a chart on which they summarize or organize important information they receive while reading this and other stories in this section of the textbook. Skill in organizing and in summarizing can also be developed in connection with activities suggested earlier under "Finding the main idea."

ARRIVING AT GENERALIZATIONS. The story provides excellent opportunity to help boys and girls develop in the ability to make generalizations. Attention can be drawn to the fact that after Jan had noticed that the lens made a near-by fly look big, he had incorrectly concluded that the glass could make everything look big. Later, he rightly concluded that the lens made near-by, but not distant, objects look bigger. Discussion could also center around the question, "Besides looking at a weather vane what should the children do before they should come to the conclusion that looking through two lenses, one close to the eye and the other farther away, makes a distant object seem larger and closer?" Practice in testing a generalization could also be given by letting some of the pupils look at a distant object through two lenses held a distance apart.

PREDICTING OUTCOMES. After the pupils have read to the point where the children in the story let the cat take the blame for the broken spectacles, the pupils may tell whether they think Jan and Gretchen will tell their father that they had broken the glasses. They may be asked to give reasons for their answer.

After the pupils have finished reading the story, they may read aloud the parts that hint that the children will not let the cat take the blame.

EVALUATING CRITICALLY. The pupils can enumerate the happenings that led to the discoveries of Galileo, by arranging the events into a cause-effect relationship. For example,

1. Because the father accidentally left the door in his shop open, Jan and Gretchen had an opportunity to look through a lens at things inside the shop.

2. Because they looked at things inside the shop through lenses, they became interested in looking at things outside through lenses.

3. Because they wanted to look at things outside through lenses, they took the lenses out of the shop.

4. Because they took the lenses out of the shop, they had an opportunity to look at the rooster on the weather vane through two lenses held a distance apart.

5. Because they looked at the rooster, they had the chance to observe the effect of looking through two lenses at objects at a distance.

6. Because they discovered the effect of looking through two lenses at the rooster,

they were able to tell their father the effect of looking through the two lenses.

7. Because the children had told their father of their discovery, he was able to make the first crude telescope.

8. Because of their father's work with the telescope, Galileo was able to find out much about stars.

The ability to evaluate critically what is read may also be developed by asking the pupils whether they think comments like these made in the story, which show the effect of a guilty conscience, are true to life: "But somehow getting presents seemed to be much less fun than usual." "At supper the food did not taste very good to them, either." "Their mother's cookies tasted like dry paper in their mouths."

The boys and girls can discuss whether they think the story is true or fanciful and then decide on ways of trying to find out to what extent it is true.

ANSWERING QUESTIONS. The boys and girls could read the story to find out how the telescope was invented. Or, if they read the story part by part, they could read to answer questions like these as they proceed: "What did Gretchen do when Jan invited her to come into the workshop with him?" "What did Father do after the children had gone to bed?"

FOLLOWING DIRECTIONS. After reading the story the pupils could write directions for making a simple telescope and then follow them.

WORD MEANING. Here are several ways in which the meaning of some of the words used in the story could be made clearer.

1. To help the pupils understand the meaning of the term *magnifying lenses*, they could be asked to see whether by studying the picture on page 101 (of the reader) and reading the text on that page they could

decide what a magnifying lens is. The meaning could further be clarified for the children by letting them look through a magnifying lens.

2. By looking at the picture on page 101 (of the reader) the pupils may be helped to understand the meaning of the word *work-bench* as used in the sentence: "A fly was on the workbench and Gretchen bent over it, staring through the magnifying glass."

3. Through the picture given on page 104 (of the reader) and the sentence, "Jan looked up at the weather vane on top of the church steeple across the square," the pupils may be able to get help in deciding on a synonym for *steeple*.

4. In helping the boys and girls understand the word *courage*, the teacher may ask them what word the father used when he said he thought his children were brave to confess what they had done.

5. Examination and use of a small telescope could help the boys and girls to attach more meaning to the word *telescope*.

6. Reference to weather vanes in town could make that term clearer.

SENTENCE MEANING. Development in skill in sentence comprehension could be brought about through questions and directions like these:

1. "What do you think Father meant when he said, 'Perhaps all men will see better because of what you learned today'?"

2. "Explain this statement by Gretchen: 'The weather vane came close to us, really close.' "

3. "Give in your own words this sentence, 'He looked at the moon and no longer saw the face of a man, but the outlines of mountains and valleys.' "

A Sixth-grade Lesson

The story by Dinah Maria Mulock, "Riquet with the Tuft," given in the sixth-grade reader *All Around Me*,[4] can be used in a variety of ways to develop comprehension skills. It is the story of a very ugly but very agreeable and very clever prince and of a very beautiful but extremely stupid princess. The fairy who watched over the birth of the prince promised his mother that her son would have power to make clever and agreeable the person whom he loved most in the world. The same fairy who watched over the birth of the beautiful princess told her mother that although the fairy could not make her daughter less stupid, she could give the princess the power to make as handsome as the princess was beautiful the person with whom the princess was most pleased. In due course the prince and the princess met. Because the prince loved the princess, he was able to make her clever and agreeable. When the princess cared enough for the prince, she was able to make him handsome. Then they were married. The author comments that some people think that the change in the prince and princess was a fairy gift, but others say that to the prince the woman whom he loved only *seemed* clever and that to the princess the man she loved only *seemed* handsome.

The following are some of the ways in which comprehension skills can be developed in connection with the reading of this story.

FINDING THE MAIN IDEA. After the boys and girls have read this story, they could read other fairy tales to see if they find others that have the same theme, that love has the power to change things. They could do this, for example, in order to decide which of a series of stories with that theme they would like to use for a program on St. Valentine's Day.

SUMMARIZING AND ORGANIZING. If the boys

4 Arthur I. Gates and Mary M. Bartlett, *All Around Me.* The Macmillan Readers. New York: The Macmillan Company, 1951.

and girls decide to read a variety of fairy stories to find out which one they would like to use for a program on St. Valentine's Day, unless all the boys and girls read all the stories, someone could profitably summarize each story read on that theme so that the group could decide which one to use for the program. If a play is given on whatever story is selected, it will be important for the pupils to select the topics for the different scenes of their play and then to decide on the details to include in each scene. Furthermore, if the pupils decide that for the program this or a similar story should be told, it would be advantageous for the group to work out an outline which the storyteller should follow.

ARRIVING AT GENERALIZATIONS. Help in arriving at generalizations could be given as the boys and girls cite evidence to support one or both theories as to why the princess became clever and the prince handsome. Two lists could be headed: "Why I Think the Change Was Brought about by Means of a Fairy Gift" and "Why I Think the Princess Only *Seemed* Clever and the Prince Only *Seemed* Handsome." After noting the arguments for each interpretation, the boys and girls could be given opportunity, through illustrations based on past experience or reading, to test the second explanation. For some children, of course, it will be quickly apparent that the author intended to make the point that a person in love attributes all fine qualities to his beloved. A few, indeed, will admire the author's skill in making this point.

PREDICTING OUTCOMES. Questions that may stimulate the pupils to predict outcomes are:

1. After the pupils have read the promise of the fairy to the mother of the ugly prince and the mother of the stupid princess, the class could be asked, "How do you think the story will turn out?"

2. After the class has read the part that tells what the princess saw when she went back to the woods, the teacher could ask, "What answer do you think the princess received to her question, 'What is this all about?' "

COMPREHENSION OF WORD MEANING. Questions and comments to help build word-comprehension skills might include some of the following:

1. "In what other ways could the thought of the word *curious* be expressed in the sentence: 'He was given the name of Riquet with the Tuft, because he was born with a *curious* tuft of hair on the top of his head'?"

2. Since a twin sister of the stupid princess is referred to as *clever* and *charming*, the teacher could ask, "What words other than *clever* and *charming* could be used to show that the twin sister was the opposite of *stupid?*" Discussion of the words as well as reference to a dictionary could help answer the question.

3. Before the pupils read the paragraph that tells that the princess promised to marry Riquet "that day twelve-month" the teacher could say: "As you read the paragraph notice what expression the author uses instead of the word *year*." In connection with a study of the word *twelve-month,* the teacher could point out that it is a word more likely to be used in tales of the long ago than in writing or speaking about present times. The pupils could then be encouraged to name other expressions that help mark a story as one that deals with events that happened long ago.

PARAGRAPH MEANING. To help pupils to pupils could study the paragraph beginning is supported by two or more details, the pupils could study the paragraph beginning with the sentence, "As the young princesses grew up, the one became uglier and the other more stupid, day by day." They could then note the details enumerated in the rest of that paragraph to support the fact that the one princess became more stupid. The teacher could also help the pupils see that the topic sentence in that paragraph is developed only in part in that same paragraph and that the rest of the development of the topic is given in the subsequent paragraph.

Since a large amount of conversation is reported in the form of direct quotations, the teacher may explain that a new paragraph is begun whenever there is a change in speaker. She may wish also to make clear to the pupils how knowledge of this fact can help them read with more understanding.

The Development of Comprehension Skills in the Content Subjects

This section will show how some of the comprehension skills can be developed in the study of the content subjects. Some possibilities for improving comprehension in three learning situations are described: (1) in a fifth-grade lesson in social studies, (2) in a unit for the primary grades combining social studies and science, and (3) in fourth-grade arithmetic lessons.

Developing Comprehension Skills in a Fifth-grade Lesson in Social Studies

When a fifth-grade class is studying about the Battle of Quebec, the teacher can assist in developing the ability to read material in the social studies with better understanding. The following examples are from the textbook *Our American Neighbors.*[5]

Since the matter of specialized vocabulary is one of the problems that needs particular attention, the boys and girls should be given special help in this area.

---

[5] J. G. Meyer, William Gray, and Ralph Hancock, *Our American Neighbors.* Chicago: Follett Publishing Company, 1948.

As part of the introduction to the lesson, the teacher could teach the meaning of the phrase *Citadel of Quebec*. She could do so by asking the pupils to look up the word *citadel* in their dictionaries and then to supply the meaning that they thought was required in this sentence (written on the board beforehand), "The *Citadel* of Quebec was located on a high cliff." Next, through the context of the sentence, supplemented by help from the teacher, the pupils could determine the meaning of the word *scaled* in the sentence, "It was doubtful for a while whether the steep cliff could be *scaled* by the British." Discussion before reading the words in italics in the following sentences might also help to make the meaning clear: (a) "General Wolfe had ordered his men not *to open fire* until the French were within forty *paces*." (b) "Both generals were *mortally wounded*."

So that the names of persons and places may not interfere with comprehension but add to it, the teacher should write on the board the words *St. Lawrence River, Quebec, Montcalm,* and *Wolfe*. During the introduction to the lesson she might help the pupils find the St. Lawrence River and Quebec on a map in the front of the room. She could tell them that the two men who played the most important parts in the battle were Montcalm and Wolfe, the two generals. She might ask the pupils which one, judging from the names Montcalm and Wolfe, they thought was the French general and which one the British general.

When the pupils are about ready to read the description of the Battle of Quebec, the teacher may ask them to name some questions that they think would be answered in the selection. Suggested might be: "Were the British able to scale the cliff?" "Where was the battle fought?" "Was it a long and hard battle?" "Who won?" The teacher could suggest that the pupils also look for an answer to the question, "What did Montcalm and Wolfe say at the close of the battle?"

To help the young readers to visualize the story, the teacher could show them a picture of the Plains of Abraham and a copy of the picture "The Death of Wolfe" by Benjamin West. To help them develop in ability to read critically, she could have them discuss, after they had read the selection, the question, "Why was the Battle of Quebec such an important one in history?"

Other ways in which the teacher may develop comprehension skills during a class period devoted to the Battle of Quebec are: (1) asking the boys and girls to give a summary of the important happenings discussed in the lesson, (2) having the pupils make an outline of the Battle of Quebec, using main topics and subtopics, (3) helping the pupils plan a frieze on events leading up to the war, the war itself, and its results, and (4) having the pupils indicate on maps the territorial possessions in North America of European countries both before and after the war.

Developing Comprehension Skills in a Primary Grade Unit in Social Studies and Science

The following are some of the ways in which a teacher can help primary grade children to develop skills that improve comprehension in a unit on aviation.

ENRICHING VOCABULARY. The pupils could make a chart with pictures illustrating words like *runway, counter, checking bag, control tower, pilot, safety belt, hostess, helicopter, propeller*. They could construct a model airport labeling the various parts. Or they could make a chart telling some of the facts that they learned on a trip to an airport. If the chart contains words that the children learned in connection with the trip, special attention could be drawn to those words.

FINDING THE MAIN IDEA OF A SERIES OF PARAGRAPHS. If the class is planning to write a series of paragraphs on "How We Travel by Plane," the children could acquire learnings, through writing, that would help them find the main ideas of a series of paragraphs. First they could decide on the important points to include in their reports. Then they could construct the paragraphs for their reports, supplying the details to support the main points.

Sometimes the pupils could read a paragraph to find out whether it deals with a topic on which they want further information. Skill in finding the main ideas of paragraphs can also be developed in connection with putting on a dramatization of an airplane activity.

SELECTING IMPORTANT DETAILS. If the pupils make plans for construction of a "movie," they will need not only to have in mind the main ideas, but they will also need to recognize details that explain or illustrate the main ideas.

FOLLOWING DIRECTIONS. In a unit on aviation much opportunity can be provided for developing skill in following directions. As the boys and girls construct model airplanes, they can receive excellent practice in following directions given either orally or in writing. Simple experiments on questions like "Why do planes stay up?" or "In what ways does weather affect aviation?" can be read by the pupils or, in other cases, recorded by the group after the experiment has been performed.

MAKING GENERALIZATIONS. The pupils can be helped in arriving at sound generalizations in connection with experiments that they perform or read about. They can be impressed with the fact that basing conclusions on too limited data is likely to result in error. The importance of the steps in formulating generalizations can also be noted. Furthermore, they can be helped in realizing the significance of testing generalizations through application.

DEVELOPING SENTENCE MEANING. As the pupils find statements that are difficult to comprehend, the teacher can ask questions that will help make the meaning clear. For example, when about to perform an experiment to show that air can lift things, they may need to read instructions such as these: "Place a large paper bag, of which the open end has been twisted, flat on a table so that the twisted end hangs over the edge of the table. Blow into the bag after placing a book on the top of the bag. The book will then rise because the air blown into the bag will lift the book." The teacher could ask questions like the following to aid in comprehension of these sentences: (a) "What should be done with the bag before it is placed on the table?" (b) "What should be done right after the bag has been placed on the table?" (c) "What should be done next?" (d) "What made the book rise?"

EVALUATING CRITICALLY. The pupils may discuss which statements like the following are based only on fact and which state, at least in part, an opinion: (a) "The Wright brothers are known for their work in aviation." (b) "Lindbergh made the first solo nonstop plane flight from the United States to Europe." (c) "The airplane is the most important invention of modern times." (d) "It is more fun to travel by plane than by train."

Developing Comprehension Skills in a Fourth-grade Arithmetic Lesson

Many arithmetic textbooks, with accompanying guides for the teacher, are now set up to cope with the special problems of comprehension in arithmetic. For example, in the *Row-Peterson Arithmetic, Book Four*,[6]

---

[6] Harry G. Wheat, Geraldine Kaufman, and Harl R. Douglass, *Row-Peterson Arithmetic, Book Four*. New York: Harper and Row, Publishers, 1954.

one lesson, entitled "Understanding a Problem," suggests that after a pupil has read each of a series of problems carefully, he should state the problem in his own words. An illustration is given how one of the problems can be restated. Another lesson, called "The Important Facts," explains that some facts given in a problem are very important because they are used in the solution of the problem but that other facts are not so important because they are not needed in the solution. An explanation is given of which facts in one stated problem are important and which are not. Then the pupil is asked to tell, after reading each of the problems on the page, which facts are needed and which are not needed for working the problem. One page, headed "Facts Hidden in Certain Words," gives help in learning the vocabulary of arithmetic. It explains the importance in a given problem of knowing that a dozen means twelve things. It refers to *dozen* as a word in which the fact that twelve things make a dozen is hidden. Then it asks the boys and girls to tell which word in each of the problems that follow is a word in which there are hidden facts. In the problems that are given, these words are thought of as words that have "hidden facts": *pints, quarts, bushels, pecks, yards, feet, inches, hour,* and *minutes.*

FOR FURTHER STUDY

Betts, Emmett A., *Foundations of Reading Instruction,* rev. ed., pp. 556–576. New York: American Book Company, 1954.

Bond, Guy L., and Miles A. Tinker, *Reading Difficulties, Their Diagnosis and Correction,* pp. 229–260, 348–372. New York: The Macmillan Company, 1957.

Bond, Guy L., and Eva Bond Wagner, *Teaching the Child to Read,* pp. 200–228. New York: The Macmillan Company, 1960.

Carter, Homer L. J., and Dorothy J. McGinnis, *Teaching Individuals to Read,* pp. 104–135. Boston: D. C. Heath and Company, 1962.

Durrell, Donald D., "Development of Comprehension and Interpretation," *Reading in the Elementary School,* pp. 193–204. Forty-eighth Yearbook of the National Society for the Study of Education. Chicago: The University of Chicago Press, 1949.

———, *Improving Reading Instruction,* pp. 285–308. New York: Harcourt, Brace and World, Inc., 1956.

Gray, Lillian, and Dora Reese, *Teaching Children to Read,* pp. 374–400. New York: The Ronald Press Company, 1957.

Hester, Kathleen, *Teaching Every Child to Read,* pp. 194–237, 255–261. New York: Harper and Row, Publishers, 1955.

Michaelis, John U., *Social Studies for Children in a Democracy,* pp. 314–332. Englewood Cliffs, N.J.: Prentice-Hall, Inc., 1956.

Russell, David H., *Children Learn to Read,* pp. 333–358. Boston: Ginn and Company, 1961.

Smith, Henry P., and Emerald V. Dechant, *Psychology in Teaching Reading,* pp. 212–221. Englewood Cliffs, N.J.: Prentice-Hall, Inc., 1961.

Yoakam, Gerald A., *Basal Reading Instruction,* pp. 162–190. New York: McGraw-Hill Book Company, Inc., 1955.

8a
―――――

Reading Rates

How fast should I be able to read?" is one of the questions about reading most frequently asked of teachers. It is asked from the elementary school through college. Not only are pupils and students concerned about the rate of reading, but parents, too, want to know how many words a minute their child reads and how he compares with the average for his grade. Inquiries concerning the reader's rate of reading are often accompanied by the question, "How can I improve my rate?"

The concern about rate of reading is understandable. The person who can read a selection rapidly and still accomplish his purpose has a distinct advantage over the one who cannot. In school the slow reader is often unable to do the work required of him. In the professional and business world, too, the ability to perform activities quickly—and these include reading—is an important asset. The individual who always reads slowly will not have time to read as much interesting and significant material as the one who reads rapidly. The sheer volume of printed matter available today, much of it essential to a knowledge of new developments in the world of ideas and of events, makes extensive reading mandatory for the educated person and the responsible citizen.

Ideally, one's rate of reading would approximate one's rate of thinking. Obviously such a standard would be unrealistic in the case of difficult material, but a serious lag between rate of reading and rate of thinking not only results in waste of time but tends to reduce a person's pleasure and interest in reading. Slow, cumbersome methods of reading start a vicious circle from less reading to less efficient reading to still less reading.

Professional interest in speed of reading first rose sharply in the 1920's with the shift of emphasis from oral to silent reading. It was discovered that the average child entering the intermediate grades could read more rapidly in silent than in oral reading. At first it was widely believed that reading speed was a unitary ability and that improvement in rate was automatically reflected in all kinds of reading. Only gradually did the relation between rate and type of reading material come under intensive study.

The difference in rate between oral and silent reading is dramatically illustrated in the eye-movement studies of Judd, Buswell, and others. Buswell's study of the "eye-voice span," for example, showed that in oral reading the eyes of the good reader run well ahead of his voice. In studies of silent reading it was found that the eyes of the efficient reader move across the line in a series of rhythmical leaps. He makes few, if any, aimless regressions. He makes relatively few fixations per line, and these are of short duration. He is not delayed by the mere physical act of articulation. Obviously the silent reading rate of the good reader must exceed that of his oral reading. In the intermediate grades the average pupil may read silently from one and a half to twice his oral reading rate.

Reading Rate and Comprehension

Much discussion has centered on the question of the relationship between rate of reading and comprehension. The question would be clarified if we substituted the term "rate of comprehension" for "rate of reading." Reading without adequate comprehension cannot properly be called reading. Therefore, if we believe that a good reader is one who can most quickly grasp the meaning of a passage, the fast reader is necessarily the best reader. We can then dispense with any debate about rate *vs.* comprehension.

Good readers differ in their rates of comprehension. It takes some good readers a little longer than others to discover the literal and implied meanings of a passage. An individual's temperament and rhythm of learning sometimes account for these differences. Standardized tests of reading are usually based on the assumption that speed of comprehension is an essential aspect of reading competence. For this reason they may frequently obscure a pupil's real reading potential. Standardized test scores should be interpreted with this fact in mind. In order to assess the reader's true capabilities we need to go behind the scores and analyze the specific nature of his performance on a test.

There are important interrelationships between speed and comprehension in reading. On the one hand, improved comprehension facilitates growth in speed. On the other hand, habits of more rapid reading often aid comprehension by shifting attention from individual words to the larger word-patterns that carry the meaning. The development of comprehension, which is primary, may therefore be cultivated in some children, especially in the intermediate and upper grades, by encouraging faster reading.

While the teacher's aim should be to develop maximum speed of reading within the limits of the child's comprehension, a special effort should be made to teach him how to adjust his rate to his purpose and to the type of material he is reading. When the material is difficult and a high degree of accuracy is required, a very slow rate is appropriate. Many readers, even very good ones, assume that all materials must be read at a "normal" rate. They must be taught how to "shift gears" when they attack a verbal problem in arithmetic or a difficult passage in science. Thus, although superior readers tend to excel in both speed and comprehension with ordinary narrative material, they employ slower rates when these are needed for maximum comprehension. The experiment of Shores and Husbands with a group of intermediate grade pupils studying science led them to suggest that speed depends to a large extent upon the purpose set for the reading and upon the nature of the reading material. "With some purposes and some materials," they believe, "fast readers are the best readers. With other purposes and materials, the best readers will read as slowly or even more slowly than the inefficient readers."[1]

Causes of Unduly Slow Reading

LACK OF WORD-RECOGNITION SKILLS. The person who has difficulty in recognizing words quickly and accurately is likely to be a very slow reader. He is at a special disadvantage when he wishes to find the answer to a question. He is also handicapped when he tries to read study-type materials that contain words not easily recognized by him.

Often the methods by which an individual has been taught to recognize words play an important role in reading rate. The person who habitually analyzes all words phonetically will have slower habits of word recognition than one who has learned to analyze words only if he cannot quickly identify them as wholes. This fact should not be interpreted to mean that a knowledge of phonics is detrimental to speed of reading. Rather it suggests that misuse of phonic analysis may have an undesirable effect on rate. It must be remembered, also, that phonics can be used in recognizing words through synthesis as well as through analysis. As a rule, word study by methods of synthesis is slower than recognition by means of analysis. Phonics is an important aid to word recognition only when faster methods fail to bring results. However, the person who can identify a large number of words through effective use of other than phonic methods of word attack, like recognition of a sight word or use of context clues

---

[1] J. Harlan Shores and Kenneth L. Husbands, "Are Fast Readers the Best Readers?" *Elementary English,* 27 (January 1950), 52–57, and "Are Fast Readers the Best Readers? A Second Report," *Elementary English,* 38 (April 1961), 236–245.

or structural analysis, is more often the one who can more speedily accomplish his purpose in reading.

VOCALIZATION. Early stress on speech sounds in reading instruction inevitably creates strong associations in the mind of the child between the sight of a word and its sound. The sound image is intended to serve as a bridge between visual perception and the apprehension of meaning, and normally the child becomes less and less conscious of language sounds as he seeks meaning on the printed page. Exclusive preoccupation with sounding in the initial stages of reading tends to cause lip-movements and subvocalization in later stages. Speed of reading is then frequently restricted to the rate of oral reading. Under these conditions the child is obliged to unlearn habits deeply fixed in the beginning. Suppressed oral reading is not conducive to the development of desirable rates of silent reading.

Closely related to the habit of vocalization is the feeling some readers have that they must "read" every word in order to comprehend. In many types of reading, as in skimming and scanning, the good reader finds the key words and supplies the intervening words with sufficient accuracy to derive the meaning intended by the author. In these cases the reading materials are not simply a continuity of symbols intended to correspond to the spoken language; they are rather a set of clues, a sort of shorthand, designed to communicate meaning without the need for vocal articulation of all the words.

POINTING TO WORDS. Another practice likely to arrest development in reading rates is that of pointing to each word as it is being read. In the early part of reading instruction in the first grade, when it usually takes the reader longer to recognize a word than to say it, pointing with the finger may not reduce reading rate. However, the practice can have a detrimental effect later on speed of reading, for the habit may become established, with the result that the pupil persists in its use after he should be reading at faster rates than are possible with pointing.

Many first-grade teachers supply the children with markers in the form of rather heavy strips of paper, often about the length of a line of print and about an inch in width. With these markers, which the boys and girls keep under the line being read, the children can often keep their place more easily than they otherwise could. Probably, if a marker is used only for a very limited length of time, it can serve as a helpful crutch. The danger is that children may get into the habit of needing some means other than their eyes and mind to keep the place. Like all other crutches, markers should be discarded as soon as they have helped a person over a difficult situation.

OVEREMPHASIS ON ORAL READING. Oral reading has its proper place in primary reading, but a program dominated by oral reading practice is almost certain to produce habits of slow silent reading. Even in the initial reading period, children should be encouraged to read words silently much of the time. In general, it is recommended that children be required to read a passage silently before they are called upon to read it orally. By this means silent reading habits are established, and the subsequent oral reading will be improved because of increased comprehension of the material read.

LACK OF INTEREST AND PURPOSE. The ability to read rapidly is only in part a matter of habit and skill. Perhaps even more important is the attitude of the reader. If the pupil knows what he is looking for on the printed page, he will be impatient until he finds his quarry. He will not dawdle over the passages that are only secondary to the goals he is seeking or that are irrelevant to them. Clear purposes are therefore basic to the improvement of both comprehension and rate.

The daydreaming pupil makes little progress in reading. But when his interest has been kindled, when the action in a story moves toward a climax, when the narrative brings smiles or tears, he races down the lines to learn the outcome. The scene before him will not be obscured by laborious struggles with printed words. With the well-selected story, the words, the page, even the immediate environment, fade from consciousness and only the people and the places and the actions in the story remain. For many children the key to reading speed is interest. Abundant, highly motivated reading will do what no tachistoscopes or flashmeters can.

Appraisal of Reading Rates

In order to plan an effective program of reading instruction that will help each child learn to read at appropriate rates, careful appraisal should be made of every pupil's reading rates.

Since an effective reader has more than one reading rate, it is not a simple matter to make an appraisal. Consequently a variety of means needs to be used. *Informal observation* is one. The classroom teacher has many opportunities to note the characteristics of a pupil's reading rates. She can observe whether the child wastes time while reading. By studying the child in reading situations she can gather evidence as to whether the pupil is able to adjust his rate of reading to his purpose and to the difficulty of the material. She can note whether he skims parts of it and reads other parts more carefully.

Sometimes important evidence about a pupil's reading habits as they affect rate of reading can be secured through *conferences*. The teacher can often discover by this means whether the pupil knows that variations in rates are necessary to good reading. Answers to questions as to the type of situations in which skimming or slow reading is required can also be illuminating to the teacher desirous of learning more about a pupil's rates of reading.

Tests, too, can furnish valuable data. Many standardized reading tests contain a subtest for determining rate. These have their limitations, however. Tests in which rate is measured in only one type of situation do not give a clear index of an individual's reading rates. For this reason tests need to be supplemented by other means of appraisal.

Because of these limitations in the measurement of rate, many teachers like to make tests of their own. One type is described in Chapter 8B, "Developing Appropriate Reading Rates." Tests similar to the one there described can be used to record the pupil's reading rate in a variety of situations.

Whenever a pupil is timed while reading, whether he is taking a standardized or nonstandardized test, allowance should be made for the fact that the results may be inaccurate because the pupil knows he is being timed. No matter how hard a teacher may try to keep the testing situation free from strain, some children, as soon as they know they are being timed, show the effects of working under pressure. There are many children who cannot do their best under such conditions.

One type of record that the teacher may find it advantageous to keep is a *check list* on which she indicates change or persistence in attitudes or habits or skills concerned with the improvement in reading rates. By means of a check list the teacher can be spared the necessity of depending upon her memory as to the reading skills of each of her pupils. On such a check list may be questions like the following: (1) Does the child recognize the need of variation in rate? (2) Is he able to adjust his rate to his purpose and to the material he is reading? (3) Does he know when to skim?

Charts, graphs, and tables are useful in the appraisal of growth in the ability to employ appropriate reading rates. In keeping this type of record, the teacher should be sure to compare only those data which are truly comparable. Rate in skimming an article should not be compared with rate in reading a selection of similar difficulty when more detailed examination is required. For skimming, a reading rate of 400 words per minute may be slow, while a work-type rate of 200 words per minute may be fast. Rate of reading two selections that are unlike in difficulty or type cannot be directly compared.

Another point is that, if rates in reading are charted, they should be recorded over a relatively long period of time. In many situations there are too many rather insignificant variations in rate from day to day to make a short-term study of rates of reading of much value. It often takes more than a few days of successful practice to show measurable improvement, even when real progress is being made from the beginning.

Furthermore, the learner himself should be informed of his progress. If a child is old enough to try to improve his rate of reading, he is old enough to understand the simple record of his performance. The learner's concern should be the improvement of his own skill, not a desire to equal or surpass others or to attain a norm.

National norms on standardized tests are not extremely helpful to teachers who wish to evaluate their pupils' reading rates. Different tests show different median rates for the various school grades, probably because of the wide variation in the difficulty and type of content they present. For example, Harris listed rates of reading in the elementary grades (in words per minute) as derived from leading standardized tests. For Grade 2 he found median rates ranging from 35 to 118; for Grade 3, from 75 to 138; for Grade 4, from 120 to 170; for Grade 5, from 145 to 195; for Grade 6, from 171 to 230.[2]

Because of the wide range of individual differences among both the children and the reading materials, it is inadvisable to prescribe specific goals for individuals or even whole classes. The reading rate of the average adult reader, with non-study-type materials, has been estimated at approximately 250 words per minute, and this figure can be substantially raised through deliberate practice in reading speed. Pupils who approach this standard by the end of the sixth grade can therefore not be regarded as deficient in reading speed. Many pupils will exceed it. The teacher of the primary grades should not be concerned with speed in terms of words per minute.

Controlled Reading

Various machines for regulating the speed at which the printed page is exposed to the reader are commercially available. The basic principle of most of these devices is that of an instrument known in psychological laboratories as a "tachistoscope." This is a contrivance that flashes words or phrases on a screen at a controlled rate. The method in which the tachistoscope and similar instruments are used in reading instruction is sometimes called "controlled reading."

The chief purpose of these instruments is to increase the reader's ability to perceive whole words and phrases quickly in a single fixation. Through intensive and prolonged practice, a child may be able to perceive—that is, recognize and identify—words and phrases with progressively greater speed. The theory is that such training will transfer to the printed page and will result not only in improved reading rate but also in better comprehension, because meaning is usually derived from whole words and words in combination rather than from individual letters.

Among the well-known pacing devices are the Harvard Reading Films, developed by Walter F. Dearborn and his colleagues. These films, however,

---

[2] Albert J. Harris, *How to Improve Reading Ability*, 4th ed., p. 508. New York: David McKay Company, 1961.

have not as yet been made in an edition usable in the elementary school. The films present reading material through bright exposures of part or a line of print at a time. Regressive movements of the eyes are thus discouraged, since the reader is forced to move his eyes more and more rapidly in left-to-right movements in order to comprehend the meaning. Tests are available with each film to test the reader's comprehension.

Other devices which employ "pressure" methods are the SRA Reading Rate Accelerator, made by Science Research Associates (Chicago, Illinois) and the Keystone Reading Pacer, made by the Keystone View Company (Meadville, Pennsylvania). The Keystone Tachistoscope is a device for increasing rate of perception of individual letters and words. All of these and similar machines present printed matter at controlled rates of speed. Faced with a gradually increasing rate of exposure, the reader is pressed to "take in" meaningful units on the line at a pace that can be constantly accelerated.

Unquestionably, the "reading machines" have been effective in improving reading rate in many cases. How permanent the improvement has been is a matter of conjecture. Quite possibly the machines have an initial advantage in that they provide novelty and interest in the improvement of reading. Unfortunately, after a time the novelty may wear off, and consequently one of the chief reasons for the success reported with instruments of this type may no longer operate.

In this connection, a study by Dr. Eloise Cason is of interest. She undertook to determine the relative effects upon third-grade children of three programs. One of these employed the Metronoscope; another followed a program which employed artificially phrased materials such as texts in which alternate phrases were underlined, separated by a blank space, or printed in a different color; and the third was one in which the pupils engaged exclusively in free library reading. In commenting on this study, her sponsor, Arthur I. Gates, reported:

> There is . . . , I believe, a growing tendency to recognize that a well-rounded, varied program of normal reading activities nicely adjusted to individual needs is a more fruitful remedial or preventive procedure than any one of the more specialized artificial types of remedial devices or stunts. . . .
>
> For the reading disability we rarely need anything more than the best and richest normal program applied with particular care and intelligence to the individual case. The remedial reading expert who is dependent upon a special kit of tricks, stunts, devices, and gadgets is rapidly being driven out of fashion by the brute force of careful study and experimentation.[3]

Mrs. Cason herself commented as follows:

[3] Arthur I. Gates, "Diagnosis and Remediation in Reading," *The Elementary English Review*, 19 (December 1942), 239–240.

It is reasonable to assume that the burden of proof rests with those who favor the introduction of such mechanical or artificial methods into the classroom. The point to be demonstrated is the effectiveness of the methods in meeting particular needs. Effectiveness implies not only that good results are produced but also that they are secured in the simplest and most economical manner. The evidence presented in this study showed that, at the level studied and under the limitations of the experimental conditions, these procedures were ineffective in the sense that results commensurate with the effort were not obtained. The results, moreover, showed that the reading habits of certain children were disorganized by subjecting them to this type of procedure. This evidence is not an indictment of the use of such methods under all circumstances. It is entirely possible that such methods may produce improvement in selected individuals who do not respond to other methods of treatment, or help pupils older or younger than those studied.[4]

In "controlled reading," emphasis is placed primarily upon the improvement of rate. Programs of improvement in reading should also place stress on comprehension. Although research studies indicate either that there was no loss in comprehension or that slight gains were made, the little increase in power in comprehension has not been commensurate with the amount of time and energy spent on attempts at improvement of reading.

The use of mechanical aids for controlling the rate of reading does not eliminate the need for an attack on the underlying causes of inappropriate rates of reading. The machines may discourage dawdling habits of reading, but in themselves they do not eliminate the chief causes of unsatisfactory rate of comprehension, such as lack of skill in methods of word recognition, lack of skill in selecting details, difficulty in organizing what is read, failure to read material critically, and inability to locate information rapidly. In fact, "controlled reading" can even have a detrimental effect upon some of these factors. For example, the person whose chief reason for slow reading is a difficulty in recognizing words may develop even poorer habits of word recognition because he is not given time to apply sound means of word identification. Nor can the efficient reader employ the flexible habits of reading that are needed to get meaning quickly. When he comes to a word that he must analyze, he wants to stop for a longer pause. He may find it advisable to make regressive movements if he discovers that he has just finished reading a point that he should note carefully. He will want to vary his rate in accordance with his purpose in reading, rather than follow the operation of mechanical shutters that compel him to read every line or part of a line in the same time as preceding ones.

Undoubtedly the eye movements that are forced by "controlled reading"

---

[4] Eloise B. Cason, *Mechanical Methods for Increasing the Speed of Reading—An Experimental Study at the Third Grade Level.* Columbia Contributions to Education No. 878. New York: Bureau of Publications, Teachers College, Columbia University, 1943.

resemble those of successful readers. Simulating these movements, however, will not necessarily produce good reading. The positive correlation between efficient reading and efficient eye movements is not caused by the effect of eye movements upon reading; rather, good eye movements are the result, not the cause, of efficient reading. The attack, consequently, should not be made directly upon eye movements.

Guidelines for the Improvement of Rate

To assist the teacher further in helping boys and girls to read at appropriate rates, guidelines that should be kept in mind by the teacher are now discussed. Only those generalizations are presented on which there is little, if any, disagreement among specialists in the teaching of reading.

1. *Growth in ability to read at appropriate rates is subject to training.* Assistance can be given the person who is not reading at appropriate rates. Studies show that remarkable increases in rate have been achieved in a brief period of time in many clinical situations, supervised reading courses, and classroom situations where this phase of reading has been stressed. In fact, there is reason to think that almost all readers could make valuable increase in the speed with which they read, without loss in comprehension, if they were given appropriate help.

2. *Reading rates should vary with the purpose of the reader and the type and difficulty of the material.* Both the teacher and the learner should be aware of this fact. In the first grade the teacher will usually set the purpose of reading. She may tell a pupil to read the next page to find out what Bobby did when his mother told him what she wanted for her birthday, or she may ask him to glance over the next page to find the new word *mother*, which has been presented on the board or on a word card. She may show the pupil that in the latter assignment it is not necessary for him to read every word and that consequently it should not take him as long to read that page as it would if he read the page to answer a question about it. Thus an early beginning can be made in helping boys and girls to read at different rates for different purposes.

Later in the development of skill in reading, the learner should be given increasing opportunity to decide on suitable purposes himself and to determine what rate of reading he will need in order to accomplish his objective.

A somewhat arbitrary classification of the rates of reading may help to clarify for pupils the ways of adapting speed to the nature of the reading material and the purpose for reading it. Reading rates have often been divided into three categories: rapid reading, moderately fast reading, and slow reading. Skimming is probably the fastest kind of reading. In skimming, the reader glances rapidly over a page without reading every word and moves his eyes quickly along the lines and down the page. He may be skimming in order to see if a certain topic is discussed or to find out what topic is taken up. Skimming is also needed when a person glances through a table of contents to find a given chapter title so that he can tell on which page it begins or when he looks over the words on a page in the dictionary in order to locate an entry word.

Fast reading is also appropriate, usually, when the reader looks at a newspaper to find out what is going on in the world or reads a magazine article just for fun. Moderately fast reading is called for when the reader wishes to absorb details. Slow reading is often advisable in a study-type situation or when appreciation of the beauty of style or of the unfolding of the details of a situation or the personality of the characters is desired.

3. *Teachers and pupils should have clearly defined goals for the improvement of reading rates.* General objectives are not enough. The teacher should try to find out the needs of the pupils in order to help them overcome their difficulties. The aims should be specific—for example, to learn when to read at the different rates, to read study-type material more slowly so as to have an opportunity to get the thought of the selection, and to read fiction rapidly while maintaining the desired amount of comprehension.

The pupil, too, should have clear-cut objectives. Results are better when the learner is consciously seeking specific goals.

4. *Development of ability to read at appropriate rates should not interfere with development of other reading skills.* Rates of reading should not be increased at a sacrifice of comprehension. To be sure, when a pupil has been reading more slowly than his immediate purpose warrants, rate should be increased. Increase in rate sometimes brings about a better degree of comprehension, if teaching methods eliminate defects in rate and comprehension simultaneously.

Much of what has been said about the effect of improvement in rate on comprehension can also, in general terms, be said of the relationship that should exist between increase in rate and other reading skills. In the case of skill in locating information, for instance, it would be unfortunate if greater speed in finding an entry in an index caused the reader to become less accurate in doing so. The goal is to spend less time in finding an entry without sacrificing accuracy.

5. *Neither haste nor undue tension should characterize the efforts to read at appropriate rates.* All practices in an effective program of developmental or remedial reading should be in harmony with the principles of mental health. Studies of child development have shown the harmful effects of creating pressures which result in anxiety and fear of failure. However, this does not mean that at times measures should not be taken to prod a person whose poor achievement, below his expected level, is due to dawdling habits or to lack of effort. Not only are haste and undue tension undesirable from the point of view of maintaining an emotional equilibrium; they are also detrimental because they interfere with success in learning. Consequently the child should be encouraged to do his best without becoming frantic when he fails to achieve his goal.

6. *The marked difference in children's ability to read at appropriate rates should be recognized.* Part of the variation among children results from differences in training received in school and practice outside of school. A further cause lies in the variations in innate capacity of individuals to master the intricacies of learning to read at the appropriate rates. Some will never become as skillful as others in reading at desirable rates.

An effective program for helping pupils to acquire skill in reading at appropriate rates recognizes these variations among individuals. The teacher needs to know what stage of learning to read each child has reached, and she must work out a program that is adapted to the needs of individual children. She should not be satisfied with averages. Some children who read with less than average speed for their grade in all types of reading situations may still be working up to capacity or even straining themselves to do good work beyond their capacity. On the other hand, some children, although surpassing norms in rate of reading, may still be reading below their potential.

8b

Developing
Appropriate Reading Rates

The purpose of this chapter is to show how the teacher can help children to develop reading rates appropriate to the various types of materials and purposes for reading.

Methods of Developing
Appropriate Rates

In this chapter reading rates are grouped for convenience into three categories: rapid reading, moderately fast reading, and slow reading. Each of these types of reading is desirable under certain circumstances and undesirable under others. The efficient reader knows not only how to use these but also when.

Some of the following suggestions are given for the improvement of rate in connection with the regular reading lessons in the basal reading textbook. Also included are recommendations that can be used in the content fields, and others that can serve as practice exercises. Samples of a few practice exercises are given. No attempt has been made, however, to designate the type of situation in which the suggestions can best be used. Nor are all the methods recommended for use with all groups or individuals. Selection should be made on the basis of the principles set forth in the preceding chapter. It is hoped that the list of recommendations will suggest to the teacher many others that are especially adapted to her pupils.

Some activities performed by pupils can be helpful for increasing rate whether fast, moderately fast, or rather slow reading is called for by the purpose of the reader and the material. The following are illustrative:

1. Discussing the importance of reading at the fastest rate possible in keeping with the aim of the reader and the nature of the material.

2. Discussing the importance of maintaining a desired level of comprehension as rate is increased.

3. Explaining that some readers read too fast to achieve the comprehension level they wish to attain.

Boys and girls practice self selection in reading

Winnetka, Illinois, Public Schools
Children use the "reading laboratory"
to strengthen reading skills

4. Explaining the importance of purpose in reading, in order to help pupils understand the optimum speed at which the material should be read.

5. Explaining the relation between type and difficulty of material and the optimum speed at which the material should be read.

6. Estimating the speed (in terms of fast, moderately fast, and slow) at which materials of designated types and difficulty should be read.

7. Reading while being timed and later checked for comprehension.

8. Practicing reading of words, phrases, or sentences that are exposed for varying lengths of time either by a commercially produced reading machine or by a teacher-made tachistoscope. The teacher can make a tachistoscope by cutting a slit in a piece of tagboard and sliding the words or groups of words, listed in column form, through the slit, at varying intervals.

9. Listing in one column possible speeds at which the pupils might read and in a second column topics on which they may be reading for stated purposes. Lines can then be drawn between the columns, matching the speed with the corresponding topic.

10. Listening to the teacher reading in meaningful phrases.

11. Reading silently material in which the phrases have been marked or separated.

12. Matching words given in two columns which when combined make meaningful phrases.

13. Marking the meaningful phrases that occur in a selection.

14. Indicating orally the meaningful phrases in a selection.

15. Keeping a record of progress in reading at appropriate rates.

16. Reading a selection in which varying rates are appropriate and indicating where and why the variations should occur.

17. Engaging in any activities that help attain the level of comprehension demanded by a situation. (For suggestions, see Chapter 7B.)

18. Engaging in activities that help improve skill in word recognition.

Developing Skill in Reading at a Fast Rate

Skill in skimming can be developed through additional activities.

1. Explaining in what situations skimming can properly be used—for example, when the reader wishes to get only a general impression of a passage or when he wishes to glance at it to see if it furnishes a certain item of information.

2. Explaining how the eyes move across the page when skimming. (It may help some of the boys and girls to know that in skimming the eyes do not always need to move from the end of one line to the beginning of the next. The eyes often take in only a part of each line as they move rapidly across and down a page.)

3. Skimming a selection while consciously moving the eyes rapidly across and down a page, without stopping to note details.

4. Skimming a table of contents to find out on what page a chapter on a given topic begins.

5. Skimming parts of an article in an encyclopedia to find a desired fact.

6. Skimming a page in a book to find a given "new" word that has been presented.

7. Skimming a page to find the answer to a question based on that page.

8. Skimming a page to see if it gives information on a given topic.

9. Skimming a page to find a sentence to be quoted.

10. Skimming a newspaper to find a report on a social activity which took place.

11. Skimming through books in the library to find one dealing, at least in part, with a specified topic.

12. Skimming a book to find out whether one would like to read it.

13. Finding as rapidly as possible the topic sentences of paragraphs.

14. Skimming a selection in order to find answers to a list of questions as quickly as possible.

15. Skimming a selection after a more thorough reading to see if any points to be remembered have been forgotten.

16. Timing oneself or being timed while engaging in many of the types of activities that have been suggested.

17. Skimming the index of a book to locate an entry in order to secure a specified item of information.

18. Finding a word in a dictionary.

19. Skimming a telephone directory to find the name of a person whose telephone number is desired.

20. Reading a paragraph in which some words have been omitted, words without which a reader can get the general thought of the paragraph. The pupils can be told not to try to guess the missing words but to see if they can understand the paragraph as it is written while reading it rapidly.

Ways which can bring about improvement in reading at an effective rate when fast reading, but not skimming, is desired include:

1. Explaining when fast reading other than skimming should be used.

2. Identifying situations in which fast reading, other than skimming, is desired.

3. Getting practice in reading rapidly easy material or material with which the reader has some familiarity.

4. Getting practice in selecting the main idea of a paragraph, without intent to note details, as rapidly as possible.

5. Timing oneself or being timed while reading rapidly.

PRACTICE EXERCISES. Some pupils can be helped to acquire appropriate rates for reading by means of practice exercises. Many workbooks, some accompanying basal textbooks and others independent of them, provide such practice exercises. However, the teacher may often find it desirable to construct exercises of her own. The teacher will find suggestions of possible practice exercises in the lists in this chapter and in preceding "B" chapters.

The following samples of exercises are representative of some that may encourage either skimming or rapid reading without skimming.

1

An exercise like the following, especially if timed, is particularly helpful to pupils inclined to use too much time in locating the main thought in a paragraph or longer selection.

Directions: This exercise is to help you learn to locate rapidly a certain sentence in a paragraph. You will be timed while you are doing this exercise. Preceding each paragraph there is a sentence. You are to find the sentence in the paragraph that expresses the thought of that sentence. When you have located the sentence in the paragraph, draw a circle around the first word of it and continue with the next paragraph.

1. Sentence: The Indian elephant has a lighter skin than the African.

There are many differences between the two kinds of elephants, the African and the Indian. The African elephants grow larger than the Indian elephants. As a rule both the male and the female of the African elephant have tusks, but only the Indian male has them. The tusks of the African elephant are larger than those of the Indian. The ears of the African elephant are also larger. The elephant in Africa has two knobs at the end of its trunk, but the Indian has only one. The elephants from Africa are darker than those from Asia. Even the texture of skin of the two animals is different, for that of the Indian elephant is not as rough as that of the African.

2

An exercise like the following, in which the child's rate during the first two minutes is checked, is valuable in stimulating him to begin reading promptly and to read at his maximum rate. The figure at the beginning of each line indicates the cumulative number of words that the child reads, not including the title. It should be explained that the pupils do not need to read the figures. The teacher may wish to tell the class what the numbers represent. The beginning or all of a selection like the following may be read by the pupils. If only part of a story is included in the exercises, the teacher should tell the pupils how it ends.

Directions: The following exercise is to help you get started reading rapidly when the material is easy for you and when all you need to know is the general idea of what you are reading. When you are told to begin, read as rapidly as you can while still getting the general idea of what you are reading. At the end of two minutes you will be asked to stop. As soon as you hear the word *Stop*, draw a circle around the last word you read. Then finish the story and answer the questions given at the end of the story.

THE BUNNY WHO DIDN'T BELIEVE IN SANTA

6 Once there was a little Bunny
12 named Winkie who didn't believe in
19 Santa Claus—if you can imagine such
26 a thing! Of course this made his
34 mother feel very sad, and, for a time,
41 it looked as if Winkie might feel
49 worse than sad. In fact, he got into
55 very serious trouble and might even
64 have lost his life if it hadn't been for
71 ——. But that part should come at
77 the very end of the story.
83 It was Christmas Eve and Mother
89 Cottontail and her nine bunnies were

96 doing all the things that everyone else
103 does on that jolliest of eves. They
108 were trimming the Christmas tree,
114 hanging up the stockings and singing
116 Christmas carols.[1]

Developing Skill in Reading at a Moderately Fast Rate

In order to develop skill in reading moderately easy material with the purpose of finding the main ideas as well as numerous details, activities like the following may prove helpful:

1. Discussing in what situations moderately fast reading should take place.

2. Identifying situations in which reading of this type is appropriate.

3. Getting much practice in reading this type of material.

4. Getting practice in selecting the main ideas and some supporting details rapidly.

5. Timing pupils or letting them time themselves as they read material of this type.

6. Reading a page of a book to find the words that complete sentences written on the chalkboard or on a sheet of paper.

7. Reading a paragraph in which one or two words do not fit the meaning of one or more sentences. When these words are located, the children should circle each incorrect word and write a more suitable word in the margin.

PRACTICE EXERCISE. Stories are well adapted for use as exercises, like the following, in fairly rapid reading of rather easy material. The story should be one that the children do not already know.

Directions: Read as rapidly as you can the story of "The Shoemaker and the Elves" so as to be able to answer fairly easy ques-

[1] Mabel Harmer, "The Bunny Who Didn't Believe in Santa," *Grade Teacher*, 72 (December 1954), 25. (Adapted.)

tions that you will be asked on it. Your teacher will time you while you are reading the story.

Questions on the story. (These questions are to be answered in as few words as possible.)

1. How many pairs of shoes did the shoemaker find the morning after the night when he had cut out leather for just one pair of shoes? _____

2. Why did the shoemaker and his wife decide to sit up one night shortly before Christmas? _____

3. Where in the room were the shoemaker and his wife hiding the evening when they sat up?_____

4. How many elves came to do the work for the shoemaker? _____

5. What did the shoemaker and his wife do to show their gratitude like their elves?

_____

6. How did the elves like their presents?

_____

Developing Skill in Reading at a Relatively Slow Rate

Many elementary school children, especially in the intermediate grades, need help in reading for study purposes. Often they also need to learn how to adjust their reading rate for directions which they are asked to follow. Although the rate of reading for such purposes necessarily is relatively slow, the pupils should be helped to read as rapidly as possible to attain their objectives. Many can profit from taking part in activities like the following:

1. Discussing in what situations slower reading is called for.

2. Identifying situations in which slower reading should take place.

3. Reading, under timed conditions, materials that require careful understanding of what is read.

4. Finding, quickly, a statement that proves or disproves a given statement.

5. Selecting all points that support a stated main topic.

6. Outlining a selection that has been read.

7. Finding a word or group of words that expresses a detail stated by the teacher.

8. Repeating directions that have been exposed for only a brief time.

9. Following directions that have been exposed for only a brief time.

10. Reading, under timed conditions, a difficult work-type selection on which detailed questions are later to be answered.

11. Reading a selection to determine whether the writer is sympathetic or unsympathetic toward a particular cause or person.

12. Reading a selection in order to find a generalization developed in the writing.

13. Reading a selection in order to answer a thought question on it.

14. Reading a selection in order to report on it.

15. Reading literary material in order to find points particularly interesting to the reader.

16. Answering questions on the details of an arithmetic problem.

17. Arranging in correct sequence the details of a story that have been listed out of order.

18. Contrasting an editorial with an objectively written news article.

19. Memorizing a significant line or longer part of a paragraph.

Reading Lessons and the Development of Appropriate Rates

The teacher has many opportunities to help pupils develop appropriate rates of reading through the use of the basal textbook. Excellent suggestions are given in the manuals that accompany basal reading series.

Improving Reading Rates in the Second Grade

Although less emphasis should generally be placed on speed in the primary than in the intermediate grades, some attention should nevertheless be paid to it even in the earlier grades.

The story chosen here for illustration is "The Rooster Who Would Not Listen," pages 2 to 11 in *Just for Fun.*[2] It is the story of a rooster who gets into trouble again and again because he does not follow the solid advice of his good friend, a little hen, who keeps helping him out of his difficulties. Because the rooster does not listen to the little hen, he becomes sick from eating green strawberries and later from drinking cold water when he is very hot. He gets pelted with cobs of corn when, against the advice of the little hen, he goes into a barn into which men are throwing corn for storage. Another time he might have been drowned while trying to walk on ice that was too thin, if the little hen had not rescued him.

In connection with this story, the teacher may use techniques like the following that will help pupils read some parts rapidly, some with moderate speed, and others slowly enough to note important details. The teacher should always aim to promote the greatest speed possible without sacrificing comprehension.

1. After the word *sometimes* has been presented on the board, the teacher may ask the pupils to glance at page 2 to see how quickly they can locate the places where the word is used.

2. The teacher may tell the class to read pages 2 through 5 as rapidly as they can to find out what was the first thing that the rooster did against which the little hen had warned him.

[2] Guy L. Bond and others, *Just for Fun.* Developmental Reading Series. Chicago: Lyons and Carnahan, 1949.

3. After the pupils have read silently pages 6 and 7, which tell how the rooster became sick from drinking water that was too cold, they may be asked to find the exact words with which the little hen warned the rooster not to drink the cold water.

4. The pupils can be asked to read page 8 carefully in order to tell in their own words exactly what happened when the men decided to throw corn into the barn for winter storage.

5. The teacher can ask the pupils to read pages 9 through 11, which tell about the rooster's experiences on the ice, in order to answer questions like the following: (a) How did the rooster feel when he looked out of the window and saw that winter had come? (b) Where did he decide to go? (c) What did the little hen say when the rooster said he would slide on the ice? (d) What happened after the rooster went on the ice? (e) Who kept the rooster from drowning?

6. Before the pupils read pages 9 and 10, they may be told to read the pages as rapidly as they can while still reading them carefully enough to find the answers to the questions. They may be asked to answer the questions orally. Or they may be asked to answer multiple-choice statements like these:

One morning when the rooster looked out and saw that winter had come, he was
> happy
> sad
> tired.
The rooster wanted to slide on the ice
> on the lake
> on the river
> in the back yard.

After the answers have been checked, a pupil may be asked to reread silently the part that gives the answer to any question he may have missed.

The following are suggestions for group activities that involve reading at various rates:

1. The teacher can place on a library table other stories about roosters or other animals that had adventures like those of the rooster. Time can then be provided for the pupils to skim these stories to decide which one each would like to read.

2. If the pupils decide to dramatize parts of the story, they may choose the main events that should be included in their dramatization. First they may dictate, as the teacher writes on the board, the points that they remember that should be in the play. Then they may reread the story rapidly to see if they have omitted any that they think should be included.

3. After reading the story, the group may decide to make a "movie" of it. When the pictures drawn for the story have been chosen and the sequence determined, the class may be asked to find as quickly as possible the parts in the story on which the pictures are based. Slower reading will be needed to get the full benefit of suggestions for drawing suitable pictures.

Improving Reading Rates in the Sixth Grade

In order to teach intermediate grade pupils to note details, the following procedure may be helpful. One teacher who taught lessons of this type, on an average of about one a week, based them on the selections within the basal reading textbooks. The first time that the reading period was devoted to work like this the boys and girls discussed some ways in which they could read at the optimum rates materials that were fairly easy for them when they wished to note rather carefully quite a number of details. Some points discussed were: (a) need for concentration; (b) suitable posture; (c) reading as fast as possible while maintaining or increasing the ability to understand at the required level of comprehension; (d) timing oneself while reading; and (e) reading a great deal. In later lessons reference was

again made to these points and further suggestions were given for making effective use of them.

A SUGGESTED TEACHING PLAN. In order to make clear how a lesson like this can be taught in such a way as to test the boys and girls on rate and comprehension in reading material of the type indicated for a specified purpose, a copy of a plan that could be used for teaching the story, "Sacajawea of the Shining Mountains," on pages 13 through 27 in *All Around Me*,[3] is described here. It is followed by further explanation of the plan.

The plan for using the story "Sacajawea of the Shining Mountains" for a silent-reading-test lesson should not be followed rigidly. Instead, whatever procedure is followed for this or any other story should be determined by the needs of the boys and girls. This plan is merely to serve as a sample of one way in which a story could be used to help children test themselves and improve in ability to read at a satisfactory rate rather easy story material with the aim of remembering details.

A. TOPIC: Silent reading of "Sacajawea of the Shining Mountains"

B. PUPILS' AIMS
  1. To test our rate in reading a story like "Sacajawea of the Shining Mountains" when wanting to remember details
  2. To get practice in improving our rate of reading story material and still accomplish our purpose
  3. To find out why Sacajawea is given much credit for the success of the Lewis and Clark expedition

C. MATERIALS
  1. Material on the board
    a. Words for pronunciation: *Sacaja-*

[3] Arthur I. Gates and Mary M. Bartlett, *All Around Me*. The Macmillan Readers. New York: The Macmillan Company, 1951.

*wea, Meriwether, Shoshone, Charbo-
neau, negotiation, annual, precipices.*

b. Sentences for study of word meaning:

(1) In May the sixth grade will have a picnic. It is an *annual* event in that grade.

(2) The trusty horse stood motionless at the edge of the seemingly bottomless *precipice.*

(3) The Indians and the white men were willing to carry on *negotiations* in order to avoid fighting.

c. Directions: (1) Read from page 13 to the top of page 21.

(2) Record your rate.

(3) Answer the questions.

(4) If you have time, finish the story.

d. Reading rates for a 1300-word passage (beginning with four minutes and ending with fourteen, with erasing of figures to be done every quarter of a minute)

325	*217*	*163*	*130*	*108*
306	208	158	127	106
289	200	153	124	104
274	193	149	121	102
260	*186*	*144*	*118*	*100*
248	179	141	116	98
236	173	137	113	96
226	168	133	111	95
				93

2. Outline map of the United States on which is traced the route of Lewis and Clark

3. Books dealing with the Lewis and Clark expedition

James Daugherty, *Of Courage Undaunted: Across the Continent with Lewis and Clark.* New York: The Junior Literary Guild and Viking Press, 1951.

Frances Joyce Farnsworth, *Winged Moccasins: The Story of Sacajawea.* New York: The Junior Literary Guild and Julian Messner, 1954.

Flora W. Seymour, *Bird Girl: Sacajawea.* Indianapolis: The Bobbs-Merrill Company, Inc., 1945.

4. Paper and pencil

5. Individual graphs (see illustration on p. 190).

6. Mimeographed test questions
Silent Reading Test on "Sacajawea of the Shining Mountains" in *All Around Me*

Directions: After you have read from page 13 to the top of page 21, number from one to ten on a slip of paper given to you. After each number write the letter before the word or group of words in the parentheses that will make the corresponding sentence correct.

1. Sacajawea was a (a. Blackfoot, b. Sioux, c. Shoshone) Indian.

2. The name *Sacajawea* means (a. Bird Girl, b. Bird Woman, c. Bird Lover).

3. Sacajawea was given her name (a. for an unknown reason, b. because she loved birds, c. because her mother loved birds).

4. The (a. Rocky Mountains, b. Cascade Mountains, c. Sierra Nevada Mountains) were called the Shining Mountains.

5. When Sacajawea was (a. two or three, b. four or five, c. ten or eleven) years old, she was captured.

6. Sacajawea was the wife of (a. an Englishman, b. an Indian chief, c. a Frenchman).

7. At the time when Lewis and Clark first met Sacajawea she lived in what is now (a. Wyoming, b. Washington, c. North Dakota).

8. An Indian wife (a. did not expect much kindness, b. expected much kindness, c. expected to have a rather easy life).

9. Lewis and Clark wanted to find the source of the (a. Columbia River, b. Missouri River, c. Snake River).

10. Sacajawea and her husband left the

camp of Lewis and Clark before the winter was over (a. because Sacajawea thought she was too ill to make the trip, b. because her husband had quarreled with the white men, c. because Lewis and Clark thought that Sacajawea would not be able to make the trip with her little papoose).

D. PROCEDURE

1. Introduction

a. Introduction to the story

(1) Review of facts about Lewis and Clark expedition that pupils have previously learned

MY PROGRESS IN READING

Tests

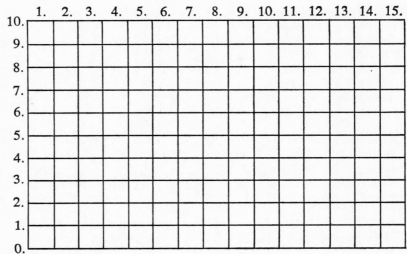

Number right

TEST NUMBER	NUMBER RIGHT	RATE
1.	————	————
2.	————	————
3.	————	————
4.	————	————
5.	————	————
6.	————	————
7.	————	————
8.	————	————
9.	————	————
10.	————	————
11.	————	————
12.	————	————
13.	————	————
14.	————	————
15.	————	————

(2) Tracing on an outline map of the United States the route of Lewis and Clark

(3) Statement of the third aim under *Pupils' aims,* namely, "To find out why Sacajawea is given much credit for the success of the Lewis and Clark expedition"

b. Statement of the first two aims under *Pupils' aims,* namely, "To test our rate in reading a story like 'Sacajawea of the Shining Mountains' when wanting to remember details" and "To get practice in improving our rate of reading story material and still accomplish our purpose"

2. Word study

a. Pronunciation of words

(1) Presentation through these methods: phonetic analysis, syllabication, or sight-word method

(2) Practice on pronunciation

b. Study of meaning of the words written in italics under *Materials*, through study of context clues and explanation by the teacher and pupils (See C-1-b.)

3. Directions for taking test

a. Reference is made to the directions listed under *Materials* (See C-1-c.)

b. Pupils place a marker between pages 20 and 21 and note that they are to stop reading for the test at the end of the second line on page 21.

4. Taking the test

a. Reading from page 13 to the top of page 21, while teacher erases rates on the board every quarter of a minute beginning with four minutes and ending with fourteen (See C-1-d.)

b. Recording the time

c. Answering the question

d. Doing the additional work, namely, reading silently the rest of the story, if time permits

5. Correcting papers

Pupils check their papers as the teacher does the following:

a. Gives the number of the sentence

b. Gives the letter of the word or group of words that forms the correct answer

c. Names the word or group of words that forms the correct answer

d. Reads the sentence supplying the correct answer

6. Recording marks on individual graphs, showing rate and comprehension (See C-1-5.)

7. Report on pages 21 to the end of the story, by a pupil who has finished the story

8. Forward look

a. Plans for further progress in development of adequate reading rates

b. Reference to books on library table (See C-3.)

1. *Length of the selection tested.* The test, both for rate and comprehension, is only on part of the selection chosen for the teaching plan, since there are approximately 2300 words in the entire story. The reason for limiting the test to only part of the story is that the reading period would need to be considerably longer than most are if the pupils were to read and be tested on all 2300 words. The number of words that the teacher will want to include in the test will vary with the selection and with the length of the class period. If the story were 1500 words in length, the teacher might wish to include the whole story. On the other hand, she may not want to exclude a story with only about 800 words. If, however, a much shorter number of words is chosen for the test, it may be difficult to select enough significant points for testing comprehension.

In estimating the number of words for the selection, the following procedure was used. The number of words in the first full ten lines of the story was found to be 86. Consequently it was known that the average number of words for those ten lines was 8.6. If, as in this case, a selection of about 1300 words was wanted for testing, the number of lines on which the test should be given can be found by dividing 1300 words by 8.6 words, which is 151. In counting the lines, it is recommended that at times part of a line should be counted and at other times a fractional part should not be counted, so as to keep the estimate of words approximately correct. When the entire selection is to be used for the test, the average number of words per line can be multiplied by the number of lines to get the estimated number of words in the selection.

2. *Computation of rate.* The rates listed

under *Materials* in this plan are the rates per minute for the 1300-word selection, beginning with four minutes and extending through fourteen, exact to the quarter of a minute. The count was begun with four minutes because in most sixth-grade classes there are few who would read material of this type at more than 325 words per minute. The counting was discontinued after 14 minutes because only very few sixth-grade pupils would read the selection at a rate slower than 93 words a minute. If it takes an individual longer than this time or if he finishes reading in less than four minutes, the teacher should, of course, take note of that fact.

In the table given under *Materials* the first entry, *325,* can be obtained by dividing 1300 words by four. Thus the rate is secured for a person who requires only four minutes to read the selection. The next entry, *306,* is the quotient when dividing 1300 words by $4\frac{1}{4}$, and so on.

If the teacher writes on the board before class a table similar to the one given in the teaching plan, she may erase a figure every quarter of a minute. She would begin erasing when the pupils had read for four minutes. She would start with the first entry in the column farthest to the left, continuing down that column and then proceeding similarly with the next column. The boys and girls should be given the instruction that, as soon as they have completed the required reading, they should look at the board and copy the highest figure left as their rate of reading. If anyone finishes the selection in less than four minutes, the starting time for the recording of rate, he may be asked to write on his paper a plus sign after the number of words per minute computed for four minutes. In this instance he would then write *325+.*

3. *The test.* If a test of this type is to be given more than once and if the results are to be compared, as suggested earlier, it is desirable to keep the questions in all the tests of the same type. Multiple-choice ques-

tions were selected for this plan because they are easier to check than completion statements and because they usually form a more reliable test than a small number of true-false statements. To be comparable, the number of choices provided in each multiple-choice statement should be kept the same. Ten was chosen for the number of questions because ten is so small a number that many significant questions can quite easily be asked on a selection. For purposes of comparison of results, it is suggested that the number be kept constant from test to test.

4. *Keeping a record.* Suggestions for using a graph like the one given on page 190 of this chapter have already been given. These, or similar graphs, should not be posted, for each pupil should be competing with himself, not with others. Frequent conferences between the teacher and each pupil should be held so that the pupil can get aid in interpreting the results of his efforts and so that he can receive suggestions for further improvement. The pupil should recognize the fact that a slight fluctuation in the score for rate is not necessarily significant, because of the inaccuracy of the tests and the fact that the rate of learning varies with circumstances.

5. *Additional work.* If the test is on only part of the selection, pupils should be encouraged to finish the story for themselves or the teacher may wish to tell the ending.

Other types of additional work for those pupils finishing earlier may be: (a) checking, by rereading parts of the selection, on any question in the test about which the pupil was not certain, (b) engaging in additional interesting and significant activities based on the story read, or (c) reading in a "library" book that the pupil already has at his desk.

6. *Supplementary reading.* If the teacher wishes to encourage children to read more on a topic related to the theme of the selection studied, she should have some additional books at hand. Telling the boys and girls briefly about the books and making provisions for their withdrawal can help stimulate more reading. Sometimes reference can be made to books in the library. If the books are not at that time in the classroom, it is recommended that the titles and the authors be written on the chalkboard or bulletin board so that the pupils will not forget the names by the time they go to the library.

Developing Appropriate Rates When Reading in the Content Subjects

Reading in the content areas, such as social studies, science, mathematics, and literature, affords much opportunity for the teacher to help pupils to become more skillful in reading at various rates appropriate to the purpose and the material. Even in the lower grades, children can learn when to employ the various rates of reading. In this section a few ways are pointed out in which, in an intermediate grade unit on Mexico, the pupils can acquire additional skill in reading at the optimum rates.

Developing Skill in Rapid Reading

Some of the ways in which the boys and girls could get helpful practice in skimming or other rapid reading when working on a unit on Mexico are:

1. Glancing at books like the following to see which ones they would like to read: *The Watchdog* by Laura Bannon, *My Pet Peepelo* by Ellis Credle, and *Let's Read About Mexico* by Stella Burke May.[4]

2. Reading one or more books on Mexico rather rapidly, merely to get the story.

---

4 Laura Bannon, *The Watchdog.* Racine, Wis.: Whitman Publishing Company, 1948.

Ellis Credle, *My Pet Peepelo.* New York: Oxford University Press, 1948.

Stella Burke May, *Let's Read About Mexico.* Grand Rapids, Mich.: The Fideler Company, 1949.

3. Skimming an article in an encyclopedia to see if it contains information about the observance of September 16.

4. Skimming a page in an index of a social studies book to find out if there is an entry on Miguel Hidalgo.

5. Glancing at the table of contents in the book *The Real Book About Explorers* by Irvin Block[5] to see if a chapter is devoted to Hernando Cortez.

Developing Skill in Reading When a Moderately Fast Rate Is Required

The boys and girls can get practice in reading material at the optimum rate when moderately fast reading is desirable in the following ways:

1. Reading a selection in a social studies textbook on Mexico City in order to find the answer to a set of relatively easy questions that the reader has seen before beginning to read.

2. Reading a section, in a book that is moderately easy to read, on Mexican art in order to be able to tell the rest of the class a few points of interest on the subject.

3. Reading the writing under a picture of a Mexican housewife grinding corn on a huge stone to find out what the woman in the picture is doing.

Developing Skill in Reading When a Slow Rate Is Required

Opportunity to help pupils read at the maximum efficiency when a rather slow rate is required can be provided in situations like the following:

1. Reading preparatory to giving a talk showing the Mexican and the American sides of issues leading up to the Mexican War.

2. Studying directions in order to make a Mexican dish like tortillas.

---

5 Irving Block, *The Real Book About Explorers.* New York: Garden City Books, 1952.

3. Studying the history of Mexico in order to be able to make a frieze portraying important events in its history—for example, the arrival of Cortez in Mexico, the conquest of the country by Cortez, the attitude of the European settlers who came to Mexico, the work of the missionaries, the long struggle for freedom, the war with the United States, and finally the progress Mexico is making in the present century.

FOR FURTHER STUDY

BLAIR, GLENN M., *Diagnostic and Remedial Teaching*, pp. 94–101. New York: The Macmillan Company, 1956.

BRAAM, LEONARD, "Developing and Measuring Flexibility in Reading," *The Reading Teacher*, 16 (January 1963), 247–251.

DURRELL, DONALD D., *Improving Reading Instruction*, pp. 190–192. New York: Harcourt, Brace and World, Inc., 1956.

GRAY, LILLIAN, AND DORA REESE, *Teaching Children to Read*, 2d ed., pp. 255–259. New York: The Ronald Press Company, 1957.

HILDRETH, GERTRUDE, *Teaching Reading*, pp. 102–105. New York: Holt, Rinehart and Winston, Inc., 1958.

McKIM, MARGARET G., AND HELEN CASKEY, *Guiding Growth in the Modern Elementary School*, pp. 338–343. New York: The Macmillan Company, 1963.

SMITH, HENRY P., AND EMERALD V. DECHANT, *Psychology in Teaching Reading*, pp. 224–236. Englewood Cliffs, N.J.: Prentice-Hall, Inc., 1961.

STRANG, RUTH, *Making Better Readers*, pp. 117–121. Boston: D. C. Heath and Company, 1955.

9a

Locating Information

The development of the ability to locate information in printed sources has become an increasingly important concern of the school. In earlier, simpler days, pupils used relatively few books, and were usually directed to the exact locations of the material to be studied. In our day of abundant newspapers, magazines, encyclopedias, dictionaries, almanacs, and other kinds of printed matter, skill in finding information is becoming ever more imperative. The increasing complexity of modern life, too, has brought this new need into focus.

Unfortunately, many children as well as adults, including college graduates, have only limited skill in locating information. For this reason, many people simply make no effort to look for information which they need or desire. Often people who have access to dictionaries and who want to know the meaning of a word do not look it up because they have difficulty in making efficient use of this indispensable reference aid.

Happily, teachers are beginning to meet the challenge presented by changing needs, by making a persistent effort to help boys and girls receive the needed information and practice in locating materials economically and efficiently. Almost all professional books on the teaching of reading stress the importance of these skills and make suggestions for their development. Basal textbook series for boys and girls provide for growth in these skills, and the teachers' guidebooks which accompany the children's books abound in excellent recommendations as to how these skills can be developed. Many of the workbooks provide helpful exercises.

The abilities to be developed in relation to the location of material are here classified under four categories: (1) the ability to find information in nonreference books, (2) the ability to use the dictionary, (3) the ability to use reference books other than the dictionary, and (4) the ability to locate books and magazine articles in the library.

Basic Locational Skills

Several of the locational skills basic to effective use of reading materials deal with the finding of information.

Skill in Finding Words Arranged in Alphabetical Order

One of these basic skills, that of finding words that are arranged in alphabetical order, is needed in many types of situations, as in locating information in the index of a book, in the card catalog, in the dictionary, in an encyclopedia, and in other reference books. Unfortunately, elementary school teachers have often wrongly assumed that the pupil has the following skills or learnings essential to locating words arranged in alphabetical order:

1. Knowledge of the sequence of letters in the alphabet.

2. Ability to tell which letter precedes and which follows another without repeating part or all of the alphabet either orally or silently.

3. Instant knowledge of the part of the alphabet—the first, middle, or last—in which a letter occurs.

4. Knowledge of the fact that in indexes, dictionaries, and card catalogs the words are arranged in alphabetical order.

5. Understanding of and skill in arranging words in alphabetical order when the first letter of each word is different.

6. Understanding of and skill in arranging words in alphabetical order when the first letter of the words is alike but the second different.

7. Understanding of and skill in arranging words in alphabetical order when the first and second letters of the words are alike but the third is different.

8. Understanding of and skill in arranging any words in alphabetical order, when the first three or more letters are alike.

9. Knowledge of how to arrange words in alphabetical order when problems like these and others exist: (a) words beginning with the syllable *Mc* or *Mac*; (b) titles beginning with *the, a,* or *an*; (c) words like *grand* and *grandmother,* in which all the letters of one word are given in the same sequence in the first part of a second word; (d) names of persons if both the first and the last names are given.

Skill in Finding a Specified Page

Another skill basic to many types of reading is that of finding quickly a given page in a book or magazine. Many pupils need to be taught that there are quicker ways of finding a page than to start at the beginning of the book and to leaf through it till they come to it. Also, they need practice in opening a book in the vicinity of the page that they want.

Skill in Finding an Entry Word

Skill in finding an entry word is needed in using a dictionary, an encyclopedia, and other reference books. In order to find an entry word quickly, pupils should know the following facts about guide words: (1) In dictionaries, guide words are listed on each page of the book proper, usually in the columns at the top of the page. (2) These words indicate the first and the last entry words listed on a given page or, in the case of some dictionaries, on two facing pages. (3) By glancing at the guide words in a dictionary the reader can tell whether the word for which he is looking is on that page or, in some dictionaries, on one of the two facing pages. (4) Similar provisions are made in some of the other reference books, so that the reader can quickly ascertain whether the topic for which he is looking belongs between the first and last topics discussed on a given page.

It is not enough, however, for children to know what guide words are and where they are found. They should also develop skill in using guide words to locate entries quickly.

Skill in Deciding on Key Words

Another locational skill needed is that of knowing under what word to look for the needed information. This skill is often referred to as the ability to decide on key words. Lack of it causes much waste of time and frequently is the reason why reference books are not used more. Skill can be developed step by step through a gradation of difficulties, beginning with work on finding a topic in an index or reference book when the topic is worded in the same manner as the entry in the book. Later, pupils should be given practice in deciding which one of a variety of words is the most likely entry under which the needed information would be found. Use of subtopics in indexes should also be taught as an aid in finding the key words.

Knowledge of Content of Reference Books

Many pupils need guidance in learning what type of information is contained in different kinds of books and magazines. For example, a pupil will need to learn what types of information to look for in geography books, in history books, in science books, and in health books. He will also need to learn what types of information he can expect to find in various encyclopedias for children, in the *World Almanac,* in an atlas, in a dictionary, and in other reference books. As he develops skill in the use of these books, he will continue to discover new types of information. He cannot, of course, learn about them all at once. In the case of the dictionary, for example, he will usually first learn that it yields the meanings of words. Only later will he discover that he can find the pronunciation of words in it and, still later, that it contains information about syllabication and other matters.

Interpreting Information

After the reader has located information, he must be able to interpret it. Sometimes interpretation is an easy process, requiring neither special effort nor skill. At other times particular alertness is needed.

Pupils need to develop skill in learning to interpret the abbreviations given in reference material. Knowledge of many is essential to effective reading of reference books. Furthermore, the pupils should know where to look for a key to the abbreviations and how to apply the information given in the key.

Common to several types of reference materials are the references to additional material designated by *See* or *See also*. The boys and girls need to know before they leave the elementary school what is meant by these directions as well as how to use them. It is also important for them to know when they should follow the *See* or *See also* direction. Speed in locating the cross reference and in deciding whether it contributes to the topic also needs to be developed.

Another problem in the use of reference materials is that of selecting the points that have bearing on the purpose that the reader has in mind. How to interpret charts, tables, maps, graphs, and diagrams given in reference books is only part of the task. The pupil needs to know also how to find speedily and correctly the information given in words, groups of words, sentences, or paragraphs.

Making Use of Information

After the reader has found and interpreted the information that he wants, he may use it for a variety of purposes. He may compare what he has learned in one reference with what he has read in another or with what he already knows. He may take notes on it, write a summary, or make an outline in order either better to remember the data himself or to assist him as he tries to impart the information to others through informal conversation, reports, panel discussions, or illustrations. Sometimes he may compile a bibliography for his own or others' use. How to take notes, make summaries and outlines, and perform some of the other activities for purposes of retention and comprehension are discussed in other parts of this book.

Ability to Find Information in Nonreference Books

Elementary school children should learn to use the following parts of books or features in books effectively in order to locate information quickly in their textbooks and in trade books:

1. The preface
2. The introduction
3. The table of contents
4. Lists of maps and illustrations
5. Chapter headings, center headings, and side headings
6. The index

The pupils should know where each of these parts is found, what its function is, and how to make effective use of it. Furthermore, the teacher should try to develop in them the desire to make effective use of the several parts.

The Preface

The boys and girls should learn the following facts about the preface: (1) It is found in the front part of the book. (2) It is written either by the author or the editor of the book. (3) It tells the author's purpose in writing the book and often indicates any special features of the book. (4) It is useful in indicating whether a given topic or question is likely to be treated in the book.

The Introduction

If the introduction is studied, the pupils should know that the terms *introduction* and *preface* are sometimes used interchangeably. They should learn that some books contain both a preface and an introduction. As they examine these two parts of a book, they should know that, although a study of the introduction may help them to decide whether information that they want is given in the book, its primary purpose is not to serve as a locational aid.

The Table of Contents

The pupil can use the table of contents almost as soon as he begins reading books. If a new book has no table of contents, the teacher can indicate what the book deals with. When a simple table of contents is given, as in many primers, the pupil can find the new story in the table of contents with the help of the teacher. Reference can also be made to the page, if the pupil cannot read the page number by himself. The teacher may say, pointing to the page, "This number, *10,* tells us that our story is on page 10." Thereupon she can help the pupils find the page.

Lists of Maps and Illustrations

Pupils should acquire the following learnings about maps and illustrations: (1) A list of maps and illustrations included in a book may be found either in the front part of the book or in the back. (2) Textbooks in social studies, science, and health are more likely to provide a list of maps or illustrations than trade books. (3) The list of maps and illustrations gives the titles used with the maps and illustrations, and also the page on which they are found.

Chapter Headings, Center Headings, and Side Headings

Pupils should be taught the value of various kinds of headings in locating material and given practice in their use. As soon as side and center headings are given in the textbooks that the pupils read or in the reference books they use, simple help should be given in making effective use of these aids as means of locating information.

The Index

The following are some of the points that pupils should learn about the index of a book: (1) The index is in the back of the book. (2) The topics are arranged alphabetically, not in order of appearance in the book as in a table of contents. (3) In many books subtopics are given under the main entries.

The following skills should be developed: (1) deciding under what entry information on a given topic or question is likely to be given; (2) speed in finding an entry; (3) locating a topic when it appears as subtopic in the index; (4) ability to turn quickly to the pages on which the information, according to the index, is given; and (5) ability to find quickly the lines on a page that give the information on the desired topic.

Ability to Use the Dictionary

One of the outstanding developments in materials of instruction for the elementary school in recent years has been the dictionary for children. Before that, if boys and girls used any dictionaries, they had to use those planned for adults. Pupils in the early part of this century often had access only to a large, unabridged dictionary or to one or two less complete ones that were also compiled for adults. In some schools the children in the intermediate grades were urged or required to have their own abridged dictionary. Because of the price and the convenience of handling, many children brought to school pocket-sized dictionaries that in many respects were more difficult to understand than the unabridged dictionaries. Those who thought that these abbreviated dictionaries would be suitable for children were wrong, for often only one short line was allowed per entry. Obviously there was little chance for explanation when no more space than this was devoted to a word. At times the entry word was defined by a synonym even more difficult for the child to understand than the word he had looked up.

Dictionaries for the Elementary School

In addition to the picture dictionaries to which reference is made in Chapter 6B, "Developing Skill in Word Recognition," the following are commonly used in the elementary school:

Basic Dictionary of American English. New York: Holt, Rinehart and Winston, Inc. 848 pp.
Giant Golden Illustrated Dictionary, Stuart A. Courtis and Garnette Watters, eds. New York: Golden Press, Inc., 1961. Six volumes, 109 pp. each.
Illustrated Golden Dictionary for Young Readers, rev. ed., Stuart A. Courtis and Garnette Watters, eds. New York: Golden Press, Inc., 1956. 544 pp.
Thorndike-Barnhart Beginning Dictionary, Edward L. Thorndike and Clarence L. Barnhart, eds. Chicago: Scott, Foresman and Company, 1959. 720 pp.
Thorndike-Barnhart Junior Dictionary, Edward L. Thorndike and Clarence L. Barnhart, eds. Chicago: Scott, Foresman and Company, 1959. 784 pp.
Webster's A Dictionary for Boys and Girls. New York: American Book Company, 1962. 739 pp.
Webster's Elementary Dictionary, Gold. New York: American Book Company, 1961. 579 pp.
The Winston Dictionary for Schools, Thomas K. Brown and William D. Lewis, eds. New York: Holt, Rinehart and Winston, Inc., 1963. 941 pp.

Dictionary Skills

The skills to be learned in using a dictionary even in the elementary school are so complex that the teacher should have clearly in mind the sub-skills about which she should give information and for which she should provide practice. The following skills are needed for the efficient use of the dictionary in the elementary school:

1. Ability to locate a word quickly
2. Ability to learn the pronunciation of a word
3. Ability to find the spelling of a word

   a. syllabication
   b. hyphenation
   c. abbreviations
   d. capitalization
   4. Ability to learn the meaning of a word
   5. Ability to use the parts of the dictionary preceding and following the main part of the dictionary, both in the pupil's dictionary and in an unbridged dictionary

   LOCATING A WORD IN THE DICTIONARY. In order to locate a word in the dictionary quickly, the pupil needs to know more than how to find a word in a list arranged alphabetically and how to make use of guide words. The difficulty in which one fifth-grade girl found herself illustrates the need for more information. This girl's teacher had told her pupils that the unabridged dictionary in their room contained every word in the English language. One day, while the teacher was busy with another group, this girl ran across the word *busied* in her reading and was puzzled as to the meaning of the word. Had the word been *busy* she would have recognized it in print, and had she heard the word *busied* pronounced, she would have had no difficulty with its meaning. However, when she saw the word *busied* in context, she thought it would be pronounced *bu si' ed,* giving the *s* an *s* instead of a *z* sound and the *i* a long sound. She therefore went to the big dictionary and looked for the entry *busied.* When she could not find *busied* listed as an entry word, she had no idea that she might find it under another form. Consequently she could hardly wait until she could tell her teacher about her amazing discovery that the dictionary did not contain every word in the language. When the teacher asked her which word she did not find, she told her *busied,* pronouncing the word as *bu si' ed.* Many boys and girls have difficulty in finding a word in a dictionary when it is not given as an entry word in the form in which they meet the word in their reading. However, teachers are increasingly trying to show pupils how inflected forms can be located in the dictionary. In some schools, too, more emphasis is being placed on structural analysis, which serves as an aid in recognizing the inflected forms.

   LEARNING THE PRONUNCIATION. The elementary school child should learn to find the pronunciation of a word by means of respellings and diacritical marks, as interpreted in the key to pronunciation at the bottom of the page in a dictionary. The significance of the syllabication of words and the markings of the accent should be clear to him. He should understand that if two pronunciations are given for the same word, each pronunciation is used, as, for example, in the word *record,* which as a noun has the accent on the first syllable but as a verb on the second. Furthermore, he should bear in mind that if no specification is given as to which of two pronunciations should be used under given circumstances, in most dictionaries the first of two indicated is usually the preferred one. However, it should also be made clear that often two pronunciations are equally acceptable, but, since one has to be written before the other, the preferred pronunciation cannot always be determined from the order.

FINDING THE SPELLING. It is a difficult feat for many individuals, even adults, to find a word in the dictionary without being sure of the spelling. The pupil should therefore be given guidance and practice in this skill. Merely to say to a child, "Look up in the dictionary the word that you do not know how to spell," is inviting frustration. Pupils should learn how the plurals of nouns and other inflected forms are indicated. They need to know that some words pronounced alike—homonyms—have different meanings for different spellings. For spelling purposes it is also often necessary to know how words can be divided into syllables and whether they are hyphenated. Consequently the pupil needs to know the key for the division into syllables and hyphenation. Some dictionaries show syllabication by means of a space left between syllables; others show it by a hyphen, which must not be interpreted as a sign that the word is a compound word. The symbols for hyphenation also vary. In some dictionaries the hyphen is used to show hyphenation, and in others the double hyphen, one line above the other, is used for that purpose. Often the pupils need help in finding out what the symbols in a given dictionary indicate.

Another problem in spelling deals with the abbreviation of a word, if it can be abbreviated. Boys and girls should know that the dictionary gives the abbreviations of words, and they should learn where they can be found.

By means of the dictionary the pupils in the elementary school should be able to find out whether a word is always written with a capital letter. They should know where and how the dictionaries give information about capitalization.

LEARNING THE MEANING. Pupils need to develop the following skills for understanding the meaning of words through the use of a dictionary:

1. They should, when the word is used in context, be able to select the meaning that fits into the setting in which it is used.

2. They should be able to make effective use of the pictorial illustrations given for some words.

3. They should be able to make effective use of the verbal illustrations given, knowing which meaning of a word a given illustration fits.

4. They should understand information given about inflected forms.

5. They should know the interpretations of the symbols for the parts of speech they have studied.

6. They should know how to make use of information given about idiomatic expressions in which some words are commonly used.

7. They should understand what is meant by synonyms and antonyms, and they should know how the dictionaries they use give this type of information.

MAKING USE OF INFORMATION GIVEN IN THE PARTS THAT PRECEDE AND FOLLOW THE MAIN PART OF THE DICTIONARY. If there is an unabridged dictionary in the schoolroom, the teacher in a fifth or sixth grade may wish to introduce the pupils to some of the types of information given in the part preceding and following the main section of the dictionary. They will be interested to know that by turning to an unabridged dictionary they can find illustrations of flags of all the countries of the world, that the dictionary gives bibliographical data on important persons, and that it has a very helpful section dealing with geographical locations. Even some of the dictionaries designed for boys and girls in the elementary school contain materials of great value in the front and back portions. Familiarity with all the parts of one's own dictionary should be an objective that is accomplished some time during the elementary school.

Ability to Use Reference Books Other Than the Dictionary

Encyclopedias and other suitable reference materials for boys and girls can serve at least two very important purposes—that of helping the child gain needed information and that of opening for him a source of information that can continue to serve his needs throughout life. More and more schools are ordering for the various rooms in their school system sets of encyclopedias as well as other reference material. If there are no adequate reference books in an intermediate grade room, the teacher should discover whether some can be obtained for her classroom. However, even if the desired reference books are not available in the classroom, they may often be found either in school or public libraries. Some boys and girls have sets of encyclopedias or other reference books at home which they should utilize.

The quality of reference materials for boys and girls in the elementary school has greatly improved. There are the well-known *Compton's Pictured Encyclopedia, The World Book Encyclopedia, Junior Britannica,* and *Our Wonderful World.* One set of encyclopedias that is filling a real need for children in the primary and lower intermediate grades as well as for the teachers of those grades is *Childcraft,* published by Field Enterprises, Incorporated. All these encyclopedias give information on persons, places, and things, as well as on important events. An encyclopedia limited in scope, but excellent, is the *Junior Book of Authors,* written on a level that many boys and girls in the intermediate grades can comprehend. It contains biographies or autobiographies of the famous writers of books for children, illustrated with a picture of the writer. It also gives a list of the works of each author.

There are several types of reference materials other than encyclopedias or dictionaries that boys and girls in the upper elementary-school grades can learn to use effectively. One is the *World Almanac,* published yearly, which gives concise data, chiefly in the form of isolated facts, on a large variety of topics, such as government, sports, and industry. It is especially valuable for the statistics recorded in it. The child can find the answer to many questions of interest to him, like "What is the population of the United States?" or "Which is longer, the Mississippi River or the Congo River?" Parts of *Goode's School Atlas,* with its variety of types of maps, constitute an excellent supplement to maps given in geography books. Familiarity with the *Subject Index to Poetry,* if a copy of it is available, can also serve the needs of many boys and girls in the fifth and sixth grades. Many pupils in the intermediate grades would profit from an introduction to *Who's Who* and *Who's Who in America.*

In the first part of this chapter there is an enumeration of skills basic to the use of many types of reference material—for instance, ability to find words when they are arranged in alphabetical order, ability to use cross references, and ability to utilize information found in reference books. All of these skills are needed for effective use of encyclopedias and other specialized reference books. In addition to these skills pupils need the following in order to use materials of this type efficiently:

1. Knowledge of what is contained in the reference books.

2. Knowledge of the organization of the reference books.

3. Ability to decide in which reference book the desired information is likely to be found.

4. Skill in finding the information.

Ability to Locate Materials in the Library

In order to be able to locate materials effectively in a library the pupil needs to know how to use the card catalog, how to locate books on the shelves (if the library has open shelves, and how to use sources like the *Reader's Guide to Periodical Literature.* The help given in learning how to locate books in a library should be in terms of the library to which children have access. If none is located in the community, a miniature classroom library can serve as substitute.

Using the Card Catalog

Almost all libraries have card catalogs that serve as indexes to their book collections. Pupils should know that the term *card catalog* is applied to the collection of drawers in which are filed 3- by 5-inch cards which give data on all the books in the library. They should learn that the cards are arranged alphabetically in the drawers and that the progression of the drawers is from the top toward the bottom drawer of one stack of drawers to the top drawer in the next stack.

In order to have skill in the use of a card catalog, boys and girls must be familiar with the common types of cards used. They should know at least three of the cards that the card catalog contains—namely, the author card, the title card, and the subject card. They also need to know that on an author card the alphabetical arrangement is according to the last name of the author, on a title card according to the first significant word of the title, and on a subject card according to the subject of the book. The pupils should also realize that if an individual knows the first and last name of the author of a book, it is usually timesaving to look for the book under the author card. If the name of the author is not known, but the exact title is known, it is often expedient to look for the title card. If neither the name of the author nor the exact title is known, it is usually best to look for the subject card. The children should also learn that by means of the subject card they can find out what other books are available in the library on a given subject. These statements will seem quite obvious to the college student and the young teacher, but they often need to be explained to elementary school pupils.

Guidance should be given in observing the data found on all three types of cards. The terms *B* for *biography* and *J* for *juvenile,* if these are used, should also be explained. The pupils should learn the significance of the call number and the use they can make of it in locating a book in the library.

Finding Books on Shelves

If the library accessible to the child has open stacks, the pupil should learn something about the arrangement of the books.

Most small libraries use an adaptation of the Dewey Decimal System of Classification. If the library has that system of classification, the pupil should learn to use it. While pupils should not be asked to memorize the categories, they should have general familiarity with the system. The Dewey Decimal System employs the following number classifications:

000–099	General works, including bibliography and general periodicals
100–199	Philosophy, psychology, ethics
200–299	Religion, Bible, mythology
300–399	Sociology, economics, education, political science
400–499	Philology, dictionaries, grammars
500–599	Natural science, including mathematics, chemistry, physics
600–699	Applied science, including useful arts, medicine, agriculture, manufacturing
700–799	Fine arts, music, recreation
800–899	Literature
900–999	History, biography, travel

Using the Reader's Guide to Periodical Literature

Some boys and girls in the upper grades of the elementary school can be taught how to locate magazine articles by means of the *Reader's Guide to Periodical Literature*. The teacher, possibly with the help of the librarian, may decide to teach the child such facts as the following:

1. Where the *Reader's Guide to Periodical Literature* is located.
2. How often it is published.
3. Method of cumulation.
4. Type of information it contains.
5. Method of locating information in it.

Pupils should also find out where a list of the magazines the library has is posted and where both the bound and unbound periodicals are kept.

Principles Underlying the Teaching of Locational Skills

For teaching boys and girls how to acquire skill in locating information, there is a large variety of procedures from which to choose. They should be selected in terms of principles like the following:

1. *Readiness for a locational skill facilitates learning.* In part, readiness for this type of skill, as for other learnings, is a matter of maturation. However, to a considerable extent it is closely related to the experience background of the learner. Fortunately, the background of experience can be broadened, and the teacher is in a key position to help. No teacher needs to wait complacently for a child to become ready to learn how to locate material in print. Readiness can be achieved through a well-planned sequence of activities, preferably those which relate to problems which call for functional use of printed sources.

Readiness can also be thought of in terms of a felt need to learn a skill. Because of the role of purpose in arousing a state of readiness, the teacher should set the stage for the acquisition of the skill. She can do this either by making use of a situation or by creating one in which the child feels a need for a given skill. For example, if the class is uncertain as to the pronunciation of a word, an occasion could be provided for teaching how the pronunciation of a word is indicated in the dictionary. Or if the pupils are planning to make a list of the persons in the room, in connection with the assignment of responsibilities, the teacher may give the pupils instruction and practice in writing words in alphabetical order.

The optimum grade placement of a skill either for initial presentation or for practice purposes has not been ascertained. It is generally agreed, however, that although the bulk of the work in developing skill in locating information should be done in the intermediate grades, work in the primary grades can make a significant contribution in this area. In the first three grades, help can be given in locating some of the information that children wish to find in books and magazines. Furthermore, in the primary grades a stable foundation can be laid for skills that can be developed in the intermediate grades.

The following are some of the skills in locating information that are developed, at least in part, in many primary grades:

    a. Looking at the pictures to get an idea as to the content of a book.

    b. Noting the titles of stories as they appear in the main part of the book.

    c. Finding page numbers.

    d. Reading the titles of stories as listed in the table of contents.

    e. Looking at the titles of stories in order to see which ones are likely to deal with a given topic.

    f. Knowing where, in the room or school or public library, books of interest can be found.

    g. Learning alphabetical order.

    h. Arranging letters and words in alphabetical order.

    i. Knowing how to use a picture dictionary.

    j. Using a glossary in a textbook.

    k. Learning a few facts related to using a dictionary for children.

    l. Finding material and looking at pictures in an encyclopedia for younger children—for instance, *Childcraft.*

    m. Looking at pictures and getting information through the teacher's reading from encyclopedias like *Compton's Pictured Encyclopedia, The World Book Encyclopedia, Britannica Junior,* or *Our Wonderful World.*

    n. Getting information from atlases, yearbooks, and the *World Almanac.*

    2. *Opportunity should be provided to make use of skills learned.* Closely related to the problem of readiness for learning a skill is that of making use of what is learned. Since the pupil is, as a rule, more receptive to learning if he knows that he finds it of value, only those abilities of real worth to a child before he is an adult should be developed. Fortunately, many skills that are needed by adults are also important to children. By providing the child with opportunity to make real use of his skill, the teacher helps furnish the child with distributed practice, important in the learning of any skill.

The children should be stimulated to make use of the skills that they are acquiring and to recognize situations in which they can do so. The teacher can also lead discussions in which the group decides what use can be made of the skills. In addition, as the teacher sees boys and girls make application of the recently acquired skills, she can call such activities to the attention of the class. She can also encourage pupils themselves to report ways in which their new abilities proved helpful to them.

Since the skills to be learned should generally be limited to those which the pupils can use in the near future, the *Reader's Guide to Periodical Literature* should not be stressed in the teaching unless it is generally available to children. Of course, the teacher may explain to the pupils that such a guide exists, but detailed information on its use would under most circumstances be inappropriate.

3. *Provision should be made for evaluating skill in locating information.* One way of appraising the skill of intermediate grade boys and girls to locate information is by means of standardized tests. Unfortunately, most standardized reading tests for the elementary school do not test skill in locating information. Two of the tests that do devote sections to this skill are "The Iowa Silent Reading Test" and the "Iowa Every Pupil Tests."

The teacher can also appraise skill through more informal means, such as teacher-made tests, observation of pupils while doing practice exercises designed to develop skills in locating information, and observation of pupils when they look up information when not taking tests or doing practice exercises.

In making evaluations it is important to observe these criteria: (1) Evaluation should be made in terms of the objectives. To be sure, before a teacher begins instruction in locating information a survey test giving information on the pupil's abilities in a variety of locational skills may be given. (2) Both teacher and pupils should take part in evaluation procedures. If the pupil has a voice in planning the means of appraisal, he is more likely to try to improve in the skills that are being taught. Furthermore, his attitude toward the tests will probably be more favorable. (3) Evaluation should be a continuous process. It should not be confined to appraisal when work on a skill is begun and when the time to be spent on working on it systematically is ended. Throughout the period of learning, checks on the successfulness of the teaching and learning should be made.

4. *Systematic instruction should be given in the development of the locational skills.* While possibly for a small minority of the boys and girls in the elementary school no instruction beyond the incidental will be essential, in many instances even these children will profit from lessons definitely planned to help them acquire greater facility in the locational skills. For a large number of pupils, much floundering and inefficiency will result unless they are given direct help in the development of the ability to locate information. How these skills can be developed incidentally in the content subjects is discussed in part of Chapter 9B. To supplement such instruction, direct assistance can, and in most cases should, be given by providing presentation lessons in which the pupils are taught locational skills, and practice exercises in which they can strengthen their command of the skills. In the following chapter suggestions as to types of practices desirable are also given.

5. *Materials of instruction should fit the needs of the individuals.* Many teachers are not aware of the excellent materials that are available for the development of locational skills. Through the sensible application of the many suggestions given in the teachers' guides accompanying most of the basal text-book series in reading, the teacher can utilize many stories and articles in the reading books. Textbooks and workbooks in the language arts also frequently devote a sizable number of pages to the development of these skills. Of late some of the publishers of dictionaries for children have supplied exercises to help develop skill in the use of the dictionary.

9b

Developing
Ability To Locate Information

Anyone with ordinary intelligence and average reading ability should have no difficulty in acquiring the locational skills, but unfortunately, because of inadequate instruction, many persons who have graduated from high school are deficient in them. A teacher who puts into practice the principles set forth in the preceding chapter can do much to help pupils to attack their problems of finding information in printed materials successfully. The following pages will illustrate ways of putting these principles into effect.

Developing the Basic Skills

Basic to the development of skill in locating information in various types of books and magazines are skills in: (1) finding words in alphabetical order, (2) finding a given page in a book quickly, (3) deciding on key words, and (4) utilizing information gained.

Finding Words in Alphabetical Order

Finding words in lists arranged alphabetically is a basic skill in locating information. The following methods are illustrative of the means by which this skill may be developed:

1. Having the pupils memorize the letters in alphabetical order.

2. Writing the letters in alphabetical order on the board with some letters missing and asking the pupils to supply the missing letters.

3. Asking pupils to name or write the letter that immediately precedes or follows a given letter.

4. Having the pupils state in what part of the alphabet—first, middle, or last—given letters are found. Some teachers may prefer making the division of the alphabet into the first, second, third, and fourth quarters.

5. Having the pupils arrange letters in alphabetical order.

6. Asking the pupils to arrange in alphabetical order a series of words in which the first letters are different; in which the first and second letters are different; and in which the first three or more letters are different.

7. Explaining to the pupils that persons' names are usually listed according to the last names, and that when two or more persons have the same last name, their names are arranged according to the first names.

8. Asking the pupils to arrange in alphabetical order the names of the boys and girls in their class.

9. Explaining to the class that as the teacher shows each word card of a set, a pupil is to respond by naming a word beginning with the letter immediately preceding, in alphabetical order, the letter with which the word on the card begins. A variation of this procedure is to have a pupil give a word beginning with the letter immediately following, in alphabetical order, the letter with which the word on a given card begins.

10. Explaining to the pupils that on each page of the dictionary and in many other reference books two words known as guide words are given. The pupils should learn that the first guide word, written in the upper left-hand corner, designates the first entry word on that page and that the second guide word, usually appearing in the upper right-hand corner, indicates the last entry word on that page. They should also learn that looking at the guide words can help the reader to determine quickly which words are found on a given page.

11. Having the pupils indicate whether a given word comes between two stated guide words.

12. Asking the pupils to name words that are expected to be found as entry words on a page in the dictionary for which the guide words are stated.

13. Providing the pupils with a list of numbered sets of guide words from a dictionary, opposite which there is a list of words, arranged in a different order, each of which appears between one of the pairs of guide words. On the line to the right of each word in the second column the pupil writes the number of the matching guide words.

PRACTICE EXERCISES. Practice exercises can be used to advantage in teaching boys and girls to find words in alphabetical order. Samples of a few follow.

1

Explanation. Preparatory to finding words in alphabetical order is skill in knowing the arrangement of letters in alphabetical sequence.

Directions: Write the letters that come immediately before and after, in ABC order, each of the letters.

LETTERS

1. ____ t ____   2. ____ o ____
3. ____ f ____   4. ____ w ____
5. ____ d ____   6. ____ v ____
7. ____ q ____   8. ____ k ____

2

Directions: Supply the missing letters.

1. a ____ c d ____ f ____ g h ____
2. r s ____ u ____ w ____ y z

3

Directions: Write *yes* on the line to the left of each number if the words in that item are arranged in alphabetical order. Otherwise write *no*.

WORDS

____1. camel; cat; lion; fox
____2. bay; gulf; lake; ocean
____3. talk; tear; tease; take
____4. James; Jones; Johnson; Jacobson

4

Explanation. In providing pupils with practice in arranging words in alphabetical order, the easiest type of exercise is one in which the first letters of the words are different. More difficult is an exercise in which only some of the first letters of the words are different, so that the alphabetical order of the word needs to be determined in part by the second letter of the words; still more difficult is an exercise in which the third and fourth letters of a word help to determine the alphabetical order. In the exercise that follows the third letter of *bluebirds* and *blackbirds* determines which word comes first.

Directions: Write *1* to the left of the word that should come first in alphabetical order, *2* to the left of the word that should come second, and so on.

_____bluebirds   _____doves
_____blackbirds   _____chickadees
_____bobwhites   _____cardinals
_____ducks   _____cranes

5

Directions: Each of the following lists of names are in alphabetical order. Number the words as they should appear if the two lists were to be combined into one alphabetical list:

_____Albright, Marian
_____Ayres, Harold
_____Fleischer, Susan
_____Fleming, Gertrude
_____Manton, Cecil
_____Meier, Roberta
_____Otto, Charles
_____Owen, James
_____Spoerr, Geraldine
_____Staples, Daniel

_____Alexander, Marjorie
_____Douda, Helen
_____Foster, Arthur
_____Gordon, Evelyn
_____Miller, John
_____Nelson, Nels
_____Nelson, Samuel

_____Sutton, Maria
_____Wright, Jean
_____Young, Richard

6

Directions: On one page of a dictionary the guide words are *Nashville* and *nature.* Write *yes* to the right of the following words that you would expect to find on that page. Write *no* to the right of the others.

LIST OF WORDS

1. narrow_____   6. net_____
2. nail_____   7. neck_____
3. nature_____   8. needle_____
4. nation_____   9. nurse_____
5. name_____   10. navy_____

Finding a Given Page in a Book Quickly

Pupils can be given help in quickly finding a given page in books of various types by means of activities like the following:

1. Telling the pupils in the first grade where to find page numbers in a book.

2. Teaching the pupils how to turn the pages of a book.

3. Having the pupils try to open a book as near as possible to a given page before they begin turning pages.

4. Giving the pupils practice in finding a given page quickly by having them keep a record during a short period of time of how many attempts they had to make before getting the right page.

5. Having the pupils estimate to which page you have opened a book.

Deciding on Key Words

One of the more difficult locational skills is to decide on the key words under which certain information can be found. Through a progression of activities from the less to the more difficult and from the known to the unknown, this ability can be developed.

Some methods that can prove helpful in developing this skill are:

1. Asking the pupils to tell under what key word in an index a reference may be found for a question such as "In what year did George Washington become president of the United States?"

2. Providing the boys and girls with an exercise in which they will choose the one of three or four words under which a reference is the most likely to be listed that gives information on a stated topic.

3. Having the pupils explain the relevancy of cross references to the subject matter being read.

PRACTICE EXERCISE. This sample shows one of the ways in which practice in deciding upon key words can be provided. The value of such an exercise can usually be greatly increased if the pupils are given a chance to discuss their reasons for making their selections.

Directions: Draw a line under the word or group of words in parentheses which you would choose as the most likely key word in an index to give information about the question.

QUESTIONS

1. In what year did George Washington become president of the United States? (Washington; George; president; United States)

2. In what year did the Mexican War, which was fought between the United States and Mexico, begin? (wars; Mexican War; United States; Mexico)

3. What were the provisions of the Kansas-Nebraska Bill? (Kansas-Nebraska Bill; Nebraska; provisions; bill)

Discovering What Types of Information Are Given in Various Kinds of Books

As each new type of reference book is introduced, help should be given to the boys and girls to decide what type of information they should look for in it. Possible procedures are:

1. Encouraging the pupils to look through the various parts of a reference book to find out what information it contains.

2. Having the pupils make a chart to indicate in what reference books they would try to locate information on specific problems.

3. Asking the pupils in what reference books they would look if they wanted stated types of information—for instance, data on the life of Hans Christian Andersen.

4. Having the pupils look up data on a given topic in a variety of books to compare the type of information given in each.

5. Asking the pupils to read parts of the table of contents or index of several reference books, and to note the various types of information given.

6. Explaining the differences between an encyclopedia and a dictionary.

7. Asking the pupils when giving reports to tell from what references they received their information if reference books were consulted.

8. Providing the pupils with opportunity to report on any topic of interest to them on which they found information in a reference book and to state what reference book they consulted.

9. Having a "quiz program" based on information found in reference books. It would be helpful, in some instances, to have the pupils indicate in which reference book the answer to each question was found.

10. Explaining the means used to keep a reference book up-to-date, such as supplements to encyclopedias.

PRACTICE EXERCISE. After the boys and girls have had experiences in learning what types of information are given in various kinds of books, they might do an exercise similar to the following. The books listed should be those with which the pupils are familiar.

Monkmeyer Press
Photo Service
The game is the thing.
Early experiences with
the printed word
should be fun (left)

Cedar City, Utah,
Public Schools
The story chart helps
to build reading
vocabulary (below)

Directions: Below the questions is a list of different kinds of books that are lettered from (a) through (g). On the line to the right of each question, write the letter or letters given to the books in which you would expect to find an answer to the question.

QUESTIONS

1. What was the population of Delaware, Ohio, during the past year? _____

2. What were the chief exports of France during the past year? _____
_____

3. How often should a person clean his teeth? _____

4. What causes a dental cavity? _____
_____

5. What is the origin of the word *belfry*?
_____

6. What part of speech is the word *produce* when the accent is on the second syllable? _____

BOOKS

a. *Compton's Pictured Encyclopedia*
b. *The World Almanac*
c. *Junior Book of Authors*
d. *Reader's Guide to Periodical Literature*
e. a dictionary
f. an atlas
g. a hygiene book

Interpreting Punctuation Marks, Diacritical Marks, Abbreviations, and Symbols

Since in indexes, dictionaries, and other reference books punctuation marks are used in different ways, and since the abbreviations and symbols used vary somewhat from one book to another, it is suggested that, although there are common problems, most work on this topic be taken up as each new reference book is studied. The following are ways in which these interpretative skills can be developed:

1. Helping the pupils find out how syllabication of words is indicated in their own

dictionaries and how the hyphen between compound words is written.

2. Asking the pupils to look up in the dictionary words like *bluejay, Sunday school,* and *good-bye* to find out which are hyphenated.

3. Helping the pupils to find the key to the diacritical marks, abbreviations, and symbols used in a reference book.

4. Providing practice in pronouncing words according to the respelling indicated in a dictionary.

5. Helping the pupils learn how division into syllables is shown in their dictionaries and asking them to divide words into syllables after consulting a dictionary.

6. Providing practice in interpreting accent marks by having pupils pronounce words that are not always accented in the same way, like *pres' ent* and *pre sent'*.

7. Asking the pupils to give words illustrating the various sounds of letters and of letter combinations like *a, e, c, th*.

8. Teaching the abbreviations for words commonly used and then testing the pupils on them.

9. Explaining to the group that when a word has two correct pronunciations, both are usually indicated in a dictionary, and that if one is preferred, that is given first. Also, however, it should be pointed out that it must not be taken for granted that if there are two pronunciations given, the second one is not as desirable as the first, for the two may be equally desirable.

10. Explaining to the boys and girls that if every letter in the alphabet stood for but one sound and every sound were represented by but one letter, there would probably be no need to have the pronunciation of a word indicated in a dictionary.

11. Helping the boys and girls discover that one and only one vowel sound is heard in each syllable. The pupils might give the vowel sound in each syllable of a group of words listed on the chalkboard.

Selecting Points That Have Bearing on a Given Problem

After the necessary reference pages have been located, skill in selecting points that have bearing on a given problem can be developed through various activities, such as:

1. Asking the class questions that are phrased in words similar to those used in the text that serve as an answer to them and asking questions when the answers are not phrased in the same way.

2. Asking the pupils to find the answer to a question or a direction like the following, in which the answer consists of two or more sentences referred to in various parts of a paragraph: "Name three reasons why many cranberries are produced in Massachusetts."

3. Providing practice in formulating problems, so that the pupils know specifically what information they are looking for. This might be done by having the boys and girls write the question or questions that they want answered.

4. Providing practice in skimming by having the pupils read as rapidly as possible, while they are being timed, a selection to spot certain words, sentences, or thoughts.

5. Asking the pupils to list items they would expect to find under a certain topic.

PRACTICE EXERCISE. To provide practice in deciding which points have bearing on a given problem, the teacher might ask the pupils to write an *x* on the line to the left of each sentence that gives information on the topic stated.

1. Topic. How to make molds of footprints

_____a. Before making a mold, clean the footprints.

_____b. Detectives often study the footprints of human beings.

_____c. Plaster of Paris can be used to make a mold.

_____d. The footprint should be thoroughly dry before the plaster of Paris is poured into it.

2. Topic. Where the robin migrates in winter

_____a. The robin is larger than the house wren.

_____b. Robins usually breed more than once during a season.

_____c. In the winter robins fly as far south as Mexico.

_____d. Robins stay in the northern states till November.

Utilizing Information Gained

After the exact information needed has been located, skill in utilizing it can be acquired through activities like the following:

1. Having the pupils judge whether a statement is reliable by considering who wrote it or in what book it appeared.

2. Giving the pupils practice in deciding which of a series of statements are relevant to their problem.

3. Having the pupils compile a bibliography of information helpful on a topic.

4. Providing opportunity for the pupils to give a talk or write a paper on information they have gathered.

5. Giving the pupils opportunity to explain to others what they learned, by putting on puppet shows or making friezes or "movies."

6. After the pupils have looked up a topic in an encyclopedia, giving them time to write a small number of interesting and significant facts that they learned and then having others in the class read these sentences.

7. Giving the pupils an opportunity to compare facts read in an encyclopedia with their own experiences.

8. Having pupils compare the information on a given subject gained from one encyclopedia with that on the same topic in another encyclopedia.

Developing Skill in Using Nonreference Books

Skill in using the various parts of a book for locating information can be acquired by means of the following methods:

1. Having the pupils examine the various parts of a book to find out where they are located, what they contain, and how the data given in them are arranged.

2. Providing practice for the pupils in examining the preface of a book to see if the book is likely to contain information needed on a given topic.

3. Having the pupils find answers to questions about the various parts of a book, such as "What is the purpose of the preface?"

4. Helping the pupils make a chart on which they list the important points to remember about each part of a book, such as "The index is found in the back part of the book."

5. Even in the first grade, having the pupils turn to the table of contents of their reader to find the page of the story they will read.

6. Giving the pupils the opportunity to answer questions like the following as they examine the table of contents in their textbook in the social studies: "How many chapters are there in the book?" or "In which chapter would you expect to find information about the fire department?"

7. Through examination of the table of contents of several books, having the pupils make a list of books in which information is given on a topic in which they are interested.

8. Asking the pupils to tell the chief differences between a glossary and a dictionary.

9. Explaining to the boys and girls the meaning of the word *appendix*.

10. Having the pupils look up cross references quickly.

11. After making and distributing dupli-cate copies of a table of contents and an index, asking the pupils questions answered in these.

12. When discussing a place of special interest, having the pupils look in the index of their geography books to find out where, if at all, it is shown on a map in these books.

13. Having the pupils make a table of contents and an index for a class notebook they are making—one on "Famous Modern Americans," for example.

14. Helping the boys and girls write a preface for a class notebook on a topic such as "Autobiographies of Boys and Girls in Our Fifth Grade." They could also include in it an appendix giving name, date of birth, and place of birth of each pupil.

15. Having the pupils compile a list of words that have interesting origins (*neighbor* is such a word) and letting them explain the etymology of these words to the class. An illustrated chart might be made to help the pupils remember the information.

Practice Exercises

These three samples of exercises show how practice exercises can be used to develop skill in locating information in nonreference books:

1

Although work on the table of contents can be begun in the first and second grades, in these lower grades, as a rule, the work should be done only as it is a help in finding an entry in the table of contents. In the intermediate grades, however, exercises such as the following can be used. Since the questions are based on the table of contents given in *New Streets and Roads*,[1] if this specific exercise were used each pupil

---

[1] William S. Gray, A. Sterl Artley, and May Hill Arbuthnot, *New Streets and Roads*. Chicago: Scott, Foresman and Company, 1952.

would have to have access to a copy of this reader. The exercise can, of course, be adapted for use with any reader.

Directions: This exercise is to help you learn to make good use of a table of contents in a book. Find and write the answers to these questions by using the table of contents of *New Streets and Roads.* Your teacher will time you as you do this exercise.

QUESTIONS

1. Into how many main parts are the stories divided? _____

2. What is the first word of the first story listed in the part on "Animals in Town and Country"? _____

3. Who wrote the story "A Halloween Surprise"? _____

4. On what page does the story "Paddle Tail" begin? _____

5. On what page does a story about deer begin? _____

Directions: Draw a line under the correct word or group of words in parentheses.

1. The index of a book is arranged (alphabetically; by chapters; in the order in which the points are taken up in the book).

2. The preface is found in the (front; middle; back) part of the book.

3. The glossary (tells the purpose of the author in writing the book; gives the list of chapters in a book; gives the pronunciation and meaning of some of the words used in the book).

4. The table of contents is arranged (alphabetically; by chapters; in the order in which the points are taken up in the book).

Developing Skill in Using the Dictionary

Some procedures that can help in the development of skills essential to the effective

2

Directions: To help you find out what types of material are found in appendixes of books, study the appendixes of five books and fill out the following form.

1. *Name of author:* _____ *Title:* _____
   Type of materials: _____
   _____

2. *Name of author:* _____ *Title:* _____
   Type of materials: _____
   _____

3. *Name of author:* _____ *Title:* _____
   Type of materials: _____
   _____

3

After the boys and girls have studied the parts of a book, a list of questions similar to the following might be used as a means of review and evaluation.

use of the dictionary are listed earlier in this chapter under "Finding Words in Alphabetical Order," on page 211, and under "Interpreting Punctuation Marks, Abbreviations, and Symbols," on page 215. Additional ones are given here.

1. Providing practice in deciding which inflectional forms are likely to be treated as distinct words in a dictionary and given separate entries and which forms are likely to be treated as run-on entries.

2. Having the pupils make a list of the types of information given for an entry word.

3. Providing practice in which the pupils select from a dictionary the meaning of a word that is appropriate in a given context.

4. Providing practice in looking up the spelling of a word in the dictionary by helping the pupils decide on probable spellings of it and then looking for these in the dictionary.

5. Providing practice in pronouncing words that according to the dictionary have two correct pronunciations.

6. Helping the pupils really learn the meanings of words they look up, so that they are not satisfied with knowing a synonym without knowing the shade of difference in meaning between the two synonyms.

7. Providing the pupils with sentences in each of which a word is in italics and asking the boys and girls to restate each sentence without using the italicized word. An example of such a sentence is: "The boys and girls did not *anticipate* a big crowd."

8. Providing practice in using the abbreviations and arbitrary signs in the dictionary.

9. Helping the pupils discover how the thumb index may help them in locating a word.

10. Having a pupil from one of two teams into which the class is divided give two guide words from a page in a dictionary and write them on the chalkboard while a pupil from the other team names a word that would be expected to be found on that page of the dictionary and writes it on the board. This practice could be provided in somewhat the same way that spelldowns are sometimes conducted.

11. Providing practice in finding out through the dictionary the possible parts of speech of a word like *effect* and in using it in those ways in sentences.

12. Giving help in finding the various definitions of a word that may be used as different parts of speech, like *effect* as a noun or as a verb.

13. Asking the pupils to find the answers to questions like the following through using the dictionary: "Are the American robin and the European robin alike?"

14. Having the pupils make a composite list of sentences illustrating all the meanings of a word of which they can think or which they can find in a dictionary, like "I can *run* fast" or "I have a *run* in my stocking."

15. Having the pupils explain with the help of the dictionary the meanings of words that are homonyms and then having them use the words in sentences.

16. Asking the pupils to look up the meaning of the words *prefix* and *suffix* and then asking them to learn the meaning of common prefixes and suffixes.

17. Having the pupils give words containing common prefixes and suffixes.

18. Asking the pupils to look up in the dictionary a list of words often mispronounced, like *handkerchief*, and giving them practice in pronouncing them correctly.

19. Having the pupils make their own picture dictionaries or make one as a class project.

20. Asking the pupils to look up words like the following to find out which should begin with a capital letter, whatever their use in a sentence may be: *river, history, Bible, Indian.*

21. Having the pupils find the meaning of words that are often confused—for example, *suppose* and *expect.*

22. Teaching the pupils the most frequently used rules for syllabication and having them divide words according to these rules and check their work in the dictionary.

23. Helping the children get meaning from illustrations in a dictionary by asking them questions about the picture or by having them explain how a given picture supplements the verbal explanation.

24. Drawing the attention of the pupils to aspects of an illustration that give an indication of the size of what is pictured.

Practice Exercises

The following are six samples of exercises for developing skill in using the dictionary.

1

Directions: Decide in which part of the dictionary you would look for each of the following words. Write a *B* (for Beginning) if it is found near the beginning of the dictionary. Write an *M* if it is found near the middle and an *E* if it is found near the end.

1. shoemaker _____   4. theater _____
2. memory _____   5. discovery _____
3. correct _____   6. whales _____

2

Directions: Look up in your dictionary the following list of words which are often mispronounced. On the line to the right of each write the respelling of the word with markings, including the accent, as given in the dictionary. Your teacher may give you an opportunity to pronounce some of the words to your classmates.

1. athletic _____
2. adult _____
3. handkerchief _____
4. little _____
5. often _____
6. library _____

3

Directions: To the right of each sentence write the spelling of the italicized (or underlined) word. If necessary, consult your dictionary to get the correct spelling.

1. I think that this trip was really *necess_ry.* _____
2. Did you *rec_ve* my message? _____
3. The boys and girls will leave in two *sep_rate* groups. _____

4

Directions: Some of the following compound words, which are here divided into syllables, should be separated by a hyphen and others should not. Consult your dictionary before you write the words correctly on the lines left for the purpose. Study the spelling of the words so that you can write them if your teacher dictates them to you.

1. an y bod y _____
2. green house _____
3. out of date _____
4. sis ter in law _____
5. shell fish _____
6. steam ship _____
7. two edged _____
8. ex pres i dent _____

5

Directions: Here are some of the meanings and illustrations given for the word *way* in a dictionary.[2] (1) manner; style: *Mary is wearing her hair in a new way.* (2) means; method: *Men of science are trying to find ways to prevent disease.* (3) respects; particulars: *The plan is bad in several ways.* (4) direction: *Look this way.* (5) coming or going; progress: *The beggar made his way from door to door.* (6) distance: *The moon is a long way off.* (7) path; road: *The hunter found a way through the forest.* (8) space for passing or going ahead: *Automobiles must make way for a fire engine.* (9) habit; custom:

[2] Edward L. Thorndike and Clarence L. Barnhart, eds., *Thorndike-Barnhart Junior Dictionary.* Chicago: Scott, Foresman and Company, 1952.

Don't mind Joe's teasing; it's only his way.
(10) one's wish; will: *A spoiled child wants his own way all the time.*

Use the word *way* in ten sentences to show each of the ten meanings given above.

1. _____
2. _____
3. _____
4. _____
5. _____
6. _____
7. _____
8. _____
9. _____
10. _____

6

Directions: Look up the answers to the following questions in your dictionary and answer them by writing *yes* or *no* on the line to the left of the questions. On the line to the right of each question write the page in your dictionary on which you found the answer.

_____1. Did the English obtain the Magna Carta from King Alfred?_____

_____2. Should the word *English* always begin with a capital letter? _____

_____3. Can the word *affect* be used as a noun? _____

_____4. Is *gotten* a word? _____

_____5. Is it correct to place the accent on the second syllable in *theater?* _____

Developing Skill in Using Reference Books Other Than the Dictionary

Skills needed in order to locate material in reference books other than the dictionary can be developed through activities like the following:

1. Providing opportunity to use as many as possible of the following reference books: *Childcraft, Compton's Pictured Encyclopedia,* the *World Book Encyclopedia, Junior Britannica, Our Wonderful World,* the *Junior Book of Authors,* the *Index to Poetry,* the *World Almanac,* and a standard atlas.

2. Having the pupils answer a list of questions, the answers to which are to be found in one or more of the reference books listed in the preceding item.

3. Having the pupils give information found on one or more of the maps contained in an atlas to which they have access.

4. Asking the pupils to tell in which volume of a set of encyclopedias information on a specified topic would be likely to be given. For this purpose the information on the labels on the back of the encyclopedias should be written on the board or duplicated on paper.

5. Showing the pupils the filmstrip, "How to Use an Encyclopedia."[3]

6. Explaining the use of the index volume of a set of encyclopedias and providing the pupils with practice in using it.

7. Providing the pupils with a list of topics on which they are to check those that are likely to be found in an encyclopedia.

8. Giving the pupils a list of questions to answer in one word or a few words after consulting an encyclopedia.

Practice Exercises

The following are two of the many types of practice exercises that can be used in order to develop skill in using reference books.

1

Directions: Find the answers to these questions in the *World Almanac.*

1. Is the population of the village, town, or city in which you are living given in the

---

[3] "How to Use an Encyclopedia." New York: Popular Science Publishing Company.

World Almanac? If so, what was it according to the last edition of the *World Almanac?*

2. Where was Thomas Edison born?
_____

3. What is the state flower of Minnesota?
_____

4. What state leads in the production of cotton? _____

5. When was Florida admitted to the Union? _____

6. What is the state bird of Ohio? _____

7. In what building did Abraham Lincoln die? _____

2

Directions: Below each entry taken from the *Reader's Guide to Periodical Literature* are given some parts of the entry. On the lines provided explain what each means or represents.

1. *Entry:* Another spring project: birdhouse building. S. Miller. il Audubon Mag 57:94 Mr '55
   a. Another spring project: birdhouse building _____
   b. S. Miller _____
   c. il _____
   d. Audubon Mag _____
   e. 57 _____
   f. 94 _____
   g. Mr _____
   h. '55 _____

2. *Entry:* ABC's of flower arrangement. F. Hullenlocher. il Bet Hom & Gard 24: 62-5 Je; 74-7 Jl '56
   a. F. _____
   b. 62-5 _____
   c. 74-7 _____

Developing Skill in Locating Material in the Library

Some procedures effective in learning to locate material in the library are:

1. Taking the children on a trip to the library.

2. Helping the pupils to draw a diagram showing the location of materials in their library.

3. Displaying and explaining to the children a chart giving the Dewey Decimal System of Classification if that method of classification is used in their library.

4. Asking the pupils to write a subject card, an author card, and a title card as you give them the necessary bibliographical data on a book.

5. Asking the pupils to list the facts given in a card catalog in addition to the author and title of a book.

6. Asking the pupils to suggest subjects under which they may be able to find on a subject card references to the answer to a given question, such as "What was travel like in the country in 1865?"

7. Having the pupils put on a skit which illustrates "do's and don't's" of library behavior.

8. Having a pupil act as librarian and explain to his audience the meaning and use of a call number.

9. Explaining to the boys and girls the plan of cumulation followed in the *Reader's Guide to Periodical Literature* and having them find entries on articles included in various volumes.

10. Asking the pupils to explain every part of an entry found in the *Reader's Guide to Periodical Literature*.

11. Helping the pupils make a card catalog of the books in their own room library. Guide cards should be included in the catalog and "See also" cards.

12. Having the pupils gather from reference books information needed for work on a unit in science or social studies.

13. Providing time for pupils to examine and read various magazines in the library and then to give reports on them.

Practice Exercises

1

Directions: Find the answer to the following questions by consulting the card catalog in your library.

1. What is the call number of the book *Heidi?* _____

2. What books written by the author of *The Singing Tree* are in your library?_____
_____

3. What is the title and call number of a book in your library on early pioneer life?
_____

4. What facts other than the title and author are given on the subject card for the book *Little Women?* _____
_____
_____

2

After the pupils have finished the following exercises, opportunity should be provided for their checking the correctness of their answers by consulting the card catalog.

Directions: What is a broader subject under which you might find a reference listed in your card catalog on each of the following subjects?

1. Thomas Edison _____
2. Description of Yellowstone National Park _____
3. Tennis _____
4. Recipes for cakes _____
5. The settlers of Plymouth, Massachusetts _____

3

The pupils could be given a diagram of the library they are using which shows the location of the various stacks and tables and racks where books or magazines are kept. The various positions should be numbered so that the pupils can refer to them by number. Make certain that the pupils understand the diagram.

Directions: On the diagram showing the arrangement of your library, the bookshelves and tables are numbered. Answer the following questions by writing the number of the bookshelf or table used in the diagram. If you do not know the answer to a question, study the arrangement of the library before you try to write an answer.

1. Where are the books for the very young children kept? _____
2. Where are the books on biography kept? _____
3. On what table are some of the newest books for boys and girls placed? _____
4. Where are books on American history placed? _____
5. Where are the encyclopedias for boys and girls kept? _____

Developing Locational Skills in Reading in the Content Subjects

The content subjects afford excellent opportunity for teaching skill in locating information. They serve two types of purposes in that they present situations which require knowledge of how to locate information, thereby furnishing an incentive for learning, and they can provide practice needed for perfecting a skill that is being learned.

In unit work carried on in the social studies and science many situations arise in which the need for locational skills becomes evident and in which practice in improving these skills can be provided through finding information needed for the solution of problems that arise in the work. The descriptions that are given in this chapter show how locational skills can be developed in unit work in both the primary and intermediate grades.

Development of Locational Skills in a Unit on Community Helpers

Even in a unit planned for the primary grades many locational skills can be developed as problems that arise in connection with the unit are being solved. As the possibilities for the development of the locational skills in connection with a unit on community helpers are discussed, it is important for the teacher to bear in mind that only those activities dealing with locational skills should be performed that really help toward the accomplishment of the objectives set for the work on the unit. If more work on any of the skills is needed than is provided by activities that help attain the objectives of the unit, this practice should usually be given at other times through exercises and lessons specifically designed for the development of these skills. Otherwise it is probable that the work on the problem of study will lack the unity which the very name *unit* implies.

The following list of activities shows some ways in which a unit on community helpers can help develop skill in locating information.

1. The boys and girls could place in a file mounted pictures of community helpers. The pictures could be arranged alphabetically by groups, with those of firemen preceding those of postmen, because the *f* of *firemen* precedes the *p* of *postmen*. Guide cards could be made similar to those used in a card catalog.

2. The pupils could look for books on the various community helpers they are studying.

3. They could examine the table of contents of some of the books on community helpers to find out on what page information is given on a helper.

4. The members of a committee or one individual could look for information in a book that will give them the answer to a specific question, such as "What does a fireman do when he hears a fire alarm?"

5. They could compile a list, arranged in alphabetical order according to the last name of the author, of books on community helpers. They could do this on 3-by-5-inch cards to be filed or on sheets of paper on which they could list a number of references.

6. Before drawing pictures for a "movie" or a frieze on community helpers they could look in books for pictures that would give them some needed background information.

7. As a group project they could make a picture dictionary containing new words learned while working on the unit.

8. For a booklet that the group could make, the pupils could write a table of contents, a preface, and an appendix. In the appendix they might give information like this: (a) a table showing the work of each of the helpers studied; (b) a picture of each community helper, showing the type of uniform or clothes he wears; and (c) a diagram showing where the helpers in the community work. This diagram could indicate, for example, the location of the post office, the fire station, bakeries, and police headquarters.

9. The more mature pupils could find information that deals with the topic in *Compton's Pictured Encyclopedia* or the *World Book Encyclopedia*. Younger ones could find information in *Childcraft*.

10. As the pupils notice that the teacher finds information in encyclopedias, they can learn some of the uses of these books.

11. Skill in learning to make use of information located can be provided as the boys and girls give talks to their classmates or others about what they have read.

12. The pupils could be helped to find in their picture dictionary the spelling of words needed for writing.

13. They could look for poems useful for the unit and make an index of poems found.

14. They could collect songs about community helpers and make a file showing in which books the songs are printed.

15. They could get help in interpreting charts and graphs that are of value in connection with the unit and show graphically such data as (a) the number of milkmen, policemen, postmen, firemen, bakers, and doctors in the community; (b) the number in each of the categories of community helpers who are fathers or mothers of the boys and girls in the room; and (c) the increase in number of firemen in the community during various intervals during the last century. Pictorial graphs could be made to show some of the suggested data.

Development of Locational Skills in a Unit on the Western States

Skill in the location of information can be developed in a large variety of situations in connection with a unit on the Western States, work typically taken up in the fifth or sixth grade. The following ways in which locational skills can be learned in such a unit will, it is hoped, be suggestive of many others:

1. A committee of boys and girls could look up material in history books other than the textbook and in encyclopedias, preparatory to putting on a skit on an interesting episode in the settlement of the West. Topics might be the work of Sacajawea, the building of the first transcontinental railroad, traveling westward by covered wagon, or the discovery of gold in California. An activity of this type could provide the boys and girls with practice in such locational skills as the following: (a) clarifying the problem that they wish to look up; (b) deciding in what books to look for information; (c) learning to locate the books they wish to use; (d) using the table of contents; (e) deciding on possible key words and looking for these words in an index or in an encyclopedia; (f) locating the information needed on a page; (g) making an outline of the information gathered from various sources; (h) and using the outline to prepare the skit.

2. The pupils could make a collection of pictures dealing with the Far West and file them alphabetically, using guide cards to indicate their position in a filing drawer.

3. Individuals, committees, or an entire class could make a notebook on some phase of the Western States and include in it a preface, an introduction, an appendix, and an index. Some topics that might be chosen are beauty spots of the West, the opening of the West, the coming of the missionaries, and famous men and women in the settling of the West. A few suggestions for the content of appendix pages are: (a) a list of important dates; (b) a page giving brief bibliographical data about the famous people connected with the Far West; and (c) a sheet giving data in tabular form about the national parks of the West.

4. Many locational skills could be used in making a frieze showing the means of communication used in pioneer days of the West: wagon, clipper ship, stagecoach, pony express, overland stage, railroad, and telegraph. These are some of the locational skills that could be used in a project of this type: (a) finding pictures of the various means of communication; (b) using encyclopedias and other history and geography books for wide reading; (c) selecting the points that have bearing on a given problem; (d) finding the dates when a given means of communication was used so that the correct sequence of events will be known; and (e) making use of the information found.

5. A large variety of locational skills could be used in giving a talk on topics on the Western States like the following: any one of the states of this section of the country; famous pioneers, such as John C. Frémont, Kit Carson, John McLoughlin, Marcus and Narcissa Whitman, and Buffalo Bill; and important events, such as the discovery of gold in California.

6. The pupils coud make a card file of books of value in connection with the study of the West. They could make subject cards, title cards, and author cards. Guide cards, similar to those used in the card catalog, could also be made.

7. When drawing pictures to show, for instance, the life history of a salmon, they could consult various textbooks and reference books—for example, encyclopedias, *The World Almanac,* an atlas, and history and geography books.

8. Making an illustrated dictionary of words and phrases learned while studying the unit could involve such locational skills as: (a) arranging words in alphabetical order; (b) looking words up in a dictionary or other reference books; (c) finding illustrations of the terms; and (d) using a dictionary to find out the spelling of words.

9. If a pageant or play were given showing, as a culminating activity, the development of the Western States, each of the various skills named earlier in this chapter in the classification of skills could be used— namely, (a) finding words in alphabetical order, as the pupils locate words in an index or encyclopedia; (b) finding quickly a given page in a book; (c) deciding on key words under which needed information might be expected to be found; (d) deciding on the type of book in which needed information would be likely to be found; (e) interpreting punctuation marks, diacritical marks, abbreviations, and symbols used in the various references; (f) selecting points that have bearing on a given problem; (g) utilizing information gained; (h) using the parts of the usual type of book, like preface, introduction, main part, index, appendix, and glossary; (i) using encyclopedias, dictionaries, and other reference books; and (j) locating material in the library.

FOR FURTHER STUDY

Cleary, Florence Damon, *Blueprints for Better Reading*, pp. 177–203. New York: The H. W. Wilson Company, 1957.

Dolch, E. W., *Psychology and Teaching of Reading*, 2d ed., pp. 415–479. Champaign, Ill.: The Garrard Publishing Company, 1951.

Gray, William S., *On Their Own in Reading*, pp. 200–242. Chicago: Scott, Foresman and Company, 1960.

Hester, Kathleen B., *Teaching Every Child to Read*, pp. 238–254. New York: Harper and Row, Publishers, 1955.

Hildreth, Gertrude, *Teaching Reading*, pp. 497–501. New York: Holt, Rinehart and Winston, Inc., 1958.

McKee, Paul, *The Teaching of Reading in the Elementary School*, pp. 425–457. Boston: Houghton Mifflin Company, 1948.

McKim, Margaret G., and Helen Caskey, *Guiding Growth in Reading in the Modern Elementary School*, pp. 363–376. New York: The Macmillan Company, 1963.

Wagner, Guy, and Max Hosier, *Reading Games*. Darien, Conn.: Teachers Publishing Corporation, 1960.

10a

Oral Reading

Fifty years ago, reading instruction in most elementary schools was instruction in oral reading. Numerous educators had, indeed, called attention to the sterility of the exclusively oral approach. Thus Edmund B. Huey wrote in 1908:

> Reading as a school exercise has almost always been thought of as reading aloud, in spite of the obvious fact that reading in actual life is to be mainly silent reading. The consequent attention to reading as an exercise in speaking . . . has been heavily at the expense of reading as the art of thought-getting. . . .[1]

In this statement he confirmed the views of earlier educational leaders like Horace Mann and Francis W Parker. It was not until the early 1920's, however, that a widespread shift of emphasis from oral to silent reading took place. In this period a great quantity of published materials, including a yearbook of the National Study for the Study of Education, numerous research reports, textbooks on the teaching of reading, reading manuals, and series of basal readers, stressed the need for instruction in silent reading.[2]

The arguments in favor of silent as against oral reading were based chiefly upon two considerations: (1) Most reading outside of school is silent reading and (2) Silent reading emphasizes meaning rather than sound. Psychologists of many schools—behaviorist, gestalt, organismic, and others—were concerned with the ways in which communication takes place between the writer and the

---

[1] *The Psychology and Pedagogy of Reading*, p. 359. New York: The Macmillan Company, 1908.

[2] Ada V. Hyatt, *The Place of Oral Reading in the School Program*. New York: Bureau of Publications, Teachers College, Columbia University, 1943.

reader. Experimentation with various methods of teaching reading, and the rise of the tests and measurements movement further strengthened the trend toward silent reading instruction.

The Values of Oral Reading

All this is not to say that the schools should neglect instruction in oral reading. It may be true that not more than one percent of out-of-school reading is oral, but frequency of use is not the sole determiner of emphasis upon any one skill. Such factors as the value of a skill and the relative difficulty of mastering it also play a part in any decision as to what is to be included in the curriculum. Oral reading is a valuable skill, one that is not automatically learned in an effective program of silent reading instruction. Rather, it requires specific attention on the part of the teacher.

Some examples of the uses of oral reading in school and everyday life are contained in a useful compilation by Hyatt:

1. Reading orally to present information toward the solution of a problem.
    a. Reading notes from newspapers, magazines, and pamphlets about some subject of interest when this particular topic is being discussed.
    b. Reading the area figures of certain states to people when the relative size of these states is desired.
2. Reading aloud to inform an audience or to provide general knowledge.
    a. Reading an informational news item or magazine article to others.
    b. Reading a speech on some topic to a group.
    c. Reading current events to others.
3. Reading aloud to clarify meanings.
    a. Reading material from a pamphlet, newspaper, magazine, or book to contribute information about the importance of some product in the world today.
    b. Pooling information on a particular subject from a variety of sources.
    c. Reading to contribute information needed in the production of a cantata or a play.
4. Reading orally to share material with another for entertainment, recreation, and appreciation.
    a. Reading an entertaining story to a group.
    b. Reading a popular play to others.
    c. Reading a beautiful poem for others to appreciate and enjoy.
5. Reading aloud to recall past action of private interest to a group.
    a. Reading the minutes of a club to the members of that club.
    b. Reading a statement concerned with the financial status of an organization to the members of that organization.
    c. Reading an old newspaper account of past activities of a group to the members of that group.

6. Reading orally to prove or disprove a statement.
   a. Reading passages to others to support the position taken in a discussion.
   b. Reading passages to others to substantiate a statement previously made to them.
   c. Reading passages aloud to disprove an assertion made by another of the group.
7. Reading aloud to others for the purpose of providing instructions, directions, announcements, invitations, and the like.
   a. Reading to others instructions which supply information concerning work to be done.
   b. Reading to others directions for making something.
   c. Reading to a group announcements of future meetings of the group.
8. Reading orally to others a part in preparation for or in participation in a play, a dramatic dialogue, a radio program, a talkie, a shadowgraph, a puppet play, a pantomime.
   a. Reading to an audience a part in a puppet play.
   b. Reading to an audience a poem as others engage in pantomime.
   c. Reading to a group a part in a dramatic dialogue.
9. Combining reading orally and speaking from notes.
   a. Combining reading and speaking from notes in providing information about the stage setting for a play.
   b. Making a report in which parts are spoken and parts are read.
   c. Sketching the closing situation of the plot of a story, telling portions of the story, and reading interesting or exciting parts.
10. Reading aloud to get criticism for the purpose of improving one's oral reading.
   a. Reading aloud a story or poem to get criticism in order to be able to read it very well before a group of people.
   b. Reading a part in a play to get criticism in order to act the part in the final production.
   c. Reading selections to get criticism so that enough improvement will result that the person will be asked to read oftener to the group.
11. Reading aloud for personal pleasure.
   a. Reading aloud a selection to enjoy sudden changes or sharp contrasts.
   b. Reading aloud a poem to make vocal adjustment to rhythm of poetry.
   c. Reading aloud to develop confidence in one's ability to entertain an audience.
12. Reading aloud to provide a good standard of oral reading for others.
   a. Reading a poem aloud to give a complete picture.
   b. Reading a poem aloud to give the correct interpretation.
   c. Reading a poem aloud to create a liking for poetry and to offer stimulation for the reading of more poetry.[3]

---

[3] *Ibid.*, pp. 99–101.

Good oral reading can produce beneficial results in the social and emotional development of children. The growth in literary appreciation that comes as the young people read orally to each other is in itself a justification for instruction in oral reading. Furthermore, sympathetic relationships among the members of a group may often be created by means of the oral reading experience. A boy or girl may acquire a much-needed feeling of "status" in his group by being able to contribute a story, a joke, or an interesting fact by reading aloud from a book, a magazine, or a newspaper. Children who do not excel in other activities may find recognition in superior performance in oral reading. On the other hand, it should be remembered that a boy or girl may be hindered in emotional development as a result of unfortunate experiences in oral reading. Reading aloud to a group involves so much more than accurate word recognition and good articulation. Unlike silent reading, it is basically a social experience, and all the fears and uncertainties that a child may experience in the presence of his fellows are involved in the process of reading aloud to them.

Relation between Oral and Silent Reading

Almost all the skills that are important in silent reading are also needed in effective oral reading, because in a certain sense all oral reading is preceded by silent reading. A word in print cannot be given orally unless the reader has recognized the word and by that very act has read it silently. Consequently skill in word recognition, possession of a suitable meaning vocabulary, and the ability to comprehend what is read are essentials of both oral and silent reading. Even rate of reading is a factor in both types, because the individual who cannot read silently as rapidly as he can say the words he is reading is handicapped in his oral reading.

The effective oral reader possesses many of the silent reading skills and, in addition, many abilities peculiar to oral reading. One of these is correct pronunciation of words. In silent reading the pupil must recognize the word and know its meaning, but it is not essential that he should know how to pronounce it. Clear articulation, a pleasing and well-modulated voice, and proper contact with the audience are additional concerns of the oral reader. Furthermore, in oral reading, thought getting, common to both oral and silent reading, must be followed by vocal interpretation, because it is necessary to convey to the audience the reader's grasp of the meaning of the passage. Thus oral reading, if done well, becomes a highly complex skill.

A convenient term frequently used to describe what goes on in oral reading is the "eye-voice span." The eye-voice span is the distance between the word which the reader is uttering and the word on which his eyes rest at the same moment. In good oral reading the eyes run ahead of the voice. This is necessary if the reading is to be connected, fluent, and meaningful. Many children can learn to avoid "word calling" by being encouraged to let their eyes move ahead of their voices.

Oral reading, when well done, can serve as an aid to silent reading in many ways, some of which are illustrated later in this chapter and in the B chapter that follows. Oral reading, for example, helps in the diagnosis of difficulties in silent reading. As a pupil reads a selection orally, the teacher can frequently detect the types of errors that keep the pupil from reading well silently. Difficulties like the following, common to both oral and silent reading, often are revealed: omission of words or phrases; insertion of words or phrases; substitution of letters, words, or phrases; skipping lines; repeating lines; and phrasing so inadequately that it interferes with thought getting and interpretation.

Learning to read well orally, then, is more difficult than learning to read well silently. Not only must the oral reader have a good grasp of the meaning of the material he reads, but he must have many abilities besides. He must know his audience—their interests and probable attitudes toward the material read, as well as their capacity to understand it—and he must be sensitive to their reactions as he reads to them. He must be fluent enough to focus his mind on the thought rather than the recognition and pronunciation of individual words. He must reproduce in his reading the mood and intention of the author, recognizing irony or pathos, happiness or depression, excitement or pensiveness. He must know how to use pauses effectively.

Except for oral reading intended for diagnostic purposes, material for children's oral reading in group situations should ordinarily be restricted to selections that they can read with understanding and fluency. The activity of oral reading should be one of communication to others, not a drill exercise in the improvement of word recognition or comprehension.

Proportion of Time for Oral and Silent Reading

What should be the proportion of oral to silent reading? To this question a precise answer cannot be given for each grade, for the apportionment depends upon a variety of factors. One of these is the length of the reading period in schools that set aside time daily for reading instruction. There is wide variation in the same grades in various schools, and often there are differences within the same building if there is more than one room of the same grade. Moreover, even when the reading periods in the two rooms of the same grade are of equal length, the time spent in oral reading may vary greatly. In one room more time may be spent in silent reading during study periods than in the other. Furthermore, the amount of oral and silent reading done during other class periods, such as social studies or science, will influence the question of the proportion of time to be devoted to each. Reading at home, too, will affect the division of the reading period between the two types of reading. Factors like individual differences among children, their past training, the methods used by the teacher, and her skill in teaching reading will also need to be considered.

In the first grade and the first part of the second grade, when most children cannot read more rapidly silently than orally, oral reading will not ordinarily affect the rate of silent reading unfavorably. However, even in beginning reading an undue amount of vocalization in silent reading may result from over-emphasis on oral reading.

Oral reading in the lower grades is abundantly justified by the extreme pleasure which many children experience when they read to others or listen to others read to them. Although oral reading exercises can prove boring to all concerned, most children look forward to the opportunity to read aloud to the teacher or classmates when there is an atmosphere of approval. It would seem unwise to deprive children of a satisfying experience which strengthens the desire to learn to read. Every avenue to genuine reading interest should be utilized.

A teacher may ask a child to read aloud to her in order to learn the child's specific needs in reading. Children may read aloud to each other to share a pleasurable reading experience or to pass on desired information. Group drills in oral reading, however, with all members of the group following on the page, should generally be avoided.

Appraising Skill in Oral Reading

The teacher who undertakes to evaluate children's growth in oral reading skill looks for such familiar signs as these:

1. The pupil recognizes the common words at sight.
2. He pronounces the words correctly.
3. He shows that he knows the meaning of the words.
4. He uses variety and appropriateness of tone, pitch, force, and speed.
5. He enunciates clearly.
6. He appears at ease as he reads.
7. He is responsive to the reactions of the audience.
8. He exhibits interest and enthusiasm when he reads.
9. He gives his own interpretation of the selection through his oral reading.
10. His posture is erect and dignified without being overformal.

Comprehension is, of course, a primary requisite to efficient oral reading. For this reason pupils should not ordinarily be encouraged to read a passage aloud until they have first read it silently and understood it. Good phrasing, effective expression, and appropriate emphasis all depend upon the reader's grasp of the meaning. It is sometimes possible for a skillful reader to read orally without giving full attention to the content, but for most children good comprehension is a first requirement for accurate, intelligible oral reading. Meaning will determine the correct selection of word accents, the sound values of letters, and the intonation appropriate to the purpose of the writer.

The physical behavior of the oral reader, while distinctly secondary to the problem of comprehension, requires some attention on the part of the teacher. Formal restrictions which were once imposed with respect to the position of the feet and hands are no longer observed. Children are encouraged to stand erect, to assume a natural, relaxed position, and to avoid leaning against a desk, table, or chair. The book or magazine should not shield the face of the reader. Ideally, contact with the audience is maintained by frequent upward glances toward the listeners, but such contact is the result of a feeling of ease and an eagerness to communicate rather than conscious effort or deliberate drill.

The appraisal of growth in oral reading skills is necessarily an informal process. Standardized tests in "oral reading" are in reality devices to determine a pupil's skill in silent reading. They are valuable in revealing to the teacher the specific difficulties which he encounters in dealing with words and sentences. The data yielded by such tests as the Gray Standardized Oral Reading Paragraphs and the Gray Oral Reading Check Tests,[4] the Gates Oral Reading Test,[5] the Durrell Oral Reading Test,[6] the Jenkins Oral Reading Test,[7] and the oral sections of the Diagnostic Reading Tests[8] are valuable in the diagnosis of reading problems, but they do not purport to measure the specific skills of *oral* reading. The teacher must rely on her own careful observation of pupil performance and such cumulative anecdotal records as she may find time to keep.

Informal observation of a pupil's performance in the oral reading situation, especially with the aid of a checklist such as the one suggested earlier, remains the best method of evaluating growth in the skills peculiar to oral reading. Bad posture, finger pointing, and poor intonation are easily noted by the alert teacher who is interested in improving the oral reading performance of the pupil.

General Observations on the Teaching of Oral Reading

Principles of teaching oral reading are suggested in the list of general observations which follows. The teacher may wish to discuss these principles

[4] Bloomington, Ill.: The Public School Publishing Company.

[5] New York: Bureau of Publications, Teachers College, Columbia University.

[6] New York: Harcourt, Brace and World, Inc.

[7] Cincinnati, Ohio: The C. A. Gregory Company.

[8] New York: Committee on Diagnostic Reading Tests.

with her class; she should not be surprised if the pupils express disagreement with some of them.

1. Learning to read silently takes priority over learning to read orally. In our society it is desirable that everyone be able to read for meaning. Although in the early stages of learning to read, oral reading can be, and usually is, a great help in learning to get meaning from the printed page, the teacher must bear in mind that the aim always is to get or convey the meaning.

2. Most children enjoy reading aloud to each other and should be given many opportunities to do so. The fact that apparently it is possible for children to learn to read for meaning without oral reading experiences in the classroom does not justify depriving them of such experiences. Children's motives for oral reading may be of many kinds: they may read aloud to the teacher to show their progress in mastering the printed page; they may do so to share a poem or a story with other children; they may do so to prove a point or to raise a question. Oral reading is essentially a form of communication between one person and another, and as such ought to be encouraged.

3. The skills of oral reading can be improved through instruction. Successful experiences in oral reading will give needed self-confidence to the shy child. Approval by teacher and class will help him to take further, perhaps timid, steps toward self-assured oral reading. Teachers can help boys and girls to overcome monotony of rate or pitch and to read literary materials aloud with feeling and animation.

4. Most instruction in oral reading is necessarily incidental. There is a proper place for formal exercises in oral reading in rehearsal for assembly programs or for special events in the classroom, but throughout the year the instruction is likely to consist of helpful suggestions as the child undertakes to communicate with his classmates from the printed page. Such suggestions are of course always made in such a way as not to embarrass the reader. Usually they are made privately, and they should always be given along with praise for those good qualities which the child displays.

5. The teacher herself can give an example of good oral reading. Not all teachers are skillful oral readers, but all can learn to read aloud with good enunciation, appropriate volume and emphasis, and an interesting variety of pitch and rate. Teachers in all grades should cultivate this ability.

6. Ordinarily the pupils should be encouraged to listen to the reader without following him in their own books. On some occasions and for some purposes such "following" of the reader is natural. As a daily routine, however, it is to be avoided. Every teacher knows how frequently pupils "lose their place" and how impatient the good readers become when the poor oral reader stumbles through the words.

7. Children should have access to a wide variety of suitable materials for oral reading. Such materials should be easy and interesting, often including much dialogue. They should include stories and poems, both published mate-

rials and the children's own work. Stories or articles cut out of discarded books and magazines make excellent material for oral reading. On special occasions, such as holidays or the birthdays of famous persons, stories about the exploits of national heroes and the meaning of the holidays may be used. Humorous anecdotes are especially suitable for oral reading.

8. The oral reading should take place only when there is a receptive audience. The reader must be eager to communicate, and the audience must be eager to listen. Until such conditions exist, it would be better to postpone the oral reading. Under no conditions should members of the audience be encouraged to criticize or in any way publicly evaluate the quality of the reading, unless the reader sincerely welcomes criticism of his performance. Occasional favorable comment by the teacher can do no harm, and certainly private suggestions given the pupil by the teacher are in order. The aim should be to relieve the pupil of self-consciousness so far as possible.

9. The cooperation of the parents should be enlisted whenever possible. Parents should not be expected to help teach the skills of oral reading, but they can encourage children to read aloud to them and to each other. Such home experiences effectively supplement the limited opportunities the school can provide for oral reading.

10b

Developing
Skill in Oral Reading

The purpose of instruction in oral reading is to help the child to interpret the printed page effectively to others. In order to attain this ability, the child must have abundant opportunity to read aloud meaningful materials. He must be encouraged to read in such a way that meaning is truly communicated to the listener. For this reason, especially in the case of beginners, the child should first read a passage silently in order to understand it. The slow, word-by-word, oral deciphering of the printed page, except perhaps in diagnosis, helps neither oral nor silent reading.

Instructional Practices

Although experience in reading in purposeful situations is basic, some direct instruction is usually necessary. Following are some illustrative teaching practices which may be used in direct instruction in oral reading:

1. Stressing the importance of correct pronunciation.

2. Requiring pupils to check pronunciation before reading orally, and giving them help when necessary.

3. Teaching the interpretation of diacritical marks in the dictionary.

4. Stressing the importance of clear enunciation.

5. Practicing the enunciation of words in which the endings *ing, ed,* and *t* are often slurred.

6. Teaching pupils to note the number of syllables in a word, using a dictionary if necessary.

7. Having pupils divide assigned words into syllables.

8. Using rhyme to illustrate correct pronunciation, as: "*Just* rhymes with *must,* not with *best!*"

9. Having pupils make a list of words which they habitually enunciate poorly.

10. Listening to records to note examples of excellent enunciation.

11. Having pupils make tape recordings of their voices to note the quality of enunciation.

12. Having pupils listen to the teacher

read a sentence with good phrasing and say it back to her. (This should be done individually, of course, with different sentences.)

13. Contrasting good and poor phrasing in the reading of a sentence.

14. Exposing for very short duration phrases to be read orally.

15. Having pupils read passages silently to note proper places for pausing and then read them orally.

16. Teaching the use of punctuation marks in determining where the pauses should come.

17. Reading orally a selection without pausing for punctuation marks and asking the class to supply them where they are needed.

18. Having pupils look for answers through silent reading of a passage and then read the appropriate parts aloud.

19. Having pupils summarize a selection after reading it aloud.

20. Preparing in advance questions to be answered by the pupil after reading orally.

21. Explaining to the pupils the role of the reader as interpreter.

22. Explaining some of the rules of good interpretation, such as (a) reading a selection beforehand, (b) making certain that one understands what is to be read, and (c) reading with expression.

23. Choosing materials that pupils will be able to interpret adequately.

24. Emphasizing the importance of having a clear purpose for the oral reading.

25. Helping pupils overcome individual mannerisms that draw attention away from the message.

26. Having pupils read orally in order to create various moods.

27. Demonstrating to the class the need for variety of tone, pitch, and rate in oral reading, by contrasting monotonous with varied expression.

28. Demonstrating, and having pupils practice, the use of different types of tone, pitch, and rate with different materials.

29. Giving practice in expressing different moods through changes in voice qualities.

30. Having pupils listen to speakers who use their voices effectively.

31. Having pupils find the words in a sentence that are especially significant in the context and then read the sentence to emphasize the important words.

32. Arranging for pupils to read in concert with others, as in choral reading.

33. Having the class formulate standards for good oral reading, including ways of holding a book or magazine.

34. Making and encouraging the pupils to help make displays that will emphasize points to observe in oral reading.

35. Getting class participation in deciding upon appropriate times and materials for oral reading.

36. Listening to pupils, individually, read for diagnostic purposes.

37. Having pupils reread a short selection orally as an aid to comprehension.

38. Discussing with a class what a reader can do to make it easy for an audience not to be restless.

39. Encouraging pupils to prepare a sketch in which varying inflections are used to say the same expression in order to produce different meanings. For example, the sentence "What a day!" could be given so as to express more than one reaction to the day.

40. Helping the class draw up standards for oral reading of the minutes of a club meeting.

Most of the practice in oral reading should be provided through meaningful situations like the following in which the pupils could engage:

1. Giving oral reports or reading stories orally, including original ones by the boys and girls, to another group, possibly within the context of a program consisting of a variety of activities.

2. Putting on a make-believe radio or television program.

3. Rereading orally short selections that have been read silently, with the purpose of clarifying the meaning.

4. Reading orally to prove a point.

5. Reading orally to give one's interpretation of a selection.

6. Participating in a panel that is reading a series of short stories or one longer story in parts.

7. Giving a puppet play in which the "conversation" is read.

8. Reading new reports.

9. Taking part in choral reading. (Suggestions for choral reading are given on pages 240 to 242.)

10. Putting on a program in which a narrator reads orally the "conversation" of "characters" made by pupils through *origami* (the Japanese art of paper folding).

Following are a few books helpful to the teacher who wishes to learn more about paper folding:

Harbin, Robert, *Paper Magic, the Art of Paper Folding.* Newton Center, Mass.: Charles T. Branford Company, 1957.

Honda, Isao, *All about Origami.* Tokyo, Japan: Toto Bunka Company, 1960. (Distributed by Japan Publications Trading Company, Tokyo, Japan)

Lewis, Shari, and Lillian Oppenheimer, *Folding Paper Puppets.* New York: Stein and Day, 1962. (Distributed by J. B. Lippincott Company, Philadelphia, Pa.)

Murray, William D., and Francis J. Rigney, *Paper Folding for Beginners.* New York: Dover Publications, Inc., 1960.

Additional suggestions on paper folding can be obtained from The Origami Center in New York.

Oral Reading by the Teacher

Some persons insist that a day should never pass during which the elementary school teacher does not read something orally to the class. While this may be an extreme view, certainly frequent oral reading by the teacher is highly desirable. By means of such reading, pupils can be acquainted with literature of genuine worth that is too difficult for them to read by themselves. Moreover, the teacher is able by this means to set standards of performance to which the pupils can aspire.

Naturally, not all teachers are equally skillful in oral reading. For many, it is desirable to precede the reading with careful preparation through prior silent reading of the selections, or even rehearsal of the oral reading activity itself. Such preparation includes also a careful consideration of the material to be used. Stories read to children should be of high quality but on the level of the children. They should be of the kind that lend themselves to oral reading. For younger children, especially, stories with much conversation in them are likely to have the greatest appeal. In addition to fiction, the reading material may include selections from poetry, social studies, current events, and even science.

Teachers sometimes ask, "When and how should the pictures be shown when a book is read to the class?" The answer must, of course, depend upon the circumstances. Many picture-story books are poorly adapted to reading to a group. Such books are more suitable for individual reading or reading shared by two or three children. Most of the modern picture books for young children have more illustrations than text; indeed, the central message is in the pictures while the text is only commentary. In such cases, it is best to have the pupils grouped as closely as possible around the teacher. The teacher reads the text material on a page and holds up the book to show the picture, turning it in all directions so that everyone may see. The children should have time to see and enjoy each scene as the story progresses. To help the pupils' observation, the teacher points out details in each picture as the story goes along. If the class is too large for convenient showing of the pictures to all pupils, the story should be read to children in smaller groups. No child should be made to feel neglected because he was unable to see the pictures. And, of course, after the reading, the book should be added to the room collection, where individual pupils can reexamine it at leisure.

Oral Reading by Children in Small Groups

In both primary and intermediate grades, the children can be divided into small groups of three or four or five who will meet in various parts of the room to read orally to one another. If this procedure can be carried out effectively in a room, much of the problem of finding time for everyone to get as much practice in oral reading as is desirable can be solved. Care must be taken that the material read is very easy and very interesting. Furthermore, in each group there should be at least one person who can serve as chairman and help the others with words they cannot recognize. So that bedlam does not result, it is usually necessary to work out rules of procedure for the group reading, designating such points as order of reading, responsibilities of the chairman, responsibilities of the reader, and duties of the listeners. If possible, there should be a rotating chairmanship, but no child who is unable to perform the duties of a chairman should be appointed to the post. The teacher can spend her time going from group to group, observing points that she may wish to bring up at a later time so as to provide for improvement in routine. This plan works only when pupils can read fairly well the material they have and when the teacher is able to maintain the desired orderliness even when she is not at all times in direct contact with each group.

Miss Marguerite Goens, first-grade teacher in Indianapolis, worked out an excellent plan for small-group reading through the help of the third grade in her building. In this cooperating third grade several of the best readers went to the first-grade room twice a week for twenty minutes to take charge of oral reading groups consisting of three or four pupils each. While the assistants were working with the children, the room teacher circulated from group to group giving needed assistance. In order to make certain that the reading material was of worth and on the level of the readers and that it fulfilled the requirements for oral presentation, everything that was to be read, including material which pupils brought to school, had to be approved by the teacher before it was read orally. The group work did not take the place of the developmental reading classes, but it did serve as a very vital adjunct to it.

Reading Poetry Orally

One of the neglected areas of oral reading in many schools is that of poetry reading by the boys and girls. It is an art so filled with rich opportunities for developing appreciation that much more emphasis should be placed upon it than is commonly the case. Unfortunately, when poetry is read orally, it is often done so poorly that the results actually interfere with its enjoyment.

As a rule, the child who does the reading should be well prepared. There are occasions when the boys and girls might read, without preparation beforehand, in order to be given specific help in reading poetry more effectively. But when the aim of the teacher is to have the audience get enjoyment from the reading, the pupils should be able to read the poetry so as to arouse appreciation in his listeners. At all such times the pupil should practice reading his poem orally before he appears in front of his audience. If possible, the teacher should help him while he is practicing. She can do so by assisting the reader to get the meaning of the poem through questioning, through comments, and through reading orally part or all of the poem herself. All the other elements essential to effective oral reading of prose, such as skill in word recognition and handling the book with facility, are also requirements for reading poetry. Because pupils are more accustomed to prose than poetry and because difficulties in interpretation of poetry are often greater than those in interpretation of prose, to achieve as good results when reading poetry as when reading prose is difficult for many boys and girls. The child must have a feeling of confidence and poise as he comes in front of his audience, a becoming self-assurance that results from knowledge of being well prepared and having a worthwhile contribution to make. Some pitfalls in reading poetry that the teacher must try to help the child avoid are "sing-song" reading, lack of discrimination between commas that represent grammatical structure and those that represent rhetorical phrasing, and overdramatic reading.

The poetry should be well selected. Even for young children there is much poetry of superior quality. An examination of the excellent anthologies of literature for children will suggest many poems and will give the names of poets whose work, other than that quoted in the anthology, is worth investigating. At times the teacher may choose the poems to be read, but no pupil should be forced to read a poem that he himself does not enjoy or one that he does not want to read to the group. When a girl or boy has a voice in choosing the poem, however, the selection should not be left entirely up to him. The teacher is responsible for seeing that no poem chosen is of poor quality. Furthermore, in the choice of poems the ability of the reader to interpret and of the audience to enjoy must be considered.

The reading of poetry should be done in a suitable setting. Sometimes the teacher will need to help create the mood needed for enjoyment even before the pupil begins reading. The teacher can at times do this by means of questions or discussion. For example, before a child reads the poem "The Swing" by Robert Louis Stevenson, the teacher may give the audience a chance to tell whether they like to be up in a swing and how they feel when they are swinging. At other times a picture may help the children get into the right mood for a poem. Before a pupil reads orally "The Duel" by Eugene Field, a picture of a gingham dog and a calico cat with a discussion as to how the two look at each other, may get the pupils interested in finding out how the gingham dog and the calico cat in the poem got along. Printed pictures that express the mood of the poem well are sometimes available. At other times the reader may wish to draw beforehand a picture that he thinks will help the audience want to hear his poem. Interest in the poem may be aroused by posting the picture on a bulletin board even as long as a few days before the poem will be read. A question written near the picture, such as "What is happening in this picture?" might arouse curiosity.

The audience should often have more access to a poem than is afforded by one reading. The poems that are read orally may be posted on a bulletin board so that everyone can read them. Or they may be put into a booklet placed on the library table, easily accessible to all the children. Oral rereading of the poem by the person who had prepared it is often effective. When a series of poems has been read, the pupils may be asked to specify a few that they would like particularly to hear again.

Choral Reading

Choral reading, in its simplest terms, can be defined as the speaking of poetry or prose by several or many voices either in unison or by parts, as solos or as group work.

Many values may be found in choral reading at its best. One of these is the beneficial effect it can have on personality development. The shy child becomes more self-confident when he can quite inconspicuously, in group work, get the assurance that comes from knowledge of a contribution to a shared undertaking. Similarly the "show-off," even in solo parts, can learn to submerge himself for the good of the group and find satisfaction in so doing. Another value that can result from choral reading is an understanding and appreciation of poetry and poetic prose. This, obviously, can be expected only if literature of enduring quality is used for choral reading purposes.

A third value is the beneficial effect choral reading can have on the speech and the oral reading of the child. The emphasis placed in choral reading upon voice quality, interpretation of meaning, enunciation, and articulation can affect oral reading favorably. Furthermore, the poise and self-assurance that it aims to develop, and under favorable conditions achieves, are essentials of effective oral reading of any type.

It is not the purpose of this chapter to give a comprehensive treatment of how to teach choral reading. The brief description that is given, as well as the few suggestions for teaching it that are included, will serve chiefly to help make clear the relationship between choral reading and other oral reading.

There is considerable variety of pattern that choral reading can follow. First of all, the poem or prose selection can be read in unison, with all individuals saying all lines. Or the reading may be done in a solo-chorus combination, as, for example, when the teacher or other leader reads alone all parts excepting the chorus parts, in which the entire class participates. The dialogue type of choral reading can be done either by two individuals who take the parts or by two choruses saying alternate lines or groups of lines. The line-a-child casting differs from the dialogues by two persons in that lines are assigned to three or more individuals. Similarly, line-a-choir reading differs from dialogues participated in by two choruses in that three or more groups say the lines. The use of various combinations of these types in reading a single long selection makes possible considerable variation of pattern of reading. Which type should be used will be determined in part by the ability of the group, the selection itself, and the objectives to be accomplished. Frequently the children, under the guidance of the teacher, should have a voice in deciding upon the choice of the selection, the type of casting to be done, and the assignment of parts.

The following are some of the points that the teacher should bear in mind as she helps boys and girls in choral reading.

Choral reading should be fun. If it is not, the major reasons for doing it will probably not be accomplished. This does not mean that hard work may not be necessary in order to get the desired results, but it does mean that if appreciation of good literature is to result, the pupils must enjoy the work.

The choral reading should be kept on the pupils' level. In the primary grades it should be kept simple and, with beginners, there is no place for long drill periods. The reading should be done for the sake of the activity and for what is attained through participation in it, rather than for a performance in front of parents or others. Nothing is wrong, however, with having children do choral reading in front of an audience if the major aim is not the program but the learning and enjoyment that come from taking part in choral reading.

In the primary grades the teacher should help boys and girls develop an appreciation of poetry by reading or speaking to them poems that appeal to them; these should be, at the same time, poems of worth. As the teacher gives the poems more than once, the boys and girls should be encouraged to come in on the lines wherever they can. A sense of rhythm can be developed by having the children beat time as they give some poems. One child or a few of the children might skip or walk or run to portray the mood suggested by appropriate poems given by the group in chorus. Casting is not usually advisable in the lower grades, except occasionally of the very simplest poems. Then often the most appropriate method is to have one child serve as leader and the rest as chorus. The poem "Baa, baa, black sheep" could be cast so that one child asks the questions to which the remainder of the class responds in chorus.

In the intermediate grades, if the pupils have not had a background of enjoyment of poetry, the teacher should begin the work in a way similar to that used in the primary grades and then proceed to more difficult casting and to a more mature interpretation. It is there that dialogues, with parts taken either by individuals or groups, play an increasingly significant role. Line-a-child reading, in which three or more pupils take parts, as well as line-a-choir reading, in which more than two choirs participate, is appropriate in the intermediate grades if the necessary prerequisites have been met.

The pupils should usually be encouraged to keep their voices light and soft, and overdramatic effects should be avoided. While children in the primary grades frequently respond naturally to what they are saying by physical movements, in the intermediate grades gestures in choral reading usually are forced, not spontaneous. Occasionally a gesture can appropriately be made, but where it cannot, it should be guarded against. In "Seein' Things" by Eugene Field, if the person or persons saying the line "A-lookin' at me cross-eyed an' p'int'n' at me—so!" can add to the interpretation by pointing ominously at someone in the audience, then the gesture is desirable. However, pointing of this type will often detract from the meaning, not enhance it.

A Prepared Oral Reading Program

In this last section of this chapter is presented a teaching plan that illustrates how a class period devoted to oral reading that has been prepared beforehand can be conducted. An explanation of phases of the plan follows.

Teaching Plan

This plan for a fourth-grade class, like all other teaching plans, should not be thought of as a model that should be followed exactly; rather it is hoped that it will serve as one concrete illustration of what can be done. The needs of the boys and girls should determine the procedure to be followed in any one situation.

A. *Topic:* Prepared oral reading of Christmas stories
B. *Pupils' aims*
   1. To see if we will like the Christmas stories that will be read to us
   2. To try to read so that our listeners will enjoy hearing us read
   3. To be good listeners
C. *Materials*
   1. Board work
     a. "Old Hans and the Toyshop Twins"
      Kenneth Jackson
      Betty Thurston
      Lois Roth
      Jean VanSickle
     b. "The Christmas Tree"
      Jimmie Reed
      Beverly Myers
     c. "The Snow Santa Claus"
      Doris Gale
      Ted Hershey

d. "A Christmas Friend"
   Ted Gardner
   Norma Staley
2. Copies of the stories listed under 1 above

Gardner, Ted	Oral Reading						
Dates :							
1. Posture							
2. Voice							
3. Pronunciation							
4. Enunciation							
5. Getting the message across							
6. Remembering the audience							
7. Listening							

3. Chart entitled "Oral Reading" with these points listed on it:
   Posture
   Voice
   Pronunciation
   Enunciation
   Getting the message across
   Remembering the audience
   Listening
4. Individual cards like that illustrated above

D. *Procedure*

1. Motivation

The teacher says: "How many of you like to hear or read Christmas stories? A committee has prepared several stories which they will read to you."

2. Noting points to watch when reading orally

a. The teacher, referring to the chart mentioned under C-3 above, states that the boys and girls have tried hard to watch those points as they practiced their reading.

b. Two pupils put on a two-minute skit in which they demonstrate good and poor posture while reading orally, and the class briefly names points of excellence and of criticism in the two types of posture demonstrated.

c. The pupils tell what "remembering the audience" means, stressing the fact that while "looking at the audience" is important, it should not be done mechanically.

d. The pupils indicate what a good listener does.

3. Statement of the procedure to be followed in reading the stories

The teacher explains to the boys and girls that after a few introductory remarks the boys and girls whose names are written on the program on the board, under C-1, will read the stories listed there.

4. Reading of the stories by the children preceded by an introductory remark or a question on each story by the teacher or by the reader

5. Brief discussion of the content of the stories

6. Pupils' evaluation of the reading

a. Pupils name the points on the chart that they think were watched particularly well.

b. Pupils name the points on the chart that they think need to be improved upon.

c. Group discusses means by which they can improve upon the points referred to under b above.

d. Teacher explains that individually later on she will discuss with those who read the quality of their reading.

At that time cards like the one illustrated below can be used for making an analysis of each pupil's reading.

Explanation of the Plan

In a lesson of this type the following procedure might be followed: (1) preparation before class, (2) deciding upon the aims for the period, (3) reference to the points to be observed in the oral reading, (4) announcement of the plan of procedure in the reading, (5) reading of the selections, (6) discussion of the story, and (7) evaluation of the reading. Each of these points is here discussed to clarify it in relation to the teaching plan presented and to indicate a few of the possible variations from it that the teacher may wish to make.

1. *Preparation before class.* Preparation should include choosing the readers, selecting the materials to be read, practicing reading the selections, providing for the materials needed during classtime and making seating arrangements.

a. Choosing the readers. The teacher who made the plans for the reading program described earlier was in the habit of choosing no pupil for a second turn at participating in an oral reading program before everyone in the room had had the opportunity to take part in one. She also made certain that

pupils of varying ability appeared on each program. She took this precaution because she realized that while it would be relatively easy to keep a program interesting if all participants were good readers, it would be difficult to hold the interest of the audience if only the poorer readers performed.

The question is often asked, "Should the poor reader really be expected or allowed to take part in an audience reading program?" The answer is, "Yes, as a rule." If a pupil is not permitted to read because he has decided difficulties in reading, he may feel slighted, even though often he may act as if he were pleased that he did not have to read. Moreover, it is the poorer reader, rather than the excellent one, who needs the practice. The teacher can help save the former from feelings of inadequacy in the oral reading situation by giving him shorter selections than most others in the group so that he can prepare thoroughly what he reads. It is probably good policy to give some of the better readers relatively brief selections, too, so that the one who is less able will not think of the brevity of his reading as a stigma attached to his performance. Also, the teacher can see to it that the child who cannot read as well orally as the others has very easy material to read. Help from the teacher in preparation for the reading can often preserve the ego of the reader, with a minimum of undesirable emotional reactions. At the same time, in this way the pupil can get real help in becoming a better reader. Some teachers, rather than depriving a poor reader of the opportunity to read orally, wisely help him all but memorize his selection before class so that he may perform well before his peers.

There are, however, undoubtedly some pupils in the intermediate grades who should be excused at least for a part of the year from participating in oral reading. A child who is so shy that he will be harmed rather than helped through reading orally should not be required to read. Great care should be taken, of course, in deciding when a child should not be asked to read. For example, Jim, a fourth-grader with approximately third-grade reading ability, complained to his tutor that his teacher never called on him to read orally.

b. Selection of material. The material to be read orally should be selected with particular care. Sometimes the teacher will make the selection by herself, always remembering that the material should be at the level of the child's interest. At other times pupils should have the opportunity to select from a variety presented by the teacher. When children make their own suggestions, the teacher, perhaps in consultation with a pupil committee, will advise as to the suitability of the selections.

The material selected should be easy for the reader to read orally and easy for the audience to comprehend. Often it is advisable to select material for audience reading that is a grade or so lower in difficulty level than the reader's silent reading level. Effective oral reading requires ability in silent reading plus the complex skill of interpreting to others what is read.

A variety of suitable materials is available. Stories, both humorous and serious, fanciful and realistic, are one source. Anecdotes make very good reading. Work-type materials of the kind that requires more than one reading or very careful attention have no legitimate place in an oral reading program. Sometimes each child on the program may have a separate, very short, selection to read. At other times a longer one may be apportioned to two or more, or even all, of the persons who will be reading. Appropriate selections are easily available in most situations because only one copy of a book or magazine article is needed. This is true even if more than one pupil is preparing material out of the same book or magazine, since they can practice at different times and since no one should be reading silently while someone is reading orally. Many teachers like to cut materials out of books that are ready to be discarded

or magazines that are not being saved. The stories used in the teaching plan were cut out of a magazine in columns and then mounted on tagboard 9 inches by 12 inches. Mounted material can often be handled better while it is being read and can be kept in better condition when filed for later use.

c. Preparation of the reader. Each reader should be thoroughly prepared for the reading. As a rule, silent reading of the selection beforehand is not enough. The pupil should read it orally one or more times, either to the teacher or to someone else who can help him not only with word recognition but also with problems of interpretation. If several children are to read parts of the same selection, at times they can help each other during the practice period. But the teacher is always responsible for seeing that no one comes before the class inadequately prepared. Furthermore, each pupil should know exactly where his selection is to begin and end if he is to read only part of an article or story.

d. Provision for materials. Careful provision should be made, often with the help of the boys and girls, so that supplies and equipment needed during the class period will be available. Included may be material placed on the board, as in the case of the plan reproduced in this chapter. If a plan like this one were used, the program for the period could be listed on the board, with the title of each story to be read and the names of the persons who were to read each, in the order of appearance. Sometimes, instead, boys and girls like to make duplicates of the program on paper to distribute to the audience at the beginning of the class period.

A chart similar to the one referred to in the plan, giving the points the pupils plan to watch in their oral reading, can be displayed. So that the pupils may wholeheartedly accept the skills for the improvement of which they will work, it is usually advisable to have the list worked out cooperatively by the pupils and the teacher. The wording should be meaningful to the pupils. If the word *enunciation* is used, as it is on the list given in the plan, the teacher should make certain that the boys and girls know what it means. The list can be drawn up early in the school year and then it can be reproduced on chart paper. For easy reference, it could be either kept posted in the room at all times or else exhibited whenever the pupils give reading programs.

Each pupil could be provided with a card similar to the one illustrated on page 243. These cards could be kept by the teacher or the child. The record should not be kept for competitive purposes, and only the teacher and the owner of a card should have access to it. A check can be placed on the chart after each item on which the child does well and a minus sign after each item on which he needs to improve. Although on the card reproduced, provision is made for checking seven different items, the number could vary. A place is left for the date of each reading. Space for comments is on the back of the card.

Sometimes other materials may be needed. A map often adds to the value of the reading by enabling the pupil to locate places about which he reads. At times pictures help the audience to visualize what will be read. Realia, too, may profitably be exhibited, if they help accomplish the purpose set for the oral reading. For example, pupils in the fifth or sixth grades can be aided in getting into the mood of the story about Nancy Hanks, the mother of Abraham Lincoln, if a replica of a log cabin is shown as representative of the type in which Lincoln lived when he was a boy.

e. Room arrangements. Arrangements should be made before class for proper seating of the audience and of the participants in the program. Sometimes all that is needed is to reserve seats near the front of the room for those who will read. At times, if there are portable seats, they can be rearranged so as to make it as easy as possible to have a desirable audience situation. If, as in the plan that is reproduced, Christmas stories are being read, someone can see to it that the shades are pulled and the lights are lit on the Christmas tree in the room before class begins.

2. *Deciding upon the aims for the period.* The aims can be suggested by the pupils who prepare the oral reading or by the teacher. No matter who states them, it is important that they are objectives that the class can wholeheartedly accept. In the teaching plan given on page 242 three aims were listed. The second aim, the aim of the readers, "To try to read so that our listeners will enjoy hearing us read," should be determined before class as the boys and girls practice reading. The first and last are suggested objectives for the members of the audience. It will be noted that the first aim, as stated, is not that each child should enjoy the story. There can be nothing mandatory about appreciation. A person does not enjoy something because he sets out to enjoy it or because he is told to enjoy it. In the plan described, the aim that deals with appreciation leaves the final choice explicitly with the audience, for all that is suggested is that they find out whether or not they will enjoy the stories. That is as far as the recommendation should be made when appreciation type of teaching is done. The third aim is brought out in *2-d* under "Procedure," which states, "The pupils indicate what a good listener does."

The audience is entitled to have a reason for listening. If the children have no purpose, they will often pay inadequate attention to what is read. Therefore, a suggestion as to what the purpose might be should be given either by the pupils who will read or by the teacher. At times the purpose may deal with entertainment and at other times it may be to get information. It is not necessary that in every oral reading lesson the audience specifically decide that they will try to be good listeners. After a while it should be taken for granted that that will always be an objec-

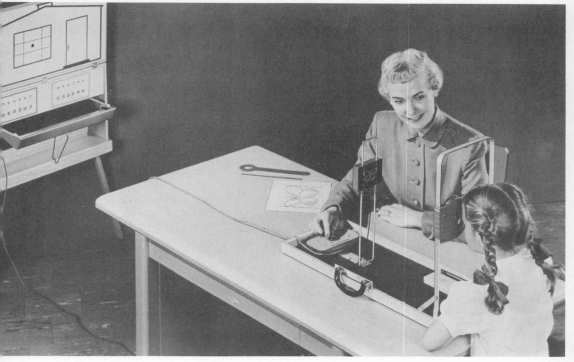

Chicago Public Schools
The reading accelerator steps up the reading rate

American Optical Company
Massachusetts Vision Test in use

An imaginative teacher makes creative use of the natural environment

tive. Nevertheless, occasionally additional elements may well be stressed for observation as far as the conduct of the audience is concerned. It is often advisable that each person who reads have in mind a particular point that he wishes to observe especially well.

As a rule, the number of expressed aims should be greatly limited, probably to three at the most. It is to be assumed that the pupil will always have certain objectives in mind in reading of this type, without mention being made of them. A large number of stated aims is likely to result in diffusion of effort. There is much to be applied to educational practice in the quotation that says, "This one thing I do." Multiplicity of aim can be decidedly disadvantageous under some circumstances.

3. *Reference to the points to be observed.* It is not necessary that the points to watch in oral reading should be discussed in each audience reading situation before the boys and girls begin reading. Sometimes they may be taken up after the reading only, and at other times no class mention needs to be made of them. Several factors should enter into the decision as to whether they should be discussed either before or after the reading. One is the time available for discussion during the lesson. Another is whether the mood to be portrayed through the reading can better be created if no mention is made of the skills to be developed.

4. *Announcement of the plan of procedure.* Although in the plan given, the teacher made the announcement, often the teacher can remain entirely in the background and a pupil, appointed as chairman of the meeting, can make the announcement. At other times, when the pupils are handed copies of the program, no mention of the order needs to be made.

5. *Reading of the selections.* It is essential that the atmosphere of a program should be maintained throughout the time set aside for reading. The teacher should not correct or prompt the reader unless it is absolutely necessary for the continuance of the program. Interruptions should probably be made no more often than in an assembly program. Possibly the only occasion when the teacher is justified in intervening arises when the child stops reading because he does not know the next word even though previously he had been instructed to proceed as best he could.

6. *Discussion of the story.* Sometimes the discussion of the story may be omitted—certainly in cases in which the mood created by the story might be destroyed by talking about it. Usually, if there is discussion, it should be brief. It might be led by the teacher or by a pupil. Occasionally, if the aim is to see how well the boys and girls have acquired the information given, they might check themselves on their ability to answer written questions on what was presented.

7. *Evaluation of the reading.* It is not recommended that the teacher check the individual "score" card while the child is reading. Some pupils may not be made self-conscious by such a practice, but others will surely either concentrate on technique rather than thought or become tense. It is just as easy for the teacher to check the cards periodically after class and discuss the record with the pupils individually.

Hard and fast rules about evaluation should not, of course, interfere with occasional informal comments upon the success with which a pupil has mastered specific skills of oral reading. However, usually it is most effective to discuss group progress in general terms at the end of the reading period. Individual pupils should be encouraged to keep their own scores and compare them with the teacher's judgments in private conference. No child should feel that he is going on trial when he rises to read.

FOR FURTHER STUDY

Arbuthnot, May Hill, *Children and Books,*

pp. 208–228. Chicago: Scott, Foresman and Company, 1957.

Bond, Guy L., and Eva Bond Wagner, *Teaching the Child to Read*, pp. 249–254. New York: The Macmillan Company, 1960.

Eisenson, Jon, and Mardel Ogilvie, *Speech Correction in the Schools*, pp. 136–140. New York: The Macmillan Company, 1963.

Gray, Lillian, and Dora Reese, *Teaching Children to Read*, pp. 214–246. New York: The Ronald Press Company, 1957.

Hester, Kathleen B., *Teaching Every Child to Read*, pp. 262–278. New York: Harper and Row, Publishers, 1955.

Kovas, Helen, "The Place of Oral Reading," *Elementary English,* 34 (November 1957), 462–466.

Robinson, Helen M., ed., *Oral Aspects of Reading.* Proceedings of the Reading Conference of the University of Chicago. Chicago: The University of Chicago Press, 1955.

Russell, David H., *Children Learn to Read,* pp. 122–127. Boston: Ginn and Company, 1961.

White, Margaret, "Oral Reading in the Modern Curriculum," *A Report of the Third Annual Conference on Reading, University of Pittsburgh,* pp. 50–57. Pittsburgh: The University of Pittsburgh, 1947.

Yoakam, Gerald A., "Problems of Oral Reading and Speech," *A Report of the Third Annual Conference on Reading, University of Pittsburgh,* pp. 14–23. Pittsburgh: The University of Pittsburgh, 1947.

11a

Children's Interests in Reading

The development of keen and continuing interests in reading is not only one of the basic aims of reading instruction, but also an essential condition for sturdy growth in reading ability. Successful reading depends on the drive, the motive that comes from within the learner. The use of outward compulsion achieves little in the way of reading progress and may in fact inhibit the growth of reading interest. Only as the abundant energies that are resident in all normal children are released may we expect rapid and enduring gains in reading skill and interest. We must therefore discover and nurture the interests that impel the child to seek meaning from the printed page.

For this reason, what is variously called "free" reading, "recreational" reading, and "personal" reading has come to occupy a place of first importance in the school program. While not long ago teachers tended to regard this kind of reading as peripheral to the instructional program—a kind of extracurricular activity—today "reading for fun" is considered a legitimate and desirable activity for school hours. The systematic study of children's interests has thus become a central part of the instructional program in reading.

The Aims of Guidance in Wide, Voluntary Reading

How great the importance of wide, voluntary reading is can be seen from an examination of some of the major purposes of this type of reading.

1. *Providing leisure-time activities.* Perhaps the first, though not necessarily the most important, purpose is the development of the habit of reading in

leisure time. Children should have much leisure time, and they should have abundant resources for its constructive use. Certainly some of these resources should take the form of sports, hobbies, and social activities. But there are many occasions when children and young people do not have the opportunity to pursue hobbies or take part in games and social activities. These are the times when good books and good magazines should be a source of pleasure. Developing the love for good reading is one of the greatest benefits that we can provide for children.

The leisure hour is the time for fairy tales, folk tales, fables, myths, tall stories, and the sagas of heroes. It is the time for *Winnie the Pooh*, for the stories of Dr. Seuss, for *Mary Poppins*, for *Mother Goose*, for *Alice's Adventures in Wonderland*, for the *Arabian Nights*. For some children it is the time for poetry —for the nonsense verse of Lewis Carroll and Edward Lear, the humor and pathos of Rose Fyleman and Eugene Field. The leisure hour can be an hour of magic, enchantment, relaxation, and relief. It can help the child to see the wonder and the beauty in the "commonplace" world all around him.

2. *Expanding the horizons of children in space and time.* Most children, like most adults, live in a circumscribed world. It is true that radio, television, and motion pictures have expanded the world measurably in our generation, but the new media have not supplanted print as a means of broadening our horizons. Each of the new media has something unique to give, but each has its limitations. Only the printed word can offer to the reader the world of the past in the mood of reflection and reminiscence and interpretation. New symbols evoke, through the various electronic media, the excitement of the possibilities of the future. But only the book can fully unfold the meaning of that future in words which supply the reader with the means to communicate to others his aspirations for the life of tomorrow.

We should prefer Dick or Jane to visit Rome or the English Lake Country or New Orleans or Mexico City rather than merely to read about these places. But even when they are fortunate enough to do so, their direct observation of the new scenes will have clearer purpose and yield more abundant rewards if they have first read about them, and their subsequent reading will in turn be heightened in vividness and color.

Some day perhaps our schools will be supplied with air buses to take classes on guided tours to Gettysburg and Valley Forge, perhaps even to Jerusalem and the Nile Valley. For the present we are grateful if the schools have a few books with settings in these places. Since most boys and girls cannot see all of their world firsthand, it is of the greatest urgency that they be given the key to the medium of books, through which they can learn about that world. Eleanor Hoffman's *Mischief in Fez* can take them in spirit to Morocco to share in the enchantment of its hypnotic folklore. Evelyn Stefansson's *Here Is Alaska*, Reba Mirsky's *Seven Grandmothers*, Leonard Clark's *Explorers' Digest*, Augusta Baker's *Talking Tree: Fairy Tales from Fifteen Lands*, Beatrice Liu's

Little Wu and the Watermelons, Anna Louise Strong's *Peoples of the U.S.S.R.,* Irmengarde Eberle's *Big Family of Peoples,* Ann Nolan Clark's *Secret of the Andes,* and Denis Clark's *Life of a Kangaroo* are examples of the many hundreds of books which can lay the foundations of a broad world view. Sonja Bleeker's factual accounts of several American Indian tribes, such as *The Navajo,* extend the horizons of children with respect to a subject often obscured by distorted narrative or fanciful inventions.

So also the child's vision of the world of science can grow through the reading of the many fine new educational books. The numerous nature books of Herbert Zim, Reed's *Stars for Sam,* Schneider's *You Among the Stars,* Lewellen's *You and Atomic Energy,* and Selsam's *Play with Plants* are illustrative of the type. Informational books on subjects other than science are increasing in number and variety each year. They serve for fortunate children as "windows upon the world" of people and things. They help boys and girls to dwell in a constantly expanding world and to achieve a constantly expanding comprehension of that world.

3. *Providing vicarious experience.* Closely related to the objective of the widening horizon is that of the vicarious enrichment of experience. The materials and methods employed in the achievement of this objective will be substantially the same as those used in the effort to expand young people's intellectual horizons, but the direction which the instruction will take will vary in essential particulars. Here the purpose will be to build a stock of impressions which the child's direct experience cannot provide. It is by means of the rapidly growing, well-organized mass of experience with people, places, things, and processes that the child or youth develops the ability to comprehend what he reads, to converse interestingly, to discuss intelligently, to make constructive use of his leisure, to live comfortably with himself in hours of solitude.

We are dealing here with a fundamental principle of learning, one that emphasizes the overriding importance of a wide contact with the best in children's literature. The generalized concepts that the learner encounters in history and geography textbooks are the products of the author's systematic experiences. They cannot become the child's unless the child has first had an abundance of first-hand experiences on which generalized notions can be built. Textbooks, because they must be comprehensive, cannot supply these, or at best they can supply only a few of them. The chronology of the life of Lincoln will have little meaning for the reader unless he has first lived vicariously with Lincoln in his log cabin at New Salem, accompanied him on his circuit in Central Illinois, paced the floor with him in the White House, or visited General Grant with him in the general's tent. Reading the D'Aulaires' *Abraham Lincoln,* Enid Meadowcroft's *Abraham Lincoln,* Carl Sandburg's *Abe Lincoln Grows Up,* Augusta Stevenson's *Abe Lincoln: Frontier Boy,* Genevieve Foster's *Abraham Lincoln's World,* Clara Ingram Judson's *Abraham Lincoln, Friend of the People,* or the picture book *Abe Lincoln and His Times, 1809–1865* will be worth a hundred readings of a section of a chapter in a history text, however useful the text may be. These can provide the wealth of personalized contacts with the man Lincoln which will illuminate the larger patterns of history with which the textbook deals.

The peculiar advantage of children's literature is that it can offer an emotionalized approach to reality which enables the reader to identify himself personally with his subject. Carol R. Brink's *Caddie Woodlawn* and Laura Ingalls Wilder's "Little House" books do not merely list the facts about frontier life; they enable young readers actually to live it, endure its hardships, and rejoice in its simple, homely, but authentic delights. Statistics about casualties in the American Civil War will have significance in the development of a unit in the social studies, but they will not have personal meaning for young people until the pupils have read such books as Delight Ausley's *Sword and the Spirit: A Life of John Brown,* Arna Bontemps' *Chariot in the Sky,* Samuel and Beryl Epstein's *Andrews Raid,* or, in the case of early adolescents, Elsie Singmaster's *Swords of Steel,* a story of Gettysburg. Figures about exports take on meaning when young readers share in spirit in the life of the farmer or factory worker who produces them, the railroad or airplane worker who transports them, the stevedore who trucks them on the dock, the seaman who looks after their safe delivery. Children's literature is a means of seeing the world through other people's eyes for a time, and it multiplies a hundredfold the experiences and insights of each person who reads.

4. *Developing esthetic sensitivity.* Many complaints have been made about the general level of taste of the American people. The banality, transparency, and even venality of typical radio and television programs have been widely commented upon. The public taste in motion pictures has been criticized with equal severity. The run-of-the-mill picture makes its appeal to people of limited intelligence and crude taste, and producers say that these are the only films that can profit at the box office. There is reason to believe that the case has been overstated, since the public has often responded enthusiastically on those rare occasions when a really superior picture is offered. Nevertheless, it is clear that for multitudes of people the area of esthetic sensitivity has scarcely been cultivated. Good literature for children can help in the development of discrimination among esthetic values if the children can be introduced to it in an atmosphere conducive to such development.

Many boys and girls will at first find it difficult to obtain a deep pleasure from such a lovely but quiet, somewhat slow-moving book as Kenneth Grahame's *Wind in the Willows.* For some children, especially if it is read to them a chapter at a time, its humor, its receptiveness to the more subtle physical sensations, and its beautiful, simple style will prove irresistible. For others, it should be preceded by other stories more obvious, more dramatic. Hugh Lofting's *Dr. Dolittle,* Pamela Travers' *Mary Poppins,* Louisa May Alcott's *Little Women,* Dr. Seuss' *The 500 Hats of Bartholomew Cubbins,* or Robert

Lawson's *Rabbit Hill* will for some boys and girls be worthy preliminaries. For each child, certainly each group, the "literary escalator" will be different.

The development of esthetic appreciation was the earliest of the school's stated objectives in the teaching of literature, and for a long time it was the only one. Today, although we see many other valuable uses for literature, literary judgment, enjoyment, and appreciation remain among the most important.

5. *Helping children to understand themselves and others.* Evelyn Wenzel, in *Elementary English*, discussed the "Little House" books of Laura Ingalls Wilder. This fine series of stories certainly possesses great literary merit, but Professor Wenzel in this article considers them from another viewpoint. She has recognized these books as being a means of helping young people to accomplish their developmental tasks and to recognize how to meet their personal needs. She finds in Mrs. Wilder's work many situations dealing with (1) young people's need for security: material security, emotional security; (2) young people's need for achievement: physical, intellectual, spiritual, and moral achievement, growing up, overcoming fears and misunderstandings, overcoming sister troubles, meeting the problems of an expanding world, dealing with adolescent problems and the problems of courtship and marriage, and gaining insight into some of the mysteries of life; and (3) young people's need for change and escape. Professor Wenzel's is a valuable analysis—one that might be made of many other writers whose work has hitherto been considered from the point of view of literary excellence alone.

While this function of literature—that of promoting self-understanding—has been referred to as "bibliotherapy," there is legitimate objection to the use of this term, just as there is to the term "remedial reading." Therapy implies illness, and the existence of personal and interpersonal problems in the life of children is not an illness, but a normal condition. When the problems become serious enough they may require therapy, but the teacher is not a therapist.

Almost any kind of book can help young people in gaining insight into themselves and others, provided it is written at the level of their abilities and is an honest and skillful portrayal of life. Helen Sewell's *Jimmy and Jemima* portrays with appropriate humor for primary grade children the destructive effects of sibling rivalry. Even Eleanor Estes' "Moffat" stories, with their delicate nonsense, have their value in steadying the emotions of children who have frustrations and troubles great enough to test adult endurance.

As children grow up, they have the need to understand and accept differences in others. They must learn to accept the handicapped member of the class without derision or condescension. Actually, most children can do this quite unconsciously, but often their attitudes have been poisoned by adults. Teaching good human relations, therefore, is not so much a matter of developing new attitudes as of having children unlearn acquired ones.

The problem is of course especially serious in the case of differences in race and national origin. Many fine books have been written for children of various ages to develop an appreciation of differences and a respect for other cultures. Lorraine and Jerrold Beim's *Two Is a Team,* for the primary level, and Jesse Jackson's *Call Me Charley,* for the intermediate grade level, illustrate the many excellent books portraying the Negro. Laura Armer's *Waterless Mountain,* for younger children, and Florence Crannell Means' *Whispering Girl* and Sonja Bleeker's well-written anthropological studies, for older children, are examples of sympathetic portrayals of the American Indian. Many of us are familiar with Mrs. Means' *Moved-Outers,* about a Japanese relocation camp in California, and with Eleanor Estes' *Hundred Dresses,* a poignant story of an immigrant girl. Books about people in other countries are constantly increasing in number and improving in quality.

Fortunately for the teacher, there are now appearing many new guides to children's literature dealing with personal and human relations problems. *Reading Ladders for Human Relations,* published by the American Council on Education, provides a graduated list of children's and young people's books dealing with eight human relations themes. The Children's Book Center of the University of Chicago publishes a monthly list of the best new children's books, annotated and classified according to theme. Charlemae Rollins has written an excellent brochure, called *We Build Together,* listing young people's books about the Negro and suggesting criteria for the evaluation of such books.

Studying the Interests of Children

In order that we may effectively guide the reading of children, we must know a great deal about their interests. Reading interests are the product of the general interests of children and youth. Often, therefore, the process of stimulating reading interests involves the expansion and enrichment of the child's general interests. In the following sections we shall examine the various interests that have been found to be characteristics of boys and girls at various age levels.

Hobbies

Many children progress through a series of hobbies and diverse intellectual interests. One talented boy, for example, was successively preoccupied with the following topics from ages five to fourteen: animals, stamps, rocks, magic, chemistry, medieval heraldry, military strategy, photography, maps, hunting and fishing, navigation, locksmithing, and science fiction. Subsequently he developed an interest in hot rods, but fortunately pursued it only in magazines. In the fishing stage, his involvement was limited to the purchase of equipment with the small sums he earned as a newspaper carrier, because no fishing waters could be found in a reasonable distance from his home. His fishing hobby was strictly an activity of the imagination. But what is important is that during this phase he read *Field and Stream* and other outdoor-life magazines. In each of these stages his hobby was enriched through the reading of weekly armloads of library books which opened new worlds to him in his chosen field of interest. Only in his sports interests did he confine himself generally to the physical activities themselves.

Play Interests

Many studies have been made of the play interests and reading interests of boys and girls in the successive stages of their development. These studies reveal that while the individual differences among children are wide, certain interests tend to be persistent at given age levels from one generation to another. For example, all adults will recognize the lists of leisure time interests listed in Tables I and II as characteristic of most normal, able-bodied boys and girls.

TABLE I
Interests of Pupils in Grades 1 and 2

BOYS	PERCENT	GIRLS	PERCENT
Activity Preferences (95 Percent Return)			
Play outdoors	29.7	Play outdoors	28.7
Watch TV	27.7	Watch TV	22.5
Go to the movies	15.6	Go to the movies	16.7
Read stories	9.9	Listen to stories	13.7
Listen to stories	9.9	Read stories	10.3
Read comics	5.6	Read comics	6.1
Listen to radio	1.6	Listen to radio	2.0
Pets Owned (60 Percent Return)			
Dog	50.0	Cat	47.0
Cat	16.1	Dog	37.9
Bird	15.3	Bird	19.1
Fish	14.4	Fish	15.4
Turtle and parakeet	13.5	Parakeet	13.2
Attendance at Movies (88 Percent Return)			
Seldom or never	32.7	Seldom or never	29.6
Three to six times a year	22.9	Three to six times a year	22.9
Once a month	15.8	Once or twice a year	20.8
Once or twice a year	14.5	Once a month	16.1
Twice a month	8.8	Once a week	6.8
Once a week	5.3	Twice a month	3.8

TABLE I *Continued*
Interests of Pupils in Grades 1 and 2

BOYS	PERCENT	GIRLS	PERCENT
	Vocational Choices (97 Percent Return)		
Policeman	32.0	Nurse	36.5
Doctor	20.0	Teacher	33.9
Pilot	12.0	Mother and housewife	15.2
Baseball player	12.0	Ballerina	6.1
Scientist	7.3	Secretary	1.8
Fireman	3.3	Airline hostess	1.8
	Things Feared (95 Percent Return)		
Snakes	19.2	Dogs	22.2
Dogs	18.6	The dark	14.9
The dark	13.8	Storms	11.8
Fire	10.8	Snakes	11.3
Wild animals	5.4	Wild animals	9.5
	Games Liked Best (96 Percent Return)		
Baseball	27.6	Playing house	14.6
Cowboys and Indians	14.9	Playing school	12.6
Tetherball	7.5	Hide-and-seek	9.3
Monopoly	6.0	Tag	6.0
Checkers	6.0	Checkers	5.3
Duck-duck-goose	5.2	Playing with dolls	5.3

SOURCE: The data in tables I, II, III, and IV are selected, by permission of the author and the publishers, from a report by Professor Paul A. Witty, "Studies of Interests of Children," in *The Packet*, 16 (Winter 1961–1962), 15–23. *The Packet* is a Heath Service Bulletin for elementary teachers, published by D. C. Heath and Company, Boston, Mass.

Only the newer media of mass communication are peculiar to the interests of children today.

Television

The mass media of communication, especially television, are extremely popular with school children of all ages. In summarizing a series of annual reports on television viewing, Witty and Kinsella noted that, contrary to what many expert observers anticipated, television has maintained its popularity with elementary school children throughout the years that it has been available on a large scale.[1] It is the favorite leisure-time activity of young boys and girls. Regardless of intelligence or school success, children spend upwards of 20 hours

---

[1] Paul Witty and Paul Kinsella, "Televiewing: Some Observations from Studies 1949–1962," *Elementary English*, 39 (December 1962), 772–779, 802.

TABLE II
Interests of Pupils in Grades 3 Through 6

BOYS	PERCENT	GIRLS	PERCENT
Activity Preferences (95 Percent Return)			
Watching TV	29.4	Watching TV	24.8
Playing indoors	21.7	Reading	24.8
Reading	20.8	Playing indoors	15.9
Playing outside	13.5	Playing outside	7.0
Playing baseball	4.0	Ice skating	2.9
Playing football	4.0		
Movie Attendance (86 Percent Return)			
Once a week	34.5	Once a week	26.8
Once a month	24.4	Once a month	24.3
Twice a month	12.5	Less than once or twice a year	13.2
Three to six times a year	9.6	Three to six times a year	12.3
Once or twice a year	9.6	Twice a month	10.9
Less than once or twice a year	6.6	Once or twice a year	7.7
Twice a week	2.8	Twice a week	4.8
Vocational Preferences (96 Percent Return)			
Doctor	13.2	Teacher	22.7
Scientist	8.6	Nurse	18.7
Baseball player	7.0	Secretary	10.9
Engineer	5.4	Mother and housewife	6.4
Soldier	4.9	Airline hostess	6.2

SOURCE: Paul Witty, "Studies of Interests of Children," *The Packet,* 16 (Winter 1961–1962), 15–23.

a week in staring at the television screen. The continued hypnotic effect of this new medium has caused justified concern among those who believe that reading is still the most rewarding of all the methods of making vicarious contact with reality and of spending one's leisure time.

Complaints about the quality of television offerings for both children and adults are numerous and vigorous. For example, in 1954 the National Association for Better Radio and Television found that crime and violence on children's programs had increased 400 percent during the preceding three years. However, in 1955 it was able to point to the increased availability of other types of programs. Teachers and parents also blame television for such problems as neglect of homework, mealtime disturbance, increased nervousness, fatigue, impoverishment of play, disinterest in school, reduction in reading, and eyestrain.[2]

Does television stimulate or inhibit the development of interest in reading?

---

2 Paul Witty, "A Sixth Report on TV," *School and Society,* 83 (May 1956), 166–168.

The answer probably is that for some children it stimulates and for others it inhibits such interest. While many parents and teachers report that children on the whole read less today than they did before the advent of television, many librarians report an increase in the reading of children's books. Certainly the many long hours that children spend with television each week are diverted from time that in an earlier day might have been spent with good books. On the other hand, some television programs open new avenues of interest to children, who thereupon seek books on these subjects and read them with increased interest and comprehension. The relation between television and reading appears to depend upon the nature of the program and the nature of the individual child. *Zoo Parade, Disneyland,* travelogues, science programs, and biographical and historical presentations probably serve to encourage some children to read more widely.

Witty and Kinsella point out:

> We should, of course, not close our eyes to some unfortunate weaknesses in TV. Too many children's programs feature crime, horror and violence. Commercials, too, are sometimes not only absurd, but misleading. Too few programs are developed with a concern for the interests and welfare of children. Greater resourcefulness and imagination are certainly needed in planning and developing children's programs. The scheduling of children's programs is often unfortunate since adult programs, frequently inappropriate for children, predominate at the favorite viewing times.
>
> Despite limitations, this gigantic new instrument can provide worthwhile entertainment. There are some genuinely informative programs and occasionally inspiring presentations of great beauty. There are untapped possibilities for utilizing the interest engendered by TV to foster constructive individual and group endeavor. It is well to remember that the pleasures and satisfactions children derive from TV afford strong motivation for worthy accomplishment. For it often follows as John Masefield has said: "The days that make us happy are the days that make us wise."[3]

The Comics

The widespread popularity of the comic books is properly deplored by parents and teachers. Nearly one billion copies of comic books are distributed every year in the United States alone. They range from the informative type, the genuinely creative type ("Pogo" is an example), to the amusing and harmless type ("Nancy" is an example), to the Western, mystery, detective, and crime type, to the horror and pornography type. Contrary to the popular notion, there are hundreds of comic book series that make desirable or at least harmless reading. Moreover, the comic book industry itself appears to have made some headway, under public pressure, in improving the quality of their product. Never-

---

[3] Witty and Kinsella, *op. cit.,* pp. 779, 802.

theless, the ready availability of comic books which depict horror, violence, invasion of civil liberties, and contempt for law is rightly considered a menace. Even when a comic book does not openly portray killing, maiming, torture, stealing, or frightening monsters and machines, it may reflect, directly or by implication, unwholesome attitudes and ideals such as greed, unworthy ambition, selfishness, and the worship of material success.

There has been much debate as to the effects of the crime comics upon the personality of the child and upon juvenile delinquency. A number of serious writers have held the comics responsible for misbehavior and crime on the part of children. For example, Fredric Wertham, senior psychiatrist at Bellevue and Queens General Hospitals in New York City, has associated much cruel or

TABLE III
Reading Interests of Pupils in Grades 1 and 2

BOYS	PERCENT	GIRLS	PERCENT
Kinds of Books Preferred (95 Percent Return)			
Animals	34.2	Animals	52.4
Stars, planets, space	28.2	Children of other lands	28.6
Pilots	17.1	Children at home	21.7
Children at home	5.3	Fairy tales	9.7
Children of other lands	4.6	School	9.0
Series Books Read (61 Percent Return)			
Golden Books	58.4	Golden Books	62.5
I Want To Be Books	14.3	True Books	5.5
True Books	7.8	I Want To Be Books	4.2
Oz Books	6.5	Wonder Books	2.8
First Books	2.6	Oz Books	2.4
		First Books	2.4
Magazines Preferred (51 Percent Return)			
Humpty Dumpty	46.3	*Humpty Dumpty*	46.8
Jack and Jill	20.4	*Jack and Jill*	26.6
Highlights	9.3	*Highlights*	7.6
Children's Digest	5.5	*Children's Digest*	3.8
Boys' Life	3.7	*Child Life*	2.5

SOURCE: Paul Witty, "Studies of Interests of Children," *The Packet,* 16 (Winter 1961–1962), 15–23.

criminal behavior of children with the reading of comic books. On the other hand, juvenile court judges appear to be divided as to the influence of the comic book upon the actual behavior of children.

Certainly we cannot be led to the conclusion that all comic books should be outlawed. Even the legal censorship of comic books raises serious constitu-

TABLE IV
Reading Interests of Pupils in Grades 3 Through 6

BOYS	PERCENT	GIRLS	PERCENT

Kinds of Stories Liked (92 Percent Return)

BOYS	PERCENT	GIRLS	PERCENT
Adventure	20.3	Mystery	18.3
Westerns	17.1	Adventure	16.1
Mystery	17.0	Animal	14.3
Science fiction	12.9	Humor	10.8
Humor	9.3	Westerns	10.3

Preferred Storybooks (93 Percent Return)

Black Beauty	*Little Women*
Davy Crockett	*Cinderella*
Daniel Boone	*Snow White*
Robin Hood, Thirty Seconds over Tokyo,	*Heidi*
and *Custer's Last Stand*	*Black Beauty*

Nonfiction Reading (84 Percent Return)

BOYS	PERCENT	GIRLS	PERCENT
Space travel	28.7	Famous people	25.0
Famous people	18.5	People from other lands	17.7
Handicrafts	12.8	Handicrafts	16.1
Travel	12.7	Travel	12.7
Careers	10.3	Space travel	11.5

Series Books Read (99 Percent Return)

BOYS	PERCENT	GIRLS	PERCENT
Landmark	28.0	First Books	12.8
First Books	16.3	Landmark	7.8
Teen-Age Tales	10.2	Bobbsey Twins	7.8

Magazines Read by Pupils in Grades 3 Through 6 (86 Percent Return)

BOYS	PERCENT	GIRLS	PERCENT
Life	28.8	*Life*	26.3
Boys' Life	22.5	*Look*	14.1
Look	12.0	*Saturday Evening Post*	6.9
Saturday Evening Post	6.5	*Jack and Jill*	6.7
Sports Illustrated	3.0	*American Girl*	4.6
Ebony	3.0	*Better Homes and Gardens*	4.6

SOURCE: Paul Witty, "Studies of Interests of Children," *The Packet*, 16 (Winter 1961–1962), 15–23.

tional questions. Parental and public pressure may help a great deal in cleaning up the magazine stands, but in the final analysis the solution lies in developing among children genuine interests in the better reading materials—including comic books—of which there is such a rich abundance. The comic book is a highly popular new medium. It appeals because of its color, action, suspense, romance, and adventure. As in the case of the motion picture, radio, and television, we have no choice but to accept it, to improve it if possible, and to develop discrimination in its use.

Children of course differ widely in their interests in comic books. Wolf and Fiske[4] described three types of comic readers. The first are the "fans" (37 percent), the second the moderate readers (48 percent), and the third the indifferent or hostile (15 percent). The interest of the first group is violent and excessive. The "fan" may be described as a "compulsive" reader. He tends to be or become a neurotic. He has a tremendous need for the "invincible hero," the superman. Wolf and Fiske tell about a 17-year-old girl, dreaming of being in mortal danger, crying, "Superman! Where are you?" and of a 12-year-old boy reporting, "When I am sick, when my nerves are all twisted, when I am worried, I read comics and they help me." Physically inferior children are more likely to be "fans" than tall and strong children. "Fans" in general avoid books because the action is slower and the pictures fewer. But for such children we should probably regard excessive reading of comic books either as a symptom or a cause of emotional maladjustment, or both.

Comic book reading generally passes through three stages. Children under eleven like the "funny animal" comics, the Donald Ducks and Bugs Bunnies who walk and talk and act like human beings in familiar situations. This age group tends to read more comic books than older children. Eleven- and twelve-year-olds specialize in fantastic adventure comics—"Superman," "Batman," "Captain Marvel," "Captain Video." Children over twelve increasingly read *True* and *Classic* comics, if they read comics at all. Since the total amount of comic book reading declines sharply after ages eleven and twelve, these, then, are the critical ages in the reading of comics, from the standpoint of both the number and the quality.

Sports and crime comics are of course more popular with boys than with girls; both sexes like humor when it is available. Strangely enough, there is little difference in the amount and character of the general reading of those who read comic books extensively and those who do not. Nor is there any great difference in comic book reading habits between good readers and poor. Vocabulary development is on the whole no less rapid among comic book readers than among nonreaders of these books.

The popularity of comic books may probably be attributed in large part to their low cost and ready availability. New and used copies may be purchased for a few cents; a flourishing exchange market exists in many schools. On the other hand, good books, attractive books, may cost upwards of $2.00 each.

---

[4] Katherine M. Wolf and Marjorie Fiske, "The Children Talk About Comics," *Communications Research, 1948–1949*, Paul Lazarsfeld and Frank Stanton, eds., pp. 3–50. New York: Harper and Row, Publishers, 1949.

When libraries and classrooms provide boys and girls with well-illustrated books about adventure, animals, space travel, science, humor, and other themes that appeal to them, the battle with the comic book can often be won.

Magazines

Since comic books appear in magazine form, one valuable method of combating undesirable comics is to introduce the children to the many fine magazines addressed to them. Children's magazines have many features in common with the comic books. The selections are short and usually well illustrated. Like comic books, they are expendable, timely, varied. It is therefore not astonishing that magazines are very popular with elementary school children beyond the second grade. They represent a much-neglected resource of the school.

The following list of magazines was compiled by Professor Thomas D. Horn:[5]

PERIODICALS FOR CHILDREN AND YOUTH

American Childhood. Springfield, Massachusetts. (5–9 years) Educational magazine published for kindergarten and primary grades, 10 months of the year, Sept.-June. 1 year, $4.

American Farm Youth. Danville, Illinois. (Boys, 14–24 years) Published nine months of the year, Sept.-May.

American Girl. New York. (Girls, 10–16 years, whether they belong to Girl Scouts or not) Published by the Girl Scouts of America.

American Junior Red Cross Journal. Washington, D. C. (Junior High and High School) Not church connected. Published by the American National Red Cross and distributed mainly to schools enrolled in the Junior Red Cross. Subscriptions accepted, but actually publications are designed as program material for the membership.

American Junior Red Cross News. Washington, D. C. Same as *American Junior Red Cross Journal,* but on elementary school level.

Arts and Activities. Skokie, Illinois. (5–12 years) Published 10 months of the year —not July and August.

Audubon Magazine. New York. (15 years and up) Published by the National Audubon Society.

Boys' Life. New York. (Scouts and others, 8–18 years) Published by Boy Scouts of America.

Child Life. Boston, Massachusetts. (3–10 years) Published 10 months of the year.

Children's Digest. New York. (7–12 years)

Children's Play Mate Magazine. Cleveland, Ohio. (6–12 years)

Current Biography. The H. W. Wilson Company, New York.

---

[5] Compiled by Thomas D. Horn and published in *Elementary English,* May 1959, pp. 342–344. Reprinted by permission. This list does not include the many excellent children's magazines published by religious organizations.

Current Events. American Education Publications, Education Center, Columbus, Ohio. (Grades 6, 7, and 8) Eight-page current events paper.

Current Science and Aviation. American Education Publications, Education Center, Columbus, Ohio. (Grades 7–12) Weekly science newspaper, eight pages.

Every Week. American Education Publications, Education Center, Columbus, Ohio. (Grades 9 and 10) Especially designed for use in world history, civics, and geography classes.

Explorer. Scholastic Magazines, New York. (Grade 4) Stories, news, and activities. Published weekly during school year.

Field and Stream. New York. Not a children's magazine, but the magazine is read by many teen-age boys, because they find a great deal in each issue that guides them in sportsmanship.

Flying. Davis Publishing Company, New York. Average age of reader 31 years.

Flying Models. New York. (12–21 years) Aimed at model builders of all ages.

Forest and Outdoors. Montreal, Canada. No particular age range.

Geographic School Bulletins. National Geographic Society, Washington, D.C. Weekly bulletin used by children from Grades 5 and 6 on up through college, but there are more readers in junior and senior high than in elementary grades.

Highlights for Children. Columbus, Ohio. Varied reading and other activities. Spiritual and patriotic emphases.

Humpty Dumpty. New York. (3–7 years)

Jack and Jill. Curtis Publishing Company, Philadelphia, Pennsylvania. (5–10 years) Boys and girls of primary and intermediate grades.

Junior Bazaar for Children. New York. *Harper's Junior Bazaar* no long exists as such, but was incorporated into *Harper's Bazaar.* Consists of fashions for children, and appears every odd month. No less than four pages.

Junior Natural History Magazine. American Museum of Natural History, New York. (8–15 years) Not church connected. Popular introduction to all phases of natural history.

Junior Review. Civic Education Service, Washington, D.C. (Junior High School) Eight-page paper. Gives students a clear, stimulating introduction to national and world problems.

Model Airplane News. New York. Junior aviation science. Not a child's publication, but about 30,000 8–12-year-olds read this magazine.

My Weekly Reader. Columbus, Ohio. Six editions for the elementary school, one in Braille.

National Geographic Magazine. National Geographic Society, Washington, D.C. Issued monthly, no religious affiliation.

Nature Magazine. Washington, D.C. Actually an adult publication, but goes into over 15,000 elementary schools and libraries to be used for reference on elementary science, biology, nature study, etc.

Newstime. Scholastic Magazines, New York. (Grade 5) Language arts, social studies, science.

Our Times. American Education Publications, Education Center, Columbus, Ohio. (Grades 11 and 12) Eight-page paper designed to meet needs of U.S. history, economics, advanced civics, and senior problems courses.

Read. American Education Publications, Education Center, Columbus, Ohio. (Grades 6–9) Balanced variety of the best in current reading for both English and social studies classes. 32 pages, two times each month.

Scholastic Magazine. New York. *Junior Scholastic* for Junior High School, English and social studies, *Senior Scholastic* for Senior High School, social studies.

Sports Afield. Hearst Magazines Division of the Hearst Corp., New York. No fiction —editorial format designed for hunter, fisherman, and boating enthusiast. Not a child's magazine primarily, but many young people find it interesting and informative.

Straight. The Standard Publishing Foundation, Cincinnati, Ohio. *Straight* replaces *Boy Life* magazine (last issue Sept. 30, 1951). (12–15 years) Published weekly.

World Week. New York. (Grades 8–10) Social studies.

Wee Wisdom. Lee's Summit, Missouri. (Children 5–13 years of age)

Young Perfectionist, The. Harper's Junior Bazaar incorporated into *Harper's Bazaar.* New York. Consists of about 10 pages of fashions for the younger set every month.

TABLE V
Choices of Magazines
Ranked According to Frequency of Mention

	BOYS N = 1038			GIRLS N = 989		
Rank	*Type*	*Number*	*Percent*	*Type*	*Number*	*Percent*
1	Detective and mystery	303	29.2	General story	198	20.0
2	Science and mechanics	241	23.2	Movies and theater	185	18.7
3	Children's	124	11.9	Children's	155	15.7
4	Adventure	117	11.3	Detective and mystery	113	11.4
5	General story	97	9.3	Household	90	9.1
6	Aviation	77	7.4	Serious—popular	88	8.9
7	Serious—popular	61	5.9	Science and mathematics	80	8.1
8	Comics	39	3.8	Literary	53	5.4
9	Sports	33	3.2	Comics	30	3.0
10	Movie and theater	31	3.0	Adventure	16	1.6
11	Literary	26	2.5	Lodge	13	1.3
12	Household	19	1.8	Religion	6	0.6
13	Religion	5	0.5	Sports	5	0.5
14	Lodge	4	0.4	Musical	4	0.4
15	Health	2	0.2	Health	3	0.3
16	Musical	..	..	Aviation	..	..

SOURCE: May Lazar, *Reading Interests, Activities, and Opportunities of Bright, Average and Dull Children.* Contributions to Education, No. 707. New York: Bureau of Publications, Teachers College, Columbia University, 1937.

One of the best known and reliable sources of information is Laura K. Martin's *Magazines for School Libraries.*[6] *101 Magazines for Schools,* by Ruby E. Cundiff, is available from the Tennessee Book Company.[7] The National Council of Teachers of English has published a committee report entitled *Using Magazines.*[8] A monthly mimeographed periodical called *Subject Index to Children's Magazines* serves as a kind of juvenile *Reader's Guide to Periodical Literature.* It is edited by Meribah Hazen at 301 Palomino Lake, Madison, Wisconsin.

Newspapers

Elementary school children read the newspapers. Many of them read only the comic strips, but large numbers of elementary school boys read the sport section, and a considerable number of both boys and girls read news stories. Table VI shows the ranks of different sections of the newspaper according to the expressed preference of the children.

TABLE VI
Sections of Newspaper Liked
Ranked According to Frequency of Mention

	BOYS N = 990			GIRLS N = 955		
Rank	*Section*	*Number*	*Percent*	*Section*	*Number*	*Percent*
1	Comics	793	80.1	Comics	852	89.2
2	Sport	223	22.5	News	73	7.6
3	News	68	6.8	Crossword puzzles	53	5.5
4	Crimes	36	3.6	Stories	40	4.2
5	Stories	26	2.6	Crimes	23	2.4
6	Crossword puzzles	25	2.5	Sport	23	2.4
7	Front page	21	2.1	Editorial	16	1.7
8	All	14	1.4	Theater and screen	11	1.2
9	Editorial	14	1.4	All	10	1.0
10	Rotogravure	11	1.1	Front page	8	0.8
11	Magazine	3	0.3	Society	8	0.8
12	Political	3	0.3	Rotogravure	8	0.8

SOURCE: May Lazar, *Reading Interests, Activities, and Opportunities of Bright, Average, and Dull Children.* Contributions to Education, No. 707. New York: Bureau of Publications, Teachers College, Columbia University, 1937.

[6] New York: The H. W. Wilson Company, 1950.
[7] Nashville, Tenn., 1954.
[8] Champaign, Ill., 1950.

Books

As every teacher knows, children differ widely in the degree to which they are interested in the reading of books. Some children read no books at all on their own, while others read several books a week. In order to discover what kinds of books will interest children, it is necessary to examine the voluntary choices of those who do like to read. Many such studies have been made.

Dunn,[9] for example, studied the interests of primary grade children more than forty years ago. She found that in these early years the interests of boys and girls were very similar. She listed among the strong interest factors the following: "childness," familiar experience, surprise, plot, liveliness, conversation, and "animalness." Of course, the first two elements ranked highest. For this reason, most modern primary basal readers stress stories about children having familiar experiences.

Some very interesting facts about the reading interests of middle and upper grade elementary school children have been reported in recent years. It has been found,[10] for example, that reading, in spite of radio and television, ranks fourth among the major recreational interests. At this level, stories and fiction —especially stories about animals—seem to have the greatest appeal to children. Moreover, children tend to choose books by a relatively small number of authors; if they like a book, they will look for other books by the same author. Some studies show that there is an increase in free reading from age 7 to 10 and 12 to 13, but a decline as pupils approach high school and enter the high school years. Perhaps the growing influence of social activities, parties, dating, and more diversified forms of recreation is responsible for this.

In the middle and upper grades children choose mystery and adventure stories and stories about children, horses, and dogs. As they progress through grades four to seven, they become increasingly interested in mystery stories and show decreasing interest in cowboy stories and fairy tales. They like animal stories throughout the period, but boys become interested in sports stories as they move toward the upper grades. Boys in the upper grades enjoy informational books about science, airplanes, space travel, Indians, boats, and rockets. Girls like stories about mythology, mystery, teen-agers and children, famous people, boy-girl relationships, and school.[11] These preferences are illustrated in Tables VII and VIII.

----

[9] Fannie W. Dunn, *Interest Factors in Primary Reading.* Teachers College Contributions to Education, No. 113. New York: Bureau of Publications, Teachers College, Columbia University, 1921.

[10] Inez L. Manck and Esther J. Swenson, "A Study of Children's Recreational Reading," *Elementary School Journal,* 50 (November 1949), 144–50.

[11] Herbert C. Rudman, "The Informational Needs and Reading Interests of Children in Grades IV through VIII," *Elementary School Journal,* 55 (May 1955), 502–16.

As one might expect, pictures help a great deal to interest children in books. Children especially prefer colored pictures. However, the picture merely serves as a bridge to the content of the book. If the subject of the picture interests the reader, it will lure him to the book; if it does not, it will be ineffective.

TABLE VII
Five Kinds of Books Liked Best by Boys

PERCENT BRIGHT		PERCENT AVERAGE		PERCENT DULL	
Adventure	33.0	Mystery	23.4	Mystery	30.8
Mystery	19.7	Adventure	22.1	Detective	29.2
Detective	14.2	Detective	18.1	Adventure	9.8
Science	10.4	History	13.6	History	7.9
History	7.0	Invention	8.2	Nature and animal	7.9

SOURCE: May Lazar, *Reading Interests, Activities and Opportunities of Bright, Average, and Dull Children.* Contributions to Education, No. 707. New York: Bureau of Publications, Teachers College, Columbia University, 1937.

TABLE VIII
Five Kinds of Books Liked Best by Girls

PERCENT BRIGHT		PERCENT AVERAGE		PERCENT DULL	
Mystery	27.1	Mystery	32.3	Fairy tales	38.3
Adventure	21.0	Fairy tales	21.1	Mystery	21.8
Fairy tales	14.4	Adventure	14.1	Detective	8.6
Novels	9.6	Home and school	7.0	Adventure	7.6
Home and school	9.3	History	6.2	Home and school	6.6

SOURCE: Lazar, *op. cit.*

In judging whether a book will interest a child, we must be careful not to be limited to adult standards. Children obviously do not always like books that adults consider superior. It is possible for adults to remember books they liked as children, and to assume that modern children will like them too. In some cases, of course, this is true. *Little Women, Heidi, Black Beauty, The Five Little Peppers,* and *Treasure Island* are perennially popular with children; *Robinson Crusoe, A Christmas Carol, Hans Brinker,* and *Tom Sawyer* also fall in this category. But other children's books of the past deal with topics and express attitudes that were of interest in their day but seem inappropriate or even ludicrous in our time. The same holds true for the element of literary style.

Many of the Newbery Prize books, for example, while chosen by competent librarians for their literary excellence, are not popular with children.[12] They are lacking in the elements of adventure and excitement that children like.

When we read these generalizations about children's interests in books and reading, we must always keep in mind that each child has his own individual pattern of voluntary reading. Some average children read more than some bright children. Some boys read more than some girls. Some able readers read very little; some children of limited reading ability read a great deal. Some children continue to increase in the amount of reading as they reach adolescence. Some children read excessively, or "compulsively," because of emotional maladjustment; others avoid reading, for the same reason. It is the particular combination of cultural and personality factors that come together in the life of an individual child that determines his voluntary reading habits. There can be no substitute for the painstaking study of individual children to discover the extent and nature of their reading interests.

---

[12] Marie Rankin, *Children's Interests in Library Books of Fiction*. New York: Bureau of Publications, Teachers College, Columbia University, 1944.

11b

Developing
Children's Interests in Reading

The preceding chapter discussed the importance of the interest factor in the teaching of reading, the purposes of the voluntary reading program, and the developmental stages in the unfolding interests of boys and girls. In this chapter we shall consider ways in which the classroom teacher can extend the range and elevate the quality of children's interests in reading.

Although the term "free" reading is commonly used to distinguish it from assigned reading, in a sense it is a misnomer. The child who reads freely and widely in the pulps and worthless or harmful books is in great need of guidance by teachers and parents. It is one of the aims of the reading program to influence his preferences so that he will choose more worthy and more rewarding books to read. Perhaps the term "voluntary" reading or "personal" reading would be better. In "directed reading," the teacher guides the reading choices of children in the direction of books of specific types or books that have certain themes. Such guidance may be desirable in the case of children who are too steadily absorbed in a single subject or who have never discovered that poetry or biography can be fun, too. In this chapter, for the sake of uniformity, we shall employ the term "voluntary" reading.

Principles Underlying the Voluntary Reading Program

Before describing specific classroom practices in the guidance of voluntary reading, we shall enumerate certain principles which will help us to devise and evaluate our procedures. There are no doubt others, but these are among the most fundamental of the governing principles:

1. Interests are acquired and, like other acquired traits, are amenable to training or teaching. They are responsive to the home and school environments and are conditioned by experience.

2. In any group of children, there will be wide variations in the children's tastes and interests. It is the task of the teacher to dis-

269

cover, so far as possible, what these tastes and interests are.

3. Reading interests and life interests bear a reciprocal relation to each other. A child will read, or can be induced to read, about the things he is interested in; through reading he will become interested in more things.

4. In order that we may improve a child's interests and tastes in reading, we must begin at his present level. No matter how limited or immature his interests may be, they are all we have to build upon. We cannot usually advance the child from Mickey Mouse to *Robinson Crusoe* in one leap. Normally we progress by easy stages. The speed will depend upon the child and the circumstances.

5. The program in voluntary reading should be a balanced program. It should include many themes and areas of interest, many literary types, many media, and both factual and imaginative material. It should appeal to many different types of pupil purposes.

6. Many children who read widely will oscillate between books of high and of low literary merit. All printed matter is grist to their mill. The measure of their growth is the highest literary level to which they respond with comprehension and pleasure. The reading of material of lesser quality is in itself no evidence of immaturity.

7. In the evaluation of children's reading interests, every effort should be made to ascertain the child's genuine preferences rather than his perception of what the teacher considers worthwhile.

8. The techniques of improving a child's voluntary reading habits should in general be those of enticement and persuasion, rather than those of coercion. "The fact of *choosing* a certain book invites something of a child's own living into what the words and pictures say. And just as strongly, the fact of being *assigned* a certain book makes it difficult for a child to bring his own zest and enthusiasm to the written symbols."[1]

9. The aim of the voluntary reading program should be, not the reading of certain specific books, or a certain number of books, but the development of enduring interests in reading.

10. Home and school cooperation is of great value in the cultivation of desirable reading interests on the part of children.

Conditions Needed for Effective Guidance

The Teacher

In the development of reading interests, as in all other instruction, the teacher is the key factor. If the teacher feels affection for the children, exhibits a sincere interest in their problems and their interests, is accepting, gives encouragement, and demonstrates genuine enthusiasm for books, she can create an atmosphere that is favorable to voluntary reading. The teacher who exercises a rigid discipline will get from many only such reading as she demands, and no more. The reading is unlikely to be accompanied with pleasure, and it will end when the assignments end.

The teacher's attitude toward the pupils should be, within limits, a permissive one. Children should be free to go from their seats to the book table or to read a story to a classmate or to go to the teacher with a comment or a call for help. All this presupposes, of course, a class size which will permit mobility and a certain amount of intercommunication. Crowded classrooms necessarily require a degree of regimentation and formal "discipline."

A generalized attitude of friendliness and good *rapport* with children are not enough. Since the task of the teacher is to bring child and book together, she must know a great

[1] Peggy Brogan and Lorene K. Fox, *Helping Children Learn*, p. 107. New York: Harcourt, Brace and World, Inc., 1955.

deal about the child, and she must have a wide acquaintance with children's books. Her knowledge of the child should include information about his home background, his intelligence, his general maturity, his personal adjustment, his reading ability, his play interests, and his reading interests. School records, tests, interviews with parents and other teachers, and particularly a careful observation of individual children are ways through which the teacher can know the child.

The teacher's preparation for the cultivation of children's interests in books includes a wide acquaintance with the rapidly growing supply of juvenile literature. While a good background in the reading of adult literature and acquaintance with the best in the theater, movies, radio, and television will be of great assistance, wide reading in children's books is essential. Reliance upon recollection of favorite books of one's own childhood will not do. So much has happened in this field, even in the last ten years, that a new look at children's books is imperative. The reading of the new books can be a really delightful experience. It is impossible for a teacher to be familiar with even a small fraction of the new titles, but she should be on speaking terms with the best of them. Fortunately she may have access to numerous publications which will acquaint her with recommended children's books. A list of such publications is found in the latter part of this chapter.

The Physical Environment

No studies, to our knowledge, have been made of the effect of the physical environment in the classroom upon the development of reading interests in children. Nevertheless, experienced teachers believe that attractive surroundings help in encouraging children to read. For most children, especially those who have little interest in reading, an attractive room provides a setting in which reading seems the natural thing to do. Some children will, of course, develop strong reading interests almost regardless of the physical surroundings. An inviting reading corner, with table, comfortable chairs, and perhaps a reading lamp, may attract children who have completed their other work. Movable tables and chairs, plenty of shelf space, a book display table, a bulletin board, and above all, a colorful display of books, frequently changed, will help to create the reading environment in which the love of books can flourish.

The Curriculum

When we speak of voluntary reading, we refer to reading that is personal, individual, and therefore not necessarily related to any units of work that may be in progress in the classroom. Nevertheless, the kind of curriculum that is pursued may have a great influence upon children's voluntary reading activities. If the curriculum is inflexible, totally prescribed, and textbook centered, it is likely to dampen the enthusiasm of many children for books and to blunt the edge of their curiosity. On the other hand, if the curriculum is vital and stimulating, if it encourages child initiative, if it encourages exploration in many directions, it will provide an abundance of "leads" for pleasurable personal reading. In this process almost every subject of study may have a part.

ACTIVITIES THAT PROMOTE WHOLESOME VOLUNTARY READING. The teacher who is both a lover of books and a lover of children will be resourceful in finding new ways of bringing children and books together. However, there are many standard techniques which skillful teachers frequently use on appropriate occasions. Here are some of them:

1. *Utilizing children's experiences.* Young children in modern schools enjoy a great variety of experiences. In some classrooms

there is a "discovery" table on which may be found a constantly changing collection of interesting objects, contributed by both teacher and pupils—shells, rocks, tropical fish, twigs, models of trains or planes, textile samples, parts of Indian or foreign costumes, and the like. Each day the children go to the table to see what is new there. Questions come thick and fast, and the teacher is ready to suggest and to display fine children's books that will help to answer them. One teacher,[2] who had recently returned from a Mexican trip, placed numerous Mexican souvenirs on the table, told stories about her trip, and started many boys and girls on reading books about Mexico.

Class visits to places of interest in the community or in nearby towns may also be a source of inspiration for voluntary reading. Classes, under the supervision of a teacher and with the consent of the parents, often go to the zoo, the museum, historical shrines, the bakery, the dairy, the farm, a factory, a newspaper plant, an airport, a railway station (sometimes children may talk with trainmen or inspect the cab of the engine), and radio and television stations. The alert teacher will arrange to have many good books about these places ready for children to read on their return. If children have become really interested, they will usually not be deterred by vocabulary which would ordinarily be too difficult for them.

The active classroom provides the setting for many other kinds of experiences. Primary grade children are fascinated by many kinds of pets. Hamsters, kittens, raccoons, white mice, goldfish, snakes, and rabbits have all found comfortable homes and eager audiences in primary grade schoolrooms. Fortunately on all of these there is much interesting material for children to read.

2. *Reading and telling to children.* Perhaps

the most popular time of the school day is the Story Hour. If it is to be successful, however, it requires careful thought and preparation on the part of the teacher. The story chosen for the day should possess literary merit. It should be one that the teacher herself enjoys and can read aloud with enthusiasm. The children should be grouped about the teacher, sitting on the floor or on comfortable chairs, not too crowded but close enough to the teacher to hear with ease. The group should not be too large; if necessary the class should be divided into subgroups to help create an atmosphere of intimacy and to permit the teacher to read in a quiet though animated voice. The teacher first shows the children the book—the jacket, the cover, the title page. As she reads, she will pause occasionally to ask a question, make a comment, or answer the inevitable exclamations and questions of the children. She will take time to show the illustrations as the story proceeds, and she will accede to the noisy requests to look at them again after the story is over. She will take pains to make it possible for *all* the children to have a good view of the pictures.

Well-liked stories may be read again and again. Children like to hear the familiar tales repeated, and they are likely to learn something new at each reading. In the second and third grades, moreover, the children are often interested in the names of the author and the illustrator, and will look for other books by the same authors and artists. Some of the authors and illustrators are themselves interesting enough personalities to tell about.[3]

Sometimes, especially with older children, the teacher will stop short of the climax and invite the children to read for themselves how the story turned out. Or she will stop and ask the children to guess at the outcome

[2] Described by Frank M. Durkee in "Why Johnny Reads," *Elementary School Journal,* 61 (April 1956), 363–365.

[3] Clara Evans, "Enjoying New Books with Children," *Elementary English,* 29 (November 1952), 419–420.

before she reads to the end. If she asks the pupils to finish the story by themselves, she will arrange, if possible, to have several copies of the book available in order to avoid the tantalizing and frustrating effect of indefinite suspense.

In the lower grades children are often encouraged to read stories to each other. The reader should be a fairly good oral reader, enthusiastic about the story, and the listener must be a willing one.

Storytelling by the teacher is one of the most ancient of all the means by which young people become aware of the heritage of books. While good storytelling is an art, it is one that can be successfully cultivated by any teacher of young children. Valuable hints may be found in the recent pamphlet, *Once upon a Time,* prepared by the Picture Book Committee of the Children's and Young People's Section of the New York Library Association. It may be obtained for 25 cents from Anne Izard of the New York City Public Library. Also, the entire March 1957 issue of the magazine *Elementary English* is devoted to the subject of Listening and Storytelling. Another source is *Stories to Tell to Children,* compiled by Laura E. Cathon and others (Pittsburgh: Carnegie Library, 1949). An excellent book on the subject of storytelling, containing many examples of good stories to tell to children, has been written by Ruth Tooze, director of the Children's Book Caravan.[4]

3. *Using the browsing table.* One of the most influential factors in the development of reading interests is that of accessibility. Perhaps the widespread popularity of the paperbacks, both good and bad, is attributable to the fact that they may be secured so easily and inexpensively at any drugstore. Many people will not make the effort to go to the library and the bookstore to get a

book, but will purchase a paperback along with a newspaper, a railroad ticket, or a candy bar. Thus, unfortunately, we seldom find a queue at the charging desk of a library.

So it is with children. Until a keen appetite for reading has been aroused, it is necessary to bring the books to the children. The book display on a browsing table should be attractive and colorful. It should be varied in subject matter, and changed frequently to lend new interest from week to week. At appropriate times during the school day, the children should be permitted and encouraged to go to the table, page through the books, look at the pictures, and select a book to read in school and to borrow for home use. When new books are added to the collection, the teacher should take a few minutes to call the children's attention to them.

4. *Pupil selection and management of books.* Nowhere does the principle of teacher-pupil planning operate with more effectiveness than in the guidance of voluntary reading. If the children have a voice in the selection of the books for the room collection, they are more likely to feel a proprietary interest in them and may be motivated to read them, or at least to become acquainted with them.

Methods of acquiring books for the room collection vary from one school system to another. In some schools a certain sum of money is periodically allotted to each teacher, who may order the book titles she believes she needs. In other schools all general book purchases are made through the principal's office or the school library. In almost all instances, when books are available for room collections, the teacher has the opportunity to make the selection of titles. In any case, whether the books are newly purchased or borrowed from a central collection, the teacher has the opportunity to consult her pupils about the books to be requested.

Preparing the book order is an exciting event in the elementary school classroom.

---

[4] Ruth Tooze, *Storytelling: How to Develop Skills in the Art of Telling Stories to Children.* Englewood Cliffs, N.J.: Prentice-Hall, Inc., 1959.

Children who have enjoyed books by certain authors will ask about other titles by the same writers and request that they be included in the order. "May we have some more books about dogs (horses, sports, adventure, fairy tales, magic, space travel)?" will be a common question. The teacher herself, of course, should have many titles to recommend. She will describe these to the children, telling them something of the theme and story of each. When the final order is ready to send in, the teacher makes a last-minute inspection to be sure that all the selections are appropriate for her class.

The children will be impatient for the books to arrive. The time when they finally come is a red-letter day. If they are new and arrive by mail, the children should have the pleasure of opening the packages. In any event, the arrival of the books should be some kind of ceremony, followed by a quiet period of browsing.

Children will take pleasure, too, in preparing the books for the shelves (it is to be hoped that the room is equipped with an abundance of open shelf space). Under the guidance of the teacher, they will arrange the books on the shelves and on the browsing table. Pupil committees will assist in the work of charging out books and keeping the records. They will help in returning books to the central library and in bringing back new titles. Through taking care of and handling books, children will come to regard them as precious possessions.

5. *Book discussions and informal book reports.* When a child likes a book, he wants to talk about it with someone. He should therefore have opportunity to talk with the teacher about it and be encouraged to tell the class about it during the discussions in Story Hour. Sometimes he can be encouraged to stand before the group and recapitulate the story.

Care should be taken not to allow the oral book reports to become a tedious succession of routine summaries. First, there should probably be no more than two or three reports in a period. Second, children should be taught how to make an effective report. It is possible to explain to them how to select the significant details of a story, to arrange them in proper order, and to build up suspense. Third, the class should be given opportunity to ask questions and to discuss the story. Such oral reports are not intended to serve as a check on whether the boys and girls have read the minimum number of books. Their purpose is to introduce other children to new books they will like.

6. *Dramatizations.* Children who have read the same book may wish to dramatize scenes from it. The dialogue may be taken directly from the book, or it may be improvised. This latter, "creative," kind of dramatics is usually more fun and is less likely to be stilted and overformal. However, the nature of the story and especially the vocabulary employed in the quotations should determine the type of dramatization selected. Other children may wish to reproduce in costume a particularly striking illustration from a book. Guessing games, too, are popular with children. A pupil, or a group of pupils, will act out characters from a story with the aid of pantomime and simple costume, while the rest of the class guesses the identity of the characters. If large sections of a book or an entire book is made into a play, it may be possible to record the final performance on tape, to be replayed for other classes.

7. *Use of audio-visual aids.* Visual aids are a very effective means of awakening the children's desire to read. These aids may include phonograph records, radio and television programs, films, filmstrips, slides, and pictures.

Dramatic recordings of books that have won the Newbery Award are now available. The discs, which are $33\frac{1}{3}$ r.p.m., sell for $5.95 and may be obtained direct from

Newbery Awards Records, New York. Complete teaching aids, including background information, vocabulary lists, suggestions for prelistening and follow-up activities, and other data, accompany the records. The dramatizations are expertly directed and are performed by professional actors. The famous Landmark Book Series, published by Random House, is accompanied by dramatizations based upon the books. The records may be secured from Enrichment Records, Inc., New York. Other publishers similarly produce records that dramatize children's books. Thomas Y. Crowell, for example, has issued a record of *Harriet Tubman, Conductor on the Underground Railroad,* by Ann Perry, and Ginn and Company has an album of LP recordings entitled, "Let's Listen." Record companies have issued recordings of many of the children's favorites. Camden (R.C.A.-Victor) has one on *The 500 Hats of Bartholomew Cubbins,* by Dr. Seuss, read by Paul Wing, and another on *A Christmas Carol.* Spoken Arts Records provides unusual recordings of literature. Of particular interest to teachers of young children are the *Just So Stories* of Kipling, *You Read to Me, I'll Read to You,* by John Ciardi, and *Grimm's Fairy Tales.* A catalog may be obtained from Spoken Arts, New Rochelle, New York. Folkways Records presents songs, folktales, and poetry. A catalog may be secured from Folkways Records, New York.

The playing of such records, both before and after the reading of the books, gives the children a sense of the reality of the story and often makes the reading itself an irresistible activity.

The use of records and recordings has numerous advantages. First, it is possible for the teacher to listen in advance to a record in order to determine its suitability for a class. Second, it is possible to stop a record at any time to discuss aspects of a story or to answer children's questions. Third, it is possible to play a record over and over, as often as the teacher or the children may desire.

As the record appeals to the ear, so the slide, filmstrip, and film appeal to the eye. Like the phonograph record, however, the visual media require careful preplanning by the teacher. Especially in the case of the slide and the filmstrip, the teacher should be familiar with the content in advance. While some filmstrips are accompanied by a record that is synchronized with the pictures on the screen, for others, the teacher must supply the sound element that is lacking—the explanation and the commentary. Often the filmstrips come provided with a teachers' manual, which explains each frame and focuses attention upon the significant ideas in the series. As a rule, it is desirable to discuss with the class in advance what is to be looked for in the still or moving pictures and to follow up the presentation with questions, interpretations, and summaries.

An example of filmstrips suited to the elementary grades is the series "Our American Heritage of Folk Music," produced by the Society for Visual Education, Inc., Chicago, Illinois. This is a series of long-playing records accompanied by filmstrips on Songs of the Sea, Songs of the Cowboy, Songs of the Mountains, Songs of the Plains, Songs of the Railroads, and Songs of the Civil War. Each filmstrip consists of about 50 frames. The records and filmstrips together provide a pleasant stimulus to the reading of children's books dealing with these themes.

Certain radio and television programs can be recommended in connection with developing children's interest in reading. Many stations throughout the country conduct regular "book hours" to which we can call children's attention. The National Broadcasting Company, for example, offers a regular weekly radio series entitled "Carnival of Books." Two books recently presented are *The Mighty Soo,* by Clara Ingram Judson (Follett) and *Santiago,* by Ann Nolan Clark.

Although television is a new medium, it has grown with unprecedented speed. The annual surveys by Paul Witty in *Elementary English* effectively dramatize the phenomenal development of this industry. Already a large body of professional literature on the subject of children and television has come into being. Two interesting pamphlets may be recommended: *Children and TV—Making the Most of It,* a publication of the Association for Childhood Education International, Washington, D.C. (75 cents); and *Your Child, Radio, and TV,* by Paul Witty, published by Science Research Associates, Chicago, Illinois.

Not all audio-visual aids are as formal as those described in the preceding paragraphs. Many miscellaneous aids may be used to good advantage. Attractive bulletin board displays, colorful wall maps, pictures, and book jackets may frequently be used to serve as an avenue to the reading of books.

Although schools are still not making adequate use of audio-visual aids, they are beginning to recognize the value of such aids in teaching. In an N. E. A. survey, it was found that school appropriations for audio-visual equipment and supplies had risen from 35 cents per pupil in 1946 to 65 cents in 1954. The N. E. A. reported that 25 percent of American classrooms were well adapted to audio-visual methods, 38 percent moderately well adapted, and 37 percent completely unadapted.

Following are some lists of sources for audio-visual materials. These lists are highly selected, for the field of audio-visual methods in teaching has become so large that a whole book would be required to do justice to it. Fortunately there is a growing supply of literature on the subject. A comprehensive book concerning it is the attractive volume by Edgar Dale, *Audio-Visual Methods in*

Teaching, rev. ed., published by Holt, Rinehart and Winston, Inc.

AUDIO-VISUAL MATERIALS—GENERAL

Audio-Visual Materials for Teaching Reading. A very extensive listing of films, filmstrips, slides, pictures, recordings, and special devices for the teaching of reading. Compiled by Robert Leestma of the Audio-Visual Education Center of the University of Michigan. Slater's Bookstore, Inc., Ann Arbor, Mich. ($1.50)

Audio-Visual Catalog. Materials for Learning, Inc., Brooklyn, N.Y.

SELECTED INFORMATION SOURCES FOR EDUCATIONAL FILMS

Catalog of Frith Films. Hollywood, Calif.

Instructional Films and Filmstrips. 16 mm. Catalog of Universal-International and J. Arthur Rank features. United World Films, New York.

Library of Congress, Card Division, Washington, D.C. Price lists of catalog card service for films and records.

UCLA Children's Film Series. Children's Theatre Committee, Theatre Arts Department, University of California, Los Angeles. Self-addressed, stamped envelope.

SELECTED LIST OF SOURCES OF EDUCATIONAL FILMS

Coronet Films, Chicago.

Education Film Library Association, New York.

Encyclopaedia Britannica Films, Inc., Wilmette, Ill.

International Film Bureau, Chicago.

Jam Handy Organization, Detroit.

McGraw-Hill Filmstrip Catalog, McGraw-Hill Text-Films, New York.

Teaching Film Custodians, New York.
United World Films, New York.
Many state universities also operate rental libraries of educational films.

SELECTED INFORMATION SOURCES FOR EDUCATIONAL RECORDS AND RECORDINGS

Annotated List of Phonograph Records. Materials for Learning, Inc., Brooklyn, N.Y. (10 cents)
Catalog of Recorded Tape and Catalog of Children's Records. M. and N. Harrison, Inc., New York.
Folkways Record and Service Corporation, record catalog, New York.
National Tape Recording Catalog, 1962–1963. Department of Audio-Visual Instruction, N. E. A., Washington, D.C.
Spoken Arts Records, New Rochelle, N.Y.
The Tape Recorder in the Elementary Classroom. Minnesota Mining and Manufacturing Company, St. Paul, Minn.

SELECTED LIST OF SOURCES OF EDUCATIONAL RECORDINGS

American Friends Service Committee, Philadelphia.
American Library Association, Chicago. (Folk tales)
Children's Record Guild, New York.
Columbia Records, Inc., New York.
Decca Records, New York.
Educational Record Company of Illinois, Charleston, Ill.
Enrichment Landmark Records, to accompany Landmark Books (Random House). Enrichment Teaching Materials, New York.
Instructional Films, Wilmette, Ill.
Library of Congress, Washington, D.C.
National Council of Teachers of English, Champaign, Ill.
World Wide Records Corporation, New York.

SELECTED INFORMATION SOURCES FOR EDUCATIONAL FILMSTRIPS AND SLIDES

Educational Filmstrip Catalog. Society for Visual Education, Inc., Chicago.
Educator's Guide to Free Slidefilms. Educators Progress Service, Randolph, Wis.
Enrichment Filmstrips. Enrichment Teaching Materials, New York. Based on such Landmark Books (Random House) as *Paul Revere and the Minute Men, The Winter at Valley Forge, The California Gold Rush.*
Eye Gate House, Inc., Jamaica, N.Y.
Filmstrip Catalog. From 21 companies, arranged by subjects. Also a catalog of educational record albums. Stanley Bowmar Company, Valhalla, N.Y.
Filmstrip Guide. The H. W. Wilson Company, New York. Classified by subjects. Alphabetical index. Found in many libraries.
Jam Handy Organization, Detroit.
Keystone View Company Catalogs. Meadville, Pa. Extensive listing of slides.
Society for Visual Education, Inc., Chicago.
Young America Filmstrip Catalog. Young America Films, New York.

MISCELLANEOUS AUDIO-VISUAL AIDS

Baited Bulletin Boards, prepared by Thomas A. Koskey. Fearon Publishers, San Francisco, Calif. Design, color, grouping, eye movement, texture, shape. Illustrated. Examples. ($1.50)
Better Bulletin Board Displays, by J. Preston Lockridge and Ernest F. Tiemann. Bridges for Ideas Series, Visual Instruction Bureau, Division of Extension, University of Texas, Austin, Tex. Designed so that every page can be used as resource material for the preparation of bulletin boards.
Bulletin Boards, by Martha Dallmann. Teachers Publishing Corporation, Dar-

ien, Conn., 1959. Planning, use, materials, procedures; suggestions for various subjects. 114 illustrations. ($1.95)

Graphic Tools for Teachers, by R. A. Frye. E. and J. Printing Company, Austin, Tex. Using graphic materials in the classroom.

Portrait of the real Davy Crockett, by S. S. Osgood, lithographer. 10″ x 15″. State Teachers Magazines, Inc. Chicago. (3 cents)

FREE AND INEXPENSIVE MATERIALS— GENERAL

Catalog of Free Teaching Aids. Riverside, Calif. ($1.25)

Choosing Free Materials for Use in the Schools. AASA, Washington, D.C. (50 cents)

Educators Guide to Free Films. Educators Progress Service, Randolph, Wis. ($9.00) Annual.

Educators Guide to Free Slidefilms. (Same as above) ($6.00)

Elementary Teachers Guide to Free Curriculum Materials. (Same as above)

Free and Inexpensive Learning Materials. Division of Surveys and Field Services, George Peabody College for Teachers, Nashville, Tenn. ($1.50)

8. *Book programs by children on radio and television.* Radio and television stations, especially in the smaller communities, welcome school groups to their programs. The opportunity to present a discussion of children's books on radio or television can serve as powerful motivation for children to read the best of the current books for young people. Both large city schools and schools in smaller towns have successfully produced children's book programs in this manner, sometimes as single projects and sometimes in a regular series during the winter months.[5]

One enterprising teacher organized a Children's Radio Workshop with boys and girls from ages nine to fourteen. Every Saturday morning different members of the group give an unrehearsed program in which they cooperatively develop an original story. Wide reading of an abundance of excellent books for children and young people supplies background for this creative experience.[6]

With primary grade children it is sometimes effective to have a storytelling period with a make-believe microphone. Such simulated "broadcasts" may serve to encourage the shy child who normally would hesitate to speak before a group. Programs may take the form of dramatizations, interviews, or direct storytelling. Visits to local radio studios will furnish ideas for procedures and physical settings. Later on, the children will be ready to participate in real broadcasts on radio and television. Meanwhile the focus will be on the books themselves and on the exciting activity of sharing book experiences.

9. *Book Week activities, book festivals, and book fairs.* In order to stimulate interest in children's books on a nation-wide scale, the Children's Book Council each year sponsors the National Children's Book Week. The Council, composed of the children's book editors of 60 leading publishing houses, is located in New York. It supplies schools with a Book Week poster, usually designed by a distinguished illustrator of children's books, streamers with children's book themes, full-color bookmarks reproducing the Book Week posters, records, picture quizzes, and other Book Week aids. Local schools throughout the country celebrate Book Week with special assemblies, open house, plays, radio programs, and other activities.

Recognizing that fall Book Week activities often tended to result in neglect of book

---

[5] Louise E. Sheppard, "Fun with Books," *Elementary English,* 31 (December 1954), 468–471.

[6] Margaret G. Mercille, "Creating on the Air," *Elementary English,* 27 (December 1950), 507–510.

Films are effective allies of the reading teacher

A small group of first graders learns the sound and meanings of printed words
Winnetka, Illinois, Public Schools
Librarian and teacher cooperate in cultivating children's interest in reading

projects during the rest of the year, the New York *Herald Tribune* established in 1937 the Spring Book Festival. It began by awarding two prizes of $250 each, one for the best book for younger children and one for older children. The newspaper issues each May a special Spring Book Festival number corresponding to the Children's Book Week number in the fall. Spring Book Week is observed in cooperation with bookstores from coast to coast.

Another development in the field of children's books is the book fair, or book bazaar. The book fair is usually a community project involving the schools, libraries, churches, civic groups, and various organizations interested in literature and the arts. Interest in local book fairs has been stimulated by the Children's Book Council, which also publishes a volume, *The World of Children's Books,* that includes a chapter on "How to Run a Book Fair." The book fair is usually set up in cooperation with a local bookseller or jobber who supplies the books and allows a commission on direct sales and orders taken at the fair. Such proceeds from book sales are commonly applied to some educational project, often the expansion of the school library. An extensive list of books for display in the fair has been compiled by the Publisher's Liaison Committee. It may be secured without cost from the Children's Book Council.

In 1954 the first Midwest Book Fair, with 2600 titles, was co-sponsored by the Children's Book Council, the *Chicago Tribune,* and the Chicago Public Library. Held at Chicago's Museum of Science and Industry, it attracted 44,000 visitors. Trained children's librarians were on hand to answer questions. One booth exhibited a model children's home library. Other book fairs were held that same year in New York (the *Times's* "Reading Is Fun" exhibit toured the schools in the New York area), Cleveland, Buffalo, Detroit, Washington, Minneapolis, Philadelphia, and Hampton, Virginia. Distinguished

children's authors appeared at some of the fairs. Storytelling programs were held mornings and afternoons. At one, Ferdinand the Bull made a personal appearance, along with clowns who entertained the young children.[7]

Book fairs need not be planned on the grand scale of those held in the great cities. In one school[8] the project is sponsored annually by two fourth-grade classes. One year, library tables usually arranged for small groups were placed around the room for displays of new books. Book Week posters and pupil-made murals of scenes from the books lined the walls of the room. Prize-winning books, along with displays of jackets and facsimiles of the medals, were featured. Original new-book illustrations loaned by the publishers were mounted on the upper shelves, and the exhibit also included photographs of authors and illustrators. A puppet show featuring characters from favorite books was shown to the children of other grades and to parents. In all these activities, the PTA cooperated closely.

10. *Miscellaneous procedures.* The teacher who is enthusiastic about books and reading will of course find many new ways of interesting children in books. Teachers can cooperate with children's librarians who organize reading clubs that meet regularly in the public library or branch library. The activities of such reading groups may include film showings, book reviews by the members or by adult counsellors, tours of historical sites or places of local interest, record sessions, arranging for guest speakers, parties, and the discussion of reviews in magazines and newspapers.

Classroom activities may include recommending favorite books to children in lower grades, conducting imaginary conversations among well-known characters from different

7 Lucy Tompkins, "Let's Have a Book Fair," *Top of the News,* 10 (May 1954), 18–21.

8 Gladys Jacobson, "Book Fair at Daniel Webster," *Elementary English,* 27 (October 1950), 356–367.

books, visiting the public library, writing letters of appreciation to authors of books that were especially well liked (one class was delighted to receive a cordial reply from E. B. White),[9] writing brief reactions to stories that had a special impact, identifying story sites on a world map, making theme posters from books, and having each child assemble his own poetry anthology.

Other activities that have been suggested[10] include decorating book jackets; writing a movie script for an adventure story; giving an illustrated lecture about a travel book, using postcards, slides, magazine clippings, and other pictorial matter; making a "movie" of a book by means of a series of pictures on a paper roll attached to rollers; supplying a different ending to a story; selecting the most humorous or exciting incident from a book to tell to the class; writing a letter to the librarian or a friend recommending a book; making a scrapbook about a subject treated in a book; giving a puppet show based on a book; stretching a cord across the room and mounting on it paper cloths decorated with titles and pictures of book characters; modeling clay or soap figures from illustrations in books; making a diorama on a sand table to reproduce the setting of a story; making a mural from a story; listening to radio or television reviews of children's books; selecting poems for choral reading; collecting pictures to illustrate a book of verse.

Puppet shows can be very effective, but they require advance planning and some specialized knowledge. The following are some reference sources for work with puppets and marionettes:

Fletcher, Helen Jill, and Jack Deckter, *Puppet Book*. New York: Chilton, 1947.

---

[9] Lucy Nulton, "Eight-Year-Olds Tangled in *Charlotte's Web*," *Elementary English*, 31 (January 1954), 11–16.

[10] Amy Elizabeth Jensen, "Attracting Children to Books," *Elementary English*, 33 (October 1956).

Hoben, Alice M., *The Beginner's Puppet Book*. New York: Noble and Noble, 1938.

Nau, Elizabeth, "Making Marionettes for the Classroom," *Elementary English*, 29 (January 1952), 19.

Pels, Gertrude, *Easy Puppets*. Illustrated by Albert Pels. New York: Crowell, 1951.

Rhodes, M., "Pupils and Puppets," *The Grade Teacher*, 69 (November 1951), 48.

Although cumulative reading records are commonly regarded as evaluation devices, they can serve also as incentives to reading. Cumulative records take many forms. Some teachers ask children to keep card files of books they have read. Others provide each child with a large card with spaces for authors, titles, and a one- or two-sentence description of each book. A four-page leaflet called *My Reading Design* provides for listing of book titles and insertion of numbers in a pie graph representing different themes and types of books.[11]

Developing Interest in Poetry

Leland B. Jacobs, in an article, "Making Poetry Live with Children," in *Literature with Children*, edited by Margaret Rasmussen, a publication of the Association for Childhood Education International, has many valuable suggestions for the development of children's interest in poetry:

POETS EVERY CHILD SHOULD MEET

Perceptive teachers constructively set about to enrich school living through poetry. In the first place, they know intimately the appeals of many poets whose work is attractive to children. Such teachers are well acquainted with the writings of poets with whom chil-

---

[11] Published by *The News Journal*, North Manchester, Ind.

dren should have the opportunity to get acquainted:

Dorothy Aldis
Mary Austin
Harry Behn
Rosemary and Stephen Benét
William Blake
Margaret Wise Brown
Lewis Carroll
Marchette Chute
John Ciardi
Elizabeth Coatsworth
Walter De La Mare
Paul Laurence Dunbar
Ivy O. Eastwick
Eleanor Farjeon
Eugene Field
Rachel Field
Aileen Fisher
Frances Frost
Rose Fyleman
Edward Lear
Vachel Lindsay
Myra Cohn Livingston
A. A. Milne
Laura E. Richards
James Whitcomb Riley
Elizabeth Madox Roberts
Christina Rossetti
Carl Sandburg
Robert Louis Stevenson
James S. Tippett
Winifred Welles
Annette Wynn

Of course, there are many other poets whose one or two or handful of poems are appealing to children and should be at the teacher's fingertips for use at the right time. In addition, if the teacher possesses several outstanding anthologies for children, he will be rich in resources for making poetry time a happy time for youngsters.

Anyone who is well read in poetry for children soon discovers that there never can be graded poetry lists. To say "These are fifth grade poems" is unfair to children and to poetry. The teacher should not be concerned with "leveling" poetry. Rather, he should select poetry, whether it be primarily written for children or adults, which meets children's mind and spirits at the present gradients of their development as personalities, as thinking persons and as consumers of the arts.

WHAT CHILDREN ENJOY IN POETRY

A perceptive teacher knows that children develop taste in poetry only as the adults in their lives guide that development of taste. The teacher capitalizes on what children like in poetry but at the same time whets their taste with good poetry which is the work of sensitive, original writers. Children enjoy good poetry that:

gives them an exhilarating sense of melodious movement

makes the everyday experiences of life vibrant

tells wonderful stories

releases health-giving laughter

carries them into extravagant or fanciful situations

extends their appreciation of their natural world

creates memorable personages or characters

sings its way into their minds and memories.

Pleasurable responses to poetry are evoked when poetry selections are neatly gauged to the maturity and interests of the youngsters. In the poetry of their workday world, children respond well to poems about pets, play activities, occupations, transportation and interesting people. In their natural world they enjoy poems about seasons, weather, animals, flowers, trees. In humorous poetry they respond to ludicrous situations, peculiar people, tongue-tickling words, absurdities, oddities and nonsense. In narrative poetry they listen enthusiastically to adventure on sea and land, patriotic achievements, courageous deeds, historical personages and events and rousing heroism. In the fanciful, they enjoy fine make-believe, the poetic interpretation of preternatural creatures, and at times the grotesque. In lyric poetry they feel akin to poetry that is rich in sensory imagery, creates moods, calls forth pictures in the mind, makes the commonplace distinctively uncommon.

POEMS MUST BE READ WELL

Then, too, the modern teacher knows that poems do not look particularly inviting on a printed page. But when the poem is read well, all its melody, its vibrance, its feeling tone, its movement, its unique quality leap into life. So the teacher learns how to read poetry well. A good reader is one who:

appreciatively comprehends the psychological content and emotional intent of the poem which he is reading

knows that as he reads a poem to children he must both reveal what seem to be the poet's thoughts and communicate the poet's moods and nuances of meaning to the listeners

helps the listener to think, sense, and feel with the poet

sympathetically interprets the full esthetic appeal and quality of mood which the poem possesses

takes his clues for the actual oralization from the patterning of the poem: its variety, its images, its symbols, its rhythms, its rhymes, its symmetry

employs effective variety in timing in his reading and uses the eloquence of appropriate pauses

so utilizes tonal quality in volume, pitch, and force that, through cadenced reading, enjoyment is enhanced

avoids elocutionary, declamatory or other forms of artificial oral interpretation in favor of wholesome naturalness

acts as a medium through which the ideas and feelings of the poet touch deeply the ideas and feelings of the listener. . . .[12]

The School Library

Since the textbook has ceased to dominate instruction in modern elementary schools,

greater reliance than ever is being placed upon the library. The library provides an extensive and well-selected variety of recreational books, geared to many interests and levels of reading ability.[13] It has fine reference books such as *Compton's Pictured Encyclopedia*,[14] *The World Book*,[15] and the *Britannica Junior*,[16] as well as such sets as *The Pictorial Encyclopedia of American History*.[17] The library helps children to develop new interests and hobbies, and introduces them to the use of community libraries and bookstores. It serves also as a central repository for books that are loaned to teachers for classroom use.

The mere existence of a school library is no guarantee that it will be effectively used. Wherever possible, it should be administered by a full-time, trained librarian, not left to some teacher to care for after school. The librarian should have as many assistants as are necessary to take care of mechanical and routine details so that she can devote her main energies to book selection and reading guidance. A good system of classifying and cataloguing should be put into operation. The librarian should be a member of school-wide curriculum committees in order that she can cooperate fully in carrying out educational policy. Provision should be made for all pupils to go to the library regularly. Children should feel that they are welcome in the library and that the librarian is a very useful friend and helper.

In some schools the library has been made into a "materials center" for the school. This means that it serves as a central clearing house for all instructional materials, includ-

---

[12] Reprinted by permission of the Association for Childhood Education International, 3615 Wisconsin Avenue, N.W., Washington 16, D.C. From Bulletin No. 3-A, *Literature with Children,* Copyright 1961; "Making Literature Live with Children," by Leland B. Jacobs. The student is urged to read this entire excellent pamphlet.

[13] Jewel Gardiner, "The Library in the Elementary School Program," *Elementary English,* 27 (May 1950), 312–319.

[14] F. E. Compton Company, Chicago.

[15] Field Enterprises, Educational Division, Chicago.

[16] *Britannica Junior,* Chicago.

[17] Childrens Press, Inc., Chicago.

ing audio-visual aids, pamphlets, textbooks, and the like. Since library books are only one kind of instructional material, it seems logical that the library should be a center for all kinds of teaching aids. The library should be a vital, busy educational unit, not a museum.

Some objections, however, have been raised to the use of the library as a materials center.[18] It is pointed out that the work of a materials center may become a purely mechanical and routine activity and will add to the already great burden of the librarian. Moreover, fears are expressed that appropriations for audio-visual and other materials will be deducted from the expenditures for books. Further, the expert handling of instructional material will add to the training needed by the qualified librarian. These are valid objections. The idea of the materials center should therefore not be introduced unless the school is prepared to add a specialist in audio-visual aids and sufficient clerical staff, and to provide the necessary additional space and equipment without reducing in any way the appropriation for library books and library maintenance.

In view of the great importance of the school library in every good reading program, it is regrettable that so large a percentage of American elementary schools have inadequate libraries, or none at all. When pressures from increased enrollments call for ever more classroom space, the library room, if one has been provided, is often the first to go. Administrators and teachers should do all in their power to convince Boards of Education and the public that a good library is essential to a good school. Far from being a luxury, it is a facility without which the school cannot function efficiently.

Requirements for an elementary school library will vary with the size of the school. If the school has no library, the staff should

see that a beginning, however modest, is made and that improvement and expansion are provided for each year. The school should be provided with the statement of school library standards of the American Library Association (*Standards for School Library Programs,* by the American Association of School Librarians, Chicago). This report describes standards for personnel, equipment, and materials for school libraries in schools of various enrollments.

The American Library Association recommends, for example, that schools with 200 to 1,000 pupils have a library of 6,000 to 10,000 books, and that schools with 200 to 250 pupils appropriate $1,000 to $1,500 per year to the library, exclusive of reference books, binding costs, and salaries. It recommends that six-grade elementary schools subscribe to 25 magazines. It advocates the employment, in schools of small enrollment, of a librarian one day per week; provision for the storage and classification of pamphlets, newspapers, films and film-strips, pictures and slides, and realia; a professional collection for teachers, including books and magazines, supported by an annual appropriation of not less than $200; in larger schools, in addition to the reading room, one or more conference rooms and a workroom.

Choosing Books for the Room and School Libraries

With the exception of those who are experts in children's literature, few teachers are able to keep up with the great outpouring of children's books, and fewer still can judge with ease which of the new titles are suitable for children. Teachers are therefore dependent in great degree upon the recommendations of the specialists. The numerous booklists now available will therefore be sources or valuable aids to teachers in planning their periodic requests for books. There are a few standard lists that should be part of the

---

[18] Helen R. Sattley, "The School Library," *ALA Bulletin,* 50 (June 1956), 373–376.

reference collection of every elementary school library. These will include:

A Basic Book Collection for Elementary Grades. Chicago: American Library Association, 1943.

A Basic Collection for Junior High Schools. Compiled by Elsa R. Berner and Mabel Sacra. Chicago: American Library Association, 1950.

Bibliography of Books for Children. Washington, D.C.: Association for Childhood Education International, 1947.

The Children's Catalog. Compiled by Ruth Giles and others. Standard Catalog Series. New York: The H. W. Wilson Company. Supplements.

A comprehensive list of references and booklists is found in an article by Barbara V. Olson in *Elementary English* for May 1961, "Aids for Librarians in Elementary Schools."

Other lists are published by the American Library Association and many other organizations. The following compilation, which includes many book lists commonly employed by teachers and librarians, is not intended to be comprehensive. By reading such magazines as the *ALA Bulletin, The Library Journal, The Horn Book,* and *Elementary English,* among other magazines of library and educational organizations, the teacher may keep abreast of the new publications in the field of children's literature. The children's book sections of such newspapers and magazines as the *New York Times,* the New York *Herald Tribune,* and the *Saturday Review* report many of the best new publications in the field of children's literature. Since the output (more than 1200 new titles per year) is so great, it is not possible for any of these periodicals to report upon and evaluate more than a small fraction of the year's products. Every elementary school should seek to be included in the regular mailing lists of the leading publishers. The professional library of every elementary school should include at least some of the following booklists:

A SELECTED LIST OF BOOKLISTS

The Junior Reviewers (Catalog of the Best Books for children). Titles grouped by ages or special subjects, arranged alphabetically by author. New Centre, Mass. (75¢ a copy, 40¢ for 20 or more, 25¢ for 100 or more, 20¢ for 1000 or more)

BOOKS ON HUMAN RELATIONS

Character Formation through Books: A Bibliography, rev. ed. Compiled by Clara J. Kircher. Washington, D.C.: Catholic University of America Press, 1952. ($1.50)

Developing World-Minded Children: Resources for Elementary School Teachers, Leonard S. Kenworthy, 1951. Copies may be obtained from Leonard S. Kenworthy, Brooklyn College, Brooklyn, N.Y. (30¢ per copy, 25¢ per copy for 10 or more copies)

"Help from Books: Bibliotherapy in the Elementary School, A Manual and Guide," *The Saint Louis Public School Journal,* 6 (November 1952). by Earl G. Herminghaus. St. Louis, Missouri, Public Schools.

Reading Ladders for Human Relations, rev. ed. Margaret M. Heaton, Helen B. Lewis. American Council on Education, Room 110, 1785 Massachusetts Ave., N.W., Washington 6, D.C., 1955.

We Build Together, rev. ed., Charlemae Rollins. Champaign, Ill.: National Council of Teachers of English, 1948. Negro life. (65¢ each)

MISCELLANEOUS LISTS

Adventuring in Literature with Children. Bulletin No. 92. Washington, D.C.: American Association for Childhood Education International, 1953. (75 cents)

Adventuring with Books. Champaign, Ill.: National Council of Teachers of English.

A Bibliography of Books for Children. Washington, D.C.: Association for Childhood Education International, 1962.

Booklist Books: a Selection. Chicago: American Library Association. (40 cents)

Books for Beginning Readers. By Elizabeth Guilfoile. Champaign, Ill.: National Council of Teachers of English, 1962.

Books for Tired Eyes. Compiled by Charlotte Matson and Lola Larson. Chicago: American Library Association, 1951.

Branch Library Book News: Books for Young People. New York: New York Public Library. (25¢ each)

Children's Books for $1.25 or Less. Washington, D.C.: Association for Childhood Education International, 1961.

Children's Books too Good to Miss. By May Hill Arbuthnot and others. Cleveland: The Press of Western Reserve University, 1948. (75¢ each)

Current Books: Junior Booklist of the Secondary Education Board. Prepared by the Committee on Junior Booklist. Secondary Education Board, Milton, Mass. (35¢ each)

"Distinguished Children's Books," *ALA Bulletin,* annual. Chicago: American Library Association. (25¢ each)

Educational Reading Guide for the Partially Seeing. Compiled by Lorraine Galisdorfer. Buffalo, N.Y.: Foster and Stewart Publishing Corporation, 1950.

Fifty Years of Children's Books. By Dora V. Smith. Champaign, Ill.: National Council of Teachers of English, 1963.

Gold Star List of American Fiction, annual. Syracuse, N.Y.: Syracuse Public Library.

Good Books for Children. Edited by Mary K. Eakin. Chicago: The University of Chicago Press, 1959. ($5.95)

Growing Up with Books. New York: R. R. Bowker Company. (10 cents each; $3.75 per 100 copies)

Recommended Children's Books of 1963. Compiled under the direction of Louise Davis. *Library Journal,* New York: Arranged by grade and subject with author-title index. ($1 net postpaid for extra copies) (Annual)

The Southwest in Children's Books. Edited by Mildred P. Harrington, Baton Rouge, La.: Louisiana State University Press, 1952.

Starred Books from the Library Journal. Edited by Peggy Melcher. *Library Journal,* New York: Arranged by grade and subject with author-title index. (50¢ net postpaid for extra copies)

Stories: A List of Stories to Tell and to Read Aloud. Compiled by Eulalie Steinmetz. New York: New York Public Library. Alphabetically arranged, followed by a subject index.

Story Telling. By Ruth Tooze. Englewood Cliffs, N.J.: Prentice-Hall, Inc., 1959.

Summary of Junior Book Awards Program. Boys' Clubs of America, New York.

A Teacher's Guide to Children's Books. By Nancy Larrick. Columbus, Ohio: Charles E. Merrill Books, Inc., 1960.

Treasure for the Taking: A Book List for Boys and Girls. By Anne Thaxter. New York: Viking Press. ($2.50)

Wisconsin Reading Circle Annual. Issued by the State Reading Circle Board. Supplements. State Reading Circle Board, State Department of Public Instruction, Madison, Wis.

Your Reading: A Book List for Junior High School. Champaign, Ill.: National Council of Teachers of English. (60¢ each)

The following are award-winning books in various competitions:

NEWBERY WINNERS

1922   *The Story of Mankind,* Hendrick Van Loon. Liveright Publishing Corporation.

1923 *The Voyages of Dr. Dolittle,* Hugh Lofting. J. B. Lippincott Company.

1924 *The Dark Frigate,* Charles Boardman Hawes. Little, Brown and Company.

1925 *Tales from Silver Lands,* Charles J. Finger. Doubleday and Company, Inc.

1926 *Shen of the Sea,* Arthur Bowie Chrisman. E. P. Dutton and Company, Inc.

1927 *Smoky, the Cowhorse,* Will James. Charles Scribner's Sons.

1928 *Gayneck: The Story of a Pigeon,* Dhan Gopal Mukerji. E. P. Dutton and Company, Inc.

1929 *The Trumpeter of Krakow,* Eric P. Kelly. The Macmillan Company.

1930 *Hitty: Her First Hundred Years,* Rachel Field. The Macmillan Company.

1931 *The Cat Who Went to Heaven,* Elizabeth Coatsworth. The Macmillan Company.

1932 *Waterless Mountain,* Laura Adams Armer. David McKay Company, Inc.

1933 *Young Fu of the Upper Yangtze,* Elizabeth Foreman Lewis. Holt, Rinehart and Winston, Inc.

1934 *The Story of the Author of Little Women: Invincible Louisa,* Cornelia Meigs. Little, Brown and Company.

1935 *Dobry,* Monica Shannon. The Viking Press, Inc.

1936 *Caddie Woodlawn,* Carol Ryrie Brink. The Macmillan Company.

1937 *Roller Skates,* Ruth Sawyer. The Viking Press, Inc.

1938 *The White Stag,* Kate Seredy. The Viking Press, Inc.

1939 *Thimble Summer,* Elizabeth Enricht. Holt, Rinehart and Winston, Inc.

1940 *Daniel Boone,* James Daugherty. The Viking Press, Inc.

1941 *Call It Courage,* Armstrong Sperry. The Macmillan Company.

1942 *The Matchlock Gun,* Walter D. Edmonds. Dodd, Mead and Company, Inc.

1943 *Adam of the Road,* Elizabeth Janet Gray. The Viking Press, Inc.

1944 *Johnny Tremain,* Esther Forbes. Houghton Mifflin Company.

1945 *Rabbit Hill,* Robert Lawson, The Viking Press, Inc.

1946 *Strawberry Girl,* Lois Lenski. J. B. Lippincott Company.

1947 *Miss Hickory,* Carolyn Sherwin Bailey. The Viking Press, Inc.

1948 *Twenty-one Balloons,* William Pene du Bois. The Viking Press, Inc.

1949 *King of the Wind,* Marguerite Henry. Rand McNally and Company.

1950 *Door in the Wall,* Marguerite de Angeli. Doubleday and Company, Inc.

1951 *Amos Fortune: Free Man,* Elizabeth Yates. Aladdin.

1952 *Ginger Pye,* Eleanor Estes. Harcourt, Brace and World, Inc.

1953 *Secret of the Andes,* Ann Nolan Clark. The Viking Press, Inc.

1954 *And Now Miguel,* Joseph Krumgold. Thomas Y. Crowell Company.

1955 *The Wheel on the School,* Meindert de Jong. Harper and Row, Publishers.

1956 *Carry on, Mr. Bowditch,* Jean Lee Latham. Houghton Mifflin Company.

1957 *Miracles on Maple Hill,* Virginia Sorensen. Illustrated by Beth and Joe Kruch. Harcourt, Brace and World, Inc.

1958 *Rifles for Matie,* Harold Keith. Thomas Y. Crowell Company.

1959 *The Witch of Blackbird Pond,* Elizabeth George Speare. Houghton Mifflin Company.

1960 *Onion John*, Joseph Krumgold. Thomas Y. Crowell Company.
1961 *Island of the Blue Dolphins*, Scott O'Dell. Houghton Mifflin Company.
1962 *The Bronze Bow*, Elizabeth George Speare. Houghton Mifflin Company.
1963 *A Wrinkle in Time*, Madeleine L'Éngle. Farrar, Straus and Company, Inc.

CALDECOTT AWARDS

1938 *Animals of the Bible*, Dorothy Lathrop. J. B. Lippincott Company.
1939 *Mei-Li*, Thomas Handforth. Doubleday and Company, Inc.
1940 *Abraham Lincoln*. Ingri and Edgar Parin D'Aulaire. Doubleday and Company, Inc.
1941 *They Were Strong and Good*, Robert Lawson. The Viking Press, Inc.
1942 *Make Way for Ducklings*, Robert McCloskey. The Viking Press, Inc.
1943 *The Little House*, Virginia Lee Burton. Houghton Mifflin Company.
1944 *Many Moons*. (James Thurber) Louis Slobodkin. Harcourt, Brace and World, Inc.
1945 *Prayer for a Child*. (Rachel Field) Elizabeth Orton Jones. The Macmilland Company.
1946 *The Rooster Crows: A Book of American Rhymes and Jingles*, Maud and Miska Petersham. The Macmillan Company.
1947 *The Little Island*. (Golden MacDonald) Leonard Weisgard. Doubleday and Company, Inc.
1948 *White Snow, Bright Snow*. (Alvin Tresselt) Roger Duvoisin, Lothrop, Lee and Shepard Company, Inc.
1949 *The Big Snow*, Berta and Elmer Hader. The Macmillan Company.
1950 *Song of the Swallows*, Leo Politi. Charles Scribner's Sons.
1951 *The Egg Tree*, Katherine Milhous. Charles Scribner's Sons.

1952 *Finders Keepers*, Nicolas Mordvinoff. Harcourt, Brace and World, Inc.
1953 *The Biggest Bear*, Lynd Ward. Houghton Mifflin Company.
1954 *Madeline's Rescue*, Ludwig Bemelmans. The Viking Press, Inc.
1955 *Cinderella*, Marcia Brown. Charles Scribner's Sons.
1956 *Frog Went A-Courtin'*, John Langstaff. Illustrated by Feodor Rojankovsky. Harcourt, Brace and World, Inc.
1957 *A Tree Is Nice*, Janice May Udry. Illustrated by Marc Simont. Harper and Row, Publishers.
1958 *Time of Wonder*, Robert McCloskey. The Viking Press, Inc.
1959 *Chanticleer and the Fox*, Barbara Cooney. Thomas Y. Crowell Company.
1960 *Nine Days to Christmas*, Marie Hall Ets. The Viking Press, Inc.
1961 *Baboushka and the Three Kings*, Nicolas Sidjakov. Parnassus Press.
1962 *Once a Mouse*, Marcia Brown. Charles Scribner's Sons.
1963 *The Snowy Day*, Ezra Jack Keats, The Viking Press, Inc.

THE CHARLES W. FOLLETT AWARD

1950 *Johnny Texas*, Carol Hoff.
1951 *All-of-a-Kind Family*, Sydney Taylor.
1952 *Thirty-One Brothers and Sisters*, Reba Paeff Mirsky.
1953 *Tornado Jones*, Trella Lamson Dick.
1954 *Little Wu and the Watermelons*, Beatrice Liu.
1955 *Minutemen of the Sea*, Tom Cluff.
1956 No manuscript submitted in the competition for the 1956 Follett Award was found worthy of the Award.
1957 *Chucks, The Boy with the Good Name*, Erela March Phillips.

1958 *Nobody Listens to Andrew,* Elizabeth Guilfoile.

1959 *The Boy Who Would Not Say His Name,* Elizabeth Vreeken.

1961 *The O'Learys and Friends,* Jean M. Berg.

1962 *Me and Caleb,* Franklyn E. Meyer.

CHILD STUDY ASSOCIATION AWARD

1943 *Keystone Kids,* John R. Tunis. Harcourt, Brace and World, Inc.

1944 *The House,* Marjorie Hill Allee. Houghton Mifflin Company.

1945 *The Moved-Outers,* Florence Crannell Means. Houghton Mifflin Company.

1946 *Heart of Danger,* Howard Pease. Doubleday and Company, Inc.

1947 *Judy's Journey,* Lois Lenski. J. B. Lippincott Company.

1948 *The Big Wave,* Pearl Buck. The John Day Company, Inc.

1949 *Paul Tiber,* Maria Gleit. Charles Scribner's Sons.

1950 *The United Nations and Youth,* Eleanor Roosevelt and Helen Ferris. Doubleday and Company, Inc.

1951 (No Award)

1952 *Twenty and Ten,* Claire Huchet Bishop. The Viking Press, Inc. *Jareb,* Miriam Powell. Thomas Y. Crowell Company.

1953 *In a Mirror,* Mary Stolz. Harper and Row, Publishers.

1954 *High Road Home,* William Corbin. Coward-McCann, Inc. *The Ordeal of the Young Hunter,* Jonreed Lauritzen. Little, Brown and Company.

1955 *Crow Boy,* Tara Yashima. The Viking Press, Inc. *Plain Girl,* Virginia Sorensen. Harcourt, Brace and World, Inc.

1956 *The House of Sixty Fathers,* Meindert de Jong. Harper and Row, Publishers.

1957 *Shadow Across the Campus,* Helen Sattley. Dodd, Mead and Company, Inc.

1958 *South Town,* Lorenz Graham. Follett Publishing Company.

1960 *Jennifer,* Zoa Sherburne. William Morrow and Company, Inc.

1961 *Janine,* Robin McKown. Julian Messner, Inc.

1962 *The Road to Agra,* Aimee Somerfelt. Criterion Books, Inc.

SPRING BOOK FESTIVAL AWARD

(New York Herald Tribune)

1937 Younger age: *Seven Simeons,* Boris Artzybasheff. The Viking Press, Inc. Older age: *The Smuggler's Sloop,* Rob White, III. Little, Brown and Company.

1938 Younger age: *The Hobbit,* J. R. R. Tolkien. Houghton Mifflin Company. Older age: *The Iron Duke,* John R. Tunis. Harcourt, Brace and World, Inc.

1939 Younger age: *The Story of Horace,* Alice N. Coats. Coward-McCann, Inc. Older age: *The Hired Man's Elephant,* Phil Strong. Dodd, Mead and Company, Inc.

1940 Younger age: *That Mario,* Lucy Herndon Crockett. Holt, Rinehart and Winston, Inc. Older age: *Cap'n Ezra Privateer,* James D. Adams. Harcourt, Brace and World, Inc.

1941 Picture Book: *In My Mother's House,* Ann Nolan Clark. The Viking Press, Inc. Eight to Twelve: *Pete,* Tom Robinson. The Viking Press, Inc. Older boys and girls: *Clara Barton,* Mildred Mastin Pace. Charles Scribner's Sons.

1942 Picture Book: *Mr. Tootwhistle's In-*

vention, Peter Wells. Holt, Rinehart and Winston, Inc.

Eight to twelve: *I Have Just Begun to Fight,* Commander Edward Ellsberg. Dodd, Mead and Company, Inc.

Older boys and girls: *None but the Brave,* Rosamond Van Der Zee Marshall. Houghton Mifflin Company.

1943 Picture Book: *Five Golden Wrens,* Hugh Troy. Oxford University Press.

Eight to twelve: *These Happy Golden Years,* Laura Ingalls Wilder. Harper and Row, Publishers.

Older boys and girls: *Patterns on the Wall,* Elizabeth Yates. Alfred A. Knopf, Inc.

1944 Picture Book: *A Ring and a Riddle,* M. Illin and E. Segal and the illustrator, Vera Bock. J. B. Lippincott Company.

Eight to twelve: *They Put Out to Sea,* Roger Duvoisin. Alfred A. Knopf, Inc.

Older boys and girls: *Storm Canvas,* Armstrong Sperry. Holt, Rinehart and Winston, Inc.

1945 Picture Book: *Little People in a Big Country,* Norma Cohn. Oxford University Press.

Eight to twelve: *Gulf Stream,* Ruth Brindze. Vanguard Press, Inc.

Older boys and girls: *Sandy,* Elizabeth Janet Gray. The Viking Press, Inc.

1946 Picture Books: *Farm Stories,* Kathryn and Bryan Jackson, shared with illustrator, Gustaf Tenngren. Simon and Schuster, Inc.

Eight to twelve: *Thirteenth Stone,* Jean Rothwell. Harcourt, Brace and World, Inc.

Older boys and girls: *The Quest of the Golden Condor,* Clayton Knight. Alfred A. Knopf, Inc.

1947 Picture Book: *Oley: The Sea Monster,* Marie Hall Ets. The Viking Press, Inc.

Eight to twelve: *Pancakes—Paris,* Claire Huchet Bishop. The Viking Press, Inc.

Older boys and girls: *Twenty-one Balloons,* William Pene Du Bois. The Viking Press, Inc.

1948 Picture Book: *My Father's Dragon,* Ruth Stiles Gannett. Random House, Inc.

Eight to twelve: *Daughter of the Mountains,* Louise Rankin. The Viking Press, Inc.

Older boys and girls: *Crimson Anchor: A Sea Mystery,* Felix Riesenberg, Jr. Dodd, Mead and Company, Inc.

1949 Picture Book: *Bonnie Bess: The Weathervane Horse,* Alvin Tresselt and Marilyn Hafner. Lothrop, Lee and Shepard Company, Inc.

Eight to twelve: *Bush Holiday,* Stephen Fennimore. Doubleday and Company, Inc.

Older boys and girls: *Start of the Trail,* Louise Dickerson Rich. J. B. Lippincott Company.

1950 Picture Book: *Sunshine,* Ludwig Bemelmans. Simon and Schuster, Inc.

Eight to twelve: *Windfall Fiddle,* Carl Cramer. Alfred A. Knopf, Inc.

Older boys and girls: *Amos Fortune: Free Man,* Elizabeth Yates. Aladdin.

1951 Picture Book: *Jeanne Marie Counts Her Sheep,* Françoise. Charles Scribner's Sons.

Eight to twelve: *Ginger Pye,* Eleanor Estes. Harcourt, Brace and World, Inc.

Older boys and girls: *Americans Before Columbus,* Elizabeth Baity. The Viking Press, Inc.

1952 Picture Book: *Big Mutt,* John Reese.

Eight to twelve: *The Talking Cat*, Natalie Savage Carlston. Harper and Row, Publishers.

Older boys and girls: *Looking for Something*, Ann Nolan Clark and Leo Politi. The Viking Press, Inc.

1953 Picture Book: *The Ark*, Margor Benary-Isbert. Harcourt, Brace and World, Inc.

Eight to twelve: *Captain Ramsey's Daughter*, Elizabeth Fraser Torjesen. Lothrop, Lee and Shepard Company, Inc.

Older boys and girls: *Pet of the Met*, Lydia and Don Freeman. The Viking Press, Inc.

1954 Picture Book: *Alphonsi, That Bearded One*, Natalie Savage Carlson. Harcourt, Brace and World, Inc.

Eight to twelve: *Winter Danger*, William O. Steele. Harcourt, Brace and World, Inc.

Older boys and girls: *Engineers' Dreams*, Willy Ley. The Viking Press, Inc.

1955 Picture Book: *Frog Went A-Courtin'*, John Langstaff, Harcourt, Brace and World, Inc.

Eight to twelve: *Crystal Mountain*, Belle Dorman Rugh. Houghton Mifflin Company.

Older boys and girls: *The Buffalo Trace*, Virginia Eifert. Dodd, Mead and Company, Inc.

1956 Picture Book: *Lion*, William Pene Du Bois. The Viking Press, Inc.

Eight to twelve: *Beaver Water*, Rutherford G. Montgomery. Harcourt, Brace and World, Inc.

Older boys and girls: *Cold Hazard*, Richard Armstrong. Houghton Mifflin Company.

1957 Picture Book: *Madeline and the Bad Hat*, Ludwig Bemelmans. The Viking Press, Inc.

Eight to twelve: *Gone-Away Lake*,

Elizabeth Enright. Harcourt, Brace and World, Inc.

Older boys and girls: *Because of Madeline*, Mary Stolz. Harper and Row, Publishers.

1958 Picture Book: *Crictor*, Toni Ungerer. Harper and Row, Publishers.

Eight to twelve: *Chúcaro: Wild Pony of the Pampas*, Francis Kalmay. Harcourt, Brace and World, Inc.

Older boys and girls: *Sons of the Steppe*, Hans Baumann. Oxford University Press.

1959 Picture Book: *Sia Lives on Kilimanjaro*, Ann Riwkin-Brick and Astrid Lindgren. The Macmillan Company.

Eight to twelve: *The Long Nosed Princess*, Priscilla Hallowell. The Viking Press, Inc.

Older boys and girls: *An Edge of the Forest*, Agnes Smith. The Viking Press, Inc.

1960 Picture Book: *The Secret Hiding Place*, Rainey Bennett. Harcourt, Brace and World, Inc.

Eight to twelve: *The Trouble with Jenny's Ear*, Oliver Butterworth. Atlantic Monthly Press.

Older boys and girls: *The Wells of Windy Troy*, Marjorie Braymer. Harcourt, Brace and World, Inc.

1961 Picture Book: *Gwendolyn the Miracle Hen*, Nancy Sherman. The Golden Press.

Eight to twelve: *Norwegian Folk Tales*, Peter Christian Asbjornson and Jorgen Moe. The Viking Press, Inc.

Older boys and girls: *Adventures in the Desert*, Herbert Kaufman. Ivan Obolensky, Inc.

1962 Picture Book: *Adam's Book of Odd Pictures*, Joseph Low. Atheneum Publishers.

Eight to twelve: *The Orphans of*

Simatra, Paul-Jacques Bonzon. Criterion Books, Inc.
Older boys and girls: *Dawn Wind*, Rosemary Sutcliff. Henry Z. Walck, Inc.

FOR FURTHER STUDY

American Library Association Bulletin, 57 (February 1963), 153–174.

Arbuthnot, May Hill, *Children and Books*, rev. ed. Chicago: Scott, Foresman and Company, 1957.

——, "Evaluating Books for Children," *Reading in Action: International Reading Conference Proceedings*, Vol II, pp. 64–69. New York: Scholastic Magazines, 1957.

Commission on the English Curriculum, National Council of Teachers of English, *Language Arts for Today's Children*, pp. 162–180. New York: Appleton-Century-Crofts, 1954.

Dallmann, Martha, "Year Round with Books," *Grade Teacher*, 75 (November 1957), 34, 98–99.

Dees, Margaret, "Easy to Read: For Beginning Independent Readers," *Elementary English*, 39 (May 1962), 418–420.

"Developing Lifetime Habits in Reading." *The Reading Teacher* (Theme Issue), 12 (April 1959).

Gates, Arthur I., and Frank G. Jennings, "The Role of Motivation," *Development in and Through Reading*, pp. 109–126. Sixtieth Yearbook of the National Society for the Study of Education, Part I. Chicago: The University of Chicago Press, 1961.

Hofer, Louise B., "What Do Sixth Graders Really Like in Poetry?" *Elementary English*, 33 (November 1956), 433–438.

Huus, Helen, "How a TV Program Can Be Used as a Springboard to Further Reading," *Elementary English*, 34 (February 1957), 81–88.

Jacobs, Leland B., "Developing Ongoing Interest in Reading in the Primary Grades Through Stories and Poetry," *Reading in Action: International Reading Conference Proceedings*, Vol. II, pp. 19–21. New York: Scholastic Magazines, 1957.

Jenkins, Marion, "Self-Selection in Reading," *The Reading Teacher*, 11 (December 1957), 84–90.

Jensen, Amy Elizabeth, "Attracting Children to Books," *Elementary English*, 33 (October 1956), 332–339.

Larrick, Nancy, *A Teacher's Guide to Children's Books*. Columbus, Ohio. Charles E. Merrill Books, Inc., 1960.

Martin, Marvin, "*Fifty Books They Can't Resist*," *Elementary English* 39 (May 1962), 415–417.

Rasmussen, Margaret, ed., *Literature with Children*. Washington, D.C.: Association for Childhood Education International, 1961.

Robinson, Helen M., ed., *Developing Permanent Interests in Reading*. Supplementary Educational Monographs, No. 84. Chicago: The University of Chicago Press, 1956.

——, *Materials for Reading*, pp. 86–98. Supplementary Educational Monographs, No. 86. Chicago: The University of Chicago Press, 1957.

Sawyer, Ruth, *The Way of a Storyteller*. New York: The Viking Press, Inc., 1942.

Shedlock, Marie, *The Art of Storytelling*. New York: Dover Publications, Inc., 1951.

Smith, Dora V., *Fifty Years of Children's Books*. Champaign, Ill.: The National Council of Teachers of English, 1963.

Smith, Nila B., ed., *Developing Taste in Literature*. Research Bulletin of the National Conference on Research in English. Champaign, Ill.: The National Council of Teachers of English, 1963.

Strang, Ruth, "Interest as a Dynamic Force in the Improvement of Reading," *Ele-*

mentary English, 34 (March 1957), 170–176.

Tooze, Ruth, *Story Telling.* Englewood Cliffs, N.J.: Prentice-Hall, Inc., 1959.

Witty, Paul, *Reading in Modern Education,* pp. 21–54. Boston: D. C. Heath and Company, 1949.

————, and David Kopel, *Reading and the Educative Process,* pp. 25–66. Boston: Ginn and Company, 1939.

————, and Robert A. Sizemore, "Reading the Comics: A Summary of Studies and an Evaluation," *Elementary English,* 31 (December 1954), 501–506; 32 (January 1955), 43–49; and 32 (February 1955), 109–114.

————, and Associates, *Studies of Children's Interest—A Brief Summary.* Reprinted from *Elementary English,* 37 (November, December 1960). Champaign, Ill.: The National Council of Teachers of English, 1961.

Wolfson, Bernice J., "Reading about Emotions in the Primary Classroom," *Elementary English,* 31 (March 1954), 146–149.

12

Providing for Individual Differences

Throughout this book we have had frequent occasion to refer to the problem of individual differences among children and the need to adapt instruction to those differences. Much research has been done on the extent of human variability and upon the effect of various methods of dealing with it. Even without the research, experienced teachers are aware that a third-grade class will usually consist of some children reading at the primer level and of others at the fifth-grade level. Moreover, the children differ in their *rate* of learning, so that a second-grade child placed with a third-grade child of equal reading achievement will probably soon outstrip him. A few distribution tables will be sufficient to illustrate the usual range of differences (Tables I, II, and III.

Children differ not only in their achievement levels and their rates of learning, but also in every identifiable human characteristic. They differ when they come into the world; they differ in their early home environments, in their physical, emotional, and temperamental characteristics, in their mental potential, in their social attitudes, in their interests and special talents. They differ also in their ways of "unlocking" words. No system of instruction could possibly do full justice to all these differences in all their aspects. The important principle to remember is that differences are normal, that in many respects they contribute to the appeal as well as the difficulty of teaching.

Methods of Dealing with Individual Differences

The methods used in dealing with individual differences are concerned primarily with (1) grouping and classification and (2) teaching technique.

293

TABLE I

Distribution of Reading Grades for Pupils in the Second Through Sixth Grades of a Small Suburban School System

READING GRADE*	NUMBER OF PUPILS ACTUAL GRADE				
	2	3	4	5	6
10.6 – 11					1
10.1 – 10.5					2
9.6 – 10.0					2
9.1 – 9.5				2	2
8.6 – 9.0		1	1	5	11
8.1 – 8.5		1	0	6	7
7.6 – 8.0		1	3	9	6
7.1 – 7.5	1	0	2	11	8
6.6 – 7.0		1	5	8	6
6.1 – 6.5	1	3	7	4	6
5.6 – 6.0	5	6	18	7	7
5.1 – 5.5	8	8	7	9	2
4.6 – 5.0	8	10	14	9	4
4.1 – 4.5	12	10	10	4	1
3.6 – 4.0	20	11	10	2	
3.1 – 3.5	27	20	7		
2.6 – 3.0	11	16	2		
2.1 – 2.5	3	5	1		
1.6 – 2.0		1			
1.1 – 1.5					
Total Number†	96	94	87	76	65
Mean Reading Grade‡	3.9	4.2	5.1	6.5	7.4

* Scores based on end-of-the-year testing with the Iowa Test of Basic Skills, Reading Comprehension Section, in the third through sixth grades, and Gates Advanced Primary in the second grade.

† Larger numbers of pupils in the lower grades were due to an influx of families with young children into the district.

‡ Computed on ungrouped data. Small change in mean score from second grade to third grade may reflect differences in norms of tests used.

SOURCE: Walter W. Cook and Theodore Clymer, "Acceleration and Retardation," *Individualizing Instruction,* p. 187. Sixty-first Yearbook of the National Society for the Study of Education, Part I. Chicago: University of Chicago Press, 1962.

Grouping within the Class

A widespread method of dealing with individual differences within a single class is to subgroup children according to ability, usually on three levels. This is the procedure suggested in earlier chapters. The effort to reduce the range

TABLE II

Distribution of 2212 Third-grade Pupils in Omaha Public Schools
According to Grade Scores on Chicago Reading
Test B, Form 3

GRADE	PUPILS	
	Number	*Percent*
6.6 – 7.5	51	2.3
5.6 – 6.5	60	2.7
4.6 – 5.5	193	8.7
3.6 – 4.5	497	22.5
2.6 – 3.5	742	33.6
1.6 – 2.5	630	28.5
0.5 – 1.5	39	1.7
TOTAL	2212	100.0

SOURCE: William H. Waite, "The Improvement of Reading in the Omaha Public Schools," *Elementary School Journal,* 48 (September 1948), 306.

TABLE III

Distribution of Eighth-grade Pupils by Reading Grade Stanford Reading Test,
Intermediate and Advanced Levels, Form F, Test I, 1940 Norms,
New York City, February 7, 1951

READING GRADE	NUMBER OF PUPILS	PERCENT OF TOTAL
12.0	3,818	6.9
11.0 – 11.9	4,277	7.8
10.0 – 10.9	5,231	9.5
9.0 – 9.9	5,918	10.7
8.0 – 8.9	7,641	13.9
7.0 – 7.9	8,662	15.7
6.0 – 6.9	7,151	13.0
5.0 – 5.9	7,681	13.9
4.9 and below	4,761	8.6
TOTAL	55,140	100.0

Intelligence: Pintner General Ability Tests, Verbal Series, Intermediate Test, Form A

Mean CA	13 yrs., 4 mos.
Mean MA	13 yrs., 6 mos.
Mean IQ	101

SOURCE: Staff of the Reading Guidance Center, Division of Instructional Research (editor, May Lazar; director, J. Wayne Wrightstone), *The Retarded Reader in the Junior High School: A Guide for Supervisors and Teachers,* p. 6. Publication No. 31, September 1952. New York: Board of Education, City of New York, Bureau of Educational Research, 1952. (This table has been adapted from the original, supplying only the combined figures and omitting the separate statistics for the junior high schools and the eight-year elementary schools.)

in instructional groups is justified by the facts about the composition of grade groupings, as reported by Wrightstone:[1]

At the first-grade level, the range of achievement in the average class is between three and four years.

At the fourth-grade level, the range of achievement in the average class is between five and six years.

At the sixth-grade level, the range of achievement in the average class is between seven and eight years.

The method is, of course, not without its limitations. The three-group plan may make the children and their parents conscious of differences in achievement and create pressure on one child to measure up to others in reading. The teacher is required to plan activities and materials for three different groups instead of one. Individual differences remain within the groups, and there is some danger that the teacher will assume that the differences have been cared for by the mere fact that the three-level plan is in operation. Certainly the problem is not solved if the teacher uses the same material with all pupils, allowing only for a difference in the speed with which the groups are expected to read them.

Much of the effectiveness of subgrouping within the class will depend on the teacher's understanding of the purpose for which the children are assigned to the groups. As Wrightstone has pointed out, great importance should be attached to how the teacher and the children feel about the group. All writers emphasize the need to keep the groups flexible. Classification of children in groups should be determined by specific purposes. For example, groups may be organized for the express purpose of providing instruction in developmental reading, and individual children should be regrouped as their performance requires. In other cases, a group may be devoted to the study of specific skills, regardless of the general proficiency of the members. Research groups may be formed for pupils who wish to investigate a similar problem. Other groups, interested in the same theme, such as pets, airplanes, plants, farm life, railroads, and the like, may plan presentations to the whole class. In some instances, a group may be formed in which the better readers help the slower ones—all, of course, under the supervision of the teacher.

Especially in the case of the beginning teacher, there is the problem of what to do with groups not under the immediate direction of the teacher. No group should be left to itself without some specific task. If a group is asked to spend a period in silent reading, the teacher should make sure that each child has found a suitable book to read or is in process of finding one at the book table. If a group is planning a display or a report to the class, the nature of the task should be clear to everyone, and the questions to be asked and

---

[1] J. Wayne Wrightstone, *Class Organization for Instruction,* p. 13. What Research Says to the Teacher, No. 13. Washington, D. C.: National Education Association, 1957.

answered should be well-formulated in advance. In no case should a group be left with mere busywork. Games and seatwork should be carefully planned to provide needed practice in skills previously taught.

Teachers who follow the practice of subgrouping within the class should be keenly aware of the limitations and dangers of the method. First, it has been estimated that dividing pupils into three groups reduces variability in achievement only to about 83 percent of that in normally organized groups. Second, the tests commonly employed in the classification of pupils measure only a small, although significant, number of the desired competencies. Third, the relative performance of individuals within the groups will change as the instruction proceeds. Fourth, studies have shown that academic progress under a system of ability grouping is only slightly greater than under a system of heterogeneous grouping.

More important, perhaps, than any of the foregoing caveats is a concern for the over-all psychological effect of grouping on the child. If the grouping is flexible and if the child understands why he is a member of a certain group at any specified time, grouping may be quite harmless, even helpful. If the grouping stigmatizes a child with himself or others, the effect may be more serious than any loss in reading progress. Speed in learning to read is certainly no more important than growth in social maturity. Reading ability is valuable only insofar as it contributes to the general happiness and well-being of the individual and his functioning in society. We must not sacrifice the child to our desire to exhibit favorable reports of reading scores.

To summarize: some kind of grouping or system of individualization is necessary in view of the large number of children with whom the average teacher must deal. But whatever the system, priority should be given to the general developmental and social needs of individual children.

Systems of Completely Individualized Instruction

Silent reading is essentially an individual activity. The communication is not between one pupil and another, but between author and reader. The development of silent reading skills, although possibly accompanied by oral reading activities, is necessarily individual in nature; no two children have exactly the same needs, no two children progress at exactly the same rate. For this reason efforts have long been made to devise means by which reading and other skills could be taught by individualized means.

Among the more famous plans of individualization of past years are those of William T. Harris of St. Louis, Preston W. Search of Pueblo, Colorado, Frederic Burk of Santa Barbara, William Wirt of Gary, Indiana (the platoon school), Helen Parkhurst of Dalton, Massachusetts (the contract plan), Carleton W. Washburne of Winnetka, Illinois, and James E. McDade of Chicago. Although such research as we have has favored the individualized plans, most of them were discontinued after a time, and none of them has enjoyed widespread acceptance in American schools. Distinguishing features of all of these plans have been the use of the classroom as a laboratory instead of a lecture and recitation room; the use of diagnostic and achievement tests, practice materials, and record forms; the adaptation of learning tasks to the achievement levels of the pupils; and pupil participation in the management of the system. All of them, while making effective use of the teacher, stressed the idea of self-teaching, suggestive of the modern vogue of programed instruction. All of them provided, in addition to the individualized work, for a rich program of socialized activities.

The vigor and diversity of the plans enumerated in the preceding paragraph probably explain why the idea underlying them has not died. We are witnessing today a widespread resurgence of interest in programs of individualized instruction in reading. Scores of articles describing such programs have appeared in recent years. Hardly a single reading conference is without one or more papers dealing with the subject.

One example of the current interest in individualized instruction in reading is the popularity of the Science Research Associates Reading Laboratories. These "laboratories" consist of cases of practice materials for each of the elementary school levels. They contain, in addition to the reading selections, answer keys, check test pads, student record books, and a teacher's handbook. Materials in each grade vary in difficulty from easy to hard. Phonics surveys, word games, and colored pencils corresponding to the colors of the reading selections are included. Pupils are expected to move ahead as far and as fast as their learning rates and capacities will permit. The plan is essentially a variation and refinement of those used in Washburne's and McDade's systems. Emphasis is placed upon the successful response and on the use of intrinsically interesting materials.

PROGRAMED READING INSTRUCTION. Programed instruction, while not a new idea in education, has been receiving extraordinary attention in recent years. Often erroneously referred to by the term "teaching machines," it is considered by many to be the application of the industrial use of automation to the teaching-learning process. Actually the idea, so far as reading instruction is concerned, does not differ fundamentally from the plans of individualization described in foregoing paragraphs. The machines that are being perfected are by no means essential or, at the present stage, always appropriate to the plan.

In programed instruction, the pupil is presented with instructional materials that enable him to learn on his own. The exercises, prepared after careful editing and experimentation, are graduated in very small steps, so that even the slowest learner can, at his own rate, arrive at the desired generalization. An exercise, or "frame," usually presents an explanation followed by a sentence containing a blank to be filled in. The correct answer, given immediately below or on a page to which the pupil is referred, enables the pupil to compare his own answer with the correct answer, so that he is "reinforced" if the answer is right or corrected if the answer is wrong. A program, or sequence of frames, is selected for the individual in terms of his specific stage of learning. The method is one of self-teaching. In the case of reading, the programs may deal with the basic skills of word recognition, such as phonetic analysis, context clues, and structural analysis, or with comprehension and critical reading.

Following is one example of a "frame":

> Q46. The bird's nest fell from the tree.
> We see the ending *'s* on the word *bird.*
> The nest *belongs to* the _____.
> A46. bird.[2]

Since the programed material is self-teaching, the work of the teacher differs from that required in the conventional classroom. Her task is primarily that of a counselor, guide, and motivator, once she has provided each pupil with the materials appropriate for him.

Programed reading instruction is still largely in the experimental stage. Large-scale studies, for example, are now going on in the public schools of New York City under the direction of the Center for Programed Instruction.

Without doubt, the plan should and will be the subject of spirited debate among educators before it is widely adopted. It will be examined not only from the point of view of its efficiency in achieving academic objectives, but especially from the point of view of its total effect upon the pupil. Certainly in theory it has much to commend it, particularly in its stress upon the principle of success in learning and upon self-activity. In any case, teachers and administrators should acquaint themselves with programed materials as they appear and with the growing body of research on this subject.

INDIVIDUALIZED READING: SEEKING, SELF-SELECTION, AND PACING. The term "individualized reading" has many possible meanings. For convenience, the method described in the following paragraphs is spelled with initial capital letters: Individualized Reading.

The common elements that underlie Individualized Reading as practiced in numerous schools and school systems are (1) the use of many books, diversified as to interest appeal and ability level; (2) little or no reliance upon basal readers as instructional tools; (3) major emphasis on children's preferences in the selection of reading materials. In general, the skills of reading are taught in connection with problems which the child actually encounters in his read-

---

2 P. Kenneth Komoski, "Teaching Machines and Programed Reading Instruction," *Controversial Issues in Reading and Promising Solutions,* pp. 109–120. Compiled and edited by Helen M. Robinson. Supplementary Educational Monographs, Number 91. Chicago: The University of Chicago Press, 1961.

ing. Isolated exercises and drills for a whole group, and even for individual pupils, are rarely, if ever, used. It should be made clear, however, that Individualized Reading follows no rigid formula. The procedure is varied and supplemented in numerous ways according to the needs of the children and the creativity of the teacher.

In commenting on programs of Individualized Reading, Leland Jacobs makes the following significant observation:

> Individualized reading is no panacea for all the ills of teaching reading. It can never be effectual in improving children's abilities to read if it becomes a patent procedure, a sentimental devotion, a rite or ceremony, an exclusive ideology, a vacuous symbol, a standardization, a slogan, a dogma. Its usefulness is dependent upon well-defined purposes and values in operation and action, upon creative uses of time, materials, and procedures suitable to the content for consideration, upon critical appraisal and assessment . . .[3]

Jacobs goes on to offer practical suggestions for the organization and administration of the program:

1. The teacher provides ample time for individual reading and for various kinds of group reading.

2. He arranges for individual skills reading and for independent recreational reading.

3. He provides time for children to share their reading accomplishments.

4. The teacher provides a varied, extensive collection of reading matter from which a child can make his choices.

5. He provides a variety of practice materials.

6. He encourages the child to select reading matter that extends the learner's growing edges.

7. The teacher develops an adequate system of record-keeping.

8. He utilizes appropriate evaluation procedures.

9. He makes appropriate arrangements for independent work for others while an individual is working with the teacher.

One of the early proponents of the method under discussion was Willard C. Olson, who used the expressions *seeking, self-selection,* and *pacing* to describe the process. By pacing he meant the adjustment of teaching materials and experiences to the child's own rate of growth.[4] Since then, extensive experimentation with the plan has been carried on in the New York City public schools under the leadership of May Lazar,[4a] and by teachers in many other

---

[3] Leland B. Jacobs, "Individualized Reading Is Not A Thing!" *Individualizing Reading Practices,* Alice Miel, ed., pp. 1–17. Practical Suggestions for Teaching, No. 14. New York: Bureau of Publications, Teachers College, Columbia University, 1958.

[4] Willard C. Olson, *Child Development.* Boston: D. C. Heath and Company, 1949, and *The Packet,* Vol. 7, No. 1 (Spring 1952).

[4a] Described in the excellent brochure, *A Practical Guide to Individualized Reading.* Prepared by Marcella K. Draper and Louise H. Schwietert, and revised and edited by May Lazar.

parts of the United States. From the voluminous literature that has grown up about Individualized Reading, one gathers that both the teachers and the pupils involved are enthusiastic about the plan and that the numerous problems involved in the development of reading ability throughout the elementary school grades have been carefully considered in the planning. Readers of this book are urged to examine thoughtfully many of the references listed at the end of this chapter.

What do we know about the results of the Individualized Reading program? Hard evidence on this question is still lacking. Such studies of the program as have been made do not reveal dramatic gains in the pupil's performance on standardized tests of reading. On the other hand, it is apparent that there have been no significant losses in comparison with the results of more conventional programs.[5] It seems likely that, with teachers of comparable ability and creativity and with suitable instructional materials, no great differences are to be expected.

There are, however, other values that must be considered in evaluating the desirability of an Individualized Reading program. If, as its proponents claim, the method causes more children to like reading and to develop habits of extensive independent reading, the program will have more than justified itself. If it contributes to a happy, carefree climate in the classroom, and if it builds self-confidence in children, it must be given serious consideration by teachers and administrators. If it removes invidious distinctions between "slow" and "fast" readers, it can overcome one of the most serious dangers of individualization through ability grouping.

The inexperienced teacher not trained in the techniques of Individualized Reading and lacking the advantage of a sympathetic, able supervisor is well-advised not to plunge into the program. It is best to study the plan first, examine carefully the books, articles, and manuals on the subject, and then to make tentative beginnings. Of supreme importance, also, is a wide knowledge

---

Publication No. 40, Board of Education, City of New York, Bureau of Educational Research, October, 1960. Dr. Lazar has also described the program in *Reading in Action*, pp. 141–144. Conference Proceedings of the International Reading Association, Vol. II. New York: Scholastic Magazines, 1957.

[5] Research summaries and evaluations relating to the effectiveness of Individualized Reading programs may be found in the following sources:

Paul Witty, with the assistance of Ann Coomer and Robert Sizemore, "Individualized Reading: A Summary and Evaluation," *Elementary English*, 36 (October 1959), 401–412, 450.

George D. Spache, *Toward Better Reading*, pp. 155–157. Champaign, Ill.: Garrard Publishing Company, 1963. (Spache's entire chapter on individualized reading may be read with profit.)

David H. Russell and Henry R. Fea, "Research on Teaching Reading," *Handbook of Research on Teaching*, N. L. Gage, ed., p. 914. A Project of the American Educational Research Association. Chicago: Rand McNally Company, 1963.

Detailed descriptions of individualized reading programs may be found in books by Brogan and Fox and by Veatch, listed at the end of this chapter.

of and love for children's books. The young teacher who has not had a good course in children's literature should probably spend at least a year in reading children's books and consulting the numerous guides, commentaries, and lists now available.

The place of the basal reader in Individualized Reading is a subject of great importance at a time when, as at present, it dominates instructional practice in reading throughout the country. Clearly its use as a primary resource would violate the essential principles of the Individualized Reading plan. On the other hand, the leading basal reader series are physically attractive. They represent vast investments in research and planning. They should certainly be prominently displayed on reading tables, and children should be encouraged to make much use of them. The beginning teacher finds the basal reader a godsend.

In the case of the untrained, inexperienced teacher, a defensible compromise would take the form of a basal reader system, employing books on several levels of difficulty, supplemented with a strong program of independent recreational reading. The more mature teacher may gradually shift from the central use of the basal reader to greater reliance on the plan of "seeking," "self-selection," and "pacing."

THE UNGRADED PRIMARY SCHOOL. The introduction of the graded system about the middle of the nineteenth century was an early effort to achieve a degree of homogeneity in elementary school classes. The aim was to group children together according to chronological age, on the apparent assumption that children of the same age would be able to deal successfully with subject matter of approximately equal difficulty. Thus by graduating the difficulty of school work from one grade to the next, it was thought possible to set standards of achievement, so that those who successfully completed all the grades would have mastered all the basic requirements of the elementary school.

Of course the effort to achieve homogeneity by this means did not succeed. The range of height and weight of children of the same age remained very great. Under a system of promotion and nonpromotion, even chronological age varied considerably in the same grade. As for scholastic achievement, all one could say about a sixth-grader was that he was in the sixth grade. He might be at the second-grade or the tenth-grade level in reading or arithmetic ability. Indeed, the number of children in the sixth grade who performed at a sixth-grade scholastic level was generally below 25 percent. And this is essentially so at the present time.

The overlapping of children's abilities from grade to grade has led some school systems to abandon grade distinctions at the primary level. Milwaukee, Wisconsin, for example, introduced an ungraded primary system in 1942, and today 114 out of 116 elementary schools in that city have voluntarily adopted the plan. Under this plan, the idea of failure and promotion is eliminated. Emphasis is placed on early and continuous success. Most children remain in the primary division for six semesters. At the end of the primary period, each child's growth is evaluated to determine whether he is ready for fourth grade work. If a child spends seven or eight semesters in the primary division, his program is stretched out to accommodate his slower rate of learning, but he is not marked a failure. A few children may be passed to the fourth grade before the expiration of six semesters.[6]

When grade levels are abolished, the primary administrative problem becomes one of grouping. Usually the classroom teacher's judgment is crucial in the selection of children for instructional groups. Account is taken not only of the child's performance on tests and classroom work, but also of work habits, social adjustment, attitudes, interests, and special personal problems. Any one group may include children who have been in school for one or more semesters and who represent different learning levels. The identifying card on the door simply says, "Primary."

Careful records are kept on the progress of each child. The record includes a child's progress from one level to another and specific indications of growth in the various reading skills and attitudes. Competition is kept at a minimum, except with the child's own past performance. Great stress is therefore laid upon the individualization of instruction.

The comments made in a preceding paragraph on Individualized Reading apply also essentially to the system of the Ungraded Primary School. The creative teacher is necessary to the success of any system, however sound it may be in theory.

PROMOTION AND NONPROMOTION. Teachers of reading, particularly those in the primary grades, are vitally concerned with the question of promotion and nonpromotion. It has been found that, in schools where the practice of promotion is followed, the highest rate of failure is in the first grade. Since reading ability is so important in all school work, it is often felt that a child should not be passed on to the next grade unless he meets certain standards of proficiency in reading.

We can dispense here with the philosophical argument against nonpromotion, except to point out that to a child the failure to be promoted is usually regarded as punishment and that there is an injustice in punishing a child who has done what he could with the capacity he has. In some instances, in fact, his plight may be the result of poor teaching. The practice of nonpromotion for inadequate learning is somehow reminiscent of the colonial practice of flogging a child for giving a wrong answer.

---

[6] Jean Hutchinson, "Ungraded Primary School," *Toward Effective Grouping,* pp. 46–50. Washington, D.C.: Association for Childhood Education International, 1962.

But we are here concerned with teaching efficiency, with the welfare of the child. The question is solely whether nonpromotion is conducive to greater learning. Fortunately, on this point there is ample research evidence. After referring to the studies summarized in the *Encyclopedia of Educational Research* (3rd edition, pp. 4–10, The Macmillan Company, 1960), John I. Goodlad declares that "slow-learning children profit significantly more from promotion than from nonpromotion." He goes on to point out the following facts:

> Neither promotion nor nonpromotion, in and of itself, can change a child's basic learning rate.
>
> Very few children in a given grade approximate the grade norms for that grade in their achievement. For example, only three or four children out of a class of thirty are found to be at grade norm in all subjects at the middle of the year. And this is true even when "grade norm" is defined generously to include a one-year spread in achievement from subject to subject.
>
> A child seldom approximates arbitrary grade norms in all areas of endeavor. He may be significantly above in one and below in another and only slightly above or below in still others.
>
> The spread in mental age among a group of children, already as much as four years in the first grade, becomes greater as these children progress through the elementary school. The spread in academic attainment, in turn, will tend to keep pace with the broadening spread in mental age, especially under conditions of good teaching.[7]

The facts, therefore, do not support those critics of American education who blame all its failings on the practice of "social promotion." Actually, the concept adopted by modern schools can better be described as "continuous progress." Nor does all this mean that a child should never be "retained." There may be compelling reasons why an individual child should not pass on to a group of older children in the next grade. But the reasons should be truly compelling. The threat of nonpromotion does not result in increased learning. And in most cases the cost in terms of emotional stress is greater than any theoretical academic advantage would warrant.

FOR FURTHER STUDY

Bond, Guy L., and Bertha Handlan, *Adapting Instruction in Reading to Individual Differences.* Minneapolis: University of Minnesota Press, 1952.

Brogan, Peggy, and Lorene K. Fox, *Helping Children Read.* New York: Holt, Rinehart and Winston, Inc., 1961.

Burrows, Alvina T., *Teaching Children in the Middle Grades*, pp. 169–202. Boston: D. C. Heath and Company, 1952.

---

[7] Reprinted by permission of the Association for Childhood Education International, 3615 Wisconsin Avenue, N.W., Washington 16, D.C. From bulletin No. 5-A, *Toward Effective Grouping*, Copyright 1962; "To Promote or Not to Promote?" by John I. Goodlad, page 34.

Deterline, William A., *An Introduction to Programed Instruction*. Englewood Cliffs, N.J.: Prentice-Hall, Inc., 1962.

Draper, Marcella K., and Louise H. Schwietert, *A Practical Guide to Individualized Reading*. Revised and edited by May Lazar. Publication No. 40. New York: Bureau of Educational Research, Board of Education of the City of New York, October 1960.

Goodlad, John I., and Robert H. Anderson, *The Nongraded Elementary School*. New York: Harcourt, Brace and World, Inc., 1963.

Johnson, Eleanor, *Individualizing Reading*. Curriculum Letter No. 35. Middletown, Conn.: Wesleyan University, March 1957.

Kelly, Florence C., "Ungraded Primary School," *Educational Leadership* (November 1960), 80.

Komoski, P. Kenneth, "Teaching Machines and Programed Reading Instruction," *Controversial Issues in Reading and Promising Solutions*, Helen M. Robinson, ed., pp. 109–120. Supplementary Educational Monographs, No. 91. Chicago: The University of Chicago Press, 1961.

Lazar, May, "Individualized Reading: A Dynamic Approach," *The Reading Teacher*, 10 (December 1957), 75.

Miel, Alice, ed., *Individualizing Reading Practices*. Practical Suggestions for Teaching, No. 14. New York: Bureau of Publications, Teachers College, Columbia University, 1958.

Rasmussen, Margaret, ed., *Toward Effective Grouping*. Washington: Association for Childhood Education International, 1962.

Smith, Wendell I., and J. William Moore, *Programed Learning*. Princeton, N.J.: D. Van Nostrand Co., Inc., 1962.

Theory into Practice, Vol. I, No. 1 (February 1962). Columbus, Ohio: College of Education, Ohio State University, 1962.

Tyler, Fred. T., and Others, *Individualizing Instruction*, pp. 44–92, 177–284. Sixty-first Yearbook of the National Society for the Study of Education, Part I, Nelson B. Henry, ed. Chicago: The University of Chicago Press, 1962.

Veatch, Jeannette, ed., *Individualizing Your Reading*. New York: G. P. Putnam's Sons, 1959.

Witty, Paul, with the assistance of Ann Coomer and Robert Sizemore, "Individualizing Reading," *Elementary English*, 36 (October 1959), 401–412.

Wrightstone, J. Wayne, *Class Organization for Instruction*. What Research Says to the Teacher, No. 13. Washington: National Education Association, 1957.

13

Helping the Retarded and the Unusually Gifted Child in Reading

The Retarded Reader

School and public alike are justifiably concerned about pupils in elementary and high schools who are retarded in reading. Reading ability is essential to success in all school work and in life outside of school. In addition, therefore, to providing the developmental reading instruction that all pupils need, the school has the task of giving special attention to those who have serious difficulties in learning to read.

It is not possible to state what percentage of pupils are retarded in reading. Obviously more than 35 percent of children fall below the average for their age or grade. Averages are computed from the full range of abilities found at any given age or grade level, and the range tends to be greatest when the instruction is the most efficient. The figure 35 percent therefore tells us little. We do know that many readers—good, average, and poor—are "underachievers," that is, readers who are not performing up to their capacity. When a reader is both a slow learner and an underachiever, we may be sure that he needs special help.

Who Is the Retarded Reader?

Some writers consider a pupil retarded if his reading score is considerably below the average for his chronological age or for his grade in school. Others

306

hold that he is retarded if he falls below the norms for his mental age. Still others believe that a child, regardless of mental age, cannot be called a retarded reader if he achieves the average for his grade, even if his mental age is above average for his grade. Such a child should be spurred on to better performance, but he cannot be classified as "retarded." In this view, a child is "retarded" if he reads well below grade level but has the capacity to perform at a higher level.

For practical purposes, the term "reading retardation" as employed in this book refers to backwardness in reading that can be corrected by special instruction. The above-average reader is not considered backward—even if he fails to realize his full potentialities. All children need the kind of guidance which will lead them to full development of their powers. Moreover, the distinction between "remedial" and "developmental" reading is at best ambiguous. This chapter will therefore deal with children who fall below the average for their age group but who have the capacity to grow more rapidly in reading ability than they presently do.

Capacity for learning to read is commonly measured by group intelligence tests. These are very useful in providing estimates of children's ability to learn. They are, however, by no means infallible. For example, group intelligence tests generally require a certain amount of reading ability. Children who are handicapped in reading may not be able to show their real mental abilities in these tests. For this reason, teachers should weigh the "mental age" records of children with great caution.

The child who reads at or above his grade level but who could do better needs particular attention. The teacher should not be satisfied with the reading of a boy with an intelligence quotient of 120 who reads only as well at the age of ten as the average ten-year-old. However, the help he needs to learn to read up to his capacity is not usually the kind needed by the child who reads below both his grade level and his intellectual capacity. He is not, in our sense of the term, a retarded reader.

The strong interest in reading retardation now evident in elementary schools had its inception in the decade of the twenties and reached great heights in the thirties. When the problem of reading deficiency first attracted the attention of school people, the tendency was to organize many classes in remedial reading. Children who were one year or more below grade level were often placed in special classes or singled out for tutorial instruction. The idea of providing for individual differences in normal classes gained acceptance only slowly.

Today we recognize at least three types of "retarded" readers. One is the youngster who is not reading as well as he can but who is able to improve his performance under the guidance of his regular classroom teacher. Another has difficulties that are serious enough to require the assistance of a remedial teacher, usually in a special remedial reading class. A third type, fortunately an exception, has problems which call for intensive study by the staff of a reading clinic. When a child fails to make progress in reading, in spite of persistent efforts by the school to help him, he needs the attention of specialists who are skilled in the investigation of causes that interfere with progress in reading. For most children, however, a flexible program which takes account of the wide differences in reading ability will be sufficient to meet their varying needs.

Causes of Reading Retardation

Knowledge of the causes responsible for unsatisfactory progress in reading is valuable from two standpoints: such understanding can help the teacher (1) to prevent retardation and (2) to deal intelligently with difficulties as they arise. The task is to look behind the symptoms and to find the causes. These will usually be a combination of several elements; indeed, "multiple causation" is a basic principle of remedial reading. The causes of reading difficulty are usually numerous, complex, and interrelated.

The principle of "multiple causation" does not, however, mean that the classroom teacher cannot cope with the reading problems of most retarded pupils. Although a few children will require study by experts, the thoughtful and sympathetic efforts of the classroom teacher are usually sufficient to help meet children's needs. What is necessary is a careful study of each child's background and an analysis of the skills in which he is deficient.

Because of their interrelatedness, the search for causes should not end when one apparent cause has been found. Frequently a primary cause of retardation in reading, especially if the difficulty is one of long duration, results in one or more secondary causes, which may in turn greatly influence the effectiveness of the reading. Thus, for example, illness, with consequent irregularity of school attendance, may be at the root of a child's reading difficulty. It may result in lack of interest in learning, which by itself is significant enough to bring about serious problems in learning to read.

Reading Deficiency and Personality

Reading problems are often associated with personality problems. Since reading is so important in the life of every child, failure in this activity may be expected to cause anxieties, feelings of insecurity, and even aggressive behavior. On the other hand, children who come to school with a sense of inadequacy, a feeling of being unloved, or an unconscious hostility against the adult world may lack the necessary incentive to learn to read or may be prepared to resist efforts on the part of the teacher to teach them. The factors of personality problems and reading problems are no doubt usually reciprocal. For this reason, it is commonly necessary to provide personal guidance along with the corrective instruction in reading. Certainly the teacher needs at all times to consider the total development of the child, not merely his reading needs.

The evidence to date on the relation between language and personality development has been ably summarized by Russell. In his conclusion, he states:

> Although results are still meager, there exists some evidence that amount and type of language behavior is often closely related to other phases of personality. At present the most detailed analysis seems to be in the area of social-emotional disturbances as related to reading difficulties. A promising lead has been opened up in the influences of reading, discussion, sociodrama, etc., on personality not only as catharsis and therapy in difficult cases but as procedures with normal children. Language activities are causes, concomitants, or results of personality factors, but many detailed relationships must be explored if teachers and parents are to have the help they sometimes need in guiding growth in both language and personality.[1]

Reading Deficiency and the Home Situation

Helen M. Robinson[2] has reported on an intensive study of the causes of reading failure. She found that social, visual, and emotional difficulties appeared most frequently as causes of poor progress or failure in learning to read. Maladjusted homes or poor family relationships were found to be contributing causes in more than 54 percent of the cases studied. Her findings, based upon data from the field of social work, psychiatry, pediatrics, neurology, ophthalmology, speech correction, otolaryngology, endocrinology, and psychology, confirm conclusions by other investigators. It seems clear that home conditions may have much to do with children's reading progress in school.

The emotional stresses resulting from conflict or deprivation in the home are only one source of reading retardation in school. Indifference on the part of parents toward a child's reading may be responsible for a lack of incentive to learn to read. Paradoxically, oversolicitude on the part of parents may also create tensions which impede reading progress. If there is hostility between child and parent, the very eagerness of the mother and father to note reading progress may serve as motive for holding back. More typically, the desire of the child to gain parental approval results in fears that inhibit normal and felicitous growth in reading.

The reading background provided by the home is a potent factor in determining how well the child will succeed in school. When parents show an

[1] David H. Russell, "Interrelationships of the Language Arts and Personality," *Elementary English*, 30 (March 1953), 167–80.

[2] Helen M. Robinson, *Why Pupils Fail in Reading*. Chicago: The University of Chicago Press, 1946.

enthusiastic interest in their children's reading, when they read stories to them and show them the pictures, when they discuss the contents of the books with them, they are laying strong foundations for pleasurable, independent reading. Especially important is the presence in the home of a variety of attractive, appealing books for children. Time for quiet reading provided at home and a reasonably comfortable place for reading, too, help to start the child on the road to the enjoyment of books.

Fortunately, many children who come from impoverished or otherwise unpromising home environments nevertheless become excellent readers. Perhaps in a few instances the very lack of favorable home surroundings may serve as an incentive for greater effort in learning to read. The example of Abraham Lincoln comes to mind. Such cases, however, are exceptional. As a rule, when children from unfavorable home environments become good readers, as they often do, it is in spite of, not because of, their early deprivation.

Reading Deficiency and Early Experiences with Reading

Children's first experiences with reading will in great measure determine their later progress. If they are faced with reading tasks for which they are not ready, they may build antagonistic attitudes toward reading which interfere with normal growth. Moreover, they may develop inappropriate habits of word attack or sentence reading which will cause trouble throughout all the formative years.

Examples of such habits are many. The child may develop the habit of sounding the words without giving attention to the meaning. Or he may feel that partial recognition of words is satisfactory. Word pointing and its companion, line pointing, may serve too long as a crutch in silent or oral reading. These devices may be harmless or even helpful at the very beginning, but children should soon learn to do without them if they are to read for meaning and develop appropriate speed. The same may be said about the use of markers (strips of paper moved from line to line during reading). The child should be encouraged as early as possible to develop independence in making accurate return sweeps from line to line. Extremely slow rate of reading, word-by-word reading, and overanalytical methods of word attack may also be responsible for unsatisfactory growth in reading.

Reading Deficiency and the School Climate

The general atmosphere of the school can be an important factor in children's success in reading. If there is a feeling of tension or pressure, if the child senses that the school authorities are anxious about his reading, he may develop harmful attitudes toward the reading process. On the other hand, if there is a bright, relaxed atmosphere, reading tends to take on the aspect of a delight-

The reading corner affords a pleasing setting for explorations in books

The well-managed and well-financed school library is essential to a good reading program

The *"experience" chart is one of many approaches
to the teaching of word recognition*

ful challenge. Such an atmosphere is created primarily by the ways in which teachers talk about reading, by their reactions to children's successes and failures, and by the variety of stimulating activities going on in the school. Physical surroundings, too, play a part in forming children's attitudes toward reading. Dreary, unstimulating classrooms lacking in suitable reading materials may inhibit the reading growth of pupils who might burgeon in a more evocative environment. Overcrowded classrooms, regimented instruction, antiquated textbooks, and lack of good school libraries may be responsible to a degree for much of the reading retardation found in our schools.

Reading Deficiency and Other Factors

Basically, the causes of reading deficiency must be sought in the presence or absence of the elements requisite to growth in reading, discussed in Chapter 4. Physical well-being, visual and auditory acuity, intelligence, experience background, mental health, and interest and purpose in reading are essential factors to be investigated when the child fails to make expected progress in reading. The process of exploring causes of reading retardation is essentially one of finding out which of these essential elements are lacking in significant degree.

Diagnosing Reading Difficulties

"Diagnosis" of reading difficulty usually involves three tasks: (1) determining whether true retardation exists; (2) determining the nature of the difficulty; and (3) determining the causes that have brought about the difficulty. Very often these purposes can be accomplished in a single step. In undertaking to determine "who is the retarded reader," the teacher frequently learns much of the nature of the difficulties and sometimes something of the causes. Various procedures may be employed to secure these types of information.

Informal Observation of the Pupil

The first method in diagnosis is one that alert, sympathetic teachers have always used: a careful observation of the child's over-all performance, his attitudes toward books and reading, his play interests, his hobbies, and his reading interests. The observation may take place in nonreading as well as in reading situations. For example, a child may unintentionally reveal a dislike for reading while working with classmates on a model airplane or while discussing what he would like for Christmas. The teacher may note the kinds of book choices a child makes during the free reading period. She may observe the child's behavior as he reads a book—whether he squints, whether he stops often in his reading, whether he assumes good or poor posture as he reads.

Use of Anecdotal Records

Since few teachers are able to keep in mind the developing characteristics of many children over a period of time, it is helpful to keep an informal record of the day-by-day observations. A file folder should be kept for each pupil suspected of having difficulty in reading; in fact, teachers will find it helpful to keep such a folder for every pupil in the class. In this folder the teacher should insert, from time to time, any material that may throw light on the child's reading problems. The folder should include samples of the child's writing and drawing as well as reading exercises which he may have performed. But perhaps the most important material is the teacher's report of the child's observed behavior. This may be in the form of a sentence or two for a given day (the date should be noted), such as: "Today Axel spent 15 minutes in uninterrupted reading of *The Little House in the Big Woods*. He has never concentrated before for so long on his reading, as far as I know." The notations should usually not be of a general nature, as, "I think Axel is improving." The anecdotal record should essentially be a behavioral record. In the course of six months it should be possible to discover from the record in what direction the child is moving with respect to significant aspects of reading growth. The type of information described in this paragraph cannot be secured from even the best of the standardized tests of silent reading.

Study of Pupil Records

Many schools keep detailed records of the history of individual children. These usually include reports on health examinations, past school attendance, achievement and intelligence tests, home visits that may have been made, and other information. An examination of such records may often give the teacher important clues as to the reasons why a child is not succeeding in reading. For example, a child from a migratory family may have had to make numerous adjustments to new school situations and may have had special difficulties in following different systems of reading instruction. (Incidentally, the problem of mobility in American families poses an increasingly critical problem to American schools.) Absence from school because of illness or other causes may also be responsible for backwardness in reading among pupils who would otherwise make normal progress. The more information the teacher has about a pupil's past experiences, the more she will be able to deal intelligently with his reading problems. School records should, of course, be kept confidential and be strictly reserved for professional use.

Use of Informal Tests

The late E. W. Dolch once suggested[3] a simple, common-sense method of testing a child's reading ability with the aid of a textbook. In an interview with a pupil, the teacher selects a book from the shelf and says, "Let's see how the reading goes." The book is one that is probably not too difficult for the pupil, but it is one he has not read before. First, the teacher asks the pupil to read a passage aloud. He supplies the words the pupil does not recognize. By this means he determines whether the pupil is lacking in knowledge of common words he should know. Second, he asks the pupil to close the book and tell in brief as much as he can of what he has read. He praises the pupil for correct answers and encourages him to go on. This step is intended to reveal whether the pupil reads with any comprehension. Third, the teacher selects another passage and asks the pupil to read it, but he does not supply any words missed. He asks, "What do you *think* the word is?" Thus the teacher learns something of the pupil's ability to use context in word recognition. Fourth, in another selection the pupil is called on to tell the first letter of a word he does not recognize—then the next, and the next, until the pupil can supply the whole word. In these four steps the teacher has discovered, in a very short time, many of the kinds of difficulty which the pupil encounters in his reading.

Many periodicals and books designed for elementary school instruction in reading contain informal, nonstandardized, but more or less objective tests based upon specific reading selections. These enable the teacher to make a quick check of pupils' comprehension and vocabulary knowledge. Some of these are timed tests and thus provide the teacher with a rough measure of a pupil's reading rate for a given type of material.

Informal tests to determine a pupil's success in reading can also be constructed by the teacher herself. From time to time, the teacher may wish to discover the extent to which pupils have comprehended the meaning of an assigned passage.

Informal tests may be of many kinds: matching tests, true-false tests, best-answer tests, proofreading tests, multiple-choice tests, and many others.[3a] Among these, perhaps one of the most useful and reliable is the multiple choice. A multiple-choice item consists of (1) a "stem," which is an incomplete statement and (2) a series of three or preferably four or more alternatives, or options, from which the pupil is asked to select the expression which best completes the statement. Examples of such items are the following:

---

[3] E. W. Dolch, "Testing Reading with a Book," *Elementary English*, 28 (March 1951), 124–125, 165.

[3a] For a fuller description of such tests, the student is referred to one of the many good books on educational measurement. One of these is J. Raymond Gerberich, *Specimen Objective Test Items: A Guide to Achievement Test Construction*. New York: David McKay Company, Inc., 1956.

1. In this story Leonardo appears as
   a.) a fairy
   b.) an angel
   c.) a dwarf
   d.) Santa Claus.
2. The children were not frightened by Leonardo because
   a.) They were accustomed to seeing strange creatures
   b.) They recognized him
   c.) Their mother had told them who he was
   d.) Leonardo revealed himself to them.

The correct expression in the item is called the "key." The other alternatives should, if possible, be such that a person who had not read the passage would be unable to make an obvious choice. At the same time, they should be unambiguously incorrect responses.

Use of Standardized Tests

A common instrument in the diagnosis of reading problems is the published standardized test. The standardized test has the advantage of being based upon the responses of a large number of pupils of specified ages and grade levels. Thus it is possible to compare the performance of an individual or a group with that of a representative sample of pupils in the same age or grade classification. Standardized tests serve two important purposes. One is to relate the average reading performance of a pupil to that of other pupils over the country who are of the same age or in the same grade in school. The pupil's achievement may be compared to that of typical pupils at various levels—the median, the first quartile, the third quartile, the first percentile, or the 99th percentile. While norms for these various levels are usually supplied, they should not be regarded as infallible standards. Their value depends upon the size and representativeness of the sample. The second purpose of the standardized test is to help the teacher make an analysis of the specific skills in which the pupil is strong or weak.

Standardized tests are often classified as "survey" tests and "diagnostic" tests. The former provide an average score; the latter undertake to break down the average into specific strengths and weaknesses. The scores on a "survey" test tell the teacher how well a pupil can read a given collection of words, sentences, and paragraphs in comparison with other pupils of the same age and grade. The scores on a "diagnostic" test tell how skillful the reader is in specific aspects of reading, in comparison with other pupils of the same age and grade in school. Both types of tests, if wisely used, are valuable in dealing with the reading problems of children. In the study of children's reading ability we therefore make use of both the survey test and the diagnostic test.

In making a selection of standardized reading tests, the teacher should study carefully the teachers' manuals supplied with them. Manuals will tell of the *validity* of a test, which indicates the degree of accuracy with which the test measures what it is intended to measure, and of the *reliability* of a test, which indicates the degree to which a test yields consistent results. The teacher should keep in mind also the purpose for which she intends to use the test. For example, tests which consist chiefly of vocabulary items may not adequately measure the degree to which a pupil is able to deal with words in context. The length of the test and the time available to teachers and pupils may also be important factors. Finally, the relative recency of the test may have a bearing on the selection.

Various sources may be consulted for the names and publishers of standardized tests in reading. Catalogs of such publishers as Harcourt, Brace and World (New York), The Public School Publishing Company (Bloomington, Illinois), Educational Testing Service (Princeton, New Jersey), California Test Bureau (Los Angeles), Educational Test Bureau (Minneapolis), Bureau of Publications, Teachers College, Columbia University (New York), and Science Research Associates (Chicago) may be secured on request. Oscar Buros' *Mental Measurements Yearbooks* present, in their various editions, the necessary publication facts about standardized reading tests, along with critical reviews by experts of their general value, utility, reliability, and validity. They are published by Gryphon Press, Highland Park, New Jersey. A very comprehensive listing, with descriptions, is found in Anthony P. Witham's article, "The Index to Reading Material," in *Elementary English* for March, 1963, pp. 318–327 (available separately from the National Council of Teachers of English, 506 S. Sixth St., Champaign, Illinois).

Following is a list of the more widely used standardized tests in reading:

Basic Sight Word Test, by E. W. Dolch. Survey. Grades 1–2. Garrard Publishing Company, Champaign, Ill., 1942.

The Botel Reading Inventory, by M. Botel and others. Survey. Grades 1–12. Follett Publishing Company, Chicago, 1961.

California Reading Test, by E. W. Tiegs and W. W. Clark. Survey. Grades 1–14. California Test Bureau, Monterey, Calif., 1957.

Chapman-Cook Speed of Reading Test, by J. C. Chapman and S. Cook. Survey. Grades 4–8. Educational Test Bureau, Minneapolis, 1924.

Detroit Reading Test, by C. M. Parker and E. A. Waterbury. Survey. Grades 2–9. Harcourt, Brace and World, Inc., New York, 1927.

Detroit Word Recognition Test, by E. F. Oglesby. Survey. Grades 1–3. Harcourt, Brace and World, Inc., New York, 1929.

Diagnostic Reading Tests, by Committee on Diagnostic Reading Tests. Diagnostic. Grades K–13. The Committee, Mountain Home, N. C., 1960.

Durrell Analysis of Reading Difficulties, by D. D. Durrell. Diagnostic. Grades 1–6. Harcourt, Brace and World, Inc., New York, 1955.

Gates Reading Diagnostic Tests, by A. I. Gates. Diagnostic. Grades 1–8. Bureau of Publications, Teachers College, Columbia University, New York, 1953.

Gates Reading Readiness Tests, by A. I. Gates. Readiness. Grade 1. Bureau of Publications, Teachers College, Columbia University, New York, 1953.

Gates Reading Survey Tests, by A. I. Gates. Survey. Grades 4–10. Bureau of Publications, Teachers College, Columbia University, New York, 1958.

Gates Reading Tests: Primary-Advanced Primary, by A. I. Gates. Survey. Grades 1–3. Bureau of Publications, Teachers College, Columbia University, New York, 1958.

Gray Oral Reading Tests, by William S. Gray. Edited by Helen M. Robinson. Diagnostic. Grades 1–12. Bobbs-Merrill Company, Inc., Indianapolis, 1963.

Iowa Every-Pupil Tests of Basic Skills: Silent Reading, by H. F. Spitzer and others. Survey. Grades 3–9. Houghton Mifflin Company, Boston, 1947.

Metropolitan Achievement Tests: Reading, by W. N. Durost and others. Survey. Grades 3–9. Harcourt, Brace and World, Inc., New York, 1960.

Murphy-Durrell Diagnostic Reading Readiness Test, by H. A. Murphy and D. D. Durrell. Diagnostic. Grade 1. Harcourt, Brace and World, Inc., New York, 1949.

The Nelson Silent Reading Test, by M. J. Nelson. Survey. Grades 3–9. Houghton Mifflin Company, Boston, 1939.

Pressey Diagnostic Reading Tests, by S. L. and L. C. Pressey. Diagnostic. Grades 3–9. Public School Publishing Company, Bloomington, Ill., 1929.

Sequential Tests of Education Progress: Reading, by the staff of the Educational Testing Service. Survey. Grades 4–14. Cooperative Test Division of the Educational Testing Service, Princeton, N.J., 1959.

Standardized Oral Reading Check Tests, by W. S. Gray. Oral, diagnostic. Grades 1–8. Public School Publishing Company, Bloomington, Ill., 1955.

Stanford Achievement Test: Reading, by T. L. Kelley and others. Survey. Grades 3–9. Harcourt, Brace and World, Inc., New York, 1955.

The percentage of retarded learners appears to be much higher among children of the lower socio-economic classes than among the school population in general. In summarizing a study by Haggard,[4] Riessman emphasizes the need for giving these children directed practice and for developing new test-taking habits.

> Deprived children are less test conscious and are not accustomed to being evaluated. They have poor auditory habits, do not concentrate sufficiently on the examiner's instructions, do not pick up the examinations readily, and, in general, are lethargic, apathetic, and ill at ease in the test situation. . . . Haggard's research also demonstrates the great need for rapport. Haggard trained his examiners so that they would know how to work with deprived youngsters. . . . The clinician has to know how to elicit questions

---

[4] Ernest A. Haggard, "Social Status and Intelligence," *Genetic Psychology Monographs*, 49 (1954), 141–186.

from the deprived child, and how to provide answers that are clearly understood, are repeated often, with numerous examples. . . . Deprived children, unless they are at ease with the examiner, are much more likely to be passive in the test situation.[5]

Such advice to the teacher of culturally deprived children applies equally for many other children who are retarded readers. Standardized test scores are reliable only if those who take the tests understand what is expected of them and if their attitude toward the test situation is favorable. As in the case of all standardized testing, the instructions in the teacher's manual as to procedure and timing must be followed exactly.

Unfortunately, in many school situations the scores made by children on standardized tests are merely tabulated and filed for possible use when a special problem arises in connection with individual children or when questions are raised about the general performance of the class. Such use of tests hardly justifies the expense, time, and effort involved. Test scores can reveal the approximate performance of a class with norms for the general population in the respective age groups. They can help identify the pupils who need special instructional assistance in reading. They can reveal specific elementa of weakness on the part of individuals or whole groups. They are only a part, but a very important part, of the total program of evaluation and diagnosis.

Just as the child needs practice in taking tests, so the teacher needs experience in the interpretation of the results. With practice, the teacher soon learns to recognize characteristic patterns in the curves yielded by test scores. Some children are weak in all phases of silent reading; others are particularly in need of help in specific aspects. So also the teacher knows that the test usually measures reading at the "instructional" level and that a child's independent reading may not measure up in all respects to the level of test performance.

Use of Check Lists

Interest inventories and lists of specific reading skills are often helpful in identifying points of difficulty in children's reading. The *Witty-Kopel Interest Inventory*[6] is a valuable aid in discovering the reading interests and attitudes of boys and girls. An illustrative check list of reading skills is suggested by Wheeler and Smith:[7]

---

[5] Frank Riessman, *The Culturally Deprived Child,* p. 61. New York: Harper and Row, Publishers, 1962.

[6] Paul Witty and David Kopel, *Reading and the Educative Process,* pp. 316–334, Boston: Ginn and Company, 1939.

[7] Adapted by L. R. Wheeler from the article by Lester Wheeler and Edwin A. Smith, "A Modification of the Informal Reading Inventory," *Elementary English,* 34 (April 1957), 224–226.

SUGGESTIONS ON HOW TO FIND A CHILD'S READING LEVEL

1. Select a series of good basic readers which will, in your opinion, best suit the child.
2. Estimate roughly, from a standardized reading test, the child's instructional reading level and select a reader about one grade under the standardized test level or grade placement.
3. Have the child read the first complete sentence at the beginning of the pages sampled and keep a record of his errors. A suggested form for recording errors is given below.
4. As the child reads, count as errors mispronunciations, omissions, substitutions, hesitancies over three seconds, distortions, and word assists by the teacher. Do not count as errors mistakes on proper names.
5. If the percentage of errors per hundred words is more than 3 to 5 percent, drop down to the next grade level in the series. If the percentage of errors is less than 2 percent move up to the next grade level in the series.
6. When you have found the level at which the child's errors constitute approximately 3 to 5 percent of the running words, test his paragraph reading. Select four or five paragraphs and have the child read these, both silently and orally, noting the difficulties.
7. Remember that series differ in difficulty; therefore, teach the child in the series used to evaluate him, or retest him in the series to be used for instruction.
8. If the child passes the sentence test but not the paragraph test, teach him on the level indicated by the sentence test. This holds true *only* on the primary level because at this level few children have difficulty with the concepts offered, and the vocabulary problem is not so much one of meaning as of recognition.
9. Children who show difficulties of organization, retention, and understanding can be taught in material where they know at least 95 percent of the running words.
10. We might summarize the following practical underlying assumptions from clinical and teaching experience:
    a) A child can read materials without any assistance when he knows and understands 98-99 percent of vocabulary and comprehends 75-90 percent of main ideas. This is his independent, library, or free reading level.
    b) The child's instructional or teaching level is the point at which he knows and understands the meaning of 95-98 percent of vocabulary and comprehends about 75-90 percent of main ideas. "Instructional level" implies that the child needs word analysis of unknown words and comprehension direction.
    c) The child's frustration level is the point at which he recognizes or knows less than 95 percent of vocabulary and comprehends less than 75 percent of the main ideas. Frustration in reading generally

CONDENSATION OF THE INFORMAL READING INVENTORY
CHECK SHEET USED AT UNIVERSITY OF
MIAMI READING CLINIC

NAME_____DATE_____AGE_____GRADE_____

Series used_____Frustration level_____

Instructional level_____Probable mental level_____

Independent level_____

Vocabulary Difficulties

Phonics poor_____

Syllabication poor_____

Use of configuration poor_____

Use of picture clue poor_____

Sight vocabulary poor_____

Use of context poor_____   *Comprehension Difficulties*

                                          Sentence reading poor_____

Perception Difficulties   Paragraph reading poor_____

Reverses words_____Memory poor_____

Reverses letters_____Organization poor_____

Omits beginnings_____Detail reading poor_____

Omits endings_____Critical reading_____

Omits words_____Inference reading_____

Sounds confused_____Diagrammatic reading_____

Sounds added_____Reading for ideas_____

Omits sounds_____Reading to visualize_____

Other factors_____Ability to visualize_____

_____Ability to anticipate_____

_____Ability to follow directions_____

Rate Difficulties

Directional problem_____Scanning_____

Word-by-word reader_____Reading for ideas_____

Regression movements_____Reading to anticipate meaning_____

Points at words_____Reading materials at different rates_____

Loses place easily_____

Quick recognition of vocabulary_____Reading to visualize_____

Reading key words in sentences_____Pictorial reading_____

Reading key sentences in paragraphs_____Ability to read rapidly different

_____ materials_____

Skimming_____Ability to read under time limits_____

increases with a decrease in recognition, meaning vocabulary, and general comprehension of materials the child is reading.

11. One of the main purposes of the diagnosis is to determine the free reading, instructional levels for teaching purposes, and also to learn the frustration level where the material is too difficult for the child to read.

Another valuable check list, or profile, has been developed by the staff of

READING PROGRESS PROFILE
Level One: Reading Readiness

NAME_____ C. A. SEPT._____M. A. SEPT._____

GRADE_____RESULTS OF READING READINESS TEST_____

	Inadequate	Improved	Adequate
Ideational Facility			
Converses easily			
Uses complete sentences			
Speaks distinctly			
Uses correct English			
Solves problems independently			
Experimental Reading Skills			
Observes carefully on excursions			
Contributes to chart stories			
Reads from left to right			
Makes accurate return sweep			
Reads phrases and separate words			
Visual and Auditory Skills			
Notes variations in word patterns			
Sees details in word forms			
Hears variations in sounds			
Hears word elements			

Dates of each check: 1._____ 2._____ 3._____ 4._____ 5._____ 6._____

Notes concerning the child's progress in reading:

READING PROGRESS PROFILE
Level Two: Beginning Reading

NAME_____C. A. SEPT._____M. A. SEPT._____

GRADE_____READING AGE_____READING GRADE_____

	Inadequate	Improved	Adequate
Oral Reading Skills			
Accomplishes reading purpose			
Phrases correctly			
Uses natural expression			
Uses automatic L-R eye movement			
Makes few reversals			
Makes few regressions			
Vocabulary Skills and Abilities			
Retains sight vocabulary			
Uses context clues			
Uses visual clues			
Silent Reading Skills and Abilities			
Reads easy books voluntarily			
Makes accurate recall			
Does seat work independently			
Uses few or no lip movements			
Skill in the Use of Books			
Handles books with care			
Knows how to find a page			

Dates of each check: 1._____ 2._____ 3._____ 4._____ 5._____ 6._____
Notes concerning the child's progress in reading:

the training schools attached to the Lowell, Massachusetts, State Teachers College.[8] These teachers thought of the reading program as consisting of three parts: (1) the integrative, which emphasizes guidance in using reading as a tool in the various subject fields; (2) the recreational, which stresses reading as a way of gaining pleasure; and (3) the basic instructional, which undertakes to build foundational habits, skills, and abilities essential to reading as a means of learning. Reading was considered as one aspect of the child's total growth. The check list is based on these principles.

The use of the profile is such that a continuous record of each child's

------

[8] Mary A. O'Rourke, "The Evaluation of Reading in Terms of Child Development," *Elementary English*, 28 (January 1951), 14–18.

READING PROGRESS PROFILE
Level Three: Rapid Progress Stage

NAME_____C. A. SEPT._____M. A. SEPT._____

GRADE_____READING AGE_____READING GRADE_____

	Inadequate	Improved	Adequate
Oral Reading Skills			
Reads for meaning			
Uses natural expression			
Recognizes new words independently			
Makes use of punctuation marks			
Silent Reading Skills			
Uses supplementary books voluntarily			
Discusses content intelligently			
Reads workbook independently			
Increases silent reading speed			
Eliminates vocalization			
Vocabulary Skills			
Recognizes sight words automatically			
Recognizes consonants by ear and eye			
Uses common word endings			
Uses common blends			
Uses configuration clues			
Uses context clues			
Adds prefixes and suffixes			
Skill in the Use of Books			
Handles books carefully			
Makes use of the table of contents			

Dates of each check: 1._____ 2._____ 3._____ 4._____ 5._____ 6._____
Notes concerning the child's progress in reading:

growth is made. The essence is the child's progress, and not the achievement of an arbitrary level in a stated time. The profile or profiles accompany the child as he moves from grade to grade. Each teacher thus has a picture of the child's growth to date and of his needs. Teachers do not speak of a child as a "fourth-grade reader" if he happens to be in the sixth grade, but refer to him in terms of his achievement along the lines indicated by the levels in the profile. Children in any given room or grade vary widely, as we all know, in all types of growth and achievement. The profile ensures that each child will secure, so far as the teacher can give it, the instruction appropriate to his level of growth.

READING PROGRESS PROFILE
Level Four: Stage of Extension of Experience and Efficiency

NAME_____ C. A. SEPT._____M. A. SEPT._____

GRADE_____READING AGE_____READING GRADE_____

	Inadequate	Improved	Adequate
Oral Reading Skills			
Reads intelligently			
Uses natural expression			
Pronounces words accurately			
Observes punctuation			
Silent Reading Skills			
Strives for full comprehension			
Adjusts speed to purpose			
Eliminates vocalization			
Vocabulary Skills			
Defines many sight words			
Uses phonics			
Uses context clues			
Divides words into syllables			
Uses dictionary			
Study Skills			
Selects important facts			
Decides the main idea			
Outlines material read			
Combines material from many sources			
Uses skimming			
Interprets graphs, charts			
Discusses reading creatively			

Dates of each check: 1._____ 2._____ 3._____ 4._____ 5._____ 6._____
Notes concerning the child's progress in reading:

The problem of promotion or nonpromotion is eliminated, children progressing with their natural groups, each with an account in the profile of his level and needs.

Use of the Reading Clinic

The reading difficulties of some children are so complex and deep seated as to require the study of specialists. Their problems may often be identified by means of the combined efforts of physicians, psychologists, psychiatrists, and specially trained teachers of remedial reading. A number of reading clinics have access to the services of these and other specialists. Unfortunately, however, clinical facilities available to teachers in most parts of the country are inadequate, and where they do exist, they are often expensive and beyond the means of many parents. Most large city school systems offer clinical services. Many states support excellent clinics, which usually have long waiting lists. The principal and the teacher should be informed about the services that are available and should make use of them when they are needed.

Teaching the Retarded Reader

Perhaps the first thing a teacher should keep in mind in teaching the retarded reader is the need to enlist his enthusiastic effort in the process of improvement. Most pupils who have had severe and persistent difficulty in learning to read have developed negative attitudes toward reading. They have, for one reason or another, experienced repeated frustration in a task which they recognize as the most important challenge facing them day after day. The result may be fear or hostility or indifference. Sometimes the awareness of parents' concern or annoyance pursues them to the school door. They may feel that the good opinion of teacher or classmates depends on their performance.

Such children are in great need of "success" experiences. The school day must be a day of achievement. The teacher should patiently seek out opportunities to enable the retarded reader to excel in some activity, whether in singing or dancing, in making something or reporting an everyday experience. Sometimes a retarded reader may do very well in taking part in a dramatic activity. The child must feel that he belongs, that he is respected. He should have something good to report when he returns home.

The experience of success is, of course, of greatest consequence in his work in reading. If the materials he is called upon to read, or the phonics and other reading exercises, are chosen with a view to his abilities, he will be emotionally prepared to take the next step. He need not be praised for every correct response, but he must know when he has done well.

Related to the principle that a child's reading tasks should be adjusted to his present capacity is the often forgotten fact that a slow reader is not necessarily an inferior reader. When we use the term "retarded," we mean that the child has been slowed up by some inhibiting factor which can be removed with good instruction. It does not follow, however, that a learner whose progress in reading is slow is a poor reader. Some children with quite adequate or even superior potential simply arrive at their goals later than others. The teacher should feel at ease about them, provided they are making progress.

Every effort should be made to stimulate the child's desire to read independently in books of his own choosing. It is quite possible to cultivate in retarded readers an interest that will lead to lifetime habits of reading. The use of pictures, dramatizations, conversations about books, and other devices for arousing interest are doubly important in the case of the retarded reader. Easy, well-illustrated books and magazines should be attractively displayed on the book table and the magazine rack.

Too often the physical environment and the program for the special class in remedial reading are barren and forbidding. The overconscientious teacher feels that every moment must be spent with reading workbooks, objective tests, and laborious oral reading. The remedial reading room should be one of the most inviting rooms in the school. The program should include the showing of films, group discussions, "creative" writing, the exchange of jokes and riddles, and oral reports of personal experiences. Reading then becomes what it ought to be—a part of the communication process and the outgrowth of real life experiences. Under circumstances such as these, teachers who dread that "period with the slowpokes" may find teaching the retarded the most rewarding experience of the school day. If remedial reading instruction is to be successful, both pupil and teacher must find pleasure in it.

A word should be said at this point about the relation between pleasure and learning. The commonly used expression, "Reading for Fun," refers not to a marginal or frivolous use of reading ability but to an essential condition for learning to read. Only when the learner finds satisfaction in the activity may we look for the free and unrestrained flow of childhood energies into the task of converting visual symbols into sound and meaning. Even very difficult reading material affords satisfaction when the reader feels that he is achieving a clearly understood purpose. For the young child the appearance of too many unfamiliar words or concepts in the reading material is a distraction and a hindrance to enjoyment. For the retarded reader, especially, the prescription must be easy, abundant, interest-charged reading material.

Another consideration in the planning of work with the retarded reader is the role of the parent. Teachers who have responsibility for large numbers of children cannot be in frequent communication with all the parents, but in the case of the severely retarded reader such communication is essential. The personal interview is the most effective form, but in the absence of opportunity for face-to-face discussions the letter-report can be most useful. Parent and teacher have much to learn from each other about the child. The teacher needs to know as much as possible about the child's home situation and his behavior with respect to play, TV habits, sleeping habits, and especially his reading at home. On the other hand, the parent needs to have advice as to methods of reinforcing the efforts of the teacher in providing appropriate reading guidance.

In many instances the parents are indifferent to the child's school problems. In others, they are overconcerned and competitive and place undue pressure on the child. Sometimes the parent adopts a punitive attitude toward the child who is not doing well in reading. The parent should be informed early about any important difficulty a child is having, so that he or she will not be shocked or agitated to discover that the child needs special help. As a rule, parents should be discouraged from attempting to give reading instruction at home; they should be encouraged to provide the environment, the stimulation, and the good example that will strengthen the teacher's efforts to build constructive attitudes toward reading on the part of the child.

Finally, appropriate guidance for the retarded reader should extend to the work in the content subjects. Gains achieved in the reading period can be quickly canceled out if the child is confronted in science, social studies, hygiene, and other subjects with regimented textbook materials that yield little meaning for him. Habits of partial comprehension acquired in the course of the school day may nullify whatever has been learned in remedial reading sessions. Careful preparation in the way of concept formation, explanation of new terms and old terms with specialized meanings, and the use of diversified reading materials at many different levels of difficulty are some of the procedures required by all pupils but particularly by those who are seriously deficient in reading ability.

Guide Lines for Helping the Retarded Reader

The following are some suggestions that should govern the work in remedial reading:

1. *Be encouraging, but, of course, not beyond the point of truthfulness.* While every good teacher tries to encourage all children, optimism is especially important in the case of the backward reader. Frequently the retarded reader is a discouraged person. Again and again, without success, he has tried to learn to read. Often he has come to think of himself as a failure not only in reading but in almost everything. Consequently, primary emphasis sometimes needs to be placed upon providing an activity in which the child can perform with superior results. There is value in the procedure of the remedial-reading teacher who, before she began to teach a child to read, provided an extended period in which one of the child's activities consisted of playing checkers with her and winning many games.

The teacher must, however, guard against encouragement that belies facts. A child should not be given the impression that it is going to be easy for him to become a good reader, for, unfortunately, such is usually not the case. As a rule, learning to overcome ineffective habits of reading is a slow and laborious task. The child who has been promised an easy path to learning to read will be discouraged when he later discovers that it is difficult.

The extent to which the teacher can be encouraging as she begins to give help in remedial reading will vary greatly with the situation. In some instances it is fairly easy to predict that the task will not be an unduly arduous one. In other instances it may be a long time before the child acquires the basic skills of reading. The teacher's remarks and her attitude toward teaching a retarded reader must be greatly influenced by a large variety of facts. The more background data the teacher has, the more readily she will be able to make accurate predictions of success.

In most instances there are some points that the teacher should make clear to a pupil at or near the beginning of the work on remedial reading. She can tell the child that there is reason for believing that he can learn to read. She may wish to tell him, too, that many boys and girls who have problems like his have learned to read when taught by methods that will be followed in his case. Early in the period of giving special help it is sometimes desirable to point out to the child that much depends upon his own willingness to work hard to learn to read. Many of the children are old enough to profit from being told that they themselves need to put forth real effort if they want to become better readers.

2. *Interest the pupil in reading.* Frequently the retarded reader lacks interest in reading; repeated failure or inability to read as well as his peers is not conducive to the development of such interest. Consequently, one of the first problems, and one of the most difficult, is to inspire the reader to want to read. Sometimes an interest in reading is stimulated through assurance to the child that he will most likely be able to read. Another means is that of surrounding him with books that contain many pictures on topics in which he is interested. Since often he cannot read these books, the teacher should devote some time daily in telling him points of significance about one or more of them. Another device often used is that of having some of the pupils tell about points of special interest that they have learned from books as they are showing them to their classmates.

Everything that has been recommended earlier in this book as a means of interesting boys and girls in reading also holds, at least to some extent, in the case of the retarded reader. It should be remembered, however, that it is usually much harder to develop reading interest in the retarded reader than in the average or superior reader.

3. *Select carefully the time of day when the special help is given.* It is unwise to ask the child to do special work in reading at a time of day when he is tired. It is usually undesirable to schedule remedial work for a recess period, for the retarded reader is even more likely than the others to require the relaxation of the play period. Moreover, a child who is deprived of the activities of the recess period may become resentful toward the remedial-reading program. The same principle applies to other parts of the school day in which he would be deprived of the opportunity to take part in some activity that he likes particularly well. Usually it is not conducive to maximum achievement to keep the child, because of the special help, from participating in music, art, or other activities that particularly attract him. Special help in reading should, if possible, be given during a period regularly set aside for reading instruction.

4. *Use appropriate materials of instruction.* Teachers of retarded readers often point out that not enough suitable material is available on the child's level of development and at the same time on his reading level. The complaint is justified. A fourteen-year-old boy with a reading ability of a typical second-grade child is not going to care much about reading a second-grade reader. However, the problem is no longer quite as acute as it used to be. A large number of trade books, on subjects of great interest to children throughout the intermediate grades, are written so simply that even a retarded reader can enjoy them, especially with a little help. Some sets of readers, too, are especially designed for the retarded reader.

A number of reading lists have been prepared to aid the teacher in locating suitable books for slow readers in the elementary school. Among these are:

Belser, Danylu, "Easy Books for the Intermediate Grades," *Elementary English Review,* 17 (October, November 1940), 235–239, 285–289.

Dunn, Anita E., *Fare for the Reluctant Reader.* Albany, N.Y.: Teachers College, State University of New York, 1952.

Durrell, Donald D., and Helen B. Sullivan, *High Interest Low Vocabulary Booklist.* Boston: Educational Clinic, Boston University School of Education, 1952.

Hill, Margaret Keyser, "A Bibliography of Reading Lists for Retarded Readers." *State University of Iowa Extension Bulletin,* No. 37, April 1, 1953. Iowa City: State University of Iowa.

Hunt, J. T., "Easy Non-Fictional Materials for the Handicapped Reader," *High School Journal,* 39 (March 1956), 322–332.

———, "Easy and Interesting Fiction for the Handicapped Reader," *High School Journal,* 39 (April 1956), 378–385.

Kircher, Clara J., *Recreational Books for Retarded Readers,* Newark, N.J.: School Libraries Division, Public Library, 1951.

Matson, Charlotte, *Books for Tired Eyes.* Chicago: American Library Association, 1951.

Ramsey, Eloise (Comp.), *Folklore for Children and Young People.* Philadelphia: American Folklore Society, University of Pennsylvania, 1952.

Richards, Margaret, "Books for Retarded Readers," *Wilson Library Bulletin,* 14 (May 1940), 642–645.

Robinson, Helen M., ed., "Trade Books for Poor Readers," *Clinical Studies in Reading II,* pp. 177–181. Supplementary Educational Monographs No. 77. Chicago: The University of Chicago Press, 1953.

Rue, Eloise (Comp.), *Subject Index to Books for Primary Grades.* Chicago: American Library Association, 1943. First supplement, 1946.

———, (Comp.), *Subject Index to Books for Intermediate Grades.* Chicago: American Library Association, 1950.

Slater, Russell, *Books for Youth Who Dislike Reading.* Ohio Conference on Reading, Bulletin No. 2. Columbus, Ohio: Ohio State University Press, 1941.

Spache, George, *Good Books for Poor Readers.* Champaign, Ill.: The Garrard Publishing Company, 1962.

Strang, Ruth, *Gateways to Readable Books*. New York: The H. W. Wilson Company, 1952.

Sullivan, Helen, *Selected List of Books for Remedial Reading*. Boston: Boston University, 1948.

Wurtz, Conrad, *A Bibliography of Reading Lists for Retarded Readers*. Bulletin, 640. Iowa City: State University of Iowa, 1949.

A very brief suggested list of easy books for older children is offered by McEntee:[9]

R.L. = Reading Level   **I.L. = Interest Level**

GRADES 1–3
Boys

Anderson—*Billy and Blaze*, R.L. 3, I.L. 6–8.
Henderson—*Why Cowboys Sing in Texas*, R.L. 3, I.L. 3 up.
Meader—*Red Horse Hill*, 1930, R.L. 5–6, I.L. 7–9.
Tousey—*Steamboat Billy*, R.L. 3–4, I.L. 7–9.

Girls

Dalgliesh—*The Smiths and Rusty*, R.L. 3–4, I.L. 7–9.
Orton—*Treasure in the Little Trunk*, R.L. 3–4, I.L. 7–9.
Reely—*Seatmates*, R.L. 3–4, I.L. 5–6.
Robinson—*Little Lucia and Her Puppy*, R.L. 3, I.L. 7–9.

GRADES 4–6
Boys

Bowman—*Pecos Bill*, R.L. 5–6, I.L. 8–10.
Meader—*Will to Win*, R.L. 5, I.L. 9–10.
Tunis—*All American*, R.L. 6, I.L. high school.
Wilder—*Farmer Boy*, R.L. 5, I.L. 7–9.

Girls

Alcott—*Little Women*, R.L. 5–6, I.L. 9–12.
Boylston—*Sue Barton, Student Nurse*, R.L. 5–6, I.L. 9–12.
Jackson—*Ramona*, R.L. 11–12, I.L. 9–12.
Porter—*Freckles*, R.L. 5, I.L. 9–12.

GRADES 7–9
Boys

Booth—*Book of Modern War Planes*, R.L. 7–8, I.L. 9–12.
Petersham—*Story Book of Aircraft*, R.L. 4, I.L. 8–10.
Sperry—*All Sails Set*, R.L. 4, I.L. 8–10.
White—*Daniel Boone, Wilderness Scout*, R.L. 7–8, I.L. 9–12.

---

9 Helen S. McEntee, "When Johnny Can Read—But!" *The Reading Teacher*, 9 (February 1956), 148.

Girls

Aldrich—*A Lantern in Her Hand*, R.L. 7, I.L. 9–12.
Brink—*Mademoiselle Misfortune*, R.L. 7–9, I.L. 8–10.
Montgomery—*Anne of Green Gables*, R.L. 7, I.L. 9–12.
Singmaster—*You Make Your Own Luck*, R.L. 7, I.L. 9–12.

The problem of finding appropriate materials is more serious with respect to the child who has so small a reading vocabulary that he cannot even recognize the words in a preprimer. Books that are challenging in thought to a nine-year-old child who cannot read on the preprimer level are not available. Sometimes with the intelligent child who cannot read, the teacher can explain that at first he will find the books decidedly below his level of interest. He should also then be made to feel that his chief interest should be in the results he accomplishes on his road to becoming a good reader, rather than in the subject matter. One teacher showed a child some books in a series that she had selected for his reading, explaining that while the earlier books lacked subject matter that would be challenging to him, the later ones contained many selections of real interest. The teacher might also tell the child that he may find, too, as many adults do, that sometimes it is fun to read subject matter that is chiefly designed for younger readers.

Many teachers inquire as to the place of workbooks and other published exercises in teaching the retarded reader. No one authoritative answer can be given that will be specific in its application. Some workbooks and other exercise material furnish economically the additional practice which a pupil who has difficulty in reading often needs. The same principles in general apply to the use of workbooks with the retarded reader that have already been stated earlier in this book in connection with teaching other children. Special caution, however, should be taken to use the workbooks in such a way that they will not cause the child to lose interest in reading.

Teacher-made materials sometimes contribute to the solution of the problem of what to have the retarded child read, particularly in the early stages of learning to read. The teacher can often write material, either dictated by the pupil or written by the teacher without contributions from the child. It is too time-consuming, however, for the teacher to continue to write all the material that a child will be reading.

5. *Decide on the methods to be used on the basis of a careful diagnosis.* The teacher who uses the same methods of procedure with all retarded readers will usually not get satisfactory results. Considerable time spent on diagnosis can be very valuable if the results are utilized in planning the program.

Correct diagnosis of reading difficulties is merely a first step in helping the retarded reader. A frequently quoted story is that of the teacher who, after she had given standardized tests year after year to her pupils, complained, "I no longer believe in standardized tests. I have given them to my pupils year after

year and they are no better than they were before I started giving the tests."
Diagnosis without the intent to profit by the discoveries made is of little, if
any, value.

When we speak of corrective or remedial instruction, we do not generally
refer to the primary grade child. Here the program is predominantly developmental, and referrals to the psychologist or clinic will usually be made for
reasons other than reading. Most children should be allowed the full three
years of the primary grades to show how well they can respond to developmental instruction. Remedial reading is primarily a problem of the middle
and upper grades.

Certain common failings will usually be revealed by observation of the
pupil's reading habits and the various tests that may be employed. These
include word-by-word reading, vocalization or subvocal sounding, finger pointing, head-swinging, lip reading, backtracking, daydreaming, and limited vocabulary. Habits such as these should be noted for later work with individual
children.

6. *If a method does not seem to work with a given pupil, change your procedure after you have given your method a fair trial.* No one method is so much
superior to all others that the teacher should persist, in spite of lack of results,
in using it with any child. Even if the teacher has used a given procedure effectively with many other children whose needs seem to be similar, she should
change her plans with a specific pupil if they are not productive of results with
him. However, she should not shift from one method to another without per-
sisting long enough with the first to be sure that it will not be successful. Some
children take a long time to learn by any method at all. Too much change in
method, here as in other learning situations, is likely to result in confusion.

7. *Make appraisal of the pupil's progress and encourage him to do likewise.*
Charts or graphs, kept by either the teacher or pupil, can serve as an incentive
to learning. However, because of the complexity of the reading act, these records
often can show but one segment of the total activity. The pupil should be
aware of this fact. The records should deal with some aspect of reading on
which fairly objective data can be obtained. A record may be kept of the
number of words a child has learned during intervals of time—a week or ten
days, for example. A chart may be kept showing the number of pages in trade
books that a pupil has read. Other accomplishments that may be recorded are:
the number of questions a pupil answers correctly on teacher-made tests; the
rate of reading for stated purposes; the number of words missed when reading
orally from a designated book; the number of words recognized from a standardized word list.

The child should be helped to realized that if he fails at times to show
progress on a record, it may not necessarily indicate that he is not learning.
The nature of learning curves, including plateaus, may need to be explained
to the child, in language, of course, that he can comprehend.

8. *Use a variety of methods.* The use of one method, no matter how good, to the exclusion of others usually does not produce the best results. No one method alone is likely to be best fitted to the needs of any individual, for reading is so complex a process and retardation in reading is ordinarily caused by such a multiplicity of factors that various types of approaches are needed. It is especially important that a variety of methods should be used when several persons are being taught as a group. Frequently one method, although helpful for all, is not the most felicitous one for every individual in the group.

There is, however, also danger in too much variety of method. The number should be limited somewhat so that it will not be necessary for the child to expend an unwarranted amount of time and energy in becoming accustomed to various ways of learning to read. Best results are usually attained only after a person has had considerable experience with a particular method.

9. *If instruction is given in group situations, make certain that it is provided under the best circumstances possible.* Some work with retarded readers can be done satisfactorily only if help is given on an individual basis. At other times, however, work in small-group situations seems advisable. Further, there are instances when sheer lack of time on the part of the teacher makes it necessary to give help to two or more persons at one time.

If instruction in learning to read is given to retarded readers in a group situation, the following suggestions may prove helpful: (1) *Group the pupils in terms of their needs.* Sometimes it is advisable to group them according to level of reading ability. At other times, it is best to group the children in terms of the type of skill in which they need most help. All those of approximately the same level of reading ability who need help in word recognition may be taught in one group, while those whose major difficulty is one specific phase of comprehension may be grouped together. (2) *Keep the groups flexible so that changes can quite readily be made as the needs change.* The administration of any program of helping the retarded reader should allow for the maximum of change from one group to another, whenever such a shift would be to the best advantage of the learner. (3) *In group work, pay special attention to the needs of each person.* Even when the teacher is helping several children at the same time, much can be done to individualize the work. A child who has more skill than the others in his group in oral reading could be asked to read orally the more difficult parts of a selection. A child who has particular trouble with a certain word should be given the appropriate help in deciphering it. (4) *Help each individual to realize that he is an important member of the group.* The attitude of the teacher has much to do with whether a child feels important. The teacher can find many ways to show each child that she considers him of real value as a contributing member of the group. Even the boy or girl who cannot read can be helped to feel his worth if he can show pictures of interest to others or tell of experiences that his age-mates recognize as valuable contributions.

Special Methods for Remedial Reading

In general, the procedures that are most effective for the retarded reader are the same as those that can be recommended for other boys and girls. Remedial reading at its best is essentially an adaptation of the same procedures effectively used with normal readers to the individual needs of retarded persons. A child with difficulty in word recognition can, as a rule, be helped most to acquire power in this respect by the same means used with other readers. Similarly, a child retarded in skill in selecting significant details can usually progress to the best advantage if he is helped to develop this comprehension skill by means of the same general procedures used with other children, if special attention is paid to his level and his responses in learning situations.

There is no bag of tricks nor list of teaching devices that can be presented with the guarantee that these will change retarded readers to average or above average. There are, however, several methods of teaching reading that are often associated primarily with remedial reading. These are briefly described here.

THE FERNALD KINESTHETIC METHOD.[10] Although Dr. Fernald recommends her method for use with any children, it is more often used with seriously retarded readers who do not respond to other methods. Important aspects of the method are these: (1) In the earliest stage of instruction the teacher writes the word to be learned in large letters as the child watches her. Then the child traces the word with his finger as he says it part by part. Thereupon he tries to write it from memory. As he writes the word, he again says it. He then compares his copy with the original and, if he finds an error, tries again to learn the word by the same method he has employed so far. Emphasis is placed upon reading words that the pupils use as they describe experiences they have. Consequently experience charts are used often with this method. (2) When the child has learned quite a number of words, he is no longer asked to trace each new word. He is instructed to write words that he learns on cards and to file them in an individual word box. When he writes stories he is encouraged to use this file if necessary. (3) When the pupil has made considerable progress in learning a word by this method without tracing it, new words are presented to him in print, not in writing. It is then that the pupil advances to the stage at which he is able to recognize a new word through its resemblance to a known word and through the aid of context clues.

Many teachers consider this method too slow and laborious and mechanical to use in a developmental reading program. Some object to emphasis upon this method even in remedial reading. There are, however, pupils who have learned to read by the Fernald method who have encountered only failure in the use of

---

10 Grace M. Fernald, *Remedial Techniques in Basic School Subjects*. New York: McGraw-Hill Book Company, Inc., 1943.

others. It is for this reason that some teachers, who do not favor its use even with all retarded readers, try it with some of them when little, if any, progress has been made with other methods. Many adaptations of the Fernald method have been made. Use of the typewriter by the pupil is part of one of the modifications.

USE OF EXPERIENCE CHARTS. Some teachers rely heavily in work with retarded readers on experience charts, of which a detailed description and evaluation are given in Chapter 5B. Modifications of the typical procedures followed in group situations are of course required. As in the experience charts for groups of children, the teacher records in writing the sentences that are dictated to her. Then the child "reads" the sentences, often in part from memory. Sometimes these reports are in the form of book reports on picture books, on simple stories that the child has read, or on books the teacher or others have read to him. Autobiographical sketches are frequently dictated and also illustrated by the child. Since these materials are ordinarily for individual use, they are usually recorded on sheets of paper rather than on tagboard.

USE OF GAMES AND OTHER DRILLS. Special mention is made of games and drills in connection with teaching the retarded reader because with such readers it is often more necessary than with others to use these activities to a considerable degree. This is true because frequently these children need more repetitive practice than the nonretarded reader. The same criteria for drill should be observed in connection with work in remedial reading as are valid at other times. Some important points to note are: (1) The game or drill should be of value. (2) The results obtained should be commensurate with the time spent on the drill. (3) The purpose of the activity should, as a rule, be recognized by the pupil and be accepted by him as worthwhile if the maximum benefit is to be gained from it. (4) There should be variety in type of drill used. (5) The spacing in practice should be in harmony with the findings of educational psychology.

Organization for Helping Retarded Readers

Help can be given to the retarded reader under a variety of plans. Most of it can undoubtedly be provided most effectively by the teacher from day to day as she adapts all her instruction to the needs of her class. Individual help given by the teacher during or just after a class period will frequently clear up the difficulties of a child who is falling behind in acquiring a reading skill. Prevention of further retardation through early attention to problems is the keynote of this informal plan. Those boys and girls who have some special difficulty in reading can sometimes be put, for a day or a week or longer, in a group by themselves for special help. Such instruction at times may be a substitute for work with the child's usual group; in other instances it may be in addition to the regular classwork in reading. Groups can be formed for longer duration, possibly for the whole year. Thus much of the problem of remedial reading can be dealt with informally in the regular classroom.

There are instances, however, when a more formal plan for remedial reading may be warranted. In some schools children seriously retarded in reading are assigned to a classroom by themselves, preferably with a teacher qualified to deal with problems in this area. Ideally such a class is kept considerably smaller in enrollment than the average. If more than fifteen pupils are placed in it, the effectiveness of the program of instruction is likely to be greatly reduced. A criticism of this organization is that all the school associations of a pupil in a class for retarded readers are with boys and girls with the same limitations. The stigma that is likely to become attached to such a class is another factor frequently raised as objection to this plan. Further objection lies in the expense of any program where classroom size is necessarily limited to the extent that it ideally ought to be in a room reserved for retarded readers. Furthermore, unless the special class serves a large district, there are not likely to be enough retarded readers of similar age and intelligence to constitute even the small number of pupils desirable for it.

Often the plan followed is that of having a specialist in reading meet with pupils from various rooms for limited parts of the school day. Under such a plan, the reading teacher ordinarily has a room of her own, often designated as the reading room. During the first half of the forenoon she may help one group of children who have been excused from their homeroom for that length of time. At the middle of the forenoon these boys and girls go back to their own rooms where they resume work with their classmates. At that time another group begins its half-forenoon session with the reading teacher. The afternoon can be divided similarly. The school day can be divided into more than four parts, possibly periods of sixty minutes' duration, to allow for more shifts of pupils during the day.

One of two plans is typically used to determine which pupils needing extra help in reading should be in the reading room at the same time. For purposes of administration, it is usually easier to assemble at one time in the reading room all the children from a given classroom who need extra help in reading work. To facilitate matters of programming, many of the homeroom teachers concurrently conduct reading classes for those of their children who are not in the reading room; thus the retarded readers do not miss work in social studies or other areas of study. Such a plan usually interferes less with the other activities of the boys and girls than one in which the reading teacher has, at the same time, those pupils from all rooms who have the same or similar reading problems. According to this latter plan children reading on preprimer level, for instance, regardless of their homeroom or grade, would meet with the reading teacher at the same time. Not only does such a plan often create many disrupting influences in the other learning activities of the children, but frequently, too, the resulting grouping is undesirable from the point of view of the socialization of the child. Under such a plan a sixth-grade pupil may be grouped for reading with a second-grade child.

One plan of grouping children for special instruction in reading that appears to have been successful is described by Barbe and Waterhouse:

PROCEDURE

During October of the school year, each teacher rated the reading grade level of the children in her room. A standardized group reading test was administered. In addition to these ratings, each child was given an individual reading test by the staff of the local reading center. With these three scores, the teachers met and placed each child in a group according to his reading level.

Children included in the program were fourth, fifth, and sixth graders. There are two classes at each grade level at Highland Park. This provided six teachers for the program and approximately 180 children.

Seventeen children were reading on the first- and second-grade level and so they were all assigned to one reading group. About 30 children were reading at third-grade level and were assigned to another reading group. The fourth-grade group, numbering about 70 in all, was split into two groups. About 35 children were reading at fifth-grade level and were assigned to one group and about 30 were reading at sixth and above level and were assigned to another group.

Following this procedure, it was not necessary to hire any extra teachers. The regular upper elementary grade teachers were then assigned to teach the reading group at the level at which they felt themselves to be best prepared. One of the sixth-grade teachers, having formerly been a primary teacher, was assigned to teach the children in the group reading at the first- and second-grade level.

This division provided for the grouping of upper elementary school children according to their reading level, irrespective of whether they were in the fourth, fifth, or sixth grades. The group to which they were assigned, however, consisted of fourth, fifth, and sixth graders who were all reading at the same level. The groups were called reading clubs. Most children changed to another teacher at the time of the club meeting. There were a few children who had their regular teacher, for she was the one who was teaching the reading club at that child's level.

The regular Lyons and Carnahan Reading Series was introduced into the school. None of the children were familiar with the books. No mention was made of the grade level at which the children were working even though they could tell the level of the book in which they were reading. Teaching procedures outlined in the manuals were followed.

In November, soon after the program was started, the children in each group were given the Gates Reading Survey, Form I. In May, shortly before the end of school, when the children had been in the program for a six months period, the Gates Reading Survey, Form II, was administered.

SOME CONCLUSIONS AND IMPLICATIONS

The purpose of the study was to determine if upper elementary school children could be better provided for in groups in which the children were all reading at the same level. The data collected clearly indicate that a great deal of progress can be made when children are grouped for reading instruction.

The implications of this study are:

(1) The traditional lack of attention to reading instruction at the upper elementary level can be partially overcome by grouping the children for one period each day at their actual reading level and instructing them from a textbook at that level.

(2) Opposition from parents, teachers, and children to grouping according to reading level can be avoided when the program is clearly defined in terms of purpose and procedures. It is particularly necessary that the teachers themselves believe in such a program and be willing to exert the initial effort to make such a program a success.

(3) Teaching according to a developmental philosophy is more feasible when children are grouped according to reading level.

(4) Children do not object to reading materials below their actual grade placement, if they are not put in a class with children too far below their own grade placement.

(5) Where grouping is employed, more opportunity is available to provide an enriched reading program for children who are advanced in reading.

(6) The needs of children can more nearly be met when they are grouped according to reading ability.

While grouping within the regular classroom is accepted as an essential for teaching reading, there is much evidence that teachers in the upper elementary grades do not have sufficient time to give all the attention that is needed to each of the reading groups. By grouping the children by reading level at Highland Park School, it was found that it was possible to give more attention to reading and, at the same time, make the job of teaching reading easier for the teacher.[11]

No matter how effective a means of helping the retarded reader a school has, the objective should always be to prevent retardation whenever possible. Someone has aptly paraphrased an old Oriental proverb by saying, "One former is worth a thousand re-formers." That statement holds true in the area of forming effective reading habits.

---

[11] Walter B. Barbe and Tina S. Waterhouse, "An Experimental Program in Reading," *Elementary English,* 33 (February 1956), 102–104.

Helping the Bright Child in Reading

Since the school in a democratic society regards all children as of equal moral worth, it does not, in its distribution of effort, deliberately discriminate against any group because of low, average, or high academic aptitude and achievement. There are compelling reasons why all should learn to read as well as their capacities permit. Nevertheless, because teachers are human and fallible and because time and resources are not unlimited, they cannot always do complete justice to all the children in their classes. Many teachers find that work with retarded and average pupils is so time-consuming and the needs of these children so apparent that they tend to neglect those who obviously are superior in academic ability. The growing concern about the gifted child is therefore justified.

The type of instruction required by the bright child does not differ in kind from that given to other children. The physical, sensory, emotional, and other factors essential to good reading as well as the specific skills of reading are important to all. The difference is to be found in the range and level of difficulty of the materials and in special problems peculiar to the very bright child.

One difference, for example, is the fact that bright children often acquire many of the reading skills independently and almost unconsciously in the course of their extensive, highly motivated reading. Special lessons and drills in these reading skills can and should be bypassed for them. All that the teacher needs to do in such situations is to be sure that these skills have been mastered.

Specialists in the education of the gifted child recognize that social maturity does not necessarily go hand in hand with academic achievement. There is no evidence that bright children as a group are less mature socially than other children. In fact, intellectual maturity is commonly accompanied by social maturity. It would not be surprising, however, if we found that some very bright children were less conforming, that they demanded reasons for rules of behavior and exhibited some impatience with other pupils less well endowed.

A degree of nonconformity is a desirable personality trait. Independence of mind is essential to social and scientific progress and to artistic creation. But it is of the greatest importance that our ablest individuals learn early in life to act responsibly and to be concerned about the well-being and happiness of others. The codes of the physician, who places the well-being of his patient first, and the scientist, who weighs the effect of his discoveries on society, has its origin in the early face-to-face experiences of childhood. In our fascination with a child's brilliance we cannot afford to forget the great influence for good or evil that he will have upon society. Reading is one of the potent means at our disposal to lead the child on the road to responsible and constructive effort.

The present-day drive toward "academic excellence" is overdue, but it must not be permitted to distort the humanistic goals of education. The child who reads about people in other cultures and other lands should be doing more than adding to his knowledge and understanding. He should be cultivating the art of unlimited kinship with people.

Discussions of the problems of educating the gifted child rarely concern themselves with questions relating to emotional growth and attitude formation. They are concerned chiefly with the conservation of intellectual talent now so often going to waste because of unfavorable home and community environments and school programs not sufficiently adapted to the needs of the gifted child. One difficulty is that emotions are hard to discover and to measure; it is almost impossible to formulate defensible educational objectives with regard to them, except as they result in serious and persistent antisocial behavior. Nevertheless, any consideration of the teaching of reading and literature which does not embrace the emotional dimension is necessarily incomplete and distorts any valid conception of the teacher's task.

The bright child usually has little difficulty in learning to interpret the literal and figurative meaning of a selection appropriate to his general maturity. What we cannot be so sure of is that the child will know how to identify with situations he reads about or utilize what he reads in building a mental image of the social and human consequences of conditions and events. Speed and comprehension in the reading of a poem, for example, are not enough. There must be moments of contemplation in which the reader visualizes a scene, laughs or weeps with a character in a story, and thinks with wonder about a deed of heroism. Speed tests in reading do not measure these capacities for feeling. Social sensitivity and human understanding should occupy a high place among our objectives in reading instruction.

Identifying the Unusually Gifted Child

All children are gifted. Without gifts, a child would be uneducable. The gifts may be few and very small, or they may be many and very great.

What shall we call those whose gifts are many and great? Many terms have been used. These children have been called "able," "bright," "talented," "academically superior," "children of high academic aptitude," "intellectually gifted," "academically talented," and similar expressions. These terms sometimes have special meanings; in some cases they are applied to children with special aptitudes in art, music, or mechanical activity and in other cases to children whose intellectual potential amounts to genius. In Terman's famous study of gifted children, those with IQ's of 130 and higher were included. Havighurst speaks of children gifted with qualities of social leadership and of children who possess "creative intelligence." Gallagher divides the gifted into three categories: those with IQ's of 116 and over (15–20 percent of the school population); those with IQ's of 132 and over (2–4 percent of the school population); and those with IQ's of 148 and over (.1 percent of the school population). These are the academically talented, the gifted, and the highly gifted.

There are in fact no sharply defined boundaries among these groups, although the problems of instruction may differ as we go up on the scale. Any dividing lines must be arbitrary. In our discussion we shall deal with the largest group of superior learners, and for convenience draw the line at approximately 120 IQ. We shall use most of the terms mentioned above interchangeably.

The usual methods of identifying bright children involve the use of individual and group tests of intelligence, achievement tests, and teacher observation. Individual intelligence tests are probably the most accurate of the methods, but they are time-consuming and require trained examiners. Group intelligence tests and achievement tests are useful as screening devices, but they may be quite inaccurate in assessing an individual's true capabilities. Errors in these tests more often result in underestimation than in overestimation of a child's potential. Teacher observation is an essential part of the evaluation process because it may reveal aspects of a child's mental powers not reflected in any test. It is not unusual for a group test to rate as many as 25 percent of the gifted children below their true intelligence level. Nevertheless, for the average classroom teacher the best available method for identifying the gifted child is a combination of one or more group intelligence tests and careful observation of the pupil's behavior and performance.

The teacher will find it helpful to look for specific characteristics that distinguish the bright child from the average or below-average child. Numerous lists of such characteristics have been published. According to one such list, compiled by Kough and DeHaan,[12] the teacher can recognize the superior learner in her class by observing to see which of the students:

1. Learns rapidly and easily.
2. Uses a lot of common sense and practical knowledge.
3. Reasons things out, thinks clearly, recognizes relationships, comprehends meanings.
4. Retains what he has heard or read without much rote drill.
5. Knows about many things of which other children are unaware.
6. Uses a large number of words easily and accurately.
7. Can read books that are one to two years in advance of the rest of the class.
8. Performs difficult mental tasks.

---

[12] Jack Kough and Robert DeHaan, "Identifying Children Who Need Help," *Teacher's Guidance Handbook*. Chicago: Science Research Associates, 1955.

9. Asks many questions. Is interested in a wide range of things.
10. Does some academic work one to two years in advance of his class.
11. Is alert, keenly observant, responds quickly.

Teachers' judgments of pupils are often clouded by the fact that a gifted pupil may be restless, complete his work quickly and turn to "mischief" to amuse himself, and thus appear to the teacher as a behavior problem rather than simply a child lacking in challenge or interest. Sometimes, too, a child's exceptional ability may be hidden by emotional problems which interfere with adequate performance in school work. Only through conscious effort and much experience can the teacher become expert in discovering superior academic ability in those children whose giftedness is not obvious to the casual observer.

Creating the Conditions for Maximum Learning

The key to good teaching is the teacher herself. Materials and methods are important, but no amount of pedagogical theory, library resources, audio-visual aids, laboratories, auditoriums, or testing programs can compensate for the lack of the competent, resourceful teacher. This fact is doubly significant in the case of the academically superior pupil.

The bright child needs a bright teacher. All children need teachers who are above average in intelligence, devoted to teaching, and sympathetic to children's educational needs. But the bright child needs a teacher who is distinctly superior in mental ability. Her IQ need not be as high as that of the brightest child in her class, but she should be bright enough to feel secure in her relations with him and to command his respect. She should be willing to learn from the bright child, and sometimes to let him teach the things she does not know as well as he.

Ruth Strang once asked a group of fifty gifted pupils in grades six through twelve to describe their best teachers.[13] Their statements revealed that gifted children want teachers who know their subject, related fields, and current events, who use humor and illustrative material to add interest to the subject, and who are skillful in relating the subject to other fields and to the pupils' lives. They want teachers who require them to learn, to work together on class projects, to discuss problems together, and to assume initiative and responsibility. They like teachers who are versatile, fair, even-tempered, and patient.

The teacher of the gifted can and should be more permissive in her assignments to gifted children than to those of more limited abilities, who usually desire and need definite and detailed instructions for a task. Gifted children are more likely to ask questions about the *why* of the methods employed by

---

[13] Paul Witty, James B. Conant, and Ruth Strang, *Creativity of Gifted and Talented Children,* pp. 43–51. Prepared for the American Association for Gifted Children. New York: Bureau of Publications, Teachers College, Columbia University, 1959.

the teacher, and the teacher should freely discuss her reasons and objectives with them. If the pupil is egotistic or immature because of coddling at home, the teacher should set challenges and require performance that will result in the development of a more accurate self-image on the part of the child. In short, the teacher of the academically superior child should have all the qualities of any good teacher, but she should have them in high degree.

Next to a good teacher in importance is the provision of abundant reading materials difficult enough and diversified enough to provide a genuine challenge and to appeal to the wide range of interests so characteristic of the bright child. For truly gifted children the book and magazine resources of most elementary schools are inadequate. Public libraries, state traveling book collections, and even the paperback selection in supermarkets and elsewhere need to be utilized to meet the need. Academically superior students tend to be omnivorous readers, particularly when suitable reading materials are readily accessible. They are attracted, also, to encyclopedias, atlases, dictionaries, and all types of reference materials. As a consequence, the school library assumes great importance in the reading guidance of gifted children. Failure to provide proper library facilities in elementary schools must necessarily result in great waste of the precious resources represented by the learning potential of these children.

The need for more and better reading materials implies also the necessity of a wide knowledge of children's literature on the part of the teacher. No teacher can possibly have read all the books that gifted children are likely to read or should read, but fortunately there are excellent guides and booklists which should be available to the teacher in the school library. Aids of this type are discussed and listed in detail in the chapters on children's interests in this book.

In providing books for individual reading, teachers should make certain that they include titles that will challenge the able reader. Many superior readers in the upper elementary grades enjoy reading books generally considered adult fare. In an excellent article on this subject, Renthal has presented a suggestive list that will help intermediate and upper grade teachers in making selections. The numbers refer to grade level:

BOOKS TO CHALLENGE THE ABLE[14]

Adamson, Joy, *Living Free*. Introduction by Julian Huxley. Harcourt, 1961. 6 and up.
Arora, Shirley, *What Then, Raman?* Follett, 1960. 4, 5.
Asimov, Isaac, *Words from the Myths*. Houghton Mifflin, 1961. 5, 6, and up.
Bauman, Hans, *World of the Pharaohs*. Pantheon, 1960. 6 and up.

---

14 Helen Renthal, "Books to Challenge the Able," *Elementary English*, 39 (December 1962), 796–798.

Direct association between whole-word symbols
and meanings is the first step toward zestful reading

National Education Association
photo by Carl Purcell
Parents can help in creating keen
interests in reading

Monkmeyer Press
Photo Service
On his own

Bonham, Frank, *Burma Rifles*. Crowell, 1960. 6 and up.

Boston, L. M., *A Stranger at Green Knowe*. Harcourt, 1961. 4, 5.

Burnford, Sheila, *Incredible Journey*. Little, Brown, 1961. 5 and up.

De La Mare, Walter, *Peacock Pie*. Illustrated by Barbary Cooney. Knopf, 1961. 4, 5, 6.

Doubleday Pictorial Library of Nature: *Earth, Plants, Animals*. Doubleday, 1961. 6, 7, 8.

Enright, Elizabeth, *Return to Gone-Away*. Illustrated by Beth and Joe Krush. Harcourt, 1961. 4, 5.

Franchere, Ruth, *Stephen Crane: The Story of an American Writer*. Crowell, 1961. 7, 8.

Godden, Rumer, *Miss Happiness and Miss Flower*. Illustrated by Jean Primrose. Viking, 1961. 4, 5.

Henry, Marguerite, *Gaudenzia, Pride of the Palio*. Illustrated by Lynd Ward. Rand McNally, 1960. 5 and up.

Life and Rand McNally, eds., *Life Pictorial Atlas of the World*. Rand McNally, 1961. 3 and up.

O'Dell, Scott, *Island of the Blue Dolphins*. Houghton Mifflin, 1960. 5, 6, 7.

Shorter, Bani, *India's Children*. Illustrated by Kurt Wiese. Viking, 1960. 6, 7.

Teale, Edwin Way, *Lost Dog*. Illustrated by Paul Lantz. Dodd, Mead, 1961. 5, 6.

Vogel, Helen, and Mary Caruso, *Ocean Harvest*. Knopf, 1961. 6.

Weaver, Stella, *Poppy in the Corn*. Pantheon, 1961. 5, 6, 7.

Planning Reading Programs for Bright Children

Studies of the reading habits of gifted children reveal that they tend to be omnivorous readers, that they spend about six hours a week in reading at age seven and up to twelve hours at age thirteen, that they have wider interests and do more voluntary reading than the average child, and that about half of the highly gifted read before they enter school. Significantly, they learn to read by a great variety of methods, and it may be assumed that in their case the method employed is far less important than the versatility and skill of the teacher and the availability of suitable reading materials.

Plans employed for meeting the needs of gifted children in general fall into three main categories: (1) enrichment, (2) acceleration, and (3) special grouping. Of these, perhaps the most popular plan is that of enrichment. In an enrichment program provision is made for individual differences in ability within the setting of the regular classroom. The gifted child remains with his age-mates, but is encouraged to take on more complex tasks. More emphasis is placed on original thinking and problem-solving. In the case of reading, the academically superior child is expected to choose books calling for higher levels of comprehension than those possessed by other members of the class.

A promising form of enrichment is the unit organization of instruction, especially in the middle grades. In this plan the teacher may propose a number of topics for study from which all the pupils make a choice. With the aid of the teacher, the class assembles a bibliography for the chosen topic, using the various reference aids in classroom and library. The teacher then assists the pupils in developing the topic. Some of the reading selections may be read and enjoyed by all the pupils, but the abler members of the class will also select reading materials commensurate with their abilities. The task of the teacher is to assist all pupils, regardless of reading ability, with the particular reading problems that may cause difficulty.

The policy of acceleration may take different forms. One of these is early admittance to school of the bright child. Certainly there is nothing sacred about age six as the earliest entering age, particularly since the differences among children of the same chronological age are so wide. In schools with an ungraded primary division it is possible to permit bright children to complete the three-year period in less time, especially if they are socially and emotionally well-adjusted. Double-promotion is another plan of acceleration, but one to be used with great caution to avoid the danger that the child will miss basic steps in skill development or the building of background information.

Many parents and school officials are reluctant to adopt a policy of acceleration because of the fear that the accelerated child will have difficulty in making a good adjustment in a group of children of higher chronological age. Research studies have indicated that, in general, pupils have benefited from programs of acceleration and that the fear of social maladjustment because of acceleration is unfounded. Nevertheless, the needs and social maturity of each child should be carefully studied before he is advanced to a group of older children.

Special classes for gifted children have been organized in a number of elementary schools. These have the advantage of enabling pupils to enjoy the opportunity of working with their intellectual peers and to benefit from the give and take of planning and discussion with other children equally alert and eager to think and to explore. The plan does not eliminate the need for attention to individual differences, but it does avoid the neglect of gifted children which is almost inevitable in heterogeneously grouped classes. In most systems employing special classes for the gifted, the children are kept with their age-mates for part of the day, usually in such classes as music, art, and physical education.

Helping the Bright Underachiever

In a sense, almost everyone is an underachiever. We tend to perform up to full capacity only under pressure. The pressure may consist of a drive or ambition, a keen but perhaps transitory interest, circumstances that demand the full exercise of our powers, or a strong desire to win the approval of others in certain situations. Some children are driven to high achievement in school subjects by a desire to compensate for a real or fancied deficiency in physical skill or in general social adjustment.

What concerns the teacher of reading, however, is persistent failure of the bright child to perform up to his full potential in reading and to achieve the kind of growth that may reasonably be expected of him. It is of great importance that the causes of his inadequate performance be discovered as early as possible.

The possible causes of underachievement in bright children are numerous, and for the most part they do not differ in kind from the causes of underachievement among average and below-average children. Among these causes is the familiar one of a lack of a strong foundation of reading skills, such as left to right reading, methods of attack on unfamiliar words, and getting the main idea of a passage. Although many able learners acquire these skills on their own, others do not. Like most children who fail to learn the basic skills early, the bright child may develop negative attitudes toward reading which persist throughout the elementary grades and beyond. Indeed, the bright child tends to be more sensitive than others to his unsuccessful efforts in reading during the initial stages.

In some instances conditions in a bright child's home may be responsible for underachievement in reading. If parents do not place a high value on academic excellence, if the home has few books or magazines of quality, if the child is not given encouragement or opportunity to read at home, he may never realize his own potential or set himself goals commensurate with his abilities. It then becomes necessary for the school to compensate for the impoverished cultural environment at home by providing intellectual and cultural stimulation through an abundance of direct and vicarious experiences.

Some bright children, perhaps *because* they are bright, enter school before they are matured sufficiently to cope with the adjustments and the tasks required by the school situation. Others are handicapped by being transported from one school situation in which they felt secure to another in which the surroundings are strange, the methods different, and the teacher's personality constrasting with that of the one he had before. Frequent absence from school because of illness or other factors is detrimental to the educational progress of most able pupils, as it is to that of average or slow learners.

Emotional problems, often stemming from discordant family relationships, may interfere with satisfactory growth in reading. Children who experience continued anxiety, feel rejected, or show hostility toward the adult world frequently suffer a lack of self-confidence that is necessary for learning; they are emotionally distracted when they should be concentrating on their reading. This is not to say that all bright underachievers are emotionally disturbed or that emotional difficulties always results in underachievement. The teacher should, however, be alert to the possible presence of emotional factors as a possible block to the full realization of the bright child's reading potential.

It has been estimated that as many as 25 percent of the gifted children in a typical class are underachievers. Whatever the true proportion may be, we cannot afford the waste of talent arising from any child's failure to reach attainable goals in reading. We must do all we can to discover the obstacles to maximum growth and, so far as possible, to remove them.

FOR FURTHER STUDY

On Problems of the Retarded Reader

Blair, Glenn Myers, *Diagnostic and Remedial Teaching*, rev. ed., pp. 3–211. New York: The Macmillan Company, 1956.

Bond, Guy L., "How to Conduct a Remedial Reading Program," *Improving Reading in the Junior High School*, pp. 101–109. U.S. Department of Health, Education, and Welfare, Bulletin No. 10, 1957.

——, and Miles A. Tinker, *Reading Difficulties: Their Diagnosis and Correction*. New York: Appleton-Century-Crofts, 1957.

Bouise, Louise M., "Emotional and Personality Problems of a Group of Retarded Readers," *Elementary English*, 32 (December 1955), 544–548.

Burton, William H., *Reading in Child Development*, pp. 550–586. Indianapolis: The Bobbs-Merrill Company, Inc., 1956.

Cleland, Donald L., "How Can Teachers Determine Pupils' Reading Status?" *Improving Reading in the Junior High School*, pp. 121–133. U.S. Department of Health, Education, and Welfare, Bulletin No. 10, 1957.

Dolch, E. W., *A Manual for Remedial Reading*, 2d ed. Champaign, Ill.: The Garrard Publishing Company, 1945.

——, "Success in Remedial Reading," *Elementary English*, 30 (March 1953), 133–137.

Fry, Edward, "Developing a Word List for Remedial Reading," *Elementary English*, 34 (November 1957), 456–458.

Gates, Arthur I., *The Improvement of Reading*, 3rd ed. New York: The Macmillan Company, 1947.

——, "What Makes a Remedial Program Effective?" *Reading in Action: International Reading Association Conference Proceedings*, Vol. II, pp. 114–117. New York: Scholastic Magazines, 1957.

——, and Miriam C. Pritchard, *Teaching Reading to Slow-Learning Pupils*. New York: Bureau of Publications, Teachers College, Columbia University, 1942.

Gray, William S., and Nancy Larrick, eds., *Better Readers for Our Times*. International Reading Association Conference Proceedings, Vol. I, pp. 120–168. New York: Scholastic Magazines, 1956.

Harris, Albert J., *How To Increase Reading Ability*, 4th ed. New York: David McKay Company, Inc., 1961.

——, ed., "New Ways of Helping Poor Readers," *The Reading Teacher*, 10 (April 1957), 195–224.

Hunnicutt, C. W., and William J. Iverson, *Research in the Three R's*, pp. 239–259. New York: Harper and Row, Publishers, 1958.

Kirk, Samuel A., *Teaching Reading to Slow Learning Children*. Boston: Houghton Mifflin Company, 1940.

Robinson, H. Alan, ed., *The Under-achiever in Reading*. Supplementary Educational Monographs, No. 92. Chicago: The University of Chicago Press, 1962.

Robinson, Helen M., "Corrective and Remedial Instruction," *Development in and through Reading*, pp. 357–375. Sixtieth Yearbook of the National Society for the Study of Education, Part I. Chicago: The University of Chicago Press, 1961.

Russell, David H., and Etta S. Karp, *Reading Aids through the Grades. Three Hundred Developmental Reading Activities*. Revised and enlarged edition. New York: Bureau of Publications, Teachers College, Columbia University, 1951.

Schiffman, Gilbert B., "How to Organize a Remedial Reading Program," *Improving Reading in the Junior High School*, pp. 110–117. U. S. Department of Health, Education, and Welfare, Bulletin No. 10, 1957.

Vernon, M. D., *Backwardness in Reading: A Study of Its Nature and Origin*. New York: The Cambridge University Press, 1957.

Witty, Paul, *Reading in Modern Education*, pp. 225–249. Boston: D. C. Heath and Company, 1949.

———, and David Kopel, *Reading and the Educative Process*, pp. 83–118, 162–293. Boston: Ginn and Company, 1939.

Woolf, Maurice D., and Jeanne A. Woolf, *Remedial Reading: Teaching and Treatment*. New York: McGraw-Hill Book Company, Inc., 1957.

On Reading Problems of the Bright Child

De Boer, John J., "Creative Reading and the Gifted Student," *The Reading Teacher*, 16 (May 1963), 435–441.

Educational Policies Commission, *Education of the Gifted*. Washington, D.C.: National Education Association, 1950.

Hildreth, Gertrude, *Teaching Reading: A Guide to Basic Principles and Modern Practices*, pp. 580–598. New York: Holt, Rinehart and Winston, Inc., 1958.

Gallagher, James J., *Analysis of Research on the Education of Gifted Children*. Springfield, Ill.: Office of the Superintendent of Public Instruction, Special Study Project for Gifted Children, 1960.

———, *The Gifted Child in the Elementary School*. What Research Says to the Teacher, No. 17. Washington, D.C.: National Education Association, 1959.

Smith, Henry P., and Emerald V. Dechant, *Psychology in Teaching Reading*, pp. 392–402. Englewood Cliffs, N.J.: Prentice-Hall, Inc., 1961.

PART THREE

The Reading
Program in Action

14

The Reading Program in
the Primary Grades

This chapter undertakes to show how reading instruction in the primary grades is integrated with the total educational program. The description is divided into three parts: (1) the prereading stage, (2) the beginning reading stage, and (3) the program in Grades 2 and 3.

The Prereading Stage

Many first-grade teachers, especially beginners, are uncertain as to how to proceed when school opens in September. They usually have some knowledge of the factors related to reading readiness and of procedures for developing readiness. Nevertheless, they have difficulty in visualizing the techniques in operation and in making the all-important decisions required on opening days.

Preparation for the First Day of School

Probably the most significant day in the pupil's entire school life is his first day of school. His attitude toward school and toward reading for months and perhaps years to come may be influenced by his initial impressions of school life. First-grade teachers are therefore quite properly concerned with the question, "How can I prepare for that crucial first day?"

It will greatly help the new teacher's self-confidence, and at the same time improve her efficiency, if she gathers a good amount of information about the school in advance. For example, if the school makes available a syllabus or course of study, a careful examination of this document may provide the teacher with clues to the expectations of the school concerning the work of the first grade and with valuable suggestions regarding instructional procedures in the early days of the school term. Early examination of the basal readers and other textbooks used in the school should likewise be a part of the preparatory process. Existing routines and materials should not be discarded until well-considered substitutes have been devised or secured. A visit by the new teacher to the classroom to which she will be assigned may reveal to her the nature of the available equipment—charts, supplies, and supplementary reading material. Certainly if it is possible she should visit the school library, the gymnasium, the playground, and other physical facilities the school may have. In her interview with the principal or supervisor before the opening of the school term, she should have numerous questions in readiness with regard to routines, facilities, procedures, responsibilities of teachers, and the relative freedom allowed teachers for the organization of instruction. She should especially make the acquaintance of those colleagues and members of the supervisory staff who can be of assistance to her.

Knowledge about the number and kind of children in her class may be difficult to gather. The administration office of the school usually has a fair, but never infallible, estimate of the size of the fall enrollment. Unless the children have been previously enrolled in the kindergarten, the school may not know even the names of the children who enter the first grade. Often only general knowledge, based on earlier experiences, can serve as a guide.

Planning in advance of the opening of school is so essential to the development of a successful instructional program that many schools and school systems now hold preschool conferences or institutes for periods extending from one or two days to several weeks. The activities of such conferences are varied. If there is sufficient time, visiting speakers are often invited. Committees of teachers, grouped by grade levels or subject interests, discuss procedures and questions of concern to them. Usually the more experienced teachers provide information and help to the newcomers in these committee meetings. In addition, time is frequently set aside for individual preparation on the part of the teacher. She can, during this period, arrange her classroom attractively by placing interesting picture books on tables and shelves, mounting attractive pictures on the bulletin boards, perhaps bringing a few flowers and a plant or two, and seeing that the furniture is in place. If the names of the children are known in advance, the teacher can prepare identification cards to be worn the first few days and other cards to label the children's desks or places at the table.

Activities on the First Day of School

As has been pointed out, success on the first day of school depends in large measure upon previous planning. It should be remembered that many of the children have not hitherto been members of so large a group and may feel somewhat insecure. Provision should therefore be made to make them feel at home at once, to make them acquainted with their classmates, and to keep them occupied with interesting activities. Pinning name cards to their clothes (the teacher should wear one, too) is a good "ice-breaking" activity and at the same time a good introduction to the concept of reading as meaningful communication. Other first-day activities might include telling or reading a story to the children, playing a simple game, drawing pictures, or learning a song. Discussion, too, is an important aid to children in making that first significant orientation to the larger group. Boys and girls may be asked, for example, to tell in turn how many brothers and sisters they have, what their father's occupation is, and where they live.

Meanwhile there is much to explain to the children about procedures. They need to learn how to take care of drawing and other supplies, where to place their wraps, what routine is followed when going to the toilet, and how to take turns when talking. These explanations should, of course, not be made in rapid succession. On the first day, only the briefest and most essential directions should be given. The routines are learned gradually over a period of many days.

At the end of the day each child should feel that he has learned something. Since many boys and girls come to school believing that they will immediately learn to read and write, the teacher should not disappoint them. She may have them "read" their names and a few words, in a functional setting, that she writes on the board, like "Good Morning," or "There are 26 children in our room." The children can be satisfied that they have been writing if, for example, the teacher asks them to copy their names from the name cards on the pictures they draw.

Testing

It is generally unwise to give intelligence or reading tests during the first week or two in a first grade. Many children, finding themselves in a completely new kind of environment, are not totally at ease in school during the first days and weeks. Their real abilities may therefore not be reflected in the standardized tests. Moreover, the tasks that are set in the standardized tests may leave the initial impression with some children that life in school can be quite difficult.

When tests are given, they should be administered in the spirit of play. The number of pupils who take them at one time should be limited—perhaps to ten or twelve—so that the teacher will have no difficulty in making the directions clear and in supervising each child's responses to the directions. Under some conditions the number should perhaps be even smaller. In order that the necessary condition of reasonable quiet may prevail during the testing, it is desirable to conduct it away from the presence of other children. If possible, the other children should be cared for at this time by some other teacher. If this is not possible, seatwork or other activities should be arranged for the other children.

Tests are often given to children individually at various times of the school day. Since the tests are relatively short, it is often possible to give them to two or three pupils a day. The testing can thereby be completed within a few weeks. In schools that do not use standardized tests, teachers are encouraged to keep particularly detailed records of their observations of pupil performance. During the pretesting and testing periods especially, all teachers should be alert to information with respect to the readiness factors discussed in Chapter 5B, such as physical health and maturity, sensory acuity and discrimination, experience background, interest in reading, language development, and ability to follow directions. Such information should whenever possible be included in anecdotal form in the pupils' folders.

Organization of the Prereading Program

Different approaches may be made to the organization of instruction during the prereading period. Those who believe in complete individualization of instruction in silent reading in the primary grades—and their number is increasing—hold that the organization should be very informal. They advocate a wide and rich variety of nonreading activities for all children. They stress the need for a great variety of attractive reading materials, and much story reading and story telling. They assert that children who are ready will soon begin to want to read to themselves and will call on the teacher for help and that others will soon want to follow their example. If the teacher has carefully observed the children, she will know which ones to encourage to read and with what reading materials to supply them. Other pupils will try, find it too hard and therefore uninteresting, and will give up for a time. With the teacher's encouragement they will return to the books when they are ready. Advocates of this plan insist that it is not a haphazard one. They believe it is the natural way to learn to read and that it will lead to the growth of sturdy habits in reading. Certainly such a plan calls for teachers of ability, but it is argued that many, if not most, teachers could learn to use it with success and satisfaction.

More formal plans are in use in most schools, especially those with large classes. In the larger elementary schools the first-grade pupils are often sectioned into more or less "homogeneous" classes. In certain of these classes, most or all of the first year is spent in "readiness" activities. In others, the formal reading instruction does not begin until after one or even several months of school. Still other classes begin reading instruction at once, if the children appear to be ready.

Since in a large number of elementary schools there is but one class for each grade level, grouping within the class is therefore common. As the teacher studies the results of her appraisals, she will usually find great variation among the boys and girls. Typically she will have a small number who are ready or almost ready for beginning reading. She is likely also to have another group, frequently a larger one, for whom it is perhaps wise to postpone beginning reading instruction for a month or longer. Almost always there will be a few pupils for whom it will be best to wait with book reading for a rather long time, probably until Christmas or longer. In addition, there may be one or more pupils who may not be ready for systematic reading instruction throughout most of the school year. The division into reading and reading readiness groups should be made after appraisal of all known factors related to beginning reading has been made. The grouping should be flexible so that no rigid barriers of administration will hinder a child from transferring easily from one group to another if his best interests are served by a change. The teacher also needs to give consideration to the size of the group. Many teachers have found groups of more than ten or twelve rather unwieldy when planning first-grade reading or prereading groups.

After the teacher has decided on desirable means of grouping, she is ready to make preliminary plans for the work both for small groups and for individuals. When making plans for those not ready to read, she will probably want to follow many of the suggestions given in Chapter 5B, "Developing Readiness for Reading."

Seatwork

Many primary-grade teachers ask, "While I am working with one reading group, how can I keep the other boys and girls engaged in worthwhile activities?"

Seatwork can be valuable if the teacher is guided by the following principles:

1. *Seatwork should help accomplish educationally sound objectives.* Mere "busy work," intended to give the boys and girls something to do, cannot be justified. School time is too valuable to squander. There are many significant activities in which boys and girls, even in the first grade, can engage independently or semi-independently.

2. *The learning acquired through seatwork should be commensurate with the time and energy expended.* For example, it is questionable to have boys and girls engage in a page of seatwork which requires them to spend most of the time cutting and pasting in order to align given printed material with corresponding pictures. The same educational objective, accomplished through practice in reading, can usually be achieved more economically if, instead of cutting and pasting, they draw lines connecting words or sentences with the appropriate pictures.

3. *The seatwork activity should be free of undesirable features.* Much of the coloring of outlines on duplicated sheets or in workbooks is not only questionable as far as the accomplishment of educational objectives is con-

cerned; it can actually be harmful if through the coloring the pupil becomes less creative in his subsequent expression of art. That such a danger exists many specialists in art as well as large numbers of classroom teachers attest.

Another undesirable feature of some seatwork is that through it the pupil loses interest in accomplishing the objective for which the work was assigned. If, for instance, the purpose of the seatwork is to provide further practice on the vocabulary of reading selections, tedious drill on vocabulary in seatwork exercises can be an interfering factor.

4. *Seatwork should be adapted to individual differences.* To require all pupils at all times to do the same seatwork is in flagrant violation of the findings of the psychology of learning. It is a waste of time to assign to a child seatwork designed to give further practice on a skill which he has already perfected. Furthermore, such practice may lead to boredom on the part of the child. Although it is often difficult to recognize what work a child needs, the teacher should try to adhere to the principle of assigning to an individual only those activities that would seem to be of value to him.

What has been said about the need of differentiated workbook activities also applies to seatwork produced by the teacher.

5. *The teacher should make certain that the boys and girls understand what is required of them in the seatwork.* Careful explanation and demonstration are often essential, especially if it is the first time that the boys and girls perform that type of activity. With children who can read directions, silent reading of the directions is often desirable. Sometimes it is helpful to have one or two examples of the type or types of activities to be performed, worked out by the pupils beforehand as the teacher or a pupil does the necessary work on the chalkboard. Or all might do the first item or two in an exercise together and report what they did before the group starts independent work on the activity.[1]

The Program for Beginning Reading

Each succeeding stage in the process of learning to read has problems peculiar to itself. The period of beginning reading, which usually starts for the child some time quite early in the first grade and continues throughout that school year and often into the next, is no exception to this rule. In fact, in some respects the problems in this stage seem more crucial than those arising at any later period.

Some of the questions pertaining to instruction in beginning reading that are often asked by teachers are: What should be the role of the textbook in beginning reading? How can the first lesson from a book be taught effectively?

---

[1] Adapted from an article written by Martha Dallmann entitled "Seatwork, Not *Busy Work*," that appeared in the October 1953 issue of *Grade Teacher*.

How can the textbook be used effectively? What provisions for directed reading beyond the use of the basal textbook can be made? How can reading be encouraged through group projects?

With these questions in mind, let us see what happens in the typical modern elementary classroom.

Classroom Procedure

The following description of activities pertaining to reading in which first-grade children engage is not based on any one classroom, but it is characteristic of an increasing number throughout the country.

Before school in the morning the boys and girls in the classroom are engaged in a variety of activities. Some are playing in the corner of the room in a playhouse made out of crates and furnished with equally rough furniture. Three boys are looking at the bulletin board on which the teacher has posted a picture of a calf, a sheep, and a dog above the question written in manuscript, "Do you have a pet?" One boy, who had previously asked the teacher what the question is, triumphantly reads it to his two classmates. Three boys and two girls are looking at picture books as they sit at the nicely arranged table in the library corner. At the same table several children are reading easy picture books with very simple text. Two other girls are asking the teacher what the text says under a picture in a book that intrigued them, which they found on the bookshelf near the library table. Two boys are feeding the rabbit according to simple directions posted on the chart. Still others are talking with one another about happenings of interest to them that took place since they had last seen each other. In this relaxed atmosphere the boys and girls begin their school day. Much of significance even for the reading program of the grade takes place during this period.

During the brief sharing time that marks the opening of school, incidental use is made of reading. As one of the boys shows small branches of two evergreen trees that his father has just planted in the yard of their new home, the teacher writes the words *pine* and *spruce* on the chalkboard and suggests that the boy attach the evergreens with binding tape at the appropriate place to the chalkboard so that all can see them. Another child, a girl, shows her new picture book and reads to the class what it says under an especially exciting-looking picture.

While plans are being made for the day's activities, opportunity for reading is again afforded incidentally. The teacher writes on the board the brief listing of events for the day as she and the children determine them. The question, "What do we do next?" as the teacher points to the words "Bob's group," attracts additional attention to the use that can be made of reading.

This is an exciting day for Bob's group. They can hardly wait for the teacher to come to their semicircle in the front of the room. The teacher had told the group yesterday that today would be a red-letter day for them, the day when they could begin reading out of books. Until this time they have confined their reading to experience charts of a variety of kinds, to labels in the room that have served a significant purpose, to notes the teacher has written on the bulletin boards or chalkboards, and to picture books that have had only little text, which from time to time the teacher read to them individually as they "followed" in the book. But now they are to have books all their own to read.

After the teacher has distributed the preprimers, the boys and girls are given time to examine the books and to make comments on pictures about which they think they will enjoy reading. After that the teacher, to use the terminology of the manuals published with this preprimer, makes the "approach" to the first lesson. Since this first story is about a boy and a girl who have a pet dog, the teacher gives the children an opportunity to tell briefly about their own pets. Reference is also made to the bulletin board on which pictures of pets are posted. Then the teacher says, "The boy and girl in our story also have a pet. It is a dog named. . . ." As she gives the name of the dog, she refers to it on the chalkboard. She then has several of the boys and girls say the name. Similarly she introduces the pupils to the names of the boy and girl. She provides for practice on words in the story that the pupils have learned through experience charts or other incidental means. Then she presents the new words in the story. The boys and girls pronounce them and find some of them in their books. The teacher asks a leading question on the story before the pupils begin reading the selection sentence by sentence, first silently and then orally. Discussion, centered on content read, on the pictures, and on some of the words, takes place as the pupils read the few simple pages of the preprimer. The reading is followed by a short period during which the pupils discuss possibilities of what may happen next. As the teacher tells them that tomorrow they will find out what does happen, she notes the reluctance with which the pupils pass in their books. The main objective of the period has been accomplished: the boys and girls are eager to continue reading their new books. The teacher hopes always to plan her reading program so that the boys and girls will leave her reading group looking forward with anticipation to the next reading period.

Before the boys and girls go to their seats the teacher explains to them a "surprise" that she has for them. She has written in manuscript the new words that can be illustrated, one each at the bottom of a sheet of paper. Each child is given four pieces of paper, with the names of the boy and girl and the dog in the story and the word *pets*. The teacher explains to the children that they can make a booklet that will help them remember the new words they will meet in their first book. Brief practice in reading the words on the papers follows and plans are laid for drawing the pictures while the teacher works with one of the other groups.

In the meantime the rest of the boys and girls have been busy. One group, which has already finished the two levels of preprimers in the basal textbook series and has just been introduced to the first readers, has spent twenty minutes reading and illustrating a simple story about children playing that the teacher has written and duplicated. In planning the story, the teacher has taken care to use no words new to the pupils, for the children are still unable to attack words independently, unless the new word presents only a minor structural difference from those they already know. For example, they may be able to figure out the word *dogs* independently since they have had the word *dog*. Similarly they probably can tell in context what the new word *playing* is because they have learned *play* as a sight word.

The boys and girls in Christine's group have been spending the same twenty minutes making new name cards for their desks. The children in the group have had no previous formal reading instruction. The teacher has suggested that they might want to practice writing first on other paper in order not to spoil the final name card. During the next twenty minutes, while the children in Maria's group are reading with the teacher, the pupils in Christine's group who have finished making their name cards are engaged in a variety of activities. Some are looking at picture books. Others are drawing pictures needed for the unit on which they are working, entitled "Our First Grade." Still others are doing some house cleaning in the playhouse. All are participating in activities filled with possibilities for growth and development.

After the boys and girls in Maria's group assemble, a few minutes are taken to discuss progress in their illustration of the storybooks on which they had been working while Bob's group was reading. The reading lesson for the period, based on a story of activities of children at school, is divided into three parts: the approach to the lesson, the silent and oral reading of the story, and more intensive study of words than was made during the approach. The approach consists of the teacher's orienting the pupils to the story, through providing opportunity for them to discuss what they think the children in the story would play during their story hour. The teacher then tells them that in the story they will meet new words. She tells them she will help them beforehand with those words that she thinks they probably will not be able to figure out by themselves, but that she will not assist them with two that she is quite certain they will be able to decipher alone.

As she helps the boys and girls with some of the new words, she makes use of various ways of presenting words, teaching some as sight words and others by means of context clues, pictures clues, and phonetic and structural analysis. Then follows the period of actual reading. This time the selection is not broken up into parts only a sentence in length, as it had been for Bob's group. These boys and girls are able to read the story in their first reader paragraph by paragraph and occasionally even more than one paragraph at a time without help from the teacher. Before each of these parts is taken up, the teacher prepares the children for reading the paragraph or group of paragraphs by asking stimulating questions, by giving the pupils purpose for reading, by directing their attention to questions on the chalkboard which they will answer later, or by having them point to a designated new word that occurs in that part.

The membership of Christine's group is made up of three boys and girls for whom, on the basis of a variety of criteria, it was deemed inadvisable, as indicated earlier, at this time to begin reading in books. During their so-called "reading" period they are engaged in work on an experience chart for which, in connection with their unit on "Our First Grade," they dictate to the teacher simple sentences describing their library corner. So that they can read the chart to the other groups, they then learn to "read" the sentences, as described in Chapter 5B, "Developing Readiness for Reading." At the same time they learn to identify a few of the new words of the chart. The words selected by the teacher are chiefly those that they are likely to need later in beginning reading.

Group Projects

Participation in group projects in connection with the classroom reading experiences can serve a two-fold purpose. It can make the children's reading more significant to them and it can help them derive the benefits inherent in activities other than reading. For example, oral reading can not only help the child become a better reader, but also enable him to gain more self-confidence in other activities.

Here are some group activities that the teacher might encourage in order to accomplish the types of objectives suggested in the preceding paragraph. Brief mention of some of them has been made earlier.

1. Dramatizations can be used to provide interesting variety in teaching methods. In the early stages of so-called dramatization in the primary grades, the children can read by parts the direct quotations given in the book. This reading can in many cases profitably be preceded by preparation like the following: (a) children indicating the exact words of each speaker; (b) several pupils reading a given quotation as each child thinks it should be read; (c) group commenting on the effectiveness of the reading; and (d) class discussing the help of quotation marks in reading a selection by parts. Later on in dramatizations the children might supplement the reading by parts with simple actions suggested by the words. A discussion of appropriate actions might either precede or follow the initial dramatization. As children become more adept at dramatization, they might get along without their books and give the content of the story in their own words. Some groups have written their own plays based on a story that they have read. How perfect a production should be before work on it is abandoned must be determined in the light of the objectives to be accomplished. Some teachers spend altogether too much time on a given dramatization; others err in that they move on to another activity before the boys and girls have received the joy and other values of desirable perfection in the undertaking.

2. One form of dramatization that deserves special explanation is the puppet play. Even in the primary grades puppet plays can serve a useful purpose. While it is impossible to state the relative values to be gained through puppetry as compared with other means of dramatization, there are doubtless advantages as well as shortcomings in puppet dramatizations. Some teachers find that through puppetry the shy youngster who feels self-conscious when he is seen by his audience can be helped in overcoming his reticence, since in puppet plays he can put dramatic quality into his voice while he himself is hidden from view. As in the case of other dramatizations, the presence of an audience lends purpose to the performance.

To use intricate puppets in the primary grades is, of course, undesirable. Some first-grade children will like to make simple paper dolls mounted on sticks as their puppets. Puppets made from paper bags admirably serve the purposes of some first-grade children.

3. The home-made "movie" is a project that has been used by many primary teachers with great success in connection with reading activities. In one first grade this procedure was followed in illustrating the story "The Circus" in the book *I Know a Secret*.[2] After the children in one reading group had read the story, they decided to make a "movie" to show to the other children in their first grade. First the teacher listed on the board the children's suggestions for pictures to be included in the "movie," along with her own. Then the group, under the direction of the teacher, worked out the sequence in which the pictures were to appear. Next, as they discussed what was to be written under each picture, the teacher jotted down the recommended comments. Thereupon each child agreed to draw one or more pictures on paper of the size to fit into the home-made stage. After the boys and girls had altered some of their pictures to incorporate suggestions that seemed helpful, the pictures, followed in each case by the appropriate sentences written in manuscript by the teacher, were fastened together with pressure-sensitive tape to form the roll to be shown on the "stage." The children next practiced reading the words of the "movie." Thereupon the "movie" was shown to the guests. The following three sentences, suggestive of the others, were used with the first three pictures:

Father is taking Bob and Nancy to the circus.
Bob is mailing a letter to Jack and Jean.
Jack and Jean are showing Mother the letter.

---

2 Gertrude Hildreth and others, *I Know a Secret,* pp. 106–131. New York: Holt, Rinehart and Winston, Inc.

4. Various methods can be employed to enrich the children's background for reading. Field trips, when well conducted, can make significant contributions to the reading program. For example, comprehension of a reading unit on the farm and interest in it can be increased through a visit to a farm. A few of the many other field trips that might be of profit in connection with reading in the primary grades are trips to the post office, the fire station, the airport, the zoo, and the grocery store. To get the most value from a field trip it is necessary to make careful preparation for the trip and, after the trip is completed, to make effective use of what was observed.

5. To give children a better background for reading, there are times when exhibits prove more profitable than field trips. Collecting and then exhibiting interesting and significant objects constitute one means of extending the children's horizons. Sometimes reproductions of objects like airplanes or silos can be made and put on exhibit. In one grade that was reading about the Arabs, objects similar to those used by those people were made and shown to the rest of the boys and girls.[3]

In these and in many other ways, activities for reading or for encouraging reading can be provided throughout the school day as the boys and girls participate in a primary grade program rich in opportunities for growth. As they experiment with the effect of water on plants, for instance, they can read the labels *water* and *no water* that are placed near the appropriate flower pots. A record that indicates on what days the one plant is to be watered also furnishes meaningful material for reading even for the child in the prereading period. Some children in that stage read the captions which, at their dictation, the teacher has written under their pictures illustrating the need plants have for water. In connection with a unit on "Our First Grade" the children could read an experience chart about their library corner which they had dictated to the teacher. Thus reading is also taught during periods not set aside for that purpose alone; in fact, some of the best opportunities for reading are afforded during parts of the school day not designated as reading periods.

Reading in Grades 2 and 3

Many boys and girls, upon entering the second grade or soon thereafter, are ready for the stage in learning to read that is described by the National Society for the Study of Education as "the stage of rapid progress in fundamental reading attitudes and habits." Throughout the time spent in the second and third grades most of the pupils continue to be on this level of development in reading. It is in these grades that there usually is rapid growth in developing independence in the identification and recognition of words, in comprehending relatively

---

[3] Adapted from an article written by Martha Dallmann entitled "You Can Teach Them to Read: Some Interesting Ways to Do It" that appeared in the January 1950 issue of *Grade Teacher.*

difficult material, in learning to read at appropriate rates, in reading a large variety of materials, and in using reference materials suited to the level.

In order to help boys and girls attain the objectives implied in the preceding paragraph, many teachers find it desirable to include within their program of reading instruction three phases—namely, (1) reading as carried on in connection with a basal reading textbook; (2) reading in connection with other areas of the curriculum; and (3) independent reading. The rest of this chapter gives suggestions as to how the teacher of the second or third grade can guide the learning in each of these parts of the reading program, so that, as a result of harmonious development in all of these aspects, the child will leave this stage of learning to read possessing the ability to read books on his level independ· ently and with enjoyment.

Use of Basal Reading Textbooks

The procedures best fitted to the use of reading textbooks in Grades 2 and 3 are different in some respects from those that can be used most advantageously during the period of beginning reading. These differences result in part from the characteristics of the average boy and girl at that stage of development and in part from the fact that boys and girls have already acquired—to only a small extent, to be sure—some of the skills of reading that were previously lacking.

USE OF THE READING TEXTBOOKS DURING SEATWORK PERIODS. Since the need for grouping and individualization of work in reading persists, the problem of providing activities for children working independently at their seats is still present. However, it no longer taxes the ingenuity of the teacher quite as much as in the preceding stage of reading, for, once the child has acquired enough independence to read without help for a twenty-minute period or longer, the seatwork can be closely related to the reading he is doing in the basal reader. The following recommendations suggest some of the ways in which the teacher can help the pupils utilize to good advantage the time during which the teacher is busy helping other boys and girls.

1. In the seatwork period set aside time for reading silently a part of the reading textbook, for which the preparation has been given during the reading period. In order to use this procedure to best advantage it is usually desirable to have the study period follow, rather than precede, the class period. In this way, the children first get the needed help on a selection as their reading group meets and then do part of the reading on that selection independently when the teacher no longer is free to help them. It is especially important that this should be the case with the poorer groups. When it is not possible to have the seatwork period immediately follow the class period, it is often necessary for the teacher to spend a few minutes with each group immediately before they begin their seatwork. The teacher will need to use these minutes to remind the group of the assignment made earlier and sometimes to review briefly the new words or in

other ways prepare the boys and girls for the silent-reading work. It is usually best to avoid using a seatwork period as preparation for the next class.

2. If during the seatwork period the pupils read some pages of the reading textbook for the first time, the last part of that period should frequently be used for testing their comprehension. For example, if the boys and girls have read a selection during this study period, the teacher may wish to tell them that when they have finished the reading they should answer questions, copies of which have already been distributed to the children. If the aim is to test recall without the use of the book to facilitate recall, the teacher should make certain that the boys and girls do not look at the questions before or while they are reading the book. The questions may be simple fact questions which require underlining, writing *yes* or *no*, or writing on a blank the correct word of a list that has been provided. (In such a method the child's concern is not with spelling the word correctly.) Some of these and other directions that the pupils might follow to show their comprehension and retention of what they read silently can well be modeled after some that are found in the better workbooks.

3. Make use of the workbooks that accompany the readers. Frequently the exercises in a workbook can be of value to many of the boys and girls. They should not be used, however, unless they will serve a worthwhile purpose. Nor should all pupils be required to do an exercise if in the best judgment of the teacher not all would profit from doing it. Two types of purposes can be accomplished by means of the workbooks. They can be used to test the pupil's comprehension as well as to provide more practice in reading, especially in reading to follow directions.

At times it is desirable, either during the preceding class period or else for a few minutes at the beginning of the seatwork period, for the teacher to help the boys and girls in getting started on the workbook exercise. As a rule, if they can read the directions silently, neither the teacher nor one of the pupils should read them orally to the group; the silent reading of the directions affords such good practice in reading directions that usually the children should not be deprived of this opportunity. To make certain that everyone knows what to do after he has read the directions silently, the teacher may at times wish to ask the pupils to tell in their own words what they are to do. Sometimes, however, mere reading of the directions and stating of them are not enough. At such times the boys and girls should be helped, as a group, to do an item written on the board that is similar to those in the exercise. It may also be helpful to have the group as a whole, under the guidance of the teacher, do the first one or two parts of the workbook exercise so that there will be no question as to procedure.

Boys and girls able to read second- and third-grade readers can often profit greatly by correcting their workbooks during the class period. The teacher, however, will usually find it desirable to check the work herself, for through her examination of the work she can determine not only whether the boys and girls are finding their errors but also what their mistakes are. The latter type of information should be utilized in planning further learning activities.

4. Have the boys and girls read orally in small groups. While the teacher is engaged with one reading group, the other boys and girls can be reading to each other quietly in other sections of the room. It is usually advisable that in the second and third grades the size of the groups reading orally without the teacher's help should be limited to three or four. Provision should be made for a pupil in each group to serve as leader. The material read at this time can be either from the textbook material that has already been read in class or from some related reading material which the pupils have had an opportunity to read silently or orally beforehand. Unless the teacher has established in the room a spirit of work, however, she should not attempt small-group work at times when she is busy with one reading group. On the other hand, in a well-organized room where orderliness conducive to work is the accepted standard, with proper guidance the boys and girls can, in this manner, be taught to get part of the needed practice in oral reading. One precaution that should be observed is that after the boys and girls have once learned to read more rapidly silently than orally, the listeners should not follow in their books while someone is reading to them.

5. Provide opportunity for the pupils to read references other than their basal textbook in order to gain information that they will need in connection with selections studied in their reader. If, for example, while reading a section on "Animal Friends" in their textbook, the group has decided to make a booklet on some of the "animal friends" in their section of the country, one animal may be assigned to each child for further study. If the work that the boys and girls are to do during the study period is well planned beforehand, many of the skills required for locating and utilizing reference material can be developed. The pupils could prepare as talks the important information that they have gathered, and later, with further help from the teacher, record it either in paragraph form or as separate sentences containing facts about the animals studied. If the boys and girls use the study period in this manner, the tasks should be on their level of development. When the children are in the earlier stages of learning to make use of such materials, the teacher will often find it advisable to select for each pupil a book in which he will find information on his topic. After the pupils have developed more skill, they can be helped to make use of more than one reference book and to find books without the teacher's help. Many suggestions for using reference materials during study periods are found in Chapters 9A and 9B, "Locating Information" and "Developing Locational Skills."

6. Set aside some seatwork periods for illustrative work on the materials taken up in the basal textbook. Sometimes this can be in the form of making a picture dictionary on words and concepts learned while reading a section of the textbook. At other times it may be work on a mural suggested by the story. Whatever the type of illustration, it is important that the work should not be done just as "busywork." If it is to be justified as an activity that extends the reading in the textbook, it must serve such purposes as the following: to interest the boys and girls further in the book; to whet their appetites for more reading on the subject discussed in the book; to stimulate the pupils to read the selections in the book more carefully; to serve as a means by which the teacher can evaluate how adequately the pupils have comprehended and retained the information given in the book.

7. Let the pupils plan dramatizations of stories in the textbook. If during the reading period the boys and girls have worked out carefully with the teacher plans for dramatizing a story given in the book, during the seatwork period they can meet independently in small groups to work out the scenes, settings, and costuming. Again, a caution should be noted: a teacher who has difficulty in maintaining a good spirit of work and cooperation in her room should not attempt to have the pupils work in groups when she is busy with a reading group, for chaos may result.

USE OF THE READING TEXTBOOKS DURING READING PERIODS. The suggestions that have been made for utilizing the seatwork period effectively can be adapted with slight modifications for use during the reading class. The following are additional suggestions for the period when the teacher is helping one of the two or three "homogeneous" reading groups.

1. During the approach to a lesson, if it seems advisable to present some of the new words before the pupils meet them in their reading, one of the aims of the teacher should be to help the boys and girls grow toward independence in word recognition as rapidly as possible, but without haste or tension. To accomplish this purpose the teacher can make use of many suggestions listed in Chapters 6A and 6B, "Word Recognition" and "Developing Skill in Word Recognition."

Other aims of the teacher during the approach should be to provide the informational background for the selection and to stimulate interest in it. In the case of a selection about Indian children, for example, the boys and girls might first discuss some of the ways in which life of Indian children differs from theirs or they might discuss a picture showing how an Indian woman taught her little daughter to weave a basket. After this discussion leading up to the selection to be read, the teacher might state the objective—in this case, "Let's read the story to find out in what ways the Indian children's education differs from ours."

2. During the reading of the selection it is not as a rule necessary, or even desirable, to break up the material for reading into the short parts suggested for the beginning reading period. In Grades 2 and 3 the pupils can often read one or two or even three pages without a break in the silent reading. For example, in a seven-page selection for reading during a class period, the teacher may decide to divide the material into only three parts, after the approach to the entire selection has been made. Preceding the reading of each of the three parts,

she can help the pupils to increase their awareness in reading by having them read silently, before they begin reading the part in the book, questions on the board to which they will find the answer in the part to be read; by giving orally an objective they should have in mind while reading that part; or by asking questions as to what they think will happen, followed by comments such as "Let's read to find out what really happens." After the pupils have read the part silently, comprehension can be increased and checked by having them answer questions on the board, discuss questions asked orally, read orally sentences that prove a point, or locate some of the new words. The part may then be read orally by one or more pupils. In these grades it is usually wise to divide the story for the period into several parts in the manner indicated, rather than to have the pupils read the whole selection for the day without any break through comments or questions or directions. The latter type of reading, which is very valuable, can as a rule be done by the pupils during periods when the teacher is not available to guide their reading more carefully.

3. The follow-up to the reading in parts in Grades 2 and 3 can be in the form of word study, which not only should emphasize the new words found in the selection but also assist the children to improve in ability to arrive at independence in word recognition. Help should be given in making use of context clues, in recognizing words by means of structural analysis, and in making use of phonics. How this can be done is suggested in Chapters 6A and 6B dealing with word recognition.

Reading in Various Curriculum Areas

Boys and girls progressing through the third stage of learning to read are becoming less and less dependent upon help in deciphering new words that they are likely to meet when reading easy materials in the field of social studies and science; hence increasingly they can profit from reading books in these areas. This independence is in marked contrast to the situation in the preceding stage of beginning reading where the pupils' reading vocabulary is greatly limited and they are almost totally dependent on others in acquiring additional words in the reading vocabulary. Very few materials in these fields are available for pupils in the period of beginning reading.

Reading in the social studies and science in the third stage of development is primarily a means of acquiring much interesting and significant information. Furthermore, when wise guidance is given as the boys and girls read both textbook material and supplementary books, they will improve in ability to read a number of types of material.

READING TEXTBOOK MATERIAL IN SOCIAL STUDIES AND SCIENCE. During the last decade there has been a considerable increase in the number of textbooks in science and social studies that have been published for use in the upper primary grades. As teachers use these with boys and girls, they should be cognizant of the various special problems connected with reading textbook material in these fields. Difficulty of concepts, problems of vocabulary, the large number of proper names in the field of social studies, the need of learning how to read intelligently the generalizations that abound in science textbooks, and the necessity for long-time recall of many facts—all these constitute problems even in the second and third grades. These are discussed in detail in Chapters 7A and 7B, on comprehension, where suggestions are also given for meeting these problems.

Use of a plan such as the following, which is for a lesson in a third grade that is using as textbook *Science Far and Near*,[4] can accomplish two important objectives of textbook reading—namely, the development of more skill in reading and the acquisition of important learnings in the field of science. The lesson for which suggestions are given is based on the material given on pages 230 to 235 in that book, the first lesson in the section entitled "Stars and Moon." The content of these pages includes: (1) reference to stories Indians made up about the moon and stars; (2) information as to how we are learning more and more about the heavenly bodies; (3) an experiment demonstrating the phases of the moon; and (4) further explanation of the phases of the moon.

No teacher should follow this plan in detail unless it fits the needs of her group better than any other procedure. It is hoped that the following outline will suggest to the teacher variations that she can make. Because of short class periods many teachers may need to spend more than one period on this lesson.

1. Begin the lesson by referring to a bulletin-board display on the phases of the moon that you have posted several days before you teach this lesson.

2. Ask the pupils what they think the Indians perhaps thought about the moon and the stars when they watched the heavens on moonlight and starlight nights.

3. Have the pupils read page 230 in order to find out what the Indians did when they could not find the answer to questions like "What makes the moon change its shape?" or "Why do the stars disappear during the daytime?" (Page 230 explains that the Indians made up stories about the heavenly bodies because they had no way of finding out many facts about them.) Either before or after the silent reading, you may find it desirable to help the boys and girls with the recognition of words that they may be unable to read without your help.

4. Give the pupils an opportunity to answer the questions that you had posed as an objective for reading page 230.

5. Have a pupil tell an Indian legend about the moon. It is usually advisable for the teacher to hear a special report before class. She can thus help the pupil to get the maximum value from the experience and can make suggestions—about organization, for example—to assure that the listeners will hear a well-prepared talk.

---

4 Herman and Nina Schneider, *Science Far and Near*. Boston: D. C. Heath and Company, 1954.

6. Ask the pupils to read page 231 to find out why we do not have to make up stories about the moon and the stars. (Page 231 explains that scientists have discovered many facts about the moon and stars.)

7. After the pupils have read page 231, have them answer questions on this page that you had written on the board before class.

8. Have the pupils tell some facts that they know about the moon.

9. Have the boys and girls read page 232 to find out more facts about the moon.

10. Give the boys and girls an opportunity to name additional points about the moon that were stated on page 232.

11. Give the pupils a short time to tell what they may already know about the phases of the moon.

12. Have the boys and girls read silently page 233 and the first half of page 234 to find out how to conduct an experiment to show the phases of the moon. Then designate one person to perform the experiment, as paragraph by paragraph the group rereads silently the steps in the demonstration. After a paragraph has been read silently, have the pupil selected demonstrate that part. (The directions given are for showing with a light and a ball the relationship between rotation of the moon and its phases.)

13. Give time for the discussion of the demonstration and the study of the illustrations of the phases of the moon on page 235.

14. Refer the pupils to questions that you have on the board that are answered on the second half of page 234 and on page 235. After they have read these questions silently, ask them to read that part of the lesson in order to find the answers to the questions. (This selection indicates the length of time of the various phases of the moon.)

15. Ask the pupils to answer the questions on the second half of page 234 and on page 235.

16. Try to stimulate the boys and girls so that they will want to try the demonstration at home, so that they will become more observant of the moon, and so that they will want to read further on the topic.

READING SUPPLEMENTARY MATERIAL IN SOCIAL STUDIES AND SCIENCE. In the modern elementary school boys and girls do much reading in connection with unit work in books other than textbooks. Typically during the planning period at the beginning of a unit, the boys and girls under the supervision of the teacher decide on questions or topics on which they will try to get information. In some instances, all of the class will read not only the material in a textbook, if a textbook is used, but also many of the other materials that will give information on their subject. In other cases committees are formed, each of which has the responsibility for finding the available data on the topic assigned to the members. It is usually advisable in the lower grades for the teacher to make available to the boys and girls many of the books on their level, for in those grades they often have difficulty in finding information in reference books. But even children at this age should be encouraged to look for additional material— in the school, at home, or in the public library. They should also be given help in developing those locational skills that will be of value to them in finding the data for which they are searching. Using the table of contents, finding a page quickly in a book, and locating a part on a page that gives the wanted information are among the skills that can be developed even in the primary grades.

Through unit work in which the boys and girls individually or in small groups look for information specifically assigned either to one person or to a committee, excellent opportunity is provided for developing skill in organizing and summarizing what is read. The teacher can give this type of help to the boys and girls individually or in small groups or to the class as a whole. Such assistance can be provided both before and after the individual or committee has reported on the findings. Rich opportunities for helping the pupils develop in power to evaluate what they read are also afforded by such work. If, for example, the class is studying a unit on Indians, questions like these, that stimulate thinking, may be asked: (1) How does the writer of this book feel toward the Indians? (2) What sentences show how he feels? (3) What sentences tell us that the Indian women had a hard life?

Work with supplementary materials also affords an opportunity for the pupils to develop ability in evaluating statements found in their reading. At times the boys and girls may find contradictory, or seemingly contradictory, statements themselves; at other times the teacher may draw attention to two sentences that do not agree or do not seem to agree. In either instance she can guide the pupils in acquiring early the ability to evaluate what they read.

Independent Reading

No program of reading instruction in Grades 2 and 3 can be considered complete if it does not make provision for extensive free, independent reading.

One of the chief problems in respect to independent reading in these grades is that of helping boys and girls find material on their level. If they cannot find books that they will enjoy reading, they are not likely to continue reading during their leisure time. It is for this reason that many primary grade teachers are constantly looking for suitable books. The teacher equipped with information about new and old books of high quality for children is then able to make specific recommendations for books to be added to the room library or to the school library. She can also be of help in guiding boys and girls to find suitable books in the public library. Furthermore, many librarians in public libraries welcome suggestions for ordering books when the recommendations are given by teachers who show that they know the field of literature for children.

An attractive library table in the classroom can be an important factor in encouraging children to do independent reading. Even in the lower grades the pupils can be given the opportunity to read at the library table not only before school and during part of the noon intermission but also at times during the school day while another part of the class is engaged in other activities. A stimulus for independent reading is often provided when the teacher sets aside, from time to time, a period of the school day during which the boys and girls can read their so-called "library books."

Thus a rich program of reading instruction can be set up for boys and girls in Grades 2 and 3 if the teacher makes adequate provision for a basal reading program, for reading in connection with units of work and with other activities in the various subject areas, and for free reading.

FOR FURTHER STUDY

Artley, A. Sterl, *Your Child Learns to Read*. Chicago: Scott, Foresman and Company, 1953.

Benjamin, Dayton, and Alice Burton, "The Experience Approach to Beginning Reading," *Elementary English*, 31 (October 1954), 346–349.

Bond, Guy L., and Eva Bond Wagner, *Teaching the Child to Read*, pp. 93–145. New York: The Macmillan Company, 1960.

Carter, Homer L. J., and Dorothy J. McGinnis, *Teaching Individuals to Read*, pp. 41–73. Boston: D. C. Heath and Company, 1962.

Dawson, Mildred A., and Henry A. Bamman, *Fundamentals of Basic Reading Instruction*, pp. 65–99. New York: David McKay Company, Inc., 1963.

Dolch, Edward W., "Four Methods of Teaching Reading," *Elementary English*, 31 (February 1954), 72–76.

Felton, Wilma, "The Values of Workbooks in a First Grade Reading Program," *Elementary English*, 34 (October 1957), 377–382.

Gray, Lillian, *Teaching Children to Read*, pp. 197–256. New York: The Ronald Press Company, 1963.

Harris, Albert J., *Effective Teaching of Reading*, pp. 43–93. New York: David McKay Company, Inc., 1962.

Hildreth, Gertrude, *Teaching Reading*, pp. 249–334. New York: Holt, Rinehart and Winston, Inc., 1958.

Leestma, Robert, "The Film-Reader Program," *Elementary English*, 33 (February 1956), 97–101.

McKim, Margaret G., and Helen Caskey, *Guiding Growth in Reading in the Modern Elementary School*, pp. 31–256. New York: The Macmillan Company, 1963.

Meeker, Alice M., *Teaching Beginners to Read*. New York: Holt, Rinehart and Winston, Inc., 1958.

National Council of Teachers of English, *Language Arts for Today's Children*, pp. 114–205. New York: Appleton-Century-Crofts, 1954.

Newton, J. Roy, *Reading in Your School*, pp. 56–71. New York: McGraw-Hill Book Company, Inc., 1960.

Petty, Walter T., "Critical Reading in the Primary Grades," *Elementary English*, 33 (May 1956), 298–302.

Russell, David H., *Children Learn to Read*, pp. 167–228. Boston: Ginn and Company, 1961.

15

The Reading Program in the Intermediate Grades

The preceding chapter has shown how some of the suggestions for developing reading growth given earlier in the book are incorporated into the primary grade reading program. This chapter similarly gives recommendations for putting into operation a well-rounded program in the intermediate grades.

Problems Confronting the Intermediate-Grade Teacher

A few of the problems that appear quite persistently with intermediate-grade teachers and their supervisors will be considered in this section of the chapter.

What Should Be Accomplished?

One reason why teaching of reading in the intermediate grades presents problems is that teachers often do not have clearly in mind what should be accomplished in those grades. Many have only a general objective in mind—for instance, "helping the child to become a better reader"—and consequently they often proceed to teach reading rather haphazardly without having valid criteria for determining methods of teaching or means of evaluation to be used.

The objectives of reading instruction in the intermediate grades can be thought of in terms of the fourth stage of reading instruction as outlined by the National Society for the Study of Education. This stage, defined as the one in which "experience is extended rapidly and increased power, efficiency, and excellence in reading are acquired," is the one through which most boys and girls pass as they are in Grades 4, 5, and 6. Some of the chief tasks of the pupil during this stage are: (1) to become skillful enough in reading so that through reading he can greatly extend and enrich his experiences and can thereby acquire much information and knowledge; (2) to continue in the development of speed in silent reading so that he will be able to read easy material on his level much more rapidly silently than orally; (3) to learn to read so well orally that it is interesting to listen to him; (4) to acquire complete independence in the ability to identify new words; (5) to develop skill in the use of the dictionary; (6) to acquire so much ability in comprehending what he reads that he can understand fairly difficult materials; (7) to achieve power in reading with discrimination; and (8) to acquire interest and skill in reading in various fields of learning.

The teacher who has in mind these clearly defined objectives for the fourth stage of reading instruction has an anchor to support her as she sets up her reading program for the intermediate grades. If she plans her reading instruction in order to help her pupils accomplish these goals, she has taken a first step toward assisting the pupils to read with understanding and at desirable rates many of the types of material read by the average adult.

Should a Period Be Set Aside for Reading Instruction?

No simple *yes* or *no* answer can be given to this question. Undoubtedly some superior teachers have attained excellent results without providing for a special period in the daily program for instruction in reading. The objectives of reading in the intermediate grades can be accomplished with or without such a period.

It is probably safe to say that generally most teachers should be advised to plan their intermediate-grade program to include a separate period for teaching of reading. This recommendation is made because many teachers do not have the time to devise an adequate program of reading instruction in which all the work on reading needed to accomplish the objectives can be done in connection with the various content areas. Furthermore, some teachers do not possess the skill needed for this type of well-planned, yet incidental, teaching. Lack of training along such lines is often one cause of this deficiency. For these reasons and others, many teachers find they can more readily achieve the objectives of reading instruction in the intermediate grades if they have a daily reading period. Even in programs that include such a period, however, it is still very important that emphasis should be placed on reading at other times of the school day, for not all the objectives can be accomplished adequately if the instruction is confined to the reading period.

What Should Be Taught during the Reading Period?

Teachers who have decided to set apart a period in the school day for teaching reading often wonder what should be taught during that period and what work in reading should be reserved for other times in the day. Again, no short authoritative answer can be given. It probably makes little difference as to what part of the school day is devoted to procedures that will help accomplish the objectives of reading instruction. The important thing is that learning-to-read activities should be done under those circumstances that are likely to be most productive of results. For example, dictionary work can be carried on effectively either during a reading period or in connection with reading in the social studies.

Even though no definite allocation of work to the reading period and to other times of the school days can be made, there are a few guidelines that the teacher may find helpful to follow. One is that it is often desirable to use the reading period when a new phase of a reading skill is to be developed or when more practice than that afforded by the incidental reading during other times in the school day seems necessary. Another guideline is that the incentive for learning a new skill can often originate in connection with work other than that taken up during the reading period. For example, real motivation to learn to use an encyclopedia can develop for a child if in science he finds he needs more information than that given in books other than encyclopedias. Application of learnings acquired during reading class also can be made when pupils are working on a unit, solving some problems in arithmetic, or studying in some other area.

Should the Class Be Divided into Reading Groups?

The intermediate-grade teacher who has decided on having a separate period in the school day for reading instruction needs to make the further decision as to whether she will teach all the boys and girls in the room at the same time or whether she will divide them into groups during the reading class. Although much can be done to adapt instruction to the needs of the boys and girls in a nongrouped situation if proper attention is paid to individual differences, nevertheless many teachers find they can work more advantageously if they have at least two groups for reading. Their decision is often based to a considerable extent on the wide variations in reading skills in the typical fourth or fifth or sixth grade. It is not at all uncommon, for example, to find in a fifth grade a pupil who reads no better than the average second-grade child and at the same time to find one or more who read on the level of the average pupil in the sixth or seventh grades.

One argument frequently advanced against grouping in these grades is that with the many other studies in the intermediate grades, not enough time is available for reading to make grouping advisable. If, for example, only forty minutes can be devoted to the reading class, and the class is divided into two groups, the teacher may be able to spend only about half of that time with each. Through skillful planning, however, the teacher can provide valuable reading activities for one group during the time when she is helping another section of the class.

Description of Classroom Procedure

In order to see how the suggestions for teaching reading in the intermediate grades can be put into practice, let us take note of what can be observed in a modern elementary classroom in which reading is taught effectively. Descriptions will be given of several types of hypothetical classroom situations that are typical of many.

A Classroom with a Grouped Reading Class

In Miss Westlund's fifth grade the 35 pupils have been divided into two sections. In Group One there are 26 pupils ranging in reading ability from beginning fifth-grade through average seventh-grade level. Group Two contains the other nine boys and girls, who are below average for a fifth grade; one of these has skills on a level with those of the typical third-grade child. The grouping was determined through the use of standardized tests as well as by means of teacher-made tests, observations by the teacher, and study of records of past progress. More pupils were placed in the upper group, in this case, because the teacher wished to have in a separate group those boys and girls whose ability was below that of their grade level. The teacher, however, recognized that the division need not necessarily have been made at that point. She was also aware of the fact that it is not necessary in all cases to place more pupils in the brighter group. She knew that there are many possible justifiable points of division if a teacher will teach each group according to the characteristics of the boys and girls as they are sectioned.

Miss Westlund did not try to hide from the boys and girls the fact that the grouping was done on the basis of ability, for she realized that if she tried to make a secret of the method of grouping, the children would soon find out for themselves why they were so divided. Rather, she discussed the situation with them frankly and thereby did much to help avoid the feeling of disgrace often experienced by a child who is placed in a lower group and learns of his placement without the sympathetic, yet factual, explanation of the teacher. The teacher tried to explain the division by telling the pupils that she had attempted to place each child in the group in which she thought he could most advantageously learn to read. A similar explanation was made to the parents. Although it would be an exaggeration to state that each child in Group Two was happy to be in that section rather than in Group One, nevertheless most of the children did not feel the stigma of the placement as they might easily have done had they learned of it through unkind remarks from classmates.

Miss Westlund set aside, as a rule, 50 minutes daily for reading class. She did not designate 25 minutes for each group, but rather kept the division of the total 50 minutes elastic so that according to the work planned for each group for a period she could decide how best to use the time. Occasionally the children in one of the groups spent the entire period reading without the teacher's help, while Miss Westlund devoted her time to the other group. At times she spent the 50 minutes helping individuals in both groups while the rest of the pupils were engaged in well-planned work on reading. At still other times she taught the entire class as a whole, either during part of the period or during the entire period. She used the latter method in presenting work on how to use an encyclopedia, a set of which belonged to the room. At the same time, however, she recognized the differences in ability of the boys and girls and adapted the instruction to those individual differences. For example, at one point a child in the lower group gave his interpretation of a picture, while another child from the higher group read to the class the short paragraph that answered a question the teacher had asked.

When the class was divided into two parts throughout the period, the teacher would sometimes help those in Group One first and at other times would first work with those in Group Two. The order was determined by the type of assignment. The following are two examples of how the 50 minutes might be divided:

9:00–9:10   *Group One:* Presentation of new work, under teacher direction
             Group Two: Silent reading of a brief selection presented the preceding day

9:10–9:40   *Group One:* Silent reading of the part presented from 9:00 to 9:10, followed by pupil answering of questions in writing, to serve as a check on comprehension of what was read
             Group Two:
             a. Oral check on interpretation of material pupils read silently during the preceding ten minutes, with oral reading of parts to prove a point
             b. Timed silent reading

9:40–9:50   *Group One:*
             a. Checking written work that pupils did during part of the preceding half hour
             b. Explanation of assignment of work pupils are to do independently at the beginning of the reading period on the following day
             Group Two: Pupil writing of answers to questions on the material they read silently at the end of the preceding half-hour period

                        *   *   *

9:00–9:30   *Group One:* Planning, under the teacher's guidance, the dramatization of a story the pupils had finished reading during the preceding day
             Group Two: Reading silently material on their level on topics assigned individually, on which they will report to the class; beginning work on planning the reports

9:30–9:50   *Group One:* Independent planning by each pupil of work for his part of the dramatization

Group Two: Further work, under teacher guidance, on reports to be given to the class

A Classroom with a Nongrouped Reading Class

In contrast to the plan adopted by Miss Westlund for her fifth-grade class, Mrs. Henricks did not divide her class into two groups, although she was aware of the fact that the range in reading ability in her class was approximately the same as that in Miss Westlund's. She realized, of course, that she would need to pay special attention to the needs of the individuals in her class if she was to make the reading class profitable for everyone.

Like Miss Westlund, she tried to discover the ability of each child. She did this through standardized tests, teacher-made tests, study of records, informal observation, and conferences. She then set varying objectives that she hoped to be able to have each child, individually, reach. She also planned how she might help each pupil most effectively. As she did so, she found that certain boys and girls had some problems in common. Six of them were markedly deficient in the ability to use phonics as a means of unlocking new words. Their problems were similar enough so that the teacher knew that at times she could meet with them in a small group to give them special help. Two of these six pupils, as well as two others, were unable to find words rapidly in the dictionary because they were not certain of the alphabetical order of letters. In the case of these four the teacher also made plans for helping them in a small group from time to time, even though she also knew that within this small group she would have to individualize the work because the problems of these pupils, though similar, were not identical.

The small-group work was often done during part of the 50-minute period that Mrs. Henricks set aside daily for reading class. While she helped either individuals or small groups, the other boys and girls were engaged in reading activities which they could do without her immediate attention. She also, at times other than reading class period, met with either the small groups or individuals needing special attention; occasionally these meetings were held before or after school. While the rest of the pupils were doing independent work in the social studies or science or arithmetic, Mrs. Henricks was alert to possibilities for helping those boys and girls who needed special attention in any field, reading included.

In addition to helping pupils individually or in small groups on their special problems, Mrs. Henricks from time to time, in a carefully planned program, tried to adapt instruction to individual differences by means such as the following:

1. When she assigned oral reading for an audience-type situation, she gave the easier selections to the children whose skill in reading was below average.

2. She often asked the easier questions of the pupils who were having some difficulty in answering harder ones. She also tried to ask questions of the better readers that would challenge them.

3. Often when she introduced new work during a reading class, she would have the entire group together at the beginning of the period. After part of the class was ready to work independently on the problem, she would assign work to them that they could do without her help. Then she would continue working with the pupils who needed more attention before they could go ahead with the new work independently.

4. While some pupils who did not need teacher help at a given time were doing independent reading, often in books of their own choice, the teacher gave additional help to those who seemed to require more guidance on the phase of learning to read on which the class was working.

A Classroom with No Reading Class

Miss Leamington's fifth grade is an example of a modern elementary classroom in which no time on the daily schedule of work is devoted to a reading class. The work is not haphazard, for Miss Leamington plans her work carefully and systematically so that it will fit the needs of the various individuals in her classroom.

Like Miss Westlund and Mrs. Henricks, Miss Leamington set out at the beginning of the school year to ascertain the abilities of each of her pupils. She, too, did this through standardized and teacher-made tests, through examination of records, through informal observation, and through conferences. Next she set up the objectives that she wanted to accomplish with each child. Roughly, too, she tried to determine what activities connected with the work in the various curricular areas each child might profitably engage in in order to acquire the skill that she hoped he would be able to achieve. She also was confronted with the problem of sequence—that is, deciding at what times the pupils could most profitably engage in each type of activity. Thus, in her plans for the year, she tried to take into account the individual needs of the children. In fact, as the class planned with the teacher what units of work should be studied in the various curriculum areas, the problems were chosen partly in terms of whether they would afford the boys and girls an opportunity to develop the necessary reading skills and abilities and attitudes.

Here are a few of the ways in which Miss Leamington helped the boys and girls to make progress in attaining greater proficiency in reading.

DEVELOPING SKILL IN WORD RECOGNITION AND WORD MEANING.

1. Before an assignment was made of work to be read in the social studies or science, the teacher at times isolated the words that she thought would cause difficulty and helped the boys and girls in learning them and, at the same time, in acquiring more skill in attacking words independently.

2. At times, after the pupils had read a selection in the content areas, she would ask the pupils to name words that they could not identify. She would then help them with these words, trying to give the help in such a way that the pupils would grow in power to learn new words independently. At times she would stop to give them aid in developing some rule of phonetic or structural analysis that they needed; at other times she would give them additional practice on the application of some generalization that they had been helped earlier to make.

3. Sometimes when the teacher talked to the class, she wrote on the board those words she thought the pupils might not recognize if they met them in writing. Occasionally she found it helpful to comment on the pronunciation of a word. For example, when a pupil mentioned on March 21 that that was the first day of spring, the teacher told the pupils that that day was called the spring *equinox.* As she told them that fact and briefly explained the concept, she wrote the word *equinox* on the board, dividing it into syllables.

4. The teacher encouraged the pupils to keep a record of new words they met in their reading. Some of the boys and girls made card files. On each card they recorded the word they had learned, indicated its pronunciation, wrote one or more common meanings, and made up sentences using the words in those meanings they had listed.

5. The teacher encouraged the boys and girls to learn new words by commenting on words that pupils had used appropriately in their speech or in their written work.

6. For a time the teacher had a bulletin board devoted to new words that the class or someone in the class was learning. The bulletin board was headed "Can *YOU* Use These Words?" Below the question were attached words cards on which the words were written large enough to be visible from all parts of the room. Rather frequently time was taken for the explanation of these words.

DEVELOPING SKILL IN COMPREHENSION.

1. As the boys and girls were reading in the content areas, the teacher tried to clarify concepts for them before they read a paragraph or longer selection of involved explanation. For instance, before the pupils read an explanation of convection, the teacher gave a demonstration of it. Then she asked the pupils to read the section to find out more about how heat travels by this means.

2. Sometimes before the boys and girls read a section containing a reference to an unfamiliar concept, the teacher would point this out and tell the pupils that she thought as they read they would be able to decipher its meaning. After the pupils had done the reading, she would make further explanation of the concept if she felt it necessary.

3. Before reading a selection the pupils were at times given questions, in written form, that they would find answered in it. After the silent reading the answers would be given by the pupils, either orally or in writing.

4. At times the teacher helped the pupils analyze difficult sentences, especially long and involved ones, that appeared in their reading.

5. Comprehension of difficult material in the content fields was improved through reading, as a preparatory activity, simple material on the same subject.

6. Learning to read critically was encouraged through: (a) discussing the qualifications of an author to write on a given subject; (b) indicating which words showed the bias of the writer when controversial subjects were under consideration; (c) comparing statements on a topic made in one book with those in another, and giving reasons for contradiction if the statements did not agree; (d) indicating whether certain statements made on a topic in science or social studies were fact or opinion; and (e) listing methods used by writers wishing to spread propaganda.

DEVELOPING SKILL IN REMEMBERING WHAT IS READ.

1. The teacher helped pupils select points worth remembering. For example, in the work in social studies she helped the boys and girls choose the names of persons they should remember. These she listed on a chart. With the guidance of the teacher the boys and girls decided upon an important statement to remember about each. From time to time they gave this statement about each person on the chart. Similarly, the class made a list of important events to remember. In this case, too, they formulated one sentence that would help them recall the event.

2. The teacher gave the pupils suggestions for improving their ability to remember. Where necessary, she explained terms. These were some of the suggestions: (a) Taking notes on points to remember sometimes helps retention. (b) Practicing recall aids retention. (c) Distributed practice is superior to nondistributed practice. (d) Overlearning is important for recall. (e) Organizing into a meaningful whole the facts to be recalled aids retention.

3. The teacher provided practice in developing retention. Some of the ways in which this was done were: (a) The pupils were tested on retention shortly after reading a passage and again after an interval of time. (b) Application was made to meaningful situations of points learned earlier.

DEVELOPING SKILL IN READING AT APPROPRIATE RATES.

1. The pupils decided before reading a selection whether it was material that should be read very carefully, at average speed, or slowly.

2. The pupils listed ways in which they could reduce the "warming-up" period that many readers have when they begin reading a selection.

3. The teacher timed the pupils as they were reading some easy materials in the content areas and had them record the rate per minute. They were also tested on comprehension of the material to determine whether they were sacrificing meaning for rate.

4. In order to provide practice in reading at various rates, the teacher gave the pupils materials of varying difficulty to be read for different purposes.

DEVELOPING SKILL IN LOCATING INFORMATION IN WRITING. Work in the social studies and science afforded many opportunities for developing locational skills. For example, pupils learned about the use of various types of reference books of value in the study of a unit on "Modern Americans." Development of skill in locating books in the library, in finding materials in reference books, and in making use of what they found was made possible throughout the work on this unit and on other study in the content areas.

DEVELOPING SKILL IN ORAL READING.

1. The pupils read orally sentences or longer selections to prove a point or answer a question.

2. Pupils read orally papers written by them.

3. Pupils read orally material that furnished information on the topic being studied.

4. Pupils took part in puppet shows that aided in learning in the content areas.

5. Pupils read a selection in a book which gives information in the content areas.

CULTIVATING INTERESTS IN READING. Miss Leamington made use of many of the suggestions for interesting children in worthwhile reading that are listed in Chapter 11A and Chapter 11B. Any of the suggestions given in those chapters can be followed in a classroom in which no time is set aside for a reading class.

HELPING THE RETARDED READER. Miss Leamington was able to help retarded readers in a number of ways without having a regular reading period daily. She helped them by adapting the instruction in the various content fields to their level of reading. In the social studies and science she at times rewrote very simply the textbook material and supplied this version to the poorer readers, who read it while the others worked with the textbook. At times she gave them written questions to answer, and at other times she asked them questions orally that were answered in their simplified version of the textbook writing.

FOR FURTHER STUDY

De Boer, John J., and Gertrude Whipple, "Reading Development in Other Curriculum Areas," *Development in and Through Reading*, pp. 54–76. Sixtieth Yearbook of the National Society for the Study of Education. Chicago: The University of Chicago Press, 1961.

Fay, Leo, Thomas D. Horn, and Constance McCullough, *Improving Reading in the Elementary Social Studies*. Washington, D.C.: The National Council for the Social Studies, 1961.

Harris, Albert J., *Effective Teaching of Reading*, pp. 94–117. New York: David McKay Company, Inc., 1962.

Huus, Helen, *Children's Books to Enrich the Social Studies*. Washington, D.C.: The National Council for the Social Studies, 1961.

Reading, Grades 7, 8, and 9: A Teacher's Guide to Curriculum Planning. New York: Board of Education of the City of New York, 1959.

Spache, George D., "Types and Purposes of Reading in Various Curriculum Fields." *The Reading Teacher*, 11 (February 1958), 158–164.

Whipple, Gertrude, "Principles for the Selection and Use of Reading Materials in Content Areas," *Materials for Reading*, pp. 104–108. Supplementary Educational Monographs, No. 86. Chicago: The University of Chicago Press, 1957.

Witty, Paul, and Margaret Ratz, *A Developmental Reading Program for Grades 6 Through 9*. Chicago: Science Research Associates, Inc., 1956.

16

The School-wide Program
in Reading

An effective program of reading instruction in the school calls for aggressive leadership and careful over-all planning. In this chapter we shall consider (1) what conditions are essential to a strong reading program; (2) what steps are needed for the development of the school-wide program; and (3) in what ways the program may be interpreted to parents. Much of what we shall say in this chapter will be a summary and review of principles discussed earlier in this book.

The Conditions Needed for an Effective Program

The teaching of reading is not carried on in a vacuum. Effective reading instruction calls for a school environment favorable to learning, to growth, to solid achievement. Teachers can do much to create the conditions which are needed for helping children to read. The following are some of these conditions:

1. *The physical surroundings should be suitable.* While it is true that some children learn to read under the most unfavorable physical conditions, if we are to get the best results with the huge numbers of children who come to us for reading instruction, we must provide schoolrooms that are light, comfortable, and colorful. The furniture should include comfortable seats, movable desks adjustable to the physical requirements of the children, a display table for books, many open shelves along the walls, and a reading corner with a table, a lamp, and an easy chair or two. Colors in the room should be bright and cheerful. Plants in the windows; bulletin boards with constantly changing ex-

hibits of pictures, announcements, information about the date, recent incidents affecting children in the room, and other subjects of interest to pupils; objects brought by teacher or pupils for reading and discussion—all these, and many other "conversation pieces" that may stimulate reading and discussion, should be a part of the elementary school classroom. Records, films, filmstrips, and other audio-visual aids should be readily available when the occasion calls for them.

2. *The children should be surrounded with an abundance of attractive reading materials.* Children's books, tastefully arranged, representing a wide range of reading difficulty and a great diversity of interests should be found on the shelves and on the tables in all classrooms. Suitable magazines, pamphlets, and pictorial matter should be displayed on racks or deposited in files to which teacher and pupils have easy access.

3. *A well-equipped and well-managed central library is essential to the school-wide reading program.* The library should have the latest reference books, an up-to-date card index, vertical files, a wide variety of children's magazines, and an abundance of books, including the great children's classics and books on hobbies, adventure, humor, science, history, biography, and fiction. The library should be the center of the "cultural" activities of the school. It should display paintings, sculpture, and other art objects which may be acquired by the school through loan or purchase. Science materials of various kinds may be exhibited here. It should, if possible, have two or more small conference rooms for pupils' committee work. It should have a librarian's office and workroom, and a storage room for back issues of magazines and other materials. It should be the repository for the visual aids to be made available to all classes in the school. Moreover, the library should be large enough to accommodate not only a whole class which may come for one or more periods during the week for browsing or for special assignments, but also small groups and individual pupils who are doing research in connection with classroom projects. Arrangements should be made for systematic use of library facilities by whole classes, and individual pupils should be encouraged to make frequent use of the library. Its use should not be reserved as a "privilege" for the bright or the "best-behaved" pupils.

4. *Reading problems should receive attention in all of the content subjects.* The teaching of reading should not be confined to a single period in the school day. The special problems of reading in arithmetic, history, geography, science, and other subjects should be dealt with at the time these subjects are studied. The special vocabularies of the various fields of study require careful, patient instruction. Not only the new words, but also the familiar words that have new meanings for the pupil require particular attention.

It is a common mistake, especially among inexperienced teachers, to assume that children know words which are familiar to most adults. The following are a few examples of words which are quite new to many young children (familiarity with these words will depend in part upon the kind of environment in which the children live):

GEOGRAPHY

cod	mines	currency	belt
copper	caravan	traffic	continent
grain	llama	occupation	region
deposit	rye	race	sphere
granite	seal	combine	zone
acre	whale	tractor	altitude
agriculture	manufacture	market	
irrigation	docks	cattle	
commerce	factories	ranch	

HISTORY

territory	election	legislature	import
veto	nominate	naturalization	blockade
treaty	convention	federal	embargo
population	persecution	declaration	domestic
frontier	enforce	petition	seizure
constitution	enemy	international	military
session	siege	surrender	naval
witness	revolution	testimony	alien
representative	intolerance	treason	repeal

ARITHMETIC

number	borrow	carry	decimal point
plus	quotient	numerator	times
minus	remainder	denominator	difference
product	fraction	reduce	
sum	total	column	

These are but a few examples of the specialized vocabularies that need to be taught directly in the content subjects. Fuller lists of the technical terms that are essential in elementary school instruction have been derived from careful research.[1]

Special problems of comprehension are presented by verbal problems in arithmetic. Since children's early experiences with reading usually involve stories, young readers will have a tendency to employ the techniques appropriate to narrative when they first encounter these verbal problems. If they are good readers, they read stories by phrases, move rapidly over nonessential details, and focus on the sequence of events. The verbal problem in arithmetic presents a quite different situation. Here the reader must note every word

---

[1] Luella Cole, *The Teachers' Word Book of Technical Vocabulary*. Bloomington, Ill.: The Public School Publishing Company, 1936.

carefully and may need to return again and again to a key word or number necessary to the solution. He may need to read a single sentence two or three or more times in order to understand the situation described. The pupil must learn how to classify in his mind the facts that are given and to define clearly to himself the task which has been set. He must give close attention to those minute differences in words which are so important in arriving at correct answers—for example, *some* versus *same, four* versus *for.*

The techniques of teaching reading in the arithmetic class will therefore differ from those used elsewhere. Arithmetic problems are usually stated in relatively few words, each one of them significant. Speed and regularity of eye movements are irrelevant in the reading of problems. Regressions are not only desirable, but for most children essential. Children need to be taught to read arithmetic problems slowly, to look for the pattern into which the facts will fall, and to reread as often as is necessary to understand the problem and to find the clues to its solution.

In other subjects the problem of *wide* reading assumes greater importance. In the social studies, for example, the development of a wide background of vicarious experience through reading is essential to the growth of understanding. Such reading involves many skills which may often be best developed in connection with social studies instruction. The ability to locate information in reference sources, to find books that deal with topics of interest to the reader, to read with reasonable speed (usually to read more rapidly silently than orally), and to adapt the speed to the nature of the material read are skills developed in the reading class and reinforced in the social studies, science, and other content subjects.

General principles of reading instruction which have been discussed in this book apply equally to the reading period and the subject fields. Thus, for example, the exclusive use of a single history textbook in a class of pupils who range from first to eighth grade in reading ability not only violates the principle of individual differences but also contributes to the development of bad reading habits in fast and slow readers alike. Moreover, the principle that an adequate experience background is essential to comprehension in reading applies with special force to the social studies and science. The use of the field trip, real objects, demonstrations, and especially audio-visual aids is essential to efficient reading in these fields of study.

The correlations between general reading ability as measured by standardized tests and ability to read materials in specialized fields have usually been low. We are faced with the fact, therefore, that the teaching of reading is an all-day job. Any plans for a school-wide attack on the reading problem must include a serious consideration of reading in the content fields. Habits of reading, good or bad, are formed wherever and whenever reading takes place. As long as our schools remain primarily "reading schools," we must regard reading as in a sense the core of the entire curriculum.

5. *The morale of the teaching staff should be high.* No school-wide program of reading improvement can be really successful if it does not enjoy the enthusiastic support of the entire teaching staff. For this reason every effort should be made to provide the conditions under which high morale may flourish. This book is not the place to discuss in minute detail the factors contributing to staff morale. These factors are complex and often elusive. Good salary levels, job security, pension funds, reasonable teacher load—all of these are essential, but by themselves they will not guarantee good morale. Strong administrative leadership coupled with sincere adherence to the democratic process on the part of everyone, respect for each other's opinions, and sympathetic concern for each other's problems are likewise important elements in the building of morale. Good communication, too, is necessary. Facts regarding the general reading situation in the school should be disseminated among the staff. In-service training of teachers by providing time, opportunity, and encouragement to study the reading problem is not the least of the factors needed to mobilize the professional resources of the school for the improvement of reading.

6. *The classroom climate should be conducive to pleasant learning experiences.* Many of the factors that contribute to good school morale are also needed in the creation of a classroom climate favorable to efficient learning. Strong teacher leadership combined with a high degree of pupil participation in decision making, a sympathetic interest in the individual needs of pupils, and an atmosphere of encouragement to explore, to question, and to discuss are needed to stimulate maximum effort on the part of pupils. In such a climate, children feel accepted. Rivalry and competition are kept on a friendly basis. Humor and spontaneous laughter are familiar experiences in each day's activities.

The nature and organization of the curriculum, too, may vitally affect the learning climate of the classroom. If there is an abundance of purposeful activities, related to problems of genuine interest to children, reading also is likely to be zestful and purposeful. Thus one fourth-grade class in New York City worked on a unit about the Statue of Liberty. This is how the children reported their experiences:

> Last Friday, Jack brought a picture of the Statue of Liberty to school. He put it on the bulletin board. Children started to ask questions. We wrote them on the blackboard. Jack told us where the statue is, but there were lots of questions we could not answer.
>
> We got our answers in many ways. Joe told us what his mother had said. Mary brought us The Guide to New York City. The pictures were good, but the words were hard. Miss Miller read parts to us. Mack went to the library and got books about the statue. Sam brought us a statue that was a paper weight, too. We all said, "Why can't we go and see the statue?"
>
> It took us several days to plan our trip. Then the day came. We rode on the subway to South Ferry. We got on a steamer called "Miss Liberty." We

stayed on the deck and watched the harbor. Karl said he wished he had two pairs of eyes so he could see more.

We got to Bedloe's Island at lunch time. We ate in the cafeteria. Jane took pictures of us looking at the statue. We walked all the way up the stairs.

When we got back to school, children asked about our trip. We decided to tell Classes 4-1 and 4-3 about it. We made slides to use with our talks. We made pictures and put them on the bulletin board outside our room. Each of us made a booklet. Other classes liked our booklets.

All of us are proud of the Statue of Liberty. We are glad we went to visit the statue.[2]

In the teacher's analysis of the activities involved in the trip, she included the following category:

Obtain information from books and audio-visual aids.

> Using index and table of contents
> Reading for information
> Interpreting pictures
> Gathering data
> Evaluating data

It was clear that the setting for meaningful and enthusiastic reading was made possible by a curriculum organization based upon strong pupil interests and purposes. Under such an organization specific reading skills are taught both in connection with their immediate functional use and, when necessary, in separate periods of direct instruction in the skills. When the school day consists of a series of relatively meaningless drills, the desired abilities are not likely to become automatic with the child. We must teach for carryover, but when the learning can be direct we may expect more and better results.

For younger children especially, the curriculum should provide rapid alternation of various types of activities. We cannot expect to achieve maximum growth in most primary grade children if we compel them to concentrate for long periods of time on one type of activity, such as doing exercises in workbooks or reading orally from the basal reader. Class work should be constantly varied: unit activities (such as those described in the Statue of Liberty project) should be swiftly followed by drawing, modeling, singing, dancing, playing games, or learning number combinations. Expert teachers sense quickly when it is time to change and they know how to make the transition smoothly. They know also how to achieve a wholesome balance of activities and learnings in the course of a day or week. And by relating the reading experiences skillfully to the fascinating variety of school activities, they lay the foundation for keen and enduring interests in reading.

---

[2] From *Curriculum Development in the Elementary Schools*, pp. 78–79. New York: Board of Education of the City of New York, 1955. Reprinted by permission of the Board of Education of the City of New York.

The way in which the children are grouped in the classroom has much to do with classroom climate. A plan of flexible grouping, described earlier in this book, is less likely to lead to hostilities and frustrations than a rigid one. It has been suggested that groups should be known by the names of their leaders, rather than by such designations as "The Bluebirds" or "The Bunnies," and that leaders should be changed often. Every child has the right to feel wanted and needed in the group in which he works.

Basically, however, the classroom climate depends upon the relations between the teacher and the class, and among the children themselves. The moods and attitudes of the teacher are quickly communicated to the children. If the teacher seems to regard her job chiefly as one of discovering the children's failures and shortcomings, the children soon come to see their own role as one of outwitting her and of doing as little work as possible. If the teacher thinks of her responsibility as one of stimulating and challenging the children, they are likely to take a positive attitude toward the work. They will find pleasure in it, and they will learn more because they enjoy what they are doing. Thus a teacher who calls on a pupil to read a paragraph aloud and then asks the class to point out the mistakes he made, is likely to produce little else than embarrassment in both the pupil and the rest of the class. A teacher who says to the class, "Let's find as many colorful words in this passage as we can," and asks a child to write them on the board as the words are called, is inviting her pupils to an exciting hunt.

The children should have the feeling that the teacher likes them, often in spite of their eccentricities and their deviation from the cultural norm. As one writer has put it,

> We need to consider . . . how the teacher sets the classroom climate for understanding differences. She herself must be a person who is not shocked or disturbed by unconventional ways of doing things—by family arrangements necessitated by meager income, poor housing, inadequate training in the use of leisure. Children must be free enough to reveal what they do and feel and think with her. She must have skill and tact to set the stage so that children talk freely with each other. . . .[3]

Steps in Planning a School-wide Program

The initiative in undertaking a school-wide program of reading instruction may come from any one or more of many sources. Sometimes a series of newspaper articles or a critical book may focus attention on the problem and hence lead to thoughtful re-examination of current practices in reading instruction. Sometimes an enthusiastic administrator, or a teacher freshly returned from a

---

[3] Margaret Heaton, "Reading to Understand Human Differences," *Elementary English* (February 1950), 83.

semester of professional study, sparks the program. Frequently a study will emerge from faculty discussions of a commonly felt need. Whatever its impetus, the program can be successfully undertaken only if a large proportion of the teaching staff sees the need for it and volunteers to participate in it.

Preparatory Steps

The introduction of a systematic school-wide program in reading calls for careful advance preparation and a continuous program of in-service training of teachers. A good example of such preparation may be found in the program inaugurated in the schools of Madison, Wisconsin.[4] While this plan was designed for a city school system, it can readily be adapted to the needs of single schools.

In Madison, a Curriculum Planning Council, consisting of one representative from each school, informally interviews teachers about their reading problems and receives suggestions from them for new curriculum practices. On the basis of these and other suggestions the council constructs a check list of items relating to such topics as public relations, teaching aids, guidance for the gifted and the retarded child, audio-visual materials, use of community resources, unit outlines, and various types of subject matter. The check lists are then distributed among all the teachers, who are invited to check those activities in which they would like to participate or those problems which they would like to select for special study. The responses from the teachers are then compiled and committees organized in preparation for group work. Meetings of the teacher committees are usually confined to the winter months, beginning in January. While in some schools teachers are released for group work, most meetings are held after school and in the evening.

The work of the committees and subcommittees varies. A committee may study published research, observe classes, interview parents or pupils, compile booklists, or conduct other kinds of investigations. Consultant service is sought from specialists in the system or from the state university. The Madison committees have produced an abundance of professional materials that testify to the productivity of these groups. The resultant changes in teaching practice are the outcome of the teachers' own thinking and work. But perhaps the greatest value of the committees consists in the satisfactions each individual derives from getting acquainted with teachers from other schools, attacking common problems together, recognizing the practical values of research, and noting improvement in the results of teaching.

The kind of curriculum planning described by Miss Leary calls for the

[4] Bernice E. Leary, "Supervisory Techniques in Improving Reading," *Keeping Reading Programs Abreast of the Times,* p. 218. Supplementary Educational Monographs, No. 72. Chicago: The University of Chicago Press, 1950.

expenditure of much additional effort and time over and above that required for the teacher's regular duties. Even to a dedicated and enthusiastic teacher it can be a considerable burden. Moreover, not all schools and school systems offer such attractive and stimulating conditions of work as those found in Madison. Most teachers have heavy teaching loads and a multiplicity of duties which cause a drain upon their nervous energies. For this reason, every effort should be made to provide teacher planning committees with adequate clerical assistance and to make available to at least one member of a planning committee some "free" time for directing and carrying forward the committee activities.

Determining the Reading Status of Pupils

"How are we doing?" is the first question to ask when we plan the school-wide program. We need to know whether our present program is getting results, whether our achievements are above or below national norms, and, especially, what our special strengths and weaknesses are. Teachers know that many of their pupils do not read as well as they should, but they will find it helpful to have specific information as to the range of pupils' reading abilities and the degree of reading retardation that exists in their schools. The first step in a general reading program, therefore, is a careful study of the existing situation with respect to pupils' reading.

Although standardized reading tests have definite limitations and should never be regarded as infallible barometers of reading ability, they are useful indicators of the presence or absence of important reading skills. They are especially valuable as general screening and classification devices and as measures of the over-all effectiveness of the reading program. They are one important means of determining the reading status of large groups of pupils.

When the testing program is designed to reveal whether a school or school system rates high or low in comparison with national averages, it is not necessary to test every pupil. It is sufficient to administer standardized reading tests to a carefully selected sample of the pupils. Thus a relatively small sample, including an equal number of boys and girls and embracing a typical range of both chronological age and mental age, is likely to reflect the situation with respect to the group as a whole. Of course, a large sample is likely to inspire more confidence among teachers and the general public; if any number less than the entire group is tested, it is of the greatest importance that the sample be truly representative.

When the data yielded by the testing program have been compiled, they should be presented to all teachers and their significance interpreted. Graphs and charts may be used to excellent advantage in this process.

The standardized tests reveal what pupils can do in a test situation. Of equal importance are the extent and quality of the voluntary reading activities of the pupils. Reading ability is of no value unless it is used. For this reason, a survey of reading attainments in a school or school system should include a study of the cumulative reading records kept by pupils of their personal, voluntary reading. Such a study does not lend itself so readily to statistical summary and analysis as data from standardized tests do, but it is no less important. In the interpretation of the records, the *nature* of pupils' choices should be given as much consideration as the number of books read.

Since so much of contemporary reading is done in the mass media, the preliminary survey should include an inquiry into the newspaper and magazine reading habits of children; indeed, perhaps the best index of the success of the reading program is the extent and quality of young people's reading in these two sources. The inquiry should deal not only with the amount of time spent in a day or week in the reading of newspapers and magazines, but especially with the pupils' preferences among the various features, and the range of their interests.

Providing Basal Reading Instruction

Having obtained the necessary background information, the staff is now ready to plan its over-all strategy. First it must decide whether special classes in basal reading instruction will be needed. While some teachers believe that reading instruction can best be carried on in connection with other learning experiences, chiefly on an incidental basis, the great majority of American schools provide for systematic reading instruction, in scheduled periods, employing basal readers designed for such instruction. Systematic instruction in basal reading skills does not, of course, preclude incidental instruction during a school day.

While it is true that some children learn to read well without any systematic instruction, acquiring all needed skills through abundant and highly motivated reading, the vast majority of children need instructional assistance if they are to learn to read at their best. The regularly scheduled reading period and the basal reader will continue to be indispensable for most teachers and with most children if essential skills are to be developed. Extensive reading may be sufficient for bright children under the guidance of skillful teachers, and it is likely to produce rapid readers, readers who readily grasp the total meaning of a passage. For most pupils, however, it should be supplemented with intensive instruction for the continuous development of increasingly difficult skills such as word recognition, comprehension of sentence meaning, and following directions.

Certain general cautions should be observed in the planning of the basal reading program. These cautions grow out of facts and principles developed earlier in this book. For example, reliance should not be placed upon a single basal reader for the whole class; indeed, it should not be placed upon an entire single series. In any given class, basal readers designed for many levels of reading ability and containing many different kinds of material should be provided. Basal readers should not be labeled according to grade level of difficulty, although the publisher's estimate of difficulty level may be indicated by some code device. All basal readers should be amply supplemented with general reading materials on many subjects and representing many levels of reading difficulty. In the primary grades every effort should be put forth to make the initial experiences with books pleasurable and rewarding. In the intermediate grades, the teacher should try to relate specific reading skills to the reading situations arising in the various curricular areas. The reading in basal readers should be accompanied by reading activities in other textbooks calling for similar skills, such as locating information, summarizing a paragraph, or using the dictionary. Basal readers should not be used for mere oral drill, in smaller or larger groups, in which everyone marks time while one pupil struggles through a passage. Pupils who are able to complete the material in the basal readers rapidly and without instructional assistance should be permitted to go on to more difficult materials. Basal readers, while building skills in word recognition, finding information, organizing ideas, applying what is learned to problems and questions discussed by the group, and similar abilities, should offer satisfaction and pleasure to the boys and girls using them.

Setting Developmental Goals in the Content Subjects

While the foundation of reading ability for most children is laid in the "reading" class, the progressive development of this ability must take place chiefly in the study of the special subjects and in free, personal reading. Teachers can give guidance and encouragement to pupils who encounter reading difficulties in the specialized materials in the subject areas. They can and they should set up clearcut goals for the development of specific skills called for in the content areas. Dealing with specialized vocabularies, reading charts and graphs, analyzing verbal problems in arithmetic and science, looking for crucial details in technical explanations, noting the organization of paragraphs, slowing down to read the more difficult passages, carrying on supplementary research in the library, building background through extensive easy reading in such magazines as *Popular Science* and *Popular Mechanics*—these and other special skills can be cultivated by the teacher who is alert to reading problems in the content fields.

Teachers of the content subjects, especially those working in a departmental organization, often hesitate to give attention to reading problems because they feel unprepared to deal with them. Sometimes they will rationalize their neglect of the reading needs of children by pleading that they lack time to do more than communicate the necessary subject matter. It is of course quite true that specific training in the teaching of reading is highly desirable. However, any competent teacher who is thoroughly familiar with her subject can, if she wishes, learn a great deal about the reading problems children encounter in the content areas and about ways of helping them. As to the additional time required, no more effective way of "communicating subject matter" could be conceived than to promote in the learner the habits and skills needed for efficient reading in the special subject areas.

Establishing Relations with the School and Public Libraries

Essential to any well-planned school-wide reading program is a well-functioning, well-coordinated central library. Good room collections are useful in supplementing the basal reading program, but they cannot fully meet the demands created by the endlessly varying interests of young people. School administrators should so far as possible resist the temptation, in times of rapidly increasing enrollments and shortage of space, of converting library rooms into classrooms. The library is an educational essential, not a luxury.

Helpful also is a friendly working relationship with the local public library. Representatives of the public library may be invited to visit classes, to explain the workings of the public library, and to encourage children to take out library cards. Teachers may take their classes on excursions to the public library. In some communities teachers inform public librarians about the reading abilities of their pupils. On the basis of this information the librarian often is able to annotate the children's library cards and can thus provide intelligent guidance for each child in the selection of books.

Organizing "Readiness Classes"

Not all children who enter first grade are, as we have seen, "ready to read." When the initial testing program reveals that a considerable number of boys and girls are not as yet likely to succeed in a program of formal reading instruction, it may be desirable to organize one or more "readiness classes," or, as they are sometimes called, "transition units." In such classes many nonreading experiences such as construction activities, rhythm games, art work, listening to records, and especially oral language communication are provided.

Organizing an Ungraded Primary Unit

In many schools the primary school unit is left ungraded. While normally the primary school period extends over three years, in the ungraded unit the child progresses at his own rate and remains in the primary school for as long as he requires to master the initial skills of reading or for as long as he seems to benefit socially from association with primary school children. There are no "promotions" or "failures." Tasks set for children will be commensurate with their abilities, not dictated by arbitrary grade standards. In large schools or school systems it is possible to follow a dual plan, in which some children are assigned to ungraded units, while others enter conventional graded classes.

Organizing Remedial Classes

Even under ideal conditions, in which differentiated instruction in reading is given in regular classes, some pupils will be so severely retarded that they will require special help in separate classes. The classrooms in which remedial instruction is carried on should be attractive, well lighted, and colorful, and equipped with tables, bookshelves, magazine and newspaper racks, a motion picture screen and opaque curtains, a reading corner, radio or television or both, a phonograph, files, and storage cases. The walls and chalkboard should be done in bright colors. There should be ample bulletin-board space. Newly constructed buildings should generally include rooms especially equipped for remedial reading instruction. Rooms in old school buildings have frequently been remodeled and redecorated at moderate cost.

Assignment of pupils to remedial classes will present problems. At what point on the scale should pupils be classified as "remedial"? Should superior pupils who are not reading up to their potential capacity be assigned to remedial classes? What type of tests should be used for screening pupils? What adjustments need to be made in the time schedule of the regular classes to allow for the work of the remedial classes? How long should the remedial class periods be? Who should determine what pupils are to be assigned to the special classes and when they are to be returned to regular instruction? How large should remedial classes be?

These and many other questions will occur to the administrator and the teacher who are concerned with the reading problem. The solution of most of them will depend upon local conditions. Generally speaking, the superior pupil who is not reading up to his capacity should not be assigned to a remedial class. He should be given individual attention in regular instruction and provided with new challenges in the form of more difficult reading materials and more demanding classroom tasks. The point on the table of reading scores at which pupils should be assigned to special classes will usually be determined by the number of teachers and classrooms available for remedial work. Quite probably the pupils who fall in the lowest 10th percentile will require the skilled help of the special teacher, regardless of their general learning capacity. When the general achievement of the school population is low, the number may be greater. Screening tests should be of the survey type because the diagnostic type of test is expensive and time consuming. However, diagnostic tests, including one such as the Gray Oral Reading Paragraphs, should be given in the remedial classes to determine specific instructional needs, and in regular classes when reading instruction is planned. Most survey tests include some diagnostic features which will be useful in any reading instruction. In general, remedial class periods should not extend beyond 30 to 45 minutes in length, and the class size should not exceed 15; 10 pupils is probably an ideal number. Assignment to remedial sections should be based on consultation between the classroom teacher and the remedial teacher or principal.

Establishing a Reading Center

In every school system there will be some pupils who do not respond to instructional guidance, either in regular or special classes. In a few cases such lack of progress may be due to extremely low mental ability, but pupils so deficient are rare and will normally be entered in special schools. More commonly the difficulty will stem from some physical, emotional, or other handicap which can be at least partially overcome through expert diagnosis and guidance. The problem is chiefly one of intensive and patient study.

Because most teachers have neither the time nor the specialized training to make such diagnoses or to plan such guidance, expert help is needed. Unfortunately, however, the supply of highly trained personnel is as yet severely limited. Many universities and some hospitals conduct psycho-educational clinics in which help in reading is given. Some governmental agencies, such as the Institute for Juvenile Research in Illinois, provide diagnostic service, but they usually have long waiting lists and are seriously understaffed. Most clinics are obliged to charge a fee. Large school systems generally operate reading centers, but small town and rural schools are lacking in clinical facilities. There is great need for county units to provide the service which the small school cannot give.

The staff of the reading clinic should include, if possible, psychologists, physicians, family visiting teachers, remedial reading teachers, and secretaries, the number of each of these depending on the enrollment in the clinic. The clinic should be equipped with bookshelves, files, audio-visual materials, and such mechanical devices as the staff may require for diagnostic or remedial purposes.

One of the values of the reading center is the opportunity it provides for the in-service training of teachers. Although the nucleus of the center must necessarily be the technically trained clinic staff, the great amount of individual instruction required by children referred to the clinic will call for the aid of a number of qualified teachers. In some cities, teachers are relieved of regular teaching duties in the classroom for a year or two to serve as teaching assistants in the reading center. After their work with severely retarded readers in the center, they return to their classrooms with a better understanding of the problems of retarded readers and with more skill in dealing with reading problems in the classroom. Teachers who have served in reading centers are often qualified to act as reading supervisors and to aid in developing remedial programs in elementary schools.

Interpreting the Reading Program to Parents

The Role of Parents in Reading Instruction

In any school-wide reading program, careful consideration needs to be given to the role of the parent. In the first place, parents have a right to know what the school's objectives in reading are, and why it is using the particular procedures which it has adopted in reading instruction. The intelligence and good judgment of parents should be respected. Most parents who are interested in their children's schooling are perfectly able to understand the principles upon which the school's policies are based when these are clearly explained to them. The school should make clear that it regards the education of children as a team project in which the home and the school have a common interest. It is no accident that in those communities where there has been friendly cooperation and good communication between home and school, the recent unreasonable criticisms of modern reading practices have had least effect.

Moreover, the school very much needs the help of the home in teaching the child to read. Parents can do much in creating a home atmosphere favorable to the development of reading ability. They are often in a better position than teachers to discover children's interests and to perceive the emotional reactions that children have toward the reading situation. By surrounding the young child with good books adapted to his level of ability, by setting the example of silent reading, by reading aloud to him and talking with him about stories and pictures, and in general by making reading an enjoyable experience for him from the earliest years, parents can lay the indispensable foundation for later success in reading.

Most parents, however, do not have the needed training for developing specific reading skills. While they should be kept informed about the changing trends in reading instruction, they should normally leave the formal instruction to the classroom teacher. When children ask questions about words or ideas encountered in the reading, they should of course not hesitate to give needed help. Reading drills, except perhaps occasionally at the request of the teacher, have no place in the home. Reading "games," yes; easy, attractive books for pleasurable reading, yes; but word drills and phonics (except in play) at home, no. The best contribution parents can make to the reading progress of their children is to provide them with a secure and happy home, an abundance of love and encouragement, a great variety of play, creative and constructive experiences, and unlimited opportunity for free reading in good books and magazines. Time to read, encouragement to read, and materials to read are necessary; pressure and a sense of urgency may be dangerous.

The following list of suggestions was given to parents on the basis of questions put to teachers:[5]

1. Give children plenty of experiences—not necessarily complex but meaningful and interesting ones.
2. Maintain a relaxed, comfortable atmosphere at home.
   a. Make the child feel important.
   b. Give him a chance to talk.
   c. Talk with him—not always to him.
3. Be enthusiastic about school. Talk encouragingly about it. Build up an interest.
4. Answer your children's questions. Answers needn't be involved or detailed.
5. Develop a feeling of independence in the child. Praise him often.
6. Encourage your child to participate in games and to play with other children.
7. Interest your child in things in which he should be interested.
8. Teach children the correct names of people and things.
9. Read to the children often. Sing with them and play with them.
10. Encourage children to associate people and places, times and events.
11. Let the children see you reading often. Let them feel that you enjoy it.
12. Provide materials similar to those in school—paste, paper, scissors, paint. . . .
13. Encourage and, if necessary, be forceful in teaching children to follow directions and to pay attention.
14. Show the child that books aren't the only kind of reading. Magazines, packages, letters, road signs, etc., are other sources.
15. Accept and respect your child. You will be proud of him some day. (Most parents are already so!)
16. Be patient. Remember that these little folks have a lot to learn. Make this learning enjoyable.

Concepts of Special Interest to Parents

Parents can be helped to understand a number of important concepts of modern reading instruction. One of these is the concept of readiness, which has been discussed earlier in this book. We know that not all children are ready to begin learning to read at the same chronological age. Since most parents assume that first grade is the time for all children to learn to read, it becomes necessary to explain to them that children vary in their readiness for initial

---

[5] Dolores Elinsky, Mary E. Farrell, and M. Dorothy Penn, "Parents Learn About First-Grade Reading," *The Reading Teacher*, 8 (April 1955), 232–233.

reading instruction. Delay in any of these processes is by no means evidence of backwardness. The important thing to remember is that the first experiences with reading should be happy, successful ones. If for any reason a child is not ready to read with fluency and satisfaction, he should be given the opportunity to develop the needed maturity.

A second concept that frequently needs to be explained to parents is the importance of meaningful reading from the very outset of instruction. Parents are frequently puzzled by the practice of confronting the beginning reader with large units which may even include whole sentences, for they may remember their own instruction which possibly began with the alphabet or with phonograms. While modern schools vary in the type of initial experiences in reading provided for young children, all stress the thought approach from the beginning. This principle can usually be understood and appreciated by parents of children who are impatient to begin "reading." Others may need to be shown through explanation and illustration that the appetite for reading can be whetted more effectively in children by meaningful reading than by the repetition of meaningless sounds.

A third concept concerns the role of oral reading. Modern schools teach children to read orally, and most of them use a certain amount of oral reading in the initial stages of reading instruction. However, they recognize that most reading outside of school is silent, that adult silent reading should usually be at least twice as rapid as oral reading, and that the skills of silent reading differ in important respects from those of oral reading. Schools therefore stress silent reading throughout the grades, giving attention to oral reading as a significant separate skill or using it as an aid in the improvement of silent reading. Parents in whose own recollections school reading is associated with oral communication or sounding of words may be interested in the reasons for the new emphasis. Most of them will be pleased to note the increased use of purposeful oral reading and the decline of oral reading exercises which required the class to mark time while one pupil recited.

Finally, parents should be informed about the more recent techniques of teaching word recognition. A great many parents believe, or have recently been convinced by popular publications, that the chief weakness of modern reading instruction is the neglect of phonics. Such complaints have been heard for a long time. They were especially vigorous in the decade of the '20's, when the importance of silent reading began to be stressed in many quarters. Parents should be assured that phonics instruction is still given in school; that it relies less upon mechanical and memorization methods and more on natural analytic methods; that it is given at strategic times and to pupils who need it; and that it occupies an important place in the total reading program, in the basal readers and in the teachers' manuals. They should also be made to realize, however, that phonics is only one of many helps to the recognition of words. The use of additional methods, involving context clues, general configuration, and syllabication, has strengthened pupils' ability to recognize new words. Parents will be pleased to know that the schools have not stood still in their efforts to teach children the diverse skills of word recognition.

Methods of Communicating with Parents

The best of all the methods of promoting home-school cooperation is the personal interview. In one elementary school, for example, the principal systematically interviews one or both parents of every child entering school for the first time. In the course of his conferences, he tries to discover the viewpoints of the parents and their assessments of their children's needs and capacities, for he believes he has much to learn from parents. At the same time, he explains to the parents the plan of reading instruction followed in the school and the major considerations that led to the adoption of the plan. Since he is able to show that the plan is getting good results in terms of national averages, the great majority of parents are enthusiastic, in spite of the fact that the reading program in the particular school is unconventional.

In other schools, certain days are set aside each year for teacher-parent conferences. On these days all teachers meet individually with parents of pupils in their classes. In these conferences teachers report the progress that the children are making in school and answer parents' questions about the instructional procedures employed. While the method is time consuming, it recognizes the important fact that parents are most intimately concerned with the progress of their children and hence should be both consulted and informed.

Some school systems, such as that in Seattle, Washington, publish attractively illustrated leaflets, addressed to parents, setting forth the rationale of the reading program in the schools. Parents in many communities are invited, even urged, to visit the schools and to observe the reading program in action. In some schools, as in Grand Island, Nebraska, colored slides illustrating the use of modern reading techniques are shown at PTA meetings and to civic groups. Tape recordings made in the classroom are played at such meetings to demonstrate progress that has been achieved in certain aspects of reading.

In the Fulton Elementary School, in Pittsburgh, an afternoon program is given in the school auditorium each year for the benefit of parents of first-grade children. All first-grade teachers participate. The auditorium stage is arranged like a classroom. A portable chalkboard, colorful posters, a table with a book display, and copies of basal and supplementary readers in use in the school help to make the presentation attractive and realistic. Parents have an opportunity to examine the books in use in the classroom and to go over lists of children's books which they may wish to purchase for the child's home library. The formal program deals with three topics: Reading Readiness, Beginning Reading, and Techniques of Developing Skills.[6]

---

[6] Dolores Elinsky and others, *op. cit.,* pp. 227–228.

Frequently parents can and will take an active part in schoolroom work itself. Mrs. Mildred Borton, a teacher in the Roosevelt School, Kalamazoo, Michigan, has described an interesting project in which the parents of the children participated. The father of one of the children had come to school to tell the second-grade boys and girls about the manufacture of paper, and the children subsequently developed an interest in the kinds of occupations their parents pursued. Each child prepared a brief story of his father's or mother's work, to be placed on a large chart at the front of the room. The children were delighted to read about the great diversity of services represented—the work of the paper makers, the hot-water heater makers, the printers, the switchboard operators, the riveters, the transmission makers, the housekeepers, the truckers, the shoe salesmen, the welders, and the soldiers. With the aid of their parents, the children wrote an illustrated book about the various occupations. Parents came to school—to talk to the children, to advise them about the contents of their book, and to arrange class visits to places of work. Not only the executives came. The driver of the lumber truck found a few minutes to stop by the school and answer questions. These parents could not be aloofly critical of the educational program. They were partners in the enterprise.[7]

Another valuable device for involving parents in the work of the school is the occasional chatty newsletter, written by the teacher especially for the parents of her children. Such a newsletter, as employed by some teachers in Denver, Colorado, can include the names of the children, some information about the teacher herself, references to the principal, clerk, nurse, custodians, and their duties, notes of appreciation for things parents have done for the school, and announcements of PTA meetings. Succeeding newsletters can report plans for various class activities, invite parents to visit the class, request materials for baking, construction, nature study, and the like, and, particularly, explain the educational significance and purpose of the activities.[8]

FOR FURTHER STUDY

Betts, Emmett A., and Ralph C. Preston, "The Role of the Community," *Development in and through Reading*, pp. 92–108. Sixtieth Yearbook of the National Society for the Study of Education, Part I, Nelson B. Henry, ed. Chicago: The University of Chicago Press, 1961.

Causey, Oscar S., ed., *The Reading Teacher's Reader*, pp. 47–168. New York: The Ronald Press Company, 1958.

Gray, William S., "Is Yours an Effective Reading Program?" *University of Kansas Bulletin of Education*, 12 (February 1958), 41–50.

---

7 Mildred Frey Borton, "Parents as Partners," *Elementary English,* 32 (November 1955), 450–454.

8 Mayme A. Sweet and Deane P. Dixon, "Readable Newsletters for Parents of Kindergarten Children," *The Elementary School Journal,* 52 (February 1952), 351–354.

Larrick, Nancy, *A Parent's Guide to Children's Reading*. New York: Doubleday and Company, Inc., 1958.

McKee, Paul, *A Primer for Parents: How Your Child Learns to Read*. Boston: Houghton Mifflin Company, 1957.

Murphy, George, "What Should Be the Objectives of a Schoolwide Developmental Program?" *Improving Reading in the Junior High School*, pp. 47–51. U.S. Department of Health, Education, and Welfare, Bulletin No. 10, 1957.

Robinson, Helen M., ed., *Evaluation of Reading*, pp. 153–185. Supplementary Educational Monographs, No. 88. Chicago: The University of Chicago Press, 1958.

Strang, Ruth, and Dorothy Kendall Bracken, *Making Better Readers*, pp. 157–202. Boston: D. C. Heath and Company, 1957.

17

The Social Uses of Reading

We have attempted in this book to describe the reading process, the ways in which children learn to read, and the procedures which are most effective in cultivating sturdy growth in reading. Although we have emphasized the self-evident importance of reading in any advanced society, especially a democratic society, in this book we have been concerned primarily with the *how*, rather than the *what*.

It would, however, be a mistake to assume that the sole task of the school is to develop proficiency in reading and that it should be indifferent to the uses to which reading is put. Reading does not and cannot occur in a social vacuum. We are still lacking in detailed knowledge about the short-term and long-term effects of reading upon the reader, but both our experience and our observation lead us to a strong belief that reading makes a difference in how we think, feel, and act. Further, we believe that this difference may be greatest in the early years of life.

Beyond the development of reading skill and interest, therefore, schools must be concerned about the total impact of the reading program upon the child as a person and upon his outlook on life. We cannot and should not attempt to control all the diverse influences which a child's encounters with reading outside of school exert upon him. We should, however, be sure that the reading materials made available to him in school will contribute to a balanced and realistic view of the world about him. If the comics and the drug store fiction present a distorted image of that world, we can at least try to provide a corrective in school.

Notwithstanding the growing use of diversified "trade" books in reading programs, the great majority of American children receive their essential training in reading from the reading textbook. The basal reading series are still the "best sellers" among children. It is therefore worthwhile to examine these books from the point of view of the picture of the world which they present.

From a technical point of view, the leading series of basal readers represent an extraordinarily high level of excellence. They are durable, attractively designed, and appealingly illustrated. Their contents are based on extensive research in vocabulary and teaching method. The editors and authors are experienced practitioners in the field of reading instruction. Whatever may be one's philosophy of educational administration, curriculum, and method, one must acknowledge the enormous contribution that these textbooks have made to the successful teaching of reading in the United States.

Because of the wide distribution of these books, they are made available to schools at relatively low cost. But, at the same time, the need for wide distribution of a given book or series of books creates serious problems. It seems difficult for publishers, for example, to avoid the dangers of uniformity and conformity. Uniform sets of books cannot possibly reflect the wide diversity of ethnic groups and social situations found in a country such as ours.

A well-known social psychologist, Otto Klineberg, recently examined fifteen widely used readers for content relating to cultural differences. He reported that the Americans in these readers are almost exclusively blondes. The characters are well-to-do. Their homes with their furnishings are attractive; the children are clean and well-dressed. Father has a new car; the farmer has his own tractor. There are television sets, bicycles, plenty of toys. The kitchen is modern. Father takes the children to the circus, or the entire family on long trips. There is no poverty; everyone can find work, which is not only easy but fun. If there is reference to religion, it is to the Christian religion. Certainly this is a picture of a world that well over a fourth of the children of the nation never knew.[1]

It is not difficult to imagine the effect that such a picture must have on Negro, Jewish, Puerto Rican, Mexican, or Oriental children. In this happy world, in which there is no frustration, no insecurity, no anger, no ugliness, no unpleasant work, no unemployment or poverty, many a child must ask himself, "But where do I fit in? Do I belong to this world?" In any case, children are left with a distorted impression of the nature of the society in which they are growing up.

It is not suggested that reading materials for children should be depressing. There would, however, seem to be no good reason why the content of readers should not include appreciative and favorable reference to people of many

---

[1] Klineberg's findings are reported in his article in the *Saturday Review*, February 16, 1963, p. 75 ff.

races, religions, occupations, nationalities, and socio-economic backgrounds. The first grade is not too early to introduce the idea of brotherhood and of friendly cooperation of many different kinds of people.

If the basal readers present a bland and essentially unrealistic portrait of the world of reality, can we not turn to the general trade books, so important in all modern reading programs, to secure more representative descriptions? Admittedly general reading, if extensive enough, will cover a wider canvas of personality, emotion, action, and scene than can be accommodated in any basal reader. However, general reading materials for children of elementary school age which give attention to the diverse nature of the American people are relatively rare. Shepard, for example, made a content analysis of sixteen popular books for children, including works by Louisa Alcott, John R. Tunis, Kate Seredy, Lois Lenski, and E. B. White. He reported:

> And what are the characters like in these books? In summary, heroes and heroines tend to be clean, white, healthy, handsome, Protestant Christian, middleclass people. Villains much more often turn out to be ugly, physically undesirable persons of non-Caucasian races, often either poor or of the wealthy classes.

Shepard asks the question, "Are we moving toward a carefully controlled environment for children in their schools and libraries that is upsettingly different from the truth of the city street?"[2]

There is no implication, of course, that these sixteen books are not highly desirable reading or that they are necessarily typical of all the books available to children in school and library. *Reading Ladders,* for example, lists numerous titles relating to pattern of family life, community contrasts, economic differences, differences between generations, adjustment to new places and situations, how it feels to grow up, belonging to groups, and experiences of acceptance and rejection.[3] Moreover, among the more than 10,000 new books for children which have appeared in the last decade are an increasing number which deal with intercultural themes. Our difficulty still is that most such books which deal with children of different cultures are concerned with life in foreign countries. Certainly we need such books, but more authors should be encouraged to deal with the cultural differences in the environments in which our children live, in somewhat the same way that John R. Tunis has dealt with them in his books for adolescents.

Promising efforts are being made to create suitable materials for culturally "deprived" children. Recently the Ford Foundation has financed programs in ten large cities, under the title Great Cities Gray Areas School Improvement

---

2 John P. Shepard, "The Treatment of Characters in Popular Children's Fiction," *Elementary English,* 39 (November 1962), 672–676.

3 Margaret M. Heaton and Helen B. Lewis, *Reading Ladders for Human Relations,* rev. ed. Washington, D.C.: American Council on Education, 1954. A new edition is in preparation.

Program. Similar projects related to reading are found in the Higher Horizons Program in New York and the Banneker Program in St. Louis.[4] In describing standards for the preprimers developed in the Detroit Great Cities project, Whipple pointed out:

> The characters in the stories should represent different races because we live in an interracial society. It is not realistic to present all-white settings even in a first preprimer. Gradually a variety of races should be presented so that all pupils may see characters with whom they can identify.
>
> Negroes in text and illustration should be shown in just as favorable a light as white people are in current reading series. Implications of inequality of any race are harmful. Because children associate themselves with the characters in the stories they read, such implications may predispose Negro children to a sense of inferiority and white children to a sense of superiority.[5]

Although the problems of society loom larger in the reading of secondary than of elementary school pupils, teachers at all levels must have a sense of urgency about the development of habits of serious reading on the part of the general public. Many of the facts contained in the reading of intermediate grade pupils are of vital significance to the adult, but all too often they are taught in isolation from the great issues that confront mankind.

For example, in the days before World War I, geography was largely a matter of memorizing place names. The significance of the names and locations was not pointed out because at that time most of them *had* little significance to us. Today Iraq is important, as are Israel, Egypt, the Congo, South Africa, Viet Nam, Kashmir, and all the Latin American countries. It has suddenly become imperative that American children and youth be made vividly aware of the rest of the world and how it looks at the United States. Since the world has become one great interdependent community, our intellectual vision must extend to the remotest regions, our sympathies must encompass all peoples, our vicarious experiences must have their settings in all kinds of cultures. Not only are all people kin to each other, but they are now all near neighbors.

Intelligent reading for the citizen of today requires an understanding of the forces that in one or two generations have changed the face of the earth. The awakening of the backward nations, with their starving populations, the decline and near-disappearance of colonialism, the growth of Communist power in many parts of the world, and the growth of neutralism among the uncommitted nations are factors to be understood if news and commentary in

---

4 Samuel A. Kirk, "Reading Problems of Slow Learners," *The Under-achiever in Reading.* Compiled and edited by H. Alan Robinson. Supplementary Educational Monographs No. 92. Chicago: The University of Chicago Press, 1962. The Higher Horizons Program is described and evaluated in Frank Riessman, *The Culturally Deprived Child*, pp. 38–111. New York: Harper and Row, Publishers, 1962.

5 Gertrude Whipple, *The Under-achiever in Reading, op. cit.,* p. 135.

newspapers and magazines are to be intelligible. And along with this understanding must come a keener realization of the dangers of modern war, made
infinitely more destructive by the "knowledge explosion" of the last two dec-
ades. Our century has already dwarfed all the thousands of years of previous
history in its capacity for the destruction of human life and the creation of
human misery. The recent history of mankind has been called a history of
deepening horror. Not only the leaders, but all reasonable men need knowledge and a sense of moral responsibility to halt our swift descent toward anni-
hilation. Informed discussion, made possible through wide reading, can help
to provide these.

At this point it is pertinent to inquire to what extent the general population
is able to read and thus to inform itself about issues. Illiteracy in the old sense
of not being able to read or write one's own name has all but disappeared in this
country. *Functional* illiteracy is a different matter. By functional illiteracy we
mean the inability to read with reasonable comprehension those materials which
are intended for the general public—popular magazines and nonfiction, for
example. Gray[6] defines functional literacy as the ability to engage in all those
reading activities essential to the welfare of all citizens in a culture. "Further
study," he writes, "led to the tentative conclusion that the minimum ability in
reading needed by adults was the equivalent of that possessed on the average by
pupils who had completed the fourth grade." Accordingly, "persons completing
fewer than five years of schooling were called functionally illiterate." This
statement is indeed an advanced formulation of the concept of literacy. Today,
however, we cannot settle for less. According to the standard suggested by the
Census report cited by Gray, 11 percent of the adults in this country are functionally illiterate, but the *average* reading ability of adults is about equal to the
average ability of pupils in the early part of the ninth grade. The percent of
functional illiteracy varies from 3.0 percent in some states to 28.7 in others.

Not all the complexities of the reading problem today arise from political
and social change. Ours is an age of science, of medical advances, of automation,
of greatly expanded interests in music and the arts. In any issue of the Sunday
New York Times, one can find terms from the fields of finance and investment,
medicine, theater, ballet, opera, movies, and literature. In science, many of the
terms relate to antibiotics, atomic energy, electronics, photosynthesis, immuniza-
tion, astronomy, space travel, and entomology. While it is probably true that
the *Times* addresses itself to an audience above average in intelligence, it is
designed for the general, nonspecialist reader. Intelligent reading of the news
in these areas whether in newspapers, magazines, or books, whether factual or
interpretive, is a challenge today.

---

6 William S. Gray, "How Well Do Adults Read?" *Adult Readings.* Fifty-fifth Yearbook
of the National Society for the Study of Education, Part II, p. 36. Edited by Nelson B. Henry.
Chicago: The University of Chicago Press, 1956.

How much does our nation read? Roughly one half of our adult population read no books. About 25 percent read from one to nine books per year, and another 18 percent read ten or more books per year. Seven percent of our vast population read 50 or more books per year.[7] These figures do not, of course, provide any information as to the quality of the books read. Apparently most of the books read by people in all categories are fiction, either good, bad, indifferent, or all three.

The output of books in this country is great enough to satisfy all needs and all tastes. In 1961, for example, 14,238 new titles were published, including 1,626 for children. Well over 300 million hardbound and about 500 million paperbound books are sold in a single year. The sale of inexpensive paperbound books has been skyrocketing and continues to increase. While it is true that many of these books may be described as trash, it is also true that through this medium many of the world's greatest classics have become available to the average reader for the first time.

Another significant development in the United States has been the increase in pamphleteering. Since the days of Tom Paine, whose *Common Sense* and *The Crisis* are credited with having contributed measurably to the success of the American Revolution, pamphlets have been a favorite means of shaping public opinion. Religious organizations, labor groups, business associations, political parties, government agencies, voluntary organizations, and individuals disseminate their views by means of pamphlets, leaflets, bulletins, reports, "flyers," and "newsletters." Although it is impossible to estimate the precise number of such publications in circulation today, it is reported that in one year alone 402.3 million pamphlets were published. They are perhaps one of the most characteristic of the efforts of a free society to keep the channels of communication open.

We know also that newspapers and magazines are widely read by the American people. Except for the Depression years, the reading of these publications has rapidly increased since 1910. Two hundred seventy magazines, with a combined circulation of 190 million copies per issue, are published in this country today. Among the 40 leading magazines, *Reader's Digest* reports a circulation of over 13 million, and *Motion Picture* Magazine, the smallest of this group, reports over one million. There are at the present time 1,761 daily newspapers in the United States, with a total circulation of nearly 60 million, and 558 Sunday newspapers, with a total circulation of nearly 50 million. The total circulation of weekly newspapers is about 23 million. The fact that the number of newspapers increased at the rate of the population increase between 1850 and 1880, while they increased 500 percent as compared with an 80 percent population increase between 1880 and 1910, the period of the early growth

---

[7] *Public Use of the Library*. Ann Arbor: Survey Research Center, University of Michigan, pp. 1–14.

of the public school movement, may suggest that schools and adult readership are closely related.

It is clear that functional literacy is on the increase. But literacy is not enough. Our great task is the development of taste and discrimination, not only in the selection of reading materials, but also in the critical evaluation of what is read. Never before has popular enlightenment been so essential to the welfare of our own country and of the world. Teachers of reading thus have the twofold task of raising the cultural level of a people and of creating the widespread understanding needed to make that culture viable in an age of unexampled peril. To accomplish this task, they must themselves be well-read, critically minded participants in the social scene.

Index

Abilities, reading, cultivating growth in, 39–347
 public interest in, 5
Age of Communication, 3
Allerton House Conference on Education, 4
Almy, Millie C., 38, 81
American Association for Gifted Children, 341
American Association of School Librarians, 283
American Educational Research Association, 6
American Library Association, 283, 284, 285, 291
Ames, Maurice U., 13
Anderson, Irving H., 42
Anderson, Robert H., 305
Anecdotal records, use in diagnosing reading difficulties, 312
Arbuthnot, May Hill, 217, 248, 285, 291
Arthur Performance Scale, 46
Artley, A. Sterl, 81, 217, 371
Association for Childhood Education International, 103, 280, 282, 284, 285, 291, 304
Audiometers, 49
Audio-visual aids, 274–278, 283
Auditory discrimination, developing, 68–69
 testing, 53–54
Austin, Mary C., 90, 128

Author's Word List for the Primary Grades, 104
Awards, book, 285–291

Baker, Emily D., 81
Bamman, Henry, 38, 371
Bannon, Laura, 193
Barbe, Walter B., 536–537
Barnhart, Clarence, 92, 201, 220
Bartlett, Mary M., 165, 188
Basal reading textbooks, 363–367
Basic Sight Vocabulary, A, 105, 106
Basic Sight Word Test, 315
Basic Vocabulary of Elementary School Children, A, 104–105
Bazaars, book, 279
Beery, Althea, 128
Beginning reading, program for, 356–362
Behavior, symbolic, reading as, 19–20
Belser, Danylu, 328
Bendick, Jeanne, 13
Benjamin, Dayton, 371
Berner, Elsa R., 284
Bernstein, David, 35
Betts, Emmett A., 42, 48, 49, 81, 128, 169, 401
Blair, Glenn, 42, 194, 346
Block, Irving, 193
Bloomfield, Leonard, 22, 92
Bloomster, Maurine, 85, 114

Blough, Glenn O., 154
Bobbitt, Franklin, 9
Bond, Guy L., 81, 128, 162, 169, 187, 248, 304, 346, 371
Boney, C. DeWitt, 81
Book awards, 285–291
Book discussions, 274
Book fairs, 279
Book reports, 274
Book Week activities, 278
Booklists, 284–291, 328–330, 342–343
Books, children's interests in, 266–268
       choosing, for school libraries, 283–291
       comic, 258–262
       dramatizations of, 274
       finding, in library, 205–206
       handling, increasing skill in, 74
       nonreference, ability to find information in, 199, 217–218
       on human relations, 284
       parts of, 199–200
       picture, 288–291
       pupil selection of, 273–274
       reference (see Reference materials)
Borton, Mildred, 401
Botel, M., 315
Botel Reading Inventory, 315
Bouise, Louise M., 346
Braam, Leonard, 194
Bracken, Dorothy Kendall, 402
Bright children, reading and, 338–346
Brogan, Peggy, 270, 301, 304
Brown, Margaret Wise, 13
Brown, Thomas K., 201
Brownell, William A., 10
Burk, Frederic, 297
Buros, Oscar K., 315
Burrows, Alvina T., 304
Burton, Alice, 371
Burton, William H., 38, 128, 346
Buswell, 84, 171
Butler, Elsie, 62

Caldecott Awards, 287
California Reading Test, 315
California Test of Mental Maturity, Pre-Primary Battery, 46

Campbell, Marjorie, 155
Campion, Nardi Reider, 12
Card catalog, 205–206, 222, 223
Carnegie Corporation, 89
Carroll, Marjorie W., 81
Carter, Homer L. J., 81, 128, 169, 371
Caskey, Helen, 129, 194, 226, 371
Cason, Eloise B., 177–178
Causey, Oscar S., 9, 38, 128, 401
Center, Stella, 5, 33, 121
Chapman, J. C., 315
Chapman-Cook Speed of Reading Test, 315
Charts, experience, 75–81, 129
       use in remedial reading, 334
       reading, 138, 156
       reading readiness, 45
       Snellen Letter, 48
       Snellen Symbol E, 48
Check lists, diagnosing reading difficulties with, 317
Chicago, University of, 5
Child development, reading and, 1–38
Child Study Association Awards, 288
Childcraft, 204, 208, 221, 224
Children, bright, reading and, 338–346
       interests of, 254–268
Children's Book Council, 278, 279
Choral reading, 240–242
Citizenship, reading and, 9
Claremont College, 5, 17
Clark, Willis W., 315
Classification Test for Beginners in Reading, 52
Classroom, modern elementary, 12–16
Cleary, Florence Damon, 226
Cleland, Donald L., 346
Clemens, Elizabeth, 121
Clinics, reading, 323–324
Clymer, Theodore, 128, 294
Cody, William, 15
Cole, Luella, 385
Comic books, 258–262
Comprehension, content subjects and, 140–143, 166–169
       developing, 146–169, 379–380
       difficulties in, causes of, 132–134
       intelligence and, 132

Comprehension (*continued*)
   long selections and, 139, 159–160, 162
   oral reading and, 133, 232
   paragraphs and, 139, 158–159, 162
   phrases and, 138–139, 157
   physical factors and, 132
   rate of reading and, 131, 171–174
   reading and, 130–169
   retention and, 131
   sentences and, 139, 157–158, 162
   skill in using reference materials and, 131
   skills, 134–139
      improvement in, 143–145
      interrelationships of, 130–132
      word recognition and, 131, 132–133
Compton's Pictured Encyclopedia, 11, 204, 208, 215, 221, 224, 282
Conant, James B., 88, 89, 341
Conferences on reading, 5–6, 17
Consonant blends, 97
Content subjects, comprehension in, 140–143, 166–169
      developing locational skills in reading in, 223
Context clues, use of, in learning words, 86–88, 111–113
Controlled reading, 176–179
Cook, S., 315
Cook, Walter W., 294
Cooke, David C., 13
Coomer, Ann, 301, 305
Cordts, Anna D., 128
Courtis, Stuart, 121, 201
Cowin, Shirley H., 81
Credle, Ellis, 193
Critical thinking, stimulating growth in, 73–74
Cuddy, Marjorie, C., 162
Cumulative reading records, 280
Cundiff, Ruby E., 265
Curriculum, and development of reading interests, 271–280

Dallmann, Martha, 277, 291, 356, 362
Daugherty, James, 189
Davis, Louise, 285

Davis-Eells Test of General Intelligence or Problem-Solving Ability, Primary-A, 47
Dawson, Mildred A., 38, 371
Dearborn, Walter F., 42, 84, 176
DeBoer, John J., 347, 381
Dechant, Emerald V., 25, 27, 42, 82, 129, 169, 194, 347
Deckter, Jack, 280
Dees, Margaret, 291
Deficiency, reading (*see* Retardation, reading)
DeHaan, Robert, 340
Desire to read, 34
Deterline, William A., 305
Detroit Beginning First Grade Intelligence Test, 47
Detroit Reading Test, 315
Detroit Word Recognition Test, 315
Development, child, reading and, 1–38
      locational skill, 211–226, 381
      see also Emotional development; Social development; Speech development
Developmental reading, 37
Dewey Decimal System, 206, 222
Diagnostic Reading Tests, 233, 315
Dictionaries, picture, 121–122
Dictionary, use of, 103, 200–204, 218–221
Differences, individual, 6–7, 293–305, 356
Difficulties, reading, diagnosing, 311–324
Digraphs, 96
Diphthongs, 96–97
Discrimination (*see* Auditory discrimination; Visual discrimination)
Dixon, Deane P., 401
Dolch, Edward W., 84, 85, 105, 106, 114, 124, 226, 313, 315, 346, 371
Douglass, Harl R., 168
Dramatizations of books, 274
Draper, Marcella K., 300, 305
Dunn, Anita E., 328
Dunn, Fannie W., 266
Durkee, Frank M., 272
Durkin, Dolores, 41, 128
Durost, W. N., 316
Durrell, Donald D., 91, 169, 194, 315, 316, 328

Durrell Analysis of Reading Difficulties, 315
Durrell Oral Reading Test, 233

Eakin, Mary K., 285
Eames Eye Test, 48
Edison, Thomas, 14
Education, 6, 10, 129
Educational factors, reading readiness and, 50–55
Educational Leadership, 305
Educational Policies Commission, 347
Educational Testing Service, 89
Eisenson, Jon, 248
Elementary English, 6, 7, 38, 62, 81, 82, 128, 129, 248, 262, 272, 276, 279, 280, 282, 284, 291–292, 305, 315, 317, 321, 328, 346, 371, 401, 405
Elementary School Journal, 6, 81, 82, 85, 114, 129, 266, 272, 295, 401
Elinsky, Dolores, 398, 400
Emotional development, fostering, 60–61
    reading readiness and, 50
Encyclopedia of Educational Research, 42, 304
Encyclopedias, 11, 204, 208, 226
English Journal, 6
Ephron, Beulah Kanter, 38
Evaluation, reading readiness, 41–55
Experience, child's background of, enriching, 61–64
    reading and, 31–33
Experience charts, 75–81, 129
    use in remedial reading, 333
Eye movements in reading, 20–21
Eyesight, reading and, 29–30, 48–49

Fairs, book, 279
Farnsworth, Frances Joyce, 189
Farrell, Mary E., 398
Fay, Leo C., 382
Fea, Henry R., 301
Felton, Wilma, 371
Fernald, Grace M., 333
Fernald Kinesthetic Method for remedial reading, 333–334
Field trips, 63, 387–388

Films, film strips and slides, 275, 276–277, 278
First day of school, activities on, 352–353
    preparation for, 351–352
Fiske, Marjorie, 261
Fitness, physical, reading readiness and, 47–50
Flesch, Rudolf, 88
Fletcher, Helen Jill, 280
Follett, Charles W., Awards, 287–288
Ford Foundation, 405
Fox, Lorene K., 270, 301, 304
Fries, C. C., 92–93
Fry, Edward, 346
Frye, R. A., 278

Gág, Wanda, 12
Gage, N. L., 129, 301
Galisdorfer, Lorraine, 285
Gallagher, James J., 347
Games, reading and, 123–128
    remedial reading and, 334
Gardiner, Jewel, 282
Gatcher, Dorothy, 121
Gates, Arthur L., 84, 104, 129, 165, 177, 188, 291, 316, 346
Gates Oral Reading Tests, 233, 316
Gates Reading Diagnostic Tests, 316
Gates Reading Readiness Tests, 51, 316
Gates Reading Survey Tests, 316
Gates Reading Tests, 316
Gerberich, J. Raymond, 313
Gifted children, reading programs and, 338–346
Giles, Ruth, 284
Gilmore, H. H., 13
Goode's School Atlas, 205
Goodlad, John I., 304, 305
Grade Teacher, The, 280, 291, 362
Graphemes, 97
Graphs, reading, 138, 156
Gray, Lillian, 169, 194, 248, 371
Gray Oral Reading Paragraphs, 233
Gray Oral Reading Tests, 233, 316
Gray, William S., 4, 9, 37, 38, 44, 45, 129, 166, 217, 226, 316, 346, 401, 407

Group projects, beginning reading and, 360–362

Grouping, individual differences and, 294–297

Grover, C. C., 52

Guild, Marion, 121

Guilefoile, Elizabeth, 285

Guralnick, David B., 121

Haggard, Ernest A., 316

Hancock, Ralph, 166

Handlan, Bertha, 304

Harmer, Mabel, 185

Harrington, Mildred P., 285

Harris, Albert J., 25, 81, 346, 371, 382

Harris, Chester W., 42

Harris, Theodore L., 42

Harris, William T., 297

Harrison, M. Lucille, 81

Harvard Reading Films, 176–177

Hazen, Meribah, 265

Headings, in books, 200

Health, reading and, 27–29, 47–50

Hearing ability, reading and, 30–31, 49–50

Heaton, Margaret, 284, 389, 405

Henig, Max S., 81

Henry, Nelson B., 305, 401, 407

Herminghaus, Earl G., 284

Hester, Kathleen, 36, 38, 129, 169, 226, 248

Hildreth, Gertrude, 9, 25, 33, 129, 194, 226, 347, 361, 371

Hill, Margaret Keyser, 328

Hinkle, Thomas C., 33

Hobbies, 254–255

Hoben, Alice M., 280

Hofer, Louise, B., 291

Holston, E. T., 33

Homer, J. Roy, 82

Homonyms, 142

Hook, J. N., 5

Horn, Thomas D., 382

Hosier, Max, 129, 226

Huey, Edumund B., 227

Human relations, books on, 284

Hunnicutt, C. W., 346

Hunt, J. T., 328

Husbands, Kenneth L., 172

Hutchinson, Jean, 303

Huus, Helen, 291, 382

Hyatt, Ada V., 227, 228

Illustrations, list of, in books, 200

Independent reading (see Voluntary reading)

Index, book, 200

Individual differences, 6–7, 293–305, 356

Individualized instruction, 297–304

Individualized reading, 299–302

Informal observation, diagnosing reading difficulties by, 311–312

Information, interpreting, 198
    locating, 195–226
    making use of, 198

Instruction, individualized, 297–304

Intelligence, comprehension and, 132
    reading and, 31
    tests, 44, 46–47

Interest in reading, 35–36, 249–292
    developing, 75, 249, 269–292, 381
    maintaining, 75

Interests, children's, 254–268

Intermediate grades, reading program in, 372–382

International Kindergarten Union List, 84, 103

International Reading Association, 6

Introduction, to book, 199

Iowa Every-Pupil Tests of Basic Skills, 209, 316

Iowa Silent Reading Test, 209

Iverson, William J., 346

Jacobs, Leland B., 280, 291, 300

Jacobs, Nina, 121

Jacobson, Gladys, 279

Jenkins, Marion, 291

Jenkins Oral Reading Test, 233

Jennings, Frank G., 291

Jensen, Amy Elizabeth, 280, 282, 291

Johnson, Eleanor, 305

Jones, R. Stewart, 42

Journal of Developmental Reading, 6

Journal of Educational Research, 6, 42
Judd, Charles H., 84, 171
Junior Britannica, 11, 204, 208, 221, 282
Junior Natural History Magazine, 11

Karlin, Robert, 82
Karp, Etta S., 347
Kaufman, Geraldine, 168
Kelley, Truman L., 316
Kelly, Florence C., 305
Kenworthy, Leonard S., 284
Keystone Reading Pacer, 177
Keystone Tachistoscope, 84, 176, 177
Keystone Visual Survey Tests, 49
Kinesthetic method in remedial reading, 333–334
Kinsella, Paul, 256, 258
Kircher, Clara J., 284, 328
Kirk, Samuel A., 129, 347, 406
Kirk, Winifred D., 129
Klineberg, Otto, 404
Knipp, Helen Bachmann, 84
Knowledge, reading and, 7–8
Koehler, Alvin, 121
Koehler, Cynthia, 121
Komoski, P. Kenneth, 299, 305
Kopel, David, 38, 292, 317, 347
Koskey, Thomas A., 277
Kough, Jack, 340
Kovas, Helen, 248
Krantz, L. L., 104
Kuhlmann-Anderson Intelligence Test, 47

LaBrant, Lou, 9
Language, abilities, stimulating growth in, 64–65
    knowledge of, reading and, 33
Larrick, Nancy, 285, 291, 346, 402
Larson, Lola, 285
Lazar, May, 129, 264, 265, 267, 295, 300, 301, 305
Lazarsfeld, Paul, 261
Learning, maximum, creating conditions for, 341–343
Leary, Bernice E., 37, 390
Leder, Ruth, 121

Lee-Clark Reading Readiness Test, 52
Leestma, Robert, 276, 371
Lenski, Lois, 13
Lessons, reading, development of comprehension skills through, 160–166
Letters, shapes of, 21
Lewellen, John B., 13
Lewis, Helen B., 284, 405
Lewis, William D., 201
Libraries, ability to locate materials in, 205–207, 222–223
    card catalog in, 205–206, 222, 223
    finding books on shelves in, 206
    public, 394
    school, 282–291, 384, 394
        choosing books for, 283–291
Linguistics, reading and, 91–94
Listening, 66–67
Lists, book, 284–291, 328–330, 342–343
    check, diagnosing reading difficulties with, 317
    word, 84, 103–108
Literature with Children, 280
Locational skills, 195–226
    development of, 211–226, 381
    teaching of, principles underlying, 207–210
Lockridge, J. Preston, 277
Lorge, Irving, 104
Low-voice tests, 50

MacBean, Dilla W., 121
McCullough, Constance M., 129, 382
McDade, James E., 23, 297, 298
McEntee, Helen S., 329
McGinnis, Dorothy J., 81, 128, 169, 371
McIntire, Alta, 121
McKee, Paul, 226, 402
McKim, Margaret G., 129, 194, 226, 371
Madden, Margaret, 121
Magazines, children's, 262–265
Manck, Inez L., 266
Mann, Horace, 227
Maps, list of, in books, 200
    reading, 138, 156
Martin, Laura K., 265

Martin, Marvin, 291

Materials center, 282–283

Matson, Charlotte, 285, 328

Maximum learning, creating conditions for, 341–343

May, Stella Burke, 193

Meeker, Alice M., 9, 371

Melcher, Peggy, 285

Mental ability, subjective data on, 47

Mental age, reading readiness and, 44–47

Mental health, reading and, 27–29

Mental Measurements Yearbooks, 315

Mental tests, 44, 46–47

Mercille, Margaret G., 278

Metropolitan Achievement Tests: Reading, 52, 316

Michaelis, John U., 169

Miel, Alice, 128, 305

Monroe, Marion, 38, 129

Moore, J. William, 305

Moore, Lillian, 121

Moore, Patrick, 13

Morrison, Coleman, 128

Murphy, George, 402

Murphy, H. A., 316

Murphy-Durrell Diagnostic Reading Readiness Test, 316

My Weekly Reader, 11

National Association for Better Radio and Television, 257

National Children's Book Week, 278

National Conference on Research in English, 6, 7, 82

National Council of Teachers of English, 5, 7, 265, 285, 291, 292, 315, 371

National Society for the Study of Education, 5, 10, 372

Nau, Elizabeth, 280

Nelson, M. J., 316

Nelson Silent Reading Test, The, 316

Newbery Awards, 268, 274, 285–287

Newspaper reading by children, 265

Newton, J. Roy, 371

Nonreference books, ability to find information in, 199, 217–218

Nulton, Lucy, 280

Observation of pupils, diagnosing reading difficulties by, 311–312

O'Donnell, Mabel, 121

Oftedahl, Laura, 121

Ogilvie, Mardel, 248

Oglesby, E. F., 315

Olson, Barbara V., 284

Olson, Willard C., 300

Ophthalmograph, 20

Oral reading, 227–248

    by children in small groups, 239

    by the teacher, 238–239

    comprehension and, 133, 232

    developing skill in, 381

    overemphasis on, 173–174

    poetry, 239–240

    program, 242–248

    proportion of time for, 231–232

    relation between silent reading and, 230–231

    skill in, appraising, 232–233

        developing, 236–248

    teaching of, observations on, 233–235

    tests, 233

    values of, 228–230

O'Rourke, Mary A., 321

Orr, E. M., 33

Orthorater, The, 49

Osgood, S. S., 278

Osswald, Edith, 121

Our Wonderful World, 11, 204, 208, 221

Ousley, Odille, 160

Pacing, 299

Paragraphs, 139, 158–159, 162

Parents, interpreting the reading program to, 397–401

Parke, Margaret B., 121

Parker, Claudia M., 315

Parker, Francis W., 229

Parkhurst, Helen, 297

Peeler, Ruth B., 82

Pels, Albert, 280

Pels, Gertrude, 280

Penn, M. Dorothy, 398

Personality, reading and, 8–9

    reading deficiency and, 308–309

Petersham, Maude and Miska, 13
Petty, Walter T., 371
Phonemes, 96
Phonetics, 24, 96
Phonic analysis, word recognition through, 88–98, 113–119
Phonics, 22–24, 88–98
    elements of, to be taught, 96–98
    instruction, evaluation of role of, 94–95
    teaching, 95–98
Phonograms, 22, 97
Phrases, comprehension of, 138–139, 157
Physical environment, effect on development of reading interests, 271
Physical factors, comprehension and, 132
Physical fitness, reading readiness and, 47–50
Physical health, reading and, 27, 47–50
Pictorial Encyclopedia of American History, The, 282
Picture books, 288–291
Picture dictionaries, 121–122
Pintner-Cunningham Primary Test, 46
Pintner Non-Language Primary Mental Test, 46
Pittsburgh, University of, 5, 248
Play interests of children, 255–256
Poetry, developing interest in, 280–282
    oral reading of, 239–240
    what children enjoy in, 281
Preface, of book, 199
Prereading stage, 351–356
    first day of school, 351–353
    program, organization of the, 354–355
    seatwork, 355–356
    testing, 353–354
Pressey Diagnostic Reading Tests, 316
Pressey, L. C., 316
Pressey, S. L., 316
Preston, Ralph C., 401
Price, O. M., 12
Primary grades, reading program in, 351–371
Pritchard, Miriam C., 346

Program, reading, 349–409
    bright children and, 343–344
    intermediate grades, 372–382
    interpreting, to parents, 397–401
    primary grades, 351–371
    school-wide, 383–402
Programed reading instruction, 298–299
Progress Profile, Reading, 320–323
Psychological tests, 44, 46–47
Publisher's Liaison Committee, 279
Pupil records, use in diagnosing reading difficulties, 312
Puppet shows, 280

Radio programs, 275, 278
Ramsey, Eloise, 328
Rankin, Marie, 268
Rasmussen, Margaret, 280, 291, 305
Rates, reading, 170–194
    appraisal of, 174–176
    appropriate, developing, 182–194, 380–381
    comprehension and, 131, 171–174
    guidelines for improvement of, 179–181
Ratz, Margaret, 382
Readers, retarded, 306–337
    defined, 306–308
    helping, 326–337, 381
    teaching, 324–334
Reader's Guide to Periodical Literature, 207, 215, 222, 265
Readiness, reading, 41–82
    activities, 56
    chart, 45
    developing, 60–82
    educational factors, 50–55
    emotional development and, 50
    guidelines, 55–59
    informal means of evaluation, 53–55
    mental age and, 44–47
    physical fitness and, 47–50
    social development and, 50
    tests, 50–53
Reading, abilities (*see* Abilities, reading)
    approach to, 18–19, 21
    as symbolic behavior, 19–20

Reading (*continued*)

  basal textbooks, 363–367

  beginning, program for, 356–362

  challenge of, 3–10

  child development and, 1–38

  choral, 240–242

  citizenship and, 9

  clinics, 323–324, 396

  complexity of, 7

  comprehension (*see* Comprehension)

  controlled, 176–179

  cumulative records, 280

  deficiency (*see* Retardation, reading)

  defined, 17

  desire for, 34

  developmental, 37

  difficulties (*see* Difficulties, reading)

  eye movements in, 20–21

  games, 123–128, 334

  grades 2 and 3, 362–371

  graphs, tables, charts, and maps, 138, 156–157

  growth in, elements essential to, 26–38

  improvement of, efforts at, 5–6

  in various curriculum areas, 367–370

  individual differences in (*see* Individual differences)

  individualized, 299–302

  instruction, programed, 298–299

  interest in, 35–36, 75, 249–292

    developing, 75, 249, 269–292, 381

    maintaining, 75

  kinds of, 24

  knowledge and, 7–8

  lessons, development of comprehension, skills through, 160–166

  linguistics and, 91–94

  meaningful, 22, 130–169

  nature of, 17–25

  oral (*see* Oral reading)

  personality and, 8–9

  process of, 17–19

  program (*see* Program, reading)

  Progress Profile, 320–323

  purpose of, 34–35

  rates (*see* Rates, reading)

Reading (*continued*)

  readiness (*see* Readiness, reading)

  remedial, 333–334, 395–396

  retardation (*see* Retardation, reading)

  sequence in, 74–75

  setting for, 11–16, 36

  silent (*see* Silent reading)

  skills (*see* Skills, reading)

  social uses of, 403–409

  tests, 209, 391–392

  to answer questions, 135–136, 149–150, 161, 164

  to arrive at generalizations, 136–137, 153–154, 161, 163, 165, 168

  to evaluate critically, 137–138, 154–155, 161, 163–164, 168

  to find main idea, 135, 146–149, 161, 163, 165, 167–168

  to follow directions, 137, 153, 162, 164, 168

  to select significant details, 135, 161, 163, 168

  to summarize and organize, 136, 150–153, 161, 163, 165

  unduly slow, causes of, 172–174

  values of, 3–5

  vocabulary, developing a, 67–68, 103–108

  voluntary (*see* Voluntary reading)

Reading center, 396–397

Reading Ladders, 405

Reading Teacher, 6, 82, 128, 129, 194, 281, 305, 347

Reading Vocabulary for the Primary Grades, 104

Recognition, word (*see* Word recognition)

Records, anecdotal, use in diagnosing reading difficulties, 312

  pupil, use in diagnosing reading difficulties, 312

Records and recordings, 274–275, 277

Reed, Mary, 121

Reese, Dora, 169, 194, 248

Reference materials, knowledge of content of, 197–198, 205, 214–215

  skill in using, 204–205

Reference materials (*continued*)
  comprehension and, 131
  developing, 221–222
Remedial reading, 333–334, 395–396
Remembering, improving ability for, 70–73, 380
Renthal, Helen, 342
Reports, book, 274
Retardation, reading, 306–337
  causes of, 308–311
  defined, 307
  early experiences with reading and, 310
  home situation and, 309–310
  personality and, 308–309
  school climate and, 310–311
Retarded readers, defined, 306–308
  helping, 326–337, 381
  teaching, 324–334
Retention, comprehension and, 131
Rhodes, M., 280
Richards, Margaret, 328
Riessman, Frank, 316–317, 406
Rinsland, Henry, 104, 105
Robinson, H. Alan, 347, 406
Robinson, Helen Mansfield, 28, 248, 291, 299, 305, 309, 316, 328, 347, 402
Rogers, Bernice, 4
Rollins, Charlemae, 284
Rudman, Herbert C., 266
Rue, Eloise, 328
Russell, David H., 38, 82, 129, 160, 248, 301, 309, 347, 371

Sacra, Mabel, 284
Sawyer, Ruth, 291
Schiffman, Gilbert B., 347
Schneider, Herman, 13, 368
Schneider, Leo, 13
Schneider, Nina, 13, 368
Schonell, Fred J., 44, 114
School libraries (*see* Libraries)
School-wide reading program, 383–402
Schubert, Delwyn G., 38, 48
Schwietert, Louise H., 300, 305
Science, reading supplementary material in, 369–370

Science (*continued*)
  reading textbook material in, 367–369
  Scott, Alice, 121
Search, Preston W., 297
Seatwork, 355–356, 363–366
Self-selection, 299
Sentences, comprehension of, 139, 157–158, 162
Sequence, in reading, 74–75
Sequential Tests of Education Progress: Reading, 316
Seymour, Flora W., 189
Shedlock, Marie, 291
Sheehan, David Vincent, 35
Shepard, John P., 405
Sheppard, Louise E., 278
Shores, J. Harlan, 172
Sight, reading and, 29–30, 48–49
Sight method, of learning words, 85–86, 109–111
Sight words, 83, 84, 109–111
Silent reading, 297
  proportion of time for, 231–232
  relation between oral reading and, 230–231
Sizemore, Robert, 94, 292, 301, 305
Skills, comprehension (*see* Comprehension)
  locational, 195–226
  reading, 36–38
    check list of, 317–323
Slater, Russell, 328
Smith, Dora V., 285, 291
Smith, Edwin A., 317
Smith, Henry P., 25, 27, 42, 82, 129, 169, 194, 347
Smith, Nila B., 82, 129, 291
Smith, Wendell I., 305
Snellen Letter Chart, 48
Snellen Symbol E Chart, 48
Sochor, Elona, 7
Social development, fostering, 60–61
  reading readiness and, 50
Social studies, reading supplementary material in, 369–370
  reading textbook material in, 367–369

Sounds, 21–22

Spache, George D., 301, 328, 382

Speech development, 65–66

Speed of reading (*see* Rates, reading)

Spitzer, H. F., 316

Spring Book Festival Awards (New York *Herald Tribune*), 279, 288–291

SRA Reading Rate Accelerator, 177

Standardized Oral Reading Check Tests, 316

Stanford Achievement Test: Reading, 316

Stanton, Frank, 261

Steinmetz, Eulalie, 285

Stevenson, Augusta, 15

Stone, Clarence R., 52, 104

Stone's 1941 Graded Vocabulary for Primary Reading, 104

Storytelling, 278

Strang, Ruth, 194, 291, 329, 341, 402

Structural analysis of words, 99–103, 119–120

    developmental program in, 101–102

    teaching, 99–101

Subject Index to Poetry, 205, 221

Subjects, content (*see* Content subjects)

Sullivan, Helen B., 328, 329

Sweet, Mayme A., 401

Swenson, Esther J., 266

Symbolic behavior, reading as, 19–20

Table of contents, 199–200

Tables, reading, 138, 156

Tachistoscopes, 84, 176, 177

Teachers, intermediate-grade, problems confronting, 372–374

    role of, in development of reading interests, 270–271

Teacher's Wordbook of 20,000 Words, 104

Teacher's Wordbook of 30,000 Words, 104

Teaching, defined, 26

    oral reading, 233–235

    phonics, 95–98

    retarded readers, 324–334

    structural analysis of words, 99–101

Telebinocular, 48

Television, 256–258, 275–276, 278

Temple University, 5

Terman Revision of the Stanford-Binet Intelligence Scale, 44, 46

Tests, eye, 48–49

    hearing, 49–50

    mental ability, 44–47

    of skill in locating information, 209

    oral reading, 233

    prereading stage and, 353–354

    reading, 209, 391–392

    reading readiness, 50–53

    use in diagnosing reading difficulties, 313–317

Textbooks, basal reading, 363–367

    reading, in social studies and science, 367–369

Thaxter, Anne, 285

Thinking, critical, stimulating growth of, 73–74

Thorndike, Edward L., 104, 201, 220

Tiegs, Ernest W., 315

Tiemann, Ernest F., 277

Tinker, Miles A., 169, 346

Tomlinson, Ethel, 82

Tompkins, Lucy, 279

Tooze, Ruth, 82, 273, 285, 292

Townes, Willmina, 121

Travers, John F., 10

Traxler, Arthur E., 129

Tyler, Fred T., 10, 305

Unusually gifted children, reading and, 338–346

Van Wagenen Reading Readiness Test, 51–52

Veatch, Jeannette, 301, 305

Vernon, M. D., 347

Vision, reading and, 29–30, 48–49

Visual aids, 274–278, 283

Visual discrimination, developing, 68, 69–70

    testing, 53

Visual Sensation Tests, 48

Vocabulary, development of, 67–68, 103–108

    specialized, 141–142

Voluntary reading, aims of guidance in, 249–254
    developing interests in, 269–292
    in grades 2 and 3, 370–371
    principles underlying program of, 269–270

Wagner, Eva Bond, 81, 128, 169, 248, 371
Wagner, Guy, 129, 226
Waite, William H., 295
Walpole, Ellen Wales, 121
Warner, Jane, 121
Washburne, Carleton W., 297, 298
"Watch-tick" test, 50
Waterbury, Eveline A., 315
Waterhouse, Tina S., 336–337
Watters, Garnette, 121, 201
Watts, A. F., 114
Wechsler-Bellevue Intelligence Scales, 44, 46
Wertham, Fredric, 259
Wheat, Harry G., 168
Wheeler, Lester, 317
Wheeler-Howell List, 84
Whipple, Gertrude, 381, 382, 406
Whisper tests, 50
White, Margaret, 248
Who's Who, 205
Who's Who in America, 205
Williams, Gertrude, 7, 82
Wirt, William, 297
Witty, Paul, 10, 38, 94, 256, 257, 258, 259, 260, 276, 292, 303, 305, 317, 341, 347, 382
Witty-Kopel Interest Inventory, 317
Wolf, Katharine M., 261

Wolfson, Bernice J., 292
Woolf, Jeanne A., 347
Woolf, Maurice D., 347
Word lists, 84, 103–108
Word recognition, 83–129
    comprehension and, 131, 132–133
    defined, 83
    developing skill in, 109–129, 378–379
    independence in, skills needed for, 83–103
    workbooks as aid to, 122–123
Words, learning, sight method of, 85–86, 109–111
    use of context clues in, 86–88, 111–113
    use of phonic analysis in, 88–98, 113–119
    use of structural analysis in, 99–103, 119–120
    sight, 83, 84, 109–111
Workbooks, as aid to word recognition, 122–123
World Almanac, 205, 208, 215, 221–222, 226
World Book Encyclopedia, 11, 204, 208, 221, 224, 282
World of Children's Books, The, 279
Wright, Wendell W., 121
Wrightstone, J. Wayne, 129, 295, 296, 305
Writing, development of, 68
Wurtz, Conrad, 329

Yates, Elizabeth, 12
Yoakam, Gerald A., 169, 248